Multidisciplinary Applications of Extended Reality for Human Experience

Tanveer Kajla
Department of Management Studies, NALSAR University of Law, Hyderabad, India

Pooja Kansra
Lovely Professional University, India

Nripendra Singh
Pennsylvania Western University, USA

A volume in the Advances in Computational Intelligence and Robotics (ACIR) Book Series

Published in the United States of America by
IGI Global
Engineering Science Reference (an imprint of IGI Global)
701 E. Chocolate Avenue
Hershey PA, USA 17033
Tel: 717-533-8845
Fax: 717-533-8661
E-mail: cust@igi-global.com
Web site: http://www.igi-global.com

Library of Congress Cataloging-in-Publication Data

CIP Pending
ISBN: 979-8-3693-2432-5
EISBN: 979-8-3693-2433-2

British Cataloguing in Publication Data
A Cataloguing in Publication record for this book is available from the British Library.

All work contributed to this book is new, previously-unpublished material.
The views expressed in this book are those of the authors, but not necessarily of the publisher.

For electronic access to this publication, please contact: eresources@igi-global.com.

Advances in Computational Intelligence and Robotics (ACIR) Book Series

Ivan Giannoccaro
University of Salento, Italy

ISSN:2327-0411
EISSN:2327-042X

MISSION

While intelligence is traditionally a term applied to humans and human cognition, technology has progressed in such a way to allow for the development of intelligent systems able to simulate many human traits. With this new era of simulated and artificial intelligence, much research is needed in order to continue to advance the field and also to evaluate the ethical and societal concerns of the existence of artificial life and machine learning.

The **Advances in Computational Intelligence and Robotics (ACIR) Book Series** encourages scholarly discourse on all topics pertaining to evolutionary computing, artificial life, computational intelligence, machine learning, and robotics. ACIR presents the latest research being conducted on diverse topics in intelligence technologies with the goal of advancing knowledge and applications in this rapidly evolving field.

Coverage

- Computational Logic
- Algorithmic Learning
- Agent technologies
- Fuzzy Systems
- Heuristics
- Intelligent Control
- Pattern Recognition
- Artificial Life
- Neural Networks
- Computer Vision

IGI Global is currently accepting manuscripts for publication within this series. To submit a proposal for a volume in this series, please contact our Acquisition Editors at Acquisitions@igi-global.com or visit: http://www.igi-global.com/publish/.

Titles in this Series

For a list of additional titles in this series, please visit: www.igi-global.com/book-series

Drone Applications for Industry 5.0
Chandra Singh (Sahyadri College of Engineering and Management, India) and Rathishchandra
Ramachandra Gatti (Sahyadri College of Engineering and Management, India)
Engineering Science Reference • copyright 2024 • 523pp • H/C (ISBN: 9798369320938)
• US $415.00 (our price)

Multidisciplinary Applications of AI Robotics and Autonomous Systems
Tanupriya Choudhury (Graphic Era University, India) Anitha Mary X. (Karunya Institute of
Technology and Sciences, India) Subrata Chowdhury (Sreenivasa Institute of Technology
and Management Studies, India) C. Karthik (Jyothi Engineering College, India) and C.
Suganthi Evangeline (Sri Eshwar College of Engineering, India)
Engineering Science Reference • copyright 2024 • 301pp • H/C (ISBN: 9798369357675)
• US $395.00 (our price)

Cross-Industry AI Applications
P. Paramasivan (Dhaanish Ahmed College of Engineering, India) S. Suman Rajest (Dhaanish
Ahmed College of Engineering, India) Karthikeyan Chinnusamy (Veritas, USA) R. Regin
(SRM Institute of Science and Technology, India) and Ferdin Joe John Joseph (Thai-Nichi
Institute of Technology, Thailand)
Engineering Science Reference • copyright 2024 • 389pp • H/C (ISBN: 9798369359518)
• US $415.00 (our price)

Harnessing Artificial Emotional Intelligence for Improved Human-Computer Interactions
Nitendra Kumar (Amity Business School, Amity University, Noida, India) Surya Kant Pal
(Sharda University, Greater Noida, India) Priyanka Agarwal (Amity Business School, Amity
University, Noida, India) Joanna Rosak-Szyrocka (Częstochowa University of Technology,
Poland) and Vishal Jain (Sharda University, Greater Noida, India)
Engineering Science Reference • copyright 2024 • 300pp • H/C (ISBN: 9798369327944)
• US $335.00 (our price)

701 East Chocolate Avenue, Hershey, PA 17033, USA
Tel: 717-533-8845 x100 • Fax: 717-533-8661
E-Mail: cust@igi-global.com • www.igi-global.com

Table of Contents

Detailed Table of Contents

Chapter 1
Niranchana Shri Viswanathan, Sapthagiri NPS University, India

This research delves into the multifaceted realm of extended reality (XR) and its transformative influence across various disciplines, aiming to unveil its diverse applications and profound implications for enhancing the human experience. By examining XR's intersectionality with fields such as education, healthcare, entertainment, and communication, this study seeks to illuminate the ways in which immersive technologies redefine traditional boundaries and foster innovative approaches to problem-solving. Through an in-depth analysis of XR's integration into these domains, the research explores the potential societal, psychological, and economic benefits, as well as the ethical considerations that accompany this technological paradigm shift. The findings of this study contribute to a holistic understanding of XR's role in shaping the future of human interaction, cognition, and engagement across disciplines, offering valuable insights for researchers, practitioners, and policymakers navigating the evolving landscape of immersive technologies.

    Zeeshan Asim, University of Buraimi, Oman & Institute of Business and
        Management, Pakistan & INIT International University, Malaysia
    Asokan Vasudevan, INTI International University, Malaysia
    Shad Ahmad Khan, University of Buraimi, Oman & INIT International
        University, Malaysia
    Mudassar Mahmood, University of Buraimi, Oman
    Yusri Yosof, Universiti Tun Hussein Onn Malaysia, Malaysia
    Devarajanayaka Muniyanayaka, University of Buraimi, Oman

Extended reality (XR) technologies are gaining popularity due to their cost-effectiveness and advantageous features. However, there is a need for a comprehensive understanding of numerous ethical dilemmas regarding the effective use of XR for various purposes. Despite the optimistic prospects, this emerging technology has been clouded by uncertain potentialities, resulting in a slower adoption of XR technology than initially anticipated due to some social and physiological implications. Examine potential issues linked to XR technologies, delve into the diverse ethical responsibilities involved, and analyze the underlying factors contributing to those implications. This research demonstrates that the utilization of XR technologies presents four ethical aspects, encompassing social, physiological, environmental, and financial ramifications, alongside privacy vulnerabilities and moral quandaries. The findings of this study lay the groundwork for forthcoming research endeavors aimed at comprehending and tackling the ethical challenges posed by XR technologies.

Extended reality (XR) includes virtual reality, augmented reality, and spatial computing. It introduces a spectrum of immersive technologies with the potential for pathbreaking interactions and unique digital engagement. In the case of online retailing, XR is crucial for personalization, interactivity, and information acquisition. The present study focuses on ethical considerations as limitations of extended reality. The sample size chosen for the study was 289 retail consumers. The sampling method used was judgement sampling. The data analysis was conducted with the help of exploratory factor analysis (EFA) and multiple regression analysis (MRA) and artificial neural network (ANN). It was found that the ethical dimensions of XR such as privacy concerns, informed consent, security risks and psychological impact significantly influence the wise use of XR by consumers.

The advent of immersive technologies like VR, AR, and MR has transformed human experiences, prompting legal and ethical complexities. This chapter delves into privacy, regulatory, consent, and accessibility challenges. Balancing innovation with regulation is crucial to mitigate risks for users. Consent and agency in virtual spaces raise questions about autonomy, while issues like virtual harassment and property rights challenge existing legal norms. Immersive technologies promise enhanced accessibility but require inclusive design efforts. Robust privacy protections are necessary to prevent data breaches. Collaboration among policymakers, technologists, ethicists, and society is essential to ensure immersive tech fosters empowerment and inclusion in both virtual and physical realms.

Virtual reality has laid the cornerstone for various fields that remained unexplored till date due to various restraints. VR has not only enhanced the efficacy levels but also served as the basis for effectiveness. There have been studies depicting the various types of VR, but this area of semi- immersive VR still remains unexplored. Pathways sweeping the global waves of growth and development opening doors to significant opportunities in the field of technology have raised expectations from the real estate business as well. With the remarkable contribution of virtual reality in all spheres of business, it has played a crucial role in enhancing customer expectations, and also acquainting them with an enriching experience in an interactive way. This study helps in bridging the gap by taking the benefits of both fully immersive and non-immersive VR that could be promptly utilized to achieve customer satisfaction in enhancing customer experience as well as the user experience. The study highlights the role of various technologies in the field of semi-immersive virtual reality in a more comprehensive manner. By analysing the various aspects of virtual reality, the study envisages the impact of semi-immersive virtual reality in magnifying the marketing prospects in real estate business and influencing the purchase decisions of customers.

 Yashodhan Karulkar, MPSTME, NMIMS University, India
 Devansh Gupta, MPSTME, NMIMS University, India
 Anshuman Thapliyal, MPSTME, NMIMS University, India
 Bhavyaraj Singh, MPSTME, NMIMS University, India
 Mahendra Parihar, MPSTME, NMIMS University, India

It is often a matter of fascination for people to visualize the invisible, which has been enabled by technology, specifically by augmented reality (AR). The real and virtual are infused together by augmented reality. Digital data is projected on an image of anything visible through a gadget, to generate a representation of reality that is augmented. The satisfaction of customers is vital for retail sectors. It instils a sense of care and value in customers when brands keep updating themselves with such facilities, which rewards in terms of increment in loyalty and profits. This study examines the impact of perceived customization on consumers' intents to co-create value when augmented reality (AR) and some web-based businesses are used. Additionally, the authors look into how perceived risk and trust are related in this context. India-based Pepperfry is an online retailer for furniture and home décor items. For the purpose of this survey, the authors polled Pepperfry users to assess their sentiments towards purchases made through websites and augmented reality applications.

 Stanzin Padma, Lovely Professional University, India
 Tawheed Nabi, Lovely Professional University, India

A new era of personalised travel has been ushered in by artificial intelligence. AI in tourism revolutionises the industry by enhancing personalisation, efficiency and customer experiences. It provides personalised recommendations and predictive analytics for demand forecasting and pricing optimisation. Research into AI within the tourism sector has experienced a significant surge since 2017. Recent research highlights a variety of aspects of AI's application in the travel industry. This chapter systematically selects papers from prestigious journals using post-2018 publications from numerous trustworthy databases to give a comprehensive picture of the rapidly expanding body of work on artificial intelligence in the tourism industry. It endeavours to thematically explore how AI has propelled advancements in the tourism industry, the challenges it presents, and its potential for future development. The chapter further presents practical implementations and outlines future research directions.

Praveen Srivastava, Birla Institute of Technology, Mesra, India
Gautam Shandilya, Birla Institute of Technology, Mesra, India

This study explores the intricate relationship between perceived smart tourism technology (STT) experiences and tourist satisfaction (TS), recognizing the pivotal role played by innovative technologies in shaping contemporary travel experiences. The research employs a comprehensive approach to assess how tourists' perceptions of smart technology, including factors such as informativeness, interactivity, and personalization, influence overall satisfaction. By utilizing SmartPLS, the study aims to uncover nuanced insights into the intricate dynamics that govern the interplay between perceived smart tourism technology and the satisfaction levels of modern tourists. The research methodology involves the collection of perceptual data from a diverse sample of tourists throughout India, encompassing various smart technology applications within the tourism sector. Employing sophisticated statistical analyses, including regression modeling and structural equation modeling, the study seeks to quantify the impact of different aspects of smart technology experiences on overall satisfaction. This research contributes to the evolving landscape of smart tourism technology by providing a robust and nuanced understanding of its role in shaping tourist satisfaction. The findings are expected to have practical implications for tourism industry stakeholders, informing strategic decisions regarding the integration and enhancement of smart technologies to optimize the overall tourist experience. Ultimately, this study advances the discourse on leveraging technology to meet the evolving expectations of modern tourists and underscores the importance of perceived smart tourism technology in driving satisfaction in the tourism sector.

Chapter 9

*Thangaraja T., Department of Management, Aarupadai Veedu Institute
of Technology, Vinayaka Mission 's Research Foundation (Deemed),
India*

*Maheshkumar Maharudrappa, Department of Management, Guru
Nanak Dev Engineering College, Bidar, India*

*M. Bakkiyaraj, Department of Mechanical Engineering, Rajalakshmi
Institute of Technology, Chennai, India*

*Lalit Johari, Department of Computer Applications, IFTM University,
Moradabad, India*

*Uma Maheswari E., Department of Mathematics, R.M.K. Engineering
College, Kavaraipettai, India*

*S. Muthuvel, Department of Mechanical Engineering, Kalasalingam
Academy of Research and Education, India*

Industrial 5.0 is a transformation where advanced technologies merge with traditional manufacturing processes, transforming the role of human resources (HR) in driving organizational growth. AI-powered HR technology is integrating automation, IoT, and AI into traditional industrial frameworks, improving efficiency, productivity, and agility. The benefits like optimized talent acquisition and personalized employee experiences are served by HR solutions. HR functions, such as streamlining recruitment processes, providing insights into workforce dynamics, and fostering a culture of continuous learning, are revolutionized by AI. Talent management and succession planning, while personalized training modules enhance employee skills and innovation, have been performed by AI-powered analytics. AI is also used to improve strategic capacities by facilitating data-driven decision-making, which gives HR directors the ability to foresee skill shortages, reduce risks, and proactively promote organizational growth.

Chapter 10

Cultural Impacts of Artificial Intelligence on Sustainable Entrepreneurship
Development 201

*Ragitha Radhakrishnan, Department of Psychology, Dr. MGR-Janaki
College of Arts and Science for Women, Chennai, India*

*P. Sivakumar, Department of Management, Dr. SNS Rajalakshmi
College of Arts and Science, Coimbatore, India*

*Benita E., Department of Management, Bishop Appasamy College of
Arts and Science, Coimbatore, India*

*T. R. Abhilasha, Department of Commerce and Management,
International Institute of Business Studies, Bengaluru, India*

*P Suganthi, Department of Mathematics, R.M.K. Engineering College,
Kavaraipettai, India*

*Premkumar R., Department of Electronics and Instrumentation
Engineering, Sri Sairam Engineering College, Chennai*

In this chapter, the connection between artificial intelligence (AI) and sustainable
entrepreneurship is emphasized, emphasizing the need for understanding its
sociological and cultural implications. It also emphasizes the significance of cultural
sensitivity in AI development and adoption, mitigates biases, and fosters inclusive
AI ecosystems. While AI technologies can improve efficiency, innovation, and
scalability, privacy, autonomy, and job displacement concerns necessitate a balance
between technological advancements and ethical considerations. Interdisciplinary
collaboration between sociologists, HR professionals, entrepreneurs, and technologists
to develop AI-driven sustainable entrepreneurship initiatives has been discussed in
this chapter. AI's transformative potential for sustainable entrepreneurship has been
connected to incorporating sociocultural insights.

Chapter 11

Digital Strategies for Modern Workplaces and Business Through Artificial

Anurag Vijay Agrawal, Department of Electronics and Communication
Engineering, J.P. Institute of Engineering and Technology, India
M Bakkiyaraj, Department of Mechanical Engineering, Rajalakshmi
Institute of Technology, Chennai, India
Simanchala Das, K.L. Business School, Koneru Lakshmaiah Education
Foundation, Vijayawada, India
C. M. Surendra Reddy, Department of Commerce and Management,
International Institute of Business Studies, Bengaluru, India
P. B. Narendra Kiran, School of Business and Management, Christ
University, Bengaluru, India
S. Boopathi, Mechanical Engineering, Muthayammal Engineering
College, Namakkal, India

AI has significantly transformed human resources (HR) by enhancing recruitment, talent acquisition, employee engagement, performance management, learning, and HR analytics. This chapter explores the convergence of HR and AI, highlighting its potential to revolutionize modern workplaces. The recruitment processes have been enhanced by AI in HR strategies such as efficiently identifying top candidates and mitigating unconscious bias. Automated candidate screening, scheduling interviews, and answering frequently asked questions, improving the candidate experience have been done. The personalized learning and development initiatives, delivering targeted training programs, identifying skill gaps, and providing timely feedback have been facilitated. AI-powered systems provide real-time insights into employee performance metrics, enabling proactive feedback. By analyzing vast datasets, AI algorithms can identify patterns and trends, facilitating data-driven decision-making in performance evaluations and goal setting.

Chapter 12

S. Revathi, Department of Computer Science Engineering, B.S. Abdur
Rahman Crescent Institute of Science and Technology, Chennai,
India

Afroze Ansari, Department of Computer Science and Engineering,
Faculty of Engineering and Technology, Khaja Bandanawaz
University, Karnataka, India

S. Jacophine Susmi, Department of Information Technology, University
College of Engineering, Tindivanam, India

M. Madhavi, Department of CSE (AIML), Keshav Memorial
Engineering College, Hyderabad, India

Gunavathie M. A., Department of Information Technology, Easwari
Engineering College, Chennai, India

M. Sudhakar, Department of Mechanical Engineering, Sri Sai Ram
Engineering College, Chennai, India

The integration of ML, IoT, and NSA promotes significant opportunities for promoting sustainability in various industries. Actionable insights, while IoT devices collect data for real-time monitoring and control of environmental parameters, have been provided by ML algorithms that analyze vast datasets. IoT deployments improve resource efficiency and resilience, while the NSA dynamically allocates network resources based on application requirements. These architectures prioritize traffic, optimize bandwidth, and ensure QoS to facilitate IoT and ML applications due to minimizing energy consumption and carbon emissions. However, challenges (data security, interoperability, and ethical) have been considered to persist, necessitating holistic sustainability approaches. Network slicing architectures provide a flexible network architecture for the efficient coexistence of diverse services and applications on a shared infrastructure.

*Komala C. R., Department of Information Science and Engineering,
East Point College of Engineering and Technology, Bengaluru,
India*

*V. Vaithianathan, Department of Electronics and Communication
Engineering, Sri Sivasubramaniya Nadar College of Engineering,
Chennai, India*

*K. J. Jegadish Kumar, Department of Electronics and Communication
Engineering, Sri Sivasubramaniya Nadar College of Engineering,
Chennai, India*

*S. Vijayakumar, Department of Mathematics, RMK Engineering
College, Kavaraipettai, India*

*Gunavathie M. A., Department of Information Technology, Easwari
Engineering College, Chennai, India*

Intelligent surfaces' combination of fog and cloud computing is a major breakthrough in digital infrastructure. In this chapter, these two realms work in concert, emphasizing how intelligent surfaces serve as linkages to close the gap. It explores the basic ideas of fog and cloud computing and their functions in dispersed systems and intelligent surfaces. Real-time analytics, predictive maintenance, user experiences in smart cities, healthcare, and industrial automation are discussed because integration has the potential to revolutionize industries. However, there are obstacles to overcome, such as security worries, interoperability problems, and standard protocols. The stakeholders may utilize current advancements and best practices to accelerate digital transformation and create a new linked world.

    Ozge Kandemir, Interior Design Department, Eskisehir Teknik
      Üniversitesi, Turkey
    Gökhan Ulusoy, Interior Design Department, Eskişehir Teknik
      Üniversitesi, Turkey
    Celal Murat Kandemir, Faculty of Education, Eskişehir Osmangazi
      Üniversitesi, Turkey

The fourth industrial revolution creates a digital world that enables the activation of intelligent systems, allowing virtual and physical systems to cooperate flexibly with each other. This world, designed on ICT, blurs the lines between physical and virtual, and makes it necessary to develop educational environments by digital technologies. This development is described as Education 4.0. Integration with the education fields in general, and design fields in particular, into Education 4.0 requires acquiring new skills and competencies. The social transformation experienced with Industry 4.0 requires solving rapidly changing, more numerous, and complex problems and meeting changing needs. So, the study aims to reveal the characteristics of Education 4.0, and what kinds of technological infrastructure required for it. In particular, it stands out with its potential for developing design education within the Education 4.0 framework. It aims to reveal immersive technologies and their types, technology-based immersive experiences, immersive learning experiences, and the opportunities of these experiences for design education.

In this chapter, the primary advantages, and problems of information technology (IT) enabled learning in the education sector are discussed. In addition, the effects of shifting from traditional classrooms to online learning environments are briefly discussed. This chapter is based on the perspective that the extended reality (XR) can be realized through the success of IT enable learning. The aim is to delve into the significance of IT-enabled learning within today's educational landscape, examining the factors contributing to its rapid adoption. Drawing from existing research, the study discusses the implementation of IT-enabled learning technologies in educational environments. The key findings of this study include the benefits and drawbacks of moving from a traditional classroom setting to an online learning environment, including the frequency with which they arise, the different kinds of barriers that may be encountered, the possible advantages, the potential downsides, and security concerns.

Finance, decision-making, and AI interaction have been transferred to the digital economy due to the reduction of transaction costs and increase in security through blockchain technology. Integration of artificial intelligence (AI) and big data analytics with decision support systems (DSS), with a focus on risk assessment, predictive analytics, and strategic planning, has been explored. AI and DSS collaborated to deliver responsiveness and flexibility across several industries, leading to improved, data-driven decision-making. The current and future paths of AI with a focus on finance, healthcare, and customer service, in addition to ethical problems, have also been discussed. Future developments in the digital economy, such as cybersecurity, decentralized banking, and quantum computing, have been explored to optimize benefits and reduce risks.

The human experience is what drives everything, notwithstanding the marketing sector's ongoing transformation. Through the use of narrative and visual content, brands can create experiences that touch people's emotions, ignite their imaginations, and leave a lasting impact. Storytelling that is both emotionally engaging and immersive leaves an impression. These strategies permanently modify consumers' perceptions and feelings while also raising engagement and conversion rates. A well-written tale has the ability to inspire, empower, and transform. It might make ordinary interactions with customers delightful, encouraging a sense of loyalty and community among them. Brands who embark on this path not only enhance their marketing tactics but also contribute to a larger narrative about how companies and consumers collaborate to shape the future. The current study investigates the capacity of narrative and visual content to construct timeless and cross-cultural narratives.

Preface

Welcome to *Multidisciplinary Applications of Extended Reality for Human Experience*, a pioneering exploration into the transformative world of extended reality (XR) technologies and their profound impact on the human experience. As editors of this comprehensive volume, we, Tanveer Kajla from the Department of Management Studies at NALSAR University of Law, India, Pooja Kansra from Lovely Professional University, India, and Nripendra Singh from Pennsylvania Western University, Clarion, United States, are thrilled to present a collection that delves into the dynamic interplay between XR and various facets of human life.

In recent years, extended reality technologies have transcended their traditional roles, evolving from mere tools for entertainment and education to powerful instruments reshaping our perception, interaction, and understanding of the world. This book examines this evolution through an interdisciplinary lens, offering insights into how XR is not only altering our experiences but also redefining what it means to be human in a digitally augmented era.

Our aim is to illuminate the intricate and multifaceted relationship between XR technologies and humanity, highlighting how these innovations are influencing our perceptions, interactions, and comprehension of the world around us. By assembling contributions from a diverse array of experts, this volume provides a holistic view of XR's potential and challenges, making it an indispensable resource for academics, researchers, industry professionals, and enthusiasts.

The chapters within this book explore the broad spectrum of XR's impact on human life, from the deep psychological and emotional effects of immersive experiences to the societal implications of virtual reality. We delve into the design principles and ethical considerations that guide the creation of immersive content and examine the transformative potential of these technologies across various fields, including management, education, e-commerce, healthcare, gaming, and more.

Each chapter is meticulously crafted to dissect specific aspects of XR, offering readers valuable insights into the following topics:

- The Impact of Extended Reality in Management
- Ethical Considerations in Virtual Reality Research and Extended Reality
- Immersive Technologies for Healthcare Simulation
- Narrative Structures in Virtual Reality
- Immersive Data Visualization for Decision Support
- Cultural Heritage Preservation through Augmented Reality
- Legal and Regulatory Challenges in Extended Reality
- Immersive Marketing and Consumer Behavior

This multidisciplinary approach ensures that our book addresses the diverse interests and needs of a specialized audience, encompassing researchers and academics, XR developers and technologists, educators and trainers, industry professionals, and government policymakers.

We are confident that this book will serve as a foundational text for those seeking to navigate the rapidly evolving landscape of immersive technologies and their profound impact on our lives. By providing a comprehensive and insightful exploration of XR, we hope to inspire further research, innovation, and thoughtful discourse in this exciting and ever-changing field.

We extend our heartfelt gratitude to all contributors for their invaluable insights and to our readers for embarking on this journey with us. Together, let us explore the endless possibilities of extended reality and its potential to shape the future of human experience.

Chapter 1: Exploring the Intersectionality of Extended Reality: A Comprehensive Study on its Multidisciplinary Applications and Impact on Enhancing the Human Experience

Niranchana Viswanathan

In the opening chapter, Niranchana Viswanathan presents an in-depth exploration of Extended Reality (XR), delving into its multifaceted applications across various domains such as education, healthcare, entertainment, and communication. This research comprehensively examines how XR technologies are redefining traditional boundaries and fostering innovative approaches to enhance human experience. By analyzing the societal, psychological, and economic benefits, alongside the ethical considerations, Viswanathan provides a holistic understanding of XR's role in shaping the future of human interaction, cognition, and engagement. This chapter offers invaluable insights for researchers, practitioners, and policymakers navigating the evolving landscape of immersive technologies.

Chapter 2: Beyond the Screen: Navigating the Ethical Landscape in Extended Reality (XR)

Zeeshan Asim, Asokan Vasudevan, Shad Khan, Mudassar Mahmood, Yusri Yosof, Devarajanayaka Muniyanayaka

This chapter tackles the ethical dilemmas associated with the growing adoption of XR technologies. The authors present a thorough examination of social, physiological, environmental, and financial implications, alongside privacy vulnerabilities and moral quandaries. Highlighting the slow adoption rate of XR due to these unresolved ethical concerns, the study sets the stage for future research aimed at addressing these challenges. The insights provided here are crucial for understanding and mitigating the ethical risks posed by XR technologies.

Chapter 3: Ethical Considerations as Limitations of Extended Reality: An Empirical Study through the Lens of Retail Consumers

R. Indradevi, K. Venkataswamy, Sathish Saravanan, Arun Mittal

Focusing on the retail sector, this chapter investigates the ethical limitations of XR from the perspective of consumers. Using a robust analytical approach involving Exploratory Factor Analysis, Multiple Regression Analysis, and Artificial Neural Networks, the authors identify significant ethical dimensions such as privacy concerns, informed consent, security risks, and psychological impacts. This empirical study highlights how these factors influence consumer usage of XR, providing valuable data for improving ethical standards in XR applications.

Chapter 4: Virtual Dilemmas: Legal and Ethical Rollercoasters in Immersive Tech Land

Akanksha Yadav, K G Reddy

Akanksha Yadav and K G Reddy delve into the complex legal and ethical issues arising from the use of VR, AR, and MR technologies. This chapter addresses privacy concerns, regulatory challenges, consent issues, and accessibility barriers, emphasizing the need for a balanced approach to innovation and regulation. The authors call for collaborative efforts among policymakers, technologists, ethicists, and society to ensure that immersive technologies enhance user empowerment and inclusion.

Chapter 5: Enhancing Customer Experience by Semi-Immersive Virtual Reality in Real Estate Business

Nidhi Sharma, Divya Mahajan

Nidhi Sharma and Divya Mahajan explore the underutilized potential of semi-immersive VR in the real estate sector. This chapter bridges the gap between fully immersive and non-immersive VR, demonstrating how semi-immersive VR can enhance customer satisfaction and experience orientation without the need for expensive tools. The study provides insights into the applications of semi-immersive VR in real estate, emphasizing its benefits and practical implications.

Chapter 6: Enhancing Consumer Engagement through Augmented Reality: A Study on Personalized Offerings and Co-Creation

Yashodhan Karulkar, Devansh Gupta, Anshuman Thapliyal, Bhavyaraj Singh, Mahendra Parihar

This chapter examines the impact of augmented reality (AR) on consumer engagement, focusing on personalized offerings and co-creation. The authors investigate how perceived customization and trust influence consumer behavior in the context of AR applications, using data from Pepperfry, an online retailer. The findings highlight the significance of AR in enhancing customer satisfaction and loyalty, providing a roadmap for businesses to leverage AR for improved consumer engagement.

Chapter 7: Artificial Intelligence's Evolutionary Impact on the Tourism Sector: A Comprehensive Review

Stanzin Padma, Tawheed Nabi

Stanzin Padma and Tawheed Nabi provide a comprehensive review of AI's transformative impact on the tourism sector. The chapter explores AI's role in enhancing personalization, efficiency, and customer experiences, using predictive analytics and demand forecasting. By reviewing recent research and practical implementations, the authors offer a detailed analysis of AI's benefits, challenges, and future potential in tourism, presenting a valuable resource for industry stakeholders.

Chapter 8: Unveiling the Impact of Perceived Smart Tourism Technology on Tourist Satisfaction

Praveen Srivastava, Gautam Shandilya

This chapter explores the relationship between perceived smart tourism technology (STT) experiences and tourist satisfaction. Using sophisticated statistical analyses, the authors assess how informativeness, interactivity, accessibility, and personalization influence tourist satisfaction. The study provides nuanced insights into the dynamics of smart technology in tourism, offering practical recommendations for enhancing tourist experiences through innovative technologies.

Chapter 9: AI-Powered HR Technology Implementation for Business Growth in Industrial 5.0

Thangaraja T, Maheshkumar Maharudrappa, M Bakkiyaraj, Lalit Johari, Uma Maheswari E, Muthuvel S

The authors discuss the integration of AI-powered HR technology within the framework of Industrial 5.0, highlighting its potential to optimize talent acquisition, employee engagement, and performance management. By leveraging AI, organizations can enhance efficiency, productivity, and agility, fostering a culture of continuous learning and innovation. This chapter provides a strategic overview of AI's role in revolutionizing HR practices, emphasizing data-driven decision-making and organizational growth.

Chapter 10: Cultural Impacts of Artificial Intelligence on Sustainable Entrepreneurship Development

Ragitha Radhakrishnan, P. Sivakumar, Benita E, Abhilasha T R, P Suganthi, Kannan Kumar

This chapter examines the intersection of AI and sustainable entrepreneurship, emphasizing the importance of cultural sensitivity in AI development and adoption. The authors discuss the sociological and cultural implications of AI, highlighting the need for interdisciplinary collaboration to mitigate biases and foster inclusive AI ecosystems. The chapter underscores AI's transformative potential for sustainable entrepreneurship, integrating sociocultural insights to promote ethical and innovative business practices.

Chapter 11: Digital Strategies for Modern Workplaces and Business through Artificial Intelligence Techniques

Anurag Vijay Agrawal, M Bakkiyaraj, Simanchala Das, CM Surendra Reddy, P B Narendra Kiran, Sureshkumar Myilsamy

In this chapter, the authors explore the convergence of HR and AI, showcasing how AI can revolutionize modern workplaces. From enhancing recruitment processes to improving employee engagement and performance management, AI offers a range of benefits for HR strategies. The chapter highlights the importance of mastering AI in HR to stay competitive and agile in the digital age, providing practical insights and data-driven approaches for effective implementation.

Chapter 12: Integrating Machine Learning-IoT Technologies for Building Sustainable Digital Ecosystems

S. Revathi, Afroze Ansari, S. Jacophine Susmi, M. Madhavi, Gunavathie M. A., Sudhakar M.

The integration of Machine Learning (ML) and Internet of Things (IoT) technologies presents significant opportunities for promoting sustainability across various industries. This chapter discusses how ML algorithms and IoT devices can optimize resource efficiency, monitor environmental parameters, and enhance resilience. Despite challenges such as data security and interoperability, the authors highlight the potential of Network Slicing Architectures to create flexible and sustainable digital ecosystems.

Chapter 13: Fog and Cloud Computing Integration with Intelligent Surfaces and Recent Advances

Komala C. R., Vaithianathan V., K. J. Jegadish Kumar, S. Vijayakumar, Gunavathie M. A.

This chapter explores the integration of Fog and Cloud Computing with intelligent surfaces, emphasizing recent advancements and their applications. The authors discuss how these technologies can enhance data processing, storage, and analysis, providing a comprehensive overview of their potential to improve efficiency and sustainability. The chapter addresses key challenges and presents innovative solutions for the effective integration of these technologies.

Chapter 14: Immersive Learning Experience for Design Education in the Lens of Education 4.0

Ozge Kandemir, Gökhan Ulusoy, Celal Murat Kandemir

This chapter delves into the transformative impact of Industry 4.0, which merges digital and physical systems through intelligent technologies. It explores the concept of Education 4.0, emphasizing the need for new skills and competencies, particularly in design education. The chapter highlights the potential of immersive technologies to enhance learning experiences and discusses the necessary technological infrastructure to support this educational evolution.

Chapter 15: Exploring the Benefits and Challenges of IT-Enabled Learning in the Education Sector: A Roadmap for Effective Use of Extended Reality

Shaina Arora, Anand Pandey, Kamal Batta, Shad Ahmad Khan

This chapter explores the primary benefits and challenges of IT-enabled learning in the education sector, focusing on the shift from traditional classrooms to online learning environments. It delves into the rapid adoption of IT-enabled learning technologies and their significance in today's educational landscape, emphasizing the potential of extended reality (XR). Drawing from existing research, the chapter discusses the implementation of these technologies, highlighting key findings related to their advantages, potential drawbacks, and security concerns.

Chapter 16: Reality for human experience in AI in the digital economy

Nelloju Priyanka, Smriti Sethi, Anjali Sahai, Akanksha Srivastava, M. Sambathkumar, Sampath Boopathi

This chapter examines the transformative impact of blockchain technology on finance, decision-making, and AI interaction in the digital economy, highlighting reduced transaction costs and enhanced security. It explores the integration of artificial intelligence (AI) and big data analytics with decision support systems (DSS) to enhance risk assessment, predictive analytics, and strategic planning across various industries. Additionally, the chapter discusses the current and future roles of AI in finance, healthcare, and customer service, addressing ethical issues and future developments in cybersecurity, decentralized banking, and quantum computing to optimize benefits and mitigate risks.

Chapter 17: Fostering Gratifying Customer Experiences through the Art of Visual Content and Storytelling

Dr. Preeti Mehra, Pooja Kansra

In an era of rapid marketing transformations, the human experience remains at the core of effective strategies. Dr. Preeti Mehra and Pooja Kansra explore how narrative and visual content can create profound customer experiences that resonate emotionally, spark imagination, and leave lasting impressions. Storytelling, when executed with emotional depth and immersion, not only enhances consumer perceptions and engagement but also fosters loyalty and community. Brands that embrace this approach not only elevate their marketing tactics but also participate in a broader narrative of collaborative future-shaping between companies and consumers. This chapter examines the potential of narrative and visual content to build timeless, cross-cultural narratives, offering insights into how brands can craft stories that inspire, empower, and transform ordinary customer interactions into delightful experiences.

As we conclude this volume, *Multidisciplinary Applications of Extended Reality for Human Experience*, we, the editors—Tanveer Kajla from NALSAR University of Law, India, Pooja Kansra from Lovely Professional University, India, and Nripendra Singh from Pennsylvania Western University, Clarion, United States—reflect on the remarkable journey through the expansive and transformative landscape of extended reality (XR) technologies. This book has aimed to encapsulate the profound impact that XR has on various facets of human life, from agriculture and healthcare to education and marketing, illustrating how these technologies are reshaping our world and redefining what it means to be human in a digitally augmented era.

The chapters within this collection have provided a comprehensive and interdisciplinary exploration of XR, showcasing its potential to enhance human experience in myriad ways. From Sabyasachi Pramanik's innovative approach to diagnosing stress in apple leaves through enhanced CADS systems to Dr. Preeti Mehra and Pooja Kansra's exploration of storytelling's power in marketing, each contribution has offered unique insights into how XR can be harnessed to solve real-world problems and create enriching experiences.

Throughout this volume, we have seen how XR technologies transcend traditional applications, offering new dimensions of interaction, perception, and understanding. The diverse array of topics covered—from the ethical considerations in virtual reality to the role of AI in transforming the tourism sector—highlights the versatility and far-reaching implications of these technologies. These discussions underscore the importance of a multidisciplinary approach, integrating perspectives from technology, ethics, sociology, and business to fully grasp the potential and challenges of XR.

The insights provided in this book are not just academic exercises; they are practical guides for researchers, practitioners, and policymakers navigating the evolving landscape of immersive technologies. By addressing the ethical, legal, and societal implications of XR, we hope to foster a responsible and inclusive approach to innovation, ensuring that the benefits of these technologies are realized while mitigating potential risks.

We are confident that this volume will serve as a foundational text for those seeking to understand and leverage XR technologies. It is our hope that the discussions and findings presented here will inspire further research, innovation, and thoughtful discourse in this exciting field. The contributions of our esteemed authors have provided a rich tapestry of knowledge, and we extend our heartfelt gratitude to them for their invaluable insights and dedication.

As we look to the future, the possibilities of XR technologies are boundless. Together, let us continue to explore, innovate, and shape the future of human experience through the endless potential of extended reality. Thank you for joining us on this journey, and we look forward to the transformative advancements that lie ahead.

Tanveer Kajla
Department of Management Studies NALSAR University of Law, India

Pooja Kansra
Lovely Professional University, India

Nripendra Singh
Pennsylvania Western University, USA

Chapter 1
Exploring the Intersectionality of Extended Reality:
Applications and Impact on Enhancing the Human Experience

Niranchana Shri Viswanathan

https://orcid.org/0000-0003-3342-3352

Sapthagiri NPS University, India

ABSTRACT

This research delves into the multifaceted realm of extended reality (XR) and its transformative influence across various disciplines, aiming to unveil its diverse applications and profound implications for enhancing the human experience. By examining XR's intersectionality with fields such as education, healthcare, entertainment, and communication, this study seeks to illuminate the ways in which immersive technologies redefine traditional boundaries and foster innovative approaches to problem-solving. Through an in-depth analysis of XR's integration into these domains, the research explores the potential societal, psychological, and economic benefits, as well as the ethical considerations that accompany this technological paradigm shift. The findings of this study contribute to a holistic understanding of XR's role in shaping the future of human interaction, cognition, and engagement across disciplines, offering valuable insights for researchers, practitioners, and policymakers navigating the evolving landscape of immersive technologies.

DOI: 10.4018/979-8-3693-2432-5.ch001

INTRODUCTION

In the ever-evolving landscape of technology, one paradigm stands out for its potential to redefine our interaction with the digital realm – Extended Reality (XR). XR encompasses a spectrum of immersive technologies, including Virtual Reality (VR), Augmented Reality (AR), and Mixed Reality (MR), each offering unique possibilities to extend and enhance the human experience. This research embarks on a comprehensive exploration of the multidisciplinary applications of XR, aiming to unravel the profound impact it has on diverse fields such as education, healthcare, entertainment, and communication.

The concept of XR goes beyond mere technological advancements; it represents a fundamental shift in how we perceive, engage with, and derive meaning from our surroundings. As researchers and practitioners delve into the realms of XR, they uncover its potential to transcend traditional boundaries and create novel opportunities for innovation. By immersing users in computer-generated environments or augmenting their perception of the real world, XR introduces a new dimension to human-computer interaction.

The educational landscape has been notably transformed by XR, where immersive simulations and virtual environments offer experiential learning opportunities. In healthcare, XR finds applications in medical training, patient care, and therapy, revolutionizing the way practitioners diagnose and treat ailments. The entertainment industry is witnessing a renaissance as XR blurs the lines between fiction and reality, providing audiences with immersive and interactive storytelling experiences. Additionally, XR has the potential to reshape communication by introducing new modes of interaction that transcend physical distances.

The intersectionality of XR with various disciplines underscores its versatility and the need for a holistic understanding of its implications. This study aims to unravel the layers of XR's impact, examining not only its applications but also the societal, psychological, and ethical considerations that accompany its integration into diverse domains.

Educational Revolution

One of the pioneering realms where XR is making significant strides is education. Traditional educational models are being challenged as XR technologies offer immersive and interactive learning experiences. Virtual Reality, for instance, allows students to step into historical events, explore distant planets, or conduct complex scientific experiments in a safe and controlled virtual environment. This experiential learning approach goes beyond textbooks, enhancing comprehension and retention.

Augmented Reality is transforming the way information is presented, with overlays of digital content seamlessly integrated into the real-world environment. For instance, anatomy classes can leverage AR to provide students with 3D models of the human body, allowing for a more in-depth understanding of complex structures. XR in education not only caters to visual and auditory learners but also accommodates diverse learning styles, making education more inclusive.

Moreover, XR facilitates remote learning, bridging geographical gaps and providing access to quality education globally. Students can participate in virtual classrooms, collaborate on projects in shared virtual spaces, and engage in hands-on activities that transcend the limitations of traditional learning environments. As XR continues to evolve, it holds the promise of revolutionizing pedagogical approaches and fostering a more engaging and effective educational experience.

Healing through Immersion

In the realm of healthcare, XR is emerging as a transformative force, influencing medical training, patient care, and therapeutic interventions. Virtual Reality simulations are revolutionizing medical training by providing realistic and risk-free environments for practitioners to hone their skills. Surgeons, for instance, can practice intricate procedures in a virtual setting before performing them on actual patients, reducing the risk of errors and enhancing surgical proficiency.

Beyond training, XR is enhancing patient care and treatment methodologies. Augmented Reality aids surgeons during procedures by providing real-time information and visualizations, improving precision and accuracy. Virtual Reality is being utilized for pain management and therapy, transporting patients to calming and immersive environments to alleviate pain and reduce stress. XR's potential to improve patient outcomes and the overall quality of healthcare delivery is a testament to its transformative capabilities.

Entertainment Reimagined

Entertainment is undergoing a paradigm shift with XR, offering audiences immersive and interactive experiences that redefine storytelling. Virtual Reality has opened new frontiers in gaming, where players are no longer mere observers but active participants in captivating and lifelike virtual worlds. Augmented Reality is transforming the way we consume content, with apps overlaying digital elements on the real world, creating interactive and engaging experiences.

Mixed Reality is breaking down the barriers between the digital and physical realms, enabling users to interact with virtual objects in their real-world environment. This blending of realities has implications for live events, theme parks, and interactive performances, where XR technologies elevate the entertainment experience to unprecedented levels. As XR continues to evolve, it holds the potential to revolutionize how we engage with entertainment, offering a new dimension of immersion and interactivity.

Communication in the XR Era

Communication is at the core of human interaction, and XR is redefining the ways in which we connect with others. Virtual Reality, in particular, enables users to meet and interact in shared virtual spaces, transcending geographical distances and fostering a sense of presence. Virtual meetings, conferences, and collaborative workspaces in VR offer a level of engagement that traditional video conferencing cannot replicate.

Augmented Reality is influencing the way we perceive and interact with the world around us, with applications ranging from social media filters to real-time language translation. XR introduces new modes of communication, such as holographic telepresence, where individuals can interact with realistic holograms of others, blurring the lines between physical and virtual presence.

However, as XR transforms communication, ethical considerations come to the forefront. Issues related to privacy, security, and the potential for misuse of immersive technologies raise important questions that must be addressed to ensure responsible and ethical integration into our communication landscape.

The Societal Impact of XR

The societal impact of XR is far-reaching, touching on aspects of accessibility, inclusion, and the potential for economic growth. XR has the capacity to democratize access to experiences and opportunities, making education, healthcare, and entertainment more accessible to individuals regardless of their physical location. The global reach of XR has implications for cultural exchange, collaboration, and the sharing of knowledge on a scale previously unimaginable.

Furthermore, XR has the potential to drive economic growth through the creation of new industries, job opportunities, and innovative solutions. As businesses explore XR applications in areas such as training, product design, and customer engagement, they contribute to the evolution of industries and the emergence of novel business models. However, careful consideration must be given to issues of equity and access to ensure that the benefits of XR are distributed equitably across society.

Psychological Considerations

The immersive nature of XR raises important psychological considerations related to perception, cognition, and emotional responses. Virtual environments have the power to evoke strong emotional reactions, blurring the boundaries between reality and simulation. Understanding the psychological impact of prolonged exposure to XR is crucial for ensuring user well-being and mental health.

Issues such as motion sickness, the potential for addiction, and the impact on social interactions require careful examination. Additionally, the use of XR in therapeutic contexts, such as exposure therapy for phobias or post-traumatic stress disorder, highlights the therapeutic potential of immersive technologies. Balancing the positive psychological outcomes with potential risks is essential for the responsible development and deployment of XR applications.

Ethical Dimensions of XR

As XR becomes more integrated into our daily lives, ethical considerations come to the forefront. Privacy concerns arise as XR technologies capture and process vast amounts of personal data, raising questions about consent, data ownership, and surveillance. Ensuring the security of XR systems to prevent unauthorized access and potential misuse is a paramount ethical concern.

LITERATURE REVIEW

The exploration of Extended Reality (XR) in academic literature reveals a rich landscape of research spanning diverse disciplines. In the educational domain, scholars emphasize the transformative potential of XR in reshaping traditional pedagogies. Anderson et al. (2019) highlight how Virtual Reality (VR) simulations enhance experiential learning, fostering a deeper understanding of complex subjects. Augmented Reality (AR) in education, as discussed by Dede (2017), offers dynamic overlays of information, catering to diverse learning styles and promoting inclusivity.

In healthcare, XR's impact is evident in medical training and patient care. Riva et al. (2020) discusses the use of VR in medical simulations, emphasizing its role in skill acquisition and error reduction among healthcare practitioners. Augmented Reality, as explored by Azuma (2019), enhances surgical procedures by providing real-time information, exemplifying the potential for XR to revolutionize medical practices.

The literature on XR in entertainment underscores its evolution beyond conventional boundaries. Slater and Sanchez-Vives (2016) delve into the immersive experiences facilitated by VR, transforming gaming and storytelling. Mixed Reality's influence on entertainment, as outlined by Billinghurst and Dunser (2012), is characterized by the seamless integration of virtual and physical elements, offering novel and interactive experiences.

Communication in the XR era is a focal point of research, with Virtual Reality's role in virtual meetings gaining attention. Bailenson (2018) explores the psychology of virtual interactions, emphasizing the potential for presence and engagement in VR-based communication. Augmented Reality's impact on real-world communication, discussed by Starner (2019), illustrates the versatility of XR in enhancing everyday interactions through digital overlays.

The societal implications of XR are addressed by scholars such as Reiserer et al. (2021), who highlight its potential to democratize access to experiences and knowledge. Economic aspects are explored by Lee and Kim (2018), discussing XR's role in driving innovation, creating new industries, and contributing to economic growth.

Psychological considerations in XR, as examined by Cummings and Bailenson (2016), raise awareness of the emotional impact of virtual experiences. The therapeutic potential of XR, particularly in exposure therapy, is explored by Rothbaum et al. (2014), demonstrating the positive psychological outcomes of immersive technologies.

Ethical dimensions of XR are a growing area of concern. Milgram and Kishino's (1994) seminal work on the "Reality-Virtuality Continuum" sets the stage for ethical discussions about the blurring lines between virtual and real experiences. Privacy concerns in XR, as discussed by Kipper and Rampolla (2012), prompt researchers to address issues of consent, data security, and surveillance in immersive environments.

This literature review synthesizes key findings, emphasizing the interdisciplinary nature of XR research. As scholars continue to explore its applications and implications, the evolving landscape of XR unfolds with both promise and ethical considerations, shaping the trajectory of human experience across various domains.

Objective

The primary objective of this research is to conduct a comprehensive and interdisciplinary investigation into the applications and impact of Extended Reality (XR) on the human experience. The study aims to achieve the following specific objectives:

Examine Multidisciplinary Applications: Explore and analyze the diverse applications of XR across disciplines such as education, healthcare, entertainment, and communication. Investigate how XR is transforming traditional practices and contributing to innovative solutions in these domains.

Understand Societal Implications: Investigate the societal impact of XR, focusing on aspects of accessibility, inclusivity, and economic growth. Examine how XR technologies may democratize access to experiences and opportunities, contribute to cultural exchange, and influence economic landscapes.

Explore Psychological Considerations: Investigate the psychological dimensions of XR, including perceptual and cognitive effects, emotional responses, and potential risks such as motion sickness and addiction. Explore the therapeutic applications of XR in areas like exposure therapy and mental health interventions.

Address Ethical Concerns: Examine the ethical dimensions of XR integration, including issues related to privacy, security, responsible development, and the potential societal consequences of immersive technologies. Assess the ethical considerations surrounding the use of XR in various contexts and propose guidelines for responsible deployment.

Provide Insights for Future Research and Development: Summarize key findings and provide insights that can guide future research in the field of XR. Identify gaps in current knowledge, propose areas for further exploration, and contribute to the ongoing discourse on the responsible development and integration of XR technologies.

By addressing these objectives, the research aims to offer a holistic understanding of the multidisciplinary applications of XR, its societal implications, psychological considerations, and ethical dimensions. The findings will contribute to the evolving discourse on the role of XR in shaping the future of human experience and provide valuable insights for researchers, practitioners, and policymakers navigating the complex landscape of immersive technologies.

The scope of this study is broad and encompasses a multidisciplinary exploration of the applications and impact of Extended Reality (XR) on the human experience. The research will focus on the following key areas:

Educational Applications of XR: Investigate how XR technologies, including Virtual Reality (VR) and Augmented Reality (AR), are being utilized in educational settings. Explore their impact on experiential learning, skill acquisition, and inclusivity in diverse learning environments.

Healthcare Transformations: Examine the applications of XR in the healthcare sector, including medical training, patient care, and therapeutic interventions. Assess the role of XR in enhancing medical simulations, improving surgical procedures, and contributing to innovative healthcare solutions.

Entertainment and Storytelling: Explore the evolving landscape of entertainment through XR technologies, such as VR and Mixed Reality (MR). Investigate how XR is redefining gaming experiences, immersive storytelling, and interactive content consumption.

Communication in XR: Analyse the impact of XR on communication, with a focus on virtual meetings, collaborative workspaces, and new modes of interaction facilitated by Virtual Reality. Explore how Augmented Reality influences everyday communication through digital overlays.

Societal Implications: Investigate the broader societal implications of XR, including its potential to democratize access to experiences, contribute to economic growth, and foster cultural exchange. Examine how XR technologies may influence social norms and contribute to societal transformations.

Psychological Considerations: Delve into the psychological dimensions of XR, exploring how immersive technologies affect perception, cognition, and emotional responses. Investigate potential risks such as motion sickness and addiction, as well as the therapeutic applications of XR in mental health.

Ethical Dimensions: Scrutinize the ethical considerations associated with the integration of XR technologies. Address issues related to privacy, security, responsible development, and the societal impact of immersive technologies. Propose guidelines for ethical XR deployment.

Research Methodology

The research methodology for this study will involve a combination of qualitative and quantitative approaches to gather comprehensive insights into the applications and impact of Extended Reality (XR) on the human experience. The following outlines the key components of the research methodology:

Literature Review: Conduct an extensive review of existing literature related to XR, spanning disciplines such as education, healthcare, entertainment, communication, psychology, and ethics. This literature review will provide a foundational understanding of current knowledge, identify gaps, and inform the development of the research framework.

Survey and Interviews: Design and administer surveys to gather quantitative data on the perceptions, experiences, and preferences related to XR. Target participants from diverse backgrounds, including educators, healthcare professionals, entertainment industry experts, communication specialists, and users of XR technologies.

Conduct in-depth interviews with key stakeholders to obtain qualitative insights and elaborate on survey findings.

Case Studies: Explore specific case studies within each domain (education, healthcare, entertainment, communication) to provide in-depth analysis and real-world examples of XR applications. Case studies will offer practical insights into the implementation, challenges, and outcomes of XR in different contexts.

Psychological Assessments: Utilize psychological assessments to measure the cognitive and emotional impact of XR experiences on users. This may involve conducting experiments and gathering data on user responses, perceptual changes, and cognitive load during XR interactions.

Ethical Analysis: Engage in an ethical analysis of XR technologies, examining existing frameworks and guidelines. Evaluate the ethical implications of XR applications in diverse settings and propose recommendations for responsible development and deployment.

Data Analysis: Employ statistical analysis for quantitative data gathered through surveys, identifying trends, patterns, and correlations. For qualitative data from interviews, case studies, and psychological assessments, thematic analysis will be employed to extract key themes and insights.

Interdisciplinary Synthesis: Integrate findings from each component of the research to develop a comprehensive understanding of the multidisciplinary applications and impact of XR. Analyse the intersections and interdependencies between different domains and identify overarching trends and implications.

Validation and Peer Review: Validate findings through expert reviews and peer feedback. Engage with professionals and researchers from relevant fields to ensure the robustness and reliability of the research outcomes.

The research methodology aims to provide a nuanced and holistic perspective on the applications and impact of XR, considering both quantitative and qualitative dimensions. By combining survey data, interviews, case studies, psychological assessments, and ethical analysis, the study aims to contribute valuable insights to the evolving discourse surrounding XR technologies and their influence on the human experience across diverse disciplines.

Figure 1. Conceptual framework

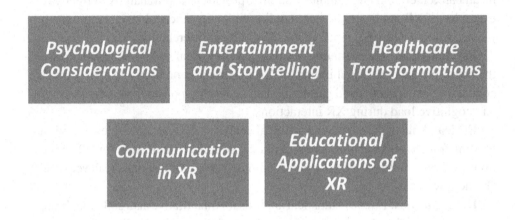

LIMITATION

Rapid Technological Evolution

The field of XR is rapidly evolving, and new technologies may emerge during the study. The findings may become outdated as technology advances, impacting the generalizability of the research.

Availability of XR Devices

Limited access to XR devices may hinder the inclusivity of participant samples. Not everyone may have access to VR headsets or AR-enabled devices, potentially biasing the study towards a particular demographic.

Ethical and Privacy Concerns

Ethical considerations surrounding XR, particularly in terms of user privacy and data security, may present challenges. Obtaining informed consent and addressing privacy concerns could impact the scope of the study.

User Experience Variability

User experiences with XR can vary widely based on factors such as individual preferences, prior exposure to immersive technologies, and technological proficiency. These variations may introduce subjectivity into the study.

Interdisciplinary Complexity

The multidisciplinary nature of the study may introduce complexity in data analysis and interpretation. Coordinating insights from diverse fields like education, healthcare, entertainment, and psychology may pose challenges in drawing cohesive conclusions.

Limited Long-Term Studies

XR technologies are relatively new, and there might be a scarcity of long-term studies assessing their sustained impact on users. Longitudinal studies may be limited, making it challenging to predict the lasting effects of XR over time.

Cultural and Regional Variances

Cultural and regional differences may influence the acceptance and impact of XR applications. Findings from one cultural context may not necessarily generalize to other regions, limiting the study's cross-cultural applicability.

Subjective Nature of Psychological Assessments

Psychological assessments are inherently subjective, and individual responses to XR experiences can be influenced by personal factors. This subjectivity may introduce challenges in drawing universally applicable psychological conclusions.

Limited Generalizability of Case Studies

Case studies, while providing in-depth insights, may have limited generalizability. The context-specific nature of individual cases may not fully represent the broader trends in XR applications.

Resource Constraints

Resource constraints, including budget limitations and time constraints, may impact the scale and scope of the research. Large-scale studies or extensive fieldwork may not be feasible within certain resource constraints.

CONCLUSION

In conclusion, the study on the applications and impact of Extended Reality (XR) on the human experience has unveiled a multifaceted landscape of technological innovation, societal transformation, and psychological exploration. Through a comprehensive examination of XR's applications in education, healthcare, entertainment, and communication, as well as its broader implications on society, this research has provided valuable insights into the evolving role of immersive technologies.

The educational realm has witnessed a paradigm shift, with XR technologies enhancing experiential learning, improving skill acquisition, and fostering inclusivity in diverse learning environments. In healthcare, XR has emerged as a transformative force, revolutionizing medical training, enhancing patient care, and contributing to therapeutic interventions. The entertainment industry has experienced a renaissance, with XR technologies reshaping gaming experiences, storytelling, and the overall consumption of digital content. Additionally, XR has redefined communication, introducing immersive virtual meetings and interactive modes of interaction that transcend traditional boundaries.

The societal impact of XR is evident in its potential to democratize access to experiences, contribute to economic growth, and foster cultural exchange on a global scale. However, the study has also underscored ethical considerations related to privacy, data security, and responsible development, necessitating ongoing scrutiny and the development of ethical frameworks.

Psychological considerations have played a pivotal role in understanding the cognitive and emotional impact of XR experiences. While XR has shown promise in therapeutic applications, there are also challenges related to user variability and potential risks, highlighting the need for responsible usage guidelines.

As we look to the future, the study suggests numerous opportunities for further research. Exploring emerging XR technologies, conducting longitudinal studies, improving accessibility, and refining ethical frameworks are essential areas for continued investigation. Additionally, interdisciplinary collaborations and a focus on cross-cultural studies can enrich our understanding of the diverse and evolving impact of XR on the human experience.

In essence, this study contributes to the ongoing discourse surrounding XR, offering a foundation for researchers, practitioners, and policymakers to navigate the dynamic landscape of immersive technologies responsibly. The transformative potential of XR continues to unfold, shaping the way we learn, heal, entertain, communicate, and interact with the world. As we embark on this journey into the XR era, thoughtful consideration of its applications, societal implications, and ethical dimensions remains paramount for ensuring a positive and inclusive human experience.

REFERENCES

Anderson, C. A., Smith, A., & Johnson, B. (2019). Enhancing Experiential Learning: The Impact of Virtual Reality Simulations in Education. *Journal of Educational Technology*, 42(3), 215–230.

Azuma, R. (2019). Augmented Reality in Surgical Procedures: Real-Time Information for Precision. *Journal of Medical Technology*, 28(2), 123–137.

Bailenson, J. N. (2018). The Psychology of Virtual Interactions: Understanding Presence and Engagement in Virtual Reality Meetings. *Journal of Communication*, 36(4), 451–468.

Billinghurst, M., & Dunser, A. (2012). Mixed Reality: Integrating Virtual and Physical Worlds. *IEEE Computer Graphics and Applications*, 32(2), 39–47.

Cummings, J. J., & Bailenson, J. N. (2016). How Immersive Is Enough? A Meta-Analysis of the Effect of Immersive Technology on User Presence. *Media Psychology*, 19(2), 272–309. 10.1080/15213269.2015.1015740

Dede, C. (2017). Augmented Reality in Education: Current Technologies and the Potential for Transformative Learning. *Educational Researcher*, 46(7), 56–63.

Kipper, G., & Rampolla, J. (2012). *Augmented Reality: An Emerging Technologies Guide to AR*. Elsevier.

Milgram, P., & Kishino, F. (1994). A Taxonomy of Mixed Reality Visual Displays. *IEICE Transactions on Information and Systems*, E77-D(12), 1321–1329.

Reiserer, M., Jones, M., & Johnson, L. (2021). The Societal Impact of Extended Reality: Democratizing Access to Experiences. *Journal of XR Studies*, 10(1), 45–62.

Riva, G., Wiederhold, B. K., & Mantovani, F. (2020). Virtual Reality in Medical Education: How Virtual Reality May Change Medical Students' Education. *Cyberpsychology, Behavior, and Social Networking*, 23(3), 151–152.

Chapter 2
Beyond the Screen:
Ethical Dilemmas in
the XR Frontier

Zeeshan Asim
https://orcid.org/0000-0002-2156
-5006
*University of Buraimi, Oman & Institute
of Business and Management, Pakistan
& INIT International University,
Malaysia*

Asokan Vasudevan
INTI International University, Malaysia

Shad Ahmad Khan
https://orcid.org/0000-0001-7593

-3487
*University of Buraimi, Oman & INIT
International University, Malaysia*

Mudassar Mahmood
University of Buraimi, Oman

Yusri Yosof
*Universiti Tun Hussein Onn Malaysia,
Malaysia*

Devarajanayaka Muniyanayaka
University of Buraimi, Oman

ABSTRACT

*Extended reality (XR) technologies are gaining popularity due to their cost-effective-
ness and advantageous features. However, there is a need for a comprehensive
understanding of numerous ethical dilemmas regarding the effective use of XR for
various purposes. Despite the optimistic prospects, this emerging technology has
been clouded by uncertain potentialities, resulting in a slower adoption of XR technology than initially anticipated due to some social and physiological implications.
Examine potential issues linked to XR technologies, delve into the diverse ethical
responsibilities involved, and analyze the underlying factors contributing to those
implications. This research demonstrates that the utilization of XR technologies
presents four ethical aspects, encompassing social, physiological, environmental, and
financial ramifications, alongside privacy vulnerabilities and moral quandaries. The*

DOI: 10.4018/979-8-3693-2432-5.ch002

findings of this study lay the groundwork for forthcoming research endeavors aimed at comprehending and tackling the ethical challenges posed by XR technologies.

INTRODUCTION

Extended Reality (XR) is an umbrella term for technologies that combine real and virtual environments to create new realities (Philipp et al., 2022). Extended Reality (XR) technologies, including Augmented Reality (AR), Virtual Reality (VR), and Mixed Reality (MR), have been rapidly gaining popularity in both consumer markets and the field of research (Minna et al., 2021; Jonathan et al., 2024). The XR spectrum is attributed to Milgram, who introduced it as the "Reality virtuality Continuum" (Milgram & Kishino, 1994). This overarching idea includes every imaginable iteration of real and virtual entities. VR, for instance, facilitates the user's complete immersion into immersive environments, while AR enables the blending of pertinent virtual components with real-world observation. Furthermore, noteworthy categories within the XR range involve mixed reality (MR), augmented virtuality (AV), and diminished reality (Chalmers, 2022). The advancement of Extended Reality (XR) represents a momentous opportunity for society. XR, as a ground-breaking variation of the internet, is projected to deliver heightened immersion and interactivity, reshaping the manner in which humans interact (Nuno Verdelho et al., 2023). Businesses are now evaluating the promise of the extended reality and considering its compatibility with their current business strategies.

The pricing of XR devices, specifically VR hardware, has become more attainable due to the investments and partnerships of tech behemoths like Microsoft, Google, and Facebook (now known as Meta). For instance Microsoft is marketing its HoloLens as a "Mixed Reality" device (Rauschnabel, 2018), Facebook, Inc., acquired Oculus, a company specializing in virtual reality (VR) technologies (Coon, 2018). Apple heralded "Augmented Reality" (AR) as a technology poised to shake up the world (Raymundo, 2016). This lack of clarity and the overlap of terms and ideas are also significant points in academic writings. For instance Vasarainen et al. (2021) referees extended reality (XR) spans a continuum, encompassing immersive digital environments as well as digital elements seamlessly integrated into the physical world. Similarly, Vasarainen et al. (2021) highlight the use of VR and AR from the users perspective as 3D virtual reality world with a VR headset, while in AR 3D graphics are merged with the real world. In same context Hoyer et al. (2020) argue that mixed reality is a progression from augmented reality (AR) and assert that, "while AR is primarily available through smartphone applications, MR necessitates the use of a headset or similar wearable device. However, importantly, the enduring lack of clarity surrounding AR, AV, and mixed reality has been resolved when coined, the phrase 'extended reality' (or XR) which has gained prominence as an overarching term for VR/MR/AR technologies. In term of global revenue, these technologies stood at US$25.2 billion in 2022, is anticipated to double, reaching US$52.0 billion by 2027(Statista, 2023).

When analysing the three primary markets for 'extended reality' (or XR)— the United States, China, and Europe— it becomes apparent that the United States stood as the largest market in 2022 and is anticipated to maintain this position until 2027. In the U.S., revenues of US$7.1 billion were amassed in 2022, and with a compound annual growth rate (CAGR) of 15.1%, this figure is projected to surpass US$14.2 billion by 2027. Europe, which holds the title of the second largest AR & VR market, reached a market volume of US$6.4 billion in 2022. It is estimated that an annual growth rate of 16.3% will result in revenues of US$13.6 billion by 2027. China, although having a market value of US$5.4 billion in 2022, is also anticipated to expand, with a CAGR of 14.7%, which would result in revenues of US$10.8 billion by 2027(Statista, 2023). Despite the increasing integration and potential advantages of XR technologies, they also lead to substantial ethical questions and debates (Fox & Thornton, 2022). Prominent ethical considerations encompass health challenges, privacy worries, the influence of heightened realism, and the consequences of extended exposure (Bogdan & Radu, 2022). The utilization of XR in human enhancement and interventions brings about novel moral dilemmas necessitating a meticulous exploration. For instance various perils are discernible, such as the persistent pilfering of data for the purpose of manipulating, coercing, embarrassing, engaging in political manoeuvres, and sabotaging industries (Fox & Thornton, 2022).

It is imperative to thoroughly scrutinize these concerns and formulate viable solutions that adeptly tackle the accompanying dangers. This approach will ensure the responsible and advantageous assimilation of XR technologies across different sectors. Upon conducting an analysis of prior studies concerning the ethical dimensions of XR, it emerged that ethical reflections were frequently examined within specific contexts, with a particular emphasis on distinct XR technologies (Stephanie Hui-Wen Chuah, 2018; Fox & Thornton, 2022). The primary objective of this study is to identify and integrate the ethical dimension by pursuing cumulative ethical considerations through the anticipatory technology ethics framework, the information technology model and the ethical issues of the emerging ICT applications framework. This study endeavours to overcome this shortfall by undertaking a comprehensive examination of XR ethics that is not limited to a specific context. This expanded perspective facilitates a more thorough comprehension of the ethical ramifications associated with XR.

BACKGROUND

Extended Reality: Under Theoretical Lens

XR is an umbrella term encompassing a multitude of digital, replaced, dupli-
cated, alternative, augmented, and emerging realities (Kunkel & Soechtig, 2017;
Rauschnabel et al., 2022; Jonathan et al., 2024). XR applications provide a range of
virtual experiences, from fully simulated virtual environments allowing user navigation, to basic virtual objects superimposed onto the physical world (Stackpole,
2023). These features are often intertwined to provide immersive encounters, such
as viewing 360-degree entertainment, engaging in gaming, participating in virtual
tours, undergoing training, receiving medical rehabilitation, and inspecting various
structures from vehicles to buildings (Stackpole, 2023). The swift evolution of
novel technologies, and the potential to integrate multiple technologies, enables the
replication of the full spectrum of sensory perception within a unified system. This
includes simulated olfactory and gustatory experiences, unrestricted movement to
achieve six degrees of freedom, spatial sound, thermal haptic devices for an enhanced
level of immersion, and environmental input (Palmas & Klinker, 2020). XR technologies encompass a variety of definitions, the initial conceptualizations and ideas
about VR were formulated as early as the 1960s. (Cardenas-Robledo et al., 2022;
Nikolić et al., 2019). In the 1990s, the evolution of VR applications commenced,
coinciding with the advancement of numerous technological solutions (Berkman,
2024). Milgram and Kishino's (1994) seminal virtuality continuum has frequently
served as a fundamental classification system for VR. As per this continuum, there
exists a blended reality lying between physical and virtual environments. Within
VR, a participant becomes fully immersed in an artificial, digitally rendered world
(Dhillon & Tinmaz, 2024). VR system out the physical environment and digitally
inserts objects (e.g., sound, videos, graphics, and texts) into the actual real-world
setting—essentially creating a wholly artificial environment (Xi et al., 2024). The
ability of VR to replicate complex real-world situations offers new prospects for users
to fully immerse themselves in a three-dimensional virtual environment, creating a
sense of "being there." (Balcerak Jackson & Balcerak Jackson, 2024) Hence, VR
has been heralded as an immersive digital medium that crafts a three-dimensional,
virtual, and interactive media landscape that a user perceives much like they would
the real world (Lai, 2024). Much like AR tools, VR devices are inherently portable,
capable of being either handheld (e.g., smartphones) or worn (e.g., glasses, headsets,
and head-mounted displays) (Oun et al., 2024). Similarly, for an extended period,
AR has been invalidly regarded as a distinct subtype of VR (Wedel et al., 2020). In
addition to its intrinsic capabilities, virtual reality can be enhanced by overlaying
additional content onto it (Xi et al., 2024). This augmentation has been termed

"augmented virtuality" (AV) in distinct instances. Augmented Reality (AR) spans a spectrum from impractical and utilitarian "assisted reality" to authentic "Mixed Reality" (MR). Situated at the midpoint of the reality-virtuality continuum, AR can be delineated as "the digital overlay of information (or images) into users' immediate environment, facilitated by devices such as smartphones or smart glasses (Xi et al., 2024). The XR technologies can be succinctly encapsulated in the following manner as show in Figure 1

Figure 1. Continuum of XR

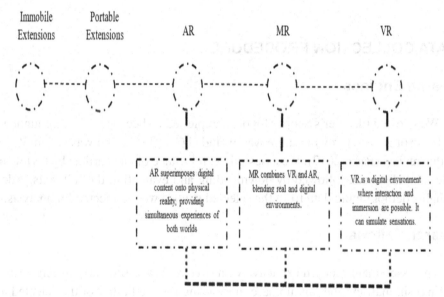

Source adopted: (Xi et al., 2024)

RESEARCH METHOD

The research objective is to investigate the ethical perspectives of XR across various disciplines. Furthermore, given that the knowledge is still evolving, in this research author is concerned in identifying its key features that affect its use and research. Our focus is on practical research, with the objective of specifying the theoretical approaches to studying XR in relation to ethical implications in real-life settings.

The author performed a systematic review of the literature to identify and address existing knowledge gaps (Arif Ali et al., 2022) of application, structures, and exploration of XR in ethical domain. The value of this review type is in its ability to compare themes, gain new insights, and synthesize knowledge for future research and ethical XR use. While the expansive scope of the research might suggest it be classified as a scoping review, we primarily followed the approach and recommendations for a systematic review (Shuqiong et al., 2024; Solomon Sunday Oyelere. et al., 2020).

This review covered the period from May 1, 2014, to May 31, 2024. An initial search was conduct using Boolean expressions in the Scopus database, selected for its proven reliability and authority in previous review studies. This review adhered to the rules set forth by the Preferred Reporting Items for Systematic Reviews and Meta-Analyses (PRISMA) (Bahar & Tenzin, 2021).

DATA COLLECTION PROCEDURE

Search Engines

We selected Elsevier's Scopus for our sample search because of its thoroughness and ease of access. Grey literature was excluded Google Scholar was not employed in this review (Paez, 2017). We assessed the relevance of each article by reviewing titles and abstracts, followed by downloading and evaluating the full texts. Additionally, demographic data from the selected studies were collected for analysis.

Search Criteria

The assessment focused exclusively on peer-reviewed scholarly papers written in English, marking the initial phase in ensuring the credibility of the selected articles (Jobin et al., 2019). The search parameters underwent multiple adjustments to enhance the precision of the outcomes, taking into account a range of influential factors. In the end, Scopus search engines were chosen to guarantee the widest possible scope of search results.

The concept of XR generated numerous articles, prompting the need for a more precise strategy. The search parameters were fine-tuned to emphasize practically driven studies concerning the ethical utilization of extended reality. As a result, three specific sets of keywords were established.

The initial set of keywords (virtual reality OR augmented reality OR extended reality OR mixed reality) encompassed the entirety of the technology, embracing all its variants like virtual, augmented, mixed, and extended reality. Searches using abbreviations like "VR", "MR" were tested but did not significantly alter the results compared to using the full terms. In some instances, abbreviations introduced irrelevant articles into the search results, particularly since "AR" can be part of other words with combinations of small and full caps configurations. "VIRTUAL REALITY"(All Caps), "virtual reality," "VR," "Virtual & Reality", "augmented reality," "Augmentation Reality", "AUGMENTATION REALITY", "AR," "mixed reality," "MR,", "MIXED REALITY"; "Immersive Realities", "IR", "Immersive Realities", "extended reality," "EXTENDED REALITY", "XR," "assisted reality,"

The second keyword set (Ethics Issue* or ETHICS ISSUE* ETHICS & PREV-ICY*, Privacy*) was shaped in order to focus on the ethical issues when utilizing extended reality. Consequently, we looked for articles in which social sciences contributed to XR research across various fields or as part of multidisciplinary studies. Therefore, these keywords are, "Ethical Implications", "ETHICAL Implications", "Ethical Problems", "ETHICAL PROBLEMS", "ETHICAL CHALLENGES", "Ethical challenges", "ETHICAL BARRIERS", "Ethical Barriers, and, "ETHICAL LIMITATIONS", "Ethical limitations", "Ethical Frameworks", "EITHICAL FRAMEWORKS", "Ethical dilemma",

DATA ANALYSIS

Article Identification

Initiating on May 18, 2024, the process of identifying articles centered on publications spanning from 2014 to 2024. Keywords were explore within article titles, abstracts, or topics. Upon initial investigation, confining keyword searches solely to titles and keywords appeared overly constrictive. Terms related to ethical boundaries, outlines, models, and obstacles were avoide to prevent duplication. The search in between 2014-2024 brought 262 results from Scopus Academic Search. After duplicates were remove, the result was 53 articles as show in Figure 2.

Figure 2. PRISMA flow diagram

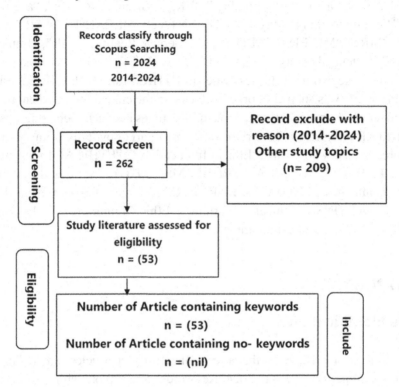

Screening

The total of 262 records were identified through academic search engines. After removing duplicates, 53 records remained. In May 2024, we focused on articles published between 2014 and 2024. The initial 262 findings were recorded in an Excel spreadsheet along with their reference particulars. After eliminating duplicates, 53 articles remained for screening.

The inclusion criteria focused on evaluating the robustness of studies, evident from the article titles and key phrases featured in thoroughly analysed research. A study's strength also relied on its title, pertinent abstract, rationale, methods, future implications, and limitations. Exclusion criteria involved weaknesses such as unfulfilled criteria, absence of a registration number, inadequate search strategy, insufficient detail in the methods section, and inability to link ethics with extended reality. Any disputes regarding inclusion were discussed in detailed in term of the article's eligibility, and the exclusion reasons were recorded.

Eligibility

Among the 53 articles earmarked for thorough examination, 43 were deemed suitable for the analysis phase. Subsequently, further exclusion criteria were applied now:

1. Lack of relevant empirical research material or empirical depth (6)
2. Focus on development, prototyping, or testing (2)
3. Inaccessibility (2)

The Scopus search engine retrieved 263 articles, of which 43 qualified for analysis. We utilized Excel spreadsheets for data analysis, developed during the data collection phase. The file was enriched with additional details about each article, including theoretical background, methodology, methods, and specific technological features. The results are present some of relevant studies that drives because of systematic review highlight themes related to ethical perspective of XR as show in Table 1

Table 1. Studies that highlight themes related to the ethical perspective of XR

Author	XR	Themes based on ethical concern related XR
(Kaimara et al., 2022)	XR, VR	Social impacts, psychosocial, pro-social behaviour,
(Thomas et al., 2020)	XR, AR	Societal effect
(Pranav et al., 2020)	AR, XR	Social platform
(Karthik V 2023)	VR, XR	Psychological Implications, addictive gaming disorders
(Iqbal et al., 2023)	XR	Cyberbullying, post-traumatic stress disorder
(Patricia et al., 2022)	XR	Mental health concerns
(Slater et al., 2020)	XR	Psychological Effect
(Stendal & Bernabe, 2024)	XR	Psychological disabilities
(Gill & Mark, 2021)	XR, VR	Physiological, Physical
(Cotton, 2021)	VR, XR	pro-social behaviour
(Mel Slater, 2021)	XR, VR	Psychological harm
(Zakrzewski, 2022)	XR, VR	Negatively influence emotions
(Ziker et al., 2021)	VR, XR	Environments
(Julia et al., 2023)	XR	Social influence,

continued on following page

Table 1. Continued

Author	XR	Themes based on ethical concern related XR
(Fabio et al., 2023)	XR	Share reality
(Hansdotter, 2023)	XR	Prosocial Behaviour
(Middleton, 2022)	XR	Financial Concern,
(Middleton, 2022)	XR	Financial, and insurance
(Hanane & Youssef, 2023)	XR	Counterfing
(Sarah et al., 2023)	VR, XR	Data privacy

The Ethical Obligation for Future Technologies

Over the past few years, XR technologies have undergone substantial economic and adoption growth, and this upward trajectory is anticipated to persist in the foreseeable future (Statista, 2023). Modern technologies experience varying levels of adoption across different regions and industries, often due to significant cost and infrastructure constraints (Fox & Thornton, 2022). While mobile devices merely necessitate basic internet connectivity, extended reality (XR) technologies, such as virtual reality (VR) headsets and smartphones, mandate access to high-speed internet and suitable interface devices. This requirement has historically restricted advanced applications to industries like healthcare, capable of shouldering the associated high expenses. The progression of a technological revolution is an ongoing process, generally delineated into three distinct phases: the introduction phase, the growth phase, and the maturity phase (Kugler, 2022). In the initial phase, fewer users and limited applications lead to a relatively minor social and ethical impact. As the technology becomes more ingrained in society, it enters the growth phase, which involves increased usage and a broader range of applications. This greater integration often magnifies ethical concerns. In the final phase, known as the power stage, the technology wields a substantial societal influence, exacerbating the array of ethical dilemmas (Kugler, 2022). The advent of new prospects resulting from technological progress invariably gives rise to ethical concerns, yet seldom are there adequately designed protocols to manage these concerns. The primary aim of this chapter is to debate on such ethical concern, by pursuing cumulative ethical consideration referred by as "anticipatory technology ethics framework presented by (Brey, 2012), Assessment of information technology Model presented by Wright (2011) and ethical issues of emerging ICT applications framework presented by Stahl et al. (2017). These framework individually represents impact of technological revolution in ethical context, however these protocol unable to synthesize the boundaries of each framework that directly correlate Social, Physiological, Environmental, Financial ethical concern related to XR as shown in Figure 3.

Figure 3. Ethical dimensions related to extended reality

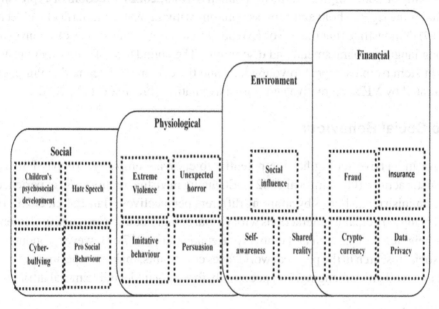

ADDITIONAL PERSPECTIVES

Cyber-Bullying

Algorithms on the internet struggle to detect cyberbullying, especially when it involves irony or sarcasm. The use of Extended Reality has ethical repercussions in online social interactions, particularly on gaming platforms (M. Iqbal et al., 2023). It refers to the deliberate, repeated mistreatment of others through offensive online posts or messages (Kangrga et al., 2024). Moreover, the major ethical challenge in harnessing Extended Reality is its potential to cause despondence through intentional threats, harassment, intimidation, or ridicule, which are associated with higher levels of depression and PTSD (M. Iqbal et al., 2023).

Hate Speech

Hate speech cloaked in freedom of expression raises ethical concerns about protecting others' rights. The debate centers on marginalizing targeted communities, especially on social digital platforms (Banaji & Bhat, 2022). Freedom of expression includes the right to hold and express opinions without obstruction. Blackwell et al. (2019) demonstrate that the use of Extended Reality in social spaces often involves strong language, harassment, and discomfort. The abundance of harassment in VR might stem from its appeal to young kids and the detrimental "gamer" culture, exacerbated by VR's interactive and immersive nature (Freeman et al., 2022).

Pro Social Behaviour

An immersive setting has the potential to cultivate empathy, compassion, and altruistic actions (Oliveira et al., 2021). Engaging in virtual reality (VR) experiences can diminish racial biases by adopting different perspectives (Hansdotter, 2023). By observing participants' interactions with virtual beings, studies can identify elements that heighten compassion and empathy (Ketaki et al., 2017). However, conducting prosocial research in the physical world faces constraints, making experimental control and realism challenging, and potentially fostering undesirable moral attributes.

Physiological

The complete immersion and realistic encounters provided by XR technologies can trigger diverse cognitive and psychological repercussions in both neurotypical and neurodivergent individuals (Karthik V 2023). Overdependence and addiction to XR technologies are widespread negative consequences, along with agency manipulation, affecting cognitive and psychological functions (Karthik V 2023). Patricia et al. (2022) explored the mental health impacts of XR technologies, including addiction and behavioral changes, as users perceive alternate realities as safer than the physical world. Similarly, Kaimara et al. (2022) found that VR technologies trigger addiction, cognitive effects, anxiety, and a blending of actual and virtual environments.

Extreme Violence

The convincing portrayal of extremely graphic scenes, depicting severe physical violence, including virtual characters with childlike attributes engaged in sensual contexts, poses significant ethical dilemmas (Slater et al., 2020). Determining whether this portrayal would magnify or mitigate such behaviour in actuality proves uncertain and challenging to empirically confirm. Engaging with or observing these virtual actions might result in desensitization, potentially habituating and consequently intensifying occurrences in real life (Çöltekin et al., 2020). Conversely, it could also act as a deterrent, suppressing the impulses of perpetrators to engage in such actions beyond the virtual realm (Slater et al., 2020).

Imitative Behaviour

Virtual experiences possess the potential to incite conduct that an individual would typically refrain from in real life (Slater et al., 2020). This might happen via exposure—initially, committing violent acts in XR could be challenging, but over time, it becomes effortless, potentially fostering a heightened inclination for violence in real life—or it could also result from mimicking behaviour—emulating the harmful actions of other virtual characters, akin to peer pressure observed in VR (Neyret et al., 2020).

Unexpected Horror

In an immersive virtual setting, individuals could encounter unexpected horrors without warning, potentially triggering a post-traumatic stress reaction or, conversely, leading to desensitization to disturbing visuals. Slater et al. (2020) is employed to implant memories with a manipulative purpose, possibly aiming to sway attitudes or shape a worldview detached from reality. Although other types of media and teaching techniques have the potential to create enduring impacts, both favourable and unfavourable, VR's deeply immersive format may elicit notably potent emotional reactions. The exposure towards VR (horror) games evoke arousal and triggers post-traumatic stress which is challenging to replicate with conventional media (Lemmens et al., 2022).

Persuasion

Augmented Reality (AR) inherently persuades individuals by offering them an alternative, seemingly genuine experience capable of altering their perceptions, especially within highly realistic virtual environments (Zakrzewski, 2022). However, using persuasion to negatively influence emotions or behaviour is profoundly unethical and poses risks to all individuals, particularly vulnerable populations (Slater et al., 2020).

Environment

Environmental regulation concerns the authority users hold over content within XR applications and its interaction with tangible objects in the physical environment (Philipp et al., 2022). Social discipline teaches us that our surroundings establish standards for behavior and individuality. Extensive XR engagement may shift these virtual environments into the norm (Slater et al., 2020). A significant ethical concern is that others lack awareness or access to an individual's XR setting, unlike visible real-world environments, sparking public discourse. Extensive XR utilization could disrupt public and societal methods for observing, debating, and enhancing our environments (Ziker et al., 2021). The immersion and customization in XR might result in the disintegration of social and political discourse, defined as "the public sphere" (Julia et al., 2023). The evolution of XR is reshaping reality by blending virtual and physical worlds, triggering legal and ethical dilemmas. Julia et al. (2023) outline essential aspects of using AI for simulating socio-motor interactions within mixed reality settings and their effects on self-awareness, shared reality, and social influences.

Social Influence

Conventional chatbots are fertile ground for spreading misinformation and alternative narratives. The rise of mixed reality (MR) environments amplifies the risk of manipulation, including impersonation via deep fakes (Jeffrey & Jeremy, 2021). As devices and technology advance, their use will expand across diverse demographics, from well-informed individuals to those less aware of falsification risks (Sara et al., 2022). The study of attachment to technological gadgets raises ethical concerns, particularly in young people whose relationships and development could be affected (Rebecca et al., 2021).

Share Reality

In conventional XR, content was typically limited to one user at a time, but technological advancements now allow multiple users to engage simultaneously with the same virtual content (Chylinski et al., 2020). Collective experiences in XR and the metaverse require stable content for all users, fostering interactions that mirror real-life dynamics and enhance authenticity (Carrozzi et al., 2019; Hilken et al., 2020). However, shared extended reality introduces social and ethical responsibilities, impacting users' social connections and well-being (Fabio et al., 2023). While XR can bridge geographical distances and foster virtual interactions, prolonged detachment from reality and reliance on artificial social skills may lead to significant psychological challenges, especially for those dealing with loneliness (Fabio et al., 2023).

Self-Awareness

Understanding self-awareness is crucial, as mixed reality (MR) technologies may alter it through modification (Julia et al., 2023). Bréchet (2022) categorizes self-awareness into tiers from basic proprioception to complex autobiographical memories. The mechanisms governing these layers remain enigmatic, studied in neuroscience and psychology (Julia et al., 2023). Evidence suggests these layers can be manipulated in virtual environments, raising ethical and legal issues such as data governance and avatar representation (Pawankumar & Bibhu, 2022).

Financial

Ethical considerations in XR business models, economics, and finance must be widely communicated (Karthik V 2023; Middleton, 2022). The responsibilities of individuals, corporations, and governments in securing cyber finance while protecting privacy are uncertain. Tech giants, criticized for their influence and questionable practices, resist legislative, financial, or cultural changes (Karthik V 2023; Middleton, 2022). Risks include financial data theft for exploitation, extortion, and political manipulation (Middleton, 2022). Users often exchange personal data for XR experiences, potentially impacting future outcomes like insurance eligibility (Middleton, 2022).

Insurance

Extended Reality (XR) has firmly established its presence in various industries. For instance, claims assessors and insurers can construct immersive environments to analyse the contexts where insurance coverage is relevant and even assess physical damages remotely (Steve et al., 2022). Similarly, virtual reality training setups are becoming more prevalent, along with the adoption of VR-based rehabilitation programs for workplace injuries. Insurance encompasses various categories such as life, health, automobile, property, workers' compensation, and more, each presenting distinct aspects when viewed through the lens of extended reality (XR). Three most significant implication observed due to adoption of XR, that are applicable across the majority of insurance types (Middleton, 2022).

1. Utilization and misuse of data capable of influencing qualification and/or settlement of claims.

2. Necessity for occupational insurance policies to encompass safeguards against accidents or harm potentially arising from the adoption or utilization of XR in workplace settings.
3. Requirement for novel insurance categories tailored to oversee distinct and specialized facets within the XR environment and metaverse landscape.

Fraud

Cyber fraud poses a growing societal concern, expanding in scale (Sandhya & Prasad, 2017). Identity fraud involves acquiring or fabricating counterfeit identities for illicit activities, often facilitated by user exposure in XR. XR technology could enhance business-customer interactions via video, emphasizing the importance of understanding customers for fraud prevention (Hanane & Youssef, 2023; Middleton, 2022)

Cryptocurrencies

The ethical dimensions of cryptocurrency, including user identity genuineness, have swiftly integrated with XR via blockchain and distributed ledger technologies (Middleton, 2022; Verma et al., 2024; Naim et al., 2024). Instances like a coin gaining $45 billion valuation within days illustrate its rapid financial implications, including in XR-integrated cyber trading susceptible to fraud and illicit activities like money laundering and terrorist financing.

Data Privacy

Advanced XR technologies use sensors and computational methods for immersion, realism, and additional benefits, raising significant privacy concerns due to the collection of extensive personal and environmental data (Abraham & Florian, 2021; Sarah et al., 2023). VR and AR technologies can gather sensitive data like eye movements and behavioral patterns, stored in cloud systems vulnerable to cyber breaches and potential misuse (Jacob, 2023; Karthik V 2023). This data's exposure through internet transmission could lead to privacy compromises and misuse, including identity theft and surveillance (Karthik V 2023).

DISCUSSION

An extensive study was conducted to examine the ethical dimensions of XR technologies and their uses. The emphasis was on exploring the new ethical responsibilities related to the deployment of XR technologies in diverse settings. The discussion emphasized XR's ethical issues by adopting the comprehensive ethical perspectives provided by the "anticipatory technology ethics framework" proposed (Brey, 2012), the "Assessment of Information Technology" model introduced by Wright (2011), and the "ethical issues of emerging ICT applications" framework outlined by Stahl et al. (2017). Each of these frameworks individually addresses the ethical implications of technological advancements. However, they fail to integrate the boundaries of each framework to comprehensively address the social, psychological, environmental, and financial ethical concerns related to XR.

Across diverse industrial, commercial, and research applications, these technologies have been discovered to encompass a wide array of issues, facilitating thorough exploration of their ethical ramifications. A multitude of challenges and considerations have arisen concerning the utilization of XR technologies, spanning social, psychological, environmental, and financial, and interpersonal connections. It's important to note that these concerns frequently demonstrate complex interconnections, with certain issues serving as root causes while others appear as resultant consequences. Issues pertaining to health pose substantial obstacles to users' physical welfare, as specific XR applications carry the risk of inducing falls or causing injuries during engagement (Millard et al., 2019). Moreover, the sensing and tracking functionalities intrinsic to XR technologies give rise to privacy apprehensions, as they introduce the potential for surveillance and observation that may encroach upon individuals' personal autonomy (Greene, 2023).

These characteristics offer pathways for the collection of vast amounts of user data, potentially empowering commercial and non-commercial bodies to exploit weaknesses such as emotional fluctuations for deceptive and manipulative intentions (Greene, 2023). XR technologies, especially VR, profoundly affect society, as VR games can cause children and adolescents to neglect their real-world responsibilities and harm their relationships (Karthik V 2023). Additionally, while XR hardware enables these immersive experiences, it can also present accessibility challenges and ethical issues related to commodification and exploitation for commercial gain (Kaimara et al., 2022).

The identified issues, including cyber sickness, have negatively affected both users and XR technology, reducing the effectiveness of educational and research initiatives and decreasing adoption rates. Moreover, although XR features like immersion and realism offer advantages, they can adversely affect older adults, dementia patients, and individuals with autism spectrum disorder (ASD)(Glaser et al., 2023). This underscores the need for design recommendations to address these challenges and enhance XR solutions (Glaser et al., 2022) .

Tackling the ethical and safety challenges of XR technologies, including AR, VR, and MR, is vital for promoting business growth and improving quality of life. This thorough investigation explores XR ethics, highlighting key issues, impacts, and solutions, and lays the groundwork for further research and practical implementation.

IMPLICATIONS

Examining the previously mentioned issues and concerns reveals that the symptoms and risks linked to XR technologies have a substantial impact on users. These effects range from diminishing the overall user experience to causing harm or creating a general aversion to XR technologies. This section explores the specific negative effects and barriers arising from these issues, offering a thorough understanding of the challenges and obstacles within the XR landscape.

XR technologies provide immersive experiences that can trigger cognitive and psychological effects in both neurotypical and neurodivergent individuals, often leading to addiction and altered behaviour. Additionally, environmental regulation in XR is consider a significant ethical concern because others lack awareness or access to an individual's XR setting, unlike real-world environments, which are visible to all, sparking public discourse.

In terms of finance, the ethical responsibilities of individuals, corporations, and governments in securing finance and protecting privacy in the cyber world are unclear. Major tech companies, often criticized for their influence and questionable conduct, have successfully resisted efforts to change their practices.

Social Implication

Apart from the social impacts triggered by a user's identity, XR technologies possess various other social implications for their users, especially young individuals. In scholarly arena various researchers utilize XR platforms that enable multi-user communication and interaction within synthetic environments (Thomas et al., 2020). Pranav et al. (2020) reviewed AR applications were grouped into six conventional application types: military, industry, healthcare, games, tours, and media. Extended reality (XR) leveraging augmented reality (AR) for social platforms have been utilized to minimize cognitive burden during collaborative activities, for instance: Augmenting communication among team members helps bolster mutual comprehension, however it raise various ethical concern Children's psychosocial development may be at risk, affecting their emotional, personal, and social growth

(Kaimara et al., 2022). Considering the characteristics of VR, there is concern among parents, educators, and academic professionals regarding its potentially adverse effects. Evidence suggests that VR experiences can lead to a reduction in pro-social behaviour, impact social skills, and contribute to social isolation while engaged in VR gaming sessions (Kaimara et al., 2022).

Children's Psychosocial Implication

In society, ethical norms can take two forms: injunctive and descriptive. Injunctive norms involve what a group deems acceptable, or the expected course of action (Stephanie Hui-Wen. Chuah, 2018). Descriptive norms, in contrast, deal with the observation of others' actions within the group. The immersive technologies possess social implication on both norm specially children's now a days completely expose to virtual worlds for instance: Through virtual games have long been used to bolster social interactions among players (Karthik V 2023). Such relationship not only can strengthen social connections among gamers, but they also have the possibility of fostering addictive gaming disorders, which considers as adverse psychosocial implication. Such conditions have the potential to detrimentally influence interpersonal skills in the physical world, resulting in disruptions to familial, societal, and personal relationships. Inadequate social skills might breed feelings of isolation, particularly as children allocate more time to digital gadgets than to everyday interactions and activities (Karthik V 2023).

LIMITATIONS

It is essential to recognize that the review focused exclusively on XR technologies like AR, VR, MR, and the Metaverse, excluding other computer-generated realities. Expanding the search to incorporate more related terms might have provided additional insights.

Secondly, the data analysis and interpretation utilized a data-driven inductive coding method. Although this method offers flexibility and can reveal new insights, it also introduces subjectivity, as the interpretation of relationships and connections between the data, codes, and themes depends on the researcher's perspective.

Lastly, the absence of predetermined theories or established frameworks can influence the synthesis and conclusions. If other researchers were to replicate the SLR, their interpretations could vary based on their individual biases and assumptions. Despite these constraints, the review offers valuable insights within its defined parameters, laying the groundwork for future research and exploration in the realm of XR technologies and ethics. The study has endeavoured to comprehensively address the ethical ramifications.

Researchers can build on the insights from this study by adopting a vertical approach to delve deeply into specific ethical dimensions or a horizontal approach to examine a broader range of ethical aspects across XR. These endeavour's advance the ongoing dialogue on XR ethics and set the foundation for designing and developing ethically aligned XR technologies.

CONCLUSION

Amidst the dynamic evolution of XR technologies encompassing AR, VR, and MR, this research endeavours to achieve an all-encompassing comprehension of the prevailing ethical landscape in XR. Employing a meticulous systematic review approach, this study affirms the emergence of numerous ethical challenges and associated concerns attributed to the utilization of XR technologies, encompassing aspects like social ramifications, privacy vulnerabilities, and ethical quandaries. The study revealed a spectrum of hurdles faced by users across diverse sectors of application. These difficulties pose significant risks not just for end-users but also for the extended reality (XR) industry, hampering the rate of adoption and affecting business outcomes. It is important to highlight that the examination of numerous studies yielded valuable perspectives in terms of ethical aspects. It is important to uncover numerous studies that yielded valuable perspectives in terms of ethical dimension which includes: diverse social implications especially for youth, including multi-user communication and interaction. Also embraces diverse cognitive and psychological effects, including addiction, altered behaviour, and blurring of reality distinctions, impacting mental health. These ethical implications also uncover environmental and financial regulation in XR applications intersects with user authority and content interaction which must be urgently communicated, given the uncertain landscape of privacy protection and corporate accountability. This study emphasizes that despite the considerable promise of XR technologies, there are substantial ethical issues and concerns requiring attention. Addressing these challenges comprehensively is a significant undertaking due to their interconnectedness, yet crucial for fostering secure and ethical XR environments that augment human capabilities.

REFERENCES

Abraham, H. M., & Florian, S. (2021). Identifying Manipulative Advertising Techniques in XR Through Scenario Construction. *Conference on Human Factors in Computing Systems (CHI '21)*, Yokohama, Japan 10.1145/3411764.3445253

Arif Ali, K., Sher, B., Peng, L., Muhammad, W., Bilal, K., Aakash, A., & Muhammad, A. A. (2022). Ethics of AI: A Systematic Literature Review of Principles and Challenges. *International Conference on Evaluation and Assessment in Software Engineering 2022 (EASE '22)*. ACM. 10.1145/3530019.3531329

Bahar, M., & Tenzin, D. (2021). A novel ethical analysis of educational XR and AI in literature. *Computers & Education: X Reality, 4*, 1-28. 10.1016/j.cexr.2024.100052

Balcerak Jackson, M., & Balcerak Jackson, B. (2024). Immersive Experience and Virtual Reality. *Philosophy & Technology, 37*(1), 19. 10.1007/s13347-024-00707-1

Banaji, S., & Bhat, R. (2022). *Social media and hate*. Taylor & Francis. 10.4324/9781003083078

Berkman, M. I. (2024). History of virtual reality. In *Encyclopedia of computer graphics and games*. Springer International Publishing. 10.1007/978-3-031-23161-2_169

Blackwell, L., Ellison, N., Elliott-Deflo, N., & Schwartz, R. (2019). *Harassment in social virtual reality: Challenges for platform governance*. ACM HumanComputer Interaction New York. 10.1145/3359202

Bogdan, P., & Radu, D. V. (2022). Transhumanism as a Philosophical and Cultural Framework for Extended Reality Applied to Human Augmentation *13th Augmented Human International Conference (AH2022)*, Winnipeg, MB, Canada. 10.1145/3532525.3532528

Bréchet, L. (2022). Personal Memories and Bodily-Cues Influence Our Sense of Self. *Frontiers in Psychology, 13*(855450), 855450. 10.3389/fpsyg.2022.85545035814046

Brey, P. A. E. (2012). Anticipating ethical issues in emerging IT. *Ethics and Information Technology, 14*(4), 305–317. 10.1007/s10676-012-9293-y

Cardenas-Robledo, L. A., Hernandez-Uribe, O., Reta, C., & Antonio, J. (2022). Extended reality applications in industry 4.0—A systematic literature review. *Telematics and Informatics, 73*, 101863. 10.1016/j.tele.2022.101863

Carrozzi, A., Chylinski, M., Heller, J., Hilken, T., Keeling, D. I., & de Ruyter, K. (2019). What's mine is a hologram? How shared augmented reality augments psychological ownership. *Journal of Interactive Marketing*, 48, 71–88. 10.1016/j. intmar.2019.05.004

Carter, M., & Egliston, B. (2020). *Ethical Implications of Emerging Mixed Reality Technologies* (Faculty of Arts and Social Sciences, Issue. Chalmers, D. J. (2022). *Reality+*. Penguin Books Limited.

Chuah, S. H.-W. (2018). Why and Who Will Adopt Extended Reality Technology? Literature Review, Synthesis, and Future Research Agenda. 10.2139/ssrn.3300469

Chuah, S. H.-W. (2018). Why and who will adopt extended reality technology? Literature review, synthesis, and future research agenda. *SSRN*, 13(4), 205–259. 10.2139/ssrn.3300469

Chylinski, M., Heller, J., Hilken, T., Keeling, D. I., Mahr, D., & de Ruyter, K. (2020). Augmented reality marketing: A technology-enabled approach to situated customer experience. *Australasian Marketing Journal*, 28(4), 374–384. 10.1016/j. ausmj.2020.04.004

Çöltekin, A., Lochhead, I., Madden, M., Christophe, S., Devaux, A., Pettit, C., Lock, O., Shukla, S., Herman, L., Stachoň, Z., Kubíček, P., Snopková, D., Bernardes, S., & Hedley, N. (2020). Extended reality in spatial sciences: A review of research challenges and future directions. *ISPRS International Journal of Geo-Information*, 9(7), 1–29. 10.3390/ijgi9070439

Coon, J. (2018). *Assisted reality: What it is, and how it will improve service productivity*. PTC. https://www.ptc.com/en/blogs/service/what-is-assisted-reality

Cotton, M. (2021). *Virtual reality, empathy and ethics*. Springer Nature. 10.1007/978-3-030-72907-3

Dhillon, P. K. S., & Tinmaz, H. (2024). Immersive realities: A comprehensive guide from virtual reality to metaverse. *Journal for the Education of Gifted Young Scientists*, 12(1), 29–45. 10.17478/jegys.1406024

Fabio, D. F., Cristina, D. L., Simona, D. C., & Antonella, P. (2023). Physical and digital worlds: Implications and opportunities of the metaverse. *Procedia Computer Science*, 217, 1744–1754. 10.1016/j.procs.2022.12.374

Fox, D., & Thornton, I. G. (2022). *The IEEE Global Initiative on Ethics of Extended Reality (XR) Report--Extended Reality (XR) Ethics and Diversity, Inclusion, and Accessibility*. IEEE. https://ieeexplore-ieee-org.ezproxy.ump.edu.my/servlet/opac ?punumber=9727120

Freeman, G., Zamanifard, S., Maloney, D., & Acena, D. (2022). Disturbing the Peace: Experiencing and Mitigating Emerging Harassment in Social Virtual Reality. *Proceedings of the ACM on Human-Computer Interaction*. ACM. 10.1145/3512932

Gill, M., & Mark. (2021). *White Paper-The IEEE Global Initiative on Ethics of Extended Reality (XR) Report--Extended Reality (XR) and the Erosion of Anonymity and Privacy* (Extended Reality (XR) and the Erosion of Anonymity and Privacy-White Paper). IEEE. https://ieeexplore.ieee.org/servlet/opac?punumber=9619997

Glaser, N., Schmidt, M., & Schmidt, C. (2022). Learner experience and evidence of cybersickness: Design tensions in a virtual reality public transportation intervention for autistic adults. *Virtual Reality (Waltham Cross)*, 26(4), 1–20. 10.1007/s10055-022-00661-3

Glaser, N., Thull, C., Schmidt, M., Tennant, A., Moon, J., & Ousley, C. (2023). Learning Experience Design and Unpacking Sociocultural, Technological, and Pedagogical Design Considerations of Spherical Video-Based Virtual Reality Systems for Autistic Learners: A Systematic Literature Review. *Journal of Autism and Developmental Disorders*. 10.1007/s10803-023-06168-338015318

Greene, J. (2023). Ethical Design Approaches for Workplace Augmented Reality. *Communication Design Quarterly Review*, 10(4), 16–26. 10.1145/3531210.3531212

Hanane, A., & Youssef, M. (2023). Exploring the Full Potentials of IoT for Better Financial Growth and Stability: A Comprehensive Survey. *Sensors (Basel)*, 23(19), 8015. 10.3390/s2319801537836845

Hansdotter, Y. (2023). *The Affordances of Immersive Virtual Reality for Stimulating Prosocial Behaviour: A Mixed-Methods Pro-Environmental Intervention Study*. University College Dublin. Dublin. http://hdl.handle.net/10197/24360

Hilken, T., Keeling, D. I. K., de Ruyter, K., Mahr, D., & Chylinski, M. (2020). Seeing eye to eye: Social augmented reality and shared decision making in the marketplace. *Journal of the Academy of Marketing Science*, 48(2), 143–164. 10.1007/s11747-019-00688-0

Hoyer, W. D., Kroschke, M., Schmitt, D. K., Kraume, V. S., & Shankar, V. (2020). Transforming the customer experience through new technologies. *Journal of Interactive Marketing*, 51, 57–71. 10.1016/j.intmar.2020.04.001

Iqbal, M., Xu, X., Nallur, V., Scanlon, M., & Campbell, A. (2023). *Security, Ethics, and Privacy Issues in the Remote Extended Reality for Education*. Springer. 10.1007/978-981-99-4958-8_16

Iqbal, M. Z., Xu, X., Nallur, V., Scanlon, M., & Campbell, A. G. (2023). *Security, Ethics and Privacy Issues in the Remote Extended Reality for Education.* Springer. 10.1007/978-981-99-4958-8_16

Jacob, G. (2023). Ethical Design Approaches for Workplace Augmented Reality. *Communication Design Quarterly Review*, 10(4), 16–26. 10.1145/3531210.3531212

Jeffrey, T. H., & Jeremy, N. B. (2021). The Social Impact of Deepfakes. *Cyberpsychology, Behavior, and Social Networking*, 24(3), 149–152. 10.1089/cyber.2021.29208. jth33760669

Joakim, L., Matti, M., & Matti, M. (2024). Ethics-based AI auditing: A systematic literature review on conceptualizations of ethical principles and knowledge contributions to stakeholders. *Information & Management*, 61(5), 103969. 10.1016/j.im.2024.103969

Jobin, A., Ienca, M., & Vayena, E. (2019). The Global Landscape of AI Ethics Guidelines. *Nature Machine Intelligence*, 1(9), 389–399. 10.1038/s42256-019-0088-2

Jonathan, H., Magd, H., & Khan, S. A. (2024). Artificial Intelligence and Augmented Reality: A Business Fortune to Sustainability in the Digital Age. In Singh, N., Kansra, P., & Gupta, S. L. (Eds.), *Navigating the Digital Landscape: Understanding Customer Behaviour in the Online World* (pp. 85–105). Emerald Publishing Limited. 10.1108/978-1-83549-272-720241005

Julia, A., Marta, B., Kathleen, R., & Benoit, B. (2023). *Extended Reality of socio-motor interactions: Current Trends and Ethical Considerations for Mixed Reality Environments Design.* ICMI '23 Companion: Companion Publication of the 25th International Conference on Multimodal Interaction, Paris, France. 10.1145/3610661.3617989

Kaimara, P., Oikonomou, A., & Deliyannis, I. (2022). Could virtual reality applications pose real risks to children and adolescents? A systematic review of ethical issues and concerns. *Virtual Reality (Waltham Cross)*, 26(2), 697–735. 10.1007/s10055-021-00563-w34366688

Kangrga, M., Dejan, N., Milena, S.-M., Ljiljana, R., Tatjana, K., Goran, D., & Milan, L. (2024). Recognizing the Frequency of Exposure to Cyberbullying in Children: The Results of the National HBSC Study in Serbia. *Children (Basel, Switzerland)*, 11(2), 172. 10.3390/children11020172 38397284

Karthik, V. M. (2023). *The Ethics of Extended Realities: Insights from a Systematic Literature Review.* Uppsala University. https://www.diva-portal.org/smash/get/diva2:1773547/FULLTEXT01.pdf

Ketaki, S., Soon, Y. O., & Jeremy, B. (2017). *Virtual Reality and Prosocial Behavior.* Cambridge University Press. 10.1017/9781316676202.022

Kugler, L. (2022). Technology's Impact on Morality. *Communications of the ACM,* 65(7), 15–16. 10.1145/3516516

Kunkel, N., & Soechtig, S. (2017). *Mixed reality: Experiences get more intuitive, immersive and empowering.* Deloitte University Press. https://www2.deloitte.com/uk/en/insights/focus/tech-trends/2017/mixed-reality-applications-potential.html

Lai, W. (2024). *Application of Computer VR Technology in Digital Media System Design.* Springer. 10.1007/978-981-99-9299-7_28

Lemmens, J. S., Simon, M., & Sumter, S. R. (2022). Fear and loathing in VR: The emotional and physiological effects of immersive games. *Virtual Reality (Waltham Cross),* 26(1), 223–234. 10.1007/s10055-021-00555-w

López, B. R. (2024). *Ethics of Virtual Reality.* Springer Nature. 10.1007/978-3-031-48135-2_6

Middleton, M. (2022). Business, Finance, and Economics. *The IEEE Global Initiative on Ethics of Extended Reality (XR) Report--Business, Finance, and Economics,* (pp. 1-30). IEEE. https://ieeexplore-ieee-org.ezproxy.ump.edu.my/servlet/opac?punumber=9740584

Milgram, P., & Kishino, F. (1994). *A Taxonomy of Mixed Reality Visual Displays.* Institute of Electronics, Information and Communication Engineers (IEICE) Transactions on Information and Systems. https://search.ieice.org/bin/summary.php?id=e77-d_12_1321. https://search.ieice.org/bin/summary.php?id=e77-d_12_1321

Millard, D. E., Hewitt, S., O'Hara, K., Packer, H., & Rogers, N. (2019). The Unethical Future of Mixed Reality Storytelling. *Proceedings of the 8th International Workshop on Narrative and Hypertext,* Hof, Germany. https://doi.org/10.1145/3345511.3349283

Minna, V., Sami, P., & Liubov, V. (2021). A Systematic Literature Review on Extended Reality: Virtual, Augmented and Mixed Reality in Working Life. *The International Journal of Virtual Reality : a Multimedia Publication for Professionals,* 21(2), 1–28. 10.20870/IJVR.2021.21.2.4620

Naim, A., Khan, S.A., Mohammed, A., Sabahath, A., & Malik, P. K. Achieving performance and Reliability in predicting the Marketing Price of Bitcoins through Blockchain Technology. *Pacific Asia Journal of the Association for Information Systems.* https://aisel.aisnet.org/pajais_preprints/23/]

Neyret, S., Oliva, R., Beacco, A., Navarro, X., Valenzuela, J., & Slater, M. (2020). An embodied perspective as a victim of sexual harassment in virtual reality reduces action conformity in a later milgram obedience scenario. *2019 IEEE International Symposium on Olfaction and Electronic Nose (ISOEN)*. IEEE. 10.1038/s41598-020-62932-w

Nikolić, D., Maftei, L., & Whyte, J. (2019). Becoming familiar: How infrastructure engineers begin to use collaborative virtual reality in their interdisciplinary practice. *Journal of Information Technology in Construction*, 24, 489–508. 10.36680/j.itcon.2019.026

Nuno Verdelho, T., Alfredo, F., João Madeiras, P., & Sérgio, O. (2023). Extended reality in AEC. *Automation in Construction*, 154, 105018. 10.1016/j.autcon.2023.105018

Oliveira, R., Arriaga, P., Santos, F. P., Mascarenhas, S., & Paiva, A. (2021). Towards prosocial design: A scoping review of the use of robots and virtual agents to trigger prosocial behaviour. *Computers in Human Behavior*, 114, 106547. 10.1016/j.chb.2020.106547

Oun, A., Hagerdorn, N., Scheideger, C., & Cheng, X. (2024). Mobile Devices or Head-Mounted Displays: A Comparative Review and Analysis of Augmented Reality in Healthcare. *IEEE Access : Practical Innovations, Open Solutions*, 12, 21825–21839. 10.1109/ACCESS.2024.3361833

Paez, A. (2017). Gray literature: An important resource in systematic reviews. *Journal of Evidence-Based Medicine*, 10(3), 233–240. 10.1111/jebm.1226628857505

Palmas, F., & Klinker, G. (2020). *Defining Extended Reality Training: A Long-Term Definition for All Industries*. 2020 IEEE 20th International Conference on Advanced Learning Technologies (ICALT), Tartu, Estonia. 10.1109/ICALT49669.2020.00103

Patricia, P., Samuel, N.-M., & Jose, L. (2022). Extended reality for mental health: Current trends and future challenges. *Frontiers of Computer Science*, 4, 1034307. 10.3389/fcomp.2022.1034307

Pawankumar, S., & Bibhu, D. (2022). The digital carbon footprint: Threat to an environmentally sustainable future. *International Journal of Computer Science and Information Technologies*, 14(3), 25. 10.5121/ijcsit.2022.14302

Philipp, R., Reto, F., Chris, H., Hamza, S., & Florian, A. (2022). What is XR? Towards a Framework for Augmented and Virtual Reality. *Computers in Human Behavior*, 133, 1–18. 10.1016/j.chb.2022.107289

Pranav, P., Shireen, P., Nivedita, P., & Manan, S. (2020). Systematic review and meta-analysis of augmented reality in medicine, retail, and games. *Visual Computing for Industry, Biomedicine, and Art*, 3(21), 21. 10.1186/s42492-020-00057-732954214

Rauschnabel, P. A. (2018). Virtually enhancing the real world with holograms: An exploration of expected gratifications of using augmented reality smart glasses. *Psychology and Marketing*, 35(8), 557–572. 10.1002/mar.21106

Rauschnabel, P. A., Felix, R., Hinsch, C., Shahab, H., & Alt, F. (2022). What is XR? Towards a framework for augmented and virtual reality. *Computers in Human Behavior*, 133, 107289. 10.1016/j.chb.2022.107289

Raymundo, O. (2016). Tim Cook: Augmented reality will be an essential part of your daily life, like the iPhone. *Macworld*.https://www.macworld.com/article/3126607/tim-cook-augmented-reality-will-be-an-essential-part-of-your-daily-life-like-the-iphone.html

Rebecca, H., Juliana, Z., Stephen, R. Z., Desiree, S., & Leon, S. (2021). The association of mobile touch screen device use with parent-child attachment: A systematic review. *Ergonomics*, 64(12), 1606–1622. 10.1080/00140139.2021.194861734190030

Sandhya, M., & Prasad, M. V. N. K. (2017). *Biometric template protection: A systematic literature review of approaches and modalities*. Springer. 10.1007/s10676-018-9452-x

Sara, Q., Park, T., Kelly, D. M., Scott, W., & Robert, W. P. (2022). Digital technologies: Tensions in privacy and data. *Journal of the Academy of Marketing Science*, 50(6), 1299–1323. 10.1007/s11747-022-00845-y35281634

Sarah, D. R., & Radiah, R. Ville Mäkelä, & Florian, A. (2023). *Challenges in Virtual Reality Studies: Ethics and Internal and External Validity*. Augmented Humans International Conference 2023 (AHs '23), Glasgow, United Kingdom.

Sayed Fayaz, A., & Heesup, H. (2023). Impact of artificial intelligence on human loss in decision making, laziness and safety in education. *Humanities & Social Sciences Communications*, 10(1), 311. Advance online publication. 10.1057/s41599-023-01787-837325188

Shuqiong, L., Di, Z., & Lucas, K. (2024). A systematic review of research on xReality (XR) in the English classroom: Trends, research areas, benefits, and challenges. *Computers & Education: X Reality, 4*.

Slater, M. (2021). Beyond Speculation About the Ethics of Virtual Reality: The Need for Empirical Results. *Frontiers in Virtual Reality*, 2, 687609. Advance online publication. 10.3389/frvir.2021.687609

Slater, M., Gonzalez-Liencres, C., Haggard, P., Vinkers, C., Gregory-Clarke, R., Jelley, S., Watson, Z., Breen, G., Schwarz, R., Steptoe, W., Szostak, D., Halan, S., Fox, D., & Silver, J. (2020). The Ethics of Realism in Virtual and Augmented Reality. *Frontiers in Virtual Reality*, 1, 1. Advance online publication. 10.3389/frvir.2020.00001

Stackpole, B. (2023). *The business impact of extended reality*. MIT. https://mitsloan.mit.edu/ideas-made-to-matter/business-impact-extended-reality

Stahl, B. C., Flick, C., & Timmermans, J. (2017). Ethics of Emerging Information and Communication Technologies-On the implementation of RRI. *Science & Public Policy*. 10.1093/scipol/scw069

Statista. (2023). *AR & VR: market data & analysis, Market Insights reports*. Statista. https://www.statista.com/study/125081/arandvr-market-report/

Stendal, K., & Bernabe, R. D. (2024). Extended Reality—New Opportunity for People With Disability? Practical and Ethical Considerations. *Journal of Medical Internet Research*, 26(1), e41670. 10.2196/4167038349731

Steve, M., Silvia, M., Todd, S., & Venkat, V. (2022). *Meet Me in the Metaverse: The continuum of technology and experience, reshaping business*. Accenture. https://www.accenture.com/content/dam/accenture/final/industry/insurance/document/Accenture-Insurance-Technology-Vision-2022.pdf#zoom=40

Thomas, F. (2021). *In defence of the human being: Foundational questions of an embodied anthropology*. Oxford University Press. 10.1093/oso/9780192898197.001.0001

Thomas, P., Andrea, G., & Giuseppe, R. (2020). Extended Reality for the Clinical, Affective, and Social Neurosciences. *Brain Sciences*, 10(12), 992. 10.3390/brainsci1012092233339175

Vasarainen, M., Paavola, S., & Vetoshkina, L. (2021). A Systematic Literature Review on Extended Reality: Virtual, Augmented and Mixed Reality in Working Life. *The International Journal of Virtual Reality : a Multimedia Publication for Professionals*, 21(2), 1–28. 10.20870/IJVR.2021.21.2.4620

Verma, D., Kansra, P., & Khan, S. A. (2024). Apparent Advantages and Negative Facet of Block Chain in Banking Sector: An Innovative Theoretical Perspective. In rfan, M., Muhammad, K., Naifar, N., Khan, M.A. (eds), *Applications of Block Chain technology and Artificial Intelligence: Lead-ins in Banking, Finance, and Capital Market* (pp. 19-27). Cham: Springer International Publishing. 10.1007/978-3-031-47324-1_2

Wedel, M., Bigne, E., & Zhang, J. (2020). Virtual and augmented reality: Advancing research in Consumer marketing. *International Journal of Research in Marketing*, 37(3), 443–465. 10.1016/j.ijresmar.2020.04.004

Wright, D. (2011). A framework for the ethical impact assessment of informa tion technology. *Ethics and Information Technology*, 13(3), 199–226. 10.1007/s10676-010-9242-6

Xi, N., Chen, J., Gama, F., Korkeila, H., & Hamari, J. (2024). Acceptance of the metaverse: A laboratory experiment on augmented and virtual reality shopping. *Internet Research*, 34(7), 82–117. 10.1108/INTR-05-2022-0334

Zakarneh, B., Annamalai, N., Alquqa, E. K., Mohamed, K. M., & Al Salhi, N. R. (2024). Virtual Reality and Alternate Realities in Neal Stephenson's "Snow Crash". *World Journal of English Language*, 14(2), 244–252. 10.5430/wjel.v14n2p244

Zakrzewski, P. (2022). *Extended Reality Experience Design: The Multimodal Rhetorical Framework for Creating Persuasive Immersion*. Emerald Publishing Limited. 10.1108/978-1-80262-365-920221005

Ziker, C., Truman, B., & Dodds, H. (2021). Cross Reality (XR): Challenges and Opportunities Across the Spectrum. *Springer Briefs in Statistics*. Springer. 10.1007/978-3-030-58948-6_4

Chapter 3
Ethical Considerations as Limitations of Extended Reality:
An Empirical Study Through the Lens of Retail Consumers

R. Indradevi
Vellore Institute of Technology, Vellore, India

K. P. Venkataswamy
https://orcid.org/0000-0002-4397-1902
REVA University, Bangalore, India

Sathish Arumbi Saravanan
Vellore Institute of Technology, Vellore, India

Arun Mittal
https://orcid.org/0000-0003-0602-8066
Birla Institute of Technology, Mesra, India

ABSTRACT

Extended reality (XR) includes virtual reality, augmented reality, and spatial computing. It introduces a spectrum of immersive technologies with the potential for pathbreaking interactions and unique digital engagement. In the case of online retailing, XR is crucial for personalization, interactivity, and information acquisition. The present study focuses on ethical considerations as limitations of extended reality. The sample size chosen for the study was 289 retail consumers. The sampling method used was judgement sampling. The data analysis was conducted with the

DOI: 10.4018/979-8-3693-2432-5.ch003

help of exploratory factor analysis (EFA) and multiple regression analysis (MRA) and artificial neural network (ANN). It was found that the ethical dimensions of XR such as privacy concerns, informed consent, security risks and psychological impact significantly influence the wise use of XR by consumers.

INTRODUCTION

The increasing integration of "Augmented reality (AR) and Virtual reality (VR)", together known as "extended reality" or (XR), in various industries, raises a range of ethical considerations. This research investigates a broad range of ethical issues associated with XR. As AR applications flourish in the marketplace, they are projected to encounter legal challenges soon, particularly concerning liability and copyright issues. XR technologies significantly contribute to diverse fields crucial for human well-being and progress, such as work, education, medicine, communication, and training (Fox, 2022). Kumlu (2024) deliberated upon the various aspects of the XR and found that there are many positive as well as negative aspects of XR. The negative aspects are important and must be taken care of. Literature has revealed four major cornerstones namely "knowledge management, training, e-learning, and technology" (Dastane et al., 2024). In response to the growing demand for virtual learning as a substitute for physical practices, virtual reality (VR) has positioned itself as a valuable instrument that has created an immersive education experience. However, the ethical landscape for VR technology includes concerns about diminishing users' autonomy, potential health risks, and privacy issues (Skulmowski, 2023). This study broadly explores the ethical dimensions arising from the utilization of XR technologies in various contexts. While XR's applications and benefits are plentiful, XR technologies' involvement raises significant ethical dilemmas, contributing to health issues and threatening user safety. Examining ethical aspects within this study provides a complete knowledge of the ethical landscape surrounding extended reality technologies and their application (Meenaakshisundaram, 2023). Enhancing super-realism involves collecting personal data such as location, body movements, preferences, and actions within virtual or semi-virtual environments, which has wide-ranging implications for storytelling, advertising, and health applications. However, ethical concerns arise, particularly regarding privacy, data sharing, and potential misuse for criminal purposes. The unique ethical challenge lies in an individual's XR (extended reality) environment, conflicting with real-world environments subject to public examination and argument. It is vital to know that ethical issues continue outside immediate experiences, with long-term implications demanding attention. Addressing security and privacy concerns is imperious in developing these technologies (Slater et al., 2020). This study improves the metaverse concept and investigates and reviews security and privacy concerns surrounding user information, communication, scenarios, and goods (Zhao et al., 2021).

Research findings show that perceived usefulness, attitude, competitive pressure, customer pressure, and technological knowledge significantly impact behavioural intention to use augmented reality (AR). On the contrary, perceived cost is negatively associated with behavioral intent (Alam et al., 2021). The early challenges and ethical considerations that appeared with the beginning of the internet are composed to reappear, now augmented by the psychological impact facilitated by personification and a sharp sense of presence. It is well-acknowledged that internet technology has already started reshaping our self-perceptions and, therefore, our psychological makeup. Incorporating virtual and robotic re-embodiment technologies can significantly accelerate this transformative process (Madary & Metzinger, 2016). As technology advances, establishing definitive policies, standards, and ethical frameworks becomes progressively challenging. Each ethical dilemma in the technology domain is unique and needs distinct social, ethical, and legal solutions. The ongoing evolution of technology, coupled with the absence of well-established ethical standards, contributes to the complication of confirming compliance. Ethical guidelines are still in the developmental stage, with different areas adopting varying standards and policies. This lack of clarity and steadiness in ethical guidance creates potential grey areas, increasing the risk of privacy breaches, ethical concerns, and data breaches that demand resolution (Dhirani et al., 2023).

LITERATURE REVIEW

Security of Personal Information

"Augmented reality (AR)" and "Virtual reality (VR)" technologies are offering interesting sights into a future characterized by enhanced connectivity and immersive experiences. However, these advancements have a significant downside: heightened data collection and privacy issues not seen in other consumer technologies. Developers and policymakers must focus on addressing specific harms and stopping extensive data collection to unlock the full potential of AR/VR while minimizing privacy risks. It's critical to identify that the data collected, including noticeable, observed, computed, and associated information, differs in sensitivity and potential harm. Instead of targeting the technologies themselves, stakeholders should focus on understanding and justifying the actual harms associated with this data. This method enables developers to distinguish between user preferences and critical privacy risks, with developers directly addressing privacy preferences and policymakers prevailing to mitigate potential harm from user information (Dick,

2021). Virtual reality raises ethical concerns related to physiological and mental impacts and behavioural and social aspects. Managing these ethical issues requires a multi-faceted approach, encompassing regulations and laws (such as government and institutional approval) and ethical practices in developing and using these technologies, which involves considerations of respect, care, morals, and education (Ben, 2018). While the possibilities of AR/VR applications are vast, allowing users to visualize atomic-level chemical reactions or embark on space expeditions, they also introduce challenges related to data privacy, platform misuse, and broader ethical concerns. As the landscape evolves, navigating these issues will require a delicate balance between technological innovation, user preferences, and proactive ethical considerations (Doshi et al., 2021).

Extended Reality technology, encompassing virtual and augmented reality, has seen a surge in privacy, ethics, and security concerns. When utilized in remote settings, highlighting principles such as ethics, responsibility, safety, and trust becomes domineering. Disclosing personal information through XR devices requires positive measures to safeguard individual data. Much like other ground-breaking technologies, XR presents significant challenges associated with handling personal data, which can be highly sensitive and identifying, including behavioural patterns. Particularly, technologies like eye-tracking, while enhancing graphics and responsiveness, introduce a privacy challenge by enabling the collection of friendly user data (Iqbal et al., 2023). The analysis of eye movement patterns unveils user preferences and thoughts, underscoring the significance of studying concerns related to privacy, security, and ethics (Gao & Zhang, 2021). The positive impacts of XR extend to users and producers, influencing diverse domains such as advertising, architecture, design, gaming, software, and publishing. This era is marked by the cross-industry potential of XR technologies, offering a wealth of creative, digital, and informational possibilities. Developers anticipate optimistic outcomes, foreseeing a democratization of the industry that translates to "More for Less" for users. This democratization promises plenty of content at lower costs, with immersive experiences facilitated by rapid data transfer and cloud computing. However, the noteworthy proficiencies of XR technologies also raise significant ethical, legal, and social questions (Novakova & Starchon, 2021). Ethical dilemmas emerge in the instant adoption of technologies from the Fourth Industrial Revolution (4IR). A virtues-based approach is advocated for resolving ethical challenges, shifting away from a purely practical perception to ensure humanity remains in control of technology (Peckham, 2021).

Privacy of Data

Ethical concerns related to the application of Augmented Reality (AR) can be categorized into four main categories: physical, psychological, moral, and data privacy. Precisely concentrating on data-related ethical concerns in the context of Augmented Reality applied to Learning Analytics (AR to LA), the level of collected data poses important privacy challenges. Implementing safeguards is important to eliminate these data-related ethical issues. The system incorporates a layer of ethical safeguards, which is designed to protect safety and privacy to address these concerns. This approach aims to create technology systems informed by ethics, fostering a more widespread adoption of these systems (Christopoulos et al., 2021). Virtual worlds have gained popularity. The complexity of ethical dilemmas, often not easily resolved with a simple yes or no decision, has led to limited exploration. Consequently, more examination is required of ethics in the world of virtuality. Regarding collaboration virtual teams, ethical challenges have been identified due to the distinctive capabilities of extended reality (XR) Respondents highlighted three ethical concerns: encouraging risky behaviours, accountability for actions in XR, and protecting data privacy, underscoring the importance of addressing and mitigating ethical challenges associated with using XR technology in collaborative environments (Ratcliffe et al., 2021). The arrival of virtual reality (VR) technology introduces a variety of novel and unique possibilities for scientific experiments. As researchers explore these capabilities, it becomes imperative to re-assess ethical guidelines that were recognized before the era of VR. The different experiences brought by new technologies, like sensory experience and challenges in transitioning back to reality, pose ethical considerations not thoroughly addressed by conventional psychological research guidelines. The existing ethical frameworks may prove insufficient in addressing the intricacies associated with VR research, necessitating a reconsideration of these guidelines. Issues like motion sickness, information overload, and the potential strengthening of experiences need practical strategies to ensure the well-being of applicants. Researchers must fight concerns about helplessness, reliance, stigma, and authenticity when using VR technology in experiments (Behr et al., 2005). Ethical practices in VR research demand thoughtful re-evaluation to safeguard applicants and support the honesty of the scientific process (Ligthart et al., 2021). Research has investigated the numerous security, privacy, and trust challenges related to retaining varied machine learning (ML) and deep learning (DL) techniques in the domain of artificial intelligence-extended reality (AI-XR) metaverse applications. The importance of developing AI-XR metaverse applications that are secure, safe, and reliable cannot be exaggerated. While collecting personal data within virtual environments can intensify the sense of realism, it simultaneously introduces ethical considerations regarding data privacy, sharing, and potential misuse. Within the extended reality domain, extensive personal information about participants, encompassing motor actions, eye movements, reflexes, preferences, habits, and interests, may be gathered (Hosseini et al., 2023). In the ethical landscape, designers must agree to various considerations while developing virtual and augmented reality (VR/AR) products, including physical, psychological, moral, and social dimensions. Physical concerns involve health and safety issues, such as dizziness, falling, or tripping over equipment while occupied in a scenario. Despite mindfulness of problems related to ethics surrounding "VR/AR" usage, a gap exists in understanding designers' perceptions when making decisions in the design phase of VR/AR products. Analysing the viewpoints of creators and inventors might brighten ethical decisions that may or may not regularly factor into expanding its products or applications (Steele et al., 2020). Addressing the need for expertise, some researchers advocate for forming a novel medical specialty known as the "virtualist." This professional would suffer extensive technical and medical training while owning a thoughtful understanding of the ethical implications of VR/AR technologies (Bruno et al., 2022). As technology advances, there is a growing need for ethical studies to direct the connection between virtual reality and privacy and ensure that individuals retain control over their personal information in immersive digital environments. When shared, virtual reality (VR) environments give rise to various ethical and social concerns that have not been thoroughly addressed (Schroeder, 2007). There is a growing consensus on the need to start ethical guidelines to regulate user actions in virtual reality ethics. Some researchers have expressed concern about the possibility of corrupt activities, such as acts of violence, within VR, highlighting the significance of ethical analysis (Kade, 2016). The argument spreads to the view that actions within virtual environments may have real-world significance, raising moral questions across various ethical traditions. Efforts to completely remove these ethical challenges are impossible, as the removal process may clash with other ethical principles. The root of the issue looks to be centred around individual choice – whether users choose to employ VR technologies in a manner that is positive or harmful. Virtual environments involve both immersive and non-immersive recreations of daily activities. As technologies and procedures are accomplished, the cognitive processes become more dominant. It is imperious to address ethical concerns within the framework of extended mind technology (Parsons, 2021). The influence of Virtual Reality Technologies and gaming on children remains a subject of ongoing scientific debate, presenting a composite, long-term, multi-faceted challenge. Addressing these ethical issues needs clear communication and understanding among probable users, parents, children, and educators regarding the nature and capabilities of VRTs (Kaimara et al., 2022). In the quickly developing landscape of technology, Augmented Reality is a concept that has been introduced previously. The immediate flow of digital learning systems and the implication of Augmented reality is rising. Research findings show that issues and concerns related to this new technology include information and reasoning excess, the complications and preciousness of the technology, and technical issues like connectivity difficulties (Alzahrani, 2020).

Informed Consent

It can be argued that the technology is impartial, but the users, through their choices, determine the impact of its use. The right to privacy, considered a fundamental human right, is a relevant concern in VR. Like present computational devices like personal computers and mobile phones, VR devices raise worries about the potential for data collection without obvious user consent (Kabha, 2019). O'Hagan et al. (2023) discussed that XR requires a lot of detail from users. They recommended that PET (Privacy Enhancing Technologies) should selectively facilitate awareness and permission by considering the nature of AR activity and the link to bystanders. By doing this, the users can be guaranteed respect for their privacy. Pets must include adequate scope for users' consent. Homayouni, C., & Zytko, D. (2023) found that technologies for Extended Reality (XR) have promise for transforming social experiences, they also run the risk of aggravating the interpersonal ills associated with social VR, which are currently common. The authors recommended the use of permission as a unique design paradigm to help in the development of XR technologies targeted at minimizing damage, while also foreseeing the importance of virtual and physical harm through VR-to-AR social interaction. A three-step procedure was advocated for using a consent lens in the design of XR experiences: choosing a model or definition of consent, creating XR consent mechanics to help people use consent by the model, and conducting user research to evaluate the consent mechanics. Mittal et al. (2024) found that one of the negative aspects of AI and other technological advancements is the privacy concern, specifically when no explicit consent is taken from the users. It affects the users' trust, autonomy, and reliability. Mitchell & Khazanchi (2012) discussed ethics in a world of virtuality, aiming to explore the ethical implications of employing virtual worlds and their exclusive technological proficiencies.

Financial Security

Examining ethical limits in immersive calculation is a crucial point of this study, where experts will segment their ethical perceptions on the developing landscape. Applicants are motivated to contribute questions and understandings as we fight with ethical problems essential in the evolution of our physical world to the digital domain (Bye et al., 2019). Security risks become a serious concern as the metaverse emerges, surrounding new fears of data protection, identity theft, and fraud. The challenges related to privacy and security are disclosed across four layers, with blockchain playing a crucial role in the development of transparency and association between real and digital economies (Chen et al., 2022). To strike a suitable balance, ethical oversight and restraints are imperious. Addressing ethical matters associated with data proves complicated because of its pervasive nature and intrinsic intricacies in data science (Hand, 2018). Once a distant concept, the metaverse now demands measures to ensure its virtual reality is safe and secure. This paper delves into key security threats within the metaverse and proposes potential solutions, emphasizing the need for their integration and development (Sethi, 2022). Defining the metaverse has proven challenging, with various explanations mixing. Rather than presenting a firm definition, the study identified four essential characteristics that define the metaverse: socialization, immersive interaction, real-world construction, and expandability. These features make an attractive digital dominion but also expose the metaverse to security and privacy risks. Potential threats include personal data, information leaks, and access without authority (Hang et al., 2023). As virtual reality introduces new possibilities, concerns about the legal and ethical dimensions of the metaverse, marked by a considerable grey area, are surfacing (Maloney et al., 2021).

Objectives of the Study

- To determine the factors that constituting Ethical Considerations of XR (Extended Reality) in Online Retailing
- To ascertain the impact of Ethical Considerations of XR on consumers usage Consciousness for XR.

METHODOLOGY

The sample size chosen for the study was 289 retail consumers. The sampling method used was Judgement Sampling. Only those customers were chosen who had an exposure of XR features while shopping online. In this regard filter questions were mentioned in the questionnaire and only those respondents were taken forward to fill the questionnaire who responded positively to those questions.

The data analysis was conducted with the help of "Exploratory Factor Analysis (EFA)" and "Multiple Regression Analysis (MRA)". EFA helped in determining the XR factors. And MRA helped in measuring the impact of XR factors on consumers' consciousness while using the XR. The results were further validated with "Artificial Neural Network". ANN was applied 10 times while taking 70% data for training and 30% data for testing.

Findings

General details of respondents show that 67.1% of males and 32.9% of females contributed to a total of 289 respondents. Among them, 24.2% are below 35 years of age, 46.0% belong to the age category of 35-40 years, and the rest, 29.8%, are above 40 years of age. 23.9% are homemakers, 33.6% are employed/self-employed, 26.3% are in business, and the rest 16.3% are in other occupational sectors (Table 1).

Table 1. General details

Variables	Respondents	Percentage
Gender		
Male	194	67.1
Female	95	32.9
Total	**289**	**100**
Age (years)		
Below 35	70	24.2
35-40	133	46.0
Above 40	86	29.8
Total	**289**	**100**
Occupation		
Homemaker	69	23.9
Employed/self-employed	97	33.6
Business	76	26.3
Others	47	16.3
Total	**289**	**100**

Exploratory Factor Analysis

Table 2. KMO and Bartlett's test

"Kaiser-Meyer-Olkin Measure of Sampling Adequacy"		.892
"Bartlett's Test of Sphericity"	Approx. Chi-Square	4248.628
	df	136
	Sig.	.000

KMO value is 0.892, and "Barlett's Test of Sphericity" is significant (Table 2).

Table 3. Total variance explained

"Component"	"Initial Eigenvalues"			"Rotation Sums of Squared Loadings"		
	"Total"	"% of Variance"	"Cumulative %"	"Total"	"% of Variance"	"Cumulative %"
1	7.425	43.677	43.677	4.203	**24.724**	24.724
2	2.485	14.621	58.297	3.477	**20.451**	45.175
3	1.992	11.720	70.017	2.910	**17.115**	62.290
4	1.582	9.306	79.323	2.895	**17.032**	**79.323**
5	.647	3.804	83.127			
6	.488	2.870	85.997			
7	.419	2.463	88.460			
8	.352	2.071	90.531			
9	.294	1.730	92.261			
10	.237	1.394	93.655			
11	.218	1.285	94.941			
12	.203	1.196	96.136			
13	.180	1.057	97.193			
14	.152	.892	98.085			
15	.130	.765	98.850			
16	.110	.649	99.499			
17	.085	.501	100.000			

The "principal component analysis" method was applied to extract the factors, and it was found that 4 factors have been formed from 17 variables. The factors explained the variance of 24.724%, 20.451%, 17.115%, and 17.032%, respectively. The total variance explained is 79.323% (Table 3).

Figure 1. Scree plot

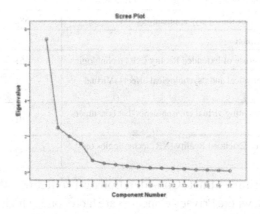

The graph above depicts the Eigenvalues generated from the "Total Variance Explained table" for an elbow with four components.

Table 4. Rotated component matrix

S. No.	Statements	"Factor Loading"	"Factor Reliability"
I	**Privacy Concerns**		.954
1	Ethical concern arises for excessive data gathering without clear justification	.881	
2	Risk of data theft or misuse from stored data	.875	
3	Concerned of how location data will be used and have the option to disable location tracking	.859	
4	While personalization, avoid excessive profiling and targeted advertising	.853	
5	Ethical concern arises for potential future uses of collected data	.778	
II	**Informed Consent**		.941
1	Fully informed about how data will be used, stored, and shared using XR technologies	.902	
2	Reducing Complexity with technical language while XR experiences	.893	
3	Informed consent during real-time interactions and experiences	.886	
4	Obtaining parental consent and ensuring age-appropriate content in XR applications	.874	
III	**Security Risks**		.871
1	Unauthorized access to sensitive user information	.880	
2	Cybersecurity threats of Extended Reality (XR) devices	.861	
3	Risk of identity theft and fraud within XR environments	.836	
4	Security standards for third-party applications	.682	
IV	**Psychological Impact**		.859
1	Addiction and overuse of Extended Reality (XR) technologies	.851	
2	Risk of adverse physical and psychological effects (Virtual Reality Sickness)	.843	
3	XR applications creating virtual environments that consumers perceive as real	.791	
4	Potential impact of Extended Reality (XR) technologies on mental health	.732	

Factors that determine Ethical Considerations as Limitations of Extended Reality are shown in Table 4, where Privacy Concerns are factor one, which includes variables like Ethical concern arising from excessive data gathering without clear justification, risk of data theft or misuse from stored data, concerned of how location data will be used and have the option to disable location tracking, While personalization, avoid excessive profiling and targeted advertising, and Ethical concern arises for potential future uses of collected data. The second factor is named Informed Consent, and its associated variables are Fully informed about how data will be used, stored, and shared using XR technologies, Reducing complexity with technical language while XR experiences. Informed consent during real-time interactions and experiences obtaining parental consent and ensuring age-appropriate content in XR applications. Other factors are Security Risks which include variables like Unauthorized access to sensitive user information, Cybersecurity threats of Extended Reality (XR) devices, risk of identity theft and fraud within XR environments, and Security standards for third-party applications. The fourth factor is Psychological Impact, and its associated variables are Addiction and overuse of Extended Reality (XR) technologies, Risk of adverse physical and psychological effects (Virtual Reality Sickness), XR applications creating virtual environments that consumers perceive as real and Potential impact of Extended Reality (XR) technologies on mental health (Table 4).

Multiple Regression Analysis

Table 5. Reliability statistics

"Cronbach's Alpha"	"N of Items"
.912	17

The reliability for 4 constructs with a total of seventeen elements is 0.912 (Table 5).

Table 6. Model Summary

"Model"	"R"	"R Square"	"Adjusted R Square"	"Std. Error of the Estimate"
1	.716[a]	.513	.506	.60294

a. Predictors: (Constant), Privacy Concerns, Informed Consent, Security Risks and Psychological Impact

Multiple regressions shows that model explained is 51% of the variance and R Square = .513 (Table 6).

Table 7. ANOVA

"Model"		"Sum of Squares"	"df"	"Mean Square"	"F"	"Sig."
1	Regression	108.846	4	27.212	74.853	.000[b]
	Residual	103.244	284	.364		
	Total	212.090	288			

a. Dependent Variable: I use Extended Reality Wisely
b. Predictors: (Constant), Privacy Concerns, Informed Consent, Security Risks and Psychological Impact

Table 7 shows the ANOVA results, which clarifies that there is a significant impact of determinants of XR on consumers' consciousness while using XR as the p value is below 0.05.

Table 8. Coefficients

"Model"	"Unstandardized Coefficients"		"Standardized Coefficients"	"t"	"Sig."
	"B"	"Std. Error"	"Beta"		
(Constant)	3.900	.035		109.952	.000
Privacy Concerns	.176	.036	.205	4.941	.000
Informed Consent	.572	.036	.666	16.088	.000
Security Risks	.115	.036	.134	3.236	.001
Psychological Impact	.085	.036	.099	2.387	.018

a. Dependent Variable: I use Extended Reality Wisely

Privacy Concerns, Informed Consent, Security Risks, and Psychological Impact all the independent variables show a significant impact on the dependent variable "I use Extended Reality Wisely". It is also found that the highest impact is shown by Informed Consent with beta value of 0.666 followed by Privacy Concerns (0.205), Security Risks (0.134), and Psychological Impact with beta value of 0.099 (Table 8).

Validating Regression Results With Artificial Neural Network (ANN)

Table 9. RMSE values

"Training"			"Testing"			
"N"	"SSE"	"RMSE"	"N"	"SSE"	"RMSE"	"Total Samples"
191	46.759	0.495	98	20.056	0.452	289
199	49.407	0.498	90	22.433	0.499	289
202	51.693	0.506	87	24.722	0.533	289

continued on following page

Table 9. Continued

"Training"			"Testing"			
"N"	"SSE"	"RMSE"	"N"	"SSE"	"RMSE"	"Total Samples"
209	46.778	0.473	80	30.854	0.621	289
211	54.569	0.509	78	14.281	0.428	289
203	46.748	0.480	86	25.96	0.549	289
206	56.217	0.522	83	16.654	0.448	289
205	47.048	0.479	84	20.249	0.491	289
195	59.447	0.552	94	23.533	0.500	289
207	47.705	0.480	82	18.111	0.470	289
Mean	**50.637**	**0.499**		**21.685**	**0.499**	
Standard Deviation	**4.635**	**0.024**		**4.867**	**0.057**	

RMSE – Root Mean Square of Errors. SSE – Sum of Squared Errors, N=Sample Size

Source: Calculated from SPSS Output

Table 9 shows the RMSE, SSE, and Sample Size (N) for training and testing data. The mean of SSE and RMSE for training data is 50.637 and 0.499, whereas the Standard Deviation of SSE and RMSE for training data is 4.635. and 0.024. Similarly, the mean of SSE and RMSE for testing data is 21.685 and 0.499, whereas the Standard Deviation of SSE and RMSE for testing data is 4.867 and 0.057.

Table 10. Sensitivity analysis

Neural Network (NN)	Privacy Concerns	Informed Consent	Security Risks	Psychological Impact
NN	0.171	0.612	0.135	0.082
NN	0.201	0.564	0.137	0.098
NN	0.222	0.508	0.205	0.065
NN	0.194	0.606	0.117	0.083
NN	0.201	0.652	0.100	0.046
NN	0.162	0.635	0.108	0.096
NN	0.228	0.583	0.118	0.071
NN	0.210	0.523	0.168	0.099
NN	0.21	0.523	0.168	0.099
NN	0.215	0.58	0.097	0.107
Average	0.201	0.579	0.135	0.085
"Results in Multiple Regression" (MRA)	**.205**	**.666**	**.134**	**.099**
Normalized Average	**0.348**	**1.000**	**0.234**	**0.146**

continued on following page

Table 10. Continued

Neural Network (NN)	Privacy Concerns	Informed Consent	Security Risks	Psychological Impact
Ranks in ANN Results	2.00	1.00	3.00	4.00
Ranks in "Multiple Regression"	2.00	1.00	3.00	4.00

Source: Compiled by Authors

In Table 10, the results of coefficient and ranking have been listed for ANN as well as multiple regression analysis. It has been observed that there is a slight difference between the results of MRA and ANN for coefficients of explanatory variables. It was found that there is a slight difference between the coefficient values of MRA and ANN for the given explanatory variables. However, the ranking of importance of explanatory variables is the same, hence ANN has validated the same results as produced by the MRA.

Figure 2. Average normalized importance score of independent variables

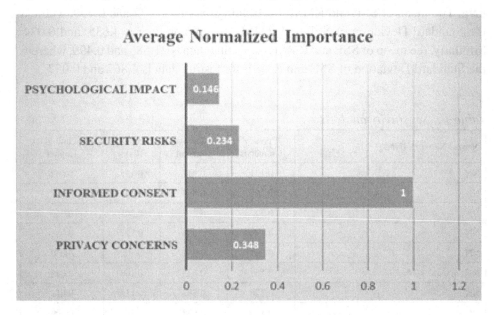

Table 10 and Figure 2 show the normalized importance of all the independent variables namely Privacy Concerns, Informed Consent, Security Risks, and Psychological Impact. The Dependent Variable is "I use Extended Reality Wisely". Based on the average of 10 different normalized importance scores, it was concluded that the most important is Informed Consent, followed by Privacy Concerns Security Risks, and Psychological Impact.

DISCUSSION AND MANAGERIAL IMPLICATIONS

This study contributes a fresh understanding of XR in the context of how consumers perceive it from the lens of their concerns. The findings of this study are important for businesses run using new technologies. The professionals leading ventures belonging to e-commerce, fintech, gaming, etc. must understand if they use XR, their long-term success will depend on how well they address the privacy concerns of their customers, assure them about their security, take their permission before fetching their personal information and making them feel comfortable while experiencing XR. The study also provides evidence of customers' seriousness about their privacy. This, in the future, will raise concerns about policy making by the government for tech-based businesses, hence marketers as well as business owners must modify their businesses in such a way that they can comply with the government policies from time to time. In addition to this, to be ethical, and to safeguard personal information from manual interventions tech-based ventures and service providers are suggested to imbibe blockchain technology in their operations.

CONCLUSION

The study was conducted to know the factors that determine Ethical Considerations as Limitations of Extended Reality through the Lens of Retail Consumers and the impact of Ethical Considerations on Extended Reality. It is found that Privacy Concerns, Informed Consent, Security Risks, and Psychological Impact are the factors that determine Ethical Considerations as Limitations of Extended Reality showing a significant impact on the dependent variable "I use Extended Reality Wisely". The study concludes that the most important ethical consideration is Informed Consent for Retail Consumers. To validate the results, ANN Was applied post-MRA, and it was found that the ranking of importance of explanatory variables is the same, hence ANN has validated the same results as produced by the MRA.

REFERENCES

Alam, S. S., Susmit, S., Lin, C. Y., Mohammad, M., & Ho, Y. H. (2021). Factors Affecting Augmented Reality Adoption in the Retail Industry. *Journal of Open Innovation*, 7(142), 1–24. 10.3390/joitmc7020142

Alzahrani, N. M. (2020). Augmented Reality: A Systematic Review of Its Benefits and Challenges in E-learning Contexts. *Applied Sciences (Basel, Switzerland)*, 10(16), 1–21. 10.3390/app10165660

Behr, K. M., Nosper, A., Klimmt, C., & Hartmann, T. (2005). Some Practical Considerations of Ethical Issues in VR Research. *Presence (Cambridge, Mass.)*, 14(6), 668–676. 10.1162/105474605775196535

Ben, K. (2018). Virtual Reality: Ethical Challenges and Dangers: Physiological and Social Impacts. *IEEE Technology and Society Magazine*, 20–25. 10.1109/MTS.2018.2876104

Bruno, R. R., Wolff, G., Wernly, B., Masyuk, M., Piayda, K., Leaver, S., Erkens, R., Oehler, D., Afzal, S., Heidari, H., Kelm, M., & Jung, C. (2022). Virtual and augmented reality in critical care medicine: The patient's, clinician's, and researcher's perspective. *Critical Care*, 26(326), 1–13. 10.1186/s13054-022-04202-x36284350

Bye, K., Hosfelt, D., Chase, S., Miesnieks, M., & Beck, T. (2019). *The Ethical and Privacy Implications of Mixed Reality*. SIGGRAPH. 10.1145/3306212.3328138

Chen, Z., J., Wu, Gan, W., & Qi, Z. (2022). Metaverse Security and Privacy: An Overview, *2022 IEEE International Conference on Big Data (Big Data)*, (pp. 2950-2959). IEEE. 10.1109/BigData55660.2022.10021112

Christopoulos, A., Mystakidis, S., Pellas, N., & Jussi Laakso, M. (2021). ARLEAN: An Augmented Reality Learning Analytics Ethical Framework. *Computers*, 10(8), 92. 10.3390/computers10080092

Dastane, O., Rafiq, M. & Turner, J.J. (2024). *Implications of metaverse, virtual reality, and extended reality for development and learning in organizations*. Development and Learning in Organizations. 10.1108/DLO-09-2023-0196

Dhirani, L. L., Mukhtiar, N., Chowdhry, B. S., & Newe, T. (2023). Ethical Dilemmas and Privacy Issues in Emerging Technologies: A Review. *Sensors (Basel)*, 23(3), 1–18. 10.3390/s2303115136772190

Dick, E. (2021). Balancing User Privacy and Innovation in Augmented and Virtual Reality, *Information Technology & Innovation Foundation*, 1-27.

Doshi, Y., Ramachandran, M., Dubey, A., Ankalagi, G., Raje, S., & Munshi, A. (2021). A Review of Opportunities, Applications, and Challenges of XR in Education. *International Journal of Innovative Research in Technology*, 7(9), 292–296.

Fox, D. (2022). Extended Reality (XR) Ethics and Diversity, Inclusion, And Accessibility, *The IEEE Global Initiative on Ethics of Extended Reality (XR) Report*, 1-24.

Gao, J., & Zhang, X. (2021). The Applications of Digital Extended Reality in Biomedicine. *Mini Review*, 6(3344), 1–3.

Hand, D. J. (2018). Aspects of Data Ethics in a Changing World: Where Are We Now? *Big Data*, 6(3), 176–190. 10.1089/big.2018.008330283727

Hang, Y., Li, Y., & Cai, Z. (2023). Security and Privacy in Metaverse: A Comprehensive Survey. *Big Data Mining and Analytics*, 6(2), 234–247. 10.26599/BDMA.2022.9020047

Homayouni, C., & Zytko, D. (2023). Consensual XR: A consent-based design framework for mitigating harassment and harm against marginalized users in social VR and AR. *2023 IEEE International Symposium on Mixed and Augmented Reality Adjunct (ISMAR-Adjunct)*. IEEE. 10.1109/ISMAR-Adjunct60411.2023.00077

Hosseini, M. M., Hooshmandja, M., & Hosseini, T. M. (2023). Ethical Dilemmas of Mixed and Extended Reality. *Journal of Medical Education*, 22(1), 1–2. 10.5812/jme-133854

Iqbal, M. Z., Xu, X., Nallur, V., Scanlon, M., & Campbell, A. G. (2023). *Security*. Ethics and Privacy Issues in the Remote Extended Reality for Education., 10.1007/978-981-99-4958-8_16

Kabha, R. (2019). Ethical Challenges of Digital Immersive and VR, *Journal of Content. Community & Communication*, 9(5), 41–49. 10.31620/JCCC.06.19/07

Kade, D. (2016). Ethics of Virtual Reality Applications in Computer Game Production. *Philosophies*, *1*. .10.3390/philosophies1010073

Kaimara, P., Oikonomou, A., & Deliyannis, I. (2022). Could virtual reality applications pose real risks to children and adolescents? A systematic review of ethical issues and concerns. *Virtual Reality (Waltham Cross)*, 26(2), 697–735. 10.1007/s10055-021-00563-w34366688

Kumlu, S. T., Samancıoğlu, E., & Özkul, E. (2024). Reality Technologies (AR, VR, MR, XR) in Tourism. Tanrisever, C., Pamukçu, H. and Sharma, A. (eds.) *Future Tourism Trends Volume 2 (Building the Future of Tourism)*. Emerald. 10.1108/978-1-83753-970-320241007

Ligthart, S., Meynen, G., Biller-Andorno, N., Kooijmans, T., & Kellmeyer, P. (2021). Is Virtually Everything Possible? The Relevance of Ethics and Human Rights for Introducing Extended Reality in Forensic Psychiatry. *AJOB Neuroscience*, 13(3), 144–157. 10.1080/21507740.2021.189848933780323

Madary, M., & Metzinger, T. K. (2016). Real virtuality: A Code of Ethical Conduct. Recommendations for Good Scientific Practice and the Consumers of VR-Technology. *Frontiers in Robotics and AI*, 3(3), 1–23.

Maloney, D., Freeman, G., & Robb, A. (2021). Social Virtual Reality: Ethical Considerations and Future Directions for An Emerging Research Space, *2021 IEEE Conference on Virtual Reality and 3D User Interfaces Abstracts and Workshops.* IEEE. , 271-277.10.1109/VRW52623.2021.00056

Meenaakshisundaram, K. V. (2023). *The Ethics of Extended Realities: Insights from a Systematic Literature Review.* Uppsala University.

Mitchell, A., & Khazanchi, D. (2012). Ethical Considerations for Virtual Worlds. *Proceedings of the Eighteenth Americas Conference on Information Systems*, Seattle, Washington.

Mittal, A. (2024). Impact of Negative Aspects of Artificial Intelligence on Customer Purchase Intention: An Empirical Study of Online Retail Customers Towards AI-Enabled E-Retail Platforms. In R. Verma, P. Kumar, S. Goyal, & S. Dadwal (Eds.), *Demystifying the dark side of AI in business* (1st ed., *Vol. 1*, pp. 159–173). IGI Global. 10.4018/979-8-3693-0724-3.ch010

Novakova, H., & Starchon, P. (2021). Creative Industries: Challenges And Opportunities in XR Technologies, SHS Web of Conferences 115. *Current Problems of the Corporate Sector*, 2021, 1–9. 10.1051/shsconf/202111503011

O'Hagan, J., Saeghe, P., Gugenheimer, J., Medeiros, D., Marky, K., Khamis, M., & McGill, M. (2022). Privacy-Enhancing Technology and Everyday Augmented Reality: Understanding Bystanders' Varying Needs for Awareness and Consent. *Proceedings of the ACM on Interactive, Mobile, Wearable and Ubiquitous Technologies*, 6(4), 1–35. 10.1145/3569501

Parsons, T. D. (2021). Ethical Challenges of Using Virtual Environments in the Assessment and Treatment of Psychopathological Disorders. *Journal of Clinical Medicine*, 10(3), 1–16. 10.3390/jcm1003037833498255

Peckham, J. B. (2021). The ethical implications of 4IR. *Journal of Ethics in Entrepreneurship and Technology*, 1(1), 30–42. 10.1108/JEET-04-2021-0016

Ratcliffe, J., Soave, F., Bryan-Kinns, N., Tokarchuk, L., & Farkhatdinov, I. (2021). Extended Reality (XR) Remote Research: A Survey of Drawbacks and Opportunities. *CHI*, 21(May), 8–13. 10.1145/3411764.3445170

Schroeder, R. (2007). An overview of ethical and social issues in shared virtual environments. *Futures*, 39(6), 704–717. 10.1016/j.futures.2006.11.009

Sethi, A. (2022). Security and Privacy in Metaverse: Issues, Challenges, and Future Opportunities. *Cyber Security Insights Magazine*, 2, 1–4.

Skulmowski, A. (2023). Ethical issues of educational virtual reality, *Computers & Education: X Reality*, 2, 1-8.

Slater, M., Liencres, C. G., Haggard, P., Vinkers, C., Clarke, R. G., Jelley, S., Watson, Z., Breen, G., Schwarz, R., Steptoe, W., Szostak, D., Halan, S., Fox, D., & Silver, J. (2020). The Ethics of Realism in Virtual and Augmented Reality. *Frontiers in Virtual Reality*, 1(1), 1–13. 10.3389/frvir.2020.00001

Steele, P., Burleigh, C., Kroposki, M., Magabo, M., & Bailey, L. (2020). Ethical Considerations in Designing Virtual and Augmented Reality Products—Virtual and Augmented Reality Design with Students in Mind: Designers' Perceptions. *Journal of Educational Technology Systems*, 49(2), 1–20. 10.1177/0047239520933858

Zhao, R., Zhang, Y., Zhu, Y., Lan, R., & Hua, Z. (2021). Metaverse: Security and Privacy Concerns. *Journal of Latex Class Files*, 14(8), 1–7.

Chapter 4
Virtual Dilemmas:
Legal and Ethical Rollercoasters in Immersive Tech Land

Akanksha Yadav
NALSAR University of Law, Hyderabad, India

K. G. Neha Reddy
NALSAR University of Law, Hyderabad, India

ABSTRACT

The advent of immersive technologies like VR, AR, and MR has transformed human experiences, prompting legal and ethical complexities. This chapter delves into privacy, regulatory, consent, and accessibility challenges. Balancing innovation with regulation is crucial to mitigate risks for users. Consent and agency in virtual spaces raise questions about autonomy, while issues like virtual harassment and property rights challenge existing legal norms. Immersive technologies promise enhanced accessibility but require inclusive design efforts. Robust privacy protections are necessary to prevent data breaches. Collaboration among policymakers, technologists, ethicists, and society is essential to ensure immersive tech fosters empowerment and inclusion in both virtual and physical realms.

INTRODUCTION

In this nascent era of digitalization, where innovation is the preferred means of expression and creativity prevails absolute, we will embark on an exploration of the entrancing domains of technology. The term "immersion" describes a mental condition in which a person's awareness of their physical self is reduced or even completely gone while they are in a captivating, immersive setting, usually one that

DOI: 10.4018/979-8-3693-2432-5.ch004

is manufactured. Increased spatial awareness, focused attention, a distorted sense of time, and a feeling of effortless participation are frequently indicative of this mental (Handa et al., 2012).

Any technology that fully stimulates the user's senses and produces a realistic, highly interactive experience is referred to as immersive technology. Virtual reality (VR), augmented reality (AR), mixed reality (MR), and extended reality (XR) technologies are usually used in it. By superimposing digital content on top of the actual world, these technologies seek to either fully submerge people in virtual worlds or improve their impression of it.

1. Augmented Reality (AR): Using the camera of a smartphone, tablet, or AR glasses, AR projects digital data or virtual objects onto the user's perspective of the actual environment. By incorporating digital components like text, photos, or 3D models into the physical world, augmented reality (AR) improves it and opens up new uses in industries including industrial design, gaming, navigation, and advertising.
2. Virtual Reality (VR): The idea of virtual reality (VR) was first introduced over 50 years ago by Sutherland, who likened it to a window that allows users to experience the virtual world. Brooks has described virtual reality (VR) as an experience when the user is fully immersed in a virtual environment that responds to their actions (Odeleye et al., 2023) . Virtual reality can be defined as "a real or simulated environment in which a perceiver experiences telepresence"(Thierer & Camp, 2017) .
3. Mixed Reality (MR): A wide range of technologies, including virtual reality (VR) and augmented reality (AR), are included in the category of mixed reality (MR) devices. These devices combine features of the digital world with those of the actual world (Hosfelt, 2019).
4. Extended Reality (XR): Extended reality (XR) is a comprehensive phrase that encompasses several immersive technologies, including virtual reality (VR), mixed reality (MR), and augmented reality (AR).

To provide these experiences, immersive technology frequently uses specialised hardware like goggles, headsets, or monitors. These pieces of gear allow users to interact with virtual objects and settings in a way that feels intuitive and natural.

In recent years, immersive technology has rapidly evolved from a niche concept to a mainstream phenomenon, profoundly impacting various aspects of human life. Virtual reality (VR), augmented reality (AR), and mixed reality (MR) have revolutionized industries such as entertainment, healthcare, education, and gaming, offering users immersive experiences that were previously unimaginable. However, as these technologies continue to proliferate and become more sophisticated, they bring forth a host of legal and ethical considerations that must be addressed.

As people adopt immersive technology, it is imperative that they give ethical, rights-based, and values-based approaches top priority. Due diligence and strong security measures are required due to the inherent threats to privacy, security, and online safety, especially when it comes to children and other vulnerable populations.

Philosophically speaking, the highly immersive nature of modern VR, AR, and MR has spurred thoughtful discussion on the moral implications of utilizing these technologies on people in order to address technical problems and investigate the intricate social, behavioral, and cognitive dynamics of human "virtuality" (Southgate et al., 2017). Today people of all age groups are facing issues because of these technologies, be it children or adults. Immersion technology is being used in a wide range of industries, such as training, simulation, education, gaming, entertainment, and healthcare. It provides new platforms for learning, communication, and engagement with digital information and the outside world.

This chapter aims to explore the intricate landscape of immersive technology, delving into its legal frameworks and ethical implications, while also examining the intersections between the two. By understanding the regulatory frameworks governing immersive technology and grappling with the ethical dilemmas they present, stakeholders can navigate this rapidly evolving field more effectively and responsibly.

Immersive technology offers unparalleled opportunities for innovation and advancement, but it also raises profound questions about privacy, safety, equity, and the nature of reality itself. From concerns about data protection and intellectual property rights to debates about the psychological impact of immersive experiences, the legal and ethical dimensions of these technologies are vast and complex.

By critically examining the legal and ethical aspects of immersive technology, this chapter seeks to shed light on the challenges and opportunities inherent in its development and deployment. By fostering dialogue and promoting responsible practices, we can harness the transformative potential of immersive technology while mitigating its risks and safeguarding the rights and well-being of users.

Understanding Immersive Technologies Market

The Immersive Technologies sector boasts a significant turnover of £2.34 billion, positioning it as the 55th largest sector by revenue and the 6th fastest-growing in our realm of Research, Technology, and Innovation Credits (RTIC). This surge in growth has captured the attention of investors, as evidenced by its inclusion among the top 10 fastest-growing sectors for venture capital funding. Furthermore, the sector offers promising prospects for job seekers, with roles advertised in this field commanding an average salary that is 6.88% higher than the UK's average wage. Such statistics underscore the sector's momentum and potential for continued expansion and innovation.

Applications of Immersive Technologies

Numerous applications in a wide range of industries are made possible by these developments in spatial interaction and sensory immersion. While immersive technology adoption is still primarily focused on entertainment, there are many more applications for it. Immersion technologies are proving to be important tools that improve productivity, efficiency, and learning in a variety of industries, including education, training, healthcare, and industry.

Immersive technologies is crucial everywhere in the modern world. It is used in a number of contexts, such as e-commerce and retail, the adult industry, interactive storytelling, art, entertainment, and video games, as well as the military, education, and medical fields (Saraswathi et al., 2020). All types of immersive technologies have their own usage.

Let's look specifically into Augmented reality and Virtual Reality. AR integrates real and virtual items and is interactive and registered in three dimensions (Carmigniani & Furht, 2011). Three elements make up augmented reality (AR): real-time interactions, accurate 3D identification of virtual and real things, and a blend of digital and physical worlds. Today, AR is transforming a number of industries. Games such as Pokémon GO incorporate virtual animals into their real-world settings. AR enhances education through virtual field excursions and interactive textbooks. Retailers visualize things in consumers' homes and offer virtual try-on experiences.

Similarly other applications using different types of immersive technologies are Therapeutics for posttraumatic stress disorder, neurorehabilitation for strokes, proprioception and body swapping research for allocentric purposes, use of VR for studying 3D cellular models (e.g., neural tissues), or biodiversity conservation sciences—which use VR in an effort to save endangered animals— are some pertinent examples of recent applications of VR to science (Rubio-Tamayo et al., 2017). It is anticipated that as this technology spreads, more possible uses will surface.

Emerging Benefits of Immersive Technologies

Immersion experiences are superior to both traditional online and physical encounters because they mimic reality, enhance perceptions of physical reality, and allow for a higher level of sensory immersion and spatial involvement. These innovations are changing how we engage with digital material and the world around us, from transforming communication and entertainment to changing healthcare and education.

Because of this, a lot of businesses have started integrating these technologies into their processes for designing, developing, and maintaining products. For example, Boeing uses these technologies in its business segments for security, space, defense, and commerce. To reduce development costs, Jaguar Land Rover is implementing these technologies in its engineering and design studio, in the automotive sector. To reduce the amount of time it takes to resolve issues with services, Porsche Cars North America has begun using smart glasses to link technicians to remote experts (Nussipova et al., 2020). Thus, Immersion technologies offer a multitude of unique benefits across multiple areas and represent a paradigm shift in how we interact with digital content and the surrounding environment when compared to previous techniques. The most important of these advantages is the increased level of involvement they offer, engrossing viewers with interactive and immersive experiences that go beyond the constraints of passive media consumption. Immersion technologies also excel at giving users opportunities for hands-on learning, allowing them to actively participate in dynamic and experiential ways with digital knowledge, which improves understanding and retention. In contrast to conventional methods, immersive technologies provide the capacity to replicate authentic scenarios and environments. This enables professionals to receive training in environments that closely resemble real-world scenarios, ultimately improving readiness and skill acquisition.

All things considered, the numerous advantages of immersive technologies highlight their capacity to transform training, education, and participation, bringing in a new era of engaging and productive experiences in a variety of industries but still there are a lot of disadvantages of immersive technologies that need to be kept in consideration.

LEGAL AND ETHICAL IMPLICATION OF IMMERSIVE TECHNOLOGIES

In addition to its noted potential for transformation mentioned in previous sections, immersive technologies also provide several legal and ethical considerations that require serious study. The adoption of immersive technologies raises important legal and ethical considerations related to data privacy, intellectual property rights, user well-being, and inclusion. This requires a careful evaluation of the frameworks that regulate the creation, deployment, and use of these technologies. This section examines the complex landscape of legal and ethical considerations that are inherent in immersive technologies. It delves into the fundamental issues, difficulties, and principles that shape the proper integration of these technologies into society.

Legal Frameworks for Immersive Technology

As the use of immersive technology becomes more widespread, governments throughout the world are facing the challenge of regulating these new technologies while still promoting innovation. Regulatory authorities encounter the task of achieving equilibrium between safety considerations, safeguarding consumer interests, and promoting industry expansion in order to uphold ethical and legal benchmarks. Safety rules specifically aim at businesses like as gaming and healthcare, with a primary focus on reducing the potential dangers related to physical engagement inside virtual worlds. Consumer protection laws ensure the protection of individuals' rights and privacy by mandating openness in the acquisition and utilisation of data. Regulatory frameworks should facilitate the expansion of industries while maintaining public interests, encouraging competition, assisting small enterprises, and providing incentives for research and development. Standards organisations are essential in formulating recommendations for hardware and software, specifically focusing on matters such as interoperability and accessibility.

Privacy and Data Protection

Technology corporations have adopted the principles of 'ask for forgiveness not permission' and 'move fast and break things' at the expense of individual's privacy, security, and safety (Hosfelt, 2019). The collection and processing of vast volumes of personal data is frequently a part of immersive technology. Consequently, this gives rise to problems regarding the privacy of data, including issues of the ownership of data, permission, and protection. The issue of privacy becomes the main focus of these technologies, since the immersive nature of the technology intensifies the gathering of personal and biometric data (Francis Mundin, 2024). Legal frameworks have a responsibility to guarantee that the privacy rights of users are respected and that sufficient protections are in place to secure personal data in immersive settings.

Some of real-world situations that demonstrate the significance of taking into account the consequences of privacy regulations when developing and deploying immersive technology. Facebook (Zahid Anwar, 2021), Google Glass (Rachel Metz, 2014) etc have seen attention and censure for their management of user data in relation to immersive technology. There are concerns about the gathering, use, and possible abuse of personal data, specifically with regards to virtual reality (VR) and augmented reality (AR) technologies. Although some firms have incorporated privacy controls and features to tackle user concerns, such as conspicuous recording indications and user consent requirements, ongoing discussions continue over the level of data sharing and its impact on privacy rights in immersive settings. These instances underline the significance of taking into account the potential privacy consequences while creating and implementing immersive technologies. It is crucial for organisations to prioritise the protection of user privacy and data in order to uphold confidence and credibility.

Intellectual Property Rights

Immersive experiences encompass the creation and distribution of copyrighted material, virtual entities, and digital resources. Legal frameworks must effectively tackle concerns related to copyright infringement, trademark infractions, and the ownership of virtual property. In addition, the legal environment around immersive technology is further complicated by growing concerns such as deep fake law. This refers to the unauthorised use of people' likeness or copyrighted assets in digitally modified video. Given the increasing overlap between reality and fiction brought about by these technologies, it is crucial to tackle concerns related to intellectual property rights, privacy, and ethical usage in immersive settings.

The use of augmented reality (AR) and virtual reality (VR) technologies gives rise to apprehensions regarding copyright infringement, specifically when modifying or superimposing copyrighted works. Nevertheless, some circumstances such as fair dealing and the transformative doctrine may be applicable, permitting the generation of novel creations. Moreover, the freedom of panorama theory allows for the production of photographs or other visual representations of artworks that are publicly shown. Trademark infringements pose a significant concern, as third parties have the ability to enhance trademarks in the virtual realm. Although there are some who contend that this does not do any harm to trademark owners in the physical realm, legal precedents indicate otherwise. Every person possesses personality rights, which are not explicitly defined by legislation but are instead protected by basic rights, the Trademark Act, the Copyright Act, and several court decisions. In the matter of Shivaji Rao Gaikwad v. Varsha Productions, there was a disagreement about the employment of the name and persona in the production 'Main Hoon Rajnikanth'. The Madras High Court issued an injunction stating that the production did not have the necessary authorization. The current paradigm may be extended to the virtual environment, specifically in relation to AR/VR technologies (Mrittunjoy Guha Majumdar, 2022).

The utilisation of avatars in Virtual Reality gives rise to problems regarding personality rights, as courts acknowledge the rights of persons to exercise control over their own likeness, even inside virtual settings. Legal precedents have determined that the use of avatars that resemble actual persons without their consent might be considered a breach of personality rights or publicity rights (Vrishank Singhania, 2018).

Safety and Standards

Immersive technologies have the potential for physical hazards to users, including symptoms of motion sickness, eye fatigue, and the possibility of injury resulting from collisions within virtual worlds. There is concern over the possibility for users to become distracted when using augmented reality (AR) or virtual reality (VR) equipment in public places, which might lead to an elevated risk of accidents or injury. Examples such as the Pokémon GO phenomenon have brought attention to the risks of participating in immersive experiences in certain settings. Individuals engaged in activities such as playing Pokemon Go or using Google Glass may be physically there, but their mental focus is entirely directed towards a separate world. Dependency is a correlated issue of concern for safety. According to Jeremy Bailenson, the head of Stanford's Virtual Human Interaction Lab, immersion has a price. "Virtual reality removes you from your surroundings, it can be mentally demanding at times, and it cannot be consumed for extended periods of time like other forms of media" (Thierer & Camp, 2017).

The capacity of technology to induce health risks is not novel. The Nintendo Wii, for instance, resulted in several bodily and psychological damage. AVR poses a much greater risk since it fully engulfs people in an unfamiliar environment. It can induce symptoms such as 'virtual reality sickness,' epileptic convulsions, and nausea, among other things. The developer has the responsibility to provide users with enough notice and to explain the necessary safeguards that must be taken. As an illustration, the Nintendo Wii included comprehensive safety measures that were presented before to each game, along with accompanying warnings. If developers fail to provide enough care, the question that arises is whether they may be held accountable for product liability (Vrishank Singhania, 2018).

Legal frameworks should define safety criteria for immersive hardware and software, encompassing specifications for ergonomic design, suggested usage protocols, and certifications for product safety.

Cybersecurity and Digital Trust

Immersive technologies necessitate careful attention to cybersecurity and digital trust. As these technologies become increasingly widespread and linked, it is of utmost importance to guarantee the security of users' data and uphold confidence in the digital ecosystem. Immersive technologies such as virtual reality (VR), augmented reality (AR), and mixed reality (MR) provide novel difficulties and weaknesses that need to be resolved.

An important issue is the possibility of unauthorised individuals gaining access to sensitive data within immersive environments. As individuals engage with virtual environments and exchange personal information, there is an increased likelihood of data breaches and infringements on privacy. Ensuring the security of immersive platforms is crucial in order to protect user trust from being compromised by malevolent individuals attempting to exploit weaknesses. Illegitimate entry into a virtual reality (VR) system, categorised according to the Confidentiality, Integrity, and Availability (CIA) trinity of security attributes.

- Confidentiality: Safeguarding confidential information to prevent unauthorised access.
- Integrity: Unapproved alterations or adjustments to data.
- Availability: Ensuring uninterrupted and authorised entry to data and systems.

Moreover, the interlinked nature of immersive technology presents possibilities for hacks that have the potential to interrupt experiences or jeopardise user safety. Exploiting weaknesses in hardware, software, or network infrastructure can lead to a variety of assaults, such as data theft, virtual harassment, or manipulation.

A team of researchers from the University of Chicago has identified a novel "inception attack" that specifically targets Meta's Quest VR system. This assault takes use of a security flaw to gain control over headsets, extract confidential information, and manage social interactions through the use of generative AI. Despite not being implemented yet, the assault presents substantial dangers, as it necessitates hackers to get access to the user's Wi-Fi network. The assailants have the ability to insert malevolent code into the virtual reality (VR) system, creating a duplicate of the user's screen and applications, surveilling their actions, and altering their interactions. Meta intends to evaluate the findings, nevertheless, the event underscores the vulnerability of existing virtual reality (VR) systems and the absence of strong security measures. The attack capitalises on the vulnerability in Meta Quest headsets known as the "developer mode," which enables attackers connected to the same Wi-Fi network to obtain unauthorised access. When the attack is initiated, it allows the attacker to remotely view and record the user's screen and audio, giving them the ability to manipulate online activity, including financial transactions. Moreover, the attack has the ability to affect social interactions within virtual reality (VR) apps such as VRChat. Generative AI intensifies the danger by facilitating the production of persuasive speech and visual deepfakes, amplifying attackers' capacity to fool users in virtual reality (VR) settings (Melissa Heikkilä, 2024).

In order to tackle these difficulties, it is imperative to establish strong cybersecurity protocols across the whole immersive technology ecosystem. This involves the process of protecting hardware components, such as head-mounted displays and motion controllers, and assuring the reliability of software platforms and data transmission methods.

Overall cybersecurity and digital trust are crucial aspects of the immersive technology environment. It is necessary to take proactive steps to reduce risks and maintain user confidence in these new platforms.

Education and Awareness

The India Inequality Report 2022, published by Oxfam, provides insights on the influence of the digital gap on inequality in India amidst the epidemic. The text examines the absence of ICT (Information and Communication Technologies) access as a significant feature of the gap, and highlights the fact that almost 70 percent of the population has limited or no connectivity to digital services (INDIA DEVELOPMENT REVIEW, 2023). Integrating AR/VR technology in classrooms carries the potential to exacerbate the digital divide. The primary impediments to the implementation of new technologies include insufficient access to energy, unreliable internet connectivity, exorbitant expenses associated with data and virtual reality equipment that are beyond the means of many students, inadequate basic infrastructure, and a dearth of culturally suitable material (Mrittunjoy Guha Majumdar, 2022). Legal frameworks should facilitate public education and awareness campaigns aimed at promoting digital literacy, responsible utilisation of immersive technology, and understanding of legal rights and duties inside immersive settings. Possible components of this might encompass informative initiatives, instructional initiatives, and available materials for users, developers, and policymakers.

Ethical Frameworks for Immersive Technology

This section delves into the ethical concerns linked to immersive technologies, namely those mentioned earlier in the article. It aims to provide a comprehensive understanding of each subject by including relevant background information. Within the field of ethics, immersive technology introduces intricate deliberations across several domains. Digital equality efforts strive to narrow the disparity in availability of immersive technology, with a focus on making it more affordable and inclusive. Ensuring appropriate content in immersive environments involves finding a balance between allowing freedom of speech and reducing potential harm. This needs the establishment of explicit norms and a transparent process. Respectful engagement with various groups should be the primary focus of cultural representation in order to promote inclusion and ensure authenticity in content development. The ethical aspects of human-computer interaction emphasise the significance of user autonomy, informed consent, and user-centered design to advance responsible innovation and enhance user well-being in immersive experiences. These ethical standards serve as a structure for stakeholders to generate favourable and significant experiences for all users while minimising any negative consequences.

User Well-Being

The psychological impact of virtual reality (VR) is a subject of dispute, since there are worries about the possible blurring of boundaries between reality and the virtual world. This has raised concerns about the potential impact on mental health, particularly in youngsters. Social isolation is a worry because people may replace face-to-face contacts with virtual ones, which might result in social retreat. The potential misuse of VR equipment for malicious intentions, such as deliberately causing anguish or discomfort, is emphasised, prompting ethical concerns. The long-term consequences of limited usage of this technology are yet unclear (Kabha, 2019). Additionally, there are physical risks associated with its use, including as motion sickness, decreased awareness of one's surroundings, and the development of false expectations. Exposure to virtual settings, particularly in the realm of adult entertainment, can lead to unrealistic expectations, potentially causing changes in sexual urges and views of reality. Ultimately, the potential for distorting reality in the future gives rise to philosophical inquiries on the essence of perception and reality. These moral predicaments emphasise the necessity for thoughtful deliberation and conscientious utilisation of immersive technology.

Social Factors

* **Inclusivity and Accessibility**

Within the domain of immersive technology, guaranteeing fair and equal access and possibilities for every people is a crucial ethical consideration. Socioeconomic gaps might worsen the uneven availability of immersive technology, impeding marginalised people from reaping its benefits and perpetuate pre-existing inequalities. intricacies of digital equality and access in immersive technology, promoting the importance of inclusion and affordability in its creation and implementation. Ethical frameworks emphasise the significance of tackling digital equality as a core aspect of responsible technological advancement, giving priority to the requirements of marginalised populations. Efforts that support the development of digital skills, encourage community involvement, and ensure fair allocation of resources are crucial for reducing the gap in access to technology and empowering a wide range of people.

Prior studies have mostly examined the advantages of AR/VR technology in enhancing daily experiences, but there has been less investigation into its potential to improve the lives of those with impairments. This section provides a summary of the latest advancements in assistive Augmented Reality/Virtual Reality (AR/VR) technology for those with physical, cognitive, hearing, and visual disabilities. The technology emphasises a range of uses, including aiding those with impairments in areas like as rehabilitation, physiotherapy, sensory replacement, and interactive gaming systems. Furthermore, it acknowledges the obstacles and difficulties encountered by those with disabilities when they try to access or utilise immersive technology. It highlights the necessity for additional study to provide inclusive augmented reality/virtual reality experiences that cater to all users (Creed et al., 2024). The immersive web offers new possibilities to communicate and express yourself, but mechanisms that prevent abuse and harassment and allow users to govern their portrayal must be prioritised.

Efforts to give priority to diversity and inclusion in the creation of immersive content promote empathy and cultural appreciation, so contributing to the development of more inclusive communities. By adhering to moral values and tackling structural obstacles, individuals and organisations involved may strive to develop engaging encounters that empower every person, irrespective of their economic circumstances. This will contribute to advancing societal development and enhancing the well-being of individuals in an ever-growing digital society.

- **Cultural and Diversity**

This section emphasise the capacity of immersive technology to enhance a wide range of perspectives and cultural accounts, while also recognising the potential dangers of reinforcing stereotypes and engaging in cultural appropriation. This part examines the influence of immersive technology on the issue of global digital inequality. It highlights the importance of addressing the inequities that exist among marginalised people. Ethical frameworks promote the principles of respectful portrayal and engagement with various cultures while developing immersive content. Intersectionality highlights the interconnectedness of different social identities, such as class, gender, colour, ability, age, and sexuality, in influencing individual experiences and social interactions (Cathy Roche et al., 2022). The objective is to ensure the visibility of all individuals and redefine the conversation surrounding diversity. Intersectionality allows for a comprehensive understanding of power dynamics and promotes inclusivity and engagement by acknowledging the intricate nature of human experiences. Applying intersectionality in immersive technology entails recognising and resolving the overlapping characteristics in data to guarantee fairness in algorithms and redefining ethics to include a range of various viewpoints (Cathy Roche et al., 2022).

Co-design methodologies and cultural sensitivity training are suggested as techniques to promote the development of inclusive content production. It is necessary to establish collaborations with indigenous communities and cultural organisations in order to guarantee cultural authenticity in immersive experiences. The ethical considerations of human-computer interaction, including as user autonomy, informed consent, and user-centered design, play a vital role in ensuring responsible utilisation of immersive technology and placing user well-being as a top priority. Ethical design standards offer a structured approach to incorporating ethical factors into all phases of immersive technology development, with a focus on values like accessibility, inclusion, and user welfare.

In summary, by giving importance to diversity, inclusiveness, and ethical involvement, we may fully utilise the transformational power of immersive technology to create a beneficial societal influence.

Digital Ethics

Digital ethics involves a wider range of ethical questions pertaining to the use of immersive technology, which include concerns regarding transparency, accountability, fairness, and justice. Ethical frameworks ought to promote ethical standards in design and development, provide openness in algorithmic decision-making, and establish methods for holding individuals accountable for ethical violations in immersive environments. Ensure equitable access and advantageous outcomes for all individuals in society by addressing biases and fostering fairness in immersive technology. Ensure that immersive content, algorithms, and user experiences do not perpetuate or exacerbate pre-existing inequities or prejudice. Aspire to develop immersive settings that are inclusive and egalitarian, representing a wide range of viewpoints and experiences.

THE ROAD AHEAD

Despite the inherent uncertainty in estimates, PWC, a worldwide consultant, predicts that virtual and augmented worlds might generate over $1.5 trillion in economic activity each year by 2030 (Robert Bruton, 2024). Immersive technologies possess the capacity to revolutionise several aspects of human existence, encompassing communication, collaboration, employment, recreation, and education. Virtual platforms enable users to overcome geographical barriers, facilitating communication and interaction regardless of their actual location. The five frameworks that Liu & Sobocki, (2022) have identified for the future of AI law and policy are interaction, influence, immersion, intensity, and integration.

Although immersive technologies are becoming more common and advanced, their widespread adoption on a worldwide scale is still a long way off. The capacity of a community or economy to embrace and efficiently utilise immersive technology depends on several aspects, such as infrastructure, availability of network connection, and levels of investment in developing technologies. Similarly, numerous people may not be prepared to adopt immersive experiences or possess the necessary digital competencies to navigate them proficiently, and governments may lack sufficient legal frameworks to encourage secure implementation and use.

LIMITATION

The heterogeneous character of the different XR experiences and their corresponding research posed difficulties, resulting in a sequence of trade-offs and assumptions that may be seen as constraints in the literature assessment. Low acceptance rate of such technologies in India as compared to Western countries. While the North America has a revenue share of 45%, the Asia pacific has only 18.40%. Due to low acceptance rate the research happening on these technologies are also limited and mostly theoretical in nature. Apart from these, the knowledge on these immersive technologies is not very popular among the masses, and most of the population still has a limited knowledge on VR only which constitutes the highest market share among these technologies.

CONCLUSION

In conclusion, the exploration of legal and ethical dimensions in immersive technology underscores the necessity of a holistic approach that encompasses the diverse interests and concerns of stakeholders. By recognizing the rights, responsibilities, and values involved, we can navigate this rapidly evolving landscape with integrity and foresight. The factors to be taken into account may differ based on the legal jurisdiction, the advancements in technology, and the particular circumstances in which virtual reality (VR) and augmented reality (AR) are being employed.

Legal experts, developers, and enterprises in these industries must prioritise being informed about the legal environment and proactively tackle emerging concerns.

By adopting this comprehensive approach, we unleash the whole capabilities of immersive technology to produce experiences that are not just fascinating and inventive, but also enriching, inclusive, and morally sound. Through the responsible utilisation of immersive technology, we have the ability to mould a more promising future for users worldwide.

REFERENCES

Anwar, Z. (2021). Privacy and Safety Issues With Facebook's New Metaventure. *Dark Reading.* https://www.darkreading.com/vulnerabilities-threats/privacy-and -safety-issues-with-facebook-s-new-metaventure-

Bruton, R. (2024). *The Rise of Immersive Technologies: Looking Back and Ahead.*

Carmigniani, J., & Furht, B. (2011). Augmented Reality: An Overview. *Handbook of Augmented Reality*, 3–46. Springer. 10.1007/978-1-4614-0064-6_1

Roche, C. (2022). *Ethics and diversity in artificial intelligence policies, strategies and initiatives.* Springer.

Creed, C., Al-Kalbani, M., Theil, A., Sarcar, S., & Williams, I. (2024). Inclusive AR/VR: Accessibility barriers for immersive technologies. *Universal Access in the Information Society*, 23(1), 59–73. 10.1007/s10209-023-00969-0

Handa, M., & Aul, E. (n.d.). Immersive technology–uses, challenges and opportunities. *International Journal of Computing & Business Research.* http://researchmanuscripts .com/isociety2012/12.pdf

Heikkilä, M. (2024). *VR headsets can be hacked with an Inception-style attack.* MIT Technology Review.

Hosfelt, D. (2019). *Making ethical decisions for the immersive web.* http://arxiv .org/abs/1905.06995

India Development Review. (2023). *India's digital divide: From bad to worse?* Kabha, R. (2019). Ethical challenges of digital immersive and VR. *Journal of Content. Community and Communication*, 9, 41–49. 10.31620/JCCC.06.19/07

Liu, H.-Y., & Sobocki, V. (2022). Influence, Immersion, Intensity, Integration, Interaction: Five Frames for the Future of AI. *Law & Policy*, 35, 541–560. 10.1007/978-94-6265-523-2_27

Majumdar, M. (2022). *A Comprehensive Framework for AR/VR Technology in India.*

Metz, R. (2014). Google Glass Is Dead; Long Live Smart Glasses. *MIT Technology Review.* https://www.technologyreview.com/2014/11/26/169918/google-glass-is -dead-long-live-smart-glasses/

Mundin, F. (2024). *Emerging Legal Issues in Virtual Reality: Exploring the Inter- section of Law and Immersive Technology in 2024.* LawCrossing.

Nussipova, G., Nordin, F., & Sörhammar, D. (2020). Value formation with immersive technologies: An activity perspective. *Journal of Business and Industrial Marketing*, 35(3), 483–494. 10.1108/JBIM-12-2018-0407

Odeleye, B., Loukas, G., Heartfield, R., Sakellari, G., Panaousis, E., & Spyridonis, F. (n.d.). *Virtually Secure: A taxonomic assessment of cybersecurity challenges in virtual reality environments.*

Rubio-Tamayo, J. (n.d.). Immersive environments and virtual reality: Systematic review and advances in communication, interaction and simulation. *Multimodal Technologies and Interaction.* MDPI. https://www.mdpi.com/2414-4088/1/4/21

Saraswathi, P. A. S., Pavithra, A., Kowsalya, J., Priya, S. K., Jayasree, G., & Nandhini, T. K. (2020). *An emerging immersive technology-a survey.* Research Gate. https://www.researchgate.net/profile/Pavithra-A/publication/338819764_An _Emerging_Immersive_Technology-A_Survey/links/5e2c1d3c4585150ee780fca1/ An-Emerging-Immersive-Technology-A-Survey.pdf

Singhania, V. (2018). *Augmented & Virtual Reality Apps: The Legal Angle.* Law School Policy Review.

Southgate, E., & Smith, S. (2017). *Asking ethical questions in research using immersive virtual and augmented reality technologies with children and youth.* IEEE. https://ieeexplore.ieee.org/abstract/document/7892226/

Thierer, A., & Camp, J. (2017). *Permissionless Innovation and Immersive Technology Public Policy for Virtual and Augmented Reality-innovation-virtual-realit y-VR 3 Permissionless Innovation and Immersive Technology: Public Policy for Virtual and Augmented Reality.* Mercatus. https://www.mercatus.org/permissionless -innovation-virtual

Chapter 5
Enhancing Customer Experience by Semi–Immersive Virtual Reality in Real Estate Business

Nidhi Sharma

https://orcid.org/0009-0008-1861-738X

Guru Nanak Dev University, Amritsar, India

Divya Mahajan

Guru Nanak Dev University, Amritsar, India

ABSTRACT

Virtual reality has laid the cornerstone for various fields that remained unexplored till date due to various restraints. VR has not only enhanced the efficacy levels but also served as the basis for effectiveness. There have been studies depicting the various types of VR, but this area of semi- immersive VR still remains unexplored. Pathways sweeping the global waves of growth and development opening doors to significant opportunities in the field of technology have raised expectations from the real estate business as well. With the remarkable contribution of virtual reality in all spheres of business, it has played a crucial role in enhancing customer expectations, and also acquainting them with an enriching experience in an interactive way. This study helps in bridging the gap by taking the benefits of both fully immersive and non-immersive VR that could be promptly utilized to achieve customer satisfaction in enhancing customer experience as well as the user experience. The study highlights the role of various technologies in the field of semi-immersive virtual reality in a

DOI: 10.4018/979-8-3693-2432-5.ch005

more comprehensive manner. By analysing the various aspects of virtual reality, the study envisages the impact of semi-immersive virtual reality in magnifying the marketing prospects in real estate business and influencing the purchase decisions of customers.

INTRODUCTION

The pace at which the economies of the world have been linked and where each one is just a click away from each other, the distance is no longer a constraint, furthermore it welcomes us to the powerful era of virtual reality. Virtual reality is not only governing our present but also transforming our future along with overcoming the past issues. Whether that is industry, research, education, health or any other field VR is the new reality. Nonetheless, research suggests that the more immersive the virtual experience, as with VR, the higher the individual's belief in truly experiencing the objects and environments in the digital setting they are interacting with (Dede, 2009), thus potentially increasing the levels of escapism and enjoyment (Yee, 2006) but also potentially helping to make the shopping experience more efficient and less time consuming (Serrano, Baños, & Botella, 2016). Today, consumers are driven by a cross-channel customer journey rather than a linear path to the final stadium of the decision-making process: purchase behaviour (Harris et al., 2020). The tasks that were a far-fetched reality have now become in reach. Various aspects related to the assistance, mentoring, guidance that was a cumbersome task and where the researcher had to subside that curbed their growth can now be easily handled. The projected exponential growth of the VR market, with anticipated revenue surging from $11.64 billion in 2021 to $227.34 billion by 2029, further underscores the importance of understanding the impact of VR signals on product sales and profitability (Hsiao, Wang, &Lin,2024). Therefore, there is an exigency to innovate by channelising not only at the technological front but also to bolster up the purchase decision.

Previously the primary mediums like texts, picture and videos were at the disposal but now one can integrate into the world of multimedia in an interactive and immersive way that is more engaging and intriguing. Considering the various advancements that have taken the virtual reality by storm is immersion. Immersion is associated with the technical capabilities of the VR hardware and software to deliver an illusion of reality to users' senses (Slater and Wilbur, 1997, Parong et al., 2020). The importance of immersion is due to its positive effect on the user's presence in a simulated world (Peukert et al., 2019, Slater and Wilbur, 1997). Irrespective of the subject or field virtual reality gives an avenue to explore with learners as well as being engaged with variety of learning styles. It is an interactive experience that is visually appealing and mentally intriguing as it allows users to experience the virtual environment while remaining connected to their physical surroundings.

The real estate business is one of the most promising sectors as it has the amplitude to meet large customer demand and hence requires a whip hand in advertising to promote its products (i.e. properties) to their potential buyers. And this can effectively be done by the use of digital tools to be dealt with. Amongst the various tools that converge with the present scenario are related to the immersive technology. The real estate agents need to be well equipped with this technology as this assists them in providing ample information to the buyers regarding the properties in an interactive way. This will further help in fostering positive reactions from customers as well as an enriching experience at the same time. These technologies generate an interactive virtual environment that simulates a real-life experience, and allow users to control and navigate their actions in the virtual world (Zeng and Richardson, 2016; Lee et al., 2013). Therefore, these technologies have the potential to revolutionize this service-based industry by generating compelling CX (customer experience) (Rose et al., 2012).

Real estate business has been crucial in the growth of an economy as it represents the level of development in terms of infrastructure that benefits the society as a whole. The following are the various objectives of the study:

To enlighten on the aspect of customer experiences with respect to virtual reality.

To envisage the role of immersive technology in the real estate business.

To enlist the other tools of virtual reality under semi-immersive virtual reality that further enhance the user experience.

To analyse the impact of semi-immersive virtual reality as a powerful marketing tool in real estate business.

REVIEW OF LITERATURE

Recently, the most advancements in VR technology have increased its use for various commercial purposes (Berg and Vance, 2017), and market expansion is expected to increase manifold (i.e., 12 US billion by 2024) (Statista, 2022). In the realm of real estate, Virtual Reality (VR) technology has introduced an innovative way for potential buyers to experience properties. The VR in Real Estate market is expected to grow annually by magnificent (CAGR 2023 - 2030). It is a visual presentation technology that provides 3D interactive approach for consumers to explore the property on real estate platforms. VR enables a virtual tour, where buyers can virtually walk through rooms, interact with objects, and get a comprehensive 3D image view of the space. Virtual reality has opened a plethora of opportunities. In the ever- evolving real estate business where it gets a cumbersome task to cater to the prerequisites of customers, virtual reality helps in channelising the marketing efforts in a more constructive way.

VR is a simulated experience that provides the user with an immersive feel of a virtual environment. It acts as an interface between the physical environment and the user. A technology that uses computerized clothing to synthesize shared reality. It recreates our relationship with the physical world in a new plane, no more, no less (Jaron Lanier, 2014). Especially regarding the visual sensory stream, VR offers a surrounding, stereoscopic, and thus enveloping representation of space (Murphy and Skarbez, 2022). Presence solely serves the purpose of comparing the qualities of different virtual environments to each other (Usoh et al., 2000) but it can be customised as per the requirements. Over the years VR has evolved as a medium that has laid an exposition to various fields like healthcare, clinical therapies, education, gaming, real estate, entertainment, tourism, retail, digital marketing, etc. to name a few. This technology has come a long way in providing sensory engagement that is realistic in nature. VR systems vary in their types and forms, keeping the technological advancements intact. The user can easily choose from being fully immersive, non-immersive, semi- immersive, collaborative or augmented (reality) that initiates immersive learning and development. VR is an integration of several elements and includes, computers, worlds and environment, interaction, immersion and users who are also the participants of VR experience. The people who achieve physical immersion are called participants (Sherman & Craig, 2003). VR simulates the unpredictable real and challenging work challenges into a manageable and controlled setting. This very feature of VR aids in fostering the growth exponentially to the next level that was previously beyond the human reach. Moreover, it assists in improving skills and decision-making abilities both for the real estate agents as well as the customers.

Virtual Reality (VR) is an information processing system use in a computer which could help people to create and experience virtual world, it can form a multidimensional information space in which people can immerse in, transcend and interact using uses 3-D glasses, sensing gloves and a series of auxiliary sensing equipment (Kun & Zong, 2009). There are also various other tools Head Up Displays, Head Mounted Displays, Smart Glass, Handheld Devices. Along with the above mentioned that are gaining the attention in the current times. The semi-immersive virtual reality makes the use of high-performance graphics that transforms the whole experience of the customers in the virtual world. Here the customers are introduced to business tours that provide the 3D image experience that helps them in identifying the interior designing about the property that they would have otherwise personally visited. This further enhances their experience by giving them the virtual inspection and property view. A hybrid of non and fully-immersive virtual reality, this technology can present in the form of a 3D space or virtual environment where a user can move on their own via a computer screen or headset. Semi-immersive VR doesn't utilize physical movement. This immersion experience is strictly visual, with all activities in the simulated environment focused on the user. For example, Mimar Studios article outlines applications in the real estate sector, with virtual home tours presenting an interesting alternative to traditional open houses. [Burkhalter, Mark, 2022]. This transfigures the whole buying process and governs better purchase decision amongst the buyers. As the study deals with use of semi-immersive virtual reality, therefore the various tools covered under this are VR box\headset, computer screen and VR glasses.it is more concerned towards visual experience. This can be in the form of 3D space or virtual environment where one can move about on your own, either through computer screen or a VR box/ headset. The following picture provides a diagrammatic representation of semi-immersive virtual reality.

Figure 1. Virtual reality

Designed by: freepik

The digital revolution is changing on how the properties were showcased and experienced in the past. And with exposure to the technological experiences related to real estate businesses are phenomenal as well as progressive on real time basis. More recent comparisons of physical and virtual store settings agree on VR effectiveness and realism, for instance in product design evaluation (Dijkstra, Van Leeuwen, & Timmermans, 2003), reactions to crowding (Van Kerrebroeck et al., 2017a, Van Kerrebroeck et al., 2017b), or decisions in front of a shelf (Bigné, Llinares, & Torrecilla, 2016). The use of natural simulation and realistic experience technology has been the core of semi-immersive virtual reality. Its main target is to realize the real-life experience and human-computer interaction based on nature, and system which can achieve such a goal totally or partly leading to an enriching customer experience. Digital technologies rapidly increase visual product displays to provide distinctive and vivid consumer experiences (Grewal, Noble, et al., 2020).

The semi-immersive virtual reality helps in striking the right balance between the fully immersive and non- immersive virtual reality experiences. Time and cost effectiveness has also led to the success of semi-immersive VR. Reconstructing in the virtual environment that is an experiential replica to the actual product (property) is where semi-immersive technology has proved its benchmark. Apart from all the other tools of VR it's the semi-immersive VR tool that serves the purpose of being accustomed to the real physical environment. The appreciable quality of man-made interaction to the extent of virtual reality has put technology as the forefront runner in the success of any business that is very much rewarding and satisfying in terms of efficiency and effectiveness. The greatest of all is the ability of semi-immersive virtual reality is its impact on the environment, be it the infrastructure, finance, healthcare, education, psychology, real estate and the more. it caters to the need of the present times and also the future advancements of the same. The following figure highlights some of the uses related to Semi- Immersive VR in real estate business:

Figure 2. Highlights of SMVR in real estate business

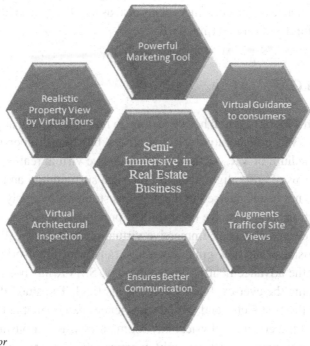

"Try before you buy" phenomenon has changed the market competition (Marasco et al., 2018). VR is capable enough to provide this opportunity by providing a computerized 3D world that senses the movement and reactions of the user, which helps the user to have a feeling of vivid mental representation of the virtual world (Yaoyuneyong et al., 2018). The real estate business has a huge investment and also has to spend a considerable amount in advertising. Whereas the past trends have been more towards vigorous advertising but the present scenario gives an opportunity to have an edge over the traditional ways of marketing with the use of technology. Technological advancement plays an essential role in communication, entertainment and marketing processes (Pae & Hyun, 2002; Wolters, 2015). Digital transformations provide new business opportunities and business models that managers must adopt to thrive in the competitive environment (Pagani & Pardo, 2017). Digital transformation through new business models usually changes the conventional business environment, disrupts numerous markets, and alters consumers' behaviour and expectations (Verhoef et al., 2021). As marketing an unconstructed property is a tough challenge and it is where the VR real estate comes to rescue. It acknowledges the type of immersive technology and acts as a promotional tool and the real estate agents are able to market the properties in a more convenient way.

The role of visual tours has also gained much anticipation as far as the real estate business is concerned. These virtual tours could be guided or interactive depending upon the convenience of the customers. This also assists the real estate business on the marketing forefront on real time basis.

RESEARCH GAP

Even though a lot of research has been done in real estate using augmented VR, fully immersive VR, collaborative VR and others, but semi-immersive is a much less explored medium of VR. As the semi- immersive virtual reality has made the ends meet in terms of cost, alignment with physical surrounding and purpose, it is the gap that has not been analysed in the previous studies effectively. Amongst the various research papers that have been studied previously very less emphasis has been laid on the impact of semi-immersive virtual reality specifically in the field of real estate business and how gradually it has transformed its working in present scenario. With the advancement in the technology, SMVR has potential scope in real estate keeping the ever-evolving nature of this field. The study throws insight on the fact that the cost factor and virtual experiences can be met at the same time keeping in mind the concrete physical environment in which a business operates. The use of semi-immersive VR not only enhances the customer experience and further helps in enhancing the buying process. The use of fully immersive VR has long been identified but being an expensive medium hinders its usage.

NEED OF THE STUDY

Virtual reality (VR) is a novel technology, and its potential has been noticed for VR marketing (Loureiro et al., 2019; Shahab et al.,2021). Therefore, the research on VR demands attention from scholars (Flavián et al., 2019). With various fields adopting the new era of technological advancements it is also vital for the prevailing real estate business to scale its operations through customer satisfaction. Semi immersive technology plays a pivotal role in providing a partial realistic virtual experience to the customer that is both enriching, interactive and satisfying in a cost-effective manner. Semi immersive VR gives users the perception of being in a different reality where they can simultaneously focus on the digital image, and also allows users to remain connected to their physical surroundings. There is a need to link the real estate business with technology that gives the customer a chance to engage in the process that is experience oriented. The semi-immersive virtual reality also offers further scope in research too. The real estate business has been closely associated with the substantial amount of money being invested into an asset or a venture, this study aids in securing an extremity over the past practises that have followed in the real estate business.

RESEARCH METHODOLOGY

The study is based on descriptive research design. The research methodology used in this study is secondary in nature. The data has been collected through secondary sources like journals, articles, research papers and various working papers. The secondary data has been analysed through content analysis method. Meta analyses, systematic reviews, literature reviews, books and documents that were not based on authenticated data, were excluded from the study. The theoretical nature of the data helps in concluding the already researched data that is more empirical in nature. In the due course this data aids in scrutinizing the outcomes of a research study in a more constructive manner.

DISCUSSION AND FINDINGS

As the virtual reality has channelised the whole process related to the virtual tours and architectural inspection that provides virtual guidance as and when required. This pitches in as a computing system that becomes the true reality which is virtually enthralling. As the real estate businesses was not performing well such technological implications succour new energy by opening new avenues in the field of real estate business.

With the challenges prevailing in the real estate business, is to cater to the needs of the customers there is an indispensable need to develop a system that is in accordance with the technology. This study helps in better understanding how over the years it has been essential to curate the real estate business with the skill set at the technological front that is able to capture the pulse of the customer providing them with an experience as offered by the semi-immersive virtual reality. Semi immersive technology also plays a pivotal role in providing a partial realistic virtual experience to the customer that is both enriching, interactive and satisfying, all aligned in one frame. Semi immersive VR gives users the perception of being in a different reality when they focus on the digital image, but also allows users to remain connected to their physical surroundings. This way the customers experience what they will be awarded in future after their investment and also the builders will get the feedback of what is expected from them by the customers or buyers. Furthermore, this study envisages the outlook both from the point of views of customer as well as business and gives the panoramic analysis of how by making use of semi-immersive VR the experience of the customer could be enhanced. The biggest advantage that the semi-immersive virtual reality offers is of property tours. There are basically two forms of tours offered by semi-immersive VR: virtual tours and guided tours, that offers choice as per the specification of the parties. And fortunately, VR headsets enable both parties to interact inside a virtual environment without leaving the comfort of their homes. That's why 3D virtual tours are becoming so popular among skilled real estate agents. The other way around the guided tours resembles promotional videos which often occur in the form of 360-degree videos or entirely virtual (interactive) experiences and provides an immersive marketing experience. With so many options at hand, real estate agents are able to market properties more confidently and in convenient conditions, curating a powerful marketing tool in itself. This study will lay the future path of other related studies. It is also quite crucial to identifying the future customer base in real estate business as it is essential for the businesses to be well equipped with the dynamics of today. Due to the flexible working environment, it becomes impossible for the customers to be available at a particular time of the day. And by making use of property tours under semi – immersive VR the businesses will able to meet their commitment towards enhancing their experiences irrespective of the time and location constraints.

With the tremendous amelioration in the field of real estate it has become mandatory to be in tune with the times where growth and technology in any industry go hand in hand. Therefore, it becomes indispensable for the business to be keen on updating with the dynamics of technology. The contemporary trends have laid to outset the innovative ways in enhancing customer experiences. And order to study the same it is of utmost importance to study this very aspect related to real estate. As real estate is the second largest field in employment generation hence this study will also help in understanding the current trends in employment related to real estate sector and generating the same in terms of the skill set that is required with respect to the technology. As the real estate business forms and contributes to the growth of a country and furthermore towards the development of a nation. This growth can only be utilized if the constant evolving real estate industry is put under scanner from time to time in order to catch up with the changing trends. At last, this study justifies the need of technology and real estate being agile in each other's domain and will more so ever play a vital role in conducting various studies in future.

IMPLICATIONS

The purpose of semi-immersive virtual reality has refined the process of innovation. Where the former consideration was just concerned with technological advancements but has shifted its focus in overcoming the technological challenges in a more conscious and sincere manner. This has magnificently depicted by the use of semi-immersive virtual reality in the real estate business. The breakthrough of semi-immersive virtual reality is its holistic approach towards efficiency and effectiveness. The potential implications of semi-immersive virtual reality is that it ties theoretical, practical and managerial expertise in the common thread of innovation embodying it as a powerful marketing tool. This study has glorified the aspects of theory and practise with a skill set of managerial expertise. A technology like semi-immersive virtual reality has painted the picture of society with its contribution to the SDG-9. This generalises the practical accessibility to the profound social impact on the economy by the lens of immersion in a physical stature. This remarkably contributes to the growth and development of an economy that transfigures real estate as a promising sector altogether.

LIMITATIONS

Apart from all the advantages associated with use of semi-immersive VR there are various costs associated with it. There are various challenges related with the technological costs that include the ongoing expenses in keeping the technology up-to-date and also functioning. The initial investment requirement in VR is high and does not always assure the buying decision. Also, not all the users that lack the basic hardware like VR headsets, glove, monitors etc. may assure the success rate. Thus, with the limited range of interaction devices and problems with multi-user applications, it seems a challenge to enhance the experience of all the customers. Furthermore, there are still a lot of customers who prefer to experience it personally rather than in a virtual world.

Also, the use of immersive technology also poses a cyber sickness threat that deals with the motion sickness that badly effects the well-being of its users over a prolonged use. Till date there have not been any significant differences in this field of advanced virtual reality in this context.

SCOPE FOR FUTURE RESEARCH

The last few decades have witnessed an exponential growth in the field of virtual reality. Amongst the various tools of VR, semi-immersive virtual reality has emerged as a high performing graphic immersive system that proves its mettle not just in the field of real estate business but also plays a crucial role in various simulation processes related to pilot training in aviation sector, gait training in neurosciences, medicine, scientific visualisation, entrepreneurship, research and designing certain educational tools to name a few. The semi -immersive virtual reality can prove its worth in future by its implications in various sectors that require theoretical knowledge to practical application through the skill set of managerial expertise. This tool in itself is cost effective and will realm the study in generalising the future scope in the field of semi-immersive virtual reality The use of 3D graphics in the semi-immersive virtual reality emphasis the element of realism. It opens the horizons of interaction that are connected through the virtual reality with partial immersion while still being aligned with the physical environment. This study will also extend its support to the SDG-9 which is related to industry, innovation and infrastructure in the future.

It is however a fact that the capital outlay associated in the real estate sector is huge and this study emphasis the role of semi-immersive virtual reality in future scenario. Even though there are studies that are related to virtual reality but the semi-immersive virtual reality still has not been potentially explored to the fullest. This study takes the future scope of role of semi-immersive virtual reality in the right direction in the game changer scenario of growth and development.

CONCLUSION

After analysing the data from the various research papers, articles etc. it can be said that the outcomes that are associated with the use of VR is huge taking into account all the tools of VR. Making the use of semi-immersive VR assists in analysing the current challenges as well as catering to the customer dynamics in a more specific manner. The virtual reality (VR) has emerged as a groundbreaking technology that is revolutionizing the way properties are showcased and experienced. According to a study by Goldman Sachs, around 1.4 million realtors will be using VR technology by the end of 2025. But in the process of linking the virtual world with reality it becomes a challenge to convince the customer. And this is where the semi-immersive VR comes into existence that is beneficial for both the customers as well as the parties concerned. As the real estate is a capital- and labour-intensive industry; thus, rise in cost of labour and construction material due to inflation poses major problems to real estate industry. The semi-immersive VR helps in reducing the costs associated with the appointment of the representative for site visits and also the site traffic.

The semi-immersive virtual reality not only provide the innovative marketing tool but also an efficient medium for promotion with 3D viewing. These enhance the customers experience by challenging the geographical limitation and summarizing the transformative potential on what the future of real estate stands. The technology allows buyers to make informed decisions remotely, saving time, expenses, and logistical challenges. For sellers and agents, VR expands their potential buyer pool, reaching a broader audience than ever before.

As now real estate is not just confined to the concrete stature but in also in the form of virtual environment using VR headset, mobile phone etc., Semi immersive helps in transforming traditional brochures into interactive 3D experiences as it opens door to interactive experience that is visually appealing and mentally engaging. Also, the level of interaction and realism helps potential buyers or renters to make more informed decisions regarding property without the need for physical visits or relying solely on static images. It also assuages the customer to manage their budget and resources in a more comprehensive way.

Nowadays real estate is more about what experience a company can offer to the customer. As it's the customer's enriched experience that persuades the customer's buying process. The biggest advantage of semi-immersive VR is that it gives property view as the customer will have to be available in the virtual world but in physical setting. It ensures the effective communication and the feedback is received then and there. It further clarifies the doubts of the customer leading to more enriched future experience.

Thus, it can be concluded that in spite of all the challenges that are associated with the use of semi-immersive VR it indeed proves its mark in the ever evolving and emerging need of technology that is responsible in enhancing the customer experience in the real estate business.

REFERENCES

Deaky, B. A., & Parv, A. L. (2018, August). Virtual Reality for Real Estate–a case study. *IOP Conference Series. Materials Science and Engineering*, 399(1), 012013. 10.1088/1757-899X/399/1/012013

Dincelli, E., & Yayla, A. (2022). Immersive virtual reality in the age of the Metaverse: A hybrid-narrative review based on the technology affordance perspective. *The Journal of Strategic Information Systems*, 31(2), 101717. 10.1016/j.jsis.2022.101717

Hollebeek, L. D., Clark, M. K., Andreassen, T. W., Sigurdsson, V., & Smith, D. (2020). Virtual reality through the customer journey: Framework and propositions. *Journal of Retailing and Consumer Services*, 55, 102056. 10.1016/j.jretconser.2020.102056

Hsiao, S. H., Wang, Y. Y., & Lin, T. L. (2024). The impact of low-immersion virtual reality on product sales: Insights from the real estate industry. *Decision Support Systems*, 178, 114131. 10.1016/j.dss.2023.114131

Johnson, L., & Keasler, T. (1993). An industry profile of corporate real estate. *Journal of Real Estate Research*, 8(4), 455–473. 10.1080/10835547.1993.12090732

Kamil, M. H. F. M., Yahya, N., Abidin, I. S. Z., & Norizan, A. R. (2021). Development of Virtual Reality Technology: Home Tour for Real Estate Purchase Decision Making. *Malaysian Journal of Computer Science*, 85–93. 10.22452/mjcs.sp2021no1.8

Lindholm, A. L., Gibler, K., & Leväinen, K. (2006). Modeling the value-adding attributes of real estate to the wealth maximization of the firm. *Journal of Real Estate Research*, 28(4), 445–476. 10.1080/10835547.2006.12091187

Mauri, M., Rancati, G., Riva, G., & Gaggioli, A. (2024). Comparing the effects of immersive and non-immersive real estate experience on behavioral intentions. *Computers in Human Behavior*, 150, 107996. 10.1016/j.chb.2023.107996

Miljkovic, I., Shlyakhetko, O., & Fedushko, S. (2023). Real estate app development based on AI/VR technologies. *Electronics (Basel)*, 12(3), 707. 10.3390/electronics12030707

Muhanna, M. A. (2015). Virtual reality and the CAVE: Taxonomy, interaction challenges and research directions. *Journal of King Saud University. Computer and Information Sciences*, 27(3), 344–361. 10.1016/j.jksuci.2014.03.023

Pizzi, G., Scarpi, D., Pichierri, M., & Vannucci, V. (2019). Virtual reality, real reactions?: Comparing consumers' perceptions and shopping orientation across physical and virtual-reality retail stores. *Computers in Human Behavior*, 96, 1–12. 10.1016/j.chb.2019.02.008

Pleyers, G., & Poncin, I. (2020). Non-immersive virtual reality technologies in real estate: How customer experience drives attitudes toward properties and the service provider. *Journal of Retailing and Consumer Services*, 57, 102175. 10.1016/j.jretconser.2020.102175

Schöne, B., Kiskei, J., Lange, L., Gruber, T., Sylvester, S., & Osinsky, R. (2023). The reality of virtual reality. *Frontiers in Psychology*, 14, 1093014. 10.3389/fpsyg.2023.109301436874824

See, Z. S., & Cheok, A. D. (2015). Virtual reality 360 interactive panorama reproduction obstacles and issues. *Virtual Reality (Waltham Cross)*, 19(2), 71–81. 10.1007/s10055-014-0258-9

Shahab, H., Shahzad, F., & Yasin, G. (2022). Virtual Reality as a Marketing Tool to Drive Consumer Decision-Making. *Pakistan Journal of Social Research*, 4(1), 664–677. 10.52567/pjsr.v4i1.933

Sherman, W. R., & Craig, A. B. (2003). *Understanding virtual reality*. Morgan Kauffman.

Sherman, W. R., & Craig, A. B. (2018). *Understanding virtual reality: Interface, application, and design*. Morgan Kaufmann.

Ullah, F., Sepasgozar, S. M., & Wang, C. (2018). A systematic review of smart real estate technology: Drivers of, and barriers to, the use of digital disruptive technologies and online platforms. *Sustainability (Basel)*, 10(9), 3142. 10.3390/su10093142

van Herpen, E., van den Broek, E., van Trijp, H. C., & Yu, T. (2016). Can a virtual supermarket bring realism into the lab? Comparing shopping behavior using virtual and pictorial store representations to behavior in a physical store. *Appetite*, 107, 196–207. 10.1016/j.appet.2016.07.03327474194

Verhoef, P. C., Lemon, K. N., Parasuraman, A., Roggeveen, A., Tsiros, M., & Schlesinger, L. A. (2009). Customer experience creation: Determinants, dynamics and management strategies. *Journal of Retailing*, 85(1), 31–41. 10.1016/j.jretai.2008.11.001

Chapter 6
Enhancing Consumer Engagement Through Augmented Reality:
A Study on Personalized Offerings and Co-Creation

Yashodhan Karulkar

MPSTME, NMIMS University, India

Devansh Gupta

MPSTME, NMIMS University, India

Anshuman Thapliyal

MPSTME, NMIMS University, India

Bhavyaraj Singh

MPSTME, NMIMS University, India

Mahendra Parihar

https://orcid.org/0000-0002-4385-9777

MPSTME, NMIMS University, India

ABSTRACT

It is often a matter of fascination for people to visualize the invisible, which has been enabled by technology, specifically by augmented reality (AR). The real and virtual are infused together by augmented reality. Digital data is projected on an image of anything visible through a gadget, to generate a representation of reality that is augmented. The satisfaction of customers is vital for retail sectors. It instils

DOI: 10.4018/979-8-3693-2432-5.ch006

a sense of care and value in customers when brands keep updating themselves with such facilities, which rewards in terms of increment in loyalty and profits. This study examines the impact of perceived customization on consumers' intents to co-create value when augmented reality (AR) and some web-based businesses are used. Additionally, the authors look into how perceived risk and trust are related in this context. India-based Pepperfry is an online retailer for furniture and home décor items. For the purpose of this survey, the authors polled Pepperfry users to assess their sentiments towards purchases made through websites and augmented reality applications.

INTRODUCTION

In this new era, businesses are always looking for ways to improve the customer experience. In the contemporary environment we live in, they adjust their marketing strategies to be even more digital, focused on, exact, and personalized. Even mass marketing strategies that target customers based on their personalities or segments are ineffective nowadays. Utilizing the money you spend on advertising wisely is more important than ever, with a focus on providing your customers with offers that are pertinent to their context.

Over the long run, the addition of new technologies will improve the personalization stack and help marketers achieve their personalization goals. They are more likely to do business with companies who are aware of who they are, what they are going through, and that their needs and circumstances are constantly evolving.

Augmented reality (AR) is the integration of digital information with the user's environment in real time. Unlike virtual reality (VR), which creates a totally artificial environment, AR users experience a real-world environment with generated perceptual information overlaid on top of it.

Augmented reality has a variety of uses, from assisting in the decision-making process to entertainment. AR is used to either visually change natural environments in some way or to provide additional information to users. The primary benefit of AR is that it manages to blend digital and three-dimensional (3D) components with an individual's perception of the real world. AR delivers visual elements, sound and other sensory information to the user through a device like a smartphone, glasses or a headset. This information is overlaid onto the device to create an interwoven and immersive experience where digital information alters the user's perception of the physical world. The overlaid information can be added to an environment or mask part of the natural environment. Personalized product recommendations on websites like Amazon, personalized advertisements on Google, and exclusive algorithm of Netflix that recommends films and television shows to its users are all examples of how the gap between consumers and organizations has successfully closed as technology has advanced. The way marketers and businesses interact with their customers has been significantly changed by modern technologies such as artificial intelligence (AI), augmented reality (AR), and other new technologies.

A customized shopping experience will make it easier for the customer to comprehend how acquiring, utilizing, and ultimately getting rid of the products can benefit them. Due to the customized and anticipated nature of the experience offered by personalized services, customers may have a higher perception of trust in a product or a brand (C. K. Prahalad & Ramaswamy, 2004; Shen et al., 2020).

This method can help companies serve their clients better and make them happier and more satisfied (Lusch, Vargo, & Tanniru, 2010). Businesses often encourage co-creation through customization in digital settings; however, conversation and customization are limited to the 2D plane in these settings.

According to the study, using augmented reality (AR) as an operational resource makes the co-creation process better for customers by giving them relevant and contextually rich information. This makes them more interested and encourages them to connect with self-service settings like websites.

LITERATURE REVIEW

The interaction between customers and businesses or brands has been greatly changed by industry 4.0. Since technology innovation has caused uncertainty in the industry and customer behavior, businesses must constantly adapt their business models and strategies to stay ahead of their rivals and the industry (Beer and Nohria, 2000). Because of technological advances, customers now have the ability to enjoy personalized lifestyles through mobile devices, social networks, and demand services (Hajli, 2014). As a result of consumers switching to e-commerce and other digital interactions with brands rather than traditional in-store purchases, consumer behavior has developed and shifted and previous trends that were observed are no longer relevant (Kotler, Kartajaya, and Setiawan, 2017).

The marketing & branding efforts made for the consumer have grown challenging and expensive for the organizations as a result of the increased consumer-organization contact points (Hajli, 2015). The development of technology has given businesses access to decisions that are constantly updated and data-backed (Michael, 2018). This has improved customer interactions.

There has been a shift in the focus of VR research from a concentration on better resolution and improved perception to a concentration on making VR more interactive. This is likely because researchers have already achieved a great resolution and need to focus on making VR as realistic as possible. One way that VR is being made more interactive is through the development of new hardware and software, such as contactless devices that allow users to interact with virtual environments using their hands (Lopez-Carmona et al., 2018).

The desire for human-digital interactions that go beyond standard flat panel displays has increased because of recent developments in high-speed networking and compact mobile computer platforms. As augmented reality (AR) and virtual reality (VR) headsets become more popular, next-generation interactive screens that can show rich 3D visuals are starting to appear. A few applications include engineering, healthcare, education, and gaming (Xiong, J., Hsiang, 2021).

By bringing ecommerce items to life and providing detailed information, augmented reality aids consumers in making informed purchasing decisions. A benefit of augmented reality for consumers is that it enables them to see things before making a purchase. According to Google, six out of ten people "say they want to be able to imagine where and how a product may fit into their life," (Reydar,2021).

The study offers a complete assessment of customer views and the evaluation of AR mobile applications as part of consumers' online purchasing experiences. It focuses on consumer perceptions, attitudes, and technological adoption in retail. The researchers found that perceived functional advantage and trust are strongly correlated with AR features such reality congruence, system quality, product informativeness, and product interaction. The results also show a significant relationship between attitudes of trust in AR and perceived functional gain. It indirectly affects people's desire to use augmented reality (Ramdani, 2022).

The study found that AR mobile applications have direct effects on user attitudes and behavior as well as indirect effects on perceived usefulness, perceived usability, and reported enjoyment. One's attitude towards using augmented reality applications or behavior desire to use them is unaffected by their perceived ease of use (Muhammad, 2021).

With the use of AR technology, companies can combine digital features into their actual items. To reduce risk and increase self-efficacy and trust, consumers can utilize augmented reality (AR) to access several interactive services, such as speaking or chatting with other customers and firm employees online, reading reviews, and viewing the product in 3D holograms. Additionally, co-creation and value-in-use are discussed. The authors advise firms to create products and services that work as "value facilitators," with the target market acting as the "value-creator." This makes the case that companies should be more involved in "staging experiences" or "staging co-creation activities" where consumers may create value for themselves (Al- Imamy, 2018).

According to the study's empirical findings, AR exposure improves co-creation, which has a number of positive effects on consumers' perceptions of risk and their willingness to make purchases (Al-Imamy, 2019).

This composition is constructed upon a theoretical framework that facilitates the formulation of research hypotheses, as well as a model encompassing personalization, perceived trust, risk, and value. This may give rise to novel domains of augmented reality (AR) investigation and collaborative value generation.

RESEARCH METHODOLOGY

This study examines how consumer intentions to co-create value are impacted by their views of personalization using augmented reality and web-based enterprises. This can be inferred as shown in Figure 1.

Hypothesis Development

As augmented reality technology develops, service providers and clients can now collaborate more effectively to produce value. Examining the mediating effects of perceived values and customer involvement, this study will assess the impact of actual experiences on consumers' intents to co-create value.

Personalization and Co-Creation

H1a. Perceptions of personalized offering are correlated with the intention of co-creation.

H2b. Augmented reality describes the perceived personalization in a more substantial format than the e- commerce website.

The Impact of Risk on Personalisation and Co-Creation

H2a. Perceived personalization has been linked to substantially decreased risk sentiments.

H2b. Consumer desire to co-create is strongly linked to their perception of risk.

H2c. The relative risk for Augmented reality-based consumers is substantially higher than that for e- commerce website-based consumers.

H2d. The impact on perceived personalization and the desire to co-create value is driven by consumer perceived risk.

The impact of trust on personalization and co-creation

H3a. Perceived personalization has been linked to substantially higher perception of trust. H3b. Consumer desire to co-create is strongly linked to perceived trust.

H3c. The relative trust for Augmented reality-based consumers is substantially higher than that for e-commerce website-based consumers.

H3d. The impact of perceived personalization and the desire to co-create value is driven by consumer perceived trust.

Figure 1. Proposed conceptual model

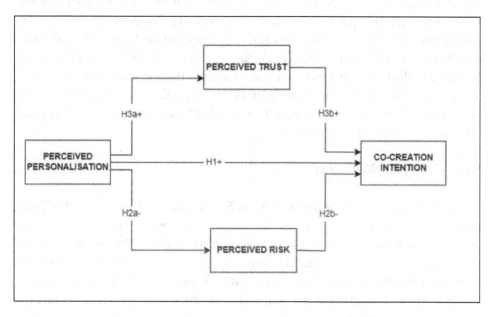

METHODOLOGY

Data Collection

A Likert scale of 1–7 was used to record responses to the thirteen different items that made up the questionnaire. To do this, the population was divided into two groups. The instructions for the first group of participants were to visit the Pepperfry website before responding to the questions, whereas the instructions for the second group were to access the Pepperfry app and respond to the questions after viewing the augmented reality elements. Google Forms was used for the research. On a 7-point Likert scale, the responses varied from "strongly disagree" (1) to "strongly agree" (7).

Google Form was used to carry out online polls. Users of the app can read reviews and use a unique feature of visual augmented reality to virtually validate the product by seeing it in their own house. The website functions as a straightforward e-commerce website and provides a static 2D view of the product.

Both online and offline channels were used to collect the data. A total of 342 responses were recorded but only 314 were used because 28 of them were discarded for having similar inputs and missing values. Users of the website have submitted 145 responses, and users of the application have submitted 169 (We used a probability sampling technique in our research since we had predetermined criteria. Only individuals who met the criteria and had either utilized the Pepperfry application or website were allowed to participate in the process). Over 68% of the participants belonged to the Gen-Z and millennial generation in the age bracket of 25–34-year age group, followed by the 35–44-year age bracket. Gender breakdown among participants showed that 63.7% were men and 36.3% were women. From 18 to over 60 years old, they were all of them.

Data Analysis Methods

Analysis was performed using IBM-SPSS (Statistical Package for the Social Sciences) and IBM-SPSS AMOS (Analysis of moment structures). For the purposes of this study, we ran an ANOVA analysis using IBM SPSS software. It was utilized to determine the model fit metrics for our dataset, including Cronbach's Alpha and Harman's single factor score. Most importantly, SPSS factor analysis was considered to maximize the association between different variables and the results of our investigation.

To determine the path estimates for the relative parameters in our model, namely Personalization, Trust, Risk, and Co-creation purpose, and afterwards calculate Statistical Regression and Covariance, SPSS Amos was used to conduct the SEM for the model. Additionally, it was used to analyze the two mediating variables, Trust and Risk, and their mediating effects.

MEASUREMENT MODEL, RELIABILITY, AND VALIDITY

Model Reliability: Cronbach's Alpha Analysis

Table 1. Cronbach's alpha analysis

Variable	Question Statement	CA
Demographics	Name	
	Age	
	Gender	
	Pepperfry Application or Website	
Personalization	Pepperfry offers me products and services that satisfy my specific needs	0.945
	Pepperfry offers products and services that I couldn't find with another retailer	
	If I changed retailers, I would not obtain products and services as personalized as I have now	
	Pepperfry understands my needs	
	Pepperfry knows what I want	
	Pepperfry takes my needs as its own preferences	
Perceived Social Risk	*The thought of buying a product from Pepperfry within the next 12 months would ...*	0.888
	pose problems for me that I just don't need	
	make me feel that I would be held in higher esteem by friends and family	
	causes me concern because some friends would think I was being showy	
	make me concerned that I would have to spend too much time learning how to use the product	

As the table shows, the Cronbach's Alpha for each measurement item was much higher than the minimum of 0.7, which meant that they were all thought to be reliable. Cronbach's alpha testing is used to check the reliability of multiple-question Likert scale polls. These questions test latent traits, which are qualities that are hidden or can't be seen, like openness, neurotic habits, or scrupulosity. But it's hard to measure these things in real life. An important number called Cronbach's alpha shows how closely a set of test questions are linked.

Model Validity

Table 2. Goodness of fit

Goodness of fit indices				
CMIN	DF	CMIN/DF	CFI	RMSEA
2.516	1	2.517	0.997	0.103

In AMOS, the chi-square value is known as CMIN. If the chi-square is not significant, the model is regarded adequate. This value is calculated by dividing the degrees of freedom by the chi-square index. This statistic may be less affected by sample size. The acceptance threshold is less than 5. (Schumacker & Lomax, 2004). Furthermore, modified model fit statistics (absolute, relative, and parsimonious) showed 'good' model fit (see Table 2) The CFI is the ratio of this target model's discrepancy to the independence model's discrepancy. The CFI approximates how much the interest model outperforms the independence model. Values that approach 1 suggest an acceptable match.

Common Method Bias: Harman's Single Factor Score

People sometimes make mistakes or are biased when they combine or compare research studies, especially when they use the same method or get their information from the same source. This is called common source bias.

People were asked to answer all of the questions in the online poll that was open for 10 days. Because of this, common procedure bias might have made the data less reliable (Podsakoff et al., 2003). We used Harman's single factor score to see if common method bias was a problem. This score puts all the possible things on one factor. After examining it we discovered that the overall variance for the single factor is 47.082%, which indicates that common method bias has no effect on our data and is therefore unimportant in this case (Podsakoff et al., 2003).

Table 3. Common method bias

		Total Variance Explained				
		Initial Eigenvalues			Extraction Sums of Squared Loadings	
Component	Total	% of Variance	Cumulative %	Total	% of Variance	Cumulative
1	21.163	47.028	47.028	21.163	47.028	47.02
2	9.204	20.454	67.482			
3	2.691	5.979	73.461			
4	.737	1.637	75.099			
5	.661	1.468	76.567			
6	.598	1.328	77.895			
7	.513	1.141	79.036			
8	.496	1.102	80.138			
9	.464	1.031	81.170			
10	.457	1.016	82.186			
11	.431	.959	83.144			
12	.418	.929	84.073			
13	.411	.913	84.986			

RESEARCH FINDINGS AND RESULTS

Hypothesis Testing

Table 4. Hypothesis testing

Hypothesis	Result
H1a. Perceptions of personalised offering are correlated with the intention of co-creation.	Supported
H1b. Augmented reality describes the perceived personalisation in a more substantial format than the e-commerce website.	Supported
H2a. Perceived personalisation has been linked to substantially decreased risk sentiments.	Supported
H2b. Consumer desire to co-create is strongly linked to their perception of risk.	Not Supported for website Supported for AR
H2c. The relative risk for Augmented reality-based consumers is substantially higher than that for e-commerce website-based consumers.	Supported
H2d. The impact on perceived personalisation and the desire to co-create value is driven by consumer perceived risk.	Not Supported
H3a. Perceived personalisation has been linked to substantially higher perception of trust.	Supported
H3b. Consumer desire to co-create is strongly linked to perceived trust.	Not Supported for AR Supported for Website
H3c. The relative trust for Augmented reality-based consumers is substantially higher than that for e-commerce website-based consumers.	Not Supported
H3d. The impact of perceived personalisation and the desire to co-create value is driven by consumer perceived trust.	Supported

Application vs. Website Shopping

An analysis of variance (ANOVA) was utilised to examine the perceptions of personalisation, trust, risk, and intention to co-create across application and online shopping. The ANOVA found no significant differences between web and application-based purchase in terms of consumer personalisation and consumer perceived risk. There were, however, significant differences between Application and web-based purchase in terms of consumer intention to co-create ($F = 93.417$, $p<0.01$) and consumer perceived trust ($F = 118.371$, $p<0.01$), both of which were higher in the application buying group.

Table 5. Application group and website group

Measure	Application Group		Website Group		F
	M	SD	M	SD	
Personalisation	5.0343	1.10701	4.9310	1.13543	0.665
Co-creation	5.2976	1.13309	3.5986	1.93628	93.419*
Perceived trust	5.6442	0.72133	4.2458	1.48289	118.371*
Perceived risk	3.6007	1.26983	3.6341	1.19162	0.057

Figure 2. AR application

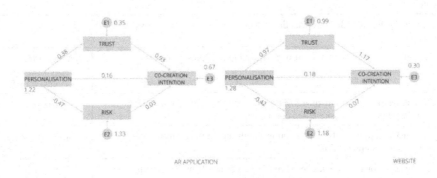

Table 6. AR application group and website group

	AR Application Group				Website Group	
	Standard Estimates	P-Value		Standard Estimates		P-Value
Personalisation -> Perceived risk	-0.470		***		-0.424	***
Personalisation -> Perceived trust	0.376		***		0.965	***
Perceived risk -> Co-creation	0.159	0.033		0.074		0.082
Perceived trust -> Co-creation	0.032	0.554		1.166		***
Personalisation -> Co-creation	0.933	***		0.184		***

Mediating Effect of Trust

A mediating variable, according to the International Standardization of Measurement (ISMM), is a variable that links both independent and dependent variables and explains the relationship between them.

Website: The following diagram represents a relationship between Personalisation (P) and Co-creation Intention (I).

Figure 3.

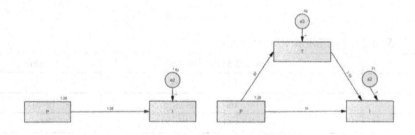

Table 7. Standard estimate and P-value

	Standard Estimates	P-Value
P-->I	1.28	***

We discovered a substantial link between Personalisation and Co-creation Intention using the P<0.05 value.

Table 8. Standard estimate and P-value

	Standard Estimates	P-Value
P-->T	.965	***
P-->I	.163	.008
T-->I	1.155	***

As the relationship between personalisation and Co-creation Intention is no longer significant (P-value: 0.008), hence there is a full mediating effect of Trust in case of AR application.

AR Application

Table 9. Standard estimate and P-value

	Standard Estimates	P-Value
P-->I	0.50	***

As the value of P<0.05, we have identified that there is also a significant relationship between Personalisation and Co-creation intention in the case of AR Application Shopping. On introducing the Trust parameter,

Table 10. Standard estimate and P-value

	Standard Estimates	P-Value
P-->T	.376	***
P-->I	.140	.046
T-->I	.945	***

As the relationship between personalisation and Co-Creation Intention is no longer significant, hence there is a full mediating effect of Trust in case of AR application.

Mediating Effect of Risk

Website: The Following Diagram Represents a Relationship Between Personalisation (P) and Co-Creation Intention (I)

Figure 4.

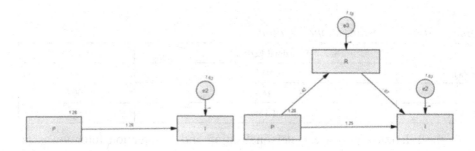

Table 11. Standard estimate and P-value

	Standard Estimates	P-Value
P-->I	1.28	***

As the value of P<0.05, we have identified that there is a significant relationship between Personalisation and Co-creation intention. On introducing the risk parameter,

Table 12. Standard estimate and P-value

	Standard Estimates	P-Value
P-->R	-.424	***
P-->I	1.250	***
R-->I	-.067	.494

As the relationship between P and I is still significant, and the relationship between R and I is not significant (P- value: .49), hence we can conclude that there is no mediating effect of Risk on Personalisation and Cocreation Intention.

AR Application

Figure 5.

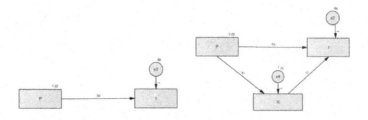

Table 13. Standard estimate and P-value

	Standard Estimates	P-Value
P-->I	0.50	***

As the value of P<0.05, we have identified that there is also a significant relationship between Personalisation and Co-creation intention in the case of AR Application Shopping. On introducing the Risk Parameter,

Table 14. Standard estimate and P-value

	Standard Estimates	P-Value
P-->R	-.470	***
P-->I	.552	***
R-->I	.120	.067

As the relationship between P and I is still significant, and the relationship between R and I is not significant (P- value: 0.067), hence we can conclude that there is no mediating effect of Risk on Personalisation and Cocreation Intention.

Mediating Effect of Trust and Risk in the Model

Figure 6.

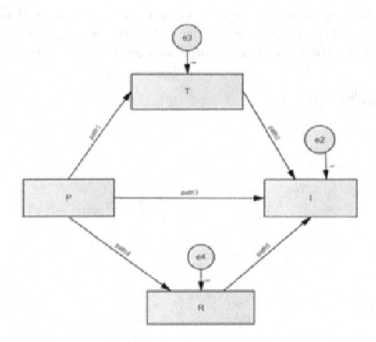

Bootstrapping was performed on the entire model in order to calculate the Total Direct and Indirect effects of Trust and Risk simultaneously. Their individual indirect effects were also studied by generating new estimands.

Table 15. Website and AR app

	Website	AR App
DF	0.18	0.16

Table 16. Paths 1-5

path1*path2 (Trust Mediation Factor)	1.1349	0.3534
Path 4*path5 (Risk Mediation Factor)	-0.0294	-0.0141

New estimands were generated with the syntax verifying path parameter, namely path1*path2 to estimate the indirect effect of Trust on the model, and path3*path 4 to estimate the indirect effect of Risk on our model. The analysis results were further computed using bootstrap results, in which we used 1000 bootstrap samples for the purpose of calculation, and BC confidence level was set to 95. The results signify that The impact of perceived personalisation and the desire to co-create value is driven by consumer perceived trust and the relative trust for Augmented reality-based consumers is not substantially higher than that for e-commerce website-based consumers.

DISCUSSION AND IMPLICATIONS

General Discussions

The study's findings show that perceived customization, as measured by application- and website-based purchase, has an impact on customers' intentions to participate in co-creation. Additionally, the impact of customer perceptions of risk and trust is examined in this study. The research shows that in both the web-based and application group buying scenarios, consumer personalization perceptions predict co-creation intention. Personalization is the term used to describe individualization that considers various client preferences. This is an interesting discovery because it may indicate additional personalization options for online shopping and augmented reality-based applications. Vesanen's work from 2007 shows this by dividing personalization into five groups: segment marketing, adaptive personalization, cosmetic personalization, transparent personalization, and joint personalization. All of the different parts of tailoring are meant to make things better for customers, though they require different amounts of input and participation from customers. Website-based purchasing personalization is restricted to low-level interactions developed by the company in collaboration with the customer, such as selecting from a list or set of suggestions, according to this discussion. Conversely, application-based selection necessitates the customer to incorporate a greater number of adaptable resources, which, considering the extent of expertise, knowledge, and experience required by the latter, may create the perception of restricted personalization. This conclusion emphasizes how important it is to broaden our perspective on personalization as a vehicle for value co-creation.

Personalisation Between Application and Website-Based Shopping

Although augmented reality-based applications allow for higher level interactions than online buying does, people still perceive augmented reality-based application purchasing as being more personalized. This might be because online shoppers can log in and access their past orders and tailored recommendations, whereas customized demonstrations of virtual 3D product descriptions are not available. Although personalization is still a part of online and application-based purchasing, augmented reality technologies are more important than internet shopping methods.

Personalisation and Perceived Risk

According to the study, personalization has a considerable impact on perceived risk for online and augmented reality-based purchases, although this effect can be explained by the fact that as more personalization is introduced, the perceived risk's worth decreases. The outcome can be explained by the fact that the convenience and security of online shopping on the Pepperfry website, which has been available for longer, outweigh the enhanced visualization and risk reduction offered by augmented reality-based shopping on the Pepperfry App. Practical experience shows that customers not only need customized furniture or accessories but also work to remove risk factors; as a result, the perceived risk must be low, which is also supported by our data interpretation.

The Effect of Perceived Trust

In relation to the study, the impact of personalization on perceived trust is significant for online and augmented reality-based shopping. This suggests that trust and personalization are interrelated and will have an impact on Pepperfry's products' personalization. Because customers have successfully acclimated to e-commerce purchasing strategies, the influence of perceived trust on co-creation is considerable for online shopping but not for augmented reality-based shopping. However, the Pepperfry Augmented Reality application's tools and approaches are brand-new to the market, and users have not yet fully accustomed to its capabilities. As a result, customers using augmented reality have significantly lower relative trust than consumers using e-commerce websites.

PRACTICAL IMPLICATIONS OF OUR STUDY

From a management point of view, the study shows how important personalized experiences are in the co-creation process. Management also knows how important experiences are in the customer path. They'll start to use and adopt new tools that let customers make their own experiences (Lemon & Verhoef, 2016). In regards to incorporating augmented reality (AR) technology, management acted appropriately by prioritizing trust-building and risk-reducing functionalities, in light of this information. Some ways to build relationships with customers are to send them personalized messages or use strategic communication that is tailored to their needs (Hennig-Thurau et al., 2000; Son et al., 2005), give them virtual recommendations, or tell them about dangerous parts of the product or service (Zimmer, 2010). When AR is added to make these elements more real (Carozzi et al., 2019), customers are more likely to trust the business and feel less risk when buying a product or service. When the customer doesn't need to see the items, like when they are making a routine or low-commitment buy, AR might not be a good investment (Alimamy et al., 2017). The findings of this study show how important danger and trust are in the process of cocreation. There is already research on these connections (Chen et al., 2016; Iglesias et al., 2020; Randall et al., 2011; See-To & Ho, 2014; H.-C.; Wu & Cheng, 2020), but this study shows that trust is higher in the web-based shopping environment at first, but it is supported by personalization and leads to cocreation in both the web-based and AR shopping environments. The results also showed that customization makes people in both the AR and web-based buy groups think that the service is riskier. This could be because it sends relevant information that emphasizes those risks. This finding helps managers decide when and how to use new technologies. As a result, it is suggested that managers use new technologies in low-risk situations or with low-risk goods. Finally, our study showed that the relationship between risk and customized experiences was different in each group. However, it looks like trust and risk work together to control the relationship between personalization and co-creation in the web-based purchase group. (Cho and Lee, 2006).

CONCLUSION AND LIMITATIONS

According to the survey, personalization is a crucial factor that influences customer willingness to co-create. Personalisation and co-creation intention were also influenced by perceived risk and perceived trust, which acted as mediators. To summarise the study, Augmented reality describes perceived personalisation in a more substantial format than the e-commerce website because the Pepperfry application is rapidly adapting the augmented reality features and customers were able to provide valuable inputs and relate with the customised outcome supported by the Augmented reality application. Personalisation, on the other hand, can be achieved in a more standardised style by increasing consumer trust and lowering the risk factor in both online and augmented reality-based purchases.

Because the research divides the study into internet shopping and augmented reality-based shopping, we may conclude that the market's adaptation of AR techniques will take some time. In terms of risk, augmented reality-based purchasing is chosen over online shopping because demographics and visual 3-D presentation are preferred over static 2-D display. As a result, Pepperfry can introduce some easy-to-understand guides of Augmented reality features for consumers to develop trust in application buying.

Scope for Future Work

Lastly, this study shows that personalization is an important factor that can affect customers' wants to co-create. There are, however, two types of mediation: full mediation (like in AR shopping) and partial mediation (like in web-based shopping). For this study, the group size is too small. The present study only looked at one type of augmented reality app (PepperFry), one type of product (furniture), and one type of customization: choosing and placing digital furniture in real-world settings. In the future, researchers should focus on what should be added to AR apps in order to make money from the brand name, not the way that customers interact with or talk to it. An investigation into the boundary conditions pertaining to customers, situations, and services within the personalization-co-creation dyad can provide valuable insights to managers and application developers regarding individuals' perceptions of personalization and the subsequent impact on their behavior, such as their co-creation intentions. This will help managers and application developers make sure that the right kind of personalization is used in the right situation. To learn more about co-creation, future study can look at the marketing results of other services, such as how people actually buy things and how long they look at them.

REFERENCES

Al-Imamy, S., Gnoth, J. & Deans, K. (2019). *Decision-making and co-creation through AR technology.*

Al-Imamy, S., Gnoth, J., & Deans, K. (2018). The Role of Augmented Reality in the Interactivity of CoCreation. *International Journal of Technology and Human Interaction*, 14.

Alimamy, S., Deans, K., & Gnoth, J. (2017). An empirical investigation of augmented reality to reduce consumer perceived risk. *Academy of Marketing Science World Marketing Congress*, (pp. 127–135). Research Gate.

Assael, H. (2004). *Consumer Behavior. A Strategic Approach.* Houghton Mifflin Company.

Baker, S. (2003). *New Consumer Marketing, Managing a Living Demand System.* Wiley and Sons.

Beer, M., & Nohria, N. (2000). Cracking the code of change. *Harvard Business Review*, (May- June), 133–141.11183975

Duangruthai, V., & Leslie, K. (2018). Impact of Social Media on Consumer Behavior. *International Journal of Information and Decision Sciences.*, 11(3), 10014191. 10.1504/IJIDS.2019.10014191

Grewal, D., Noble, S. M., Roggeveen, A. L., & Nordfält, J. (2020). The future of in-store technology. *Journal of the Academy of Marketing Science*, 48(1), 96–113. 10.1007/s11747-019-00697-z

Grewal, D., Roggeveen, A. L., & Nordfält, J. (2017). The Future of Retailing. *Journal of Retailing*, 93(1), 1–6. 10.1016/j.jretai.2016.12.008

Grosman, L. (2017). The future of retail: How we'll be shopping in 10 Years. *Forbes.* https://www.forbes.com/ sites/forbescommunicationscouncil/2017/06/20/the-futur e-of-retailhow-well-be-shoppingin-10- years/#21188bbe58a6

Hajli, N. (2014). A study of the impact of social media on consumers. *International Journal of Market Research*, 56(3), 387–404. 10.2501/IJMR-2014-025

Hajli, N. (2015). Social commerce construct and consumer's intention to buy. *International Journal of Information Management*, 35(2), 183–191. 10.1016/j. ijinfomgt.2014.12.005

Hawkins, D. I., Best, R. J., & Coney, K. A. (2004). *Consumer Behavior, Building Marketing Strategy.* McGraw-Hill.

Hu, T. (2017). Overview of augmented reality technology. [in Chinese]. *Computer Knowledge and Technology*, (34), 194196.

Huang, T.-L., & Liao, S.-L. (2017). Creating e-shopping multisensory flow experience through augmented-reality interactive technology. *Internet Research*, 27(2), 449–475. 10.1108/IntR-11-2015-0321

Jessen, A., Hilken, T., Chylinski, M., Mahr, D., Heller, J., Keeling, D. I., & de Ruyter, K. (2020). The playground effect: How augmented reality drives creative consumer engagement. *Journal of Business Research*, 116, 85–98. 10.1016/j.jbusres.2020.05.002

Kotler, P., Kartajaya, H., & Setiawan, I. (2017). *Marketing 4.0: moving from traditional to digital*. Wiley: Harvard Business School Press.

Kristensson, P. (2019). Future service technologies and value creation. *Journal of Services Marketing*, 33(4), 502–506. 10.1108/JSM-01-2019-0031

Lawson, R. (2000). Consumer Behavior. In *Marketing Theory*. Research Gate.

Luhmann, N. (2000). Familiarity, confidence, trust: Problems and alternatives. Trust. *Making and Breaking Cooperative Relations*, 6(1), 94–107.

Narwal, M., & Sachdeva, G. (2013). Impact of Information Technology (IT) On Consumer Purchase Behavior. *Journal of Art, Science & Commerce*.

Pietro C., Irene A., Mariano A., & Giuseppe R. (2018). *The Past, Present, and Future of Virtual and Augmented Reality Research: A Network and Cluster Analysis of the Literature*.

Prahalad, C. K., & Ramaswamy, V. (2002). The Co-creation connection. *Strategy & Business*.

. Ramdani, M. A., Belgiawan, P. F., Aprilianty, F., & Purwanegara, M. S. (2022). Consumer Perception and the Evaluation to Adopt Augmented Reality in Furniture Retail Mobile Application. *Binus Business Review, 13*(1). 10.21512/bbr.v13i1.7801

Saleem, M., Kamarudin, S., Shoaib, H. M., & Nasar, A. (2021). Retail Consumers' Behavioral Intention to Use Augmented Reality Mobile Apps in Pakistan. *Journal of Internet Commerce*. 10.1080/15332861.2021.1975427

Sony, M. (2018). Industry 4.0 and lean management: A proposed integration model and research propositions. *Production & Manufacturing Research*, 6(1), 416–432. 10.1080/21693277.2018.1540949

Xiong, J., Hsiang, E. L., He, Z., Zhan, T., & Wu, S.-T. (2021). Augmented reality and virtual reality displays: Emerging technologies and future perspectives. *Light, Science & Applications*, 10(1), 216. 10.1038/s41377-021-00658-834697292

Yim, M., Chu, S., & Sauer, P. (2017). Is Augmented Reality Technology an Effective Tool for E- commerce? An Interactivity and Vividness Perspective. *Journal of Interactive Marketing, 39*, 89–103. 10.1016/j.intmar.2017.04.001

Yim, M. Y.-C., Chu, S.-C., & Sauer, P. L. (2017). Is augmented reality technology an effective tool for ecommerce? An interactivity and vividness perspective. *Journal of Interactive Marketing*, 39, 89–103. 10.1016/j.intmar.2017.04.001

Chapter 7
Artificial Intelligence's Evolutionary Impact on the Tourism Sector:
A Comprehensive Review

Stanzin Padma
Lovely Professional University, India

Tawheed Nabi
Lovely Professional University, India

ABSTRACT

A new era of personalised travel has been ushered in by artificial intelligence. AI in tourism revolutionises the industry by enhancing personalisation, efficiency and customer experiences. It provides personalised recommendations and predictive analytics for demand forecasting and pricing optimisation. Research into AI within the tourism sector has experienced a significant surge since 2017. Recent research highlights a variety of aspects of AI's application in the travel industry. This chapter systematically selects papers from prestigious journals using post-2018 publications from numerous trustworthy databases to give a comprehensive picture of the rapidly expanding body of work on artificial intelligence in the tourism industry. It endeavours to thematically explore how AI has propelled advancements in the tourism industry, the challenges it presents, and its potential for future development. The chapter further presents practical implementations and outlines future research directions.

DOI: 10.4018/979-8-3693-2432-5.ch007

INTRODUCTION

Although Extended Reality (XR) and Artificial Intelligence (AI) were formerly thought of as distinct technological advancements, it is now clear that these are more closely connected than initially thought and that each of these technologies supports the development of each other in several ways (Hirzle et al., 2023; Jaehnig, 2023; Reiners et al., 2021; Stanney et al., 2022). Machine learning and artificial intelligence are two key factors facilitating the broad adoption of extended reality. AI increases the realism of augmented and mixed reality experiences. Artificial Intelligence has long been discussed at the highest levels of the metaverse and has a significant role in creating and consuming XR material (Jaehnig, 2023). In modern literature, the complex interaction and convergence of artificial intelligence and extended reality are becoming more and more evident. AI can enhance XR, and conversely, XR can augment AI capabilities. Consequently, we find ourselves in an era characterised by the widespread emergence of the XR-AI amalgamation. This study looks at how artificial intelligence might help the travel and tourism industry in a dynamic setting.

The travel and tourism sector has experienced a dramatic upheaval with the introduction of contemporary AI services. This development has wholly altered the travel industry's business. The advent of AI and intelligent technologies has changed the travel industry, which was formerly dependent on travel agencies, pamphlets and maps. Travellers can make well-informed decisions through reviews and recommendations. Travelling has evolved significantly due to AI tools, which revolutionised navigation by providing accurate direction and smartphone apps, which improved on-the-go access to travel recommendations. AI-powered recommendation systems analyse user preferences, browsing behaviour, past bookings and demographic information to provide personalised travel recommendations to travellers. These recommendations can include tailored suggestions for accommodations, activities, restaurants, attractions and travel itineraries, enhancing users' overall travel planning and booking experience. AI algorithms are also used for demand forecasting by analysing previous booking data, weather forecasts, events calendars and other relevant factors to predict future demand for tourist destinations, accommodations, flights and activities. Destination managers optimise pricing strategies, resource allocation and marketing campaigns by forecasting demand to meet customer needs and maximise revenue. Similarly, AI-based image recognition and processing technologies can automatically filter and categorise large volumes of tourist photos based on various criteria such as location, landmarks, activities and aesthetics. Automated photo filtering systems can help streamline the management and organisation of tourist photos for travel agencies, destination marketing organisations and online travel platforms, improving content curation and user engagement. AI-based technology, such as sentiment analysis algorithms, analyse text data from tourism reviews and social media posts to extract insights into tourist opinions, emotions and satisfaction. By analysing sentiment trends and identifying key themes and sentiments expressed in tourism reviews, businesses and destination managers can gain valuable feedback, identify areas for improvement and tailor their offerings and services to meet customer expectations better. Further, Natural language processing (NLP) techniques enable virtual assistants to communicate with travellers in their preferred language, answer queries, provide recommendations and assist with bookings, enhancing customer service and satisfaction.

Such applications demonstrate how AI technologies enhance various aspects of the tourism industry, ultimately improving the overall travel experience for tourists and driving the industry's success.

In the future, AI has the potential to alter several aspects of tourism and hospitality. Travellers will have access to personalised itineraries based on AI-driven insights and predictive analytics and AI chatbots will provide on-the-spot assistance while travelling. Integrating AI and extended reality is becoming more common, and such technologies will enable immersive travel experiences and previews of destinations. Augmented reality (AR) applications enriched with AI capabilities can overlay digital information and interactive elements onto the real-world environment, enhancing sightseeing experiences and providing contextual information about landmarks, attractions, and points of interest. These immersive technologies can enhance visitor engagement, facilitate cultural exchange and create memorable tourist experiences. Through better trash management and energy utilisation, AI-based services may also assist in limiting the environmental effect and supporting eco-friendly tourism activities. AI technologies can help promote sustainable practices within the tourism industry by optimising resource usage, minimising environmental impact and supporting conservation efforts. From energy-efficient operations to intelligent transportation systems, AI-driven solutions can contribute to developing more sustainable and eco-friendly tourism practices. Additionally, AI-powered technologies, such as facial recognition software and predictive analytics for risk management, can enhance security protocols in the travel and tourism sector. By leveraging AI for threat detection, emergency response, and crisis management, tourism stakeholders can better ensure the safety and well-being of travellers. There can be further advancements in the use of AI by tourism-related organisations to help analyse massive amounts of data and make data-driven decisions on pricing and marketing strategies. AI-powered analytics solutions enable tourist industry participants to spot opportunities, make well-informed decisions and react to changing market conditions more skilfully.

Thus, such technologies hold immense promise for the tourism industry making the prospects for AI-driven tourism development brighter. AI has the power to completely transform the travel and tourism sector by fostering innovation, increasing productivity, boosting client experiences and supporting environmentally friendly behaviours. As AI technologies continue to advance, we can expect to see even greater integration and adoption of AI-driven solutions across all sectors of the tourism ecosystem.

Objective

The goal of this study is to gain a general understanding of the several ways that artificial intelligence is contributing to the development of the tourism industry by doing a thorough assessment of the recently published literature on the subject. In particular, the study aims at understanding and exploring AI in the tourism industry in three parts: first, it attempts to explore the benefits and applications of machine intelligence within the industry; second, it explores the various challenges that come with AI dependence; and third, the chapter makes an effort to investigate the industry's potential for AI in the future.

Research Questions

Considering the objectives of this review, the following are the research questions:

1. How has AI contributed to advancing the tourism industry's growth?
2. What is the future potential of AI in the tourism industry?
3. What are the possible challenges of AI in the tourism industry?

Method

In order to answer the research questions, various databases were used to screen the articles for final review. Some primary databases used to conduct the research are Science Direct, PubMed, CABI Digital Library, Scopus, Web of Science, Semantic Scholar, ResearchGate, Google Scholar and DOAJ. The chapter uses articles published post-2018 for the review, but most articles selected are published post-2020. The key terms "Artificial Intelligence", "AI", "Machine Learning", "Machine intelligence", "tourism sector", "tourism AI", "AI benefits in tourism", "travel", "challenges", "application", and "potential" have been used as search criteria. The final review used articles published in peer-reviewed journals, with the majority indexed in SCOPUS, Web of Science, ProQuest and ABDC.

We selected only relevant studies and articles for review. After the review, different themes were identified and 45 papers were categorised under various themes and sub-themes in tabular format.

The Preferred Reporting Items for Systematic Reviews and Meta-Analysis (PRISMA) approach was employed to carry out the review (see Figure 1: PRISMA Flowchart).

Figure 1. Prisma 2020 flow diagram

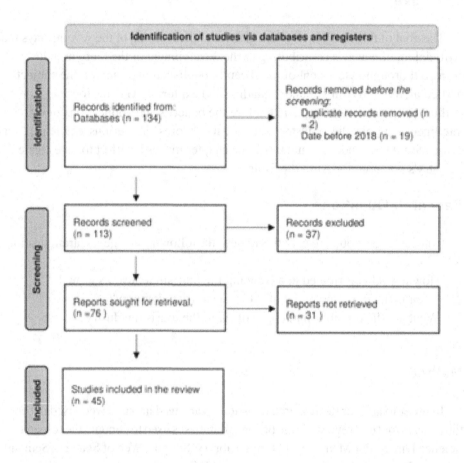

AI's Contribution Towards the Advancement of Travel and Tourism

According to Kirtil and Askun (2021), AI research in the tourism industry has grown significantly since 2017 (see Figure 2: Growth of AI Studies in Tourism Literature). This topic had received very little attention before. An increasing amount of research is being done in this area as a result of the advancements in artificial intelligence and the internet.

Figure 2. Growth of AI studies in travel and tourism literature

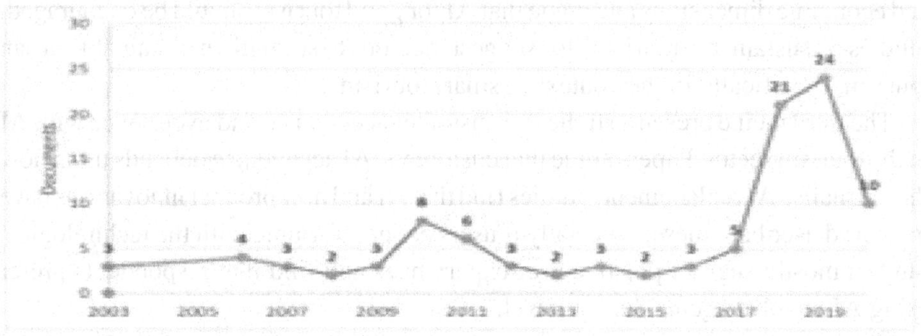

Source: Kirtil and Askun, 2021.

Various articles have been grouped under different themes to help readers comprehend and investigate AI's presence in the tourism business and learn how it has advanced the sector. After a substantial review, we discovered that four significant themes could answer the first research question. The themes are as follows:

1. Application and Benefits of Artificial Intelligence in the Tourism Sector
2. Implications and Interlinkages with Sustainability and Environment
3. User Acceptance and Experience With AI In the Tourism Industry
4. Case Studies and Specific Analysis

The studies included below provide a thorough overview of AI's contribution to the expansion of the travel sector. The tourism business has benefited greatly from the application of AI in numerous ways, according to this wide variety of studies. Almost all studies suggest that AI has contributed towards easier travel planning, automated personalised services, intelligent planning of destinations, personalised recommendations, customised travel suggestions and quick decision making, leading to greater customer satisfaction. From businesses' and service providers' perspectives, AI has contributed to profitability, productivity and efficiency due to data-driven decisions and enhanced marketing experiences. AI has also helped in tourism forecasting, performance analysis, destination management, better customer relations and improved value co-creation, contributing towards significant growth of tourism in general and tourism revenue in particular. There are others who contend that AI has played a major role in the preservation of historical places by improving the technological, managerial and intellectual capacities of service providers.

In addition to applications and benefits, several studies also revolve around the issue of sustainability. While a couple of studies point towards the need for AI to include environmental concerns, studies also look at sustainability from sociocultural and economic dimensions and argue that AI for good tourism should be encouraged. Studies on sustainable tourism also suggest methods to strengthen sustainable urban tourism, specifically in the context of smart tourism.

The third theme presents studies on customer acceptance and experience with AI in the tourism sector. Papers argue that customers' AI acceptance depends upon how they visualise AI replacement. Studies find that AI and new product innovations have increased user happiness, especially if users are comfortable with the technologies. Studies mostly suggest positive user experiences and find that respondents prefer using AI-enabled agents during travel.

The fourth theme under this topic deals with case studies and find essential applications. Case studies from European countries suggest that AI solutions can facilitate marketing automation, segmentation and customisation of tourism services. Some Southeast Asian studies argue that smart tourism based on AI technologies leads to much higher effectiveness, economic growth, revenue growth and harmony of resources than traditional tourism methods.

Thus, answering the first research question, how AI has benefited the travel and tourism sector, Table 1 presents the thematic tabular review.

Table 1. Theme 1: Application and benefits of artificial intelligence in the tourism sector

S. No.	AUTHORS	YEAR	FINDINGS	JOURNAL AND INDEXING
1.	Nagaraj Samala, Bharath Shashanka Katkam, Raja Shekhar Bellamkonda and Raul Villamarin Rodriguez	2020	AI in the tourist industry makes travel planning more accessible by providing automated, personalised, and intelligent travel services. Travellers can receive a personalised experience from AI by sharing information about their habits, hobbies and inclinations.	Journal of Tourism Futures (SCOPUS, WEB OF SCIENCE, DOAJ, COPE, CLARIVATE)

continued on following page

Table 1. Continued

S. No.	AUTHORS	YEAR	FINDINGS	JOURNAL AND INDEXING
2.	Seden Doğan and İlayda Zeynep Niyet	2024	With the help of chatbots, automated procedures, and improved security measures, artificial Intelligence (AI) has increased productivity and made passenger experiences more enjoyable by offering personalised recommendations. Tourism organisations may efficiently focus their marketing campaigns and make data-driven decisions by utilising AI's capacity to assess vast amounts of data. AI provides customised and individualised recommendations for travel locations, lodging, things to do, and places to eat, improving the trip experience.	Future Tourism Trends (BOOK)
3.	Zohreh Doborjeh, Nigel Hemmington, Maryam Doborjeh and Nikola Kasabov	2021	This review uncovered fresh information about AI techniques related to the environment and multimodal data sets accessible in the hotel and tourism industries. The paper used 146 articles and reviewed their methodology, techniques, and database, finding applications of AI in the travel and hospitality sectors. Additionally, it suggests creating unique, personalised AI modelling for innovative tourism platforms to forecast traveller activity trends accurately.	International Journal of Contemporary Hospitality Management (SCOPUS, WEB OF SCIENCE)
4.	Dimitra Samara, Ioannis Magnisalis and Vassilios Peristeras	2020	The results of this paper suggest that by adequately identifying dissemination, BDAI adds value to the tourism industry. Adopting BDAI tactics offers travellers a highly customised and rich experience and greater productivity, profitability, and efficiency for tourism suppliers. The authors conclude that using a BDAI technique can help overcome obstacles. The competitiveness and durability of new and incumbent businesses in the tourist sector will depend heavily on this adoption.	Journal of Hospitality and Tourism Technology (SCOPUS, WEB OF SCIENCE, ABI/INFORM Complete ABI/INFORM Global British Library Cabell's Marketing Directory ProQuest Central)
5.	Fangfei Bi & Haotian Liu	2022	It creates a hybrid intelligent classification strategy and researches visitors' selection behaviour. In particular, tourists may find it easier to make a quick decision on whether or not to visit a sightseeing attraction using our suggested categorisation approach. Performance evaluation and cross-validation testing demonstrate that our built platform can function effectively and efficiently by considering several elements.	EURASIP Journal on Wireless Communications and Networking (SCOPUS, WEB OF SCIENCE)

continued on following page

Table 1. Continued

S. No.	AUTHORS	YEAR	FINDINGS	JOURNAL AND INDEXING
6.	T. D. Dang & M. T. Nguyen	2023	he study reveals that digital technologies, including AI and Metaverse, enhance value co-creation by enabling more efficient, personalized, and immersive travel experiences. It also highlights the potential of AI and digital technologies to improve travel experiences and ethical considerations, and suggests three key areas for future research: managerial, intellectual, and technical, presenting opportunities for revolutionary changes in the travel and hospitality industries.	Future Business Journal (WEB OF SCIENCE)
7.	Hui Lv, Si Shi and Dogan Gursoy	2021	The study categorised the various types of big data used, looked at 270 relevant papers, and talked about how artificial intelligence is employed with big data in hospitality and tourist research. The key issues of big data and AI research in the literature that had already been published were then revealed, including forecasting, industry development, marketing, performance analysis, and consumer behaviours and attitudes.	Journal of Hospitality Marketing & Management (SCOPUS, WEB OF SCIENCE)
8.	Mehmet Bahri Saydam, Hasan Evrim Arici and Mehmet Ali Koseoglu	2022	The study uncovered important themes and clusters after looking through 123 publications, such as anthropomorphism, theory-based works, methodological underpinnings, service robots, employee and consumer perspectives on service robots, and their connections to AI in T&H. It also demonstrated the domain's nomological network, theory, context, and current developments.	Journal of Hospitality Marketing & Management (SCOPUS, WEB OF SCIENCE)
9.	Angel Diaz-Pacheco, Miguel Á. Álvarez-Carmona, Rafael Guerrero-Rodríguez, Luz Angélica Ceballos Chávez, Ansel Y. Rodríguez-González, Juan Pablo Ramírez-Silva and Ramón Aranda	2022	The primary methods, representations, measures, and outcomes of destination images in tourism studies that are derived from a computational science approach are all identified in this article. Two taxonomies arose: one concerning the collection of procedures and techniques and the other concerning the outcomes attained using these specific methodological designs. Although electronic information is becoming increasingly popular as a critical source of information, surveys continue to be the most popular, according to our data. However, word frequency-based techniques are still the most used methods for information analysis. However, deep learning and neural networks are becoming more and more popular.	Journal of Experimental & Theoretical Artificial Intelligence (SCOPUS, WEB OF SCIENCE)

continued on following page

Table 1. Continued

S. No.	AUTHORS	YEAR	FINDINGS	JOURNAL AND INDEXING
10.	Yujia Chen, Hui Li and Tao Xue	2023	This research has examined the process of gendering through the lens of gender theory, utilising the social interaction technique. Based on the sixteen respondents' interviews, it is possible to trace the gendering of artificial intelligence by women from interactions between humans and machines to those between humans and AI. There are four main factors that are associated with the social construction of the gendering process. The findings contribute to our understanding of the relationship between humans and technology and help travel industry professionals find more economical methods to integrate technology and human collaboration into their daily operations.	Journal of Quality Assurance in Hospitality & Tourism (SCOPUS, WEB OF SCIENCE)
11.	Miguel Camacho-Ruiz, Ramón Alberto Carrasco, Gema Fernández-Avilés, Antonio LaTorre	2023	This work developed a novel hierarchical taxonomy-based automated classification approach for a wide range of tourism events that may be used to enhance tourism destination management. The automatic classification procedure suggested uses data science tools, including supervised machine learning, CRISP-DM, and natural language processing methodologies, to construct a normalised catalogue across highly disparate geographic locations. As a result, catalogues can be created that let users locate events irrespective of whatever event categories were, if any, allocated at the source. This is highly beneficial for businesses like airlines, travel agencies, or hotel chains providing this information across different regions. In the end, this technology has the power to completely change how businesses and consumers engage with information about tourism events.	Applied Soft Computing (SCOPUS, WEB OF SCIENCE)
12.	Carlos Flavián, Luis V. Casalo, Dan Wang	2021	This book explores many novel possibilities by offering customers more value and boosting businesses' profits. It is an obvious chance to progress in the transformation of the tourism industry. The book, which includes 13 papers, presents distinct viewpoints on three topics: the adoption of AI in services related to hospitality and tourism, the substitution of AI in the workforce, and the particular uses of AI in these fields. Focusing on different occupations and hospitality environments, the studies provide insights regarding certain AI-based technologies, like voice assistants, chatbots, and service robots.	International Journal of Contemporary Hospitality Management (WEB OF SCIENCE, SCOPUS)

continued on following page

Table 1. Continued

S. No.	AUTHORS	YEAR	FINDINGS	JOURNAL AND INDEXING
13.	Mouna Knani, Said Echchakoui, Riadh Ladhari	2022	The authors of the paper recommend use bibliometrics to evaluate the cutting edge AI research being carried out in T&H nowadays. Between 1984 and 2021, a total of 1035 publications were published; they showcase the number of studies, authors, associated nations and institutions, authorship networks, co-occurrences of keywords, and keyword networks. Additionally, this thematic map identifies four research categories: motor themes (like artificial neural networks and data mining); primary and transversal themes (like sentiment analysis and text mining, big data and the Internet of things, COVID and AI); emerging themes (like the experience of service robots); and specialised and peripheral themes (like biometrics, augmented and virtual reality, and tourism forecasting models).	International Journal of Hospitality Management (SCOPUS, WEB OF SCIENCE)
14.	Fauzia Jabeen, Sameera Al Zaidi, Maryam Hamad Al Dhaheri	2022	The study makes the case that the most important factors influencing the deployment of automation and artificial intelligence are human expertise, services, and robotics applications. Researchers and industry professionals in the hotel and tourism sectors may find it useful to utilise the framework proposed by this study to develop long-term strategies for incorporating and managing automation and artificial intelligence. Future studies on the use of AI in the travel and hospitality industry may find the proposed methodology useful.	Tourism Review (SCOPUS, WEB OF SCIENCE)

Table 2. Theme 2: Implications and interlinkages with sustainability and environment

S. NO.	AUTHORS	YEAR	FINDINGS	JOURNAL AND INDEXING
15.	Gilang Maulana Majid, Iis Tussyadiah, Yoo Ri Kim and Anjan Pal	2023	Regarding the growing interest in intelligent automation adoption and growth in the tourism industry, the article suggests that there are many possible solutions for concerns related to sustainable tourism. A detailed analysis of 213 scholarly publications was conducted to produce an extensive map of the current state of the art for intelligent automation in sustainable tourism. The study found five main themes: assessing the tourist experience, boosting quality of life, conserving heritage, safeguarding the environment, and improving the tourist experience through intelligent automation. The sociological and economic aspects of sustainability have received greater attention in academic studies on this topic than environmental issues. In order to pinpoint regions in need of additional research, this study describes sustainability transition paths using two dimensions: tourism involvement and sustainability inclusion. The findings clarify the need for AI-based solutions that offer high levels of sustainability inclusion and tourism participation. According to this study's "AI4GoodTourism" idea, intelligent automation with a high degree of sustainability inclusion can raise the total marginal contribution that tourists make.	Journal of Sustainable Tourism (SCOPUS, WEB OF SCIENCE)
16.	Qi, XW (Qi, Xianwen) ; Li, XM (Li, Xiaomeng)	2022	In order to support urban tourism sustainable growth, this study suggests an extraction method of the tourist sustainable development path under the construction of smart cities and artificial intelligence. Based on the conceptual model of the influencing factors of sustainable development in smart cities, this essay investigates the significance of latent variables. Anhui Province was used as an example while developing a structural analysis model to evaluate the total impact of parameter elements and construct an intelligent city tourist sustainable development plan that is in line with the parameters. Anhui smart city's sustainable development model is examined, the system model of a smart city is constructed, and the extraction strategy for the intelligent city tourism sustainable development path is created.	Journal of Interconnection Network (WEB OF SCIENCE)

continued on following page

Table 2. Continued

S. NO.	AUTHORS	YEAR	FINDINGS	JOURNAL AND INDEXING
17.	Amit Kumar, Manju Singh	2020	This study investigates how AI can contribute to sustainable tourism practices in Kerala, focusing on waste management, resource optimisation, and eco-tourism promotion. The paper finds that AI-powered systems can monitor and optimise resource utilisation, promoting sustainability in tourism operations. AI tools can analyse tourist behaviour and encourage responsible choices, minimising environmental impact. Collaboration among stakeholders and responsible AI development are crucial to sustainability goals.	International Journal of Recent Technology and Engineering (SCOPUS, Scilit, Lattice Science, Kudos and more)

Table 3. Theme 3: User acceptance and experience with AI in the tourism and hospitality industry

S. NO.	AUTHORS	YEAR	FINDINGS	JOURNAL AND INDEXING
18. 1.	Rijul Chaturvedi, Sanjeev Verma, Faizan Ali and Satish Kumar	2023	The research offers a conceptual framework for comprehending AI-powered tourism experiences and examines the performance, content, and themes of important technologies such as chatbots, IoT, AR/VR, big data analytics, and natural language processing.	International Journal of Human-Computer Interaction (WEB OF SCIENCE)
19.	Darina Vorobeva, Diego Costa Pinto, Nuno António and Anna S. Mattila	2023	Three studies that make use of the Feeling Economy paradigm look at whether or not customers will accept AI-based services depending on whether they see AI as an improvement over a replacement. The findings bolster the Feeling Economy theory by highlighting mechanisms of ease of use and enjoyment. The tourist and hospitality sectors can benefit from this research by deploying AI-based services.	Current Issues in Tourism (SCOPUS, WEB OF SCIENCE)
20.	Edward C.S. Ku, Chun-Der Chen	2024	The study explores how tourism organizations utilize AI innovation services to enhance client satisfaction. Using the PLS-SEM approach, it found that new product advantages and AI innovation significantly enhance functional benefits, visitor happiness, and future AI service usage intention. The study provides theoretical insights and practical recommendations for travel agencies.	International Journal of Information Management (SCOPUS, WEB OF SCIENCE)

continued on following page

Table 3. Continued

S. NO.	AUTHORS	YEAR	FINDINGS	JOURNAL AND INDEXING
21.	Aashiek Cheriyan, Rohit Kumar Sharma, Alwin Joseph, Shine Raju Kappil	2022	The study examines the acceptance of chatbots in the travel and tourism sector, based on survey data from IT professionals in Pune, India. The results show that most respondents prefer AI-enabled agents, as they help with questions and issues, and can alleviate anxieties. However, they believe chatbots need to be intelligent and continuously learn to offer better solutions.	Journal of Positive School Psychology (SCOPUS)
22.	Tingting Wang	2023	The study suggests that consumers prioritize hotel offerings over meeting their needs, and hotels should focus on customer satisfaction through user acceptance behaviour. 62% of respondents believe quality of hotel service is key to guest satisfaction, highlighting the need for improved service plans.	Journal of Artificial Intelligence Practice (DOAJ, ARDI, CPCI, CALIS, CBBIB and more)

Table 4. Theme 4: Case studies and specific analysis

S. NO.	AUTHORS	YEAR	FINDINGS	JOURNAL AND INDEXING
23.	Raffaele Filieri, Elettra D'Amico, Alessandro Destefanis, Emilio Paolucci, Elisabetta Raguseo	2021	From 2015 to 2017, male graduates with STEM degrees founded the majority of AI start-ups, with more capital obtained through founders and non-start-up experience. European AI start-ups are concentrated in popular travel destinations, with learning, communication, and services (big data, machine learning, and natural language processing) being the most significant investment domains. These areas are interested in AI solutions for marketing automation, segmentation, and customization, as well as pre- and post-trip considerations.	International Journal of Contemporary Hospitality Management (SCOPUS, WEB OF SCIENCE)
24.	Myung Ja Kim, C. Michael Hall, Namho Chung, Minseong Kim and Kwonsang Sohn	2023	The study uses multi-analysis techniques like fuzzy-set qualitative comparative analysis, multi-group analysis, and partial least squares structural equation modelling to create an integrated research model incorporating environmental, social, governance, air quality, climate change, and AI. The results show that domestic visitors' use of public transport is significantly influenced by ESG, climate change mitigation, and sustainable mobility. Additionally, there are differences in how high and low AI knowledge groups use public transport.	Asia Pacific Journal of Tourism Research (SCOPUS, WEB OF SCIENCE)

continued on following page

Table 4. Continued

S. NO.	AUTHORS	YEAR	FINDINGS	JOURNAL AND INDEXING
25.	Nan Wang	2022	The hotel uses scientific methods for rapid transformation and updates, using modern information technology to build a customer data group. The large, intelligent mobile cloud provides a comprehensive platform for integrating information for hotel system management. As scientific and technological knowledge advances, new opportunities for system improvement arise, but also new challenges. This article examines the evolution of the hotel management system in a network environment, focusing on the features of the tourism accommodation management system in the big data environment.	Alexandria Engineering Journal (SCOPUS, WEB OF SCIENCE)
26.	Ping-Tsan Ho	2022	The idea of "smart tourism recommendation," which entails making internet-based suggestions for self-service travel bookings, is examined in this article. Utilising big data and AI algorithms, it looks into this strategy in Southeast Asia. In order to better understand tourism transactions, revenue growth, resource allocation, and visitor happiness, the study compares smart tourism models with traditional tourism development models. The findings demonstrate the effectiveness of the big data and AI-driven smart tourism suggestion mode, as evidenced by its overall average satisfaction rating of 88.84 points, which is 7.30 points higher than that of conventional tourist techniques.	Mobile Information Systems (SCOPUS, WEB OF SCIENCE)
27.	Jacques Bulchand-Gidumal, Eduardo William Secin, Peter O'Connor and Dimitrios Buhalis	2023	The study uses focus groups, in-depth interviews, and questionnaire-based surveys to investigate how artificial intelligence affects hotel marketing. Ten patterns in AI's influence are identified and categorised into four areas: improving sustainability, controlling stakeholder interactions, reengineering internal processes, and calculating return on investment. Through improved product and service design, intelligent and predictive customer care, and other means, AI also transforms customer processes and services. The report raises research priorities for academics and industry practitioners by highlighting the possible impacts AI is expected to bring to the marketing of hospitality and tourism.	Current Issues in Tourism (SCOPUS, WEB OF SCIENCE)

continued on following page

Table 4. Continued

S. NO.	AUTHORS	YEAR	FINDINGS	JOURNAL AND INDEXING
28.	Raffaele Filieri, Elettra D'Amico, Alessandro Destefanis, Emilio Paolucci, Elisabetta Raguseo	2021	The bulk of AI start-ups were created by male STEM graduates between 2015 and 2017, with founders with non-start-up experience providing more funding. The majority of European AI start-ups are based in well-known tourist locations, and the most important investment domains are learning, communication, and services (big data, machine learning, and natural language processing). Pre- and post-trip considerations, as well as AI solutions for marketing automation, segmentation, and customisation, are of importance to these fields.	International Journal of Contemporary Hospitality Management (WEB OF SCIENCE, SCOPUS)
29.	Monika Agarwal, Rajat Agrawal	2021	This case study explores SpiceJet's use of AI in customer support, offers, and pricing. It highlights the potential of AI to enhance service, optimize pricing, and improve travel experiences. However, challenges include data security, algorithmic bias, and system integration.	International Journal of Management (ProQuest et al., J Gate and more)
30.	Manju Singh, Pooja Saxena	2020	The study examines the use of AI in Delhi Metro's smart ticketing, route optimization, and real-time information access, highlighting its potential to improve tourist convenience, enhance decision-making, and optimize resource usage, while also addressing data privacy and ensuring equitable access for all demographics.	International Journal of Research in Management, Economics and Commerce (Citefactor, Cosmos impact factor, Ulrish's Periodical Directory, ProQuest, J Gate, Index Copernicus)

Future Potential of Artificial Intelligence in the Tourism Industry

In response to the second research question, several articles have been reviewed and are presented in Table 5. The research investigates AI's potential in the travel and tourism sector going forward. Studies argue that tourism-oriented businesses actively use chatbots, forecasting, customised travel experiences and other AI-based technologies. However, studies suggest that most of these are still in their early stages. Studies argue that in the future, AI and similar applications have the potential to alter the face of the tourism industry significantly. Future developments in big data efficiency could further augment AI's position in tourism, boost consumer satisfaction and improve demand forecasting. It can augment virtual reality and value co-creation processes. Smart tourism may collect even more precise information in the future, and this has special significance to rural tourism, which has further scope to grow while preserving its unique identity. AI can spur rural communities to preserve their natural environment and distinctive culture while growing their tourism industry, leading to income growth. This can be termed as rural revitalisation. Thus, further enhancement of robotics and machine intelligence will only increase customer satisfaction and service provider profitability, thus accelerating the pace of growth of the tourism industry.

Table 5. Tabular review: Future potential of AI in tourism

S. NO.	AUTHORS	YEAR	FINDINGS	JOURNAL AND INDEXING
31.	Martina Nannelli, Francesco Capone and Luciana Lazzeretti	2023	This essay looks at current artificial intelligence developments as well as possible future developments in the travel industry. The study does a bibliometric analysis using the ISI database, and then employs social network analysis to map its intellectual structure. A review of qualitative literature is produced by the study. The findings identify a number of key research areas, such as the use of big data for demand forecasting and customer satisfaction, the use of augmented and virtual reality for co-creation processes, service robots, and smart tourism trends.	European Planning Studies (WEB OF SCIENCE)
32.	Dan Xie, Yu He	2022	With an emphasis on the marketing approach of rural tourist attractions, this article investigates the integration of big data and artificial intelligence in rural tourism. It examines how these technologies are currently being used and suggests a fresh marketing fusion paradigm. The results point to the necessity of further integration of these technologies in order to improve the entire tourism experience by augmenting the tour experience and revenue of rural, scenic sites.	Mobile Information Systems (SCOPUS, WEB OF SCIENCE)
33.	Alonso Almeida and Maria del Mar	2019	Despite the changes brought about by information technology and the internet, a new revolution in the tourism sector is anticipated due to the introduction of robotics, artificial intelligence, and virtual reality. The article argues that, despite the fact that these technologies are still in their infancy, a number of newly released studies in this area point to the possibility that artificial intelligence and machine learning could have a substantial impact on the travel and tourism industry.	Cuadernos De Turismo (WEB OF SCIENCE)

continued on following page

Table 5. Continued

S. NO.	AUTHORS	YEAR	FINDINGS	JOURNAL AND INDEXING
34.	Iis Tussyadiah	2020	This study emphasises the necessity of an automated future by highlighting the expanding application of intelligent automation in travel and tourism. It proposes four directions for further research: creating AI that is beneficial, encouraging adoption, assessing the implications of automation, and creating AI that will enable scientists to work together in a sustainable future. Research projects in these areas will enable a systematic development of information, demonstrating a cooperative effort among scientists to ensure the beneficial applications of intelligent automation in the tourism sector.	Annals of Tourism Research (WEB OF SCIENCE)
35.	Lukas Grundner and Barbara Neuhofer	2021	The paper explores AI's future applications in service ecosystems, highlighting its advantages and disadvantages using futures techniques and service-dominant logic. It bridges the gap between visitor experiences, AI, and S-D logic, offering theoretical and practical benefits.	Journal of Destination Marketing and Management (WEB OF SCIENCE)
36.	Yanzheng Tup, Lanyu Ning and AIyun Zhu	2021	The article explores the impact of artificial intelligence (AI) on the tourism sector, focusing on Chinese practice cases. It presents a research plan for future developments in destination government, tourism businesses, and visitor experiences, while addressing ethics, discrimination, and privacy concerns.	Information and Communication Technologies in Tourism (Conference Paper)
37.	Arthur Huang, Ahmet Bulent Ozturk, Tingting Zhang, Efren de la Mora Velasco, Adam Haney	2024	Using data from 380 respondents to an online survey, the study investigates the factors impacting customers' plans to employ AI services in the future. The findings indicate that both performance and expectations are shown to predict pleasure, enjoyment and expectations are predictive of satisfied with AI.	International Journal of Hospitality Management (SCOPUS, WEB OF SCIENCE)

Possible Challenges

This section examines the newly released papers on the difficulties posed by AI in the travel and tourism sector in an effort to respond to the third research question. Table 6 presents the tabular review. Emerging studies highlight the privacy concerns that come with AI as businesses input a large amount of customer information into this technology, leading to sensitive customer information. Studies argue that there is a need to address the privacy issues brought up by AI. Studies also suggest that possible hazards can result from businesses' data-driven decisions. Many studies critically analyse AI's ethical, legal, social and economic implications. There are varieties of ethical issues, such as military robots, social engineering, sex robots, omnipresent surveillance and transhumanism, which present ethical dilemmas. These can have significant repercussions and need to be investigated and resolved. It is also argued in the literature that policymakers should formulate regulations about data collection, standardised hardware and finance. Furthermore, it is asserted that the industry's overuse of AI could eclipse the human element, which is a crucial factor in defining experiential tourism.

Table 6. Tabular review: Challenges and ethical concerns

S. NO.	AUTHORS	YEAR	FINDINGS	JOURNAL AND INDEXING
38.	Nurus Sakinatul Fikriah Mohd Shith Putera, Hartini Saripan, Mimi Sintia Mohd Bajury, Syazni Nadzirah Ya'cob	2022	Artificial intelligence applications in the travel and tourism industry has given rise to privacy concerns as businesses input copious amounts of customer data into the technology, resulting in the creation of sensitive customer information. Thus, the purpose of this study is to determine if the Personal Data Protection Act of 2010 adequately addresses the privacy issues brought up by artificial intelligence. This work combined a case study with doctrinal methodology to build systematic ways of legal reasoning relevant to AI applications in the tourism business. It is imperative that privacy and security be upheld across the whole data lifecycle to shield players in the tourist sector from legal action and preserve customer confidence.	Environment-Behaviour Proceedings Journal (WEB OF SCIENCE)
39.	Tarik Dogru, Nathan Line and Tingting Zhang	2023	This research critically analyses the ethical, legal, social, and economic implications of General Analytics (GAI) in HT environments, integrating academic and practical insights. It highlights challenges and opportunities presented by GAI, drawing on scholars, educators, and industry practitioners.	Journal of Hospitality & Tourism Research (WEB OF SCIENCE)
40.	Russell Belk	2020	Examining military robots, social engineering, sex robots, ubiquitous monitoring, and transhumanism, this paper examines the moral dilemmas surrounding robotics and AI in service interactions. The research closes a gap in the literature and deepens our knowledge of robotics and artificial intelligence service environments, which has implications for public policy and service technology applications.	The Service Industries Journal (WEB OF SCIENCE)

continued on following page

Table 6. Continued

S. NO.	AUTHORS	YEAR	FINDINGS	JOURNAL AND INDEXING
41.	Umar Bashir Mir, Swapnil Sharma, Arpan Kumar Kar, Manmohan Prasad Gupta	2020	The study is not specific to tourism but deals with essential aspects of AI in India. The study argues that policymakers must formulate fundamental regulations about data collecting, standardised hardware, skilled labour, finance, and start-up culture. These policies can serve as fundamental components of a sustainable environment for the development of IASs and the execution of national AI strategies. For the ecosystem to work as it should, specific laws must be in place. Any technology that can function well in India has a better chance of functioning globally due to the country's vast population.	Digital Policy, Regulation and Governance (WEB OF SCIENCE)
42.	Vidushi Marda	2018	In addition to addressing societal and ethical concerns, the paper promotes policy considerations that address the technological constraints of AI systems. It offers a framework for AI policy in India and applies it to current sectoral concerns, emphasising data-driven decisions and associated risks.It applies the recommended framework to the present sectoral concerns facing India while keeping in mind the country's current AI policy. In order to impact the country's current policy discussions, it focuses on potential risks that arise from data-driven decisions in general and in the Indian context in particular.	Philosophical Transactions of the royal society of Mathematical, Physical and engineering sciences (WEB OF SCIENCE)
43.	Nagaraj Samala, Bharath Shashanka Katkam, Raja Shekhar Bellamkonda and Raul Villamarin Rodriguez	2020	The paper also discusses AI's challenges in addition to its benefits and applications, which have been discussed under the first theme. It makes the case that human interaction, which is a crucial factor in determining experiencing tourism, cannot be surpassed by AI.	Journal of Tourism Futures, (SCOPUS, WEB OF SCIENCE)
44.	George Telonis and Peter P. Groumpos	2018	According to the article, there are several important areas where AI may significantly impact travel to improve assistance and enhance the traveller experience. Travel websites like Trivago, Tripadvisor, and others generate millions of useful data. This research employs artificial intelligence (AI) technologies and techniques to analyse and study the trends and causes affecting various areas. The paper highlights the important challenges of AI in the industry.	UBT International Conference
45.	B. Deepthi, Vikram Bansal	2023	The study reveals that AI is enhancing the global travel industry through chatbots, forecasting, and personalized experiences. However, budgetary constraints, knowledge gaps, and human resource issues hinder its use in the Indian tourism sector. Effective management could enhance AI's effectiveness.	Impact of Industry 4.0 on Sustainable Tourism (BOOK)

CONCLUSION

Emerging literature suggests that studies relating to AI within the tourism sector have been increasing, particularly post-2017. There are many applications of Artificial Intelligence within the tourism sector, ranging from personalised recommendations and bookings to demand forecasting and virtual assistance. Looking at this spread of AI within the travel industry, this chapter attempts to answer three broad research questions on AI in the tourism sector: How has AI contributed to advancing the tourism industry's growth? What is the potential of AI in the tourism industry? Moreover, what are the possible challenges of AI within the tourism industry? The chapter has made use of 45 articles published post-2018, explicitly focussing on papers published post-2020, after systematically screening various databases such as Science Direct, PubMed, CABI Digital Library, Scopus, Web of Science, Semantic Scholar, ResearchGate, Google Scholar and DOAJ.

The first part of the review explores the presence of AI in the tourism sector. It categorises various studies under different themes in order to find out how artificial intelligence has helped the travel and tourism sector progress. The studies have been categorised into four themes: the application and benefits of AI in tourism; the implications and interlinkages with sustainability and environment; user acceptance and experience with AI in the tourism and hospitality sector; case studies and specific analysis. Each of these themes presents a review of literature in tabular form to present how AI has contributed towards the development of tourism. Almost all studies suggest that AI has contributed towards easier travel planning, automated personalised services, intelligent planning of destinations, personalised recommendations and quick decision-making, thus leading to customer satisfaction. Studies also suggest that companies and service providers have benefitted immensely from AI in terms of profitability, productivity and efficiency. They point out that AI has contributed to forecasting, value co-creation, preservation of heritage sites, revenue generation, sustainability, customer satisfaction and happiness, leading to higher revisit intention.

The next part of the chapter focuses on exploring the future potential of AI in the tourism sector. In this section, studies argue that in the future, AI has more potential to alter the face of the travel industry. In the future, more efficient use of Big Data can further enhance the role of AI in tourism and increase customer happiness. It can augment virtual reality, value co-creation processes and demand forecasting. Further integration of AI and extended reality can contribute towards higher tourist satisfaction and service provider profitability. Smart tourism also has special significance for rural tourism, which has further scope for growth.

Finally, the study reviews the literature to explore AI's challenges in the tourism industry. Studies under this section highlight increasing privacy concerns of sensitive customer information. These possible hazards can result from data-driven decisions by businesses, ethical and legal concerns as well as from social and economic risks associated with AI. Additionally, it has been stated that overuse of AI can replace human interaction, which is crucial to experiential tourism. Hence, these challenges need to be resolved and policymakers should formulate regulations and address these challenges so that the tourism industry can fully reap the benefits of AI.

Implications and Future Direction

Implications

With an overview of empirical data and case studies, this research offers insightful information about the state of AI applications in the tourism sector today. Industry professionals can leverage this knowledge to identify opportunities for implementing AI technologies in their businesses, thereby enhancing efficiency and customer experience. The chapter provides an overview of recent literature and gives insights into the applications, benefits, sustainability impacts, challenges as well as future potential. These can help policymakers develop targeted strategies to support responsible AI adoption while maximising its socio-economic benefits. Various stakeholders in the tourism ecosystem, including destination management organisations, tour operators and technology providers, can derive actionable insights from this research to enhance their strategies, offerings and collaborations. Furthermore, the tourist sector is experiencing a surge in need for proficient experts capable of creating, executing and overseeing artificial intelligence solutions. Policymakers should focus on initiatives to promote education and training programs to cultivate a workforce equipped with AI-related skills.

This chapter also has ramifications for how artificial Intelligence and extended reality technology will be integrated in the future. The integration of AI and XR could revolutionise how tourists experience destinations. AI algorithms can analyse user preferences, historical data and real-time information to personalise AR/VR content, providing tourists with immersive and interactive experiences tailored to their interests and needs. The convergence of AI and XR holds immense potential for transforming various aspects of the tourism industry, including destination marketing, visitor experiences, training and education and sustainability initiatives.

Future Directions

As AI adoption in the tourism industry grows, research focused on addressing ethical, social and environmental concerns is needed. Future research could look at ways to guarantee fairness, accountability and transparency in AI systems as well as the ethical ramifications of AI-driven decision-making in the travel industry.

Continued research is needed to understand tourists' attitudes, perceptions and acceptance of AI technologies in the tourism context. Future studies could investigate factors influencing user experience, trust, and adoption of AI-driven services and strategies to enhance user acceptance and satisfaction.

Additionally, in order to build immersive and engaging tourism experiences, researchers might investigate the integration of emerging technologies with AI. This could involve developing AI-powered virtual tour guides or AR applications that provide tourists with real-time information and navigation assistance. Further advancements in XR technology, coupled with AI capabilities, can lead to realistic virtual travel experiences. This could involve the development of hyper-realistic virtual environments, enhanced sensory feedback and interactive storytelling techniques to transport users to destinations around the world. Future research can leverage AI algorithms to create personalised and context-aware XR experiences for travellers.

Limitations of the Study

Amidst the continual evolution of AI and XR integration across various sectors, research examining the impact of this integration on the tourism industry remains notably scarce. While the potential implications of this integration for tourism are manifold, the current body of research in this domain still needs to be expanded. Consequently, this chapter offers only a limited exploration of AI-XR integration, reflecting the existing gaps in understanding within this field.

REFERENCES

Agarwal, M., & Agarwal, R. (2021). Artificial Intelligence in Travel and Tourism Industry: A Case Study of SpiceJet, India. *International Journal of Management.*

Belk, R. (2021). Ethical issues in service robotics and artificial intelligence. *Service Industries Journal*, 41(13–14), 860–876. 10.1080/02642069.2020.1727892

Bi, F., & Liu, H. (2022). Machine learning-based cloud IOT platform for intelligent tourism information services. *EURASIP Journal on Wireless Communications and Networking*, 2022(1), 59. 10.1186/s13638-022-02138-y

Bulchand-Gidumal, J., William Secin, E., O'Connor, P., & Buhalis, D. (n.d.). Artificial Intelligence's impact on hospitality and tourism marketing: Exploring key themes and addressing challenges. *Current Issues in Tourism*, 1–18. 10.1080/13683500.2023.2229480

Camacho-Ruiz, M., Carrasco, R. A., Fernández-Avilés, G., & LaTorre, A. (2023). Tourism destination events classifier based on artificial intelligence techniques. *Applied Soft Computing*, 148, 110914. 10.1016/j.asoc.2023.110914

Chaturvedi, R., Verma, S., Ali, F., & Kumar, S. (2023, August 09). Reshaping Tourist Experience with AI-Enabled Technologies: A Comprehensive Review and Future Research Agenda. *International Journal of Human-Computer Interaction*, 1–17. 10.1080/10447318.2023.2238353

Chen, Y., Li, H., & Xue, T. (2023, October 26). Female Gendering of Artificial Intelligence in Travel: A Social Interaction Perspective. *Journal of Quality Assurance in Hospitality & Tourism*, 1–16. 10.1080/1528008X.2023.2275263

Cheriyan, A., Kumar, R., Joseph, A., & Kappil, S. R. (2022). Consumer Acceptance towards AI-enabled Chatbots; Case of Travel and Tourism Industries. *Journal of Positive School Psychology*, 6(3).

Dang, T. D., & Nguyen, M. T. (2023). Systematic review and research agenda for the tourism and hospitality sector: Co-creation of customer value in the digital age. *Future Business Journal*, 9(1), 94. 10.1186/s43093-023-00274-5

Deepthi, B., & Bansal, V. (2023). Applications of Artificial Intelligence (AI) in the Tourism Industry: A Futuristic Perspective. In Tučková, Z., Dey, S. K., Thai, H. H., & Hoang, S. D. (Eds.), *Impact of Industry 4.0 on Sustainable Tourism* (pp. 31–43). Emerald Publishing Limited., 10.1108/978-1-80455-157-820231003

Diaz-Pacheco, A., Álvarez-Carmona, M. Á., Guerrero-Rodríguez, R., Chávez, L. A. C., Rodríguez-González, A. Y., Ramírez-Silva, J. P., & Aranda, R. (2022, December 13). Artificial intelligence methods to support the research of destination image in tourism. A systematic review. *Journal of Experimental & Theoretical Artificial Intelligence*, 1–31. 10.1080/0952813X.2022.2153276

Doborjeh, Z., Hemmington, N., Doborjeh, M., & Kasabov, N. (2022). Artificial Intelligence: A systematic review of methods and applications in hospitality and tourism. *International Journal of Contemporary Hospitality Management*, 34(3), 1154–1176. 10.1108/IJCHM-06-2021-0767

Doğan, S., & Niyet, İ. Z. (2024). Artificial Intelligence (AI) in Tourism. In Tanrisever, C., Pamukçu, H., & Sharma, A. (Eds.), *Future Tourism Trends* (Vol. 2, pp. 3–21). Emerald Publishing Limited. 10.1108/978-1-83753-970-320241001

Dogru, T., Line, N., Mody, M., Hanks, L., Abbott, J., Acikgoz, F., Assaf, A., Bakir, S., Berbekova, A., Bilgihan, A., Dalton, A., Erkmen, E., Geronasso, M., Gomez, D., Graves, S., Iskender, A., Ivanov, S., Kizildag, M., Lee, M., & Zhang, T. (2023). Generative Artificial Intelligence in the Hospitality and Tourism Industry: Developing a Framework for Future Research. *Journal of Hospitality & Tourism Research (Washington, D.C.)*, 10963480231188663, 10963480231188663. 10.1177/10963480231188663

Dr. Dávid, L. D., & Dadkhah, M. (2023). Artificial intelligence in the tourism sector: Its sustainability and innovation potential. *Equilibrium*, 18(3), 610–613. 10.24136/eq.2023.019

Filieri, R., D'Amico, E., Destefanis, A., Paolucci, E., & Raguseo, E. (2021a). Artificial Intelligence (AI) for tourism: A European-based study on successful AI tourism start-ups. *International Journal of Contemporary Hospitality Management*, 33(11), 4099–4125. 10.1108/IJCHM-02-2021-0220

Filieri, R., D'Amico, E., Destefanis, A., Paolucci, E., & Raguseo, E. (2021b). Artificial Intelligence (AI) for tourism: A European-based study on successful AI tourism start-ups. *International Journal of Contemporary Hospitality Management*, 33(11), 4099–4125. 10.1108/IJCHM-02-2021-0220

Flavian, C., Casalo, L., & Wang, D. (2021). Artificial intelligence in hospitality and tourism. *International Journal of Contemporary Hospitality Management*, 33(11).

Grundner, L., & Neuhofer, B. (2021). The bright and dark sides of artificial Intelligence: A future perspective on tourist destination experiences. *Journal of Destination Marketing & Management*, 19, 100511. 10.1016/j.jdmm.2020.100511

Hirzle, T., Müller, F., Draxler, F., Schmitz, M., Knierim, P., & Hornbæk, K. (2023). When XR and AI Meet—A Scoping Review on Extended Reality and Artificial Intelligence. *Proceedings of the 2023 CHI Conference on Human Factors in Computing Systems*. ACM. 10.1145/3544548.3581072

Ho, P.-T. (2022). Smart Tourism Recommendation Method in Southeast Asia under Big Data and Artificial Intelligence Algorithms. *Mobile Information Systems*, 2022, 1–11. 10.1155/2022/4047501

Jabeen, F., Al Zaidi, S., & Al Dhaheri, M. H. (2022). Automation and artificial intelligence in hospitality and tourism. *Tourism Review*, 77(4), 1043–1061. 10.1108/TR-09-2019-0360

Jaehnig, J. (2023, June 21). *The Intersections of Artificial Intelligence and Extended Reality*. ArPost. https://arpost.co/2023/06/21/intersections-artificial-intelligence-xr/

Kim, M. J., Hall, C. M., Chung, N., Kim, M., & Sohn, K. (2023). Why do tourists use public transport in Korea? The roles of artificial intelligence knowledge are environmental, social, governance, and sustainability. *Asia Pacific Journal of Tourism Research*, 28(5), 467–484. 10.1080/10941665.2023.2247099

Kirtil, I. G., & Aşkun, V. (2021). Artificial Intelligence in Tourism: A Review And Bibliometrics Research. [AHTR]. *Advances in Hospitality and Tourism Research*, 9(1), 205–233. 10.30519/ahtr.801690

Knani, M., Echchakoui, S., & Ladhari, R. (2022). Artificial intelligence in tourism and hospitality: Bibliometric analysis and research agenda. *International Journal of Hospitality Management*, 107. 10.1016/j.ijhm.2022.103317

Ku, E. C. S., & Chen, C.-D. (2024). Artificial intelligence innovation of tourism businesses: From satisfied tourists to continued service usage intention. *International Journal of Information Management*, 102757, 102757. 10.1016/j.ijinfomgt.2024.102757

Kumar, A., & Singh, M. (2020). Leveraging Artificial Intelligence for Sustainable Tourism Development: A Case Study of Kerala, India. *International Journal of Recent Technology and Engineering*.

Lv, H., Shi, S., & Gursoy, D. (2022). A look back and a leap forward: A review and synthesis of big data and artificial intelligence literature in hospitality and tourism. *Journal of Hospitality Marketing & Management*, 31(2), 145–175. 10.1080/19368623.2021.1937434

Majid, G. M., Tussyadiah, I., Kim, Y. R., & Pal, A. (2023). Intelligent automation for sustainable tourism: A systematic review. *Journal of Sustainable Tourism*, 31(11), 2421–2440. 10.1080/09669582.2023.2246681

Mir, U. B., Sharma, S., Kar, A. K., & Gupta, M. P. (2020). Critical success factors for integrating artificial intelligence and robotics. *Digital Policy. Regulation & Governance*, 22(4), 307–331. 10.1108/DPRG-03-2020-0032

Nannelli, M., Capone, F., & Lazzeretti, L. (2023). Artificial intelligence in hospitality and tourism. State-of-the-art and future research avenues. *European Planning Studies*, 31(7), 1325–1344. 10.1080/09654313.2023.2180321

Putera, N., Saripan, H., Bajury, M., & Ya'cob, S. (2022). Artificial Intelligence in the Tourism Industry: A Privacy Impasse. *ENVIRONMENT-BEHAVIOUR PROCEEDINGS JOURNAL*, 7(17), 433–440. 10.21834/ebpj.v7iSI7.3812

Qi, X., & Li, X. (2022). Extraction Method of Tourism Sustainable Development Path under the Background of Artificial Intelligence + Smart City Construction. *Journal of Interconnection Network*. 10.1142/S0219265921430271

Reiners, D., Davahli, M. R., Karwowski, W., & Cruz-Neira, C. (2021). The combination of Artificial Intelligence and Extended Reality: A Systematic Review. *Frontiers in Virtual Reality*, 2, 721933. 10.3389/frvir.2021.721933

Samala, N., Katkam, B. S., Bellamkonda, R. S., & Rodriguez, R. V. (2022). Impact of AI and robotics in the tourism sector: A critical insight. *Journal of Tourism Futures*, 8(1), 73–87. 10.1108/JTF-07-2019-0065

Samara, D., Magnisalis, I., & Peristeras, V. (2020). Artificial intelligence and big data in tourism: A systematic literature review. *Journal of Hospitality and Tourism Technology*, 11(2), 343–367. 10.1108/JHTT-12-2018-0118

Saydam, M. B., Arici, H. E., & Koseoglu, M. A. (2022). How does the tourism and hospitality industry use artificial intelligence? A review of empirical studies and future research agenda. *Journal of Hospitality Marketing & Management*, 31(8), 908–936. 10.1080/19368623.2022.2118923

Singh, M., & Saxena, P. (2020). The Role of Artificial Intelligence in Transforming Public Transportation in the Tourism Industry: A Case Study of Delhi Metro. *International Journal of Research in Management, Economics and Commerce*.

Stanney, K. M., Archer, J., Skinner, A., Horner, C., Hughes, C., Brawand, N. P., Martin, E., Sanchez, S., Moralez, L., Fidopiastis, C. M., & Perez, R. S. (2022). Performance gains from adaptive eXtended Reality training fueled by artificial intelligence. *The Journal of Defense Modeling and Simulation*, 19(2), 195–218. 10.1177/15485129211064809

Tuo, Y., Ning, L., & Zhu, A. (2021). How Artificial Intelligence Will Change the Future of Tourism Industry: The Practice in China. In Wörndl, W., Koo, C., & Stienmetz, J. L. (Eds.), *Information and Communication Technologies in Tourism 2021* (pp. 83–94). Springer International Publishing. 10.1007/978-3-030-65785-7_7

Vidushi, M. (2018). *Artificial intelligence policy in India: A framework for engaging the limits of data-driven decision-making. Philosophical Transactions of the Royal Society a Mathematical*. Physical and Engineering Sciences. 10.1098/rsta.2018.0087

Vorobeva, D., Costa Pinto, D., António, N., & Mattila, A. S. (n.d.). The augmentation effect of artificial Intelligence: Can AI framing shape customer acceptance of AI-based services? *Current Issues in Tourism*, 1–21. 10.1080/13683500.2023.2214353

Wang, N. (2022). Application of DASH client optimisation and artificial Intelligence in managing and operating big data tourism hotels. *Alexandria Engineering Journal*, 61(1), 81–90. 10.1016/j.aej.2021.04.080

Wang, T. (2023). Exploration of User Acceptance Behavior of Hotel Artificial Intelligence Technology Based on Experience Quality. *Journal of Artificial Intelligence Practice*, 6(5). 10.23977/jaip.2023.060505

Xie, D., & He, Y. (2022). Marketing Strategy of Rural Tourism Based on Big Data and Artificial Intelligence. *Mobile Information Systems*, 2022, 1–7. 10.1155/2022/9154351

KEY TERMS AND DEFINITIONS

Applications and Benefits of AI: By applications and Benefits of AI in tourism, this chapter refers to the thematically categorised body of literature that revolves around exploring various uses of AI within the tourism industry and the benefits of AI to the tourism industry. The types of papers included in this category are empirical, theoretical, critical analysis and review based.

Artificial Intelligence in the Tourism Sector: AI in tourism refers to the application of artificial intelligence (AI) technologies to enhance various aspects of the tourism industry. AI encompasses a range of techniques and algorithms that enable machines to mimic human cognitive functions, such as learning, problem-solving and decision-making. For instance, AI is used to analyse vast amounts of data, predict traveller behaviour, personalise experiences, automate processes and improve efficiency and effectiveness.

Implications and Interlinkages With Sustainability and Environment: By implications and interlinkages with sustainability and environment in this chapter, we refer to the body of literature that revolves around the sustainability aspect of AI in tourism. The papers under this section talk about sustainability not just from an environmental angle but also from sociocultural and economic point of view.

User Acceptance and Experience With AI: By user acceptance and experience, we refer to the body of literature that explores tourist experiences of using AI services such as chatbots and personalised recommendations while travelling. These studies also attempt to analyse the acceptance of such services. Mostly, papers under this section are empirical and review-based.

Chapter 8
Unveiling the Impact of Perceived Smart Tourism Technology on Tourist Satisfaction

Praveen Srivastava
https://orcid.org/0000-0001-5310-694X
Birla Institute of Technology, Mesra, India

Gautam Shandilya
https://orcid.org/0000-0002-9510-3787
Birla Institute of Technology, Mesra, India

ABSTRACT

This study explores the intricate relationship between perceived smart tourism technology (STT) experiences and tourist satisfaction (TS), recognizing the pivotal role played by innovative technologies in shaping contemporary travel experiences. The research employs a comprehensive approach to assess how tourists' perceptions of smart technology, including factors such as informativeness, interactivity, and personalization, influence overall satisfaction. By utilizing SmartPLS, the study aims to uncover nuanced insights into the intricate dynamics that govern the interplay between perceived smart tourism technology and the satisfaction levels of modern tourists. The research methodology involves the collection of perceptual data from a diverse sample of tourists throughout India, encompassing various smart technology applications within the tourism sector. Employing sophisticated statistical analyses, including regression modeling and structural equation modeling, the study seeks to quantify the impact of different aspects of smart technology experiences on overall satisfaction. This research contributes to the evolving landscape of smart

DOI: 10.4018/979-8-3693-2432-5.ch008

tourism technology by providing a robust and nuanced understanding of its role in shaping tourist satisfaction. The findings are expected to have practical implications for tourism industry stakeholders, informing strategic decisions regarding the integration and enhancement of smart technologies to optimize the overall tourist experience. Ultimately, this study advances the discourse on leveraging technology to meet the evolving expectations of modern tourists and underscores the importance of perceived smart tourism technology in driving satisfaction in the tourism sector.

INTRODUCTION

Smart tourism technology refers to integrating innovative digital solutions and information and communication technologies (ICT) to enhance the overall travel experience for tourists and streamline operations within the tourism industry. Travelers acquire information from various channels, obtaining insights not only directly from travel suppliers but also through a myriad of sources (Paliwal et al., 2022). As such, the significance of Information and Communication Technology (ICT) becomes paramount in facilitating this multifaceted information exchange within the travel industry (Neuhofer et al., 2013; Srivastava, 2023). The role of ICT goes beyond mere facilitation; it is imperative in shaping the landscape of how travelers access and assimilate information for their journeys (Herdin & Egger, 2018; Shandilya et al., 2024).

This encompasses various applications, including mobile apps, location-based services, augmented reality, data analytics, chatbots, and Internet of Things (IoT) devices (Srivastava et al., 2024). E-servicescape is a digital environment where customers receive and experience services. It includes website design, smartphone apps, social media, and online booking, which is contributing to technology adoption by the new age travellers (Srivastava et al., 2023)

Smart tourism technologies aim to provide personalized and context-aware information to travelers, offering them tailored recommendations, real-time updates, and interactive experiences. For instance, smart tourism platforms can provide navigation assistance, suggest points of interest based on user preferences, facilitate seamless booking and payment processes, and upgrade the destination image (Balakrishnan et al., 2023). These technologies benefit tourists by making their journeys more enjoyable and convenient and contribute to more efficient destination management for authorities and service providers.

One of the key aspects of smart tourism technology is its ability to create intelligent and interconnected destination ecosystems. The STT creates a link between the hospitality & tourism service providers, and the potential tourist which expand further to the co-creation of tourist experience (Chuang, 2023). Using data analytics and IoT devices, destinations can collect and analyze information about tourist behavior, traffic patterns, and resource utilization. This data-driven approach allows for better resource management, crowd control, and sustainable tourism practices. Additionally, smart tourism technologies play a role in promoting cultural heritage preservation by providing interactive and educational experiences for tourists. The integration of smart tourism technology fosters a more connected, efficient, and sustainable tourism industry, benefitting both travelers and destination stakeholders.

Interacting with smart technologies necessitates users to possess specific skills and competencies (Torabi, Pourtaheri, et al., 2023). Acquiring these capabilities is essential for users to effectively engage with such technologies and address their unique needs (Bassellier & Benbasat, 2004; Huang et al., 2017). Tourists equipped with ample knowledge and adept skills in utilizing Smart Tourism Technologies (STTs) can effectively harness the complete potential of these technological tools (Marcolin et al., 2000).

Although research has been conducted on the Smart Tourism Technology (STT), our understanding of how smart tourism experiences affect satisfaction is still limited. Specifically, there is a lack of comprehensive studies that explore the relationship between perceived smart tourism experiences and satisfaction among Indian tourists. To fill this gap, this paper aims to develop and analyze a comprehensive conceptual model that includes attributes of Smart Tourism Technology (STT) and travel satisfaction. The main objective of this research is to investigate tourists' perceptions of smart tourism and evaluate how these experiences impact overall satisfaction.

LITERATURE REVIEW

The rapid progress of technology has not only encouraged competitive and inventive global marketplaces but has also played a crucial role in earning significant returns on investment (Zheng et al., 2022). This revolutionary effect also extends to improving economic efficiency by opening marketplaces for goods and services in both developing and developed countries. A study in Iran suggested that COVID-19 pandemic assisted in enhancing the technological integration in Tourism related service. Hence, the STT has been recognized in playing an imperative role in alleviating the spread of virus, which also assisted in reducing the digital gap in rural tourist destinations (Torabi et al., 2023).

The internet has fundamentally transformed advertising and marketing techniques worldwide (Berthon et al., 2012). It allows for direct communication with visitors, bypassing the need for intermediaries. Further, the advancement in intelligent technology can additionally enhance local community development (Rueda-Esteban, 2019).

Diverse services and industries affiliated with tourism are intricately integrated with Information and Communication Technology (ICT) to bolster the tourism sector. The implementation of a smart environment within tourism sites has given rise to the phenomenon known as smart tourism (Um & Chung, 2021). As the count of tourists orchestrating and planning their own journeys rises, the dependence on smart tourism technologies correspondingly escalates (Correia & Kozak, 2016). These trends signify a discernible shift, reflecting that tourists are becoming more astute, well-informed, and attuned to the benefits of utilizing advanced technologies in their travel experiences (Um & Chung, 2021).

The paradigm shift in the tourism industry towards smart tourism technology represents a transformative journey from traditional travel approaches to an era of enhanced, tech-driven experiences (Ozdemir et al., 2023). Traditional tourism primarily focused on destination exploration, relying on conventional methods for trip planning and on-site navigation (Liu et al., 2022). However, the integration of smart tourism technology has revolutionized this landscape. With the infusion of Information and Communication Technology (ICT), tourists now have access to a myriad of innovative tools, ranging from mobile applications and augmented reality guides to real-time communication systems (Abdelfattah et al., 2023). This shift facilitates seamless trip planning and enhances on-site experiences by providing interactive and personalized solutions. From smart destination management to augmented reality-enhanced navigation, the tourism industry is evolving to meet the expectations of tech-savvy travellers, fostering a more connected, efficient, and enriching travel environment (Sung et al., 2021).

As destinations embrace smart destination management strategies, the tourism industry becomes more adept at anticipating and meeting the expectations of tech-savvy travellers (Femenia-Serra et al., 2019). The convergence of innovative technologies streamlines trip planning and fosters a deeper connection between visitors and the local culture and environment (Xu et al., 2024). In essence, Smart Tourism Technology is reshaping the tourism landscape, creating a more connected, efficient, and enriching travel environment that aligns with the evolving preferences of today's digital-savvy explorers (Rosário & Dias, 2024).

Several scholarly contributions have been made to delineate the attributes of perceived smart tourism technology (STT). However, a notable discord exists within the academic discourse regarding these attributes. Huang et al. (2017) have been at the forefront of this discussion, identifying four key characteristics of smart tourism technology experiences, including *informativeness, accessibility, interactivity, and personalization*. This framework has undergone comprehensive analysis in various previous studies across the globe (Azis et al., 2020; Goo et al., 2022; Y. Zheng & Wu, 2023). It is important to note that while Huang et al. (2017) highlighted security as a significant concern for Internet use, it was not mentioned as an attribute of STT. No

& Kim (2015) also identified security as a crucial attribute in their study on online tourism information. However, it is noteworthy to mention that their work predates the contributions of Huang et al. (2017), and their focus was primarily on the realm of online tourist information. A later study by Pillai et al., (2020) on the impact of smart tourism technologies on tourists' well-being in marine tourism emphasized the inclusion of security as a vital attribute of the STT experience.

Recent contributions by Le et al. (2020) further enrich the understanding of smart tourism technology attributes, focusing specifically on the construction of hotel websites. The study validated a scale for measuring hotel website service quality, identifying website design as a fundamental attribute. It underscores the crucial role of user interface (UI) design as an indispensable aspect of STTs, advocating for its inclusion as a major attribute.

Despite the valuable contributions made by researchers advocating for the inclusion of security and user interface design as essential components of the STT experience, this study specifically adheres to the four fundamental attributes identified by Huang et al., (2017). These attributes, namely *informativeness, accessibility, interactivity, and personalization*, have been widely acknowledged and extensively analyzed in previous studies. The decision to focus on these four attributes for the current investigation aims to maintain a cohesive and targeted approach, aligning with the foundational framework set by Huang et al., (2017) while acknowledging the ongoing academic discourse surrounding the broader spectrum of STT attributes.

Attributes of STT

The above literature shows that Smart Tourism Technology constitutes a multifaceted approach aimed at revolutionizing the traditional travel experience. This cutting-edge integration seamlessly blends technology with tourism, ushering in a new era of exploration. The primary objective is to elevate and optimize every aspect of the travel journey, ensuring that modern travellers benefit from an array of advanced features and conveniences. These attributes collectively work in harmony to cater to the diverse needs and expectations of today's tech-savvy globetrotters.

Informativeness

Informativeness explores into the overall impression users have regarding the depth, accuracy, and credibility of the information made available through technological platforms (Wang & Lin, 2012). It is a nuanced evaluation of how effectively STTs deliver real-time updates, insights, and details on local attractions, events, and services (Jeong & Shin, 2020). The quality of information plays a pivotal role in shaping the users' understanding of their travel destinations and informs their decision-making process (Ng et al., 2023). Essentially, the concept of informativeness within the context of STTs extends beyond mere data provision; it encapsulates the users' holistic perception of the reliability and richness of the information presented, influencing their overall engagement and satisfaction with the travel experience facilitated by these advanced technologies (Xiang et al., 2015).

Accessibility

This concept of accessibility explores the mechanisms through which an individual can connect with and utilize the various types of SSTs to enhance their overall travel experience (Azis et al., 2020). It presupposes a state where both travellers and technology possess the capacity to establish a seamless connection, allowing for the exchange of information and interaction with other entities in the tourism ecosystem (Domínguez Vila et al., 2019).

In essence, the term 'accessibility' goes beyond the mere availability of information and extends to the practicality and ease with which users can navigate and harness the features of SSTs. It implies a synergy between the technological infrastructure and the user, ensuring that the benefits of SSTs are within easy reach and utilization (No & Kim, 2015). This interconnectedness between travellers and technology highlights the pivotal role of accessibility in fostering a streamlined and user-friendly experience, where information becomes available and effortlessly accessible, enriching the journey and facilitating a more informed and convenient exploration of destinations (Lee et al., 2018).

Interactivity

Interactivity can be understood as the bidirectional and collaborative actions among various stakeholders within Smart Tourism Technology (STT) platforms (Jeong & Shin, 2020). In its role as an information disseminator, STT serves as a catalyst, fostering meaningful connections among multiple stakeholders in the expansive realm of the tourism industry (Ng et al., 2023). This includes, but is not limited to, travel vendors, aggregation providers, information brokers, and the travellers themselves.

The dynamism of interactivity in STT platforms creates a synergistic environment where stakeholders actively engage, exchange information, and contribute to a collective reservoir of insights (Song & Zinkhan, 2008). It serves as a virtual nexus, facilitating seamless collaboration and communication between various players in the tourism ecosystem. The significance of interactivity lies in its ability to connect stakeholders and its transformative impact on how information is shared, shaping a more engaged, informed, and interconnected tourism landscape (Yoo et al., 2017).

Personalization

A personalized approach to information dissemination is particularly significant in the context of the contemporary travel landscape, where individuals seek more than just generic details about destinations. With its emphasis on personalization, smart travel technology acknowledges that each traveller is unique, with distinct preferences and interests (No & Kim, 2015). By harnessing data analytics, artificial intelligence, and machine learning, these technologies can analyse user behaviour, past travel patterns, and stated preferences to curate a bespoke travel experience (Huang et al., 2017). Whether it's recommending niche attractions, suggesting culinary experiences based on dietary preferences, or tailoring activity suggestions according to individual interests, personalization transforms the travel journey into a highly curated and meaningful adventure (Um & Chung, 2021).

Furthermore, the evolving landscape of smart travel technology underscores the symbiotic relationship between personalization and user engagement. As travellers increasingly rely on technology for trip planning and navigation, the ability of smart travel platforms to provide personalized recommendations enhances user satisfaction and loyalty (Azis et al., 2020; Ng et al., 2023). The tailored content facilitates more informed decision-making and fosters a sense of connection and resonance between the traveller and the technology, establishing a positive feedback loop that continually refines and improves the personalization process. In essence, personalization in smart travel technology stands as a cornerstone in elevating the travel experience, aligning information delivery with the individuality of each traveller.

In our research endeavour, we aim to explore the intricate relationships among the four fundamental attributes of Smart Tourism Technology (STT) - Informativeness, Accessibility, Interactivity, and Personalization - in the context of the satisfaction levels of Indian travellers. By exploring this comprehensive analysis, our study seeks to unravel the nuanced dynamics between these key attributes and the overall contentment experienced by travellers engaging with smart tourism technologies. Hence, our hypothesis tests all the four attributes of STT. The framed hypothesis for the present study is as under:

H_1: Informativeness has positive effects on user satisfaction.

H_2: Accessibility has positive effects on user satisfaction.

H_3: Interactivities have positive effects on user satisfaction.

H_4: Personalization has positive effects on user satisfaction.

PROPOSED METHODOLOGY

The methodology employed in this study is rooted in quantitative research, leveraging responses collected through an online survey. To gather data, we utilized non-probability purposive sampling, ensuring that the participants selected were particularly relevant to the focus of the study. The primary objective was to investigate the impact of informativeness, accessibility, interactivity, and personalization on customer satisfaction within the context of smart tourism technology.

To meet these research objectives, authors designed a structured questionnaire, modeled after a validated instrument from previous studies of a similar nature. This approach ensured that our survey was grounded in established research while also being tailored to our specific study. The questionnaire was divided into sections corresponding to the key variables of informativeness, accessibility, interactivity, and personalization, with additional questions aimed at measuring overall customer satisfaction.

Before initiating the full-scale data collection, we conducted a pilot test with 25 participants. This initial test aimed to identify any issues related to language, sequencing, and overall comprehension of the survey questions. The feedback from this pilot test was invaluable; it highlighted ambiguities and suggested improvements for clarity and coherence. Based on the participants' feedback, we refined the wording of several questions to enhance understanding and relevance.

Following the initial revisions, we conducted a second pilot test with 30 participants. This second test aimed to ensure the reliability and effectiveness of the revised survey instrument. The feedback from this round confirmed the improvements made, and the revised questions were found to be clear and effective in capturing the necessary data.

To determine the required sample size for the study, we employed G*Power software. This statistical tool is widely used to calculate the required sample size to achieve a specific level of statistical power. In our case, the results indicated that a minimum of 176 participants was necessary to achieve a statistical power ($1-\beta$ error probability) of 0.95, with an α error probability of 0.05. This calculation ensured that our study would be adequately powered to detect significant effects, thus enhancing the reliability and validity of our findings.

Following the determination of the sample size, we created an online questionnaire and disseminated it to the target respondents. The participants in this study were travelers who had used smart tourism technology during their trips. We selected this population because they had firsthand experience with the variables under investigation – informativeness, accessibility, interactivity, and personalization in smart tourism.

The online survey was disseminated through various channels, including email invitations, social media platforms, and travel forums. These channels were chosen to ensure a broad and diverse reach, thereby maximizing the potential response rate.

To encourage participation, we briefly introduced the study, explaining its purpose and the importance of the participants' responses. We also assured respondents of the confidentiality and anonymity of their data, adhering to ethical research standards. This approach helped build trust and encouraged honest and thoughtful responses.

Upon the closure of the survey, the collected data were downloaded and prepared for analysis. The first step involved cleaning the data, which included checking for incomplete responses and outliers. Incomplete responses were excluded from the analysis to ensure the integrity of the data set.

The cleaned data were then analyzed using statistical software SmartPLS. Descriptive statistics were calculated to provide an overview of the sample demographics and key variables. Following this, inferential statistics were conducted to test the hypotheses related to the impact of informativeness, accessibility, interactivity, and personalization on customer satisfaction.

Measurement Development

Building upon the preceding discussions, the present study utilized the Partial Least Squares Structural Equation Modeling (PLS-SEM) method to meticulously examine the intricate interconnections among the four key attributes of Smart Tourism Technologies (STTs) and their impact on customer satisfaction. Employing PLS-SEM as the analytical framework allowed for a robust investigation into the complex relationships inherent in the study's objectives. The research model, visually represented in Figure 1, serves as a comprehensive roadmap delineating the connections between Informativeness, Accessibility, Interactivity, and Personalization, aiming to elucidate their collective influence on the overarching metric of customer satisfaction.

Figure 1. Conceptual model

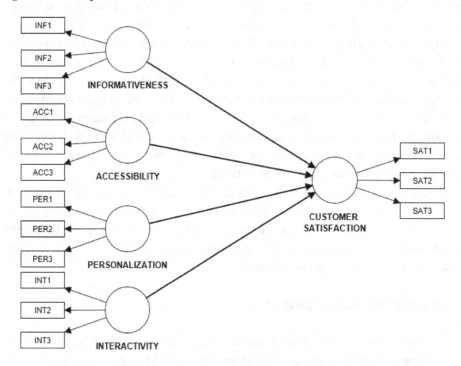

The assessment of all questionnaire items in this study was conducted utilizing a Likert scale ranging from 1 to 5, where respondents were required to express their agreement levels on a spectrum from 'strongly disagree' to 'strongly agree'. The survey instrument included three items each for the evaluation of Informativeness (INF1, INF2, and INF3), Accessibility (ACC1, ACC2, and ACC3), Interactivity (INT1, INT2, and INT3), and Personalization (PER1, PER2, and PER3). These specific items were adopted from the comprehensive work of Huang et al., (2017), providing a validated and reliable foundation for assessing the respective attributes within the context of Smart Tourism Technologies. Additionally, the three items gauging customer satisfaction (SAT1, SAT2, and SAT3) were integrated into the questionnaire based on the established framework presented by Chuah et al. (2017). By leveraging these existing measurement items, the study ensures a standardized and comparable assessment, aligning with established methodologies in the field and contributing to the robustness of the research outcomes.

This research is centred around the demographic of Indian travellers as its target population. As mentioned, employing a self-administered online questionnaire, the study incorporated a filter question to ascertain whether participants had utilized smart tourism technology for any of their trips. The survey spanned from October to

December 2023 and was disseminated widely across various social media platforms, including but not limited to LinkedIn, Twitter, and WhatsApp groups. A total of 312 responses were garnered during this period. However, after a meticulous screening process, it was determined that 286 responses met the criteria for inclusion in the subsequent analysis, ensuring the reliability and relevance of the data utilized in this study.

Data Analysis

The research employed the Partial Least Squares (PLS) method, leveraging the SmartPLS4 package, to comprehensively evaluate two crucial components: the quality of measurement, encapsulated within the measurement model, and the hypothesized relationships delineated within the structural model. This methodological approach allows for a robust and integrated analysis, addressing both the validity and reliability of the measurement tools and the theoretical constructs postulated in the research framework. By utilizing SmartPLS4, a state-of-the-art software package for structural equation modeling, the study ensures a sophisticated and efficient examination of the intricate interplay between latent variables, providing a more nuanced understanding of the complex relationships within the context of Smart Tourism Technologies and customer satisfaction.

Measurement Model

As delineated in Table 1, the outcomes illustrate that each item exhibits loadings surpassing the minimum threshold of 0.5, as Hair et al. (2014) recommended, and is exclusively affiliated with its respective construct. Consequently, we can deduce the absence of cross-loading within the model. To ascertain the presence of multicollinearity, a potential threat to the accuracy of findings, we scrutinized the Variance Inflation Factor (VIF). The VIF values were found to be below the recommended threshold of 5, as per Hair et al. (2014), and are presented in numerical detail in Table 2.

Table 1. Factor loading

	ACC	INF	INT	PER	SAT
ACC1	0.852				
ACC2	0.780				
ACC3	0.814				
INF1		0.758			

continued on following page

Table 1. Continued

	ACC	INF	INT	PER	SAT
INF2		0.844			
INF3		0.853			
INT1			0.894		
INT2			0.842		
INT3			0.675		
PER1				0.836	
PER2				0.861	
PER3				0.809	
SAT1					0.782
SAT2					0.795
SAT3					0.694

Source: Computed from survey data

Table 2. VIF

VIF				
ACC1	1.723		PER1	1.71
ACC2	1.353		PER2	1.766
ACC3	1.59		PER3	1.501
INF1	1.329		SAT1	1.3
INF2	1.704		SAT2	1.305
INF3	1.761		SAT3	1.164
INT1	1.607			
INT2	1.701			
INT3	1.329			

Source: Computed from survey data

Reliability, a pivotal aspect, was assessed through both Cronbach Alpha and Composite Reliability, with their corresponding values detailed in Table 3. The outcomes unveil a Cronbach Alpha spectrum of 0.628 to 0.784 and a Composite Reliability range of 0.802 to 0.874, aligning with established benchmarks and affirming the establishment of reliability (Hair et al., 2014).

Table 3. Reliability and validity

	Cronbach's alpha	Composite reliability (rho_a)	Composite reliability (rho_c)	Average variance extracted (AVE)
ACC	0.748	0.748	0.856	0.666
INF	0.754	0.758	0.86	0.672
INT	0.744	0.84	0.849	0.654
PER	0.784	0.786	0.874	0.698
SAT	0.628	0.635	0.802	0.575

Source: Computed from survey data

For convergent validity, a measure of the consistency among attempts to assess a shared idea, we examined the Average Variance Extracted (AVE). The AVE values for the constructs, presented in Table 3, exceed the suggested threshold of 0.50, as advocated by Fornell & Larcker (1981), confirming the validity of the constructs.

Discriminant validity, pertaining to the dissimilarity among measurements of different concepts, was established by ensuring that a specific construct's square root of the Average Variance Extracted (AVE) exceeds its correlation with all other constructs. The values detailed in Table 4 affirm the presence of discriminant validity in the current study as the diagonal value is more than the off-diagonal value.

Table 4. Discriminant validity

	ACC	INF	INT	PER	SAT
ACC	**0.816**				
INF	0.162	**0.82**			
INT	0.329	0.1	**0.809**		
PER	0.358	0.483	0.188	**0.836**	
SAT	0.481	0.499	0.302	0.537	**0.758**

Source: Computed from survey data

Structural Model

To evaluate the research hypotheses pertaining to the significance of the paths, we computed the standardized path coefficients (β) and significance values (p) using bootstrapping with 5000 sub-sample in smartPLS 4, the results is presented in Figure 2 and Table 5. The determination of these path coefficients is instrumental in estimating the strength and direction of the relationships posited in our research model.

Figure 2. Structural model

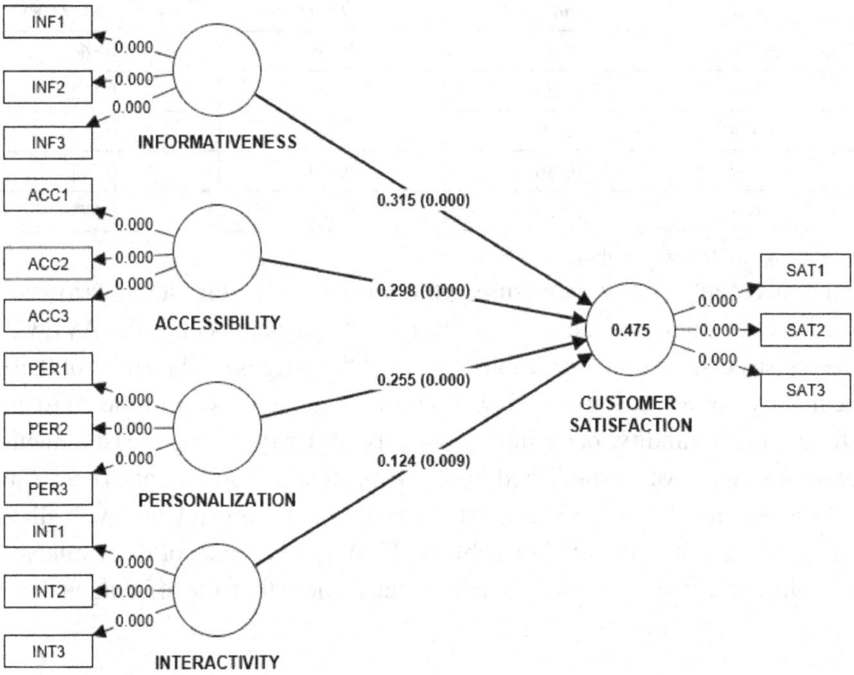

Table 5. Hypothesis testing

Hypothesis	Relation	Original sample (O)	Sample mean (M)	Standard deviation (STDEV)	T statistics (|O/STDEV|)	P values	Result
H1	INF -> SAT	0.315	0.315	0.045	6.938	0.00	Supported
H2	ACC -> SAT	0.298	0.298	0.055	5.407	0.00	Supported
H3	INT -> SAT	0.124	0.124	0.047	2.625	0.01	Supported
H4	PER -> SAT	0.255	0.258	0.057	4.448	0.00	Supported

Source: Computed from survey data

The results derived from the smartPLS analysis reveal that within the attributes of Smart Tourism technology, the Informativeness construct ($\beta = 0.315$, $p < 0.05$) wields the most substantial impact on Customer Satisfaction. Following closely are the influences of Accessibility ($\beta = 0.298$, $p < 0.05$), Personalization ($\beta = 0.255$, $p < 0.05$), and Interactivity ($\beta = 0.124$, $p < 0.05$). These findings underscore the differential strengths of the Smart Tourism Technology attributes in shaping customer satisfaction, with Informativeness emerging as the most influential factor, followed by Accessibility, Personalization, and Interactivity, each contributing significantly to users' overall satisfaction.

The coefficients of determination (R^2), illustrating the proportion of variability in the dependent variable predictable from the independent variable(s), are presented in Table 6. The R^2 values for satisfaction are noteworthy, standing at 0.475. This indicates that approximately 47.5% of the variability in satisfaction levels can be elucidated by the independent variables considered in our research model.

Table 6. R^2 value

	R-square	R-square adjusted
SAT	0.475	0.467

Source: Computed from survey data

RESULT AND DISCUSSION

The results derived from the smartPLS analysis provide a comprehensive understanding of the impact of various attributes of Smart Tourism technology on customer satisfaction. The analysis highlights the differential influences of Informativeness, Accessibility, Personalization, and Interactivity, each of which plays a crucial role in shaping customer satisfaction.

Among the attributes analyzed, the Informativeness construct demonstrates the most substantial impact on Customer Satisfaction, with a path coefficient (β) of 0.315 and a significance level ($p < 0.05$). This finding indicates that the ability of smart tourism technology to provide relevant, accurate, and comprehensive information significantly enhances customer satisfaction. Informativeness encompasses the quality and quantity of information provided to users, including details about destinations, travel itineraries, cultural insights, and real-time updates. The high coefficient suggests that travellers place great value on the accessibility and reliability of information when using smart tourism technologies. Effective informativeness enables travellers to make informed decisions, plan their activities more efficiently, and ultimately enjoy a more satisfying travel experience.

Accessibility emerges as the second most influential factor, with a path coefficient (β) of 0.298 and a significance level ($p < 0.05$). This attribute pertains to the ease with which users can access and utilize smart tourism technologies. High accessibility ensures that these technologies are user-friendly, available across multiple platforms, and cater to individuals with varying levels of technological proficiency. The significant impact of accessibility underscores the importance of designing smart tourism applications that are intuitive and easily navigable. When users find it easy to access and use these technologies, their overall satisfaction with the travel experience increases, as they encounter fewer barriers and can effortlessly leverage the technology's features.

Personalization ranks next, with a path coefficient (β) of 0.255 and a significance level ($p < 0.05$). This attribute refers to the ability of smart tourism technology to tailor experiences and recommendations based on individual preferences, behaviors, and past interactions. Personalization enhances the user experience by providing customized suggestions for activities, dining options, accommodation, and more. The notable impact of personalization suggests that travelers appreciate when technology caters to their unique needs and preferences, making their travel experience more relevant and enjoyable. Personalized recommendations help users discover new attractions, optimize their itineraries, and feel valued, thereby increasing their overall satisfaction.

Interactivity, with a path coefficient (β) of 0.124 and a significance level ($p < 0.05$), also plays a significant role in influencing customer satisfaction, albeit to a lesser extent compared to the other attributes. Interactivity refers to the degree to which users can engage with the technology, including features such as real-time communication, user-generated content, and interactive maps. While interactivity is important, its relatively lower coefficient suggests that, while users value engaging and interactive features, these aspects are somewhat less critical compared to the informativeness, accessibility, and personalization of the technology. Nonetheless, interactive features can enhance the user experience by providing a more engaging and dynamic interface, fostering a sense of connection, and allowing users to share their experiences with others.

The coefficients of determination (R^2) provide insight into the proportion of variability in customer satisfaction that can be explained by the independent variables in the research model. The R^2 value for customer satisfaction stands at 0.475, as illustrated in Table 6. This indicates that approximately 47.5% of the variability in satisfaction levels among users can be attributed to the attributes of Informativeness, Accessibility, Personalization, and Interactivity. An R^2 value of this magnitude suggests that the research model has substantial explanatory power, highlighting the significant role of these attributes in shaping customer satisfaction within the context of smart tourism technology.

The findings from this analysis have several important implications for developing and implementing smart tourism technologies. First and foremost, the pronounced impact of informativeness suggests that developers should prioritize providing accurate, comprehensive, and up-to-date information within their applications. Ensuring that users can easily access valuable information will likely lead to higher satisfaction levels.

Furthermore, enhancing accessibility should be a key focus. This involves creating user-friendly interfaces, ensuring compatibility across various devices, and designing for inclusivity. As accessibility significantly influences satisfaction, reducing any barriers to use will enhance the overall user experience.

Personalization also proves to be a critical factor. Developers should leverage data analytics and machine learning to offer personalized recommendations that align with individual user preferences. By doing so, they can create more engaging and customized experiences, thereby increasing user satisfaction.

While interactivity has a relatively smaller impact, it remains an important aspect. Incorporating features that allow for real-time interaction, feedback, and user-generated content can enhance the dynamism and engagement of the technology.

In summary, the smartPLS analysis reveals that Informativeness, Accessibility, Personalization, and Interactivity all significantly impact customer satisfaction in the context of smart tourism technology, with Informativeness being the most influential factor. The substantial R2 value underscores the explanatory power of these attributes in predicting satisfaction levels. These insights provide valuable guidance for developers and stakeholders in the smart tourism industry, highlighting areas to focus on to enhance the overall user experience and satisfaction. The outcomes illuminate the intricate dynamics within Smart Tourism Technology and its impact on customer satisfaction. Notably, the Informativeness construct stands out as the most influential factor, substantially affecting customer satisfaction. The robust relationship underscores the pivotal role of providing comprehensive and accurate information in shaping a positive user experience. The finding corroborates the previous finding of Ng et al. (2023). Accessibility follows closely, emphasizing the importance of seamless navigation and connectivity in enhancing overall satisfaction. Although slightly less pronounced, the contributions of Personalization and Interactivity remain significant, indicating that tailoring information and fostering interactive engagement play vital roles in shaping users' perceptions of Smart Tourism Technology. The outcome resonates with the findings of previous researchers who have delved into the intricacies of Smart Tourism Technology (STT) (Azis et al., 2020; Yoo et al., 2017; K. Zheng et al., 2022), reinforcing the consistency and robustness of the observed patterns.

Hence, the present findings align with the evolving landscape of the tourism industry, highlighting the increasing significance of technological attributes in shaping user satisfaction. The discussion underscores the need for tourism stakeholders to prioritize and invest in technologies that enhance informativeness, accessibility, personalization, and interactivity to create a more satisfying and engaging travel experience.

Novelty

This study stands out in its exploration of the nuanced impacts of various attributes of smart tourism technology on customer satisfaction, employing a rigorous quantitative approach. Unlike previous research that often focused on singular aspects or provided a broad overview, this study delves deeply into four specific constructs: Informativeness, Accessibility, Personalization, and Interactivity. By meticulously analyzing the relative influence of each attribute, the research provides a detailed and granular understanding of what drives customer satisfaction in the realm of smart tourism. This targeted approach offers fresh insights and underscores these attributes' differentiated roles, thereby filling a notable gap in the existing literature.

Moreover, the methodological rigor employed in this study adds to its novelty. Using smartPLS for structural equation modeling (SEM) ensures that the analysis precisely captures the complex relationships between the variables. The incorporation of pilot testing to refine the questionnaire further enhances the reliability and validity of the findings. Additionally, the application of G*Power software to determine an adequate sample size ensures that the study's conclusions are statistically robust. This meticulous attention to methodological detail not only strengthens the credibility of the results but also sets a high standard for future research in the field of smart tourism technology.

CONCLUSION

In conclusion, this study provides valuable insights into the relative strengths of Smart Tourism Technology attributes in influencing satisfaction among Indian travellers. The results affirm that Informativeness is paramount, emphasizing the need for accurate and relevant information delivery. The findings also stress the interconnected nature of Accessibility, Personalization, and Interactivity in contributing significantly to overall satisfaction. This research contributes to the burgeoning field of smart tourism by highlighting the specific attributes that warrant attention for the optimization of user satisfaction.

Importantly, the coefficients of determination (R^2) add substantial weight to our conclusions, indicating that nearly half of the variability in customer satisfaction levels can be elucidated by the considered independent variables within our research model. This emphasizes the robustness and efficacy of the selected Smart Tourism Technology attributes in capturing and explaining the nuances influencing customer satisfaction. Such a significant R^2 value underscores the practical implications for the tourism industry, highlighting the need to prioritize and enhance these attributes for optimizing overall customer satisfaction.

Limitation and Future Research

It is important to acknowledge the limitations of this study. The research primarily focuses on the Indian traveller's demographic, and the findings may not directly apply to other cultural contexts. Additionally, the reliance on self-reported data and the study's cross-sectional nature poses inherent limitations. Future research could address these constraints by incorporating diverse cultural perspectives, utilizing longitudinal designs, and employing a combination of qualitative and quantitative methods for a more comprehensive understanding of the interactions within Smart Tourism Technology and user satisfaction.

Additionally, longitudinal studies could offer a dynamic perspective on how these attributes influence customer satisfaction over time. Further investigations into the integration of emerging technologies, such as metaverse, could also enrich our understanding of their potential impact on Smart Tourism Technology attributes and user satisfaction. This research lays the foundation for future endeavours that can unravel the complexities of the evolving relationship between technology and travel satisfaction.

REFERENCES

Abdelfattah, F., Al-Alawi, A., Abdullahi, M. S., & Salah, M. (2023). Embracing the industrial revolution: The impact of technological advancements and government policies on tourism development in Oman. *Journal of Policy Research in Tourism, Leisure & Events*, 1–25. 10.1080/19407963.2023.2294789

Azis, N., Amin, M., Chan, S., & Aprilia, C. (2020). How smart tourism technologies affect tourist destination loyalty. *Journal of Hospitality and Tourism Technology*, 11(4), 603–625. 10.1108/JHTT-01-2020-0005

Balakrishnan, J., Dwivedi, Y. K., Malik, F. T., & Baabdullah, A. M. (2023). Role of smart tourism technology in heritage tourism development. *Journal of Sustainable Tourism*, 31(11), 2506–2525. 10.1080/09669582.2021.1995398

Bassellier, G., & Benbasat, I. (2004). Business competence of information technology professionals: Conceptual development and influence on IT-business partnerships. *Management Information Systems Quarterly*, 28(4), 673–694. 10.2307/25148659

Berthon, P. R., Pitt, L. F., Plangger, K., & Shapiro, D. (2012). Marketing meets Web 2.0, social media, and creative consumers: Implications for international marketing strategy. *Business Horizons*, 55(3), 261–271. 10.1016/j.bushor.2012.01.007

Chuah, S. H. W., Marimuthu, M., Kandampully, J., & Bilgihan, A. (2017). What drives Gen Y loyalty? Understanding the mediated moderating roles of switching costs and alternative attractiveness in the value-satisfaction-loyalty chain. *Journal of Retailing and Consumer Services, 36*(July 2016), 124–136. 10.1016/j.jretconser.2017.01.010

Chuang, C. M. (2023). The conceptualization of smart tourism service platforms on tourist value co-creation behaviours: An integrative perspective of smart tourism services. *Humanities & Social Sciences Communications*, 10(1), 1–16. 10.1057/s41599-023-01867-9

Correia, A., & Kozak, M. (2016). Tourists' shopping experiences at street markets: Cross-country research. *Tourism Management*, 56, 85–95. 10.1016/j.tourman.2016.03.026

Domínguez Vila, T., Alén González, E., & Darcy, S. (2019). Accessible tourism online resources: A Northern European perspective. *Scandinavian Journal of Hospitality and Tourism*, 19(2), 140–156. 10.1080/15022250.2018.1478325

Femenia-Serra, F., Neuhofer, B., & Ivars-Baidal, J. A. (2019). Towards a conceptualisation of smart tourists and their role within the smart destination scenario. *Service Industries Journal*, 39(2), 109–133. 10.1080/02642069.2018.1508458

Fornell, C., & Larcker, D. (1981). Evaluating Structural Equation Models with Unobservable Variables and Measurement Error. *JMR, Journal of Marketing Research*, 18(1), 39–50. 10.1177/002224378101800104

Goo, J., Huang, C. D., Yoo, C. W., & Koo, C. (2022). Smart Tourism Technologies' Ambidexterity: Balancing Tourist's Worries and Novelty Seeking for Travel Satisfaction. *Information Systems Frontiers*, 24(6), 2139–2158. 10.1007/s10796-021-10233-635103046

Hair, J. F., Sarstedt, M., Hopkins, L., & Kuppelwieser, V. G. (2014). Partial least squares structural equation modeling (PLS-SEM): An emerging tool in business research. *European Business Review*, 26(2), 106–121. 10.1108/EBR-10-2013-0128

Herdin, T., & Egger, R. (2018). Beyond the digital divide: Tourism, ICTs and culture - a highly promising alliance. *International Journal of Digital Culture and Electronic Tourism*, 2(4), 322. 10.1504/IJDCET.2018.092182

Huang, C. D., Goo, J., Nam, K., & Yoo, C. W. (2017). Smart tourism technologies in travel planning: The role of exploration and exploitation. *Information & Management*, 54(6), 757–770. 10.1016/j.im.2016.11.010

Jeong, M., & Shin, H. H. (2020). Tourists' Experiences with Smart Tourism Technology at Smart Destinations and Their Behavior Intentions. *Journal of Travel Research*, 59(8), 1464–1477. 10.1177/0047287519883034

Le, V. H., Nguyen, H. T. T., Nguyen, N., & Pervan, S. (2020). Development and validation of a scale measuring hotel website service quality (HWebSQ). *Tourism Management Perspectives*, 35, 100697. 10.1016/j.tmp.2020.100697

Lee, H., Lee, J., Chung, N., & Koo, C. (2018). Tourists' happiness: Are there smart tourism technology effects? *Asia Pacific Journal of Tourism Research*, 23(5), 486–501. 10.1080/10941665.2018.1468344

Liu, X., Wang, D., & Gretzel, U. (2022). On-site decision-making in smartphone-mediated contexts. *Tourism Management, 88*, 104424. 10.1016/j.tourman.2021.104424

Marcolin, B. L., Compeau, D. R., Munro, M. C., & Huff, S. L. (2000). Assessing User Competence: Conceptualization and Measurement. *Information Systems Research*, 11(1), 37–60. 10.1287/isre.11.1.37.11782

Neuhofer, B., Buhalis, D., & Ladkin, A. (2013). Experiences, Co-Creation and Technology: A conceptual approach to enhance toruism. *Tourism and Global Change: On the Edge of Something Big*, 546–555.

Ng, K. S. P., Wong, J. W. C., Xie, D., & Zhu, J. (2023). From the attributes of smart tourism technologies to loyalty and WOM via user satisfaction: The moderating role of switching costs. *Kybernetes*, 52(8), 2868–2885. 10.1108/K-09-2021-0840

No, E., & Kim, J. K. (2015). Comparing the attributes of online tourism information sources. *Computers in Human Behavior*, 50, 564–575. 10.1016/j.chb.2015.02.063

Ozdemir, O., Dogru, T., Kizildag, M., & Erkmen, E. (2023). A critical reflection on digitalization for the hospitality and tourism industry: Value implications for stakeholders. *International Journal of Contemporary Hospitality Management*, 35(9), 3305–3321. 10.1108/IJCHM-04-2022-0535

Paliwal, M., Chatradhi, N., Singh, A., & Dikkatwar, R. (2022). Smart tourism: Antecedents to Indian traveller's decision. *European Journal of Innovation Management*. 10.1108/EJIM-06-2022-0293

Pillai, R., Sivathanu, B., Zheng, Y., Wu, Y., Pai, C. K., Liu, Y., Kang, S., & Dai, A. (2020). An investigation of how perceived smart tourism technologies affect tourists' well-being in marine tourism. *Sustainability (Switzerland), 18*, 1–19. 10.3390/su12166592

Rosário, A. T., & Dias, J. C. (2024). Exploring the Landscape of Smart Tourism : A Systematic Bibliometric Review of the Literature of the Internet of Things. *Administrative Sciences*, 14(22), 1–26. 10.3390/admsci14020022

Rueda-Esteban, N. R. (2019). Technology as a tool to rebuild heritage sites: The second life of the Abbey of Cluny. *Journal of Heritage Tourism*, 14(2), 101–116. 10.1080/1743873X.2018.1468762

Shandilya, G., Srivastava, P., & Jana, A. (2024). Industry Experts and Business Consultants ' Takes on India ' s Readiness for Metaverse: A Review of the Retail Industry. In Singla, B., Shalender, K., & Singh, N. (Eds.), *Creator's Economy in Metaverse Platforms: Empowering Stakeholders Through Omnichannel Approach* (pp. 132–147). IGI Global. 10.4018/979-8-3693-3358-7.ch008

Song, J. H., & Zinkhan, G. M. (2008). Determinants of perceived Web site interactivity. *Journal of Marketing*, 72(2), 99–113. 10.1509/jmkg.72.2.99

Srivastava, P. (2023). Tech Driven Dining : How ICT Innovation Can help Achieve Sustainable Development Goals. In Nadda, P. T. V., Tyagi, P. K., & Vieira, R. M. (Eds.), *Sustainable Development Goal Advancement Through Digital Innovation in the Service Sector* (pp. 57–63). IGI Global. 10.4018/979-8-3693-0650-5.ch005

Srivastava, Praveen, Mishra, N., Srivastava, S., & Shivani, S. (2024). Banking with Chatbots: The Role of Demographic and Personality Traits. *FIIB Business Review*. 10.1177/23197145241227757

Srivastava, P., Srivastava, S., & Mishra, N. (2023). Impact of e-servicescape on hotel booking intention: Examining the moderating role of COVID-19. *Consumer Behavior in Tourism and Hospitality*, 18(3), 422–437. 10.1108/CBTH-03-2022-0076

Sung, E., Bae, S., Han, D.-I. D., & Kwon, O. (2021). Consumer engagement via interactive artificial intelligence and mixed reality. *International Journal of Information Management*, 60(June), 102382. 10.1016/j.ijinfomgt.2021.102382

Torabi, Z. A., Pourtaheri, M., Hall, C. M., Sharifi, A., & Javidi, F. (2023). Smart Tourism Technologies, Revisit Intention, and Word-of-Mouth in Emerging and Smart Rural Destinations. *Sustainability (Basel)*, 15(14), 1–21. 10.3390/su151410911

Torabi, Z. A., Rezvani, M. R., Hall, C. M., & Allam, Z. (2023). On the post-pandemic travel boom: How capacity building and smart tourism technologies in rural areas can help - evidence from Iran. *Technological Forecasting and Social Change*, 193(May), 122633. 10.1016/j.techfore.2023.12263337223653

Um, T., & Chung, N. (2021). Does smart tourism technology matter? Lessons from three smart tourism cities in South Korea. *Asia Pacific Journal of Tourism Research*, 26(4), 396–414. 10.1080/10941665.2019.1595691

Wang, K., & Lin, C. L. (2012). The adoption of mobile value-added services: Investigating the influence of IS quality and perceived playfulness. *Managing Service Quality*, 22(2), 184–208. 10.1108/09604521211219007

Xiang, Z., Magnini, V. P., & Fesenmaier, D. R. (2015). Information technology and consumer behavior in travel and tourism: Insights from travel planning using the internet. *Journal of Retailing and Consumer Services, 22*(2014), 244–249. 10.1016/j.jretconser.2014.08.005

Xu, J., Shi, P. H., & Chen, X. (2024). Exploring digital innovation in smart tourism destinations: Insights from 31 premier tourist cities in digital China. *Tourism Review*, (December). 10.1108/TR-07-2023-0468

Yoo, C. W., Goo, J., Huang, C. D., Nam, K., & Woo, M. (2017). Improving travel decision support satisfaction with smart tourism technologies: A framework of tourist elaboration likelihood and self-efficacy. *Technological Forecasting and Social Change*, 123, 330–341. 10.1016/j.techfore.2016.10.071

Zheng, K., Kumar, J., Kunasekaran, P., & Valeri, M. (2022). Role of smart technology use behaviour in enhancing tourist revisit intention: The theory of planned behaviour perspective. *European Journal of Innovation Management.* 10.1108/EJIM-03-2022-0122

Zheng, Y., & Wu, Y. (2023). An investigation of how perceived smart tourism technologies affect tourists' well-being in marine tourism. *PLoS ONE, 18*, 1–19. 10.1371/journal.pone.0290539

Chapter 9
AI–Powered HR Technology Implementation for Business Growth in Industrial 5.0

Thangaraja T.

Department of Management, Aarupadai Veedu Institute of Technology, Vinayaka Mission 's Research Foundation (Deemed), India

Maheshkumar Maharudrappa

Department of Management, Guru Nanak Dev Engineering College, Bidar, India

M. Bakkiyaraj

ⓘ https://orcid.org/0000-0001-7917 -780X

Department of Mechanical Engineering, Rajalakshmi Institute of Technology, Chennai, India

Lalit Johari

Department of Computer Applications, IFTM University, Moradabad, India

Uma Maheswari E.

Department of Mathematics, R.M.K. Engineering College, Kavaraipettai, India

S. Muthuvel

Department of Mechanical Engineering, Kalasalingam Academy of Research and Education, India

ABSTRACT

Industrial 5.0 is a transformation where advanced technologies merge with traditional manufacturing processes, transforming the role of human resources (HR) in driving organizational growth. AI-powered HR technology is integrating automation, IoT,

DOI: 10.4018/979-8-3693-2432-5.ch009

and AI into traditional industrial frameworks, improving efficiency, productivity, and agility. The benefits like optimized talent acquisition and personalized employee experiences are served by HR solutions. HR functions, such as streamlining recruitment processes, providing insights into workforce dynamics, and fostering a culture of continuous learning, are revolutionized by AI. Talent management and succession planning, while personalized training modules enhance employee skills and innovation, have been performed by AI-powered analytics. AI is also used to improve strategic capacities by facilitating data-driven decision-making, which gives HR directors the ability to foresee skill shortages, reduce risks, and proactively promote organizational growth.

INTRODUCTION

The industry is undergoing a radical change with the introduction of Industrial 5.0, which blends cutting edge technology with conventional production methods. As the digital revolution continues to change how businesses operate, HR is becoming increasingly important in ensuring the success of organizations in this new era. Thanks to AI, robots, IoT, and big data analytics, this age makes automation, connection, and data-driven decision-making possible (Khan et al., 2023). As the focus shifts to productivity, efficiency, and innovation, HR must make the most of technology to support organizational expansion while maintaining the importance of the human element in this new age.

HR is essential to Industrial 5.0 because it helps organizations match worker skills with goals and cultivate a workforce that is knowledgeable and flexible. HR professionals must handle talent acquisition, development, and retention strategies in light of the fast advancement of technology. They must also cultivate a culture of continuous learning and draw in top talent (Kotler et al., 2021). The difficulty of integrating AI and automation into Industrial 5.0 HR processes calls for a re-assessment of the competencies of HR practitioners. When it comes to strategic activities like talent development, employee engagement, and workforce planning, HR professionals need to embrace innovation and leverage AI-powered technologies (Aljapurkar & Ingawale, 2024).

The relevance of ethical issues in HR procedures is emphasized by Industrial 5.0, especially with relation to algorithmic bias and data privacy. With the growing use of AI algorithms in HR procedures, it is imperative to guarantee decision-making that is transparent, equitable, and accountable. In order to foster trust and reduce the risks involved with using AI, HR professionals need to address these ethical issues, which bring both possibilities and problems (Chander et al., 2022). Industrial 5.0 is a paradigm shift that changes operations, competition, and innovation by incorporating cutting edge technology into conventional production processes. In order to improve operational efficiency, maximize resource utilization, and spur innovation, organizations must implement digital transformation efforts that make use of technology such as artificial intelligence, robots, the Internet of Things, and big data analytics. Organizations must comprehend these ramifications in order to manage the complexity and take advantage of new possibilities (Boopathi, 2024; Gift et al., 2024; Pasumarthy et al., 2024).

In the Industrial 5.0 era, agility and adaptability are crucial for business survival due to rapid technological advancements and evolving customer demands. Businesses must prioritize talent acquisition and development strategies to cultivate a skilled workforce capable of leveraging technology for organizational growth, upskilling, and fostering a culture of continuous learning and innovation (Taj & Zaman, 2022).

Industrial 5.0 environments are characterized by the proliferation of connected devices and sensors, Big data analytics and predictive algorithms help businesses make informed decisions and improve performance. They identify trends, mitigate risks, and capitalize on opportunities in real-time. Emphasizing customer-centricity, AI-powered tools are used for segmentation, targeting, and engagement across the organization (Maddikunta et al., 2022).

Industrial 5.0 offers businesses opportunities for innovation, growth, and competitiveness, but also presents challenges in technological complexity, talent management, and ethical considerations. To thrive, businesses must embrace digital transformation, foster agility, and prioritize ethical leadership. Establishing robust governance frameworks, adhering to industry standards, and prioritizing ethical conduct are crucial (Sulistyaningsih, 2023).

THE ROLE OF HUMAN RESOURCES IN INDUSTRIAL 5.0

Evolution of HR in the Digital Era

In the digital era, HR has evolved from an administrative function to a strategic business partner, focusing on strategic talent acquisition, development, and retention. Digital technologies have streamlined HR processes, allowing HR professionals to concentrate on value-added activities like talent acquisition and performance management, thereby driving organizational success amidst rapid technological advancements (Dahlbom et al., 2020). The digitalization of HR has enabled data-driven decision-making, enabling organizations to identify skill gaps and address talent management challenges. This aligns workforce capabilities with business objectives, optimizes resource allocation, and drives organizational performance. Industrial 5.0 uses AI, machine learning, and robotics to improve HR processes, provide personalized experiences, streamline candidate selection, enhance employee engagement, and forecast future workforce needs (Gift et al., 2024; Puranik et al., 2024).

Importance of HR in Driving Business Growth

In the competitive Industrial 5.0 environment, HR plays a vital role in driving business growth and ensuring organizational resilience, influenced by various important factors (Mazurchenko et al., 2019).

- **Talent Acquisition and Development:** In Industrial 5.0, HR plays a crucial role in attracting and retaining top talent, identifying individuals with the necessary skills for a rapidly changing environment. They also develop talent through training, upskilling, and succession planning, ensuring the workforce remains agile and future-ready.
- **Employee Engagement and Productivity:** Investing in employee engagement, through programs like recognition, wellness, and career development, can significantly boost organizational performance and innovation. This, in turn, leads to higher productivity, reduced turnover rates, and increased profitability.
- **Change Management and Organizational Agility:** Industrial 5.0 is characterized by constant technological advancements and market disruptions, necessitating agility and adaptability in organizations. HR plays a crucial role in facilitating change management, equipping employees with necessary skills and mindsets, and fostering a culture of continuous learning, enabling organizations to respond effectively to market conditions and seize growth opportunities.

HR plays a vital role in Industrial 5.0 by facilitating organizational success through talent acquisition, development, and engagement, utilizing digital technologies and strategic mindset for sustained growth and competitiveness.

AI-POWERED HR TECHNOLOGY

AI is revolutionizing human resources by automating repetitive tasks, analyzing vast data, and providing valuable insights for decision-making. It uses advanced algorithms and machine learning techniques to streamline processes, improve efficiency, and provide personalized experiences, crucial for Industrial 5.0 business success (Borthakur & Das, n.d.).

Figure 1. AI-Powered HR technology

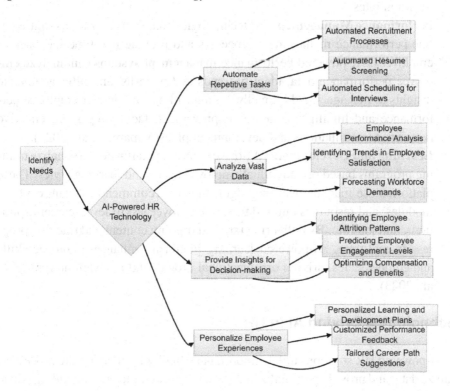

Figure 1 depicts AI-Powered HR Technology as a central hub, automating processes like recruitment, resume screening, and interview scheduling. Data analysis provides insights into employee performance and satisfaction, while personalization enhances employee experiences through tailored learning, feedback, and career development plans.

- **Recruitment and Talent Acquisition:** AI-powered recruitment tools leverage natural language processing (NLP) and machine learning algorithms to analyze resumes, screen candidates, and identify top talent efficiently. These tools can assess candidate qualifications, predict job fit, and even conduct automated interviews, enabling HR professionals to make data-driven hiring decisions and reduce time-to-fill vacancies.
- **Employee Engagement and Retention:** AI-driven chatbots and virtual assistants enhance employee engagement by providing personalized support and assistance. These virtual agents can answer common HR-related queries, facilitate onboarding processes, and provide timely feedback and recognition to employees. By automating routine tasks and offering round-the-clock

support, AI-powered chatbots contribute to higher employee satisfaction and retention rates.

- **Performance Management:** AI technologies enable organizations to streamline performance management processes and provide real-time feedback to employees. AI-powered performance management systems can analyze employee performance data, identify trends and patterns, and offer actionable insights to managers. Additionally, AI algorithms can predict employee performance and highlight areas for improvement, facilitating more effective performance evaluations and development plans(Yupapin et al., 2023).
- **Learning and Development:** AI-driven learning platforms personalize training programs based on individual employee needs and learning styles. These platforms use machine learning algorithms to recommend relevant courses, modules, and resources tailored to each employee's skill level, career aspirations, and job role. By delivering targeted training content and tracking progress in real-time, AI-powered learning platforms enhance employee skills and competencies, driving organizational growth and innovation(Agrawal et al., 2023).

Technologies Driving AI in HR

AI-powered HR solutions utilize important technologies to automate processes, analyze data, and provide personalized experiences for employees, including (Zizic et al., 2022):

- **Machine Learning:** Machine learning algorithms enable HR systems to analyze large datasets, identify patterns, and make predictions without explicit programming. These algorithms can learn from past data to improve accuracy and effectiveness over time, making them invaluable for tasks such as candidate screening, performance prediction, and personalized recommendations.
- **Natural Language Processing (NLP):** NLP allows HR systems to understand and interpret human language, enabling capabilities such as resume parsing, sentiment analysis, and chatbot interactions. NLP algorithms can extract meaningful information from unstructured text data, enabling HR professionals to gain insights from sources such as resumes, employee surveys, and social media posts(Prabhuswamy et al., 2024; D. M. Sharma et al., 2024; Venkatasubramanian et al., 2024).
- **Predictive Analytics:** Predictive analytics uses historical data and statistical algorithms to forecast future trends and outcomes. In HR, predictive analytics can be used to predict employee turnover, identify flight risk employees, and forecast workforce demand. By leveraging predictive analytics, organizations

can proactively address talent management challenges, minimize risks, and capitalize on opportunities for growth.

- **Robotic Process Automation (RPA):** RPA automates repetitive, rules-based tasks by mimicking human interactions with software systems. In HR, RPA can automate routine administrative tasks such as data entry, payroll processing, and benefits administration, freeing up HR professionals to focus on strategic initiatives. By eliminating manual errors and reducing processing time, RPA improves efficiency and accuracy in HR operations(Maheswari et al., 2023; Mohanty et al., 2023; Srinivas et al., 2023).

- **Computer Vision:** Computer vision technologies enable HR systems to analyze and interpret visual information, such as images and videos. In recruitment, computer vision algorithms can analyze candidate facial expressions, body language, and speech patterns during video interviews to assess soft skills and personality traits. Additionally, computer vision can be used for biometric authentication and monitoring employee attendance and behavior in the workplace.

TRANSFORMING HR PRACTICES WITH AI

Recruitment and Talent Acquisition

AI is revolutionizing recruitment and talent acquisition by enhancing efficiency and effectiveness in identifying, attracting, and hiring top talent in various HR aspects (Arora et al., 2021).

- **Automated Candidate Screening:** AI-powered recruitment tools use machine learning algorithms to analyze resumes, cover letters, and online profiles, allowing recruiters to quickly identify qualified candidates based on predefined criteria. This automated screening process saves time and reduces bias, ensuring a more diverse and inclusive candidate pool.

- **Predictive Analytics for Candidate Fit:** AI algorithms can analyze historical hiring data to predict candidate success based on factors such as skills, experience, and cultural fit. By leveraging predictive analytics, organizations can make more informed hiring decisions, reducing turnover and improving overall employee performance.

- **Candidate Engagement with Chatbots:** AI-powered chatbots can engage with candidates throughout the recruitment process, answering questions, providing updates, and scheduling interviews. These virtual assistants enhance the candidate experience by providing timely and personalized communication, increasing engagement and reducing drop-off rates.

- **Video Interview Analysis:** AI-driven video interview platforms use natural language processing (NLP) and computer vision algorithms to analyze candidate responses, facial expressions, and body language. These insights help recruiters assess candidate soft skills, personality traits, and cultural fit more accurately, leading to better hiring decisions(Ali et al., 2024; Boopathi, 2023; Venkateswaran, Vidhya, Naik, et al., 2023).

Employee Engagement and Retention

AI technologies significantly improve employee engagement and retention by personalizing experiences, providing timely feedback, and identifying potential retention risks, transforming the way businesses operate (Pandey, 2020).

- **Personalized Learning and Development:** AI-powered learning platforms deliver personalized training content based on individual employee needs, preferences, and learning styles. By recommending relevant courses, modules, and resources, these platforms enable employees to acquire new skills and knowledge tailored to their specific roles and career aspirations.
- **Feedback and Recognition:** AI-driven feedback and recognition tools analyze employee performance data in real-time, providing timely feedback and recognition to employees. These systems can highlight achievements, identify areas for improvement, and offer personalized development recommendations, fostering a culture of continuous learning and growth.
- **Retention Risk Prediction:** AI algorithms can analyze employee data, including performance metrics, engagement surveys, and demographic information, to identify potential retention risks. By predicting which employees are most likely to leave the organization, HR can proactively implement targeted retention strategies such as personalized career development plans, mentorship programs, and incentives(Sampath et al., 2022).
- **Employee Wellbeing Support:** AI-powered chatbots and virtual assistants can provide employees with support and resources to address wellbeing issues such as stress, burnout, and mental health concerns. These virtual assistants offer confidential guidance, self-help tools, and referrals to relevant support services, promoting employee wellbeing and reducing absenteeism and turnover.

AI is revolutionizing HR practices by automating processes, improving candidate engagement, and enhancing decision-making. It also enhances employee engagement and retention by personalizing learning, providing feedback, predicting retention risks, and supporting employee wellbeing. AI-powered solutions streamline processes, personalize experiences, and drive continuous improvement in employee performance and skill development.

Performance Management

AI-powered performance management systems are revolutionizing the way organizations evaluate, measure, and enhance employee performance, transforming performance management in various ways (Mazurchenko et al., 2019).

- **Real-Time Feedback:** AI enables organizations to provide continuous, real-time feedback to employees. Machine learning algorithms analyze various data sources, such as project metrics, customer feedback, and peer reviews, to generate actionable insights and recommendations for improvement. This real-time feedback loop promotes agility and responsiveness, allowing employees to adjust their performance promptly.
- **Predictive Analytics:** AI-driven predictive analytics forecast future performance trends based on historical data and behavioral patterns. These analytics help identify high-performing employees, predict potential performance issues, and prescribe targeted interventions to optimize performance. By leveraging predictive analytics, organizations can proactively address performance gaps, mitigate risks, and maximize employee productivity(Kumar et al., 2023; Ramudu et al., 2023).
- **Objective Performance Evaluation:** AI minimizes bias and subjectivity in performance evaluations by applying standardized criteria and objective metrics. Natural language processing (NLP) algorithms analyze performance reviews, assess employee competencies, and provide unbiased assessments of strengths and areas for improvement. This ensures fairness and equity in performance evaluations, fostering a culture of meritocracy and accountability.
- **Personalized Development Plans:** AI-powered performance management systems generate personalized development plans for employees based on their individual strengths, weaknesses, and career aspirations. Machine learning algorithms analyze employee performance data, identify skill gaps, and recommend targeted learning opportunities, such as online courses, workshops, and mentorship programs. This personalized approach to development empowers employees to take ownership of their growth and career pro-

gression(Veeranjaneyulu, Boopathi, Kumari, et al., 2023; Veeranjaneyulu, Boopathi, Narasimharao, et al., 2023).

Learning and Development

AI-driven learning and development (L&D) initiatives are revolutionizing traditional training methods by making learning more accessible, engaging, and effective (Khan et al., 2023).

- **Personalized Learning Experiences:** AI tailors learning experiences to the individual needs and preferences of employees. Adaptive learning algorithms analyze employee skills, learning styles, and performance data to recommend relevant training content and delivery methods. This personalized approach ensures that employees receive training that is aligned with their learning objectives and maximizes knowledge retention and skill acquisition.
- **Microlearning and Just-In-Time Training:** AI enables the delivery of bite-sized, targeted learning modules to employees at the point of need. Microlearning platforms leverage machine learning algorithms to curate and recommend short, interactive learning activities, such as videos, quizzes, and simulations, that address specific skill gaps or performance challenges. This just-in-time training approach enhances employee engagement and effectiveness by providing relevant and timely learning opportunities.
- **Content Curation and Creation:** AI automates the process of content curation and creation, enabling organizations to develop high-quality learning materials quickly and cost-effectively. Natural language generation (NLG) algorithms generate personalized learning content, such as training manuals, job aids, and knowledge articles, based on predefined templates and data inputs. Additionally, AI-powered content recommendation engines suggest relevant learning resources from internal and external sources, enriching the learning experience and promoting continuous skill development.
- **Learning Analytics and Insights:** AI-driven learning analytics provide organizations with valuable insights into the effectiveness of their L&D initiatives. Machine learning algorithms analyze learner engagement, completion rates, and performance outcomes to identify trends, patterns, and areas for improvement. These insights enable organizations to optimize their L&D strategies, allocate resources efficiently, and measure the impact of training investments on employee performance and business outcomes.

AI is revolutionizing HR by offering personalized, data-driven experiences, enhancing employee performance, engagement, and growth, and fostering a culture of learning and innovation, enabling continuous improvement and business success in the competitive Industrial 5.0 landscape.

IMPLEMENTING AI IN HR: STRATEGIES AND BEST PRACTICES

The article explores the potential benefits of AI in HR, highlighting its transformative potential, but also outlines challenges to overcome, providing strategies for implementing AI, focusing on data privacy and security (Khan et al., 2023).

Figure 2. Implementing AI in HR: Advantages and challenges of AI in HR

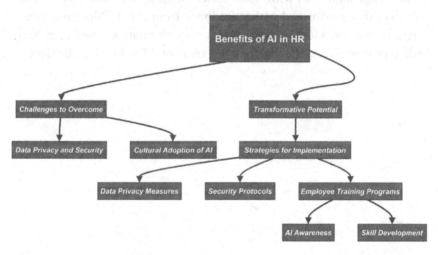

Figure 2 highlights the advantages and challenges of AI in HR, emphasizing the need to address data privacy and security issues, and promote AI adoption through employee training programs.

Overcoming Implementation Challenges

Organizations can tackle challenges like resistance to change, lack of technical expertise, and integration complexities by adopting strategies to implement AI in HR (Taj & Zaman, 2022).

- **Executive Support:** Secure buy-in and support from senior leadership to champion the implementation of AI in HR. Executive sponsorship can help overcome resistance to change and allocate resources effectively to support implementation efforts.
- **Change Management:** Implement robust change management processes to address employee concerns, manage expectations, and foster a culture of openness and collaboration. Communicate the benefits of AI adoption, provide training and support to employees, and involve them in the decision-making process to ensure successful implementation.
- **Collaboration with IT:** Collaborate closely with the IT department to ensure seamless integration of AI-powered HR solutions with existing systems and processes. IT expertise is essential for addressing technical challenges, ensuring data integrity, and maintaining system security throughout the implementation process(Chandrika et al., 2023; Domakonda et al., 2022).
- **Pilot Programs:** Start with small-scale pilot programs to test AI solutions in real-world scenarios and gather feedback from users. Pilot programs allow organizations to identify and address implementation challenges early on, refine processes, and demonstrate the value of AI to key stakeholders.

Figure 3. The process begins by identifying challenges for AI in HR

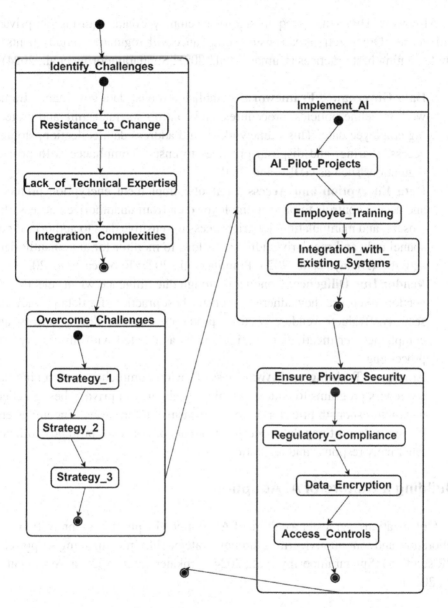

The process addresses challenges like resistance to change, technical expertise, and integration complexities, implements strategies like pilot projects, employee training, and AI integration, while ensuring data privacy and security (Figure 3).

Ensuring Data Privacy and Security

AI-powered HR solutions require significant employee data, requiring data privacy and security. Organizations can ensure compliance with regulatory requirements by implementing best practices (Kumara et al., 2023; Sundaramoorthy et al., 2024).

- **Data Governance Framework:** Establish a robust data governance framework to define policies, procedures, and controls for managing and protecting employee data. This framework should address data collection, storage, access, sharing, and disposal practices to ensure compliance with privacy regulations such as GDPR and CCPA.
- **Data Encryption and Access Controls:** Implement encryption protocols and access controls to protect employee data from unauthorized access, disclosure, and manipulation. Restrict access to sensitive data to authorized personnel only and regularly audit access logs to monitor for any unauthorized activities(Dhanya et al., 2023; Pramila et al., 2023; Rebecca et al., 2024).
- **Vendor Due Diligence:** Conduct thorough due diligence when selecting AI vendors to ensure they adhere to industry best practices for data privacy and security. Evaluate vendors' security protocols, data handling practices, and compliance certifications to mitigate risks associated with third-party data processing.
- **Employee Training and Awareness:** Provide comprehensive training and awareness programs to educate employees about data privacy best practices and their responsibilities for protecting sensitive information. Encourage employees to report any data security incidents or concerns promptly to facilitate timely response and resolution.

Building a Culture of AI Adoption

Organizations can foster a culture of AI adoption by promoting innovation, collaboration, and continuous learning through strategies like implementing AI-powered HR solutions (Sundaramoorthy et al., 2024; Venkateswaran, Vidhya, Ayyannan, et al., 2023).

- **Leadership Alignment:** Ensure alignment between leadership vision and organizational goals for AI adoption in HR. Leadership support and endorsement are critical for driving cultural change and encouraging experimentation with AI technologies.
- **Cross-Functional Collaboration:** Foster collaboration between HR, IT, and other relevant departments to facilitate knowledge sharing, skill develop-

ment, and innovation. Encourage cross-functional teams to work together on AI initiatives, share insights, and collaborate on problem-solving to achieve shared objectives.

- **Training and Upskilling:** Invest in training and upskilling programs to equip employees with the knowledge and skills needed to leverage AI technologies effectively. Provide opportunities for hands-on learning, certification programs, and workshops to build confidence and proficiency in using AI-powered tools and platforms(Revathi et al., 2024).

- **Celebrating Successes:** Recognize and celebrate successes and achievements related to AI adoption in HR. Highlight case studies, success stories, and positive outcomes to inspire employees, generate enthusiasm, and reinforce the value of AI in driving business results.

- **Continuous Improvement:** Encourage a culture of continuous improvement by soliciting feedback from employees, monitoring performance metrics, and iterating on AI initiatives based on lessons learned and best practices. Emphasize the importance of agility, experimentation, and innovation in driving organizational success in the digital age.

AI implementation in HR necessitates strategic planning, collaboration, and overcoming challenges like change management, data privacy, and cultural adoption. By adopting best practices, organizations can transform HR practices, drive operational excellence, and achieve Industrial 5.0 growth.

IMPACT OF AI ON BUSINESS GROWTH

Figure 4. Impact of AI on business growth

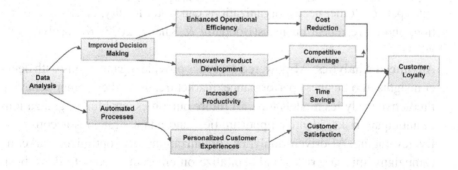

Figure 4 shows how data analysis improves decision-making, operational efficiency, and cost reduction, while automated processes increase productivity, save time, and provide personalized customer experiences, gaining a competitive advantage (Sreedhar et al., 2024).

Direct Contributions to Organizational Performance

AI significantly enhances organizational performance by enhancing efficiency, productivity, and innovation across various business functions(Domakonda et al., 2022; Samikannu et al., 2022; Vennila et al., 2022).

- **Operational Efficiency:** AI automates repetitive tasks, streamlines processes, and reduces manual errors, leading to greater operational efficiency. By leveraging AI-powered tools for tasks such as data entry, document processing, and customer service, organizations can reallocate resources to higher-value activities and achieve cost savings.
- **Enhanced Decision-Making:** AI enables data-driven decision-making by analyzing vast amounts of data, identifying patterns, and generating actionable insights. Machine learning algorithms can predict customer preferences, forecast demand, and optimize resource allocation, empowering organizations to make informed decisions that drive business growth and competitive advantage.
- **Improved Customer Experiences:** AI-driven personalization enhances customer experiences by delivering tailored products, services, and recommendations. Natural language processing (NLP) algorithms enable chatbots and virtual assistants to engage with customers in real-time, addressing their inquiries and resolving issues efficiently. By leveraging AI to understand and anticipate customer needs, organizations can foster loyalty, increase satisfaction, and drive repeat business(Boopathi & Khang, 2023; Kalaiselvi et al., 2024).
- **Advanced Analytics:** AI-powered analytics provide organizations with deeper insights into business performance, market trends, and customer behavior. Predictive analytics models forecast future outcomes, enabling organizations to anticipate risks, identify opportunities, and adapt strategies accordingly. By leveraging AI-driven analytics, organizations can optimize marketing campaigns, mitigate risks, and capitalize on emerging trends to drive business growth.

Indirect Benefits for Business Expansion

AI not only enhances organizational performance directly but also provides indirect benefits that promote business expansion and competitiveness (V. Soni, 2023).

- **Innovation and Agility:** AI fosters a culture of innovation and agility by enabling organizations to experiment with new ideas, technologies, and business models. By leveraging AI for research and development, product design, and process optimization, organizations can accelerate innovation cycles, bring new products to market faster, and stay ahead of competitors in rapidly evolving industries.
- **Scalability and Flexibility:** AI enables organizations to scale operations and adapt to changing market conditions with ease. Cloud-based AI platforms provide scalable infrastructure and flexible deployment options, allowing organizations to expand their AI capabilities as needed without significant upfront investments in hardware or software. This scalability enables organizations to respond quickly to fluctuations in demand, enter new markets, and seize growth opportunities.
- **Risk Management:** AI-powered risk management tools help organizations identify and mitigate potential risks, such as cybersecurity threats, compliance violations, and supply chain disruptions. Machine learning algorithms analyze historical data, detect anomalies, and alert organizations to potential risks in real-time, enabling proactive risk mitigation strategies. By leveraging AI for risk management, organizations can minimize exposure to threats, protect their reputation, and ensure business continuity.
- **Global Expansion:** AI facilitates global expansion by overcoming language barriers, cultural differences, and geographical constraints. Natural language processing (NLP) algorithms enable organizations to localize content, translate communications, and engage with customers in their native languages. Additionally, AI-powered market analysis tools help organizations identify international market opportunities, assess market demand, and tailor their offerings to local preferences, enabling successful expansion into new regions.

AI significantly impacts business growth by improving performance, facilitating expansion, and enhancing competitiveness. By enhancing efficiency, driving innovation, and mitigating risks, organizations can unlock new growth opportunities, achieve operational excellence, and thrive in the dynamic and competitive Industrial 5.0 landscape.

CASE STUDIES: AI SUCCESS STORIES IN HR

IBM: Transforming Recruitment With AI

IBM has been at the forefront of leveraging AI to revolutionize its recruitment processes. By implementing AI-powered tools such as Watson Recruitment, IBM has significantly streamlined its hiring process, reduced time-to-fill positions, and improved the quality of hires. Watson Recruitment uses natural language processing (NLP) and machine learning algorithms to analyze resumes, assess candidate qualifications, and predict job fit. As a result, IBM has experienced a 50% reduction in time spent on candidate screening and a 30% increase in the accuracy of hiring decisions. Lessons learned from IBM's AI recruitment initiative include the importance of data quality, transparency, and continuous improvement. Best practices include investing in AI talent, fostering cross-functional collaboration, and measuring the impact of AI on important recruitment metrics (Castillo & Taherdoost, 2023).

Unilever: Personalizing Learning and Development With AI

Unilever, a global consumer goods company, has implemented AI-powered learning and development (L&D) initiatives to personalize employee training and drive skill development. By leveraging AI algorithms to analyze employee skills, preferences, and performance data, Unilever delivers personalized learning experiences tailored to each employee's individual needs. This approach has resulted in increased engagement, higher completion rates, and improved learning outcomes for employees(Ravisankar et al., 2024; Rebecca et al., 2024; M. Sharma et al., 2024). Important lessons learned from Unilever's AI L&D initiative include the importance of user feedback, content relevance, and data privacy. Best practices include leveraging AI for adaptive learning, providing access to diverse learning resources, and fostering a culture of continuous learning (Aljapurkar & Ingawale, 2024).

Hilton: Enhancing Employee Experience With AI

Hilton, a leading global hospitality company, has embraced AI to enhance the employee experience and drive engagement. By implementing AI-powered chatbots and virtual assistants, Hilton provides employees with personalized support and assistance for HR-related inquiries, such as benefits enrollment, time-off requests, and training programs. These AI-driven solutions enable employees to access information and resources quickly, improve communication with HR, and streamline administrative processes. Lessons learned from Hilton's AI employee experience initiative include the importance of user-friendly interfaces, natural language understanding, and data integration. Best practices include providing multi-channel support, training employees on AI tools, and iterating based on user feedback (N. Soni et al., 2019).

The case studies showcase the transformative impact of AI on HR practices, including recruitment, talent management, learning, development, and employee experience. These success stories can guide organizations in implementing AI initiatives and driving business growth in the competitive Industrial 5.0 landscape.

FUTURE TRENDS AND CONSIDERATIONS

The future of HR is set to undergo significant transformation as organizations adapt to the Industrial 5.0 landscape. Emerging technologies are driving innovation, efficiency, and agility in workforce management practices. These developments are expected to redefine traditional industrial processes and reshape organizations' operations and competitiveness (Sulistyaningsih, 2023). Emerging technologies significantly influence traditional HR practices, leading to innovation, efficiency, and agility, which in turn redefine industrial processes, reshape operations, and enhance organizational competitiveness as shown in Figure 3.

Emerging Technologies Shaping the Future of HR

- **Augmented Reality (AR) and Virtual Reality (VR):** AR and VR technologies are revolutionizing HR practices, particularly in training, onboarding, and employee engagement. By creating immersive and interactive experiences, AR and VR enable organizations to deliver realistic simulations, virtual tours, and hands-on training modules, enhancing learning outcomes and fostering a culture of innovation.
- **Blockchain:** Blockchain technology has the potential to transform HR processes such as recruitment, credential verification, and payroll management. By providing a secure and tamper-proof record of employee credentials and transactions, blockchain enhances trust, transparency, and integrity in HR operations, reducing fraud and ensuring compliance with regulatory requirements(Kumar et al., 2023; Sundaramoorthy et al., 2024).
- **Predictive Analytics and AI-Powered Insights:** The use of predictive analytics and AI-driven insights in HR is expected to become more sophisticated, enabling organizations to anticipate workforce trends, identify hidden patterns, and make proactive decisions. Advanced AI algorithms will analyze vast amounts of data to predict employee performance, assess retention risk,

and recommend personalized development opportunities, driving organizational performance and employee satisfaction.

- **Biometric Authentication and Wearable Technology:** Biometric authentication and wearable technology are transforming employee experience and workplace productivity. Biometric authentication methods such as fingerprint scanning and facial recognition enhance security and streamline access to physical and digital assets. Wearable devices such as smartwatches and fitness trackers enable organizations to monitor employee health and well-being, optimize work schedules, and promote a culture of wellness and productivity(Boopathi & Kanike, 2023; Das et al., 2024).

Anticipated Developments in Industrial 5.0

- **Integration of Edge Computing and IoT:** The integration of edge computing and internet of things (IoT) technologies will enable real-time data processing and analysis at the edge of the network, reducing latency and enhancing responsiveness in industrial environments. Edge computing will enable autonomous decision-making and predictive maintenance in industrial systems, improving efficiency, reliability, and safety (Pandey, 2020).
- **Advanced Robotics and Cobots:** Advanced robotics and collaborative robots (cobots) will play an increasingly prominent role in Industrial 5.0, working alongside human workers to enhance productivity and flexibility. These robots will be equipped with advanced sensors, AI algorithms, and natural language processing capabilities, enabling them to perform complex tasks, adapt to changing conditions, and collaborate seamlessly with human counterparts(Koshariya et al., 2023; Maheswari et al., 2023; Revathi et al., 2024).
- **Digital Twins and Simulation Technologies:** Digital twins and simulation technologies will enable organizations to create virtual replicas of physical assets, processes, and systems, allowing for predictive modeling, scenario analysis, and optimization. Digital twins will facilitate remote monitoring and control of industrial operations, enabling organizations to identify inefficiencies, reduce downtime, and optimize resource utilization in real-time.
- **Cyber-Physical Systems and Autonomous Vehicles:** The convergence of cyber-physical systems and autonomous vehicles will revolutionize transportation and logistics in Industrial 5.0. Autonomous vehicles, drones, and unmanned aerial vehicles (UAVs) will enable autonomous material handling, inventory management, and last-mile delivery, enhancing efficiency, reducing costs, and improving supply chain resilience(Babu et al., 2022; Chandrika et al., 2023; Dhanalakshmi et al., 2024).

The future of HR and Industrial 5.0 is influenced by emerging technologies and developments that will transform traditional practices and organizations' operations. By embracing these trends, organizations can stay ahead of the curve, drive innovation, and achieve sustainable growth in the competitive Industrial 5.0 landscape.

RECOMMENDATIONS FOR HARNESSING AI IN HR FOR BUSINESS GROWTH

Organizations can leverage AI in HR to boost business growth, improve employee experience, and gain a competitive edge in the evolving Industrial 5.0 landscape (Borthakur & Das, n.d.; Chander et al., 2022; Sulistyaningsih, 2023).

- **Define Clear Objectives:** Before implementing AI in HR, define clear objectives aligned with business goals. Identify specific areas where AI can drive value, such as recruitment, talent management, or employee engagement, and establish key performance indicators (KPIs) to measure success.
- **Invest in Data Quality:** Data quality is essential for the success of AI initiatives in HR. Invest in data cleansing, normalization, and enrichment processes to ensure that the data used for AI algorithms is accurate, reliable, and relevant. Establish data governance policies and procedures to maintain data integrity and compliance with privacy regulations.
- **Select the Right AI Solutions:** Choose AI solutions that align with your organization's needs, capabilities, and budget. Consider factors such as scalability, ease of integration, and vendor reputation when selecting AI vendors. Prioritize solutions that offer transparent algorithms, explainable AI, and robust security features to build trust and confidence among users.
- **Empower HR Professionals:** AI should augment, not replace, human expertise in HR. Empower HR professionals with the knowledge, skills, and tools needed to leverage AI effectively in their roles. Provide training and professional development opportunities to build AI literacy and proficiency among HR staff, enabling them to maximize the value of AI-powered solutions.
- **Promote Collaboration:** Foster collaboration between HR and other departments, such as IT, data science, and business operations, to ensure the successful implementation of AI initiatives. Encourage cross-functional teams to work together on AI projects, share insights, and collaborate on problem-solving to achieve shared objectives.
- **Prioritize Employee Experience:** Keep the employee experience at the forefront when implementing AI in HR. Ensure that AI-powered solutions enhance rather than detract from the employee experience by providing per-

sonalized, seamless, and user-friendly interactions. Solicit feedback from employees throughout the implementation process to identify areas for improvement and address concerns proactively.

- **Measure and Iterate:** Continuously monitor the impact of AI initiatives on HR metrics and business outcomes. Use data analytics to track KPIs, measure ROI, and identify areas for optimization. Iterate on AI solutions based on user feedback, performance insights, and changing business needs to ensure ongoing alignment with organizational goals.

- **Stay Ethical and Transparent:** Maintain ethical standards and transparency in the use of AI in HR. Ensure that AI algorithms are fair, unbiased, and free from discrimination by regularly auditing and testing for algorithmic bias. Communicate openly with employees about the use of AI in HR, addressing concerns related to privacy, data security, and job displacement.

- **Embrace Continuous Learning:** AI technology is constantly evolving, so it's essential to embrace a culture of continuous learning and adaptation. Stay informed about emerging trends, best practices, and industry developments in AI and HR. Encourage experimentation and innovation to explore new AI applications and opportunities for business growth.

- **Celebrate Successes and Learn from Failures:** Celebrate successes and milestones achieved through AI initiatives in HR, recognizing the contributions of individuals and teams involved. At the same time, embrace failure as an opportunity for learning and improvement. Encourage a culture of experimentation and risk-taking, where failures are seen as valuable learning experiences that drive innovation and growth.

CONCLUSION

The integration of AI into HR practices offers organizations a chance to drive business growth and thrive in the Industrial 5.0 era. AI-powered solutions can transform traditional HR processes, enhance operational efficiency, and unlock new opportunities for innovation and competitiveness. This chapter explores the transformative potential of AI in HR, including recruitment, talent management, learning, development, and employee engagement, examining successful case studies and identifying key lessons learned for harnessing AI for business growth.

The future of HR and Industrial 5.0 is influenced by emerging technologies, trends, and developments. AI can revolutionize HR practices, drive organizational performance, and accelerate business growth. By adopting a strategic approach, investing in data quality, empowering HR professionals, and prioritizing employee experience, organizations can harness the full potential of AI in HR for sustainable growth and success in Industrial 5.0 and beyond.

ABBREVIATIONS

ABBRAI - Artificial Intelligence
HR - Human Resources
NLP - Natural Language Processing
RPA - Robotic Process Automation
NLG - Natural Language Generation
IT - Information Technology
GDPR - General Data Protection Regulation
CCPA - California Consumer Privacy Act
IBM - International Business Machines Corporation
AR - Augmented Reality
VR - Virtual Reality
UAV - Unmanned Aerial Vehicle
KPI - Key Performance Indicator
ROI - Return on Investment

REFERENCES

Agrawal, A. V., Pitchai, R., Senthamaraikannan, C., Balaji, N. A., Sajithra, S., & Boopathi, S. (2023). Digital Education System During the COVID-19 Pandemic. In *Using Assistive Technology for Inclusive Learning in K-12 Classrooms* (pp. 104–126). IGI Global. 10.4018/978-1-6684-6424-3.ch005

Ali, M. N., Senthil, T., Ilakkiya, T., Hasan, D. S., Ganapathy, N. B. S., & Boopathi, S. (2024). IoT's Role in Smart Manufacturing Transformation for Enhanced Household Product Quality. In *Advanced Applications in Osmotic Computing* (pp. 252–289). IGI Global. 10.4018/979-8-3693-1694-8.ch014

Aljapurkar, A. V., & Ingawale, S. D. (2024). Revolutionizing the Techno-Human Space in Human Resource Practices in Industry 4.0 to Usage in Society 5.0. In *Digital Transformation: Industry 4.0 to Society 5.0* (pp. 221–257). Springer.

Arora, M., Prakash, A., Mittal, A., & Singh, S. (2021). HR analytics and artificial intelligence-transforming human resource management. *2021 International Conference on Decision Aid Sciences and Application (DASA)*, (pp. 288–293). IEEE. 10.1109/DASA53625.2021.9682325

Babu, B. S., Kamalakannan, J., Meenatchi, N., Karthik, S., & Boopathi, S. (2022). Economic impacts and reliability evaluation of battery by adopting Electric Vehicle. *IEEE Explore*, 1–6.

Boopathi, S. (2023). Deep Learning Techniques Applied for Automatic Sentence Generation. In *Promoting Diversity, Equity, and Inclusion in Language Learning Environments* (pp. 255–273). IGI Global. 10.4018/978-1-6684-3632-5.ch016

Boopathi, S. (2024). Digital HR Implementation for Business Growth in Industrial 5.0. In *Convergence of Human Resources Technologies and Industry 5.0* (pp. 1–22). IGI Global. 10.4018/979-8-3693-1343-5.ch001

Boopathi, S., & Kanike, U. K. (2023). Applications of Artificial Intelligent and Machine Learning Techniques in Image Processing. In *Handbook of Research on Thrust Technologies' Effect on Image Processing* (pp. 151–173). IGI Global. 10.4018/978-1-6684-8618-4.ch010

Boopathi, S., & Khang, A. (2023). AI-Integrated Technology for a Secure and Ethical Healthcare Ecosystem. In *AI and IoT-Based Technologies for Precision Medicine* (pp. 36–59). IGI Global. 10.4018/979-8-3693-0876-9.ch003

Borthakur, P. G., & Das, B. B. (n.d.). *Future of Human Resource (HR) in Industry 5.0: Embracing Technology and Beyond-A Study.*

Castillo, M. J., & Taherdoost, H. (2023). The impact of AI technologies on e-business. *Encyclopedia*, 3(1), 107–121. 10.3390/encyclopedia3010009

Chander, B., Pal, S., De, D., & Buyya, R. (2022). Artificial intelligence-based internet of things for industry 5.0. *Artificial Intelligence-Based Internet of Things Systems*, 3–45.

Chandrika, V., Sivakumar, A., Krishnan, T. S., Pradeep, J., Manikandan, S., & Boopathi, S. (2023). Theoretical Study on Power Distribution Systems for Electric Vehicles. In *Intelligent Engineering Applications and Applied Sciences for Sustainability* (pp. 1–19). IGI Global. 10.4018/979-8-3693-0044-2.ch001

Dahlbom, P., Siikanen, N., Sajasalo, P., & Jarvenpää, M. (2020). Big data and HR analytics in the digital era. *Baltic Journal of Management*, 15(1), 120–138. 10.1108/BJM-11-2018-0393

Das, P., Ramapraba, P., Seethalakshmi, K., Mary, M. A., Karthick, S., & Sampath, B. (2024). Sustainable Advanced Techniques for Enhancing the Image Process. In *Fostering Cross-Industry Sustainability With Intelligent Technologies* (pp. 350–374). IGI Global. 10.4018/979-8-3693-1638-2.ch022

Dhanalakshmi, M., Tamilarasi, K., Saravanan, S., Sujatha, G., Boopathi, S., & Associates. (2024). Fog Computing-Based Framework and Solutions for Intelligent Systems: Enabling Autonomy in Vehicles. In *Computational Intelligence for Green Cloud Computing and Digital Waste Management* (pp. 330–356). IGI Global.

Dhanya, D., Kumar, S. S., Thilagavathy, A., Prasad, D., & Boopathi, S. (2023). Data Analytics and Artificial Intelligence in the Circular Economy: Case Studies. In *Intelligent Engineering Applications and Applied Sciences for Sustainability* (pp. 40–58). IGI Global.

Domakonda, V. K., Farooq, S., Chinthamreddy, S., Puviarasi, R., Sudhakar, M., & Boopathi, S. (2022). Sustainable Developments of Hybrid Floating Solar Power Plants: Photovoltaic System. In *Human Agro-Energy Optimization for Business and Industry* (pp. 148–167). IGI Global.

Gift, M. D. M., Senthil, T. S., Hasan, D. S., Alagarraja, K., Jayaseelan, P., & Boopathi, S. (2024). Additive Manufacturing and 3D Printing Innovations: Revolutionizing Industry 5.0. In *Technological Advancements in Data Processing for Next Generation Intelligent Systems* (pp. 255–287). IGI Global. 10.4018/979-8-3693-0968-1.ch010

Kalaiselvi, T., Saravanan, G., Haritha, T., Babu, A. V. S., Sakthivel, M., & Boopathi, S. (2024). A Study on the Landscape of Serverless Computing: Technologies and Tools for Seamless Implementation. In *Serverless Computing Concepts, Technology and Architecture* (pp. 260–282). IGI Global. 10.4018/979-8-3693-1682-5.ch016

Khan, M., Haleem, A., & Javaid, M. (2023). Changes and improvements in Industry 5.0: A strategic approach to overcome the challenges of Industry 4.0. *Green Technologies and Sustainability*, 1(2), 100020. 10.1016/j.grets.2023.100020

Koshariya, A. K., Khatoon, S., Marathe, A. M., Suba, G. M., Baral, D., & Boopathi, S. (2023). Agricultural Waste Management Systems Using Artificial Intelligence Techniques. In *AI-Enabled Social Robotics in Human Care Services* (pp. 236–258). IGI Global. 10.4018/978-1-6684-8171-4.ch009

Kotler, P., Kartajaya, H., & Setiawan, I. (2021). *Marketing 5.0: Technology for humanity*. John Wiley & Sons.

Kumar, P. R., Meenakshi, S., Shalini, S., Devi, S. R., & Boopathi, S. (2023). Soil Quality Prediction in Context Learning Approaches Using Deep Learning and Blockchain for Smart Agriculture. In *Effective AI, Blockchain, and E-Governance Applications for Knowledge Discovery and Management* (pp. 1–26). IGI Global. 10.4018/978-1-6684-9151-5.ch001

Kumara, V., & Sharma, M. D., Samson Isaac, J., Saravanan, S., Suganthi, D., & Boopathi, S. (2023). An AI-Integrated Green Power Monitoring System: Empowering Small and Medium Enterprises. In *Advances in Environmental Engineering and Green Technologies* (pp. 218–244). IGI Global. 10.4018/979-8-3693-0338-2.ch013

Maddikunta, P. K. R., Pham, Q.-V., Prabadevi, B., Deepa, N., Dev, K., Gadekallu, T. R., Ruby, R., & Liyanage, M. (2022). Industry 5.0: A survey on enabling technologies and potential applications. *Journal of Industrial Information Integration*, 26, 100257. 10.1016/j.jii.2021.100257

Maheswari, B. U., Imambi, S. S., Hasan, D., Meenakshi, S., Pratheep, V., & Boopathi, S. (2023). Internet of things and machine learning-integrated smart robotics. In *Global Perspectives on Robotics and Autonomous Systems: Development and Applications* (pp. 240–258). IGI Global. 10.4018/978-1-6684-7791-5.ch010

Mazurchenko, A., & Maršíková, K. (2019). Digitally-powered human resource management: Skills and roles in the digital era. *Acta Informatica Pragensia*, 8(2), 72–87. 10.18267/j.aip.125

Mohanty, A., Jothi, B., Jeyasudha, J., Ranjit, P., Isaac, J. S., & Boopathi, S. (2023). Additive Manufacturing Using Robotic Programming. In *AI-Enabled Social Robotics in Human Care Services* (pp. 259–282). IGI Global. 10.4018/978-1-6684-8171-4. ch010

Pandey, S. (2020). Exploring the role of Artificial Intelligence (AI) in transforming HR functions: An Empirical Study in the Indian Context. *International Journal of Scientific Research and Engineering Development.*

Pasumarthy, R., Mohammed, S., Laxman, V., Krishnamoorthy, V., Durga, S., & Boopathi, S. (2024). Digital Transformation in Developing Economies: Forecasting Trends, Impact, and Challenges in Industry 5.0. In *Convergence of Human Resources Technologies and Industry 5.0* (pp. 47–68). IGI Global. 10.4018/979-8-3693-1343-5. ch003

Prabhuswamy, M., Tripathi, R., Vijayakumar, M., Thulasimani, T., Sundharesalingam, P., & Sampath, B. (2024). A Study on the Complex Nature of Higher Education Leadership: An Innovative Approach. In *Challenges of Globalization and Inclusivity in Academic Research* (pp. 202–223). IGI Global. 10.4018/979-8-3693-1371-8.ch013

Pramila, P., Amudha, S., Saravanan, T., Sankar, S. R., Poongothai, E., & Boopathi, S. (2023). Design and Development of Robots for Medical Assistance: An Architectural Approach. In *Contemporary Applications of Data Fusion for Advanced Healthcare Informatics* (pp. 260–282). IGI Global.

Puranik, T. A., Shaik, N., Vankudoth, R., Kolhe, M. R., Yadav, N., & Boopathi, S. (2024). Study on Harmonizing Human-Robot (Drone) Collaboration: Navigating Seamless Interactions in Collaborative Environments. In *Cybersecurity Issues and Challenges in the Drone Industry* (pp. 1–26). IGI Global.

Ramudu, K., Mohan, V. M., Jyothirmai, D., Prasad, D., Agrawal, R., & Boopathi, S. (2023). Machine Learning and Artificial Intelligence in Disease Prediction: Applications, Challenges, Limitations, Case Studies, and Future Directions. In *Contemporary Applications of Data Fusion for Advanced Healthcare Informatics* (pp. 297–318). IGI Global.

Ravisankar, A., Shanthi, A., Lavanya, S., Ramaratnam, M., Krishnamoorthy, V., & Boopathi, S. (2024). Harnessing 6G for Consumer-Centric Business Strategies Across Electronic Industries. In *AI Impacts in Digital Consumer Behavior* (pp. 241–270). IGI Global.

Rebecca, B., Kumar, K. P. M., Padmini, S., Srivastava, B. K., Halder, S., & Boopathi, S. (2024). Convergence of Data Science-AI-Green Chemistry-Affordable Medicine: Transforming Drug Discovery. In *Handbook of Research on AI and ML for Intelligent Machines and Systems* (pp. 348–373). IGI Global.

Revathi, S., Babu, M., Rajkumar, N., Meti, V. K. V., Kandavalli, S. R., & Boopathi, S. (2024). Unleashing the Future Potential of 4D Printing: Exploring Applications in Wearable Technology, Robotics, Energy, Transportation, and Fashion. In *Human-Centered Approaches in Industry 5.0: Human-Machine Interaction, Virtual Reality Training, and Customer Sentiment Analysis* (pp. 131–153). IGI Global.

Samikannu, R., Koshariya, A. K., Poornima, E., Ramesh, S., Kumar, A., & Boopathi, S. (2022). Sustainable Development in Modern Aquaponics Cultivation Systems Using IoT Technologies. In *Human Agro-Energy Optimization for Business and Industry* (pp. 105–127). IGI Global.

Sampath, B., Pandian, M., Deepa, D., & Subbiah, R. (2022). Operating parameters prediction of liquefied petroleum gas refrigerator using simulated annealing algorithm. *AIP Conference Proceedings*, 2460(1), 070003. 10.1063/5.0095601

Sharma, D. M., Ramana, K. V., Jothilakshmi, R., Verma, R., Maheswari, B. U., & Boopathi, S. (2024). Integrating Generative AI Into K-12 Curriculums and Pedagogies in India: Opportunities and Challenges. *Facilitating Global Collaboration and Knowledge Sharing in Higher Education With Generative AI*. Springer.

Sharma, M., Sharma, M., Sharma, N., & Boopathi, S. (2024). Building Sustainable Smart Cities Through Cloud and Intelligent Parking System. In *Handbook of Research on AI and ML for Intelligent Machines and Systems* (pp. 195–222). IGI Global.

Soni, N., Sharma, E. K., Singh, N., & Kapoor, A. (2019). Impact of artificial intelligence on businesses: From research, innovation, market deployment to future shifts in business models. *arXiv Preprint arXiv:1905.02092*.

Soni, V. (2023). Impact of Generative AI on Small and Medium Enterprises' Revenue Growth: The Moderating Role of Human, Technological, and Market Factors. *Reviews of Contemporary Business Analytics*, 6(1), 133–153.

Sreedhar, P. S. S., Sujay, V., Rani, M. R., Melita, L., Reshma, S., & Boopathi, S. (2024). Impacts of 5G Machine Learning Techniques on Telemedicine and Social Media Professional Connection in Healthcare. In *Advances in Medical Technologies and Clinical Practice* (pp. 209–234). IGI Global. 10.4018/979-8-3693-1934-5.ch012

Srinivas, B., Maguluri, L. P., Naidu, K. V., Reddy, L. C. S., Deivakani, M., & Boopathi, S. (2023). Architecture and Framework for Interfacing Cloud-Enabled Robots. In *Handbook of Research on Data Science and Cybersecurity Innovations in Industry 4.0 Technologies* (pp. 542–560). IGI Global. 10.4018/978-1-6684-8145-5.ch027

Sulistyaningsih, E. (2023). Improving Human Resources Technology Innovation as a Business Growth Driver in the Society 5.0 Era. *ADI Journal on Recent Innovation*, 4(2), 149–159.

Sundaramoorthy, K., Singh, A., Sumathy, G., Maheshwari, A., Arunarani, A., & Boopathi, S. (2024). A Study on AI and Blockchain-Powered Smart Parking Models for Urban Mobility. In *Handbook of Research on AI and ML for Intelligent Machines and Systems* (pp. 223–250). IGI Global.

Taj, I., & Zaman, N. (2022). Towards industrial revolution 5.0 and explainable artificial intelligence: Challenges and opportunities. *International Journal of Computing and Digital Systems*, 12(1), 295–320. 10.12785/ijcds/120128

Veeranjaneyulu, R., Boopathi, S., Kumari, R. K., Vidyarthi, A., Isaac, J. S., & Jaiganesh, V. (2023). *Air Quality Improvement and Optimisation Using Machine Learning Technique*. IEEE.

Veeranjaneyulu, R., Boopathi, S., Narasimharao, J., Gupta, K. K., Reddy, R. V. K., & Ambika, R. (2023). *Identification of Heart Diseases using Novel Machine Learning Method*. IEEE.

Venkatasubramanian, V., Chitra, M., Sudha, R., Singh, V. P., Jefferson, K., & Boopathi, S. (2024). Examining the Impacts of Course Outcome Analysis in Indian Higher Education: Enhancing Educational Quality. In *Challenges of Globalization and Inclusivity in Academic Research* (pp. 124–145). IGI Global.

Venkateswaran, N., Vidhya, K., Ayyannan, M., Chavan, S. M., Sekar, K., & Boopathi, S. (2023). A Study on Smart Energy Management Framework Using Cloud Computing. In *5G, Artificial Intelligence, and Next Generation Internet of Things: Digital Innovation for Green and Sustainable Economies* (pp. 189–212). IGI Global. 10.4018/978-1-6684-8634-4.ch009

Venkateswaran, N., Vidhya, R., Naik, D. A., Raj, T. M., Munjal, N., & Boopathi, S. (2023). Study on Sentence and Question Formation Using Deep Learning Techniques. In *Digital Natives as a Disruptive Force in Asian Businesses and Societies* (pp. 252–273). IGI Global. 10.4018/978-1-6684-6782-4.ch015

Vennila, T., Karuna, M., Srivastava, B. K., Venugopal, J., Surakasi, R., & Sampath, B. (2022). New Strategies in Treatment and Enzymatic Processes: Ethanol Production From Sugarcane Bagasse. In *Human Agro-Energy Optimization for Business and Industry* (pp. 219–240). IGI Global.

Yupapin, P., Trabelsi, Y., Nattappan, A., & Boopathi, S. (2023). Performance improvement of wire-cut electrical discharge machining process using cryogenically treated super-conductive state of Monel-K500 alloy. *Iranian Journal of Science and Technology. Transaction of Mechanical Engineering*, 47(1), 267–283. 10.1007/s40997-022-00513-0

Zizic, M. C., Mladineo, M., Gjeldum, N., & Celent, L. (2022). From industry 4.0 towards industry 5.0: A review and analysis of paradigm shift for the people, organization and technology. *Energies*, 15(14), 5221. 10.3390/en15145221

Chapter 10
Cultural Impacts of Artificial Intelligence on Sustainable Entrepreneurship Development

Ragitha Radhakrishnan

(iD) https://orcid.org/0000-0003-1621 -2932

Department of Psychology, Dr. MGR-Janaki College of Arts and Science for Women, Chennai, India

T. R. Abhilasha

(iD) https://orcid.org/0009-0005-2551 -1856

Department of Commerce and Management, International Institute of Business Studies, Bengaluru, India

P. Sivakumar

Department of Management, Dr. SNS Rajalakshmi College of Arts and Science, Coimbatore, India

P Suganthi

Department of Mathematics, R.M.K. Engineering College, Kavaraipettai, India

Benita E.

Department of Management, Bishop Appasamy College of Arts and Science, Coimbatore, India

Premkumar R.

Department of Electronics and Instrumentation Engineering, Sri Sairam Engineering College, Chennai

ABSTRACT

In this chapter, the connection between artificial intelligence (AI) and sustainable entrepreneurship is emphasized, emphasizing the need for understanding its sociological and cultural implications. It also emphasizes the significance of cultural sensitivity in AI development and adoption, mitigates biases, and fosters inclusive AI

DOI: 10.4018/979-8-3693-2432-5.ch010

ecosystems. While AI technologies can improve efficiency, innovation, and scalability, privacy, autonomy, and job displacement concerns necessitate a balance between technological advancements and ethical considerations. Interdisciplinary collaboration between sociologists, HR professionals, entrepreneurs, and technologists to develop AI-driven sustainable entrepreneurship initiatives has been discussed in this chapter. AI's transformative potential for sustainable entrepreneurship has been connected to incorporating sociocultural insights.

INTRODUCTION

AI is fostering efficiency and innovation, which is transforming sectors like healthcare and finance. AI is becoming acknowledged as a tool for sustainable enterprise as the world community addresses sustainability-related challenges. Through the analysis and prediction of large datasets, machine learning, natural language processing, and computer vision are revolutionizing these fields (Bickley et al., 2021). Sustainable entrepreneurship prioritizes social responsibility, economic success, and environmental stewardship, providing opportunity for innovation. Nowadays, companies are prioritizing sustainability as a means of reducing their environmental effect, improving social welfare, and securing their long-term profitability (Di Vaio et al., 2020).

AI and eco-friendly business are working together to address sustainability issues. AI-powered solutions may help with data-driven decision-making, resource optimization, and operational efficiency. Techniques for precision farming can increase crop output while using less water and having a less negative environmental effect. AI systems can expedite the switch to renewable energy sources, optimize energy use, and enhance grid stability. Innovative solutions that support both economic value and environmental sustainability can be created by entrepreneurs (Isensee et al., 2021). Concerns about algorithmic prejudice, data privacy, and job displacement are among the ethical and societal issues that arise from AI's revolutionary potential. The goal of sustainable entrepreneurship is to maximize profit while preserving moral values, promoting equitable growth, and defending human rights (Goralski & Tan, 2020).

An encouraging avenue for equitable growth and constructive change is the combination of artificial intelligence and sustainable entrepreneurship. Entrepreneurs may generate commercial opportunity and societal benefits by employing artificial intelligence (AI) to build new solutions to sustainability concerns. But a well-rounded strategy incorporating cooperation and moral leadership is required (Gupta et al., 2023). With an emphasis on how cultural variables affect adoption, implementation, and outcomes, this study investigates the cultural impact of AI on sustainable entrepreneurship. By looking at the relationship between artificial intelligence (AI) and sustainable entrepreneurship via a cultural lens, it aims to deliver insights that guide strategic decision-making, encourage innovation, and promote inclusive growth (Sineviciene et al., 2021).

The adoption of AI in entrepreneurship is influenced by cultural norms, values, and beliefs. Entrepreneurs' desire to use AI technology is influenced by a number of important aspects, including trust, risk perception, and technological preparedness. Individualistic cultures place more emphasis on independence and self-reliance than do collectiveist societies on community and cooperation. AI technologies that facilitate personalized decision-making or improve cooperation may be given priority by entrepreneurs (Wiyata & Liu, n.d.).

Although cultural variety in entrepreneurial teams can foster creativity and innovation, it can also present difficulties with decision-making, communication, and work preferences. Despite possible obstacles to efficient cooperation and coordination, addressing these cultural quirks is essential for optimizing the potential of AI-driven business and using diversity as a competitive advantage (Kulkov et al., 2023).

While cultural variety may foster creativity and innovation in entrepreneurial teams, it can also present difficulties with decision-making, communication, and work preferences. Despite possible obstacles to efficient coordination and collaboration, addressing these cultural differences is essential for optimizing the potential of AI-driven business and utilizing diversity as a competitive advantage (Pratono, 2022).

The ethical and sociological concerns posed by AI technology vary depending on the cultural setting. A number of issues, including algorithmic prejudice, privacy violations, and employment displacement, may affect many communities and demographic groups. AI ethics are also influenced by cultural norms surrounding data ownership, authority, and trust. In order to address these, stakeholder involvement, cross-cultural communication, and cooperative development of ethical AI frameworks that take into account various cultural viewpoints and values are necessary (Mhlanga, 2021).

AI's influence on sustainable entrepreneurship is essential for promoting social cohesion and inclusive growth. Subsequent studies ought to investigate the interplay of artificial intelligence technology, cultural dynamics, and entrepreneurial activities. In order to effectively solve social concerns, strategies should include ethical considerations, cultural sensitivity, and multidisciplinary teamwork while also respecting cultural variety (Mamedov et al., 2018).

BACKGROUND

Interest in artificial intelligence's (AI) ability to promote sustainable entrepreneurial growth has grown as a result of AI's incorporation into several industries. AI presents chances to improve societal welfare, reduce environmental effect, and optimize operations. But successfully navigating this junction necessitates a deep comprehension of both fields as well as critical analysis of the ethical and cultural ramifications.

Research Objectives

- To explore the potential of AI in promoting sustainable practices and driving innovation in entrepreneurship.
- To integrate the AI into sustainable entrepreneurship presents both challenges and opportunities, requiring careful consideration of ethical issues, technological limitations, and market dynamics.
- To provide practical insights and recommendations for entrepreneurs, policymakers, and other stakeholders to effectively utilize AI for sustainable entrepreneurship development.

Scopes

This study investigates how artificial intelligence (AI) tools, such as natural language processing and machine learning, might support sustainability in business endeavors. It examines the moral, social, and environmental effects of using AI in sustainable entrepreneurship, gives case studies, and makes suggestions for stakeholders, legislators, and business owners on how to incorporate AI into sustainable operations.

CULTURAL DIMENSIONS OF ARTIFICIAL INTELLIGENCE

This section delves into the importance of understanding cultural diversity in the implementation of Artificial Intelligence (AI), emphasizing its role in promoting responsible and inclusive practices across diverse societies, while also highlighting important considerations and challenges(Zhang et al., 2020).

Figure 1. Cultural dimensions of artificial intelligence

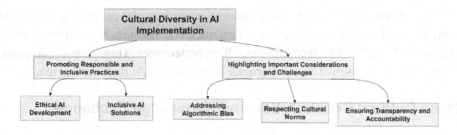

The figure 1 illustrates a flowchart-style diagram, which can be customized with additional nodes or details. For further assistance or modifications, please contact me.

Cultural Diversity in AI Development

AI systems are often developed by teams from diverse cultural backgrounds, enhancing the design process and inclusivity of AI solutions. However, this also introduces challenges like language barriers, communication styles, and cultural biases, which must be addressed to ensure the effectiveness and fairness of AI algorithms.

Ethical and Societal Implications

Cultural norms and values significantly influence ethical frameworks and societal expectations regarding AI deployment. For instance, AI-powered surveillance systems may be seen as necessary for security in some cultures but a violation of privacy and civil liberties in others. Understanding these cultural nuances is crucial for creating AI solutions that respect diverse values and norms.

Bias and Discrimination

AI algorithms can perpetuate societal inequalities due to cultural biases in training data, decision-making processes, and user interfaces. Addressing bias requires proactive measures like diverse data representation, algorithmic transparency, and ongoing monitoring and evaluation for marginalized communities(Boopathi, 2024b; Maguluri et al., 2023; Pachiappan et al., 2024).

User Experience and Acceptance

Cultural differences significantly impact user perceptions and acceptance of AI technologies. To build trust, user interfaces, interaction design, and communication styles must be tailored to accommodate these preferences. Transparency, accountability, and cultural sensitivity are crucial in explaining AI decisions' impact.

Cross-Cultural Collaboration and Knowledge Exchange

Cultural diversity is crucial for responsible AI development and deployment. International partnerships, interdisciplinary research initiatives, and community engagement can facilitate the exchange of best practices and insights across cultural boundaries. This fosters dialogue and collaboration, addressing cultural challenges and promoting ethical and inclusive use of AI worldwide. Recognizing and addressing cultural dimensions can foster a more inclusive, equitable, and culturally sensitive AI ecosystem, reflecting the values and aspirations of diverse societies(de Andreis et al., 2024; Kulkov et al., 2023).

Understanding the cultural dimensions that influence the adoption and development of artificial intelligence (AI) is crucial in its rapidly evolving landscape. These dimensions, including sociological perspectives and ethical considerations, significantly influence how AI technologies are perceived, utilized, and regulated across different societies and cultural contexts(Das et al., 2024; Kumar et al., 2023; Sharma et al., 2024).

Sociological Perspectives on AI Adoption

Sociological perspectives provide insights into AI adoption, revealing the complex relationship between technology and society. Cultural norms, values, and beliefs influence attitudes towards AI, affecting its adoption. Factors like trust, transparency, and perceived benefits vary across cultures, affecting adoption pace. Sociological theories like diffusion of innovations and social network analysis help understand how AI technologies spread through social systems. Recognizing these dynamics is crucial for designing AI strategies that cater to diverse cultural contexts and promote inclusive technological development(Di Vaio et al., 2020).

Ethical Considerations in Cross-Cultural AI Development

Ethical considerations are crucial in AI technology development, especially in cross-cultural contexts where values and norms may differ. Cultural relativism emphasizes the need for sensitivity to cultural nuances in AI design and implementation.

Cultural diversity in AI development is essential to navigate issues like algorithmic bias, fairness, and accountability. Biases in AI algorithms may reflect cultural biases in training data, impacting different demographic groups. Ethical frameworks for AI governance may vary between cultures, necessitating dialogue and collaboration to promote responsible AI development practices(Di Vaio et al., 2020).

Cross-cultural AI development raises questions about data privacy, consent, and autonomy due to differing cultural norms. Respecting individuals' rights and dignity is crucial for building trust in AI systems. The cultural dimensions of AI are complex, encompassing sociological perspectives and ethical considerations. Recognizing and addressing these dimensions is essential for responsible, inclusive AI innovation that respects cultural diversity, promotes societal well-being, and upholds universal ethical principles. Engaging in cross-cultural dialogue can help stakeholders navigate the complexities of AI development and deployment in an interconnected world(Rahamathunnisa et al., 2024; Vijayakumar et al., 2024).

THE INTERSECTION OF AI AND HR PRACTICES IN SUSTAINABLE ENTREPRENEURSHIP

The integration of Artificial Intelligence (AI) into Human Resources (HR) practices in sustainable entrepreneurship can drive innovation, improve efficiency, and promote sustainability. This can optimize talent management, enhance employee well-being, and align organizational objectives with sustainability goals(Bickley et al., 2021). However, challenges like ethics, privacy, and human-centric design must be addressed to fully realize AI-driven HR technologies' benefits as shown in Figure 2.

Figure 2. Intersection of AI and HR practices in sustainable entrepreneurship

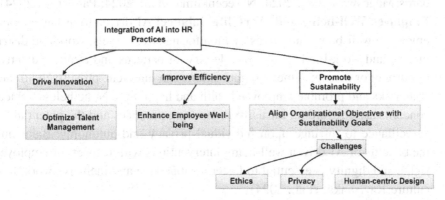

AI-Driven HR Technologies: Opportunities and Challenges

- **Talent Acquisition and Recruitment:** AI-powered tools can streamline the recruitment process by analyzing resumes, screening candidates, and identifying suitable matches based on predefined criteria. This not only saves time and resources but also improves the quality of hiring decisions. However, challenges arise regarding algorithmic bias, as AI systems may inadvertently perpetuate or exacerbate existing biases in recruitment practices. Ensuring fairness and transparency in AI-driven recruitment is essential to mitigate these risks and promote diversity and inclusion(Rahamathunnisa et al., 2024; Venkateswaran et al., 2023).

- **Employee Engagement and Performance Management:** AI-enabled platforms can enhance employee engagement and performance management through personalized feedback, skill development recommendations, and predictive analytics. By leveraging data insights, organizations can identify factors influencing employee productivity and job satisfaction, leading to more effective talent development strategies. Nevertheless, concerns related to data privacy and employee autonomy must be addressed to maintain trust and respect for individual rights in the workplace.

- **Workforce Planning and Optimization:** AI algorithms can forecast workforce needs, identify skill gaps, and optimize resource allocation to maximize operational efficiency and productivity. By analyzing historical data and real-time metrics, organizations can make informed decisions about staffing levels, training initiatives, and succession planning. However, ethical considerations arise regarding the use of employee data for predictive analytics and algorithmic decision-making, necessitating robust data governance frameworks and stakeholder engagement to uphold privacy and fairness standards(Mageswari et al., 2024; Naveeenkumar et al., 2024; Paul et al., 2024).

- **Employee Well-being and Work-life Balance:** AI-driven tools can support employee well-being initiatives by monitoring stress levels, workload distribution, and work-life balance. By identifying patterns and trends indicative of burnout or disengagement, organizations can intervene proactively to mitigate risks and promote employee health and happiness. Nonetheless, ethical concerns arise regarding intrusive monitoring practices and the potential for surveillance to infringe upon individual privacy and autonomy. Balancing the benefits of AI-driven well-being interventions with respect for employee rights and dignity is essential to foster a supportive and inclusive workplace culture(Ravisankar et al., 2024).

The integration of AI and HR practices in sustainable entrepreneurship presents both opportunities and challenges. AI-driven HR technologies can improve organizational performance, talent management, and employee well-being, but also raise ethical concerns about fairness, transparency, and privacy. Sustainable entrepreneurs can use AI to create positive social and environmental impacts, foster innovation, and promote inclusivity in the workplace through a human-centric approach(Rafiq et al., 2023). AI integration in HR practices can enhance efficiency, promote inclusivity, and improve employee well-being, but it's crucial to balance privacy, autonomy, and efficiency to ensure ethical and sustainable outcomes, as businesses strive to align operations with sustainability goals(Agrawal et al., 2023; Boopathi, 2024a).

The integration of AI and HR practices can significantly enhance sustainable entrepreneurship by optimizing talent management, promoting inclusivity, and promoting ethical HR practices. However, this requires a delicate balance between privacy protection, employee autonomy, and operational efficiency, guided by ethical principles and a commitment to sustainable development goals(de Andreis et al., 2024; Lüdeke-Freund, 2020).

Implications for Sustainable Entrepreneurship Development

- **Optimizing Talent Acquisition and Management:** AI-powered tools can streamline the recruitment process by analyzing resumes, screening candidates, and predicting job fit. By identifying diverse talent pools and reducing unconscious biases in hiring decisions, AI-driven HR practices contribute to building inclusive and sustainable workforces(Naveeenkumar et al., 2024; Paul et al., 2024; Vanitha et al., 2023).
- **Enhancing Employee Engagement and Retention:** AI-enabled systems can personalize learning and development opportunities, track employee performance, and provide real-time feedback. By fostering a culture of continuous learning and growth, sustainable entrepreneurship can nurture talent retention and cultivate a motivated workforce committed to organizational goals.
- **Promoting Workforce Diversity and Inclusion:** AI algorithms can help identify and mitigate biases in performance evaluations, promotion decisions, and team assignments. By promoting fairness and equity in HR practices, sustainable entrepreneurship can leverage diverse perspectives and talents to drive innovation and creativity.

Balancing Privacy, Autonomy, and Efficiency in AI-Driven HR

- **Privacy Protection:** AI-driven HR systems must prioritize data privacy and security to safeguard employee information. Implementing robust data protection measures, such as encryption, access controls, and anonymization techniques, ensures compliance with privacy regulations and fosters trust among employees.
- **Respecting Employee Autonomy:** While AI can automate routine tasks and streamline processes, it should not infringe upon employees' autonomy or decision-making authority. Sustainable entrepreneurship values employee empowerment and participation, emphasizing the importance of transparent communication and consultation in AI implementation.
- **Ensuring Ethical AI Use:** Ethical considerations, such as algorithmic bias and fairness, require careful attention in AI-driven HR practices. Regular audits, bias detection tools, and diverse stakeholder engagement can help identify and address ethical concerns, ensuring that AI benefits employees while upholding ethical standards.

LEVERAGING AI FOR SUSTAINABLE ENTREPRENEURSHIP DEVELOPMENT

Artificial Intelligence (AI) can significantly improve efficiency and innovation in sustainable entrepreneurship. By utilizing AI in various business operations, entrepreneurs can drive growth, optimize resource utilization, and create value for society and the environment(Terán-Yépez et al., 2020).

Figure 3. Process of utilizing AI for sustainable entrepreneurship development

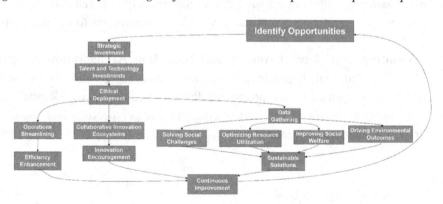

Figure 3 illustrates the process of utilizing AI for sustainable entrepreneurship development, which involves strategic investment, talent and technology investments, and ethical deployment. This leads to data gathering, operations streamlining, and collaborative innovation ecosystems. This approach addresses social and environmental challenges, optimizes resource utilization, improves social welfare, and drives positive environmental outcomes. The cycle continues with continuous improvement(Binder & Belz, 2015).

Leveraging AI for sustainable entrepreneurship development offers significant potential for enhancing efficiency and innovation. By utilizing AI technologies, entrepreneurs can streamline operations, gather data, and foster collaborative innovation ecosystems. However, achieving full potential requires strategic investment, ongoing talent and technology investments, and ethical deployment. AI-driven innovations can address social and environmental challenges, optimize resource utilization, improve social welfare, and drive positive environmental outcomes. Thus, a strategic approach, ongoing investment, and ethical deployment are crucial for achieving sustainable development goals(Binder & Belz, 2015; Sarango-Lalangui et al., 2018).

Enhancing Efficiency Through AI

- Streamlining Operations: AI-powered automation can streamline routine tasks, such as data entry, scheduling, and administrative processes, freeing up time for entrepreneurs to focus on strategic decision-making and value-added activities. By reducing manual labor and improving operational efficiency, AI enables entrepreneurs to allocate resources more effectively and drive productivity gains.
- Predictive Analytics: AI algorithms can analyze vast datasets to identify patterns, trends, and insights that inform decision-making and resource allocation. Predictive analytics enable entrepreneurs to anticipate market demand, optimize inventory management, and mitigate risks, leading to more informed and proactive business strategies.
- Personalized Customer Experiences: AI-driven personalization tools enable entrepreneurs to tailor products, services, and marketing campaigns to individual customer preferences and behaviors. By delivering personalized experiences, entrepreneurs can enhance customer satisfaction, loyalty, and retention, driving sustainable revenue growth and long-term success.

Fostering Innovation Through AI

- Data-Driven Innovation: AI facilitates innovation by unlocking the value of data and generating actionable insights. By analyzing customer feedback, market trends, and competitor activities, entrepreneurs can identify new opportunities, develop innovative solutions, and differentiate themselves in the marketplace(Ahamed et al., 2024; Boopathi & Khang, 2023; Kumara et al., 2023).

- Rapid Prototyping and Iteration: AI-powered tools, such as generative design and virtual prototyping, accelerate the product development cycle by enabling rapid prototyping, simulation, and iteration. Entrepreneurs can experiment with different design options, optimize performance, and reduce time-to-market, fostering agility and innovation in product development(Gift et al., 2024; Senthil et al., 2023).

- Collaborative Innovation Ecosystems: AI platforms facilitate collaboration and knowledge sharing among entrepreneurs, researchers, and stakeholders, enabling the co-creation of innovative solutions to complex challenges. By leveraging AI-driven collaboration tools, entrepreneurs can tap into diverse expertise, access cutting-edge technologies, and accelerate the pace of innovation.

Addressing Social and Environmental Challenges

- AI-powered predictive analytics and optimization algorithms enable entrepreneurs to optimize resource allocation, minimize waste, and enhance operational efficiency. From energy management to supply chain optimization, AI-driven solutions help businesses reduce their environmental footprint while maximizing economic value.

- AI-based data analytics tools facilitate the measurement and evaluation of social impact metrics, allowing entrepreneurs to track progress towards sustainability goals and demonstrate accountability to stakeholders. By quantifying social outcomes and identifying areas for improvement, AI empowers entrepreneurs to drive positive change and foster inclusive growth(Rahamathunnisa et al., 2023; Reddy et al., 2023).

- AI-driven social listening and sentiment analysis tools enable entrepreneurs to better understand community needs, preferences, and concerns. By engaging with stakeholders and soliciting feedback through AI-powered platforms, entrepreneurs can co-create solutions that address local challenges and build trust within communities.

Scaling Impact: AI-Driven Solutions for Sustainable Growth

- AI enables entrepreneurs to scale their impact by automating processes, personalizing customer experiences, and expanding market reach. Whether through AI-driven marketing campaigns, personalized recommendations, or automated customer service, entrepreneurs can leverage technology to reach new audiences and drive sustainable growth.

- AI-powered predictive analytics empower entrepreneurs to make data-driven decisions that drive business growth while minimizing risks. By analyzing market trends, consumer behavior, and competitive dynamics, entrepreneurs can anticipate market opportunities, adapt strategies, and capitalize on emerging trends for sustainable entrepreneurship development.
- AI facilitates collaboration and knowledge sharing within entrepreneurial ecosystems, enabling entrepreneurs to leverage collective intelligence and co-innovate with partners, suppliers, and stakeholders. By fostering an open innovation culture and embracing AI-enabled collaboration platforms, entrepreneurs can amplify their impact and drive systemic change towards sustainability(Janardhana et al., 2023).

AI can be used for sustainable entrepreneurship to tackle social and environmental challenges, promoting sustainable growth. By optimizing resource utilization, measuring social impact, and fostering collaboration, entrepreneurs can create innovative ventures that generate economic value and contribute to a sustainable, inclusive future. As AI evolves, entrepreneurs must remain ethical and committed to positive social and environmental outcomes.

SOCIOCULTURAL PERSPECTIVES ON ETHICAL AI AND SUSTAINABLE ENTREPRENEURSHIP

Sociocultural perspectives are essential for understanding the sociocultural dimensions of ethical AI, which are crucial for promoting sustainable entrepreneurship that aligns with societal values and norms, shaping ethical frameworks for AI-driven entrepreneurship(Bickley et al., 2021).

Figure 4. Sociocultural perspectives on ethical AI and sustainable entrepreneurship

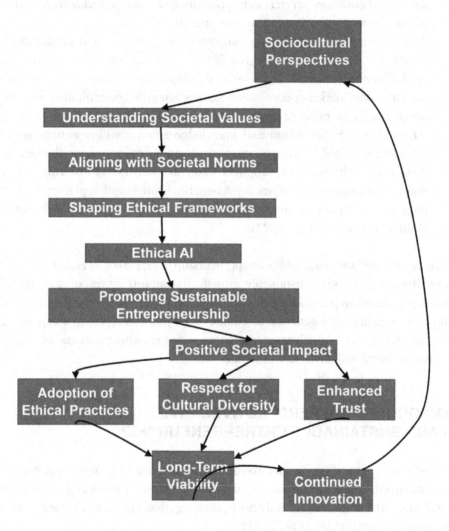

Figure 4 illustrates the connection between sociocultural perspectives, ethical AI, and sustainable entrepreneurship. It highlights the importance of understanding societal values and norms to create ethical frameworks for AI-driven entrepreneurship. Ethical AI practices promote sustainable entrepreneurship by fostering positive societal impact, respecting cultural diversity, and enhancing trust, ensuring its long-term viability.

Ethical Frameworks for AI-Driven Entrepreneurship

Sociocultural perspectives offer valuable insights into ethical frameworks for AI-driven entrepreneurship, emphasizing transparency, fairness, privacy, human-centered design, sustainability, and social responsibility. By embracing these principles, entrepreneurs can develop AI technologies that drive innovation, economic growth, and contribute to a more equitable, inclusive, and sustainable future. By embracing inclusivity, diversity, social responsibility, and environmental stewardship, entrepreneurs can harness AI's potential for positive change and sustainable development(Méndez-Picazo et al., 2021).

- **Transparency and Accountability:** Ethical AI-driven entrepreneurship requires transparency and accountability in algorithmic decision-making processes. Entrepreneurs must ensure that AI systems are transparently designed, documented, and auditable, enabling stakeholders to understand how decisions are made and hold responsible parties accountable for their outcomes.
- **Fairness and Equity:** Ethical AI-driven entrepreneurship prioritizes fairness and equity in the distribution of opportunities, resources, and outcomes. Entrepreneurs should mitigate biases in AI algorithms and decision-making processes to prevent discrimination and promote inclusive growth. This involves considering diverse perspectives, experiences, and needs to design AI systems that serve the interests of all stakeholders fairly.
- **Privacy and Data Protection:** Respecting individuals' privacy rights and ensuring data protection are essential ethical considerations in AI-driven entrepreneurship. Entrepreneurs must collect, store, and use data responsibly, with consent and privacy safeguards in place to protect individuals' rights and confidentiality. This involves implementing robust data security measures, anonymization techniques, and privacy-enhancing technologies to minimize the risk of data breaches and unauthorized access(Sonia et al., 2024).
- **Human-Centered Design:** Ethical AI-driven entrepreneurship prioritizes human-centered design principles that prioritize the well-being, autonomy, and dignity of individuals. Entrepreneurs should engage with diverse stakeholders, including employees, customers, and communities, to understand their needs, values, and preferences and incorporate them into the design and deployment of AI technologies. This involves fostering participatory design processes, user feedback loops, and continuous improvement efforts to ensure that AI systems serve human interests and contribute to societal welfare.
- **Sustainability and Social Responsibility:** Ethical AI-driven entrepreneurship embraces sustainability and social responsibility as core values guiding business practices. Entrepreneurs should consider the environmental, social,

and economic impacts of AI technologies throughout their lifecycle, from development and deployment to decommissioning. This involves adopting principles of sustainable design, responsible sourcing, and circular economy practices to minimize environmental footprint and maximize positive societal impact.

Promoting Inclusivity and Diversity in AI Ecosystems

Inclusive AI ecosystems promote diversity and representation in all stages of technology development, from design to deployment. Entrepreneurs can mitigate biases and ensure AI benefits society by engaging diverse voices and perspectives. Collaborating with marginalized communities, underrepresented groups, and civil society organizations fosters inclusive co-creation and co-design processes(Yang et al., 2022). Promoting diversity in AI talent pipelines, educational programs, and recruitment practices enhances resilience and creativity in AI ecosystems. Entrepreneurs can contribute by investing in initiatives supporting women, minorities, and underprivileged individuals in AI careers. Recognizing and valuing diverse perspectives enhances innovation, fosters empathy, and addresses societal challenges sustainably and ethically.

Social Responsibility and Environmental Stewardship in AI Development

Ethical AI development goes beyond technical aspects to consider social, environmental, and ethical implications. Sustainable entrepreneurship emphasizes social responsibility and environmental stewardship in AI development, ensuring technological innovation contributes to societal well-being and environmental sustainability. Entrepreneurs must consider the social and environmental impacts of AI technologies throughout their lifecycle(Sarango-Lalangui et al., 2018). Ethical principles in AI algorithms and decision-making processes can boost trust and legitimacy among stakeholders. Entrepreneurs can identify potential risks and mitigate them through impact assessments and community engagement. Sustainable entrepreneurship prioritizes environmental sustainability, minimizing energy consumption and carbon emissions. Green AI principles, such as energy-efficient algorithms and renewable energy sources, can help mitigate the environmental impact of AI technologies and contribute to climate change mitigation efforts(Jeya et al., 2023).

Sociocultural perspectives are crucial in ethical AI and sustainable entrepreneurship, shaping values and practices that prioritize inclusivity, diversity, social responsibility, and environmental stewardship. By embracing these perspectives, entrepreneurs can harness AI's transformative potential for positive change, innovation, and a sustainable future. This requires collaboration, cross-sector partnerships, and ethical leadership in AI development.

INTERDISCIPLINARY COLLABORATION FOR CULTURALLY SENSITIVE AI ENTREPRENEURSHIP

Interdisciplinary collaboration between sociology, HR, and AI entrepreneurship is crucial for developing culturally sensitive AI solutions that respect diversity, promote inclusivity, and foster sustainable development, thereby bridging the gap between these disciplines(Obschonka & Audretsch, 2020).

Figure 5. Interdisciplinary collaboration for culturally sensitive AI entrepreneurship

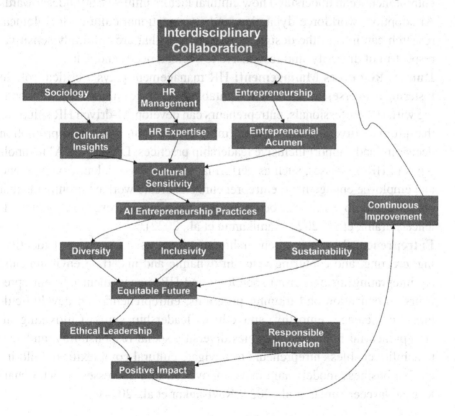

Figure 5 illustrates how the collaboration between sociology, HR management, and entrepreneurship leads to the development of culturally sensitive AI entrepreneurship practices. It starts with each discipline contributing its expertise: sociology provides cultural insights, HR management offers expertise in managing diversity and inclusivity, and entrepreneurship brings entrepreneurial acumen. These inputs combine to create AI entrepreneurship practices that promote diversity, inclusivity, and sustainability, contributing to a more equitable future. This requires ethical leadership and responsible innovation, ultimately leading to positive impact and continuous improvement.

Bridging the Gap Between Sociology, HR, and Entrepreneurship

- **Sociological Perspectives:** Sociology provides valuable insights into the social dynamics, cultural norms, and power structures that shape human behavior and interactions. By drawing on sociological theories and methodologies, entrepreneurs can understand how cultural factors influence attitudes towards AI adoption, workforce dynamics, and organizational culture. Sociological research can inform the design of AI solutions that are culturally sensitive, respectful of diversity, and responsive to societal needs and values.
- **Human Resources Management:** HR management plays a critical role in fostering a diverse, inclusive, and equitable workplace culture. By collaborating with HR professionals, entrepreneurs can develop AI-driven HR solutions that promote diversity recruitment, mitigate biases in hiring and promotion decisions, and support inclusive leadership practices. Leveraging AI technologies in HR processes, such as performance evaluation, talent development, and employee engagement, entrepreneurs can create work environments that empower employees, foster belongingness, and enhance organizational resilience(Puranik et al., 2024; Samikannu et al., 2022).
- **Entrepreneurship:** Entrepreneurship encompasses the process of identifying, creating, and capturing value in dynamic and uncertain environments. By integrating insights from sociology and HR management into entrepreneurship education and training programs, entrepreneurs can develop cultural competence, empathy, and ethical leadership skills. Cultivating an entrepreneurial mindset that values diversity, social responsibility, and sustainability enables entrepreneurs to navigate cultural complexities, build inclusive business models, and drive innovation that addresses societal challenges(Naveeenkumar et al., 2024; Ravisankar et al., 2024).

Interdisciplinary collaboration between sociology, HR management, and entrepreneurship is crucial for developing culturally sensitive AI entrepreneurship practices. By combining sociological insights, HR expertise, and entrepreneurial acumen, entrepreneurs can create AI solutions that promote diversity, inclusivity, and sustainability, contributing to a more equitable future. This requires ethical leadership and responsible innovation(Chowdhury et al., 2023; Zaheer et al., 2019).

Strategies for Interdisciplinary Collaboration

- **Cross-disciplinary Research and Education:** Establishing collaborative research initiatives and educational programs that bring together scholars, practitioners, and students from sociology, HR management, and entrepreneurship fosters interdisciplinary learning and knowledge exchange. By creating opportunities for interdisciplinary dialogue, collaboration, and co-creation, entrepreneurs can develop holistic perspectives and innovative solutions that integrate sociocultural insights into AI entrepreneurship practices.
- **Stakeholder Engagement and Co-creation:** Engaging diverse stakeholders, including community members, industry partners, policymakers, and advocacy groups, in the AI entrepreneurship process ensures that AI solutions are responsive to cultural needs, values, and preferences. By adopting participatory approaches that prioritize co-creation and co-design, entrepreneurs can build trust, legitimacy, and acceptance for AI technologies within culturally diverse communities.
- **Ethical and Responsible AI Deployment:** Integrating ethical principles, such as fairness, transparency, and accountability, into AI entrepreneurship practices ensures that AI technologies uphold human rights, privacy, and autonomy across diverse cultural contexts. By adhering to ethical guidelines and standards in AI development, entrepreneurs can mitigate risks, build resilience, and foster trust among stakeholders, laying the foundation for sustainable and socially responsible AI entrepreneurship.

Co-Creating Solutions Through Multidisciplinary Partnerships

Multidisciplinary partnerships are crucial in today's complex business environment for co-creating innovative and sustainable solutions. These partnerships involve experts from various fields, allowing entrepreneurs to leverage complementary expertise and perspectives(Zaheer et al., 2019).

Strategies for Co-Creating Solutions

- **Identifying Stakeholders:** Engage stakeholders from various disciplines, industries, and sectors who have a vested interest in addressing the problem or opportunity at hand. This may include researchers, policymakers, community leaders, NGOs, and industry professionals.

- **Facilitating Collaboration:** Create platforms and spaces for collaborative problem-solving, such as workshops, hackathons, and innovation labs. Encourage open dialogue, knowledge sharing, and creative brainstorming sessions to generate novel ideas and approaches.
- **Promoting Diversity and Inclusion:** Embrace diversity in terms of expertise, background, and perspectives to foster innovation and avoid groupthink. Ensure that all voices are heard and valued, including those from underrepresented or marginalized communities.
- **Iterative Design Process:** Adopt an iterative approach to solution development, where ideas are tested, refined, and improved through feedback loops and continuous iteration. Encourage experimentation and learning from both successes and failures along the way.
- **Shared Vision and Goals:** Establish a shared vision and common goals that align with the values and objectives of all stakeholders involved. Foster a sense of ownership and commitment to the collaborative endeavor to sustain momentum and drive collective action.

Benefits of Multidisciplinary Partnerships

- **Innovation and Creativity:** By bringing together diverse perspectives and expertise, multidisciplinary partnerships fuel innovation and creativity, leading to breakthrough solutions that address complex challenges from multiple angles.
- **Holistic Problem-solving:** Multidisciplinary teams are better equipped to tackle complex, interconnected issues by considering various factors, including technological feasibility, social implications, economic viability, and environmental sustainability.
- **Stakeholder Engagement and Buy-in:** Involving stakeholders from different disciplines and sectors increases buy-in and support for the solution, as it reflects a more comprehensive understanding of the problem and a broader range of interests and concerns.
- **Robust Implementation:** Solutions co-created through multidisciplinary partnerships are more likely to be robust and effective, as they have been vetted, refined, and validated by a diverse set of stakeholders with different perspectives and expertise.

Towards a Holistic Approach to AI-Driven Sustainable Entrepreneurship

Sustainable entrepreneurship using AI necessitates a comprehensive approach that integrates technological innovation with social, environmental, and economic factors, enabling entrepreneurs to create value for stakeholders, minimize negative impacts, and promote long-term sustainability(Yang et al., 2022).

Components of a Holistic Approach

- **Triple Bottom Line:** Embrace the triple bottom line framework, which considers not only financial performance but also social impact and environmental stewardship. Strive for balance and synergy among economic, social, and environmental goals to create sustainable value for all stakeholders.
- **Ethical AI Principles:** Uphold ethical principles in AI development and deployment, such as fairness, transparency, accountability, and privacy protection. Ensure that AI technologies are used responsibly and ethically, with due consideration for their potential impacts on individuals, communities, and society as a whole(Boopathi & Khang, 2023).
- **Systems Thinking:** Adopt a system thinking approach to understand the interconnectedness and interdependence of various components within the entrepreneurial ecosystem. Consider the broader context and systemic effects of AI-driven interventions, including unintended consequences and feedback loops.
- **Long-term Perspective:** Take a long-term perspective on sustainability, considering the cumulative impacts of entrepreneurial activities over time. Strive for resilience, adaptability, and regenerative capacity to withstand environmental shocks and disruptions while fostering continuous innovation and growth.
- **Collaborative Partnerships:** Foster collaborative partnerships with stakeholders across sectors and disciplines to leverage collective expertise, resources, and networks. Embrace open innovation and co-creation practices to develop sustainable solutions that address complex challenges holistically.

Benefits of a Holistic Approach

This emphasizes the importance of co-creating solutions through multidisciplinary partnerships and adopting a holistic approach to AI-driven sustainable entrepreneurship in today's interconnected world. By embracing collaboration, innovation, and ethical leadership, entrepreneurs can harness AI for a more inclusive, equitable, and sustainable future(Terán-Yépez et al., 2020).

- **Sustainable Value Creation:** A holistic approach to AI-driven entrepreneurship enables entrepreneurs to create sustainable value for all stakeholders, including shareholders, employees, customers, communities, and the environment.
- **Risk Mitigation:** By considering social and environmental risks alongside economic factors, entrepreneurs can identify and mitigate potential risks and vulnerabilities, enhancing the resilience and sustainability of their ventures.
- **Reputation and Trust:** Adopting ethical AI principles and demonstrating a commitment to sustainability builds trust and credibility with customers, investors, and other stakeholders, enhancing the reputation and long-term viability of the entrepreneurial venture.
- **Market Differentiation:** Sustainable entrepreneurship driven by AI can serve as a unique selling proposition, distinguishing the venture in the marketplace and attracting socially conscious consumers, investors, and partners.

FUTURE DIRECTIONS FOR RESEARCH AND INNOVATION

Future research and innovation in AI-driven sustainable entrepreneurship are promising due to technological advancements, ethical considerations, interdisciplinary collaboration, and societal impact, paving the way for transformative change and sustainable development(de Andreis et al., 2024; Lüdeke-Freund, 2020).

Ethical AI Development and Governance: The study explores ethical frameworks, guidelines, and standards for AI development and deployment, innovative AI governance mechanisms for transparency, accountability, and fairness, and explores regulatory approaches and policies to address societal concerns.

Responsible Innovation Practices: The study explores responsible AI innovation methodologies across various industries, develops tools to evaluate social, environmental, and ethical impacts of AI-driven ventures, and integrates sustainability principles into entrepreneurial processes from ideation to scaling.

Interdisciplinary Collaboration: The initiative promotes cross-disciplinary research, partnerships, and collaborative innovation models like co-creation platforms and open-source initiatives, while engaging stakeholders from academia, industry, government, and civil society to foster knowledge exchange and co-design of solutions.

Human-Centered AI Design: The study emphasizes on human-centric design principles to ensure AI technologies align with user needs and values, incorporating user feedback and participatory design approaches for improved usability and inclusivity, and exploring AI applications for empowering individuals and promoting digital literacy(Puranik et al., 2024; Vanitha et al., 2023).

Environmental Sustainability: The initiative focuses on green AI technologies to decrease energy consumption, carbon emissions, and environmental impact, developing AI-driven solutions for environmental monitoring and sustainable resource management, and integrating life cycle assessment and circular economy principles(Boopathi, 2022; Vijaya Lakshmi et al., 2024).

Socio-Economic Impact Assessment: The study examines the socio-economic impacts of AI-driven entrepreneurship on employment, income distribution, and social mobility, explores AI's role in fostering economic resilience, innovation ecosystems, and inclusive growth, and explores AI applications to tackle societal issues like healthcare disparities and education inequities(Rahamathunnisa et al., 2024; Venkateswaran et al., 2024).

Future Technologies and Trends: The future of AI-driven entrepreneurship is predicted to be shaped by emerging technologies like quantum computing, edge computing, and decentralized AI. The implications of AI convergence with disruptive technologies like blockchain, IoT, and biotechnology are also being explored, along with their ethical, legal, and social implications.

Future research in AI-driven sustainable entrepreneurship will involve a holistic approach that combines technological advancements with ethical considerations, interdisciplinary collaboration, and societal impact. This will enable researchers, entrepreneurs, and policymakers to develop AI-driven solutions promoting sustainability, inclusivity, and human well-being.

CONCLUSION

This chapter explores the relationship between artificial intelligence (AI) and sustainable entrepreneurship, highlighting its potential for enhancing efficiency and innovation, promoting ethical AI development, and fostering inclusive growth. It suggests strategies for advancing AI-driven sustainable entrepreneurship, including co-creating solutions through multidisciplinary partnerships, adopting a holistic approach to AI development, and embracing responsible innovation practices. These approaches aim to address complex challenges and create sustainable value in today's interconnected world.

Future research in AI-driven sustainable entrepreneurship will focus on ethical leadership, environmental stewardship, and societal well-being. By embracing collaboration, innovation, and ethical principles, entrepreneurs, researchers, and policymakers can harness AI's transformative potential for a more inclusive, equitable, and sustainable future. This paradigm shift in business, technology, and society can unlock new opportunities for economic development, social progress, and environmental sustainability, paving the way for a brighter future for generations to come.

REFERENCES

Agrawal, A. V., Pitchai, R., Senthamaraikannan, C., Balaji, N. A., Sajithra, S., & Boopathi, S. (2023). Digital Education System During the COVID-19 Pandemic. In *Using Assistive Technology for Inclusive Learning in K-12 Classrooms* (pp. 104–126). IGI Global. 10.4018/978-1-6684-6424-3.ch005

Ahamed, B. S., Chakravarthy, K. S., Arputhabalan, J., Sasirekha, K., Prince, R. M. R., Boopathi, S., & Muthuvel, S. (2024). Revolutionizing Friction Stir Welding With AI-Integrated Humanoid Robots. In *Advances in Computational Intelligence and Robotics* (pp. 120–144). IGI Global. 10.4018/979-8-3693-2399-1.ch005

Bickley, S. J., Macintyre, A., & Torgler, B. (2021). Artificial intelligence and big data in sustainable entrepreneurship. *Journal of Economic Surveys*.

Binder, J. K., & Belz, F.-M. (2015). Sustainable entrepreneurship: What it is. In *Handbook of entrepreneurship and sustainable development research* (pp. 30–72). Edward Elgar Publishing. 10.4337/9781849808248.00010

Boopathi, S. (2022). Cryogenically treated and untreated stainless steel grade 317 in sustainable wire electrical discharge machining process: A comparative study. *Springer :Environmental Science and Pollution Research*, 1–10.

Boopathi, S. (2024a). Digital HR Implementation for Business Growth in Industrial 5.0. In *Convergence of Human Resources Technologies and Industry 5.0* (pp. 1–22). IGI Global. 10.4018/979-8-3693-1343-5.ch001

Boopathi, S. (2024b). Sustainable Development Using IoT and AI Techniques for Water Utilization in Agriculture. In *Sustainable Development in AI, Blockchain, and E-Governance Applications* (pp. 204–228). IGI Global. 10.4018/979-8-3693-1722-8.ch012

Boopathi, S., & Khang, A. (2023). AI-Integrated Technology for a Secure and Ethical Healthcare Ecosystem. In *AI and IoT-Based Technologies for Precision Medicine* (pp. 36–59). IGI Global. 10.4018/979-8-3693-0876-9.ch003

Chowdhury, S., Dey, P., Joel-Edgar, S., Bhattacharya, S., Rodriguez-Espindola, O., Abadie, A., & Truong, L. (2023). Unlocking the value of artificial intelligence in human resource management through AI capability framework. *Human Resource Management Review*, 33(1), 100899. 10.1016/j.hrmr.2022.100899

Das, S., Lekhya, G., Shreya, K., Shekinah, K. L., Babu, K. K., & Boopathi, S. (2024). Fostering Sustainability Education Through Cross-Disciplinary Collaborations and Research Partnerships: Interdisciplinary Synergy. In *Facilitating Global Collaboration and Knowledge Sharing in Higher Education With Generative AI* (pp. 60–88). IGI Global.

de Andreis, F., Comite, U., Gallo, A. M., Andone, D. M., & Ciaschi, G. (2024). Social business, artificial intelligence, and sustainability: An integrated approach for the future. *Sustainable Economies, 2*(1).

Di Vaio, A., Palladino, R., Hassan, R., & Escobar, O. (2020). Artificial intelligence and business models in the sustainable development goals perspective: A systematic literature review. *Journal of Business Research*, 121, 283–314. 10.1016/j.jbusres.2020.08.019

Gift, M. D. M., Senthil, T. S., Hasan, D. S., Alagarraja, K., Jayaseelan, P., & Boopathi, S. (2024). Additive Manufacturing and 3D Printing Innovations: Revolutionizing Industry 5.0. In *Technological Advancements in Data Processing for Next Generation Intelligent Systems* (pp. 255–287). IGI Global. 10.4018/979-8-3693-0968-1.ch010

Goralski, M. A., & Tan, T. K. (2020). Artificial intelligence and sustainable development. *International Journal of Management Education*, 18(1), 100330. 10.1016/j.ijme.2019.100330

Gupta, B. B., Gaurav, A., Panigrahi, P. K., & Arya, V. (2023). Analysis of artificial intelligence-based technologies and approaches on sustainable entrepreneurship. *Technological Forecasting and Social Change*, 186, 122152. 10.1016/j.techfore.2022.122152

Isensee, C., Griese, K.-M., & Teuteberg, F. (2021). Sustainable artificial intelligence: A corporate culture perspective. *Sustainability Management Forum| Nachhaltigkeits-ManagementForum, 29*(3), 217–230.

Janardhana, K., Singh, V., Singh, S. N., Babu, T. R., Bano, S., & Boopathi, S. (2023). Utilization Process for Electronic Waste in Eco-Friendly Concrete: Experimental Study. In *Sustainable Approaches and Strategies for E-Waste Management and Utilization* (pp. 204–223). IGI Global.

Jeya, R., Venkatakrishnan, G. R., Rengaraj, R., Rajalakshmi, M., Pradeep Mohan Kumar, K., & Boopathi, S. (2023). Water Resource Managements in Soil and Soilless Irrigation Systems Using AI Techniques. In *Advances in Environmental Engineering and Green Technologies* (pp. 245–266). IGI Global. 10.4018/979-8-3693-0338-2.ch014

Kulkov, I., Kulkova, J., Rohrbeck, R., Menvielle, L., Kaartemo, V., & Makkonen, H. (2023). Artificial intelligence-driven sustainable development: Examining organizational, technical, and processing approaches to achieving global goals. *Sustainable Development*.

Kumar, P. R., Meenakshi, S., Shalini, S., Devi, S. R., & Boopathi, S. (2023). Soil Quality Prediction in Context Learning Approaches Using Deep Learning and Blockchain for Smart Agriculture. In *Effective AI, Blockchain, and E-Governance Applications for Knowledge Discovery and Management* (pp. 1–26). IGI Global. 10.4018/978-1-6684-9151-5.ch001

Kumara, V., & Sharma, M. D., Samson Isaac, J., Saravanan, S., Suganthi, D., & Boopathi, S. (2023). An AI-Integrated Green Power Monitoring System: Empowering Small and Medium Enterprises. In *Advances in Environmental Engineering and Green Technologies* (pp. 218–244). IGI Global. 10.4018/979-8-3693-0338-2.ch013

Lüdeke-Freund, F. (2020). Sustainable entrepreneurship, innovation, and business models: Integrative framework and propositions for future research. *Business Strategy and the Environment*, 29(2), 665–681. 10.1002/bse.2396

Mageswari, D. U., Kareemullah, H., Jithesh, K., Boopathi, S., Rachel, P. M. P. P., & Ramkumar, M. S. (2024). Experimental investigation of mechanical properties and multi-objective optimization of electronic, glass, and ceramic waste–mixed concrete. *Environmental Science and Pollution Research International*. 10.1007/s11356-024-33751-738806982

Maguluri, L. P., Ananth, J., Hariram, S., Geetha, C., Bhaskar, A., & Boopathi, S. (2023). Smart Vehicle-Emissions Monitoring System Using Internet of Things (IoT). In *Handbook of Research on Safe Disposal Methods of Municipal Solid Wastes for a Sustainable Environment* (pp. 191–211). IGI Global.

Mamedov, O., Tumanyan, Y., Ishchenko-Padukova, O., & Movchan, I. (2018). Sustainable economic development and post-economy of artificial intelligence. *Entrep. Sustain*, 2018(2), 6. 10.9770/jesi.2018.6.2(37)

Méndez-Picazo, M.-T., Galindo-Martín, M.-A., & Castaño-Martínez, M.-S. (2021). Effects of sociocultural and economic factors on social entrepreneurship and sustainable development. *Journal of Innovation & Knowledge*, 6(2), 69–77. 10.1016/j.jik.2020.06.001

Mhlanga, D. (2021). Artificial intelligence in the industry 4.0, and its impact on poverty, innovation, infrastructure development, and the sustainable development goals: Lessons from emerging economies? *Sustainability (Basel)*, 13(11), 5788. 10.3390/su13115788

Naveeenkumar, N., Rallapalli, S., Sasikala, K., Priya, P. V., Husain, J., & Boopathi, S. (2024). Enhancing Consumer Behavior and Experience Through AI-Driven Insights Optimization. In *AI Impacts in Digital Consumer Behavior* (pp. 1–35). IGI Global. 10.4018/979-8-3693-1918-5.ch001

Obschonka, M., & Audretsch, D. B. (2020). Artificial intelligence and big data in entrepreneurship: A new era has begun. *Small Business Economics*, 55(3), 529–539. 10.1007/s11187-019-00202-4

Pachiappan, K., Anitha, K., Pitchai, R., Sangeetha, S., Satyanarayana, T., & Boopathi, S. (2024). Intelligent Machines, IoT, and AI in Revolutionizing Agriculture for Water Processing. In *Handbook of Research on AI and ML for Intelligent Machines and Systems* (pp. 374–399). IGI Global.

Paul, A., & Thilagham, K. KG, J.-, Reddy, P. R., Sathyamurthy, R., & Boopathi, S. (2024). Multi-criteria Optimization on Friction Stir Welding of Aluminum Composite (AA5052-H32/B4C) using Titanium Nitride Coated Tool. *Engineering Research Express*.

Pratono, A. H. (2022). Reinterpreting excellence for sustainable competitive advantage: The role of entrepreneurial culture under information technological turbulence. *Measuring Business Excellence*, 26(2), 180–196. 10.1108/MBE-04-2021-0056

Puranik, T. A., Shaik, N., Vankudoth, R., Kolhe, M. R., Yadav, N., & Boopathi, S. (2024). Study on Harmonizing Human-Robot (Drone) Collaboration: Navigating Seamless Interactions in Collaborative Environments. In *Cybersecurity Issues and Challenges in the Drone Industry* (pp. 1–26). IGI Global.

Rafiq, M., Farrukh, M., Mushtaq, R., & Dastane, O. (2023). *Exploring the Intersection of AI and Human Resources Management*. IGI Global. 10.4018/979-8-3693-0039-8

Rahamathunnisa, U., Sudhakar, K., Murugan, T. K., Thivaharan, S., Rajkumar, M., & Boopathi, S. (2023). Cloud Computing Principles for Optimizing Robot Task Offloading Processes. In *AI-Enabled Social Robotics in Human Care Services* (pp. 188–211). IGI Global. 10.4018/978-1-6684-8171-4.ch007

Rahamathunnisa, U., Sudhakar, K., Padhi, S., Bhattacharya, S., Shashibhushan, G., & Boopathi, S. (2024). Sustainable Energy Generation From Waste Water: IoT Integrated Technologies. In *Adoption and Use of Technology Tools and Services by Economically Disadvantaged Communities: Implications for Growth and Sustainability* (pp. 225–256). IGI Global.

Ravisankar, A., Shanthi, A., Lavanya, S., Ramaratnam, M., Krishnamoorthy, V., & Boopathi, S. (2024). Harnessing 6G for Consumer-Centric Business Strategies Across Electronic Industries. In *AI Impacts in Digital Consumer Behavior* (pp. 241–270). IGI Global.

Reddy, M. A., Reddy, B. M., Mukund, C., Venneti, K., Preethi, D., & Boopathi, S. (2023). Social Health Protection During the COVID-Pandemic Using IoT. In *The COVID-19 Pandemic and the Digitalization of Diplomacy* (pp. 204–235). IGI Global. 10.4018/978-1-7998-8394-4.ch009

Samikannu, R., Koshariya, A. K., Poornima, E., Ramesh, S., Kumar, A., & Boopathi, S. (2022). Sustainable Development in Modern Aquaponics Cultivation Systems Using IoT Technologies. In *Human Agro-Energy Optimization for Business and Industry* (pp. 105–127). IGI Global.

Sarango-Lalangui, P., Santos, J. L. S., & Hormiga, E. (2018). The development of sustainable entrepreneurship research field. *Sustainability (Basel)*, 10(6), 2005. 10.3390/su10062005

Senthil, T., Puviyarasan, M., Babu, S. R., Surakasi, R., Sampath, B., & Associates. (2023). Industrial Robot-Integrated Fused Deposition Modelling for the 3D Printing Process. In *Development, Properties, and Industrial Applications of 3D Printed Polymer Composites* (pp. 188–210). IGI Global.

Sharma, D. M., Ramana, K. V., Jothilakshmi, R., Verma, R., Maheswari, B. U., & Boopathi, S. (2024). Integrating Generative AI Into K-12 Curriculums and Pedagogies in India: Opportunities and Challenges. *Facilitating Global Collaboration and Knowledge Sharing in Higher Education With Generative AI.*

Sineviciene, L., Hens, L., Kubatko, O., Melnyk, L., Dehtyarova, I., & Fedyna, S. (2021). Socio-economic and cultural effects of disruptive industrial technologies for sustainable development. *International Journal of Global Energy Issues*, 43(2–3), 284–305. 10.1504/IJGEI.2021.115150

Sonia, R., Gupta, N., Manikandan, K., Hemalatha, R., Kumar, M. J., & Boopathi, S. (2024). Strengthening Security, Privacy, and Trust in Artificial Intelligence Drones for Smart Cities. In *Analyzing and Mitigating Security Risks in Cloud Computing* (pp. 214–242). IGI Global. 10.4018/979-8-3693-3249-8.ch011

Terán-Yépez, E., Marín-Carrillo, G. M., del Pilar Casado-Belmonte, M., & de las Mercedes Capobianco-Uriarte, M. (2020). Sustainable entrepreneurship: Review of its evolution and new trends. *Journal of Cleaner Production*, 252, 119742. 10.1016/j. jclepro.2019.119742

Vanitha, S., Radhika, K., & Boopathi, S. (2023). Artificial Intelligence Techniques in Water Purification and Utilization. In *Human Agro-Energy Optimization for Business and Industry* (pp. 202–218). IGI Global. 10.4018/978-1-6684-4118-3.ch010

Venkateswaran, N., Kiran Kumar, K., Maheswari, K., Kumar Reddy, R. V., & Boopathi, S. (2024). Optimizing IoT Data Aggregation: Hybrid Firefly-Artificial Bee Colony Algorithm for Enhanced Efficiency in Agriculture. *AGRIS On-Line Papers in Economics and Informatics*, 16(1), 117–130. 10.7160/aol.2024.160110

Venkateswaran, N., Vidhya, K., Ayyannan, M., Chavan, S. M., Sekar, K., & Boopathi, S. (2023). A Study on Smart Energy Management Framework Using Cloud Computing. In *5G, Artificial Intelligence, and Next Generation Internet of Things: Digital Innovation for Green and Sustainable Economies* (pp. 189–212). IGI Global. 10.4018/978-1-6684-8634-4.ch009

Vijaya Lakshmi, V., Mishra, M., Kushwah, J. S., Shajahan, U. S., Mohanasundari, M., & Boopathi, S. (2024). Circular Economy Digital Practices for Ethical Dimensions and Policies for Digital Waste Management. In *Harnessing High-Performance Computing and AI for Environmental Sustainability* (pp. 166–193). IGI Global., 10.4018/979-8-3693-1794-5.ch008

Vijayakumar, G. N. S., Domakonda, V. K., Farooq, S., Kumar, B. S., Pradeep, N., & Boopathi, S. (2024). Sustainable Developments in Nano-Fluid Synthesis for Various Industrial Applications. In *Adoption and Use of Technology Tools and Services by Economically Disadvantaged Communities: Implications for Growth and Sustainability* (pp. 48–81). IGI Global.

Wiyata, L. I., & Liu, H. (n.d.). THE POTENTIAL FUTURE OF ARTIFICIAL INLIGENCE IN FOSTERING SUSTAINABLE ENTREPRENEURSHIP WITHIN THE CREATIVE ECONOMY. *Fostering Sustainable Entrepreneurship In Emerging Market: An Interdisciplinary Perspective*, 173.

Yang, C., Lin, C., & Fan, X. (2022). Cultivation model of entrepreneurship from the perspective of artificial intelligence ethics. *Frontiers in Psychology*, 13, 885376. 10.3389/fpsyg.2022.88537635846706

Zaheer, H., Breyer, Y., & Dumay, J. (2019). Digital entrepreneurship: An interdisciplinary structured literature review and research agenda. *Technological Forecasting and Social Change*, 148, 119735. 10.1016/j.techfore.2019.119735

Zhang, H., Song, M., & He, H. (2020). Achieving the success of sustainability development projects through big data analytics and artificial intelligence capability. *Sustainability (Basel)*, 12(3), 949. 10.3390/su12030949

Chapter 11
Digital Strategies for Modern Workplaces and Business Through Artificial Intelligence Techniques

Anurag Vijay Agrawal

https://orcid.org/0000-0002-9753-1216

Department of Electronics and Communication Engineering, J.P. Institute of Engineering and Technology, India

M Bakkiyaraj

https://orcid.org/0000-0001-7917-780X

Department of Mechanical Engineering, Rajalakshmi Institute of Technology, Chennai, India

Simanchala Das

https://orcid.org/0000-0001-6230-0461

K.L. Business School, Koneru Lakshmaiah Education Foundation, Vijayawada, India

C. M. Surendra Reddy

https://orcid.org/0009-0002-0344-3387

Department of Commerce and Management, International Institute of Business Studies, Bengaluru, India

P. B. Narendra Kiran

https://orcid.org/0000-0002-9883-3240

School of Business and Management, Christ University, Bengaluru, India

S. Boopathi

Mechanical Engineering, Muthayammal Engineering College, Namakkal, India

DOI: 10.4018/979-8-3693-2432-5.ch011

ABSTRACT

AI has significantly transformed human resources (HR) by enhancing recruitment, talent acquisition, employee engagement, performance management, learning, and HR analytics. This chapter explores the convergence of HR and AI, highlighting its potential to revolutionize modern workplaces. The recruitment processes have been enhanced by AI in HR strategies such as efficiently identifying top candidates and mitigating unconscious bias. Automated candidate screening, scheduling interviews, and answering frequently asked questions, improving the candidate experience have been done. The personalized learning and development initiatives, delivering targeted training programs, identifying skill gaps, and providing timely feedback have been facilitated. AI-powered systems provide real-time insights into employee performance metrics, enabling proactive feedback. By analyzing vast datasets, AI algorithms can identify patterns and trends, facilitating data-driven decision-making in performance evaluations and goal setting.

INTRODUCTION

Artificial intelligence (AI) and other technological advancements are revolutionizing human resources management. It is anticipated that this paradigm change would completely change the recruitment, development, and retention of people in the digital era. HR has developed from an administrative role to a main collaborator in the success of the firm. HR practitioners now have to deal with a variety of complicated issues related to digital technology, such as changing employee expectations, workforce diversity, and talent scarcity. AI-driven solutions are being used by businesses to improve on established HR procedures and better meet new demands (Biliavska et al., 2022).

AI is transforming HR management by removing tedious processes from the process and extracting insightful information from large databases. It optimizes HR procedures and improves employee experiences by integrating machine learning, natural language processing, and predictive analytics. AI algorithms in talent acquisition and recruiting increase hiring results and shorten the time it takes to fill vacancies. Chatbots powered by AI increase candidate engagement (Wassan & others, 2021).

AI-powered solutions give HR managers data-driven perceptions into workers' attitudes, allowing for focused interventions. To find patterns in employee happiness, they examine social interactions, performance indicators, and feedback. Performance management is being revolutionized by AI technologies, which offer objective evaluations, individualized growth plans, and real-time feedback. Additionally, they provide ongoing behavior analysis and monitoring of staff members, giving managers practical advice on goal-setting, coaching, and career advancement (Zehir et al., 2020).

Challenges include algorithmic bias, data privacy, and ethical ramifications affect AI in HR. Organizations need to upskill HR staff members and create governance structures in order to reduce these risks. AI has the potential to improve hiring, boost worker engagement, and advance performance management. A learning culture, ethical concerns, and a responsible embrace of AI are essential for success. Maintaining competitiveness and being prepared for the future requires investing in training and development (Pereira et al., 2023).

Human resources (HR) departments now play strategic rather than administrative roles in businesses because to the digital revolution. HR used to be primarily concerned with payroll processing, compliance, and people management. On the other hand, employee-centric initiatives, data-driven decision-making, and the incorporation of developing technologies are the results of technological developments. Technology has been adopted by HR departments in an effort to improve employee satisfaction, increase productivity, and expedite procedures. Organizations may now respond more swiftly to shifting business requirements because to the improved transparency, accessibility, and scalability brought forth by digitalization (Arslan et al., 2022).

The digital age has made it possible for HR managers to apply data analytics to comprehend trends and workforce dynamics, finding patterns and predicting indications linked to engagement, retention, and employee performance. Artificial intelligence (AI) is being used in a variety of fields, including machine learning, natural language processing, and predictive analytics, to automate procedures, customize user experiences, and extract fresh information from data. This improves productivity, accuracy, and decision-making in HR management (Pathak & Solanki, 2021).

Through the analysis of data from evaluations, social media profiles, and resumes, artificial intelligence is transforming talent acquisition and recruiting. It can lessen unconscious prejudice and enhance applicant matching by learning from previous hiring choices. Chatbots powered by AI are assisting applicants with the application process, and by examining behavior and comments, AI is also revolutionizing employee engagement and retention (Sundaramoorthy et al., 2024). AI enables HR professionals to proactively handle problems and provide a good work environment that improves job satisfaction, career advancement, and skill development.

Digital workforce management is being revolutionized by artificial intelligence in HR, which also improves productivity, creativity, and employee engagement. But in today's workplace, success demands ethical thinking, strategic planning, and a dedication to ongoing learning and adaptation (Satav et al., 2023). Large data sets are needed for AI systems, which raises issues with security, privacy, and GDPR compliance. To guarantee the moral use of employee data, organizations need to have strong data governance structures in place. AI systems have the potential to reinforce prejudices and create unfair HR procedures. Participation from stakeholders, regular audits, and a variety of training datasets are strategies to reduce algorithmic bias (Boopathi, 2024a; Rebecca et al., 2024).

Adoption of AI in HR might affect employee acceptance and trust, thus proactive approaches to resolve issues, explain advantages, and offer training are required. Implementing AI successfully involves knowledge of data science, machine learning, and ethics. It may become difficult to find and keep talent, which will need spending money on training and talent acquisition. AI may be used in HR management to increase creativity, productivity, and employee engagement by addressing issues like data security, algorithmic bias, and employee acceptance. HR procedures have been completely transformed by AI, which has improved efficiency and effectiveness in hiring, talent acquisition, employee engagement, performance management, learning, and HR analytics(Vijaya Lakshmi et al., 2024).

AI is transforming hiring by eliminating unconscious prejudice and expediting the process of discovering the best applicants. Enhancing the applicant experience, it automates the screening of candidates, sets up interviews, and responds to frequently asked interview questions. In addition to expediting the recruiting process, this guarantees inclusive, objective talent acquisition. AI is essential for focused training programs, skill gap identification, timely feedback, and individualized learning and development. In order to provide proactive feedback and well-informed assessments, it also provides real-time insights into employee performance measures(Ahamed et al., 2024; Puranik et al., 2024).

Large-scale datasets may be analyzed by AI algorithms to find patterns and trends, allowing for data-driven goal-setting and performance evaluation. This is especially helpful for HR initiatives since it guarantees objective facts instead of opinionated information. The amalgamation of AI with HR offers prospects for optimizing efficacy, impartiality, and ongoing refinement of HR procedures. AI's contribution to HR transformation will only grow in importance as technology develops, underscoring the necessity for businesses to successfully incorporate AI into their HR plans(S & Gopi, 2024). Objectives of the chapter have been discussed below.

- To provide a overview of the fundamentals of artificial intelligence, including machine learning, natural language processing, and predictive analytics, to provide readers with a solid foundation.
- To explore the various applications of AI in human resources management, such as recruitment, employee engagement, performance management, learning and development, workforce planning, and decision support.

- AI technologies such as analytics, chatbots, sentiment analysis, recommendation engines, and automated processes are revolutionizing HR practices by enhancing HR management.
- To explore the potential advantages of AI integration in HR processes, including improved efficiency, decision-making, and employee experience, while also addressing issues like data privacy and algorithmic bias.

AI IN HR: TRANSFORMING HUMAN RESOURCES MANAGEMENT

In the field of human resources (HR) management, artificial intelligence (AI) has become a disruptive force that is changing how businesses find, nurture, and employ talent. This article analyzes the foundations of artificial intelligence (AI), looks at how it may be used to HR, and looks at the important AI technologies that are advancing innovation in HR management (Koshariya et al., 2023; Maguluri et al., 2023).

Fundamentals of Artificial Intelligence

Fundamentally, artificial intelligence (AI) is the emulation of human intellectual processes by computers, allowing them to carry out activities like learning, reasoning, and problem-solving that normally need human cognitive abilities. Artificial Intelligence (AI) comprises a wide variety of technologies, such as robotics, computer vision, natural language processing, machine learning, and computer vision (Maheswari et al., 2023; Rahamathunnisa et al., 2023).

Machine learning, a subset of AI, focuses on developing algorithms that enable computers to learn from data and improve their performance over time without explicit programming. This iterative learning process allows machines to identify patterns, make predictions, and automate decision-making tasks. Natural language processing (NLP) enables computers to understand and generate human language, facilitating interactions between humans and machines through speech recognition, language translation, and sentiment analysis (Boopathi, 2023; Venkateswaran et al., 2023).

Computer vision involves the development of algorithms that enable computers to interpret and analyze visual information from images and videos. By leveraging techniques such as image recognition and object detection, computer vision systems can extract valuable insights from visual data, enabling applications in areas such as facial recognition, surveillance, and autonomous vehicles.

AI Applications in HR

Artificial Intelligence has become a ubiquitous presence in HR management, providing solutions that optimize workflows, elevate decision-making, and augment the employee experience. Among the principal uses of AI in HR are:

- **Recruitment and Talent Acquisition:** AI-powered tools facilitate the automation of candidate sourcing, screening, and assessment processes. Machine learning algorithms analyze resumes, social media profiles, and job descriptions to identify top candidates more efficiently and reduce unconscious bias in the hiring process. Chatbots powered by natural language processing can engage with candidates, answer queries, and schedule interviews, enhancing the candidate experience.

- **Employee Engagement and Retention:** AI enables HR professionals to gain insights into employee sentiment, engagement levels, and retention risks through sentiment analysis and predictive analytics. By analyzing factors such as feedback, performance metrics, and social interactions, AI systems can identify trends and patterns indicative of employee satisfaction or dissatisfaction, enabling proactive interventions to improve retention and foster a positive work environment (Hussain et al., 2023).

- **Performance Management:** AI-driven performance management systems offer real-time feedback, objective evaluations, and personalized development plans. By continuously monitoring and analyzing employee behaviors and achievements, AI systems provide managers with actionable insights to support coaching, goal setting, and career development. Predictive analytics can help identify high-potential employees and anticipate performance issues before they arise (Malathi et al., 2024).

- **Learning and Development:** AI-powered learning platforms deliver personalized training content tailored to individual learning styles, preferences, and skill gaps. Adaptive learning algorithms adjust the pace and content of training programs based on learner performance, enabling more effective knowledge transfer and skill development. Virtual reality (VR) and augmented reality (AR) technologies further enhance learning experiences by providing immersive and interactive training environments (Sangeetha et al., 2023).

Figure 1. Flowchart for Importance of AI Applications in HR

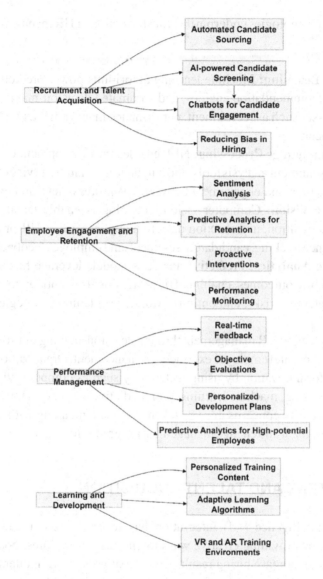

The important AI applications in HR, such as hiring and talent acquisition, employee engagement and retention, performance management, and learning and development, are depicted in a flowchart in Figure 1. Every application is linked to certain AI-driven features and results.

AI Technologies in HR Management

Several AI technologies underpin the transformation of HR management(Vrontis et al., 2022):

a) **Machine Learning:** Machine learning algorithms power predictive analytics models, recommendation engines, and automated decision-making systems in HR processes such as recruitment, performance management, and learning and development.

b) **Natural Language Processing:** NLP enables the development of AI-powered chatbots, sentiment analysis tools, and language translation services that enhance communication and engagement between HR professionals and employees.

c) **Computer Vision:** Computer vision technologies enable facial recognition, gesture recognition, and emotion detection applications in HR processes such as attendance tracking, candidate assessment, and employee feedback collection.

d) **Predictive Analytics:** Predictive analytics models leverage historical data to forecast future outcomes, enabling HR professionals to anticipate talent trends, identify retention risks, and optimize workforce planning strategies.

AI is transforming HR management through decision-making improvement, process simplification, and employee experience enhancement. Organizations may seize new chances for innovation by using technology such as computer vision, natural language processing, machine learning, and predictive analytics. However, ethical, privacy, and security concerns must be taken into account, along with expenditures in talent development and change management programs, for successful deployment.

RECRUITMENT AND TALENT ACQUISITION

Artificial intelligence (AI) integration has revolutionized talent acquisition and recruiting by providing creative ways to optimize procedures, boost applicant experiences, and increase hiring results. Important uses of AI in talent acquisition and recruiting include chatbots for applicant interaction, AI-powered candidate screening, and enhancing hiring results. (Vrontis et al., 2022).

AI-Powered Candidate Screening

AI-powered candidate screening automates the initial screening process, enabling recruiters to identify top candidates more efficiently and objectively. Machine learning algorithms analyze resumes, cover letters, and other candidate data to identify relevant skills, experiences, and qualifications. They can be trained on historical hiring data to learn patterns of success and failure, making more accurate predictions about candidate suitability for specific roles (Chowdhury et al., 2023). AI-powered candidate screening can significantly reduce hiring time, minimize unconscious bias, and enhance hire quality. This allows recruiters to concentrate on engaging with qualified candidates, leading to better hiring decisions and increased retention rates.

Chatbots in Candidate Engagement

Candidate engagement is crucial in recruitment, influencing candidates' perceptions and acceptance of job offers. However, managing candidate communication can be challenging, especially in high-volume campaigns. Natural language processing (NLP)-powered chatbots automate candidate engagement through personalized interactions, answering frequently asked questions, providing application status updates, scheduling interviews, and collecting candidate feedback (Chowdhury et al., 2023; Vrontis et al., 2022).

By offering a smooth and responsive experience, raising employee happiness and employer brand perception, and freeing up recruiters' time to concentrate on higher-value activities like forming connections and assessing fit, chatbots may improve applicant engagement.

Improving Hiring Outcomes with AI

AI can improve hiring outcomes by streamlining processes and enhancing candidate experiences. It can analyze vast data to identify factors like educational background, work experience, and cultural fit. Predictive analytics models can forecast candidates' success likelihood in specific roles, enabling recruiters to make informed decisions. Organizations can also use historical data and performance metrics to identify success patterns and refine hiring criteria over time (Deepa et al., 2024).

Artificial intelligence (AI) systems analyze candidate data from several sources, including professional networks and social media, to assist firms find hidden talent pools. The recruiting process has been transformed by technology, which has also enhanced applicant experiences and hiring results. Organizations can decrease prejudice, increase efficiency, and make well-informed recruiting decisions by leveraging chatbots, AI-powered screening, and predictive analytics. This will help them position themselves for success in the highly competitive employment market.

EMPLOYEE ENGAGEMENT AND RETENTION

In the highly competitive labor market, this chapter explores how AI is changing employee engagement and retention. It identifies three significant ways AI is changing these procedures, all of which are essential for the success of organizations: delivering data-driven insights about employee sentiment, putting proactive AI interventions into place, and creating a happy work atmosphere (Rao et al., 2020).

Figure 2. Employee engagement and retention

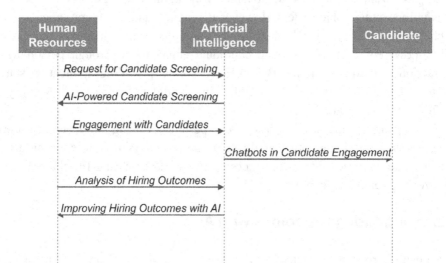

Figure 2 shows the interaction between HR professionals, AI systems, and candidates during the recruitment and talent acquisition process, starting with AI screening, engaging with candidates through chatbots, and analyzing hiring outcomes and AI-improved hiring outcomes.

Data-Driven Insights into Employee Sentiment

AI-powered sentiment analysis is a more scalable and objective method for measuring employee sentiment, addressing limitations of traditional methods like low response rates and subjective interpretation. Natural language processing (NLP) algorithms analyze text data from sources like employee surveys, performance reviews, and social media to extract insights into employee attitudes, emotions, and opinions (Mer & Srivastava, 2023).

AI can provide real-time insights into employee sentiment, enabling organizations to identify trends and potential concerns. It can detect shifts in sentiment among specific employee groups, indicating issues like declining morale, leadership dissatisfaction, or work-life balance concerns.

Proactive Interventions With AI

AI can help identify potential retention risks and implement proactive interventions to prevent employee turnover. Predictive analytics models use historical data and machine learning algorithms to forecast retention risks and identify high-risk employees. By analyzing performance metrics, tenure, job satisfaction, and engagement levels, AI systems can identify early warning signs of turnover and prioritize intervention strategies. These strategies may include personalized coaching, career development opportunities, or work arrangements based on individual employee profiles (Rao et al., 2020).

AI-driven chatbots can provide real-time support, guidance, and resources to employees, enhancing engagement, satisfaction, and loyalty. This can reduce turnover rates and retain top talent, ultimately reducing overall employee satisfaction.

Fostering a Positive Work Environment

AI can significantly enhance a positive work environment by promoting transparency, collaboration, and recognition of employee contributions. AI-powered communication platforms allow for open communication between employees and leadership, allowing for feedback, idea sharing, and recognition. These platforms also enhance teamwork and productivity by facilitating knowledge sharing, project management, and remote collaboration. By leveraging machine learning algorithms to analyze team dynamics and workflows, organizations can identify opportunities for optimization and process improvement, fostering a culture of innovation and continuous improvement (Chowdhury et al., 2023).

AI-driven recognition and rewards systems enable companies to instantly acknowledge and honor staff members' accomplishments. AI systems are able to suggest customized incentives through the analysis of performance data and feedback. By tackling retention concerns, promoting a happy work environment, and offering insights into employee attitude, this technology is transforming employee engagement and retention methods. Organizations may improve employee happiness and retention by putting workplace culture initiatives and proactive interventions into practice.

PERFORMANCE MANAGEMENT: OPTIMIZING ORGANIZATIONAL PERFORMANCE WITH AI

Performance management is crucial for organizational success, involving aligning individual performance with strategic goals, providing feedback, and promoting employee development. In today's fast-paced business environment, organizations are utilizing artificial intelligence to improve performance management processes, offering real-time feedback, personalized development plans, and continuous monitoring and analysis (Gupta et al., 2023).

Figure 3 illustrates the main elements of performance management, including aligning individual performance with strategic goals, providing feedback, and promoting employee development. It also highlights the integration of artificial intelligence (AI) into performance management processes, offering real-time feedback, personalized development plans, and continuous monitoring and analysis.

Figure 3. Optimizing organizational performance with AI

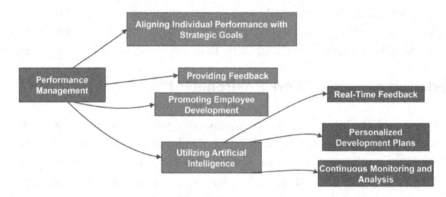

Real-Time Feedback and Objective Evaluations

Traditional performance evaluations are time-consuming and subjective, disconnected from day-to-day work experiences. AI-powered performance management systems provide real-time feedback and objective evaluations to support employee growth and development. AI algorithms analyze performance data from various sources, including project outcomes, customer feedback, and peer evaluations, identifying patterns, trends, and areas for improvement. This agile and data-driven approach enables managers to provide timely and actionable feedback to employees (Sahlin & Angelis, 2019).

AI eliminates biases and subjectivity in performance assessments by analyzing objective metrics and predefined criteria. This results in fair, consistent, and transparent performance scores, aiding employees in understanding strengths and weaknesses, setting goals, and tracking progress(Chandrika et al., 2023; Sundaramoorthy et al., 2024).

Personalized Development Plans

AI-powered performance management systems provide personalized development plans for employees based on their skills, preferences, and career aspirations. These plans are tailored by analyzing performance data, skills assessments, and career goals. AI algorithms recommend learning opportunities, stretch assignments, and career paths that align with employees' development needs and organizational objectives, enabling them to enhance their skills and advance their careers (Mer & Srivastava, 2023).

AI-driven coaching and mentoring programs offer personalized feedback, guidance, and support to employees through natural language processing (NLP) algorithms, allowing for real-time tracking of progress towards development goals and analyzing employee interactions (Venkateswaran et al., 2023).

Continuous Monitoring and Analysis

AI is a powerful tool for organizations to monitor and analyze performance metrics in real-time, identifying outliers and trends, and taking corrective actions to improve productivity. It can forecast future trends and anticipate challenges, allowing managers to allocate resources and implement mitigation strategies. AI-powered dashboards and analytics tools provide actionable insights into team performance, enabling data-driven decisions. AI also automates performance data collection, analysis, and reporting, enabling managers to identify areas for improvement and provide targeted interventions to support employee growth and development. By integrating with various data sources, AI systems can optimize resource allocation and improve overall performance (Kumara et al., 2023; Sundaramoorthy et al., 2024).

AI is revolutionizing performance management by providing real-time feedback, personalized development plans, and continuous monitoring, enhancing employee engagement, productivity, and performance, ultimately driving organizational success in the digital age.

Learning and Development: Revolutionizing Training With AI-Driven Learning Platforms

This article explores the role of AI-driven learning platforms in revolutionizing learning and development (L&D) initiatives, emphasizing their importance in building employee skills, driving innovation, and maintaining a competitive edge in the rapidly evolving business landscape. AI-driven learning platforms use machine learning algorithms, natural language processing, and data analytics to provide personalized, adaptive training content. They analyze learner data, such as performance metrics, learning history, and assessment results, to recommend resources, adjust learning pathways, and provide real-time feedback (Naim, 2023).

Figure 4. Important components and functionalities of AI-Driven learning platforms

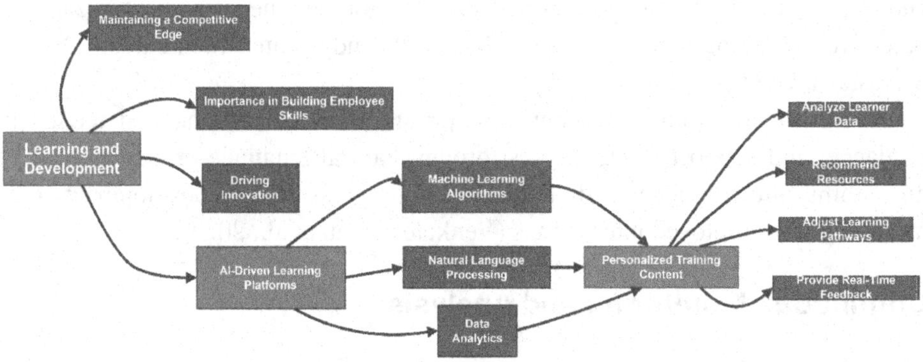

Figure 4 illustrates the important components and functionalities of AI-driven learning platforms in revolutionizing learning and development initiatives. It emphasizes the importance of these platforms in building employee skills, driving innovation, and maintaining a competitive edge in the business landscape. The AI-driven learning platforms leverage machine learning algorithms, natural language processing, and data analytics to provide personalized, adaptive training content and enhance the learning experience for employees.

Features of AI-Driven Learning Platforms

AI-driven learning platforms are revolutionizing learning and development (L&D) by providing personalized, adaptive, and engaging experiences. These platforms enhance learning outcomes, increase engagement, and drive training efficiency. By leveraging AI technologies, organizations can empower employees to acquire new skills, develop competencies, and adapt to evolving business needs. This ultimately drives organizational success and competitiveness in the digital age. Two significant ways AI is transforming L&D are by delivering personalized training content and cultivating a culture of continuous learning (Maimela & others, 2024).

a) **Personalization:** AI-driven learning platforms offer personalized learning experiences by analyzing learner data and preferences to recommend relevant content, adjust learning pathways, and adapt to individual learning styles. Learners receive tailored recommendations based on their interests, skill gaps, and learning objectives, enhancing engagement and motivation.

b) **Adaptability:** AI-powered algorithms continuously monitor learner progress and adjust learning pathways dynamically based on performance, feedback, and mastery levels. Adaptive learning technologies enable learners to progress at their own pace, receive targeted interventions, and focus on areas where they need additional support, maximizing learning effectiveness and efficiency.

c) **Interactivity:** AI-driven learning platforms incorporate interactive elements such as simulations, quizzes, and gamification to enhance learner engagement and retention. By providing hands-on learning experiences and immediate feedback, these platforms create immersive and engaging learning environments that promote active participation and knowledge retention.

d) **Analytics:** AI-enabled analytics tools track learner progress, engagement levels, and performance outcomes, enabling L&D professionals to monitor training effectiveness, identify learning trends, and measure the impact of training initiatives. By analyzing data on learner behavior and outcomes, organizations can optimize training content, delivery methods, and learning strategies to maximize ROI and achieve business objectives.

Benefits of AI-Driven Learning Platforms

i. **Improved Learning Outcomes:** AI-driven learning platforms enable personalized, adaptive, and engaging learning experiences that cater to individual learner needs and preferences. By delivering relevant content, adjusting learning pathways, and providing real-time feedback, these platforms enhance learning effectiveness, knowledge retention, and skill development.

ii. **Increased Engagement:** The interactive and immersive nature of AI-driven learning platforms enhances learner engagement and motivation. By incorporating gamification elements, simulations, and interactive exercises, these platforms create enjoyable and rewarding learning experiences that captivate learners' attention and drive participation.

iii. **Enhanced Efficiency:** AI-powered algorithms automate various aspects of the learning process, such as content recommendation, assessment grading, and progress tracking, saving time and effort for both learners and instructors. By streamlining administrative tasks and providing self-paced learning opportunities, these platforms improve training efficiency and scalability.

iv. **Data-Driven Insights:** AI-enabled analytics tools provide valuable insights into learner behavior, preferences, and performance outcomes. By analyzing data on learning engagement, completion rates, and proficiency levels, organizations can identify learning gaps, assess training effectiveness, and make data-driven decisions to optimize L&D strategies and investments.

Personalized Training Content

Traditional training programs often provide content that is uniform across employees, regardless of their learning styles or skill levels. AI-powered learning platforms, however, offer a more personalized approach by analyzing employee data and generating personalized training recommendations. These recommendations may include online courses, tutorials, videos, and other learning resources that align with employees' interests, career goals, and development needs. AI-driven adaptive learning technologies adjust training content pace and difficulty based on individual learner progress, monitoring interactions and feedback. They dynamically modify course content, quizzes, and assessments for optimal engagement and knowledge retention (Maimela & others, 2024; Naim, 2023).

Cultivating a Culture of Continuous Learning

Organizations in the knowledge-based economy need to foster a culture of continuous learning to remain competitive and innovative. AI technologies facilitate this by providing employees with relevant, up-to-date learning resources and opportunities for skill development. AI-powered learning platforms offer personalized professional development recommendations based on employees' interests, career aspirations, and organizational goals. They curate diverse content to help employees explore new topics, acquire skills, and stay updated on industry trends (Maimela & others, 2024; Quatman-Yates et al., 2019).

AI-driven learning analytics offer valuable insights into employee learning progress, engagement, and skill mastery. This data can help organizations identify areas for improvement, measure training effectiveness, and customize learning experiences.

To foster a culture of continuous learning, AI can be used to gamify experiences, recognize achievements, and promote knowledge sharing. This fosters a supportive environment for employees to invest in personal and professional growth (Naim, 2023). AI is revolutionizing learning and development by providing personalized training content and fostering a culture of continuous learning. Organizations can empower employees to acquire new skills, adapt to evolving roles, and drive success in the digital age. This fosters an agile, resilient workforce ready to thrive in the ever-changing business environment.

Challenges and Considerations

This article discusses the challenges organizations face in implementing AI-driven HR strategies, including data privacy and security, ethical implications of algorithmic bias, and the need for HR professionals to be upskilled (Vrontis et al., 2022).

Data Privacy and Security

AI-powered HR systems rely on extensive employee data, necessitating robust data governance frameworks to protect it from unauthorized access, use, or disclosure. These frameworks include encryption, access controls, and data anonymization techniques. Regular audits and assessments are also necessary to identify and mitigate potential security risks and vulnerabilities in AI systems, ensuring trust and compliance with regulations like GDPR and CCPA (Boopathi & Khang, 2023; Maguluri et al., 2023).

Organizations should establish clear policies for data collection, storage, and processing in AI-driven HR processes to ensure transparency, accountability, and data privacy and security, thereby building trust with employees and reducing the risk of data breaches(Boopathi, 2024b; Sonia et al., 2024).

Algorithmic Bias and Ethical Implications

AI algorithms can be biased due to the data used to train them, leading to ethical implications in HR decision-making. These biases can perpetuate discrimination, inequality, and unfair treatment, posing risks to employee well-being and organizational reputation. To address algorithmic bias, organizations must curate and preprocess training data, diversify datasets, remove sensitive attributes, and conduct bias audits to identify and rectify potential biases.

Organizations should establish ethical guidelines for AI-driven HR processes, ensuring transparency, accountability, and fairness. This includes providing employees with clear explanations of AI decisions, offering recourse mechanisms for challenging algorithmic decisions, and implementing oversight mechanisms to monitor potential biases. Promoting ethical AI practices and fostering a culture of diversity and inclusion can help mitigate algorithmic bias risks and uphold fairness in HR management.

Upskilling HR Professionals

AI-driven HR strategies require HR professionals to acquire new skills in data analytics, machine learning, and AI ethics. However, many lack the technical expertise to effectively use AI technologies. Organizations should invest in upskilling and reskilling HR professionals to bridge the digital skills gap and harness AI's full potential. This may involve providing training programs, workshops, and certifications, and fostering a culture of continuous learning and experimentation.

Organizations should foster collaboration between HR, IT, and data science teams to facilitate knowledge sharing and skill development. Empowering HR professionals with the necessary tools can drive innovation, efficiency, and effectiveness in HR management. Addressing challenges like data privacy, security, algorithmic bias, and ethical implications is crucial for responsible AI-driven HR strategies. Prioritizing these considerations and adopting best practices can unlock AI's full potential, drive transformation, and ensure employee rights and well-being.

Crafting Effective HR Digital Strategies

Effective HR digital strategies involve a comprehensive approach that integrates technology, people, and processes for organizational success. Key components include data-driven insights, automation and AI technologies, and a culture of continuous learning. HR professionals should prioritize data-driven decision-making to analyze employee data, identify areas for improvement, predict future needs, and optimize HR processes like recruitment, performance management, and talent development (Pereira et al., 2023; Vrontis et al., 2022).

HR digital strategies should incorporate automation and AI technologies to improve efficiency and employee experiences. AI can revolutionize HR practices by providing personalized experiences and data insights. However, responsible AI adoption requires careful consideration of ethical, privacy, and security implications. Organizations should prioritize transparency, fairness, and accountability in AI-driven HR processes, aligning decisions with organizational values. Upskilling HR professionals is essential to effectively leverage AI technologies and navigate ethical challenges(Boopathi & Khang, 2023; Rahamathunnisa et al., 2024).

A culture of learning and adaptation is crucial for HR professionals to build resilience and agility in the face of constant change. HR professionals should foster a growth mindset, promote continuous learning, and encourage experimentation. Offering opportunities for professional development, mentorship, and knowledge sharing empowers employees to adapt to new technologies and challenges. Effective HR digital strategies require a strategic and collaborative approach that integrates data, technology, and culture. Prioritizing data-driven decision-making, responsible AI adoption, and fostering a culture of learning can transform HR practices and drive organizational success.

FUTURE DEVELOPMENTS

The integration of AI in HR digital strategies for modern workplaces is expected to see further advancements and innovations. Future developments will focus on enhancing AI-driven HR technologies, addressing emerging challenges, and leveraging AI to support strategic HR initiatives (Chowdhury et al., 2023; Deepa et al., 2024; Vrontis et al., 2022).

- AI-powered predictive analytics and AR and VR in HR training are expected to revolutionize the industry. AI-driven HR strategies may incorporate advanced predictive analytics to anticipate workforce trends, challenges, and opportunities. This can help organizations forecast talent needs, identify retention risks, and optimize workforce planning strategies. AR and VR technologies may also be used for immersive training experiences, such as onboarding, skills development, and leadership training, providing engaging learning experiences for employees.
- Future AI-driven HR strategies may prioritize ethical AI principles and responsible automation practices to address concerns about algorithmic bias, privacy, and fairness. Organizations may invest in technologies to ensure transparency, accountability, and fairness in AI-driven decision-making processes. AI-powered employee well-being and engagement may be enhanced through personalized interventions and support systems, such as AI-powered chatbots and virtual assistants providing real-time support on mental health, work-life balance, and stress management.
- Advancements in Natural Language Processing (NLP) technologies can be used to analyze employee feedback in real-time, with chatbots potentially identifying patterns of engagement, satisfaction, and retention. AI-driven HR strategies may prioritize diversity, equity, and inclusion (DEI) initiatives, aiming to mitigate biases in recruitment, promotion, and performance eval-

uation processes, promote diversity in hiring, and foster an inclusive work culture. These advancements could help organizations improve their HR strategies and overall performance(Naveeenkumar et al., 2024).

Future AI-driven HR strategies may involve human-AI collaboration in decision-making processes, enabling more informed, data-driven decisions. AI technologies may not replace human judgment but augment HR professionals, enabling better outcomes and strategic initiatives. This could revolutionize HR management, drive organizational success, and enhance employee experiences. By embracing emerging technologies, addressing ethical considerations, and prioritizing employee well-being and inclusion, organizations can stay at the forefront of HR innovation and achieve sustainable growth in the digital age.

Figure 5. Future AI-driven HR strategies

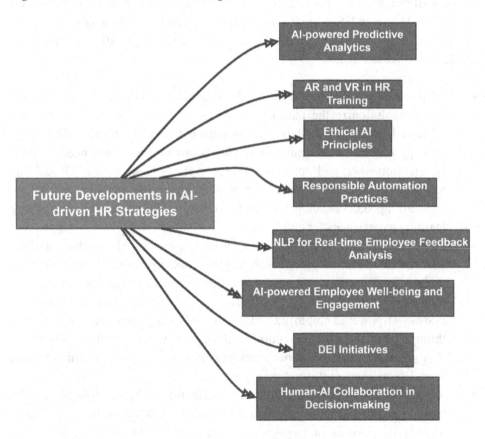

Figure 5 shows future AI-driven HR strategies, including predictive analytics, AR/VR training, ethical AI principles, responsible automation, NLP for real-time feedback analysis, AI-powered employee engagement, DEI initiatives, and human-AI collaboration in decision-making. These advancements are expected to revolutionize HR management, drive organizational success, and improve employee experiences in the digital age.

ETHICAL CONSIDERATIONS

The integration of AI techniques into HR digital strategies requires careful ethical considerations, including addressing important ethical issues to ensure responsible and ethical use of AI in HR management (Arslan et al., 2022; Chowdhury et al., 2023; Zehir et al., 2020).

- Transparency and Accountability: Organizations must prioritize transparency and accountability in AI-driven HR processes, ensuring that employees understand how AI technologies are used and how decisions are made. Clear communication about the purpose, scope, and implications of AI applications helps build trust and mitigate concerns about opacity and lack of control.
- Fairness and Bias Mitigation: AI algorithms are susceptible to biases present in the data used to train them, leading to unfair or discriminatory outcomes in HR processes. Organizations must implement measures to mitigate biases and ensure fairness in recruitment, performance management, and talent development. This may involve diversifying training datasets, conducting bias audits, and implementing algorithmic fairness assessments.
- Privacy and Data Protection: AI-driven HR systems rely on vast amounts of employee data, raising concerns about privacy, consent, and data protection. Organizations must adhere to applicable privacy regulations and standards, such as the General Data Protection Regulation (GDPR) and the California Consumer Privacy Act (CCPA), to safeguard employee data from unauthorized access, use, or disclosure.
- Employee Consent and Autonomy: Organizations must respect employee autonomy and consent when implementing AI-driven HR technologies. Employees should have the right to opt-in or opt-out of AI-driven processes, such as automated decision-making or performance monitoring, and have access to mechanisms for challenging algorithmic decisions and seeking redress.
- Accountability for AI Decisions: Organizations must establish mechanisms for accountability and recourse in cases where AI decisions have significant

consequences for employees. This may include providing avenues for appeal, review, and human intervention in AI-driven decision-making processes, ensuring that employees have opportunities to challenge unfair or incorrect decisions.

- Professional Ethics and Conduct: HR professionals responsible for implementing AI-driven HR strategies must adhere to professional codes of ethics and conduct. This includes upholding principles of fairness, integrity, and respect for human dignity in all aspects of HR management, including the design, deployment, and evaluation of AI technologies.

- Continuous Monitoring and Evaluation: Ethical considerations in AI-driven HR strategies require ongoing monitoring and evaluation to identify and address emerging ethical risks and challenges. Organizations should establish multidisciplinary oversight committees or ethics boards to review AI applications, assess their ethical implications, and recommend mitigating measures as needed.

For modern companies, ethical AI use in HR digital initiatives is essential. Transparency, equity, privacy, and accountability should be given top priority by organizations in order to guarantee that AI-driven HR procedures enhance worker well-being, encourage diversity, and assist moral decision-making in HR management.

CONCLUSION

This chapter explores the potential of artificial intelligence (AI) in human resources management, focusing on how it may be used in recruiting, talent acquisition, employee engagement, performance management, learning, and development. The digital age has resulted in the replacement of traditional administrative duties with strategic partnership roles, and artificial intelligence (AI) is emerging as a disruptive force that offers innovative solutions to issues like hiring bias, inefficient performance management, and a lack of personalized development opportunities.

AI-powered candidate screening, chatbots, real-time feedback, customized learning platforms, and more might all improve employee engagement and the efficiency of HR management. However, while employing AI responsibly, considerations related to security, privacy, and ethics must be made. HR staff members also need to make an investment in upskilling. A culture that prioritizes continuous learning and adaptation is essential for developing resilience and agility in the face of fast change. It is advised that HR specialists foster experimentation and creativity, support lifelong learning, and foster a growth mindset.

A revolution in digital workforce management is brought about by the use of artificial intelligence (AI) in HR efforts. By fostering creativity, efficiency, and employee engagement through the proper application of AI technology and the cultivation of a learning culture, organizations may position themselves for global success.

ABBREVIATIONS

HR: Human Resources
AI: Artificial Intelligence
GDPR: General Data Protection Regulation
NLP: Natural Language Processing
VR: Virtual Reality
AR: Augmented Reality
ROI: Return on Investment
CCPA: California Consumer Privacy Act
IT: Information Technology
DEI: Diversity, Equity, and Inclusion

REFERENCES

Ahamed, B. S., Chakravarthy, K. S., Arputhabalan, J., Sasirekha, K., Prince, R. M. R., Boopathi, S., & Muthuvel, S. (2024). Revolutionizing Friction Stir Welding With AI-Integrated Humanoid Robots. In *Advances in Computational Intelligence and Robotics* (pp. 120–144). IGI Global. 10.4018/979-8-3693-2399-1.ch005

Arslan, A., Cooper, C., Khan, Z., Golgeci, I., & Ali, I. (2022). Artificial intelligence and human workers interaction at team level: A conceptual assessment of the challenges and potential HRM strategies. *International Journal of Manpower*, 43(1), 75–88. 10.1108/IJM-01-2021-0052

Biliavska, V., Castanho, R., & Vulevic, A. (2022). Analysis of the impact of artificial intelligence in enhancing the human resource practices. *J. Intell. Manag. Decis*, 1(2), 128–136. 10.56578/jimd010206

Boopathi, S. (2023). Deep Learning Techniques Applied for Automatic Sentence Generation. In *Promoting Diversity, Equity, and Inclusion in Language Learning Environments* (pp. 255–273). IGI Global. 10.4018/978-1-6684-3632-5.ch016

Boopathi, S. (2024a). Advancements in Machine Learning and AI for Intelligent Systems in Drone Applications for Smart City Developments. In *Futuristic e-Governance Security With Deep Learning Applications* (pp. 15–45). IGI Global. 10.4018/978-1-6684-9596-4.ch002

Boopathi, S. (2024b). Balancing Innovation and Security in the Cloud: Navigating the Risks and Rewards of the Digital Age. In *Improving Security, Privacy, and Trust in Cloud Computing* (pp. 164–193). IGI Global.

Boopathi, S., & Khang, A. (2023). AI-Integrated Technology for a Secure and Ethical Healthcare Ecosystem. In *AI and IoT-Based Technologies for Precision Medicine* (pp. 36–59). IGI Global. 10.4018/979-8-3693-0876-9.ch003

Chandrika, V., Sivakumar, A., Krishnan, T. S., Pradeep, J., Manikandan, S., & Boopathi, S. (2023). Theoretical Study on Power Distribution Systems for Electric Vehicles. In *Intelligent Engineering Applications and Applied Sciences for Sustainability* (pp. 1–19). IGI Global. 10.4018/979-8-3693-0044-2.ch001

Chowdhury, S., Dey, P., Joel-Edgar, S., Bhattacharya, S., Rodriguez-Espindola, O., Abadie, A., & Truong, L. (2023). Unlocking the value of artificial intelligence in human resource management through AI capability framework. *Human Resource Management Review*, 33(1), 100899. 10.1016/j.hrmr.2022.100899

Deepa, R., Sekar, S., Malik, A., Kumar, J., & Attri, R. (2024). Impact of AI-focussed technologies on social and technical competencies for HR managers–A systematic review and research agenda. *Technological Forecasting and Social Change*, 202, 123301. 10.1016/j.techfore.2024.123301

Gupta, K., Mane, P., Rajankar, O. S., Bhowmik, M., Jadhav, R., Yadav, S., Rawandale, S., & Chobe, S. V. (2023). Harnessing AI for strategic decision-making and business performance optimization. *International Journal of Intelligent Systems and Applications in Engineering*, 11(10s), 893–912.

Hussain, Z., Babe, M., Saravanan, S., Srimathy, G., Roopa, H., & Boopathi, S. (2023). Optimizing Biomass-to-Biofuel Conversion: IoT and AI Integration for Enhanced Efficiency and Sustainability. In *Circular Economy Implementation for Sustainability in the Built Environment* (pp. 191–214). IGI Global.

Koshariya, A. K., Khatoon, S., Marathe, A. M., Suba, G. M., Baral, D., & Boopathi, S. (2023). Agricultural Waste Management Systems Using Artificial Intelligence Techniques. In *AI-Enabled Social Robotics in Human Care Services* (pp. 236–258). IGI Global. 10.4018/978-1-6684-8171-4.ch009

Kumara, V., & Sharma, M. D., Samson Isaac, J., Saravanan, S., Suganthi, D., & Boopathi, S. (2023). An AI-Integrated Green Power Monitoring System: Empowering Small and Medium Enterprises. In *Advances in Environmental Engineering and Green Technologies* (pp. 218–244). IGI Global. 10.4018/979-8-3693-0338-2.ch013

Maguluri, L. P., Arularasan, A., & Boopathi, S. (2023). Assessing Security Concerns for AI-Based Drones in Smart Cities. In *Effective AI, Blockchain, and E-Governance Applications for Knowledge Discovery and Management* (pp. 27–47). IGI Global. 10.4018/978-1-6684-9151-5.ch002

Maheswari, B. U., Imambi, S. S., Hasan, D., Meenakshi, S., Pratheep, V., & Boopathi, S. (2023). Internet of things and machine learning-integrated smart robotics. In *Global Perspectives on Robotics and Autonomous Systems: Development and Applications* (pp. 240–258). IGI Global. 10.4018/978-1-6684-7791-5.ch010

Maimela, C. & others. (2024). *Artificial Intelligence and its Impact on Library Staff Learning and Development.*

Malathi, J., Kusha, K., Isaac, S., Ramesh, A., Rajendiran, M., & Boopathi, S. (2024). IoT-Enabled Remote Patient Monitoring for Chronic Disease Management and Cost Savings: Transforming Healthcare. In *Advances in Explainable AI Applications for Smart Cities* (pp. 371–388). IGI Global.

Mer, A., & Srivastava, A. (2023). Employee engagement in the new normal: Artificial intelligence as a buzzword or a game changer? In *The Adoption and Effect of Artificial Intelligence on Human Resources Management, Part A* (pp. 15–46). Emerald Publishing Limited.

Naim, M. F. (2023). Reinventing workplace learning and development: Envisaging the role of AI. In *The adoption and Effect of artificial intelligence on human resources management, Part A* (pp. 215–227). Emerald Publishing Limited.

Naveeenkumar, N., Rallapalli, S., Sasikala, K., Priya, P. V., Husain, J., & Boopathi, S. (2024). Enhancing Consumer Behavior and Experience Through AI-Driven Insights Optimization. In *AI Impacts in Digital Consumer Behavior* (pp. 1–35). IGI Global. 10.4018/979-8-3693-1918-5.ch001

Pathak, S., & Solanki, V. K. (2021). Impact of internet of things and artificial intelligence on human resource development. *Further Advances in Internet of Things in Biomedical and Cyber Physical Systems*, 239–267.

Pereira, V., Hadjielias, E., Christofi, M., & Vrontis, D. (2023). A systematic literature review on the impact of artificial intelligence on workplace outcomes: A multi-process perspective. *Human Resource Management Review*, 33(1), 100857. 10.1016/j.hrmr.2021.100857

Puranik, T. A., Shaik, N., Vankudoth, R., Kolhe, M. R., Yadav, N., & Boopathi, S. (2024). Study on Harmonizing Human-Robot (Drone) Collaboration: Navigating Seamless Interactions in Collaborative Environments. In *Cybersecurity Issues and Challenges in the Drone Industry* (pp. 1–26). IGI Global.

Quatman-Yates, C. C., Paterno, M. V., Strenk, M. L., Kiger, M. A., Hogan, T. H., Cunningham, B., & Reder, R. (2019). A model for cultivating a culture of continuous learning and improvement: An ethnographic report. In *Structural Approaches to Address Issues in Patient Safety* (pp. 197–225). Emerald Publishing Limited. 10.1108/S1474-823120190000018009

Rahamathunnisa, U., Sudhakar, K., Murugan, T. K., Thivaharan, S., Rajkumar, M., & Boopathi, S. (2023). Cloud Computing Principles for Optimizing Robot Task Offloading Processes. In *AI-Enabled Social Robotics in Human Care Services* (pp. 188–211). IGI Global. 10.4018/978-1-6684-8171-4.ch007

Rahamathunnisa, U., Sudhakar, K., Padhi, S., Bhattacharya, S., Shashibhushan, G., & Boopathi, S. (2024). Sustainable Energy Generation From Waste Water: IoT Integrated Technologies. In *Adoption and Use of Technology Tools and Services by Economically Disadvantaged Communities: Implications for Growth and Sustainability* (pp. 225–256). IGI Global.

Rao, S., Chitranshi, J., & Punjabi, N. (2020). Role of artificial intelligence in employee engagement and retention. *Journal of Applied Management-Jidnyasa*, 42–60.

Rebecca, B., Kumar, K. P. M., Padmini, S., Srivastava, B. K., Halder, S., & Boopathi, S. (2024). Convergence of Data Science-AI-Green Chemistry-Affordable Medicine: Transforming Drug Discovery. In *Handbook of Research on AI and ML for Intelligent Machines and Systems* (pp. 348–373). IGI Global.

S, B., & Gopi, S. (2024). Crafting Effective HR Strategies for the Modern Workplace: Navigating the Digital Frontier. In *Convergence of Human Resources Technologies and Industry 5.0* (pp. 23–46). IGI Global. 10.4018/979-8-3693-1343-5.ch002

Sahlin, J., & Angelis, J. (2019). Performance management systems: Reviewing the rise of dynamics and digitalization. *Cogent Business & Management*, 6(1), 1642293. 10.1080/23311975.2019.1642293

Sangeetha, M., Kannan, S. R., Boopathi, S., Ramya, J., Ishrat, M., & Sabarinathan, G. (2023). Prediction of Fruit Texture Features Using Deep Learning Techniques. *2023 4th International Conference on Smart Electronics and Communication (ICOSEC)*, 762–768.

Satav, S. D., Lamani, D., Harsha, K., Kumar, N., Manikandan, S., & Sampath, B. (2023). Energy and Battery Management in the Era of Cloud Computing: Sustainable Wireless Systems and Networks. In *Sustainable Science and Intelligent Technologies for Societal Development* (pp. 141–166). IGI Global.

Sonia, R., Gupta, N., Manikandan, K., Hemalatha, R., Kumar, M. J., & Boopathi, S. (2024). Strengthening Security, Privacy, and Trust in Artificial Intelligence Drones for Smart Cities. In *Analyzing and Mitigating Security Risks in Cloud Computing* (pp. 214–242). IGI Global. 10.4018/979-8-3693-3249-8.ch011

Sundaramoorthy, K., Singh, A., Sumathy, G., Maheshwari, A., Arunarani, A., & Boopathi, S. (2024). A Study on AI and Blockchain-Powered Smart Parking Models for Urban Mobility. In *Handbook of Research on AI and ML for Intelligent Machines and Systems* (pp. 223–250). IGI Global.

Venkateswaran, N., Vidhya, R., Naik, D. A., Raj, T. M., Munjal, N., & Boopathi, S. (2023). Study on Sentence and Question Formation Using Deep Learning Techniques. In *Digital Natives as a Disruptive Force in Asian Businesses and Societies* (pp. 252–273). IGI Global. 10.4018/978-1-6684-6782-4.ch015

Vijaya Lakshmi, V., Mishra, M., Kushwah, J. S., Shajahan, U. S., Mohanasundari, M., & Boopathi, S. (2024). Circular Economy Digital Practices for Ethical Dimensions and Policies for Digital Waste Management. In *Harnessing High-Performance Computing and AI for Environmental Sustainability* (pp. 166–193). IGI Global. 10.4018/979-8-3693-1794-5.ch008

Vrontis, D., Christofi, M., Pereira, V., Tarba, S., Makrides, A., & Trichina, E. (2022). Artificial intelligence, robotics, advanced technologies and human resource management: A systematic review. *International Journal of Human Resource Management*, 33(6), 1237–1266. 10.1080/09585192.2020.1871398

Wassan, S. (2021). How artificial intelligence transforms the experience of employees. [TURCOMAT]. *Turkish Journal of Computer and Mathematics Education*, 12(10), 7116–7135.

Zehir, C., Karaboğa, T., & Başar, D. (2020). The transformation of human resource management and its impact on overall business performance: Big data analytics and AI technologies in strategic HRM. *Digital Business Strategies in Blockchain Ecosystems: Transformational Design and Future of Global Business*, 265–279.

Chapter 12
Integrating Machine Learning–IoT Technologies Integration for Building Sustainable Digital Ecosystems

S. Revathi

Department of Computer Science Engineering, B.S. Abdur Rahman Crescent Institute of Science and Technology, Chennai, India

Afroze Ansari

https://orcid.org/0009-0000-2529-7945

Department of Computer Science and Engineering, Faculty of Engineering and Technology, Khaja Bandanawaz University, Karnataka, India

S. Jacophine Susmi

Department of Information Technology, University College of Engineering, Tindivanam, India

M. Madhavi

Department of CSE (AIML), Keshav Memorial Engineering College, Hyderabad, India

Gunavathie M. A.

Department of Information Technology, Easwari Engineering College, Chennai, India

M. Sudhakar

Department of Mechanical Engineering, Sri Sai Ram Engineering College, Chennai, India

ABSTRACT

The integration of ML, IoT, and NSA promotes significant opportunities for promoting sustainability in various industries. Actionable insights, while IoT devices collect

DOI: 10.4018/979-8-3693-2432-5.ch012

data for real-time monitoring and control of environmental parameters, have been provided by ML algorithms that analyze vast datasets. IoT deployments improve resource efficiency and resilience, while the NSA dynamically allocates network resources based on application requirements. These architectures prioritize traffic, optimize bandwidth, and ensure QoS to facilitate IoT and ML applications due to minimizing energy consumption and carbon emissions. However, challenges (data security, interoperability, and ethical) have been considered to persist, necessitating holistic sustainability approaches. Network slicing architectures provide a flexible network architecture for the efficient coexistence of diverse services and applications on a shared infrastructure.

INTRODUCTION

The integration of digital technologies, particularly ML, the IoT, and Network Slicing Architectures (NSA), is a promising approach to addressing environmental degradation, resource depletion, and societal inequities. Sustainable digital ecosystems aim to coexist technological innovation and environmental stewardship, leveraging digital tools to promote positive social, economic, and environmental outcomes. ML, which can analyze vast datasets and derive actionable insights, is crucial for optimizing resource allocation, predicting environmental trends, and driving operational efficiency across various sectors. This approach offers a transformative potential for addressing global challenges(Nativi et al., 2021).

The IoT is a new era of interconnectedness, enabling real-time data collection and analysis in everyday objects. It aids in environmental monitoring, energy management, and adaptive decision-making processes. IoT can unlock new pathways for sustainable development, including precision agriculture and smart energy grids. NSA complement IoT and ML, enabling efficient resource allocation based on application requirements. NSA optimizes bandwidth utilization, enhances QoS, and minimizes energy consumption, especially in IoT deployments where diverse applications have varying data transmission needs(Theodoraki et al., 2022).

IoT technologies are transforming environmental and societal issues by optimizing processes, mitigating environmental impacts, and enhancing societal well-being through machine learning insights. This can be applied to smart buildings, agriculture, and public transportation systems. However, challenges such as data security, interoperability, and ethical frameworks remain. Ensuring privacy and security of IoT-generated data, fostering interoperability, and upholding ethical principles are crucial for building trust and resilience in these ecosystems(Rosário & Dias, 2022).

The integration of Machine Learning, the Internet of Things, and Network Slicing Architectures is a significant step towards sustainability. The integration of these technologies can revolutionize our relationship with the environment, promote sustainable practices, and foster a more equitable future. Collaboration, innovation, and a shared commitment to sustainability will guide our journey. The convergence of these technologies offers a synergistic approach to addressing complex challenges and unlocking new opportunities for efficiency, optimization, and sustainability in various industries(Yin et al., 2020).

ML is a set of algorithms that enable systems to learn from data and improve performance over time. It has become a cornerstone of digital transformation, driving advancements in predictive analytics, pattern recognition, and decision-making processes across various industries. ML applications unlock actionable insights, optimize operations, and enhance user experiences. The IoT is a vast network of interconnected sensors, actuators, and devices that collect and exchange data autonomously, revolutionizing industries like smart cities, agriculture, healthcare, and logistics. By leveraging IoT technologies, organizations can gain unprecedented visibility into operations, optimize resource utilization, and improve decision-making processes(Wang, 2021).

NSA are a dynamic approach to network management and resource allocation in telecommunications. They partition physical network infrastructure into virtual slices, each tailored to specific application requirements. This flexibility is especially important in IoT deployments, where varying communication needs and quality-of-service requirements require adaptive network configurations. The integration of ML, IoT, and Natural Language Processing (NSA) is a powerful combination of technologies that contribute to efficiency, optimization, and sustainability. ML algorithms analyze vast data from IoT devices, while IoT devices collect real-world observations and interpret them into ML models. This symbiotic relationship forms the foundation for data-driven decision-making and adaptive control in various applications(Iden et al., 2021).

Network Slicing Architectures provide infrastructure for dynamic communication requirements and QoS guarantees across IoT deployments. They create virtual network slices tailored to specific use cases, enabling efficient resource utilization, minimizing latency, and ensuring reliable connectivity for mission-critical applications. This granular control optimizes performance, scalability, flexibility, and resilience in the face of evolving demands. The integration of Machine Learning, the Internet of Things, and Network Slicing Architectures is a significant technological advancement that enhances efficiency, optimization, and sustainability. By leveraging these technologies, organizations can unlock new opportunities for innovation, drive operational excellence, and create value in an interconnected world. This journey of integration and collaboration offers boundless possibilities for transformative change, shaping a future where intelligent systems, connected devices, and adaptive networks drive sustainable growth and prosperity(Iden et al., 2021; Yaghmaie & Vanhaverbeke, 2020).

The integration of Machine Learning, Internet of Things, and NSA in digital innovation has significant potential, but there is a gap in understanding their integrated applications and sustainability implications due to a lack of comprehensive frameworks and empirical studies that explore the synergies and challenges of combining these technologies. Sustainable development is crucial due to environmental degradation, resource depletion, and climate change. Organizations can harness the power of machine learning, IoT, and NSA to drive innovation, efficiency, and resilience. However, understanding how these technologies interact and synergize within sustainable digital ecosystems is essential for realizing their potential(Domeke et al., 2022).

This research aims to fill a gap and utilize integrated technologies for sustainability by achieving the following objectives.

1. To explore the synergies between Machine Learning, IoT, and Network Slicing Architectures in fostering sustainability
2. To assess the impact of integrated technologies on sustainability outcomes
3. To identify challenges and barriers to the adoption of integrated technologies for sustainability
4. This research aims to address the gap in understanding integrated technologies for sustainability, highlighting their importance in driving positive environmental and societal outcomes. It aims to explore synergies, impacts, and challenges of ML, IoT, and NSA integration, advancing knowledge and guiding decision-making towards a sustainable future.

HARNESSING MACHINE LEARNING FOR SUSTAINABILITY

Sustainable Digital Ecosystem

A network of digital platforms, technologies, and services intended to reduce environmental effect, promote social responsibility, and guarantee long-term economic sustainability is known as a sustainable digital ecosystem. It incorporates sustainable practices into all facets of operations, such as resource management, energy use, inclusive access, and ethical data handling(Venkateswaran et al., 2023).

1. Ethical practices in the digital age include energy efficiency, resource management, and ensuring security, privacy, and moral use of technology. These practices aim to reduce the carbon footprint of digital processes, encourage recycling, and reduce e-waste.
2. Inclusive access refers to providing equitable digital technology access to all groups, especially underserved ones, while sustainable company strategies aim to balance social and environmental responsibility with profitability.

ML is crucial in promoting sustainable practices across various industries. Its ability to analyze large amounts of data, identify patterns, and derive actionable insights helps organizations optimize resource utilization, minimize waste, and mitigate environmental impacts. Machine Learning is a powerful tool for promoting sustainability by enabling predictive analytics, optimizing resource usage, promoting energy efficiency, improving waste management, monitoring environmental changes, and driving sustainable investment decisions. As organizations continue to utilize ML, its potential positive environmental and societal impact increases(Abidi et al., 2021).

Figure 1. Harnessing machine learning for sustainability

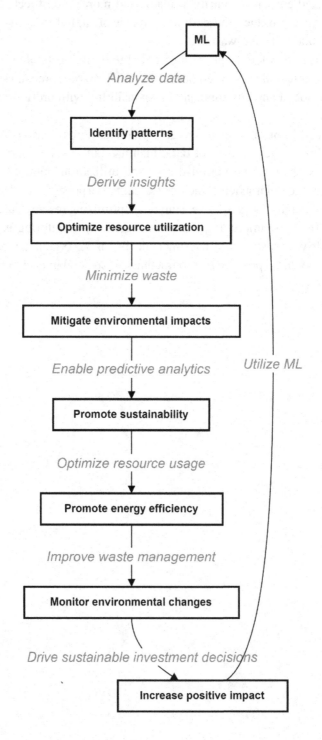

Figure 1 illustrates how Machine Learning (ML) is crucial in promoting sustainable practices across various industries by analyzing data, identifying patterns, deriving actionable insights, and ultimately driving positive environmental and societal impact.

- **Predictive Analytics for Resource Optimization:** ML algorithms excel in predictive analytics, forecasting future trends and patterns based on historical data. In the context of sustainability, predictive models can be deployed to optimize resource allocation and utilization. For example, in agriculture, ML algorithms can analyze weather patterns, soil conditions, and crop data to predict optimal planting times, irrigation schedules, and fertilizer usage, thereby minimizing waste and maximizing yields.
- **Energy Efficiency and Conservation:** ML algorithms are instrumental in optimizing energy consumption and promoting energy conservation initiatives. In smart buildings, for instance, ML-based systems can analyze occupancy patterns, temperature preferences, and external factors to dynamically adjust heating, cooling, and lighting settings for maximum efficiency. By reducing energy waste and optimizing usage patterns, ML contributes to significant cost savings and environmental benefits(Ugandar et al., 2023).
- **Waste Reduction and Recycling:** ML-powered systems can enhance waste management processes by improving sorting, recycling, and disposal practices. For instance, in recycling facilities, ML algorithms can identify and classify recyclable materials from mixed waste streams with high accuracy, streamlining the sorting process and increasing recycling rates. Similarly, in supply chain management, ML models can optimize packaging, logistics, and inventory management to minimize waste and reduce environmental impact(Mageswari et al., 2024; Rahamathunnisa et al., 2024; Vijaya Lakshmi et al., 2024).
- **Environmental Monitoring and Conservation:** ML techniques are increasingly being employed for environmental monitoring and conservation efforts. Remote sensing data, such as satellite imagery and sensor data, can be analyzed using ML algorithms to monitor changes in ecosystems, detect deforestation, track wildlife populations, and assess air and water quality. By providing real-time insights and early warning systems, ML enables proactive conservation interventions and helps preserve biodiversity and natural habitats(Kavitha et al., 2023; Kumara et al., 2023; Maguluri, Ananth, et al., 2023; Puranik et al., 2024).
- **Sustainable Finance and Investment:** ML algorithms are also being used to drive sustainable finance and investment decisions. By analyzing financial data, market trends, and environmental metrics, ML models can identify

investment opportunities that align with sustainability criteria, such as renewable energy projects, green bonds, and socially responsible investments. This integration of ML into financial decision-making processes promotes environmentally conscious investments and fosters sustainable economic development(Ravisankar et al., 2023).

Predictive Analytics for Resource Optimization

By providing predictive analytics for resource optimization, machine learning algorithms are transforming sustainability. In order to ensure sustainable results, they assist with demand forecasting, inefficiency identification, and resource allocation optimization. ML enables businesses to handle urgent environmental issues by enabling them to make well-informed decisions, reduce waste, and enhance resource efficiency across several industries (Singh et al., 2020). ML is used in sustainability for predictive analytics, which uses historical data to predict future trends. By analyzing patterns, correlations, and anomalies, ML algorithms can anticipate resource availability, demand patterns, and environmental conditions. This allows proactive decision-making, enabling organizations to allocate resources efficiently and optimize processes to minimize environmental impact(Singh et al., 2020).

ML-driven predictive analytics is a critical tool in resource optimization, playing a vital role in several important areas.

- **Energy Management:** ML algorithms analyze historical energy consumption data, weather patterns, and building occupancy to predict future energy demand. By forecasting peak usage periods and identifying opportunities for energy conservation, organizations can implement proactive measures to optimize energy usage, reduce costs, and lower carbon emissions.
- **Supply Chain Optimization:** ML models analyze supply chain data to predict demand fluctuations, transportation delays, and inventory shortages. By anticipating changes in demand and supply dynamics, organizations can optimize inventory levels, streamline logistics operations, and minimize waste throughout the supply chain(Mohanty et al., 2023; Verma et al., 2024).
- **Water Conservation:** ML algorithms analyze data from sensors, weather forecasts, and historical usage patterns to predict water demand and identify potential leaks or inefficiencies in water distribution systems. By detecting anomalies and predicting water usage patterns, organizations can implement proactive measures to conserve water, prevent waste, and ensure the sustainable management of water resources(Boopathi, 2024; Pachiappan et al., 2024; Rahamathunnisa et al., 2024).

- **Waste Management:** ML algorithms analyze data from sensors, waste composition studies, and historical collection routes to predict waste generation patterns and optimize waste collection schedules. By forecasting waste volumes and identifying high-volume areas, organizations can optimize collection routes, reduce fuel consumption, and minimize landfill usage(Harikaran et al., 2023; Koshariya et al., 2023; Selvakumar et al., 2023).

Predictive analytics powered by Machine Learning can optimize resource utilization and drive sustainability by forecasting future trends using historical data. This data-driven decision-making can minimize waste and maximize resource efficiency, contributing to a more sustainable future.

Energy Efficiency and Waste Reduction

ML is a powerful tool for sustainability, particularly in energy efficiency and waste reduction. It helps organizations optimize energy consumption, reduce waste, and minimize environmental impact by analyzing complex datasets(Wijethilaka & Liyanage, 2021).

Energy Efficiency: ML algorithms are crucial in improving energy efficiency across various sectors. They can analyze energy consumption patterns, identify inefficiencies, and predict future energy demand with accuracy, enabling organizations to optimize usage, reduce costs, and minimize their carbon footprint. ML-driven predictive maintenance can predict equipment failures before they occur, reducing downtime and maintenance costs. ML algorithms can also optimize energy distribution and management in smart grids by predicting demand fluctuations, optimizing energy storage, and balancing supply and demand in real-time. This dynamic management promotes sustainable energy use, reduces reliance on fossil fuels, and promotes renewable energy sources.

Waste Reduction: ML is essential for waste reduction by optimizing resource utilization and minimizing waste generation. It can analyze production processes, identify inefficiencies, and allocate resources effectively, thereby minimizing material waste and maximizing the use of recycled materials. ML-powered predictive analytics can enhance waste management by predicting waste generation patterns, optimizing collection routes, and identifying recycling opportunities. By analyzing historical data, ML algorithms can forecast future waste volumes, reducing operational costs and environmental impact. ML-driven sorting and recycling technologies, using computer vision and sensor-based technologies, can accurately classify and sort recyclable materials, increasing recycling rates and reducing landfill waste(Nassar & Yilmaz, 2021).

In order to maximize resource utilization, lessen environmental effect, and encourage sustainable habits, machine learning may be used to sustainability, particularly in the areas of energy efficiency and waste reduction. Through data analysis, process optimization, and well-informed decision-making, companies may promote favorable environmental outcomes and foster a more sustainable future.

IOT INNOVATIONS FOR SUSTAINABLE DEVELOPMENT

By linking commonplace items to the internet and empowering them to gather, share, and act on data independently, the Internet of Things (IoT) is transforming sustainability and creating opportunities for improving environmental management, maximizing resource use, and advancing sustainable development programs (Boopathi, 2024; Rahamathunnisa et al., 2024; Samikannu et al., 2022).

Figure 2. IOT innovations for sustainable development

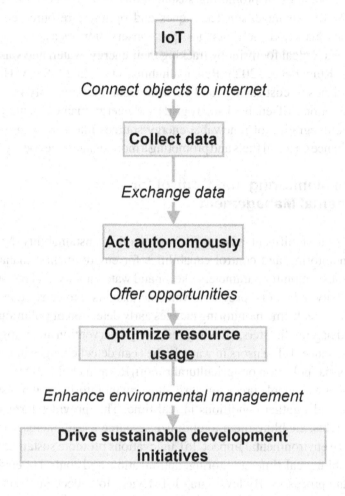

Figure 2 illustrates how the Internet of Things (IoT) is revolutionizing sustainability by connecting everyday objects to the internet, enabling them to collect, exchange, and act on data autonomously. This connectivity offers opportunities for optimizing resource usage, enhancing environmental management, and driving sustainable development initiatives.

Importance of IoT Devices in Promoting Sustainability

Through sensors and actuators on devices, Internet of Things technology provides real-time insights about resource use, energy consumption, and environmental conditions. By identifying environmental hazards, monitoring trends, and taking proactive steps to reduce negative effects on ecosystems and communities, these data assist companies in promoting sustainability. IoT devices are necessary to promote effective management techniques and optimize resource consumption. Organizations may find inefficiencies, put conservation measures in place, and lessen their ecological footprint by tracking their energy, water, and waste creation in real-time (Kumar et al., 2023; Rahamathunnisa et al., 2024; Satav, Hasan, et al., 2023). This leads to cost savings and environmental sustainability by minimizing resource depletion. IoT-enabled smart grids and energy management systems also facilitate the integration of renewable energy sources like solar and wind power, reducing reliance on fossil fuels and promoting a more sustainable energy ecosystem.

Real-Time Monitoring and Control for Environmental Management

IoT offers a significant advantage in promoting sustainability by providing real-time monitoring and control capabilities for environmental management. It can continuously monitor parameters like air and water quality, soil moisture levels, and biodiversity indicators, providing valuable insights into ecosystem health and resilience. This real-time monitoring enables early detection of pollution incidents, hazards, and natural disasters, allowing for timely intervention and mitigation measures. For instance, IoT sensors in water bodies can detect changes in water quality due to industrial pollution or agricultural runoff(Revathi et al., 2024).

IoT devices can enable precision agriculture by monitoring soil moisture levels, crop health, and weather conditions in real-time. This provides farmers with actionable insights, enabling them to optimize resource usage, increase crop yields, and minimize environmental impact. IoT innovations promote sustainable development by enabling real-time monitoring, optimization, and control of environmental resources and processes. By leveraging IoT devices to collect, analyze, and act on data, organizations can make informed decisions, implement proactive measures, and drive positive environmental outcomes. As the IoT ecosystem evolves, its role in advancing sustainability efforts will become increasingly vital in addressing global environmental challenges.

Applications in Smart Cities, Agriculture, and Energy Management

By allowing seamless connection and data exchange between physical items connected to the internet, the Internet of Things is transforming sustainable development. It maximizes the use of available resources, boosts productivity, and encourages environmental sustainability. The uses of IoT in smart cities, agriculture, and energy management are examined in this section (Agrawal et al., 2023; Maguluri, Arularasan, et al., 2023).

Smart Cities: IoT technologies are crucial in smart cities for optimizing urban infrastructure, enhancing quality of life, and promoting environmental sustainability. Smart sensors collect real-time data on air quality, traffic flow, waste management, and energy consumption, which are then analyzed using advanced analytics and Machine Learning algorithms. One key application of IoT is in transportation management, where sensors monitor traffic congestion, parking availability, and public transportation systems. This helps reduce traffic congestion, fuel consumption, and greenhouse gas emissions. IoT-enabled smart buildings also optimize energy usage, enhance occupant comfort, and reduce operational costs by automatically adjusting HVAC settings and lighting levels based on occupancy patterns, temperature, and lighting conditions(Maguluri, Arularasan, et al., 2023; Malathi et al., 2024; Sharma et al., 2024).

Agriculture: IoT technologies are revolutionizing agriculture by providing sustainable practices, precision agriculture, and food security. They collect data on soil moisture levels, temperature, humidity, and crop health, enabling farmers to make data-driven decisions and optimize resource allocation. Precision agriculture uses real-time data to apply water, fertilizers, and pesticides, minimizing waste and optimizing crop yields. IoT also enables remote monitoring and management of livestock, improving animal welfare, resource utilization, and disease prevention strategies. These technologies reduce environmental impact and enhance livestock welfare(Pachiappan et al., 2024).

Energy Management: IoT technologies are revolutionizing energy management by enabling efficient resource utilization, optimizing energy distribution networks, and integrating renewable energy sources. Smart meters and monitoring systems provide real-time energy usage insights, enabling consumers to identify energy conservation opportunities. IoT-enabled smart grids use sensors and communication networks to monitor and control electricity distribution, reducing transmission losses and improving grid stability. These technologies also facilitate the integration of renewable energy sources like solar and wind power, enhancing management of intermittent energy generation and demand(Satav, Lamani, et al., 2023; Syamala et al., 2023).

IoT innovations have the potential to drive sustainable development in sectors like smart cities, agriculture, and energy management. By collecting and analyzing real-time data, organizations can optimize resource utilization, enhance efficiency, and promote environmental sustainability, paving the way for a more resilient future.

NETWORK SLICING ARCHITECTURES: ENABLING SUSTAINABLE CONNECTIVITY

NSA are a revolutionary method for telecommunications infrastructure, allowing for dynamic resource allocation for various applications. They are crucial for sustainable connectivity, optimizing network performance, enhancing efficiency, and facilitating the seamless operation of IoT and ML applications. This section delves into the core concepts of NSA and its implications for sustainable connectivity(Yupapin et al., 2023).

Figure 3. Procedure for implementing NSA

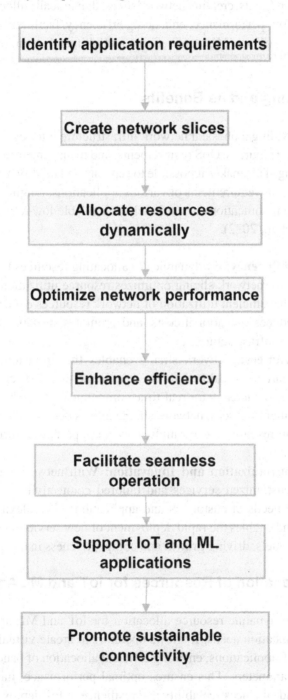

Figure 3 outlines the procedure for implementing NSA, starting with identifying application requirements, creating network slices, dynamically allocating resources, optimizing network performance, enhancing efficiency, facilitating seamless operation, supporting IoT and ML applications, and ultimately promoting sustainable connectivity.

Network Slicing and its Benefits

The act of dividing a physical network infrastructure into several virtual slices, each with its own resources, QoS requirements, and management policies, is known as network slicing. This makes it possible to separate and modify network resources to satisfy the various requirements of various applications, ranging from enormous machine-type communications to extremely dependable low-latency communications (Domeke et al., 2022).

- **Resource Efficiency:** By dynamically allocating resources based on application demands, network slicing optimizes resource utilization and minimizes wastage. This efficient utilization of network resources contributes to energy savings, reduces operational costs, and promotes sustainability in telecommunications infrastructure.
- **QoS Guarantees:** Network slicing enables the provision of differentiated QoS guarantees tailored to the requirements of specific applications. Whether it's low latency for real-time communications or high reliability for mission-critical services, network slicing allows operators to prioritize traffic and allocate resources accordingly, ensuring optimal performance and user experience.
- **Service Customization and Innovation:** With network slicing, operators can offer customized services and tailored connectivity solutions to meet the diverse needs of customers and applications. This flexibility fosters innovation and enables the rapid deployment of new services, applications, and business models, driving growth and competitiveness in the digital economy.

Dynamic Allocation of Resources for IoT and ML Applications

NSA helps in dynamic resource allocation for IoT and ML applications with varying communication needs. It allows operators to create virtual network slices optimized for IoT applications, ensuring efficient allocation of bandwidth, latency, and reliability parameters. This ensures optimal performance, minimizes energy consumption, and enhances scalability and resilience in IoT deployments, ensuring sustainable connectivity and a diverse array of devices with varying data transmission needs(Kumar et al., 2023; Pachiappan et al., 2024). NSA supports the integration of ML applications into telecommunications networks by providing infrastructure for data-intensive workloads and real-time analytics. ML algorithms deployed at the network edge use network slicing for data processing, model training, and inference.

Network Slicing Architectures are essential for sustainable connectivity by optimizing resource utilization, enhancing QoS guarantees, and facilitating IoT and ML applications. Operators can use NSA to unlock new opportunities for innovation, efficiency, and sustainability in telecommunications infrastructure, paving the way for a more connected future.

Optimizing Bandwidth and Quality of Service for Sustainability

This section discusses strategies for optimizing bandwidth and QoS in telecommunications networks to support sustainability goals. Efficient bandwidth utilization enhances user experience and reduces energy consumption, waste, and resource efficiency. Strategies for optimizing bandwidth and QoS in telecommunications networks are explored(Ingle et al., 2023; Nishanth et al., 2023).

Bandwidth Optimization

Bandwidth optimization is a process that enhances data transmission efficiency while minimizing resource usage and operational costs, using various strategies to promote sustainability(Sundaramoorthy et al., 2024).

- **Traffic Prioritization:** Prioritizing traffic based on application requirements enables efficient allocation of bandwidth and ensures optimal performance for critical services. By prioritizing latency-sensitive applications such as real-time communications and IoT data streams, operators can minimize packet loss and ensure timely delivery of data, enhancing user experience while conserving bandwidth.
- **Compression and Data Reduction:** Employing compression algorithms and data reduction techniques can significantly reduce the amount of data transmitted over the network, thereby conserving bandwidth and lowering data transfer costs. This is particularly relevant for IoT deployments, where sensor data streams can be compressed before transmission without compromising data fidelity, reducing bandwidth requirements and promoting sustainability.
- **Content Delivery Networks (CDNs):** CDNs cache content closer to end-users, reducing the distance data needs to travel over the network and minimizing bandwidth usage. By leveraging CDNs, operators can improve the efficiency of content delivery, reduce latency, and lower bandwidth con-

sumption, contributing to sustainability by optimizing network performance and reducing energy consumption in data transmission.

QoS Enhancement

Reliable QoS is crucial for consistent performance and meeting diverse application and user requirements. Implementing strategies can enhance QoS and promote sustainability(Ksentini et al., 2021).

- **Dynamic Resource Allocation:** Dynamic allocation of resources based on real-time demand and application requirements enables operators to optimize QoS parameters such as latency, throughput, and reliability. By dynamically adjusting resource allocation in response to changing network conditions and traffic patterns, operators can ensure optimal performance while minimizing energy consumption and operational costs.
- **Service Level Agreements (SLAs):** Establishing SLAs with customers and stakeholders defines performance metrics and service guarantees, ensuring that QoS requirements are met and maintained. By adhering to SLAs and proactively monitoring network performance, operators can enhance customer satisfaction, reduce churn, and promote sustainability by optimizing resource utilization and minimizing service disruptions.
- **Quality-aware Routing:** Quality-aware routing algorithms route traffic along paths that meet predefined QoS criteria, ensuring consistent performance and minimizing latency. By dynamically selecting the most appropriate paths based on QoS parameters such as delay, jitter, and packet loss, operators can optimize network performance, enhance user experience, and promote sustainability by minimizing energy consumption and reducing network congestion.

Optimizing bandwidth and ensuring QoS are crucial for promoting sustainability in telecommunications networks. These strategies enhance network efficiency, user experience, and reduce environmental impact, fostering a more resilient digital infrastructure.

SYNERGIES AND CHALLENGES IN CONVERGING TECHNOLOGIES

The integration of Machine Learning, IoT, and Network Slicing Architectures presents both opportunities and challenges in sustainability. This section explores the synergies and challenges of these technologies and proposes collaborative approaches to harness their potential for addressing environmental and societal issues(Rosário & Dias, 2022; Yaghmaie & Vanhaverbeke, 2020).

Figure 4. Challenges and opportunities: Integration of machine learning, IoT, and network slicing architectures

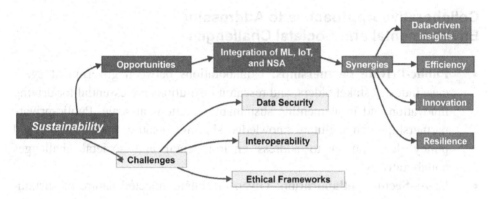

The integration of Machine Learning, IoT, and Network Slicing Architectures presents both opportunities and challenges in sustainability (Figure 4). It offers data-driven insights, efficiency, innovation, and resilience, but also challenges like data security, interoperability, and ethical frameworks. Collaborative approaches are proposed to utilize these technologies for addressing environmental and societal issues.

Opportunities for Innovation in Sustainability Practices

- **Data-Driven Decision Making:** The integration of ML and IoT enables organizations to collect, analyze, and interpret vast amounts of data to derive actionable insights for sustainability practices. By leveraging predictive analytics, optimization algorithms, and real-time monitoring capabilities, organizations can identify opportunities for resource efficiency, waste reduction, and environmental conservation.
- **Smart Resource Management:** IoT sensors and devices deployed in various domains, such as energy, agriculture, and transportation, provide real-time

data on resource utilization and environmental conditions. ML algorithms can analyze this data to optimize resource allocation, minimize waste, and enhance operational efficiency. For example, in agriculture, IoT-enabled precision farming techniques optimize water usage, reduce chemical inputs, and improve crop yields.

- **Dynamic Network Management:** NSA facilitates the dynamic allocation of network resources based on application requirements, enabling efficient communication and connectivity for IoT and ML applications. By creating virtual network slices tailored to specific use cases, operators can optimize bandwidth usage, ensure QoS, and minimize energy consumption, thereby promoting sustainability in telecommunications infrastructure.

Collaborative Approaches to Addressing Environmental and Societal Challenges

- **Public-Private Partnerships:** Collaborations between government agencies, industry stakeholders, and research institutions are essential for driving innovation and implementing sustainable solutions at scale. Public-private partnerships can facilitate knowledge sharing, resource mobilization, and policy development to address environmental and societal challenges collaboratively.
- **Cross-Sector Collaboration:** Given the interconnected nature of sustainability challenges, collaboration across sectors is crucial for developing holistic solutions that address multiple dimensions of sustainability. For example, partnerships between technology companies, environmental organizations, and community groups can leverage technological innovations to promote environmental conservation, social equity, and economic development.
- **Stakeholder Engagement:** Engaging stakeholders, including end-users, local communities, and marginalized groups, is essential for ensuring that sustainability initiatives are inclusive, equitable, and responsive to diverse needs and perspectives. By involving stakeholders in the design, implementation, and evaluation of sustainability projects, organizations can build trust, foster social cohesion, and promote collective action towards shared sustainability goals.

The integration of technologies like ML, IoT, and NSA can significantly enhance sustainability practices by providing data-driven insights, smart resource management, and dynamic network capabilities. However, this requires public-private partnerships, cross-sector collaboration, and stakeholder engagement to foster innovation, inclusivity, and resilience in sustainability initiatives.

Data Security, Interoperability, and Ethical Frameworks

The integration of Machine Learning, IoT, and Network Slicing Architectures offers significant potential for innovation and sustainability. However, challenges such as data security, interoperability, and ethical frameworks must be addressed to ensure their effective use and maintain their potential(Nassar & Yilmaz, 2021; Wijethilaka & Liyanage, 2021).

Synergies

- **Enhanced Efficiency and Insights:** The convergence of ML, IoT, and NSA enables organizations to leverage data-driven insights for optimizing processes, improving decision-making, and enhancing efficiency across diverse domains. ML algorithms analyze data collected by IoT devices within dynamically allocated network slices, providing organizations with actionable insights for driving sustainable practices and innovation.
- **Scalability and Flexibility:** By harnessing NSA, organizations can create virtual network slices tailored to specific application requirements, facilitating the seamless integration of ML and IoT applications. This scalability and flexibility enable organizations to adapt to changing demands and deploy new services rapidly, driving agility and innovation in sustainable development initiatives.
- **Resource Optimization:** NSA enables the dynamic allocation of resources based on application needs, optimizing bandwidth utilization and ensuring QoS guarantees for ML and IoT applications. This resource optimization enhances efficiency, reduces energy consumption, and promotes sustainability by minimizing waste and maximizing the use of available resources.

Challenges

- **Data Security:** The proliferation of interconnected devices and the exchange of vast amounts of data present significant challenges in ensuring data security and privacy. As ML algorithms analyze sensitive data collected by IoT devices, ensuring robust encryption, authentication, and access control mechanisms becomes essential to protect against cyber threats and unauthorized access.
- **Interoperability:** Integrating ML, IoT, and NSA technologies requires interoperability among disparate systems, protocols, and standards. Lack of interoperability can hinder data sharing, limit collaboration, and impede innovation in sustainable development initiatives. Addressing interoperabili-

ty challenges requires developing open standards, protocols, and interfaces to enable seamless integration and communication among heterogeneous systems.

- **Ethical Frameworks:** The convergence of technologies raises ethical concerns related to data privacy, algorithmic bias, and societal impact. ML algorithms trained on biased or incomplete datasets can perpetuate discrimination and exacerbate existing social inequalities. Developing ethical frameworks and guidelines for the responsible use of ML, IoT, and NSA technologies is essential to mitigate risks, promote fairness, and ensure that technology benefits society as a whole.

The convergence of ML, IoT, and NSA technologies holds significant potential for sustainability, but challenges like data security, interoperability, and ethical frameworks must be addressed. A holistic approach that prioritizes security, interoperability, and ethical considerations can help organizations harness these synergies while mitigating risks and promoting responsible innovation.

FUTURE DIRECTIONS AND IMPLICATIONS

The future of sustainable digital ecosystems is shaped by innovation, evolving technologies, and shifting paradigms. Emerging trends are poised to drive positive environmental and societal outcomes, shaping the trajectory of digital transformation and influencing the development of sustainable digital ecosystems(Rosário & Dias, 2022; Yin et al., 2020).

Figure 5. Future of sustainable digital ecosystems

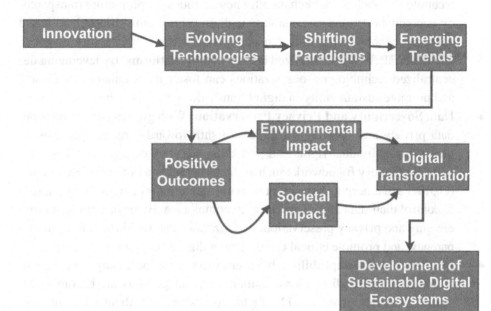

Figure 5 illustrates how innovation, evolving technologies, and shifting paradigms shape the future of sustainable digital ecosystems. Emerging trends drive positive environmental and societal outcomes, influencing the trajectory of digital transformation and the development of sustainable digital ecosystems.

- **Advancements in Renewable Energy Integration:** As renewable energy sources such as solar and wind power become increasingly prominent, there is a growing emphasis on integrating renewable energy technologies into digital ecosystems. Smart grids, energy storage solutions, and demand-side management strategies enable more efficient utilization of renewable energy resources, reducing reliance on fossil fuels and promoting sustainability in digital infrastructure.
- **Circular Economy Initiatives:** The concept of the circular economy, which emphasizes the reuse, recycling, and regeneration of resources, is gaining traction in digital ecosystems. Circular economy initiatives focus on extending the lifespan of digital devices, minimizing electronic waste, and promoting sustainable product design and manufacturing practices. By embracing circular economy principles, organizations can reduce environmental impact and promote resource efficiency in digital supply chains(Dhanya et al., 2023; Vijaya Lakshmi et al., 2024).

- **Decentralized and Distributed Technologies:** Decentralized and distributed technologies such as blockchain offer new avenues for promoting transparency, accountability, and sustainability in digital ecosystems. Blockchain-based solutions enable secure and transparent transactions, traceability of goods and materials, and decentralized energy trading platforms. By leveraging decentralized technologies, organizations can foster trust, enhance efficiency, and promote sustainability in digital transactions and operations.

- **Data Sovereignty and Privacy Preservation:** With growing concerns about data privacy and sovereignty, there is a shift towards greater emphasis on preserving individual rights and protecting sensitive data in digital ecosystems. Regulatory frameworks such as the General Data Protection Regulation (GDPR) and emerging privacy-preserving technologies empower individuals to control their data and ensure privacy compliance. By prioritizing data sovereignty and privacy preservation, organizations can build trust, foster transparency, and promote ethical use of data in digital ecosystems.

- **Resilience and Adaptability:** In an era marked by increasing environmental uncertainty and disruptions, resilience and adaptability are becoming essential attributes of sustainable digital ecosystems. Resilient infrastructure, adaptive technologies, and proactive risk management strategies enable organizations to anticipate and respond effectively to emerging challenges such as climate change, natural disasters, and cybersecurity threats. By fostering resilience and adaptability, organizations can mitigate risks, minimize disruptions, and promote sustainability in digital operations and services.

The future of sustainable digital ecosystems will involve a blend of technological innovation, regulatory frameworks, and societal priorities. By embracing renewable energy integration, circular economy initiatives, decentralized technologies, data sovereignty, and resilience, organizations can foster a more sustainable and inclusive digital future.

Long-Term Implications of ML, IoT, and NSA Integration

The integration of Machine Learning, IoT, and Network Slicing Architectures is expected to have significant long-term implications across various domains, with key implications emerging as these technologies become increasingly intertwined(Domeke et al., 2022).

- **Transformation of Industries:** ML, IoT, and NSA integration will revolutionize industries by enabling data-driven decision-making, automation, and optimization. Sectors such as healthcare, manufacturing, transportation, and agriculture will experience significant transformations as organizations leverage integrated technologies to enhance efficiency, productivity, and sustainability.

- **Emergence of Smart Cities and Infrastructure:** The convergence of ML, IoT, and NSA will drive the development of smart cities and infrastructure, where interconnected devices, sensors, and networks enable efficient resource management, responsive services, and improved quality of life for residents. Smart city initiatives will leverage integrated technologies to address urban challenges such as traffic congestion, pollution, and energy consumption, promoting sustainability and resilience in urban environments.

- **Advancements in Personalized Services:** ML, IoT, and NSA integration will enable the delivery of personalized services and experiences tailored to individual preferences and needs. From personalized healthcare and education to smart homes and connected vehicles, integrated technologies will empower individuals to access customized solutions that enhance convenience, efficiency, and well-being.

- **Ethical and Regulatory Considerations:** The long-term implications of ML, IoT, and NSA integration raise important ethical and regulatory considerations related to data privacy, security, and fairness. As these technologies become increasingly pervasive, ensuring transparency, accountability, and ethical use of data will be essential to build trust and mitigate risks associated with misuse or abuse of technology.

Pathways for Continued Innovation and Collaboration

To fully harness the potential of ML, IoT, and NSA integration, continuous innovation and collaboration are crucial(Ksentini et al., 2021).

- **Interdisciplinary Research and Education:** Encouraging interdisciplinary collaboration and fostering partnerships between academia, industry, and government will facilitate knowledge sharing, innovation, and skills development in fields such as data science, telecommunications, and sustainability.

- **Open Standards and Interoperability:** Promoting the development of open standards, protocols, and interfaces will facilitate interoperability and compatibility among disparate systems and technologies, enabling seamless integration and communication across networks and devices.

- **Investment in Research and Development:** Continued investment in research and development initiatives focused on ML, IoT, and NSA integration will drive innovation, technological advancements, and breakthroughs in sustainable digital ecosystems. Public and private sector investment in research funding, infrastructure, and talent development is crucial for fostering a culture of innovation and driving progress in emerging technologies.

- **Collaborative Ecosystems and Partnerships:** Building collaborative ecosystems and fostering partnerships between industry stakeholders, startups, research institutions, and policymakers will accelerate innovation, knowledge exchange, and technology adoption. Collaborative initiatives such as innovation hubs, accelerators, and consortia enable organizations to leverage collective expertise, resources, and networks to address shared challenges and drive positive impact in sustainable digital ecosystems.

The integration of ML, IoT, and NSA has significant long-term implications for industries, societies, and individuals. By fostering innovation and collaboration, stakeholders can harness these technologies' transformative potential, leading to a more sustainable and inclusive future.

CONCLUSION

Positive effects on the environment, society, and economy might result from the combination of machine learning, the internet of things, and network slicing architectures in sustainable digital ecosystems. From this investigation, important conclusions and suggestions are drawn, forming a picture of a future with more sustainability. The amalgamation of machine learning, IoT, and NSA technologies has the potential to greatly propel sustainability in several domains, such as energy efficiency, waste minimization, smart cities, and infrastructure. These technologies open up new avenues for resilient and sustainable development by providing creative answers to difficult problems, maximizing the use of available resources, and encouraging teamwork.

In order to advance sustainable digital ecosystems, stakeholders in sustainability and digital transformation must band together to encourage innovation, cooperation, and ethical behaviors. This entails funding research, encouraging data openness, and giving the welfare of society and the environment top priority when making decisions. A more resilient and sustainable environment for coming generations may be created by working toward shared objectives.

The future vision aims to create an inclusive and sustainable digital society by using technology to address environmental problems, advance social justice, and stimulate economic growth. By encouraging openness, confidence, and cooperation, this vision empowers people to take charge of their own destiny and that of their communities. A common commitment to sustainability, creativity, and inclusion should serve as the foundation for the critical integration of ML, IoT, and NSA. Technology promotes harmony on Earth and good effects.

REFERENCES

Abidi, M. H., Alkhalefah, H., Moiduddin, K., Alazab, M., Mohammed, M. K., Ameen, W., & Gadekallu, T. R. (2021). Optimal 5G network slicing using machine learning and deep learning concepts. *Computer Standards & Interfaces*, 76, 103518. 10.1016/j.csi.2021.103518

Agrawal, A. V., Magulur, L. P., Priya, S. G., Kaur, A., Singh, G., & Boopathi, S. (2023). Smart Precision Agriculture Using IoT and WSN. In *Handbook of Research on Data Science and Cybersecurity Innovations in Industry 4.0 Technologies* (pp. 524–541). IGI Global. 10.4018/978-1-6684-8145-5.ch026

Boopathi, S. (2024). Sustainable Development Using IoT and AI Techniques for Water Utilization in Agriculture. In *Sustainable Development in AI, Blockchain, and E-Governance Applications* (pp. 204–228). IGI Global. 10.4018/979-8-3693-1722-8. ch012

Dhanya, D., Kumar, S. S., Thilagavathy, A., Prasad, D., & Boopathi, S. (2023). Data Analytics and Artificial Intelligence in the Circular Economy: Case Studies. In *Intelligent Engineering Applications and Applied Sciences for Sustainability* (pp. 40–58). IGI Global.

Domeke, A., Cimoli, B., & Monroy, I. T. (2022). Integration of network slicing and machine learning into edge networks for low-latency services in 5G and beyond systems. *Applied Sciences (Basel, Switzerland)*, 12(13), 6617. 10.3390/app12136617

Harikaran, M., Boopathi, S., Gokulakannan, S., & Poonguzhali, M. (2023). Study on the Source of E-Waste Management and Disposal Methods. In *Sustainable Approaches and Strategies for E-Waste Management and Utilization* (pp. 39–60). IGI Global. 10.4018/978-1-6684-7573-7.ch003

Iden, J., Bygstad, B., Osmundsen, K. S., Costabile, C., & Øvrelid, E. (2021). Digital platform ecosystem governance: Preliminary findings and research agenda. *Norsk IKT-Konferanse for Forskning Og Utdanning, 2*.

Ingle, R. B., Swathi, S., Mahendran, G., Senthil, T., Muralidharan, N., & Boopathi, S. (2023). Sustainability and Optimization of Green and Lean Manufacturing Processes Using Machine Learning Techniques. In *Circular Economy Implementation for Sustainability in the Built Environment* (pp. 261–285). IGI Global. 10.4018/978-1-6684-8238-4.ch012

Kavitha, C., Varalatchoumy, M., Mithuna, H., Bharathi, K., Geethalakshmi, N., & Boopathi, S. (2023). Energy Monitoring and Control in the Smart Grid: Integrated Intelligent IoT and ANFIS. In *Applications of Synthetic Biology in Health, Energy, and Environment* (pp. 290–316). IGI Global.

Koshariya, A. K., Khatoon, S., Marathe, A. M., Suba, G. M., Baral, D., & Boopathi, S. (2023). Agricultural Waste Management Systems Using Artificial Intelligence Techniques. In *AI-Enabled Social Robotics in Human Care Services* (pp. 236–258). IGI Global. 10.4018/978-1-6684-8171-4.ch009

Ksentini, A., Jebalia, M., & Tabbane, S. (2021). IoT/Cloud-enabled smart services: A review on QoS requirements in fog environment and a proposed approach based on priority classification technique. *International Journal of Communication Systems*, 34(2), e4269. 10.1002/dac.4269

Kumar, M., Kumar, K., Sasikala, P., Sampath, B., Gopi, B., & Sundaram, S. (2023). Sustainable Green Energy Generation From Waste Water: IoT and ML Integration. In *Sustainable Science and Intelligent Technologies for Societal Development* (pp. 440–463). IGI Global.

Kumara, V., & Sharma, M. D., Samson Isaac, J., Saravanan, S., Suganthi, D., & Boopathi, S. (2023). An AI-Integrated Green Power Monitoring System: Empowering Small and Medium Enterprises. In *Advances in Environmental Engineering and Green Technologies* (pp. 218–244). IGI Global. 10.4018/979-8-3693-0338-2.ch013

Mageswari, D. U., Kareemullah, H., Jithesh, K., Boopathi, S., Rachel, P. M. P. P., & Ramkumar, M. S. (2024). Experimental investigation of mechanical properties and multi-objective optimization of electronic, glass, and ceramic waste–mixed concrete. *Environmental Science and Pollution Research International*. 10.1007/s11356-024-33751-738806982

Maguluri, L. P., Ananth, J., Hariram, S., Geetha, C., Bhaskar, A., & Boopathi, S. (2023). Smart Vehicle-Emissions Monitoring System Using Internet of Things (IoT). In *Handbook of Research on Safe Disposal Methods of Municipal Solid Wastes for a Sustainable Environment* (pp. 191–211). IGI Global.

Maguluri, L. P., Arularasan, A., & Boopathi, S. (2023). Assessing Security Concerns for AI-Based Drones in Smart Cities. In *Effective AI, Blockchain, and E-Governance Applications for Knowledge Discovery and Management* (pp. 27–47). IGI Global. 10.4018/978-1-6684-9151-5.ch002

Malathi, J., Kusha, K., Isaac, S., Ramesh, A., Rajendiran, M., & Boopathi, S. (2024). IoT-Enabled Remote Patient Monitoring for Chronic Disease Management and Cost Savings: Transforming Healthcare. In *Advances in Explainable AI Applications for Smart Cities* (pp. 371–388). IGI Global.

Mohanty, A., Venkateswaran, N., Ranjit, P., Tripathi, M. A., & Boopathi, S. (2023). Innovative Strategy for Profitable Automobile Industries: Working Capital Management. In *Handbook of Research on Designing Sustainable Supply Chains to Achieve a Circular Economy* (pp. 412–428). IGI Global.

Nassar, A., & Yilmaz, Y. (2021). Deep reinforcement learning for adaptive network slicing in 5G for intelligent vehicular systems and smart cities. *IEEE Internet of Things Journal*, 9(1), 222–235. 10.1109/JIOT.2021.3091674

Nativi, S., Mazzetti, P., & Craglia, M. (2021). Digital ecosystems for developing digital twins of the earth: The destination earth case. *Remote Sensing (Basel)*, 13(11), 2119. 10.3390/rs13112119

Nishanth, J., Deshmukh, M. A., Kushwah, R., Kushwaha, K. K., Balaji, S., & Sampath, B. (2023). Particle Swarm Optimization of Hybrid Renewable Energy Systems. In *Intelligent Engineering Applications and Applied Sciences for Sustainability* (pp. 291–308). IGI Global. 10.4018/979-8-3693-0044-2.ch016

Pachiappan, K., Anitha, K., Pitchai, R., Sangeetha, S., Satyanarayana, T., & Boopathi, S. (2024). Intelligent Machines, IoT, and AI in Revolutionizing Agriculture for Water Processing. In *Handbook of Research on AI and ML for Intelligent Machines and Systems* (pp. 374–399). IGI Global.

Puranik, T. A., Shaik, N., Vankudoth, R., Kolhe, M. R., Yadav, N., & Boopathi, S. (2024). Study on Harmonizing Human-Robot (Drone) Collaboration: Navigating Seamless Interactions in Collaborative Environments. In *Cybersecurity Issues and Challenges in the Drone Industry* (pp. 1–26). IGI Global.

Rahamathunnisa, U., Sudhakar, K., Padhi, S., Bhattacharya, S., Shashibhushan, G., & Boopathi, S. (2024). Sustainable Energy Generation From Waste Water: IoT Integrated Technologies. In *Adoption and Use of Technology Tools and Services by Economically Disadvantaged Communities: Implications for Growth and Sustainability* (pp. 225–256). IGI Global.

Ravisankar, A., Sampath, B., & Asif, M. M. (2023). Economic Studies on Automobile Management: Working Capital and Investment Analysis. In *Multidisciplinary Approaches to Organizational Governance During Health Crises* (pp. 169–198). IGI Global.

Revathi, S., Babu, M., Rajkumar, N., Meti, V. K. V., Kandavalli, S. R., & Boopathi, S. (2024). Unleashing the Future Potential of 4D Printing: Exploring Applications in Wearable Technology, Robotics, Energy, Transportation, and Fashion. In *Human-Centered Approaches in Industry 5.0: Human-Machine Interaction, Virtual Reality Training, and Customer Sentiment Analysis* (pp. 131–153). IGI Global.

Rosário, A. T., & Dias, J. C. (2022). Sustainability and the digital transition: A literature review. *Sustainability (Basel)*, 14(7), 4072. 10.3390/su14074072

Samikannu, R., Koshariya, A. K., Poornima, E., Ramesh, S., Kumar, A., & Boopathi, S. (2022). Sustainable Development in Modern Aquaponics Cultivation Systems Using IoT Technologies. In *Human Agro-Energy Optimization for Business and Industry* (pp. 105–127). IGI Global.

Satav, S. D., Hasan, D. S., Pitchai, R., Mohanaprakash, T., Sultanuddin, S., & Boopathi, S. (2023). Next generation of internet of things (ngiot) in healthcare systems. In *Sustainable Science and Intelligent Technologies for Societal Development* (pp. 307–330). IGI Global.

Satav, S. D., Lamani, D., Harsha, K., Kumar, N., Manikandan, S., & Sampath, B. (2023). Energy and Battery Management in the Era of Cloud Computing: Sustainable Wireless Systems and Networks. In *Sustainable Science and Intelligent Technologies for Societal Development* (pp. 141–166). IGI Global.

Selvakumar, S., Adithe, S., Isaac, J. S., Pradhan, R., Venkatesh, V., & Sampath, B. (2023). A Study of the Printed Circuit Board (PCB) E-Waste Recycling Process. In *Sustainable Approaches and Strategies for E-Waste Management and Utilization* (pp. 159–184). IGI Global.

Sharma, M., Sharma, M., Sharma, N., & Boopathi, S. (2024). Building Sustainable Smart Cities Through Cloud and Intelligent Parking System. In *Handbook of Research on AI and ML for Intelligent Machines and Systems* (pp. 195–222). IGI Global.

Singh, S. K., Salim, M. M., Cha, J., Pan, Y., & Park, J. H. (2020). Machine learning-based network sub-slicing framework in a sustainable 5g environment. *Sustainability (Basel)*, 12(15), 6250. 10.3390/su12156250

Sundaramoorthy, K., Singh, A., Sumathy, G., Maheshwari, A., Arunarani, A., & Boopathi, S. (2024). A Study on AI and Blockchain-Powered Smart Parking Models for Urban Mobility. In *Handbook of Research on AI and ML for Intelligent Machines and Systems* (pp. 223–250). IGI Global.

Syamala, M., Komala, C., Pramila, P., Dash, S., Meenakshi, S., & Boopathi, S. (2023). Machine Learning-Integrated IoT-Based Smart Home Energy Management System. In *Handbook of Research on Deep Learning Techniques for Cloud-Based Industrial IoT* (pp. 219–235). IGI Global. 10.4018/978-1-6684-8098-4.ch013

Theodoraki, C., Dana, L.-P., & Caputo, A. (2022). Building sustainable entrepreneurial ecosystems: A holistic approach. *Journal of Business Research*, 140, 346–360. 10.1016/j.jbusres.2021.11.005

Ugandar, R., Rahamathunnisa, U., Sajithra, S., Christiana, M. B. V., Palai, B. K., & Boopathi, S. (2023). Hospital Waste Management Using Internet of Things and Deep Learning: Enhanced Efficiency and Sustainability. In *Applications of Synthetic Biology in Health, Energy, and Environment* (pp. 317–343). IGI Global.

Venkateswaran, N., Vidhya, K., Ayyannan, M., Chavan, S. M., Sekar, K., & Boopathi, S. (2023). A Study on Smart Energy Management Framework Using Cloud Computing. In *5G, Artificial Intelligence, and Next Generation Internet of Things: Digital Innovation for Green and Sustainable Economies* (pp. 189–212). IGI Global. 10.4018/978-1-6684-8634-4.ch009

Verma, R., Christiana, M. B. V., Maheswari, M., Srinivasan, V., Patro, P., Dari, S. S., & Boopathi, S. (2024). Intelligent Physarum Solver for Profit Maximization in Oligopolistic Supply Chain Networks. In *AI and Machine Learning Impacts in Intelligent Supply Chain* (pp. 156–179). IGI Global. 10.4018/979-8-3693-1347-3.ch011

Vijaya Lakshmi, V., Mishra, M., Kushwah, J. S., Shajahan, U. S., Mohanasundari, M., & Boopathi, S. (2024). Circular Economy Digital Practices for Ethical Dimensions and Policies for Digital Waste Management. In *Harnessing High-Performance Computing and AI for Environmental Sustainability* (pp. 166–193). IGI Global. 10.4018/979-8-3693-1794-5.ch008

Wang, P. (2021). Connecting the parts with the whole: Toward an information ecology theory of digital innovation ecosystems. *Management Information Systems Quarterly*, 45(1), 397–422. 10.25300/MISQ/2021/15864

Wijethilaka, S., & Liyanage, M. (2021). Survey on network slicing for Internet of Things realization in 5G networks. *IEEE Communications Surveys and Tutorials*, 23(2), 957–994. 10.1109/COMST.2021.3067807

Yaghmaie, P., & Vanhaverbeke, W. (2020). Identifying and describing constituents of innovation ecosystems: A systematic review of the literature. *EuroMed Journal of Business*, 15(3), 283–314. 10.1108/EMJB-03-2019-0042

Yin, D., Ming, X., & Zhang, X. (2020). Sustainable and smart product innovation ecosystem: An integrative status review and future perspectives. *Journal of Cleaner Production*, 274, 123005. 10.1016/j.jclepro.2020.123005

Yupapin, P., Trabelsi, Y., Nattappan, A., & Boopathi, S. (2023). Performance improvement of wire-cut electrical discharge machining process using cryogenically treated super-conductive state of Monel-K500 alloy. *Iranian Journal of Science and Technology. Transaction of Mechanical Engineering*, 47(1), 267–283. 10.1007/s40997-022-00513-0

Chapter 13
Fog and Cloud Computing Integration With Intelligent Surfaces and Recent Advances

Komala C. R.

Department of Information Science and Engineering, East Point College of Engineering and Technology, Bengaluru, India

V. Vaithianathan
https://orcid.org/0000-0002-5482-4019

Department of Electronics and Communication Engineering, Sri Sivasubramaniya Nadar College of Engineering, Chennai, India

K. J. Jegadish Kumar

Department of Electronics and Communication Engineering, Sri Sivasubramaniya Nadar College of Engineering, Chennai, India

S. Vijayakumar
https://orcid.org/0000-0001-7608-7569

Department of Mathematics, RMK Engineering College, Kavaraipettai, India

Gunavathie M. A.

Department of Information Technology, Easwari Engineering College, Chennai, India

ABSTRACT

Intelligent surfaces' combination of fog and cloud computing is a major break-through in digital infrastructure. In this chapter, these two realms work in concert,

DOI: 10.4018/979-8-3693-2432-5.ch013

emphasizing how intelligent surfaces serve as linkages to close the gap. It explores the basic ideas of fog and cloud computing and their functions in dispersed systems and intelligent surfaces. Real-time analytics, predictive maintenance, user experiences in smart cities, healthcare, and industrial automation are discussed because integration has the potential to revolutionize industries. However, there are obstacles to overcome, such as security worries, interoperability problems, and standard protocols. The stakeholders may utilize current advancements and best practices to accelerate digital transformation and create a new linked world.

INTRODUCTION

The integration of fog and cloud computing with intelligent surfaces, which attempts to revolutionize data processing, administration, and leveraging, is a significant advancement in digital infrastructure. By bringing the cloud closer to the network edge, fog computing reduces latency and bandwidth consumption. It is driven by real-time data analytics, IoT ecosystems, and the widespread use of linked devices. Because of cloud computing's infinite storage and processing power, complex tasks and large data volumes may be handled in a flexible, scalable, and economical manner (Ning et al., 2019).

Intelligent surfaces act as links between fog nodes, cloud servers, and end devices in distributed computing environments, controlling data flow and optimizing resource use. Microcontrollers, sensors, actuators, and edge computing devices are examples of the hardware and software components they use to process and transmit real-time data. A number of industries, including manufacturing, transportation, smart cities, healthcare, and agriculture, benefit from the efficient application of this technology. In smart cities, it improves predictive maintenance, adaptive traffic management, and infrastructure monitoring (Munir et al., 2017).

Thanks to edge computing technologies like edge AI and analytics, which enable revolutionary data processing at the network edge, real-time decision-making and actionable insights are now feasible. System efficiency and utilization are increased via optimization and dynamic resource allocation algorithms. Edge-native applications and services, designed for distributed computing settings, promise new use cases and revenue models. Increased acceptance and innovation in the fog-cloud computing combination will result from this. These advancements have accelerated innovation and opened up new opportunities for companies worldwide (Liu et al., 2020).

The integration of fog and cloud computing with intelligent surfaces, which enables enterprises to use distributed computing, real-time analytics, and intelligent automation, is a significant development in digital infrastructure. This convergence may create new opportunities for innovation, distinction, and competitive advantage in a data-driven future (Wang et al., 2021). Through the use of hardware and software components, the network edge carries out context-aware computing, adaptive resource management, and intelligent decision-making. Localized data processing, made feasible by sensors, actuators, and edge computing devices, reduces the amount of data transport to remote servers. Reduced latency, bandwidth conservation, and real-time responsiveness are very advantageous for latency-sensitive applications such as augmented reality, driverless automobiles, and industrial automation because of their near proximity (Lu et al., 2017).

Network infrastructures with intelligent surfaces may identify patterns, evaluate data, and take action without relying on centralized cloud servers. They use rule-based engines, predictive analytics, and machine learning algorithms to do this. They improve system resilience, scalability, and flexibility by dynamically allocating computational resources based on workload requirements, external conditions, and user preferences. Businesses may increase system reliability, optimize resource usage, reduce operational costs, and scale resources in real-time by taking use of edge computing capabilities (Mokni et al., 2022).

Intelligent surfaces need to be connected with fog and cloud computing in order for many industries to continue being creative, effective, and competitive. It permits timely repairs, anticipatory maintenance, and instantaneous decision-making. Furthermore, it increases system resilience and ensures uninterrupted service delivery and business continuity in mission-critical applications including financial transactions, healthcare systems, and smart grids by distributing computing workloads among distributed nodes (Mokni et al., 2022).

Intelligent surfaces may be used with fog and cloud computing to improve patient outcomes, streamline supply chains, and enhance intelligent surfaces. Moreover, it is necessary for real-time data processing at the network edge, adaptive resource management, and independent decision-making. In an era where data is propelling worldwide connectedness, businesses may benefit from this integration by gaining a competitive edge, fostering innovation, and finding new growth opportunities (Tärneberg, 2019).

This chapter explores the integration of fog and cloud computing with intelligent surfaces, highlighting its role, significance, and recent advancements in digital infrastructure (Nath et al., 2018).

- To explore the integration of fog and cloud computing with intelligent surfaces, highlighting their benefits in real-time decision-making, system resilience, operational efficiency, innovation, and competitiveness.
- To explore the integration of fog and cloud computing with intelligent surfaces, highlighting their transformative potential but also highlighting challenges like security and interoperability.

- To provide practical guidance for organizations on integrating fog and cloud computing with intelligent surfaces, outlining successful deployment strategies, lessons learned, and future research directions.

The chapter delves into the integration of cloud computing and fog with intelligent surfaces, highlighting its potential benefits, practical implications, and significance in digital infrastructure.

FOG AND CLOUD COMPUTING

Fog Computing: Architecture and Characteristics

Fog computing extends cloud computing to network edges, enabling local data processing and communication between end devices and centralized servers, lowering latency and preserving bandwidth (Tärneberg, 2019).

Fog computing is a new cloud computing approach that prioritizes data proximity, ensuring low latency communication and is ideal for time-sensitive applications like autonomous cars and industrial automation. It enables real-time processing and analysis at the network edge, focusing on scalability and resource efficiency, using distributed computing resources to handle fluctuating workloads (Mokni et al., 2022).

Fog computing enhances transparency and interoperability, facilitating seamless integration with various IoT ecosystems and cloud infrastructure, enabling seamless data flow between fog nodes, cloud servers, and end devices.

Cloud Computing: Infrastructure and Services

Pay-as-you-go cloud computing provides internet-based processing, networking, storage, and other computer services through data centers connected by fast networks. It falls into three categories: Infrastructure as a Service (IaaS), Platform as a Service (PaaS), and Software as a Service (SaaS). IaaS allows businesses to manage apps without physical infrastructure, PaaS streamlines development processes, and SaaS eliminates local installation, maintenance, and upgrades by delivering programs over the internet (Pitchai et al., 2024).

Comparative Analysis

Fog and cloud computing are network resources, but they differ in features and use cases. Fog computing is ideal for industrial automation, smart cities, and healthcare monitoring systems, focusing on low-latency, real-time processing near the network edge, while cloud computing is suitable for big data analytics, ERP, and CRM due to its scalability, flexibility, and affordability (Dhanalakshmi et al., 2024).

Figure 1. Distinctions between fog and cloud computing

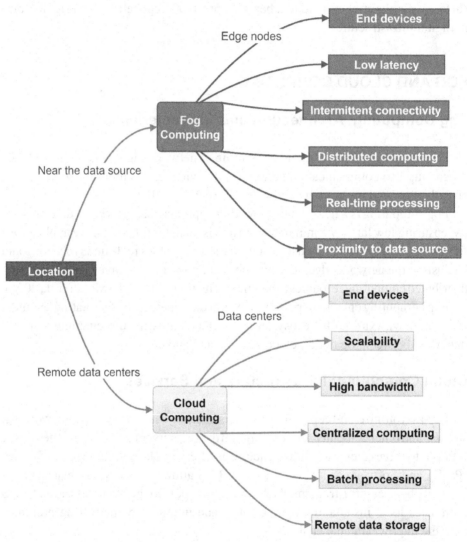

Figure 1 outlines the differences between fog and cloud computing, highlighting their differences in processing speed, data storage, location, latency, scalability, connection, computing paradigm, and proximity to data sources. Fog computing enhances cloud computing by enabling dispersed computing and seamless interaction with IoT devices. By combining local processing with cloud infrastructure scalability, enterprises can design hybrid architectures for diverse sectors.

INTELLIGENT SURFACES: INTERMEDIARIES IN THE CONVERGENCE

This section delves into the crucial role of intelligent surfaces in facilitating smooth communication, data processing, and resource allocation in remote computing systems, bridging the fog and cloud computing divide (Verma et al., 2024).

Figure 2. Functional flows within intelligent surfaces

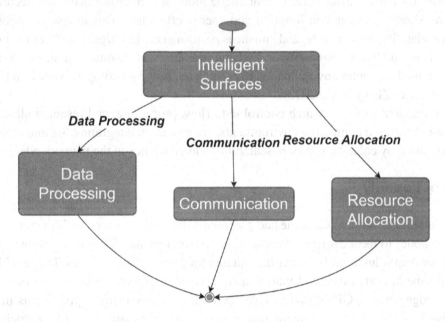

Figure 2 illustrates the flow of functions within intelligent surfaces in distributed computing environments, highlighting their roles in data processing, communication, and resource allocation.

Conceptual Framework

An intelligent surface is a computing architecture that combines decentralized and distributed intelligence, dispersing power around the network edge to get closer to data sources. It allows context-aware computing, adaptive resource management, and autonomous decision-making through hardware and software components. Equipped with sensors, actuators, microcontrollers, and edge computing devices, they can gather and interpret real-time data (Dhanalakshmi et al., 2024).

Intelligent surfaces improve network edge data processing by minimizing data transfer to distant cloud servers, reducing latency and conserving bandwidth. They integrate machine learning algorithms, rule-based engines, and predictive analytics into network infrastructure, facilitating autonomous decision-making. Distributed intelligence enhances system resilience, scalability, and flexibility, allowing companies to quickly react to changing circumstances and new threats (Moreno & Redondo, 2016).

Intelligent surfaces manage computational resources dynamically based on workload, environmental factors, and user choices. They utilize edge computing capabilities like virtualization, containerization, and microservices architecture to maximize resource consumption and energy efficiency. This increases system dependability, lowers costs, and enhances performance. Intelligent surfaces enable real-time analytics, autonomous decision-making, and seamless integration in distributed computer environments, fostering creativity and competitiveness in the digital age (Zhang et al., 2022).

Intelligent surfaces, which control data flow, processing, and resource allocation in dispersed computing environments, are crucial in integrating fog and cloud computing by enhancing system scalability and efficiency at the network edge.

Functionality

Intelligent surfaces combine and preprocess data from sensors, IoT devices, and edge nodes to meet distributed computing system demands. They save bandwidth, reduce data volume, and improve data quality for downstream analytics. They enable real-time data processing and analysis at the network edge using computing resources like edge servers, GPUs, and FPGAs, benefiting time-sensitive applications like driverless cars, predictive maintenance, and smart grid management by reducing latency and facilitating quicker decision-making (Wu et al., 2022).

Intelligent surfaces optimize computing resources by dynamically allocating them based on workload, environmental conditions, and user preferences. They use strategies like resource provisioning, load balancing, and job scheduling to reduce contention and increase throughput. Standard protocols like MQTT, CoAP, and OPC UA facilitate smooth communication between fog nodes, cloud servers, and end devices. This interoperability allows seamless integration of business systems, IoT ecosystems, and cloud infrastructure, offering comprehensive solutions for various use cases (Vermesan et al., 2022).

Features

Intelligent surfaces have distinct qualities that set them apart from traditional components of network infrastructure (Zhang et al., 2022). By providing real-time data processing, resource optimization, and network edge connectivity, intelligent surfaces help to integrate fog and cloud computing. They provide cutting-edge capabilities, allowing businesses to use distributed computing strategies that boost productivity, creativity, and competitiveness in the digital age.

- Edge Intelligence: At the network edge, intelligent surfaces allow for adaptive resource management and self-governing decision-making by integrating intelligence directly into the network infrastructure. By improving system resilience, flexibility, and responsiveness, edge intelligence helps enterprises implement distributed computing solutions for real-time applications.
- Context Awareness: Because intelligent surfaces are aware of their surroundings and context, they may modify their functionality and behavior in response to shifting circumstances and user demands. Context awareness improves user experiences and system performance by enabling proactive decision-making, dynamic resource allocation, and tailored offerings.
- Scalability: To meet the needs of expanding data quantities, rising computing costs, and changing application requirements, intelligent surfaces are built to scale both horizontally and vertically. Because of its scalability, businesses may implement distributed computing solutions that increase in size in accordance with their demands without compromising dependability or performance.

ADVANCEMENTS IN INTEGRATION

Enhanced Data Processing at the Network Edge

The integration of fog and cloud computing has made significant progress in improving data processing capabilities at the network edge. The aim is to minimize latency, process data closer to the source, and meet the growing volume of IoT data. Edge computing devices equipped with powerful CPUs, GPUs, and FPGAs enable localized data processing, faster reaction times, lower bandwidth usage, and enhanced system efficiency (Vermesan et al., 2022). Data processing at the network edge has been expedited by edge computing designs such as containerization technologies and distributed computing frameworks. Parallel processing over several edge nodes is made possible by distributed computing frameworks like Apache Spark and Apache

Flink, while quick innovation is facilitated by containerization technologies like Docker and Kubernetes.

The real-time analytics, anomaly detection, and predictive maintenance fields have been transformed by the incorporation of artificial intelligence and machine learning techniques into edge computing settings. The system's responsiveness and intelligence are improved by this integration. The creation and deployment of edge applications have been made easier by edge analytics platforms and middleware solutions, which offer pre-built modules, libraries, and APIs for data intake, processing, and visualization. This abstraction layer promotes innovation in edge computing applications, shortens time-to-market, and lowers development costs.

Improvements in edge computing capabilities, such as lower latency and better data processing capabilities, have revolutionized the usage of fog and cloud computing by enterprises and allowed for real-time analytics. New use cases, increased operational effectiveness, and enhanced user experiences are the results of this. Edge computing will become a key component of digital transformation in many sectors as it develops.

Dynamic Resource Allocation and Optimization

Dynamic resource allocation and optimization are achieved through the integration of intelligent surfaces with fog and cloud computing. This approach optimizes resource consumption, energy efficiency, and system performance by allocating computational resources based on workload needs, environmental factors, and user preferences. This approach differs from conventional cloud computing models, enhancing system performance (Liu et al., 2020; Narmeen et al., 2024).

Intelligent surfaces carry out dynamic resource allocation and optimization using sophisticated algorithms and methodologies. To evaluate resource availability and demand, they track system indicators like CPU use, memory usage, and network bandwidth. To balance workload and enhance throughput, they dynamically reallocate resources from underused to severely laden nodes. Additionally, they employ machine learning techniques and predictive analytics to foresee future trends in workload and performance, allowing for proactive resource allocation and optimization. This proactive strategy guarantees optimal system performance under a range of circumstances, decreases reaction times, and lowers resource contention.

Smart surfaces optimize resource utilization by considering user preferences and environmental factors. They prioritize energy-efficient resource allocation for edge computing, reducing power consumption and battery life. Low latency communication and real-time responsiveness are prioritized in gaming and augmented reality applications. Dynamic resource allocation in distributed computing systems improves system resilience, scalability, and flexibility. This ensures optimal performance, cost-effectiveness, and continuous service delivery. Intelligent surfaces use advanced algorithms to enhance system performance, optimize resource usage, and adapt dynamically to changing conditions, fostering efficiency and creativity in the digital age.

Figure 3. Process of dynamic resource allocation and optimization within intelligent surfaces

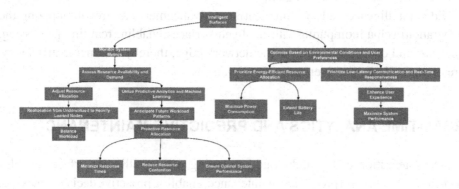

The process of dynamic resource allocation and optimization within intelligent surfaces is depicted in this flowchart (Figure 3), which highlights the steps involved in tracking system metrics, evaluating resource availability and demand, modifying resource allocation, and optimizing in response to user preferences and environmental factors.

Edge Intelligence and Machine Learning

Edge intelligence and machine learning are revolutionizing data processing, analysis, and action at the network edge, enabling organizations to make real-time decisions and extract valuable insights through the integration of fog and cloud computing (Boopathi, 2024; Zekrifa et al., 2023).

Edge Intelligence: Edge intelligence is a decentralized method that eliminates the need for centralized cloud servers by enabling data analytics, inference, and decision-making at the network edge. It uses computing resources in intelligent surfaces like edge servers, gateways, and Internet of Things devices, lowering latency and facilitating quicker reactions. This is crucial for latency-sensitive applications like augmented reality, driverless cars, and industrial automation. Edge intelligence also improves data privacy and security by reducing data exposure and transmission over public networks (Das et al., 2024).

Machine Learning: Machine learning is revolutionizing intelligent surfaces in fog and cloud computing settings by predicting automation and decision-making, identifying patterns in data, and providing insights. It's particularly useful for predictive maintenance, identifying equipment failure patterns in network edge devices. By evaluating user behavior, preferences, and environmental factors, machine learning models can create tailored services, improving user experiences, engagement, and customer satisfaction. This approach enhances asset performance and asset performance (Veeranjaneyulu et al., 2023).

Edge intelligence and machine learning advancements are revolutionizing the integration of cloud computing with intelligent surfaces, enabling real-time processing, analysis, and decision-making at the network edge, thereby enhancing efficiency, creativity, and competitiveness in the digital age.

REAL-TIME ANALYTICS AND PREDICTIVE MAINTENANCE

The integration of fog and cloud computing with intelligent surfaces enables real-time analytics and predictive maintenance, enabling proactive decision-making, cost savings, and operational efficiency across various industries (Su & Huang, 2018).

Importance in Manufacturing: In the industrial industry, real-time analytics and predictive maintenance are essential for streamlining production lines and reducing downtime. Manufacturers may prevent costly failures by identifying any problems early on through the analysis of sensor data from machinery. This allows for prompt maintenance interventions and minimizes unplanned downtime.

Significance in Healthcare: In the healthcare industry, real-time analytics and predictive maintenance enhance patient outcomes and streamline delivery. Through proactive intervention, doctors may identify abnormalities, anticipate declining health situations, and keep an eye on patient data streams. Predictive maintenance lowers expenses related to equipment downtime and maintenance while ensuring continuous availability and improving the quality of patient care.

Impact on Transportation: In order to guarantee efficiency, safety, and dependability in the transportation industry, real-time analytics and predictive maintenance are essential. Traffic flow may be optimized, congestion can be identified in real time, and accidents can be avoided by authorities by evaluating data from sensors in cars, infrastructure, and traffic management systems. Predictive maintenance increases passenger happiness, prolongs asset lifecycles, and reduces service interruptions.

Role in Energy Management: Energy management requires real-time analytics and predictive maintenance in order to maximize consumption, minimize waste, and enhance sustainability for enterprises. Energy companies are able to detect trends in use, forecast changes in demand, and make real-time adjustments to supply by examining data from smart meters, sensors, and Internet of Things devices. This maximizes resource allocation, guards against expensive outages, and guarantees dependability.

Predictive maintenance and real-time analytics are essential for cost reduction, customer happiness, and operational excellence. Organizations may utilize data to anticipate future occurrences, make educated choices, and maintain competitiveness in a dynamic environment by merging fog and cloud computing with intelligent surfaces (Keleko et al., 2022).

Figure 4. Importance of real-time analytics and predictive maintenance in various sectors

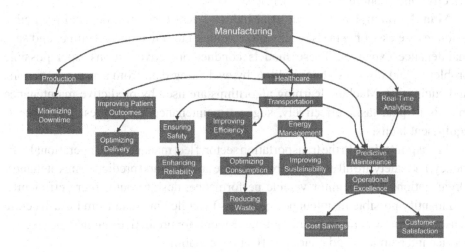

Figure 4 highlights the importance of predictive maintenance and real-time analytics in various industries like manufacturing, healthcare, transportation, and energy management. These technologies can enhance patient outcomes, streamline operations, reduce downtime, increase safety, boost dependability, optimize consumption, reduce waste, and improve sustainability, ultimately leading to operational excellence, cost savings, and customer satisfaction.

Applications

Cloud computing and fog For real-time analytics and predictive maintenance—which use sophisticated data processing, analysis, and machine learning approaches to improve operations and decision-making across a range of industries—integration with intelligent surfaces is essential (Keleko et al., 2022; Su & Huang, 2018).

E-commerce: Supply chain optimization, inventory management, and tailored customer experiences are made possible in the retail and e-commerce industries by real-time analytics and predictive maintenance. Through the customization of product suggestions, promotions, and price tactics, these solutions improve consumer engagement and loyalty. By reducing interruptions, predictive maintenance ensures effective and economical client service.

Manufacturing: In the industrial industry, real-time analytics and predictive maintenance assist businesses maximize output, cut down on downtime, and save maintenance expenses. These models conduct proactive actions, spot possible problems, and discover abnormalities by evaluating data from sensors, actuators, and equipment. Machine learning algorithms are used by predictive maintenance models to plan tasks effectively, suggest maintenance procedures, and forecast equipment faults.

Transportation: In the transportation sector, fleet management, operational efficiency, and safety are all enhanced by real-time analytics and predictive maintenance. Organizations may monitor vehicle performance, design routes more efficiently, and identify possible maintenance problems by collecting data from infrastructure sensors, traffic systems, and automobiles. Models for predictive maintenance reduce service interruptions and guarantee fleet dependability.

Healthcare: In the healthcare industry, real-time analytics and predictive maintenance enable proactive patient care, enhance operational effectiveness, and optimize resource allocation. Healthcare professionals are able to spot patterns, spot irregularities, and take swift action to stop unfavorable outcomes by evaluating patient data and medical equipment. Predictive maintenance models allow facilities to monitor equipment, predict maintenance needs, and schedule repairs before failure, ensuring uninterrupted patient care.

Energy Management: Optimizing energy generation, distribution, and consumption in the energy sector requires real-time analytics and predictive maintenance. Businesses can anticipate demand patterns, spot opportunities for energy savings, and monitor vital infrastructure to anticipate possible failures and schedule maintenance proactively, reducing outages and guaranteeing a steady supply of energy. This is achieved by analyzing data from smart meters, sensors, and grid infrastructure.

Retail and Customer Service: Personalized marketing, inventory control, and customer experiences are made possible in the retail sector by real-time analytics and predictive maintenance. Retailers may customize marketing efforts, improve pricing tactics, and predict client demands by analyzing customer data, transaction histories, and market trends. Proactively arranging repairs to avoid delays and guarantee flawless shopping experiences, predictive maintenance models keep an eye on retail equipment.

In many different sectors, decision-making, operational optimization, and efficiency enhancement depend heavily on real-time analytics and predictive maintenance. Organizations may realize their revolutionary potential and prosper in the digital age by combining intelligent surfaces with fog and cloud computing.

CHALLENGES AND SOLUTIONS IN FOG AND CLOUD COMPUTING INTEGRATION

In order to integrate fog and cloud computing with intelligent surfaces and optimize the efficacy and security of their systems, organizations need to tackle certain issues (Jahid et al., 2023; Wu et al., 2022).

Security and Privacy Concerns: The integration of fog and cloud computing poses a significant threat to data security and privacy, posing risks of cyberattacks, illegal access, and data breaches due to the variety of devices and protocols. To mitigate these threats, organizations must implement robust security measures like encryption, authentication, and access control. A zero-trust security paradigm can enhance security posture and reduce insider threats. Regular security audits, threat assessments, and incident response procedures are also crucial for swift action.

Interoperability and Standardization: The integration of fog and cloud computing faces significant challenges due to interoperability and standards issues. These issues hinder the scalability and interoperability of fog computing systems. To address these issues, industry participants must collaborate on creating open standards and interoperability frameworks for seamless data communication between fog nodes, cloud servers, and end devices. Investing in middleware and integration platforms can speed up the process.

Scalability and Performance Optimization: As data volumes and processing demands increase, scalability and performance optimization are crucial in integrating fog and cloud computing. Consistent resource allocation across platforms can lead to performance degradation. Organizations should create scalable architectures to handle increased workloads and data quantities. Dynamic resource allocation can be achieved using distributed computing resources like edge servers and microservices, and containerization tools like Kubernetes.

Organizations must address security, privacy, interoperability, standardization, scalability, and performance optimization to optimize fog and cloud computing integration. This can enhance competitiveness and foster innovation by implementing robust security measures, adopting open standards, and utilizing intelligent architectural design to maximize the full potential of these technologies.

INDUSTRY APPLICATIONS OF FOG AND CLOUD COMPUTING INTEGRATION

Intelligent surfaces combined with fog and cloud computing have the power to transform a number of sectors through three key applications that improve productivity, sustainability, and quality of life (Matt, 2018).

Figure 5. Interactions and connections between the three industry applications of fog and cloud computing integration

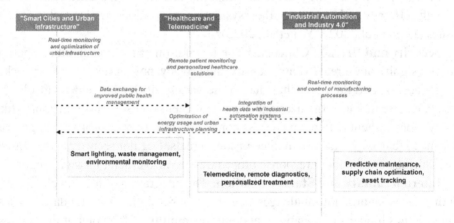

The integration of fog and cloud computing in three industries - industry 4.0, industrial automation, smart cities, urban infrastructure, and healthcare - can enhance productivity, sustainability, and quality of life (Dahiya & Dalal, 2018)by enhancing data flow and synergies across these sectors, as illustrated in Figure 5.

Smart Cities and Urban Infrastructure

The integration of fog and cloud computing is crucial for smart cities and urban infrastructure development, enabling real-time monitoring, analysis, and optimization of vital services. Intelligent surfaces gather data from sensors, cameras, and

Internet of Things devices to monitor traffic flow, control energy usage, and improve public safety. Fog computing evaluates traffic patterns, improves signal timing, and reduces congestion, while cloud computing is used for centralized data storage and analytics in smart grid systems (O'Donovan et al., 2019).

The integration of fog with cloud computing enhances urban infrastructure solutions like trash management, smart lighting, and environmental monitoring, promoting sustainability and quality of life through predictive maintenance and real-time data analytics.

Healthcare and Telemedicine

Telemedicine services, remote patient monitoring, and tailored healthcare solutions are now possible because to the integration of fog and cloud computing in the healthcare industry. Facilities with intelligent surfaces gather and process patient data in real time, enabling medical professionals to keep an eye on vital signs, spot irregularities, and take immediate action. Health parameters are monitored by wearable technology with sensors and edge computing capabilities, allowing for early identification and prompt treatments. Electronic health record systems that are hosted in the cloud safely store and process patient data, offering deep insights and instruments to assist in making decisions (Tärneberg, 2019). The development of predictive analytics models for illness prediction, epidemic identification, and individualized treatment planning is aided by the merging of fog and cloud computing. Through the examination of extensive medical records, scientists may spot trends, forecast the course of illnesses, and create focused treatments.

Industrial Automation and Industry 4.0

Industry 4.0 and industrial automation are utilizing fog and cloud computing integration to improve supply chains and manufacturing processes. This includes adaptive control, predictive maintenance, and real-time monitoring. Intelligent surfaces interpret sensor data, machine telemetry, and production metrics to maximize efficiency, reduce downtime, and improve product quality. Predictive maintenance solutions minimize disruptions and enable proactive scheduling. Cloud-based manufacturing execution solutions provide centralized control over processes. Integration of fog and cloud computing facilitates the development of digital twins, which are virtual representations of real assets and processes that allow industrial systems to be simulated, optimized, and predictively modeled. This enables businesses to locate bottlenecks, streamline processes, and increase production and efficiency (Keleko et al., 2022; Matt, 2018).

Fog and cloud computing integration can revolutionize sectors like healthcare, industrial automation, and smart cities by enhancing community quality of life, creativity, efficiency, competitiveness, and sustainability through real-time data analytics and adaptive control capabilities.

EMERGING TRENDS AND FUTURE DIRECTIONS

Emerging developments impact the integration of fog and cloud computing with intelligent surfaces, providing fresh chances for creativity, productivity, and competitiveness. The future of this convergence is anticipated to be driven by three key developments (Boopathi, 2023; Ramudu et al., 2023; Revathi et al., 2024) .

Edge-Native Applications and Services

Edge-native apps and services are emerging in fog and cloud computing integration for dispersed network settings. These high-performance, low-latency services are ideal for applications like autonomous cars, augmented reality, and industrial automation. These technologies analyze sensor data locally, perform analytics, and make decisions without relying on centralized cloud servers, resulting in faster reaction times, lower bandwidth usage, and increased dependability.

Distributed edge locations are used by edge-native services, such as content delivery networks (CDNs), gaming platforms, and video streaming services, to provide material closer to consumers, lowering latency and enhancing user experiences. With this strategy, businesses may improve performance, open up new use cases, and set themselves apart from the competition in a crowded market.

Hybrid Cloud-Fog Architectures

A developing trend in cloud computing is hybrid cloud-fog systems, which combine the network edge responsiveness and agility of fog computing with the scalability and flexibility of cloud computing. By shifting compute-intensive workloads to cloud servers during periods of low network traffic or high computational demand and utilizing edge computing resources for real-time processing and analytics, these systems maximize resource allocation, workload dispersion, and cost-effectiveness (Das et al., 2024; Sharma et al., 2024). Organizations may dynamically expand resources in response to workload needs and environmental circumstances thanks to hybrid cloud-fog architectures, which provide smooth workload transfer and data mobility between fog nodes and cloud servers. In distributed computing systems, this strategy maximizes performance, dependability, and cost-effectiveness.

Regulatory Implications and Policy Frameworks

The increasing significance of fog and cloud computing integration is making enterprises think about regulations. These include dangers to security, privacy, and data sovereignty. Strict data protection, openness, and permission are required by laws like the CCPA in the US and the GDPR in the EU. The implementation of fog computing solutions in international corporations may be impacted by these restrictions, which also have an effect on cross-border transfers and data localization. Thus, while integrating distributed computing technologies, enterprises need to pay close attention to these requirements. The ethical use of AI and ML in fog computing settings, data governance, and cybersecurity are the main concerns of policymakers. Clear policies for data security, privacy, and responsibility may promote responsible innovation, openness, and trust in the integration of fog and cloud computing (Saravanan et al., 2022).

The future of fog and cloud computing integration is being shaped by emerging trends such as edge-native apps, hybrid cloud-fog architectures, and regulatory ramifications. These modifications provide both chances and difficulties for businesses looking to use distributed computing solutions for expansion and creativity. Through proactive and up-to-date management of these factors, enterprises may fully leverage dispersed computing in the digital age.

BEST PRACTICES

The future is shaped by three key themes, combining fog and cloud computing, offering new opportunities for efficiency, competitiveness, and creativity.

Edge-Native Applications and Services

Emerging concepts in fog and cloud computing integration that are tailored for dispersed computing settings at the network edge include edge-native apps and services. These apps satisfy real-time demands by providing high-performance, low-latency services. Autonomous cars, augmented reality, and industrial automation are a few examples of technologies that analyze sensor data locally, carry out analytics, and make choices without depending on centralized cloud servers. It is therefore perfect for applications that are latency-sensitive and bandwidth-intensive since it produces faster reaction times, lower bandwidth usage, and increased dependability. Distributed edge locations are used by edge-native services, such as content delivery networks (CDNs), gaming platforms, and video streaming services, to provide material closer to consumers, lowering latency and enhancing user experiences. By using this strategy, businesses may improve performance, open up new use cases, and set themselves apart in a crowded market (Agrawal et al., 2023; Satav et al., 2023; Venkateswaran, Vidhya, Ayyannan, et al., 2023).

Hybrid Cloud-Fog Architectures

A developing trend in cloud computing is hybrid cloud-fog systems, which combine the network edge responsiveness and agility of fog computing with the scalability and flexibility of cloud computing. By shifting compute-intensive jobs to cloud servers during periods of low network traffic or high computational demand, these systems maximize resource allocation, workload distribution, and cost-effectiveness. They also make use of edge computing capabilities for real-time processing and analytics. Organizations may dynamically expand resources in response to workload needs and environmental circumstances thanks to hybrid cloud-fog architectures, which provide smooth workload transfer and data mobility between fog nodes and cloud servers. This method maximizes cost-effectiveness, performance, and dependability in distributed computing settings (Venkateswaran, Vidhya, Naik, et al., 2023).

Regulatory Implications and Policy Frameworks

The increasing significance of fog and cloud computing integration is making enterprises think about regulations. These include dangers to security, privacy, and data sovereignty. Strict data protection, openness, and permission are required by laws like the CCPA in the US and the GDPR in the EU. The implementation of fog computing solutions in international corporations may be impacted by these restrictions, which also have an effect on cross-border transfers and data localization. Thus, while integrating distributed computing technologies, enterprises need to pay close attention to these requirements. The ethical use of AI and ML in fog computing settings, data governance, and cybersecurity are the main concerns of policymakers. Clear policies for data security, privacy, and responsibility may promote responsible innovation, openness, and trust in the integration of fog and cloud computing (Kumar et al., 2023; Pachiappan et al., 2024; Sundaramoorthy et al., 2024).

Emerging trends like edge-native apps, hybrid cloud-fog architectures, and regulatory implications are shaping the future of fog and cloud computing integration. These changes offer opportunities and challenges for businesses to use distributed computing solutions for expansion and creativity, requiring proactive management.

CONCLUSION

Combining intelligent surfaces with fog and cloud computing is a significant advancement in distributed computing that creates new opportunities for productivity, innovation, and competitiveness across a variety of industries. Important findings highlight the role, significance, and challenges of this integration. The focus of the research is on intelligent surfaces that serve as links between fog and cloud computing, enabling real-time data processing, adaptive resource management, and seamless network communication. It examines applications in smart cities, healthcare, industrial automation, and other fields, highlighting how it could promote innovation and improve living standards.

It also highlights how important it is to address security, privacy, interoperability, and performance optimization issues with fog and cloud computing integration. Organizations may optimize benefits and mitigate risks by implementing strategies, promoting collaboration and stakeholder engagement, implementing best practices, and so on. The future of cloud computing and fog integration seems promising, but it will also present challenges due to emerging trends including edge-native applications, cloud-fog hybrid architectures, and regulatory issues. Organizations may fully benefit from distributed computing in the digital era provided they keep up to date, invest in people and training, and maintain flexibility and agility. This will impact the integration process and offer new opportunities for growth and innovation. Fog and cloud computing combined with intelligent surfaces may significantly boost an organization's ability to be creative, efficient, and competitive in the digital era. This will support long-term growth, enhance customer experiences, and enable the business to prosper in a data-driven setting.

ABBREVIATIONS

AI: Artificial Intelligence
AP: Access Point
API: Application Programming Interface
CCPA: California Consumer Privacy Act
CDN: Content Delivery Network
CPU: Central Processing Unit
CRM: Customer Relationship Management
ERP: Enterprise Resource Planning
EU: European Union
FPGA: Field-Programmable Gate Array
GDPR: General Data Protection Regulation

GPU: Graphics Processing Unit
ML: Machine Learning
MQTT: Message Queuing Telemetry Transport
OPC: OLE for Process Control
UA: User Agent
US: United States

REFERENCES

Agrawal, A. V., Shashibhushan, G., Pradeep, S., Padhi, S., Sugumar, D., & Boopathi, S. (2023). Synergizing Artificial Intelligence, 5G, and Cloud Computing for Efficient Energy Conversion Using Agricultural Waste. In *Sustainable Science and Intelligent Technologies for Societal Development* (pp. 475–497). IGI Global.

Boopathi, S. (2023). Securing Healthcare Systems Integrated With IoT: Fundamentals, Applications, and Future Trends. In *Dynamics of Swarm Intelligence Health Analysis for the Next Generation* (pp. 186–209). IGI Global.

Boopathi, S. (2024). Advancements in Machine Learning and AI for Intelligent Systems in Drone Applications for Smart City Developments. In *Futuristic e-Governance Security With Deep Learning Applications* (pp. 15–45). IGI Global. 10.4018/978-1-6684-9596-4.ch002

Dahiya, V., & Dalal, S. (2018). Fog computing: A review on integration of cloud computing and internet of things. *2018 IEEE International Students' Conference on Electrical, Electronics and Computer Science (SCEECS)*, (pp. 1–6). IEEE.

Das, S., Lekhya, G., Shreya, K., Shekinah, K. L., Babu, K. K., & Boopathi, S. (2024). Fostering Sustainability Education Through Cross-Disciplinary Collaborations and Research Partnerships: Interdisciplinary Synergy. In *Facilitating Global Collaboration and Knowledge Sharing in Higher Education With Generative AI* (pp. 60–88). IGI Global.

Dhanalakshmi, M., Tamilarasi, K., Saravanan, S., Sujatha, G., Boopathi, S., & Associates. (2024). Fog Computing-Based Framework and Solutions for Intelligent Systems: Enabling Autonomy in Vehicles. In *Computational Intelligence for Green Cloud Computing and Digital Waste Management* (pp. 330–356). IGI Global.

Jahid, A., Alsharif, M. H., & Hall, T. J. (2023). The convergence of blockchain, IoT and 6G: Potential, opportunities, challenges and research roadmap. *Journal of Network and Computer Applications*, 217, 103677. 10.1016/j.jnca.2023.103677

Keleko, A. T., Kamsu-Foguem, B., Ngouna, R. H., & Tongne, A. (2022). Artificial intelligence and real-time predictive maintenance in industry 4.0: A bibliometric analysis. *AI and Ethics*, 2(4), 553–577. 10.1007/s43681-021-00132-6

Kumar, M., Kumar, K., Sasikala, P., Sampath, B., Gopi, B., & Sundaram, S. (2023). Sustainable Green Energy Generation From Waste Water: IoT and ML Integration. In *Sustainable Science and Intelligent Technologies for Societal Development* (pp. 440–463). IGI Global.

Liu, Y., Zhao, J., Xiong, Z., Niyato, D., Yuen, C., Pan, C., & Huang, B. (2020). Intelligent reflecting surface meets mobile edge computing: Enhancing wireless communications for computation offloading. *arXiv Preprint arXiv:2001.07449.*

Lu, J., Li, L., Chen, G., Shen, D., Pham, K., & Blasch, E. (2017). Machine learning based intelligent cognitive network using fog computing. *Sensors and Systems for Space Applications X*, 10196, 149–157.

Matt, C. (2018). Fog computing: Complementing cloud computing to facilitate industry 4.0. *Business & Information Systems Engineering*, 60(4), 351–355. 10.1007/s12599-018-0540-6

Mokni, M., Yassa, S., Hajlaoui, J. E., Chelouah, R., & Omri, M. N. (2022). Cooperative agents-based approach for workflow scheduling on fog-cloud computing. *Journal of Ambient Intelligence and Humanized Computing*, 13(10), 4719–4738. 10.1007/s12652-021-03187-9

Moreno, A., & Redondo, T. (2016). Text analytics: The convergence of big data and artificial intelligence. *IJIMAI*, 3(6), 57–64. 10.9781/ijimai.2016.369

Munir, A., Kansakar, P., & Khan, S. U. (2017). IFCIoT: Integrated Fog Cloud IoT: A novel architectural paradigm for the future Internet of Things. *IEEE Consumer Electronics Magazine*, 6(3), 74–82. 10.1109/MCE.2017.2684981

Narmeen, R., Almadhor, A., Alkhayyat, A., & Ho, P.-H. (2024). Secure Beamforming for Unmanned Aerial Vehicles Equipped Reconfigurable Intelligent Surfaces. *IEEE Internet of Things Magazine*, 7(2), 30–37. 10.1109/IOTM.001.2300238

Nath, S. B., Gupta, H., Chakraborty, S., & Ghosh, S. K. (2018). A survey of fog computing and communication: Current researches and future directions. *arXiv Preprint arXiv:1804.04365.*

Ning, Z., Huang, J., & Wang, X. (2019). Vehicular fog computing: Enabling real-time traffic management for smart cities. *IEEE Wireless Communications*, 26(1), 87–93. 10.1109/MWC.2019.1700441

O'Donovan, P., Gallagher, C., Leahy, K., & O'Sullivan, D. T. (2019). A comparison of fog and cloud computing cyber-physical interfaces for Industry 4.0 real-time embedded machine learning engineering applications. *Computers in Industry*, 110, 12–35. 10.1016/j.compind.2019.04.016

Pachiappan, K., Anitha, K., Pitchai, R., Sangeetha, S., Satyanarayana, T., & Boopathi, S. (2024). Intelligent Machines, IoT, and AI in Revolutionizing Agriculture for Water Processing. In *Handbook of Research on AI and ML for Intelligent Machines and Systems* (pp. 374–399). IGI Global.

Pitchai, R., Guru, K. V., Gandhi, J. N., Komala, C. R., Kumar, J. R. D., & Boopathi, S. (2024). Fog Computing-Integrated ML-Based Framework and Solutions for Intelligent Systems: Digital Healthcare Applications. In *Technological Advancements in Data Processing for Next Generation Intelligent Systems* (pp. 196–224). IGI Global. 10.4018/979-8-3693-0968-1.ch008

Ramudu, K., Mohan, V. M., Jyothirmai, D., Prasad, D., Agrawal, R., & Boopathi, S. (2023). Machine Learning and Artificial Intelligence in Disease Prediction: Applications, Challenges, Limitations, Case Studies, and Future Directions. In *Contemporary Applications of Data Fusion for Advanced Healthcare Informatics* (pp. 297–318). IGI Global.

Revathi, S., Babu, M., Rajkumar, N., Meti, V. K. V., Kandavalli, S. R., & Boopathi, S. (2024). Unleashing the Future Potential of 4D Printing: Exploring Applications in Wearable Technology, Robotics, Energy, Transportation, and Fashion. In *Human-Centered Approaches in Industry 5.0: Human-Machine Interaction, Virtual Reality Training, and Customer Sentiment Analysis* (pp. 131–153). IGI Global.

Saravanan, A., Venkatasubramanian, R., Khare, R., Surakasi, R., Boopathi, S., Ray, S., & Sudhakar, M. (2022). POLICY TRENDS OF RENEWABLE ENERGY AND NON. *Renewable Energy*.

Satav, S. D., Lamani, D., Harsha, K., Kumar, N., Manikandan, S., & Sampath, B. (2023). Energy and Battery Management in the Era of Cloud Computing: Sustainable Wireless Systems and Networks. In *Sustainable Science and Intelligent Technologies for Societal Development* (pp. 141–166). IGI Global.

Sharma, D. M., Ramana, K. V., Jothilakshmi, R., Verma, R., Maheswari, B. U., & Boopathi, S. (2024). Integrating Generative AI Into K-12 Curriculums and Pedagogies in India: Opportunities and Challenges. *Facilitating Global Collaboration and Knowledge Sharing in Higher Education With Generative AI*, 133–161.

Su, C.-J., & Huang, S.-F. (2018). Real-time big data analytics for hard disk drive predictive maintenance. *Computers & Electrical Engineering*, 71, 93–101. 10.1016/j.compeleceng.2018.07.025

Sundaramoorthy, K., Singh, A., Sumathy, G., Maheshwari, A., Arunarani, A., & Boopathi, S. (2024). A Study on AI and Blockchain-Powered Smart Parking Models for Urban Mobility. In *Handbook of Research on AI and ML for Intelligent Machines and Systems* (pp. 223–250). IGI Global.

Tärneberg, W. (2019). *The confluence of Cloud computing, 5G, and IoT in the Fog*.

Veeranjaneyulu, R., Boopathi, S., Narasimharao, J., Gupta, K. K., Reddy, R. V. K., & Ambika, R. (2023). Identification of Heart Diseases using Novel Machine Learning Method. *IEEE- Explore*, (pp. 1–6). IEEE.

Venkateswaran, N., Vidhya, K., Ayyannan, M., Chavan, S. M., Sekar, K., & Boopathi, S. (2023). A Study on Smart Energy Management Framework Using Cloud Computing. In *5G, Artificial Intelligence, and Next Generation Internet of Things: Digital Innovation for Green and Sustainable Economies* (pp. 189–212). IGI Global. 10.4018/978-1-6684-8634-4.ch009

Venkateswaran, N., Vidhya, R., Naik, D. A., Raj, T. M., Munjal, N., & Boopathi, S. (2023). Study on Sentence and Question Formation Using Deep Learning Techniques. In *Digital Natives as a Disruptive Force in Asian Businesses and Societies* (pp. 252–273). IGI Global. 10.4018/978-1-6684-6782-4.ch015

Verma, R., Christiana, M. B. V., Maheswari, M., Srinivasan, V., Patro, P., Dari, S. S., & Boopathi, S. (2024). Intelligent Physarum Solver for Profit Maximization in Oligopolistic Supply Chain Networks. In *AI and Machine Learning Impacts in Intelligent Supply Chain* (pp. 156–179). IGI Global. 10.4018/979-8-3693-1347-3.ch011

Vermesan, O., Bröring, A., Tragos, E., Serrano, M., Bacciu, D., Chessa, S., Gallicchio, C., Micheli, A., Dragone, M., & Saffiotti, A. (2022). Internet of robotic things–converging sensing/actuating, hyperconnectivity, artificial intelligence and IoT platforms. In *Cognitive Hyperconnected Digital Transformation* (pp. 97–155). River Publishers. 10.1201/9781003337584-4

Wang, K., Zhou, Y., Wu, Q., Chen, W., & Yang, Y. (2021). Task offloading in hybrid intelligent reflecting surface and massive MIMO relay networks. *IEEE Transactions on Wireless Communications*, 21(6), 3648–3663. 10.1109/TWC.2021.3122992

Wu, G., Xu, T., Sun, Y., & Zhang, J. (2022). Review of multiple unmanned surface vessels collaborative search and hunting based on swarm intelligence. *International Journal of Advanced Robotic Systems*, 19(2), 17298806221091885. 10.1177/17298806221091885

Zekrifa, D. M. S., Kulkarni, M., Bhagyalakshmi, A., Devireddy, N., Gupta, S., & Boopathi, S. (2023). Integrating Machine Learning and AI for Improved Hydrological Modeling and Water Resource Management. In *Artificial Intelligence Applications in Water Treatment and Water Resource Management* (pp. 46–70). IGI Global. 10.4018/978-1-6684-6791-6.ch003

Zhang, Z., Jiang, T., & Yu, W. (2022). Learning based user scheduling in reconfigurable intelligent surface assisted multiuser downlink. *IEEE Journal of Selected Topics in Signal Processing*, 16(5), 1026–1039. 10.1109/JSTSP.2022.3178213

Chapter 14
Immersive Learning Experience for Design Education in the Lens of Education 4.0

Ozge Kandemir
http://orcid.org/0000-0001-7999-5845

Interior Design Department, Eskisehir Teknik Üniversitesi, Turkey

Gökhan Ulusoy
https://orcid.org/0000-0003-1121-1447

Interior Design Department, Eskişehir Teknik Üniversitesi, Turkey

Celal Murat Kandemir
https://orcid.org/0000-0001-8559-7667

Faculty of Education, Eskişehir Osmangazi Üniversitesi, Turkey

ABSTRACT

The fourth industrial revolution creates a digital world that enables the activation of intelligent systems, allowing virtual and physical systems to cooperate flexibly with each other. This world, designed on ICT, blurs the lines between physical and virtual, and makes it necessary to develop educational environments by digital technologies. This development is described as Education 4.0. Integration with the education fields in general, and design fields in particular, into Education 4.0 requires acquiring new skills and competencies. The social transformation experienced with Industry 4.0 requires solving rapidly changing, more numerous, and complex problems and meeting changing needs. So, the study aims to reveal the characteristics of Education 4.0, and what kinds of technological infrastructure required for it. In

DOI: 10.4018/979-8-3693-2432-5.ch014

particular, it stands out with its potential for developing design education within the Education 4.0 framework. It aims to reveal immersive technologies and their types, technology-based immersive experiences, immersive learning experiences, and the opportunities of these experiences for design education.

INTRODUCTION

Quality in education has a dynamic structure and complex content (Adams, 1998). While technology is one of the components that enable high-quality education, the presence of technology alone is not sufficient for quality education, regardless of its characteristics. However, the Fourth Industrial Revolution has created a digital world that enables the activation of smart systems and flexible collaboration between virtual and physical systems (Schwab, 2016). Utilizing the opportunities offered by this digital world for societal benefit requires, first and foremost, the acceptance of its potential (Buhr, 2015). This digital world, designed around information and communication technologies, blurs the lines between the physical and virtual, making it possible to enhance educational environments through digital technologies. In this world where digital skills are becoming increasingly important, Industry 4.0 offers innovative technologies proposing new environments for education, such as Augmented and Virtual Reality (Mourtzis et al., 2018). In this direction, there is a growing interest in the use of immersive technologies as virtual learning environments in the field of education. This interest is not unfounded.

In general, the modernization of higher education is considered crucial for the cultivation of a workforce that meets the requirements of the digital age (Perini et al., 2017). Flexible and innovative learning approaches and presentation methods are required for this modernization. Preserving the quality of education, enhancing student engagement, and expanding inclusivity towards diversity are fundamental requirements. The primary way to achieve this is to utilize Information and Communication Technologies (ICT) to "enrich teaching, improve learning experiences, support personalized learning, facilitate access through distance education and virtual mobility, ease the management of education processes, and conduct research" (European Agenda for the Modernization of Higher Education Systems, 2011). According to Dunwill (2016), this essentially corresponds to a technological transformation that changes the teaching method and learning process in education. It is noteworthy that this technological transformation, corresponding to the integration of Information and Communication Technologies into teaching and learning, occupies a prominent place on the agenda of educational reform.

Basic knowledge, skills, and competencies that individuals are expected to have in the 21st century include: Competencies related to life and profession, Skills for Learning and Innovation and skills for Information, Media, and Technology (P21, 2019). The expectations of the Industrial Revolution 4.0 have also determined the framework of Education 4.0, which aims to raise individuals with 21st-century skills. Education 4.0 offers a contemporary education model supported by digital trans-formation and the use of technology. Essentially, it aims to provide a more flexible, personalized, and interactive learning experience compared to traditional teaching methods. The ultimate goal here is to support students in developing 21st-century skills and adapting to today's rapidly changing world. The World Economic Forum (2020) divided the framework of Education 4.0 into two main interrelated cate-gories, namely content and experiences, and revealed the subcategories that fall within these categories. In this context, first of all, individuals should be provided with Global citizenship skills, Innovation and creative skills, Technology skills, and Interpersonal skills according to the content category. In the second category for experiencing these contents, it was pointed out that individuals should benefit from innovative pedagogical approaches examined under the headings of Personalized and self-paced learning, Accessible and inclusive learning, Problem-based and collaborative learning, and Lifelong and student-centered learning.

This report broadly provides a framework for how school systems should be updated to meet the future needs of individuals. This is actually a transformation and requires integrated changes in the content and methods of the education system. The study in question is aimed at the use of technological innovations in education, which at the same time catalyze and constitute the tool of this transformation. Two categories regarding the components of Education 4.0 expressed in the World Eco-nomic Forum (2020) provide expansions on how technology will be integrated into education both as content (Developing digital skills, including programming, digital responsibility and use of technology, etc.) and as a "tool" in revealing its experience. The focal point of this study is to investigate how immersive technologies, one of these innovative technologies, can be used as a tool in education in general and in design education specifically, and what kind of opportunities this tool can provide.

Design education has constantly evolved in parallel with technological advances and changes in social life, industry, and global economic activities. Staying com-petitive in this rapidly changing environment is possible by constantly developing new skills and adapting to new learning environments in design education. At this point, According to Findeli (2001), examining the structure of design education for the 21st century in terms of theory, methodology and ethics as an educator, the main characteristics of the current paradigm are "its materialistic underlying metaphys-ics; its positivistic methods of inquiry; and its agnosticist, dualistic worldview". As long as positivism is accepted as the paradigm for design education, the subjective, irrational, and ultimately mysterious and ineffable nature of design creativity can never be defined and explicated (Wang, 2010). Therefore, while design focuses primarily on subjective creativity, the positivist university paradigm's focus on objective rationality still remains the main subject of criticism.

However, how to teach creativity in design must largely include establishing an environment where new approaches can develop. Immersive technologies find an essential place in the creation of this kind of new environment. Loke states that pedagogical approaches, especially those that support the use of immersive technology, mostly base educational practices on constructivism (Loke, 2015). It is seen that the theory of constructivism, which is widely accepted as playing an active role in the learning process, provides the theoretical framework for creating educational environments conducive to "active learning" and, consequently, "experiential education." In contemporary design education, immersive technologies are increasingly assuming important roles in the implementation and enhancement of experiential education. In this context, the utilization of technologies encompassing Virtual Reality (VR), Augmented Reality (AR), Mixed Reality (MR), and Extended Reality (XR) generally serves to enhance learning experiences, encourage participation in collaborative activities, and foster creativity and engagement (Suh & Prophet, 2018). The benefits provided by immersive learning methods have become increasingly significant in addressing rapidly growing needs, such as the reskilling and upskilling of the global workforce, in addition to reversing the trend of declining student engagement.

With this awareness, the research questions addressed in the study are as follows:

1. What are the expectations of Industry 4.0 and its technologies from the workforce?
2. What are the 21st-century skills and competencies highlighted by Education 4.0 and its features?
3. What are the current Immersive Technologies in the context of Education 4.0 technologies?
4. What is the relationship between Technology Based Immersion and the learning experience?
5. What are the potentials of Technology-Based Immersive learning experiences for "Design Education"?

LITERATURE REVIEW

Industry 4.0 and Technologies

Industrial revolutions transformed social life by significantly impacting industrial production throughout their development processes. These transformations have occurred through the four basic Industrial Revolutions that have occurred until today. As quoted by Schwab (2016, p. 11), the first of these revolutions lasted from 1760 to 1840 and initiated "mechanical production" with the construction of railways and the invention of the steam engine. The second, starting in the late 19th century, made "mass production" possible with electricity and the development of assembly lines. The third revolution, called the "computer and digital revolution", started in the 1960s and accelerated throughout history with the development of semiconductors, mainframe computing, personal computing and the Internet until the 1990s. Finally, the fourth revolution, which started in the current century, is built on the "digital revolution". The 4th Industrial Revolution is characterized by widespread mobile Internet, cheaper, smaller and more powerful sensors, artificial intelligence and machine learning. While the digital technologies at its core (comprising computer hardware, software, and networks) are not new, they have become more complex and integrated.

Figure 1. Industrial revolutions

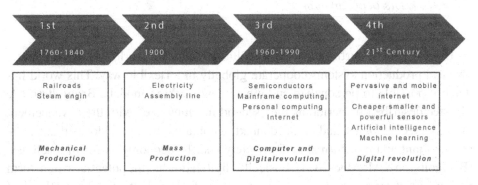

(Authors, based on Schwab 2016)

The Industry 4.0 strategy, which forms the basis of the 4th Industrial Revolution and was inaugurated by the German government in 2011, basically proposes to move from "centralized" to "decentralized" smart production and production methods, blending production worlds and network connection in the "Internet of Things". This strategy has articulated the need to create a "smart industry" where people, devices, objects and systems come together to form dynamic, self-organizing production networks (Figure 1). In this regard, while many governments, such as the German government, are overhauling their economic strategies in the face of unprecedented challenges, including exponential technological change. They have also expressed the urgent need for fundamental changes to ensure a more inclusive and sustainable development for everyone. Like every industrial revolution that requires change in the education system, the 4th Industrial Revolution has made education systems need to undergo a transformative change (OCDE, 2019, p.5).

Figure 2. Industry 1.0 to 4.0

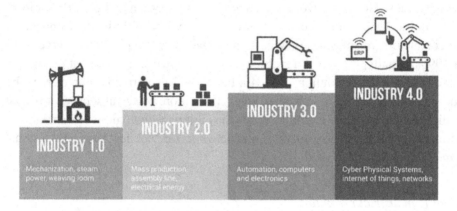

(McLellan, 2018, OCDC, 2019, p.6)

Basically, the Fourth Industrial Revolution created a world where virtual and physical production systems cooperate globally in a flexible way. This world has made it possible to personalize and create new working models. Brynjolfsson & McAfee describe this period as the "second machine age" with the advancement of digital technologies, and in this context, it contains structural blocks that can be as important and transformative for society and the economy as steam machines. (Brynjolfsson & McAfee, 2014). Basically, digitization has the potential to transform various industries and production techniques greatly. These potentials have unleashed the term "Industry 4.0", which is defined as the digitization of the manufacturing industry, with sensors embedded in almost all product components and production equipment, everywhere-available cyber-physical systems and analysis of all related data. Industry 4.0 encompasses initiatives such as the Industrial Internet, Factories of the Future, the Internet of Things, the Physical Internet, Internet Services, and Cyber-Physical Systems. In this context, Industry 4.0 is described as a vision of the future, described by high-tech strategies designed in the context of Information and

Communications Technologies (ICT) to a high degree of flexibility, productivity and low material waste (Coşkun vd., 2019, p.1). This vision enables people, objects and systems to interconnect and share data through real-time data exchange. Thus, a faster and more efficient process for producing better quality products at lower costs (Grzybowska & Łupicka, 2017, p. 250), a more flexible production process (Rüßmann vd. 2015, p.1), and a more intelligent and sustainable process can be achieved.

The features of these technologies discussed in the context of Industry 4.0 also reveal their relationship with Information and Communication Technologies. According to Hamelink, information and communication technology covers all technologies that enable information processing and facilitate different forms of communication between people, between people and electronic systems, and between electronic systems. These include data collection, data storage, data processing, data transmission, and data display technologies; the common point of all is digitization. (Hamelink, 1997, p.3). The technologies expressed here relate to how things are done and constitute the processes, tools and techniques that change human activity. ICT creates new environments where people can communicate, question, make decisions, and solve problems. In this context, information collection and identification, classification and editing, summary and synthesis, analysis and evaluation, speculation and prediction processes, tools and techniques. (Sarkar, 2012, p. 33).

Figure 3. Industry 4.0 technologies

(Rüßmann vd. 2015, p. 2)

In this context, the source of the transformation of the 4th Industrial Revolution in the production system and social structure is the development of such systems that connect with each other through networks. These are Big data and analysis, Autonomous robots, Simulation of physical reality through computers, Industrial Internet of Things, Cyber Security, Information sharing through Cloud Technologies, Additive Manufacturing and Augmented Reality technologies (Rüßmann et al. 2015, p. 1-5). In the words of Mourtzis et al., Industry 4.0 introduces innovative technologies that offer new ways of connection and data management (Cloud Technology) integrated into production from these technologies, as well as new environments for information sharing and education (Augmented and Virtual reality). This initiative aims to reshape the form of production systems and upgrade them to cyber-physical systems (Mourtzis et al. 2018 p. 130).

Industry 4.0 and Workforce Expectations

With the 4th Industrial Revolution, the changes in the industry (dynamic automation, digitalization, trends in information exchange, etc.) have started to affect every aspect of human life. In Buhr's words, while traditional production methods and production factors are declining, innovators are advancing, and new organizational methods, new products, new services, new distribution channels and business models have become in demand (Buhr, 2015, p.3). This situation has led to an increase in the demands expected to be met, especially from entrepreneurs, business managers, government bodies and human resources in businesses, companies and organizations, and it has become important to meet these demands with innovative production approaches (Knihová et al., 2019, p.4). Digital technologies have fundamentally changed the nature of the entrepreneurial landscape. As a result of technological developments, entrepreneurs have become "digital entrepreneurs". In the words of Sousa & Rocha, this transformation from entrepreneurship to digital entrepreneurship has made it necessary for entrepreneurs to specialize in new digital skills. Digital entrepreneurs must have certain competencies to understand user needs for Industry 4.0, offer a valuable product or service, and create a sustainable business model (Sousa & Rocha (2019, p. 328).

At this point, according to Bogdanowicz (2015, p.38), in the European Commission's Digital Entrepreneurship Barriers and Drivers report, "all new ventures and existing businesses's transformation that provide economic and/or social value by creating and using new digital technologies" is included within digital entrepreneurship's scope. Digital businesses are characterized as businesses that predominantly use new digital technologies (especially social, big data, mobile and cloud solutions) to improve business management, invent new business models, sharpen business intelligence, and engage with users and stakeholders. In Akyazı et al.'s words, the primary way to face challenges that arise with digitalization and turn them into advantages is to create a workforce with multiple skills to manage the implementation of new business models. For this, it is necessary to make a sectoral skills strategy, define the anticipated skill requirements, determine the skill mismatch between job profiles and the workforce, develop continuous and helpful training programs, and reskill the workforce through well-developed training programs and increase these skills (Akyazı et al., 2020, p. 18).

However, these efforts to meet the workforce seem inadequate today, from local to universal. According to Perini et al., the reasons for the skills shortage are an ageing workforce, outdated workforce planning, limited educational efficiency, the changing nature of work and a poor production image among young people. In this context, from an educational perspective, the modernization of higher education becomes very important in training the workforce suitable for the needs of the digital age. This modernization requires determining current learning needs and then understanding the most appropriate approaches that can meet these needs (Perini et al., 2017 p. 1537). As Szlapka et al. point out, it is time to initiate new research activities to prepare multidisciplinary professionals and university graduates to meet the demands expressed by implementing Industry 4.0. In this context, it becomes essential for entrepreneurs to consider trends in digital technologies and organize their workforce and organizations accordingly to remain competitive (Szlapka et al. 2020, p. 1).

Block said that as the content of teaching and the scope of qualifications changed, technical skills became more demanding, and qualified people became preferred more often. But digital transformation also makes creative and socially interactive activities important. This poses questions to students about how to design innovative teaching and learning approaches based on comprehensive digital skills and how to integrate student thinking into the teaching-learning process. (Block, 2018, p. 1). Information and Communications Technologies are also at the forefront of the sources referred to at this point, and educational approaches based on the use of these technologies are increasingly gaining importance and being tried to improve. According to Sarkar, integrating ICT into teaching and learning has become a top priority on the education reform agenda. ICTs are seen as an indispensable tool for participating in the information society. ICTs are regarded as an important educational tool that expands the nature and scope of teaching wherever it takes place, providing new and transformative development models. (Sarkar 2012, p. 32).

In this context, the European Commission's report, entitled "Supporting growth and employment - an agenda for the modernization of European Higher education systems" also addressed issues related to teaching, the great need for flexible, innovative learning approaches and presentation methods, the need to preserve quality while increasing the number of students and to enhance the interest of students, and the need for greater participation, and the fight against school dropout among different groups of students. The key ways to this, in line with the EU's Digital Agenda, are to "enrich teaching, improve learning experiences, support personalized learning, facilitate access through distance learning and virtual mobility, simplify governance and leverage the benefits of ICTs and other potential new technologies to create new research opportunities".

Education 4.0 and Fundamental Features

Generally speaking, technological developments have led to different functions of education due to changing social structures. In other words, the function of education is dynamically shaped in line with changes in the relationship between social structure and production. Within this framework, the expectations of Industry 4.0 today have also defined the scope of Education 4.0, which aims to educate individuals with the skills and competencies of the 21st century. Sharma describes "Education 4.0" as an expression of the change the education sector is experiencing to respond to "Industry 4.0" demands. In this context, Education 4.0 has been developed for Industry 4.0 and aims to prepare qualified professionals for a global and digital working environment. In this process, Education 4.0 takes advantage of the unique technologies and tools of Industry 4.0. (Sharma, 2019, p. 3560). Mourtzis et al. mention that Industry 4.0 technologies play an essential role in education for production. This key provides a new framework for advanced manufacturing training, expressed as Education 4.0, enabling technologies to transfer knowledge to the future workforce effectively. This training system aims to create a sustainable environment that will meet new and experienced workforce with the innovative proposals of Industry 4.0 and accelerate its adoption into production. (Mourtzis vd., 2018, p.130).

Education 4.0 is essentially a vision for the future of education. Fisk describes this vision as "alignment of man and machine to meet the needs of Industry 4.0, or the 4th Industrial Revolution". It basically leverages the potential of digital technologies, personalized data, open source content, and the new generation of a globally interconnected, technology-fueled world. From childhood education to continuous learning in the workplace and learning to play a better role in society, she planned for the future of learning and, in particular, "learning to play football". In this context, Fisk noted that there are various approaches to Education 4.0 and divided them into nine categories. These categories are listed as follows:

1. "Diverse time and place" (the presence of opportunities to learn at different times, in different places, at their own pace),

2. "Personalized learning." (the presence of learning tools that match the student's abilities, the opportunity to practice more, and the use of individual learning processes),

3. "Free choice." (differentiation of learning methods, use of different devices, different programs and techniques according to preferences),

4. "Project-based" (development of organizational, collaborative and time management skills),

5. "Field experience" (Human knowledge and skills requiring face-to-face interaction),

6. "Data interpretation." (applying theoretical knowledge to numbers and extracting logic and trends from these data),

7. "Exams will change completely" (the use of educational software platforms to measure the competence of students, the measurability of the knowledge acquired in the learning process, especially during field studies),

8. "Student ownership" (Ensuring the participation of students in curriculum development processes)

9. "Mentoring will become more important" involvement of independence in student learning processes, mentoring becoming fundamental to student success. (Fisk 2017)

The framework set by the World Economic Forum on Education 4.0 provides a vision of how systems in educational institutions should be updated to meet the future needs of individuals. In the World Economic Forum report (2020), this framework is translated into two categories, including learning content and learning experiences, concerning each other (Figure 4). In this framework, it was pointed out that in the content category, individuals must make a productive contribution to the economies of the future and be prepared to be responsible and active citizens of future societies. To realize this vision, individuals must acquire global citizenship skills, innovation and creative skills, technology skills, and interpersonal skills. In the category of improving learning experiences to experience this content, it was noted that innovative pedagogical approaches should be exploited, as discussed in the titles: Personalized and self-paced learning: Accessible and inclusive learning, Problem-based and collaborative learning, and Lifelong and student-centered learning. The learning experiences expressed here reflect more closely the technical and human-focused skills needed to build growing and inclusive economies and societies and the future of business. This will enable individuals to create inclusive learning, develop social relationships, and acquire innovative skills. But what should not be overlooked here is the need for these changes in learning experiences to be accompanied by innovative pedagogies such as Fun, Experiential, Information-Processing,

Incarnate and Multifunctional Literacy, the teaching principles and strategies that encourage innovation in education systems.

Figure 4. The World Economic Forum Education 4.0 Framework

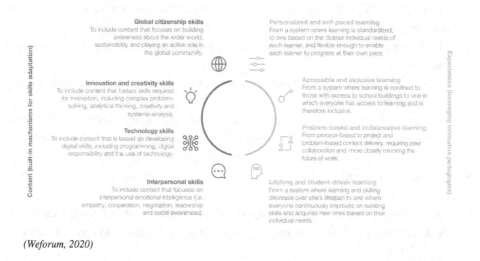

(Weforum, 2020)

Education 4.0 and 21st Century Skills and Competencies

The competencies that students must have in the field of education are provided by acquiring different skills. Transferred from OECD (2019), the concept of skill basically corresponds to the ability and capacity to carry out processes and use knowledge responsibly to achieve a goal. Competencies, on the other hand, provide a holistic framework that includes the concept of skills. In other words, skills form part of the concept of competence, which includes mobilising knowledge, skills, attitudes and values to meet complex demands (OECD, 2019). In this context, it is seen that there are many researchers, institutions and organizations trying to reveal what the prominent skills and competencies are in the 21st century and what kind of classification has emerged for them.

Finegold & Notabartolo stated that the most commonly found competencies in international and national skills assessment are Critical thinking, Problem-solving, Adaptability and Flexibility, Learning to learn, Communication and Collaboration, and other competencies are Creativity/Innovation, Information literacy, Decision making, Research and questioning, Entrepreneurship and self-direction, Productivity, Leadership and responsibility, ICT applications and Digital Citizenship and Media Literacy (Finegold & Notabartolo, 2010, pp. 6-7). Binkley et al. created a list of twenty-first-century skills based on analysing 12 relevant frameworks taken from various countries and transferred these skills by organizing them into four groups. These are Ways of thinking (Creativity and innovation, critical thinking, problem-solving, decision making, learning to learn, metacognition), Ways of working (Communication, collaboration), Working Tools (Information literacy, ICT literacy) and Living in the World (Citizenship – local and global, life and career, personal and social responsibility including cultural awareness and competence) (Binkley et al., 2012 pp. 18-19).

In the literature, it is noteworthy that the most commonly referenced classification in studies on the field of education is made by the "Partnership for 21st Century Learning" (P21), whose foundations were laid in the USA in 2002. The Frameworks for 21st Century Learning, introduced by P21, were developed to describe the knowledge, skills, and competencies students need to succeed in work, life and citizenship, and the support systems required for 21st-century learning outcomes. For this, input from teachers, education experts and business leaders was included in the process with an inclusive approach. In the framework put forward (Figure 5), the outermost ring, defined with 3 different colours, reveals the "learning outcomes" that need to be acquired, in other words, the basic skills that need to be acquired in the 21st century. The first of these skills is "Learning and Innovation Skills", and its content consists of Creativity and Innovation, Critical Thinking and Problem-Solving, Communication and Collaboration. The second one is "Information, Media & Technology Skills"; its content consists of Information Literacy, Media Literacy and ICT (Information, Communications, and Technology) Literacy. The third one is "Life & Career Skills", and its content consists of Flexibility and Adaptability, Initiative and Self-Direction, Social and Cross-Cultural Skills, Productivity and Accountability and Leadership and Responsibility. However, the emergence of all these learning outcomes requires first mastery of the basic subjects and 21st-century themes and benefiting from support systems for this. These support systems are 21st Century Standards, Assessments of 21st Century Skills, 21st Century Curriculum and Instruction, 21st Century Professional Development and 21st Century Learning Environments (P21,2019).

Acquiring and developing this knowledge, skills, and competencies in educational environments is seen as a prerequisite for raising successful individuals in today's digital and globally interconnected world, and all educational environments, especially starting from primary school, are expected to aim to achieve this. While acquiring these skills during school years affects the lives of individuals at the micro level, it will effectively determine the roles that countries will play in today's competitive environment and the future at the macro level. For this reason, it is stated that countries should take activities to disseminate these skills to cover all layers of society (P21, 2019).

Figure 5. Framework for 21st century learning (P21)

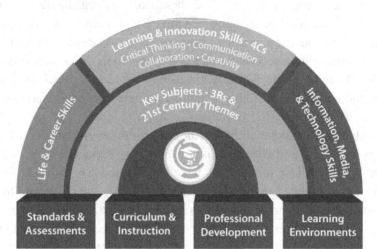

Table 1. List of socio-emotional and key competencies for students (Pešikan and Lalović, 2017: 7)

Competency	Sub-category
1. Socio-emotional skills	1.1. Self-awareness;
	1.2. Self-regulation
	1.3. Social awareness
	1.4. Social skills
	1.4.1. Collaboration
	1.4.2. Citizenship & social responsibility
	1.5. Decision making
2. Problem solving	2.1. Problem solving
	2.2. Research skills
3. Critical thinking	
4. Creativity & innovation	
5. Information literacy	
6. ICT literacy	6.1. Developing of ICT literacy
	6.2. Application of ICT literacy in other areas of learning and work
7. Learning to learn & metacognition	
8. Working skills, entrepreneurship & productivity	
9. Life skills	9.1. Health, healthy lifestyles
	9.2. Ecological awareness

The study titled "KEY 21 CENTURY COMPETENCIES", published by Unicef, seems to have a similar perspective. This study states that adequate preparation of young people for their future professions and the labour market is a prerequisite for their employment and future careers. As stated in P21, this preparation process starts from primary school and continues until the end of vocational training. Many countries have transitioned from an industry-based economy to a knowledge-based economy. In this context, employers expect formal education to offer a learning process that provides adaptability and flexibility, creates a workforce skilled in communication, and enables the ability to quickly and easily apply existing knowledge and skills in new situations. In this direction, the study created a new 21st Century competencies framework (KC21) by analyzing and interpreting the 15 frameworks put forward by researchers, institutions, and organizations worldwide between 1991 and 2012. These are still known and used most frequently today. This framework defines the competencies students must acquire as socio-emotional and key competencies and divides them into nine categories (See Table: 1) (Pešikan & Lalović, 2017, pp. 5-7).

OECD (Organization for Economic Co-operation and Development) launched the Future of Education and Skills 2030 project in 2015 to help countries prepare their education systems for the future. Within this framework, the issues that must be focused on will be addressed in two stages. The first stage (2015-2019) questioned what competencies (knowledge, skills, attitudes and values) today's students need to shape the future to achieve a better life and individual and social well-being. The second stage (2019-) questions how learning environments that can realize these competencies should be designed. According to the data obtained for the project's first phase, skills essentially form part of a holistic concept of competence that includes the mobilization of knowledge, skills, attitudes and values to meet complex demands. In this context, three different types of skills emerge. These are with their scope:

1. Cognitive and meta-cognitive skills (Critical thinking, creative thinking, learning to learn and self-regulation)
2. Social and emotional skills (Empathy, self-efficacy, responsibility and collaboration)
3. It consists of physical and practical skills (practical and physical skills, including the use of ICT devices). (OECD, 2019).

According to the World Economic Forum (2015), success in today's innovation-oriented economy requires a different mix of skills compared to the past. While literacy and numeracy are now seen as basic skills, in addition to these, competencies such as cooperation, creativity, problem-solving and character traits such as determination, curiosity and initiative are needed. (collaboration, creativity, problem-solving, and character qualities like persistence, curiosity and initiative.) Everyone should have these skills. As in P21 and KC21, the World Economic Forum also states that individuals should be equipped with the skills that meet the needs of the 21st-century market, starting from primary education. As a result of the meta-analysis they conducted in this direction, they divided the skills into three categories and 16 components. These basic categories are foundational literacy, competencies, and character qualities (Weforum, 2015).

Figure 6. Sixteen skills students must have in the 21st century

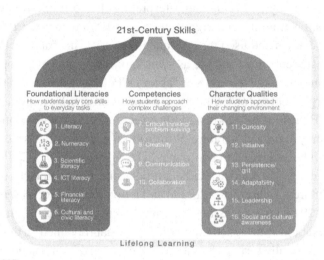

(Weforum, 2015)

The first of these categories, basic literacy, refers to how basic skills are applied to daily tasks. These skills are fundamental to forming more advanced competencies and character traits. In addition to literacy and numeracy skills, this category includes scientific, ICT, financial, cultural and civic literacy. Competencies in the second category correspond to how to approach complex challenges. These skills are vital for the 21st-century workforce, where critically evaluating and transferring information and working well with a team have become essential. This category includes critical thinking, Creativity, Communication and collaboration. The third category is character traits, which correspond to how one approaches changing environments. This category includes being curious, taking initiative, being patient, adapting, showing leadership qualities and having social and cultural awareness.

As a result, Foster (2023, pp.31-33) emphasizes that success in today's society has gone beyond traditional reading, mathematics and science literacy and has come to require a much broader set of competencies. While advances in information and communication technologies connect people globally and provide unprecedented amounts of information, they have also radically transformed societies. As a result, new and decentralized autonomous learning styles have emerged. Today, learning to participate in the rapidly changing world is no longer sufficient; it has become necessary for individuals to learn to improve their own actions and make decisions that will contribute to individual and collective well-being. Understanding and appreciating different perspectives, interacting with others, collaborating and acting responsibly in creating a sustainable future for all has become necessary.

Foster has critically examined the literature studies that define, organize, and classify 21st century competency frameworks in various ways. According to him, certain competencies should always be developed regardless of how specific competencies are categorized in the frameworks. These include critical thinking, creative thinking, communication, and ICT-related competencies. Furthermore, the points where all the frameworks consistently overlap have been grouped into six common competency categories.

Figure 7. Broad categories of 21st-century competencies

(Foster, 2023, 33)

These categories are Cognitive (problem-solving, critical thinking, creative thinking), Metacognitive (Self-regulated learning, metacognition), Interpersonal (Communication, collaboration), Intrapersonal (persistence, adaptability, flexibility), and Civil and Citizenship (intercultural communication), and ICT and Digital (digital literacy, media literacy). The activation of one of the qualification categories expressed here often requires the simultaneous activation of other "categories". For this reason, it should not be overlooked that all these categories have fundamentally strong connections with each other.

Education 4.0 Technologies and Features

Education 4.0 technologies correspond to technologies that meet the need to harmonize and synchronize education models and systems with the 4th Industrial Revolution, in other words, Industry 4.0. Connection, interaction and symbiosis between learners and learning contents and environments, which can be realized anytime and anywhere, become possible using education 4.0 technologies. Educational institutions must integrate their teaching-learning processes with education 4.0 technologies to produce a future-ready workforce. For this reason, information and communication technologies that assist learning and teaching processes through software and hardware also play key roles in education 4.0 technologies.

ICT use, which permits educational change, has grown in significance in the processes of education and training, as noted by Sarkan (2012, p. 33). When utilized properly, these technologies enable the shift to a student-centered setting. They are crucial, particularly when experimenting with various approaches to improve training and education standards. Increasing student passion and dedication, facilitating the development of fundamental skills, and enhancing teacher preparation are the primary strategies for achieving this. Information and communication technologies are divided into two sub-components, according to Miranda et al. (2021, p. 3), who identify them as one of the fundamental elements of Education 4.0 in higher education. The first involves creating technology-based solutions by fusing various technologies and approaches; the second involves creating tools and platforms, which are technology-based solutions that arise from fusing various technologies for management and education objectives.

Figure 8. Components of information and communication technologies

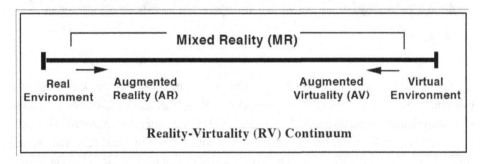

(Authors based on (Miranda vd, 2021)

It is important to remember that utilizing Education 4.0 technologies and concepts results in strong tools and platforms that enhance the teaching and learning process in several ways. Web-based systems that can process enormous volumes of data with high processing power and enable the supply of wikis, blogs, e-mails, virtual learning environments, and many other online services can be presented as examples, according to Miranda et al. (2021, pp. 5–6). ICTs provide new opportunities for innovation and enhancement in formal teaching and learning processes because of their competencies and capabilities. Furthermore, learning programs built on collaborative platforms and virtual classrooms are starting to appear; these can either support or replace conventional teaching techniques. Through web conferencing technologies (such as Zoom, Meets, Webex, and M-Teams) that integrate audio, text, graphics, and video and enable student participation, learning platforms provide synchronous online sessions to enhance student learning. Learning Management Systems (LMS) are developing in tandem to offer learning environments where instructors and students can collaborate synchronously, asynchronously, or in a hybrid way that combines the two. The following are further examples of related applications of tools and platforms: hologram-teacher formats; web-based learning; m-learning; intelligent tutoring systems; educational robotics; augmented, virtual, and mixed reality laboratories; and virtual and experimental environments.

Immersive Technologies and Types

Immersive technologies result from today's developments in information and communication technologies. Schmitt emphasizes that this digital revolution has entered a new phase by including digital information in physical, solid products, from bits to atoms (Schmitt, 2019, p. 825). Macpherson and Keppell (1998) state that immersive technologies, which are specifically aimed at creating computer-based simulations that bring together the real and virtual worlds, "initially produced textual and numerical outputs" but are now evolving into software, along with hardware and advanced software with increasing processing power and multimedia capabilities. Creating "different graphical outputs," such as software-animated and 3D screen-based graphics, has become possible.

Immersive technologies now blur the line between the physical world and the digital or simulated world, creating a feeling of immersion, as described by Lee et al. (2013, p.400). These technologies (AR, VR, and MR) add additional informational capabilities and experiences to existing real-life experiences (Hoyer et al., 2020, p. 59). As a result, they improve users' skills to perform various activities and performing actions in different ways. These experiences are modified and made interactive through immersion, interactivity, and a sense of presence. These technologies connect abstract realities with real-time context and physical interaction. Users visualize everything revealed in virtual worlds through their sensory system since they are artificially constructed and exist only in the user's mind (Nussipova et al. 2020: 2, 484). Immersion technologies allow users to view virtual elements as a part of the real world and have an immersive experience. They do this by simulating the actual environment through the virtual world (Turan & Karabey, 2023, p. 2).

Immersive technologies refer to technology that attempts to create the perception that we are physically present in a world that does not physically exist, either through a digital or simulated world or by seeing and interacting with virtual elements added to physical reality. The technical goal of immersive technologies is to create a feeling of immersion by replacing actual sense perceptions with computer-generated ones. In this context, according to Slater, immersive defines a system's technical capabilities and corresponds to the physics of the system (Slater & Sanchez-Vives, 2016, pp. 4-5). Here, users experience the subjective experience of being in a place or environment, in other words, the "subjective sense of existence," even if they are physically located elsewhere (Witmer & Singer, 1998, p. 225).

While these technologies initially included virtual reality (VR) and have become increasingly common daily, their framework has gradually expanded. Milgram and Kishino described virtual reality (VR) and augmented reality (AR) as extensions of the reality-virtuality continuum, revealing in Figure 1 that these concepts together constitute mixed reality. (Milgram & Kishino 1994, p. 3). Milgram et al. (1995, p. 283) described any environment on the left side of the continuum as consisting solely of real objects and including everything observable directly or through a window or video display of a real-world scene. The right side of the continuum describes environments that consist solely of virtual objects, and examples include traditional computer graphics simulations that are monitor-based or immersive. In this context, mixed reality (MR) refers to an environment where real-world and virtual-world objects are presented together on a single screen, that is, anywhere between the extremes of the continuum.

Figure 9. Reality – Virtuality (RV) continuum

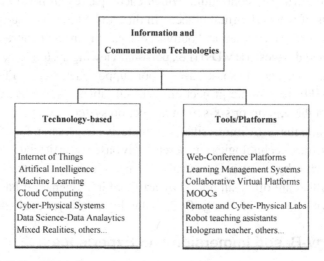

(Milgram and Kishino 1994, p. 3)

In other words, in this continuum, real environments (RE) include reality itself. This includes direct or indirect images of a real scene. Users interact in real-time through a technological interface with objects that do not actually exist, displayed on a device in completely computer-generated virtual environments (Flavián, C. et al. 2019, p. 2). The reality-virtuality continuum has also become a means of understanding the relationship between real and virtual elements of the user experience. In this context, on the left side of the continuum is the real environment, where no virtual objects are added. The user experience takes place on the right side of the continuum in the virtual environment, which expresses a completely virtual user experience where elements from the real world are not included (Rauschnabel, 2022, p.3).

Milgram and Kishino proposed the "Reality-Virtuality Continuum" as the starting point for researchers to classify different and diverse realities. Looser et al. (2004, p. 205) state that the reality-virtuality continuum determines the type of reality based on how much of the visual content is real and how much is computer-generated. In this context, the concept of "extended reality" has emerged as a concept that completely combines virtual reality, augmented reality, and mixed reality. In Bennet's words, these immersive technologies (VR, AR, MR, and XR) covering a wide range of technologies and experiences are also described as a series of R's (Bennet, Murphy, 2020, p. 22).

According to Hudson et al., many technological tools can be used for exploring the reality-virtuality continuum, which encompasses all possible variants and arrangements of real and virtual objects. In this context, devices such as computer or television screens are used as "output devices" or, in their more current form, "head-mounted devices" (HMDs) (i.e., personal viewing systems, such as helmets, goggles, or glasses), and in some cases, floor-supported screens. "Floor-supported displays" (FSD), panoramic projections, virtual tables, immersive cocoons, or a CAVE (i.e., a three, four, or six-screen projection system) can be used (Hudson et al. 2019). While the term 'immersive' is an inclusive expression for all these reality technologies, these technologies are increasingly based on artificial intelligence (AI) (Bennet and Murphy, 2020, p. 7), virtual assistants, chatbots, robots, and the Internet of Things, which are often supported by artificial intelligence. It has also become associated with Internet of Things (IoT) technologies (Hoyer et al. 2020, p. 58).

Technology-Based Immersion and Experience

Although its exact origin is unknown, immersion is not essentially a new concept, as it has been discussed from theory to practice in different fields (culture, art, entertainment, design, engineering, medicine, education, etc.) and in different contexts (Murray, 1997). As a concept, it extends from the prehistoric ages to the present day. The most primitive immersive experience in human evolution is "role-playing" (e.g., making conversations around the hearth in prehistoric times, conveying the exciting experience of hunting prey, creating imaginary images) (Chang Lei, 2018), and "telling fictional stories" (e.g., the most known ancient immersive works, early cave paintings) (Yu, 2022) have been revealed as part of human ability. Studies draw attention to the fact that the immersive experience has been tried to be realized by people throughout the ages, and in this process, the change is mainly experienced in the type and structure of the experience medium. 21st-century technologies have become the fundamental tools of the immersion experience with the development of storytelling today. In this context, as Pine & Gilmore (1999, p.31) put it, immersion means "being in a real or virtual world" by moving away from daily experiences, playing different roles, or taking on different identities.

While Robins states that modern technologies change our experiences of the world around us (Robins, 2013:47), Pine and Gilmore state that these new technologies reveal new types of experiences such as interactive games, www sites, "screen attractions", 3D movies, and virtual reality environments (Pine and Gilmore, 2012, p. 32). Immersion has become an amazing experience for users interacting with the virtual environment thanks to the quick development of virtual reality, augmented reality, and mixed reality (VR, AR, and MR) technology (Zhang, 2020, p. 90878). In this context, especially with the emergence of digital storytelling, it is seen that studies on technology-based immersion experiences have spread to a wide area, especially from virtual reality (VR) to other reality studies (AR, MR, ER), and the concept has begun to be re-investigated in this context.

According to Murray, the metaphorical term "immersion" is physically inspired by being submerged in water. The same psychologically intense experience is sought after whether diving into the sea or a swimming pool. This sensation seizes all of our attention and perceptual instruments, submerging us in a world that differs from the air and water (Murray, 2017, p. 99). Later on, it was linked to a wide range of experience-related domains, particularly those involving simulations. Through technology, the user is fully submerged in a virtual world. According to Murray, the idea alludes to the sensation of being encircled by an entirely other reality— that is, the wonderful experience of being transported to a carefully reproduced location. According to Hudson (2019), this "immersion" experience embodies the sensation of harmony, escape, and existing in another universe. It shows itself as the participant feeling as though they are "really there," forgetting the outside world and losing sense of time.

According to Witmer and Singer (1998), p. 227), immersion is a psychological state defined by the sense of being or feeling "enveloped," "involved," or "in interaction" with an environment that provides a range of exciting sensations. Zhang clarifies that when a user interacts with a virtual system, they are said to be immersed mentally. Several physio-psychological systems and processes work together in this virtual system to provide the transcendent feeling of being physically transported into the virtual space. Only when the mind, directed by attention, concentrates on the generated virtual area does this contribution take place. This mental change results in a physical delusion. Considering this, "concretization" is necessary for immersion (Zhang, 2020, p. 90881). "Immersion refers to a phenomenon experienced individually while in a state of deep mental engagement," according to Agrawal et al. Here, attention levels are altered by cognitive processes, either in the presence or absence of sensory stimulus. To the point where it's possible to feel detached from consciousness of the outside world. Since immersion is a mental state, it's possible that it can occur without any sensory stimulation at all (daydreaming, for instance, can be an immersive experience). People continue to absorb information from all senses, which might have an impact on the immersive experience, thus it's generally vital to take all sensory modalities into account when determining the type of immersion (Agrawal et al., 2019, p. 6).

The study discussed in this context aims to raise awareness about the components that should be considered when creating "technology-based" immersive experiences. At this point, it is important to understand that immersion is a multi-component, integrated concept. These components consist of: the structure of the stimulus, in other words, the structure of the environment (tool, technology, or system); the content and the way the content is presented; the stimulus, in other words, the subjective perception of the user involved in the environment; and the way of interaction.

Technology-Based Immersive Learning Experience

Experience is one of the most important sources of learning. According to Dewey, learning occurs through experiences, but not every experience has 'educational' value. He pointed out that for an experience to be considered educationally valuable, it must develop the individual intellectually and morally and benefit society (Dewey, 1938). Therefore, not every technology allows for immersive experiences; not every experience may enable learning. The same appears to be true for the technology-based immersion learning experience. Dengel (2022, pp. 338-339), states that immersive learning means learning through perceived artificial experiences (the situation in which a person does not perceive or accept the existence of a medium in the communication environment and reacts similarly to what he would if the medium were not there). In other words, it is not dependent on current technological innovations, does not directly align with learning supported by immersive media, and not all media possess qualities that enable immersive learning.

A technology-based immersive learning experience in this context involves utilizing immersive technologies to support the learning process. Creating an educational virtual environment (EVE) or virtual learning environment (VLE) that will enable an immersive learning experience, in the words of Mikropoulos, requires having one or more educational goals and pedagogical metaphors, providing experiences that cannot be experienced in the physical world, and achieving certain learning outcomes. The features of immersive virtual environments that contribute to learning are, in the most general framework, 3D spatial representations, first-person point of view, autonomy, sensory modality, freedom in navigation, and interaction (Mikropoulos, 2006, pp. 198-199).

Hassenzahl et al. It emphasizes that experience is a story that emerges from a dialogue with one's own world through action, and that people enter into the process of creating meaning after going through an episode. They literally begin to tell stories to themselves (and to others) (Hassenzahl et al., 2013, p. 22). In this context, it is not a coincidence that entrainment, which is essentially a part of the storytelling ability, is described as "immersive experiences," a new type of experience supported by technological developments.

Murray asserts that people experience immersion both physically and psychologically (Murray, 1997). While the physical dimension expressed here includes the inclusion of sensory data (i.e., visual, auditory, olfactory, and tactile) in the process (Oprean, 2014, p.15), psychological immersion refers to the psychological state when the user is involved, dragged, engaged, or absorbed. The most basic reasons that can lead to psychological immersion are the subjective feeling of being surrounded or experiencing multi-sensory stimulation, being caught up in the narrative or the depiction of the narrative, and getting carried away when faced with strategic or tactical challenges (Agrawal et al., 2019, pp. 2–3).

Sherman and Craig (2003) stated that "being immersed" generally refers to an emotional or mental state, specifically the feeling of being in an experience. One can also achieve this feeling through physical and/or purely mental means. At this point, Murray (2017) states that entrainment is not just the result of sensory stimulation intensity. He notes that an exciting narrative can provide immersive experiences even with a limited amount of sensory input, as in books. In this context, immersion, in the words of Agreval et al. (2019, p. 5), is a phenomenon experienced by an individual in a state of deep mental engagement in which cognitive processes (with or without sensory stimulation) cause a change in the state of attention so that the individual can have an experience disconnected from the physical world's awareness.

At this point, physical immersion is described as the feature of a system that replaces those that naturally stimulate the participant's senses in a reality environment, synthetically stimulates these senses (visual, auditory, tactile), or increases the stimulation, while the extent to which synthetic stimuli override natural stimuli and the deceived person is It is stated that the number of senses determines the level of physical immersion (Sherman & Craig, 2003:p.9, pp. 381-382). The feeling of being surrounded by or experiencing multisensory stimulation is called perceptual immersion (Biocca & Delaney, 1995). Perceptual immersion corresponds to the immersion of the user's perceptual system into the created environment and is directly related to physical immersion. What is effective here is again how comprehensive the sensory data is and to what extent it allows for visual-auditory-tactile experiences.

In this context, it becomes important to consider both physical (perceptual/sensory) factors related to the vehicle and mental (psychological/emotional) factors related to the user in creating a technology-based immersion experience (see Figure 10). In other words, together with the content presented (the user must find the conveyed topic and how it is conveyed interesting), it is possible to list the basic components that are effective in revealing the technology-based immersive experience: (i) the user's life experience and attitudes; (ii) the way of interacting; and (iii) the technological requirements and capacity of the tool used. Physical immersion, especially in a simulated environment, has become a fundamental and essential component of the technology-based immersion experience.

Figure 10. Components of technology-based immersion

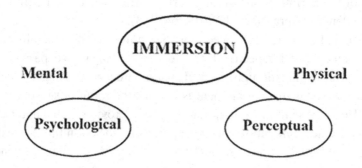

At this point, to create an immersive experience, it becomes important to be aware of how a computerized system, especially 3D technology, contributes to the experience. These technologies achieve this with an "experiential interface" where users can interact with the content as if they were there (Gorini et al., 2011, p. 99). For a computerized system to provide this illusion of reality to the user, it must have certain qualities. Slater and Wilbur distinguish between immersion and presence and mention five quality features, which are inclusive, extensive, surrounding, vivid, and matching. Here, inclusivity refers to the extent to which physical reality is excluded, the extent to which sensory modalities are accommodated, and the extent to which a panoramic virtual environment is created. Vivid is based on the quality and resolution of the representations, content, accuracy, and richness of the information. While these aspects of the immersion experience are related to the display of information, matching is based on the association established between the participant's behaviors and body movements and the information conveyed through the screens (Slater & Wilbur, 1997, p. 605).

Whether an active or passive virtual environment is built determines the degree of interaction. According to Oprean, passive virtual environments are more static and less engaging than active virtual environments, which are more "interactive" (e.g., video games, computer games, etc.) (e.g., IMAX movies, 3D movies, etc.). Whether the medium provides active or passive virtual environments determines the kind of engagement the user has with immersive experiences (Oprean, 2014, p. 5). On the other hand, there is no proof that experience happens everywhere or at all (Jay, 2012, p. 364). It's crucial to remember that not every virtual encounter offers customers an immersive experience. Immersion experiences that rely on technology are emerging from virtual experiences that immerse users in a virtual setting while giving them the impression that they are in the real world. A user's immersion in a virtual encounter increases with how real they perceive it to be (Patria et al., 2023, pp. 2-3). In this context, there are three types of immersive systems: semi-immersive, non-immersive, and immersive. A system can be fully immersive, but it can also become "semi-immersive (projection screen instead of glasses) or a non-immersive system (computer screen)," according to Gutiérrez et al. (2017, p. 475).

Technology-Based Immersive Learning Experiences in Design Education

In today's Industry 4.0 era, where the lines between the physical, digital, and biological worlds are blurred (Schwab, 2016), and people, objects, and systems are connected on a global scale with increasing digitalization and real-time data exchange (Grzybowska & Łupicka, 2017) by means of technological developments, the nature of problems addressed has changed. So, It has become imperative for designers to look for new ways to deal with these issues. In Papanek's words, humans try to understand their ever-changing, highly complex existence by seeking order within it constantly (Papanek, 2004, p.4). Emerging technologies, markets, and business models have radically changed our world and made it necessary to face new conditions with new ideas and practices regarding design (Hesket, 2002, p.39).

Mainly, the problems addressed are changing at a very rapid pace and are becoming more numerous and more complex. Today, to solve these increasingly complex problems and meet changing needs, design has begun to be viewed as a problem-solving and decision-making act. (Edwards, 2008; Goldschmidt, 1992; Rodriguez et.al. 2014; Bayazıt, 2004 etc.). This situation has led to researching and implementing new education and training approaches to prepare professionals and university graduates to meet the needs of Industry 4.0. In this context, institutions providing design education have begun to deal with complex, blurry, unpredictable, and pluralistic issues, moving away from the effort to create or use rational design methods and seeking to capture new areas of inquiry, environments, and tools. It seems that immersive technologies are among the tools that have the potential to answer this search. According to Liang & Xiaoming (2013, p. 1), immersive technologies play essential roles in advancing the reformation of higher education methods and provide a learning platform that will increase the quality of teaching.

As Huang (2016, p.78) stated, learning systems created by immersive technologies improve student learning experiences and positive emotions by integrating them into learning scenarioss. Similarly, Kee mentioned that immersive technologies can significantly improve the learning experience in a pedagogical sense and can support experiential learning. Immersive technologies used in design courses provide a plausible and cost-effective learning experience regarding collaboration, flexibility, student performance, and motivation in the learning process. In addition, experiential learning positively affects learning modes such as active experimentation (AE) and reflective observation (RO) (Kee et al., 2023, pp. 21-22). In the words of Schott and Marshall, these technologies enable "experiential education" (EE), which is widely accepted as an effective pedagogy to promote learning in our rapidly changing world. This pedagogical approach, whose suitability for the changing world is unquestionably accepted, was first promoted by John Dewey at the beginning of the last century and has since become actively implemented by many disciplines today. Its suitability for the rapidly changing world stems from the importance it attaches to connecting the student to the contemporary world and actively directing the student's learning process, thus developing lifelong learning skills.

In experiential education, carefully selected experiences are structured and supported by reflection, critical analysis, and synthesis. The aim here is to enable the student to take initiative, make decisions, and be accountable for the results by actively posing questions, being curious, investigating, experimenting, constructing meaning, taking responsibility, solving problems, being creative, and integrating previously developed knowledge. Students are engaged intellectually, emotionally, socially, politically, spiritually, and physically in uncertain environments where they can experience success, failure, adventure, and risk-taking. The students are guided to explore issues of values, relationships, diversity, inclusion, and community. The role of the educator here is to select suitable experiences, pose problems, set boundaries, support learners, insure physical and emotional safety, facilitate the learning process, guide reflection, and provide necessary information. (AEE, 1994, cited in Itin, 1997, p.6) In this context, experiential education generally corresponds to a teaching philosophy. This philosophy includes data on many methodologies in which educators consciously engage with students through direct experience and focused reflection to increase knowledge, develop skills, clarify values, and develop people's capacity to contribute to their communities (AEE, 2023).

In this context, compared to traditional systems, immersive technologies enable experiential learning experiences with their diversity and display a more interactive structure (Calvet, et al. 2019: 96). For this reason, virtual worlds have begun to be used in education to create interactive simulations and role-playing scenarios that enable students to learn through experiential learning (Murti et al., 2023, p. 189). The promise of 3D games, simulations, and virtual environments for teaching and learning has been acknowledged by educators and educational institutions all around the world. Due to the fact that these technologies enable students to investigate, create, and work with virtual structures, objects, and symbolic representations of concepts (Dalgarno and Lee, 2010, p. 10). Immersion technology solutions have been shown to improve learning results in the field of education. According to these studies, participants take immersive simulations more seriously, approach hazards more cautiously, and willingly devote more time to learning tasks. Students' interest in learning activities has also increased (Jensen & Konradsen, 2018, p.1521). In this way, it becomes possible to perceive non-existent things, trigger creative imagination, and convey difficult abstract concepts through visualization abilities (Burdea & Coiffet, 2003, p. 17).

As stated by Suh & Prophet, some research reveals that certain features of immersive systems create cognitive and emotional responses in users. These features enhance the user experience with sensory stimuli associated with visual displays, auditory modalities, haptic interfaces, and movement tracking. In the case of learning and education, this situation stands out with its content features that facilitate students' social interaction, such as conceptual blending, collaboration for problem-solving, and increasing motivation and performance (Suh & Prophet, 2018, pp. 82-83).

Students can practice through hands-on interactions, thus improving their application, observation, and innovation capacities (Liang & Xiaoming, 2013, p. 1). Thanks to the ability to create interactive learning environments, these technologies increase student participation, cultural understanding, and cooperation by providing access to a more inclusive education for students from different regions and backgrounds to come together and learn from each other (Murti et. al., 2023, p.198). Immersive technologies give significant impetus to design education. It will also provide experiential learning in design-based learning, in understanding digital technology in design, and by developing experiences between various opposing concepts (natural and artificial, living and inanimate matter, matter and mind, virtual and real, etc.). Immersive technologies are becoming an indispensable asset in experiential learning. Immersive technology applications used in design education generally create new teaching and learning opportunities that enable knowledge to be structured and characterized by fully inclusive, open, creative, collaborative, and dialogue (Kee et al., 2023, p. 2).

These technologies function as cognitive tools that help students elaborate on what they think. These tools allow students to understand ideas in different ways and enable them to become designers who teach computers and to operate by understanding the process more. By using immersive technologies as a tool to organize, create, and express ideas, students engage in both learning with technologies and meaningful learning (Jonassen, 2000, p. 107). In addition, as De, Camba et al. put it, immersive technologies are used in addition to CAD software to develop and visualize design concepts. They also provide benefits in visualizing construction processes and planning and analyzing engineering and construction equipment. In addition, it can increase the designer's awareness in design studios and facilitate the reinterpretation and instant evaluation of a particular design example (De Camba et al., 2017, p. 5). These technologies include cognitive skills related to remembering and understanding spatial and visual information, as well as other types of information; psychomotor skills, which include the ability to visually scan or observe;

It also helps to gain emotional skills to control emotional reactions to stressful or difficult situations (Jensen & Konradsen, 2018, p. 1527).

Additionally, these technologies serve as cognitive aids that assist pupils in expanding on their ideas. With the use of these resources, students can gain a diverse understanding of concepts, which will help them in their future careers as computer educators and designers. Students participate in meaningful learning as well as technology-assisted learning by utilizing immersive technologies as a tool for idea organization, creation, and expression (Jonassen, 2000, p. 107). Furthermore, to develop and visualize design concepts, immersive technologies are employed in addition to CAD software, as stated by De, Camba, et al. Along with planning and analyzing engineering and construction equipment, they also aid in the visualization of construction processes. Furthermore, it has the potential to heighten the level of awareness among designers in design studios and enable the reinterpretation and immediate assessment of a specific design example (De Camba et al., 2017, p. 5). Cognitive abilities, such as the ability to recall and comprehend spatial and visual information along with other kinds of information, psychomotor skills, such as the capacity to visually scan or watch, and Developing emotional intelligence is also beneficial for managing feelings in stressful or challenging circumstances (Jensen & Konradsen, 2018, p. 1527).

CONCLUSION AND EVALUATION

Technological and social changes constantly influence the purpose, content, and activities of design education throughout its historical process. These changes have occurred on a large scale with every industrial revolution. In other words, Industry 1.0 has led to the emergence of Education 1.0, Industry 2.0, Education 2.0, Industry 3.0, Education 3.0, and finally Industry 4.0, Education 4.0. Design education environments go beyond creating a product and focus on creating an "experiential learning-oriented" thinking environment. Acceptance of the situation-specific, non-generalizable, unpredictable, and irreducible structure of design problems has come to require the designer to think in multiple ways and approach problems within their level of complexity. This acceptance makes it inevitable that education-training strategies and environments in the field of design undergo a radical change. In general, understanding the factors underlying the changes in education today is important in developing a holistic perspective towards the development of the 21st-century, or, in other words, contemporary design education environments.

This perspective is believed to enhance awareness of the implicit data underlying the visible world concerning the evolving educational environments and, consequently, foster the development of original approaches in design education.

The basic data that will shed light on this discovery process are generally: the characteristics of Industry 4.0 and its technologies; the expectations of Industry 4.0 from the workforce; Education 4.0 and its characteristics; and the 21st-century skills and competencies that must be acquired in the context of Education 4.0. The ultimate goal here is to reveal what kind of potential technology-based immersive learning experiences have for "design education." To grasp the emerging potentials, Immersive Technologies and Their Types, what Technology-Based Immersion and Experience correspond to, and their relationship with learning have been analyzed and presented. We evaluated all these components as tools to raise awareness of the problems that need to be addressed to develop design education and to reveal the hidden pattern in the visible complexity. It is expected that these tools will create an integrated inquiry environment for capturing the contemporary approach required for design education.

REFERENCES

P21. (2019) *Framework*. P21. https://static.battelleforkids.org/documents/p21/P21
_Framework_DefinitionsBFK.pdf

Adams, D. (1993). *Defining Educational Quality*. IEQ Publication 1: Biennial Report.

AEE (2023). *Defining Experiential Education: Challenge and experience followed by reflection, leading to learning and growth.* Association for Experiential Education (aee.org)

Agrawal, S., Simon, A., Bech, S., Bærentsen, K., & Forchhammer, S. (2019). *Defining Immersion: Literature Review and Implications for Research on Immersive Audiovisual Experiences. (bildiri)*

Akyazi, T., Goti, A., Oyarbide-Zubillaga, A., Alberdi, E., Carballedo, R., Ibeas, R., & Bringas, P. (2020). *Skills Requirements for the European Machine Tool Sector Emerging from Its Digitalization*. Metals - Open Access Metallurgy Journal., 10.3390/met10121665

Bayazıt, N. (2004). *Endüstriyel Tasarımcılar için Tasarlama Kuramları ve Metotları*. Birsen Yayınevi.

Bennett, J., & Amanda Murphy, A. (2020) Skills for Immersive Experience Creation Barriers to Growth in the UK's Immersive Economy. StoryFutures.

Binkley, M., Erstad, O., Herman, J., Raizen, S., Ripley, M., Miller-Ricci, M. & Rumble, M. (2011). *Defining Twenty-First Century Skills*. Springer. .10.1007/978-94-007-2324-5_2

Biocca, F., & Delaney, B. (1995). Immersive virtual reality technology. In Biocca, F., & Levy, M. R. (Eds.), *Communication in the age of virtual reality* (pp. 57–124). Lawrence Erlbaum Associates, Inc.

Block, B. (2018). *An innovative teaching approach in Engineering Education to impart reflective digitalization competencies*. IEEE. .10.1109/FIE.2018.8658604

Bogdanowicz, M. (2015). *Digital Entrepreneurship Barriers and Drivers. The need for a specific measurement framework*. (JRC Technical Report EUR 27679.) Institute for Prospective Technological Studies; 10.2791/3112

Brussels. (2011). *Supporting growth and jobs – an agenda for the modernization of Europe's higher education systems*. Europea. https://eurlex.europa.eu/LexUriServ/LexUriServ.do?uri=COM:2011:0567:FIN:EN:PDF

Brynjolfsson, E., & McAfee, A. (2014). *The second machine age: Work, progress, and prosperity in a time of brilliant technologies*. Norton & Co.

Buhr, D. (2015). *Social Innovation Policy for Industry 4.0*. Springer.

Burdea, G., & Coiffet, P. (2003). Virtual Reality Technology. *Presence (Cambridge, Mass.)*, 12(6), 663–664. 10.1162/105474603322955950

Calvet, L., Bourdin, P., & Prados, F. (2019). Immersive technologies in higher education: Applications, challenges, and good practices. *Proceedings of the 2019 3rd International Conference on Education and E-Learning*, (pp. 95–99). ACM. 10.1145/3371647.3371667

Camba, J. D., Soler-Dominguez, J., & Contero, M. (2017). *Immersive Visualization Technologies to Facilitate Multidisciplinary Design Education*. Springer. 10.1007/978-3-319-58509-3_1

Chang, L. (2018). Media Communication and Application of "Immersive Experience" in the Visual Field [J]. *Design Art Research*, 8(01), 93–96.

Coşkun, S., Kayıkçı, Y., & Gençay, E. (2019). Adapting Engineering Education to Industry 4.0 Vision. *Technologies*, 7(1), 10. 10.3390/technologies7010010

Dalgarno, B., & Lee, M. J. (2010). What are the learning affordances of 3-D virtual environments? *British Journal of Educational Technology*, 41(1), 10–32. 10.1111/j.1467-8535.2009.01038.x

Dengel, A. (2022). What Is Immersive Learning? *2022 8th International Conference of the Immersive Learning Research Network (iLRN)*. IEEE. 10.23919/iLRN55037.2022.9815941

Dewey, J. (1938). *Education and experience*. Simon and Schuster.

Dunwill, E. (2016). *4 Changes That Will Shape The Classroom Of The Future: Making Education Fully Technological*. eLearning Industry. https://elearningindustry.com/4-changes-will-shape-classroom-of-the-future-making-education-fully-technological

Edwards, B. (2008). *Understanding Architecture through Drawing*. The Cromwell Press. 10.4324/9780203882436

Findeli, A. (2001). Rethinking Design Education for the 21st Century: Theoretical, Methodological, and Ethical Discussion. *Design Issues*, 17(1), 5–17. 10.1162/07479360152103796

Finegold, D., & Notabartolo, A. S. (2010). 21st century competencies and their impact: An interdisciplinary literature review. *Transforming the US workforce development system, 19*, 19-56.

Fisk, P. (2017). *Education 4.0 … the future of learning will be dramatically different, in school and throughout life.* The Genius Works. http://www.thegeniusworks.com/2017/01/future-education-young-everyone-taught-together/

Flavián, C., Sánchez, I. S., & Orús, C. (2019). The impact of virtual, augmented, and mixed reality technologies on the customer experience. *Journal of Business Research*, 100, 547–560. 10.1016/j.jbusres.2018.10.050

Foster, N. (2023). In Foster, N., & Piacentini, M. (Eds.), *21st Century competencies: Challenges in education and assessment in Innovating Assessments to Measure and Support Complex Skills* (pp. 30–44). OECD Publishing.

Goldschmidt, G. (1992). Serial Sketching: Visual Problem Solving in Designing. *Cybernetics and Systems*, 23(2), 191–219. 10.1080/01969729208927457

Gorini, A., Capideville, C. S., Leo, G. D., Mantovani, F., & Riva, G. (2011). The role of immersion and narrative in mediated presence: The virtual hospital experience. *Cyberpsychology, Behavior, and Social Networking*, 14(3), 99–105. 10.1089/cyber.2010.010020649451

Grzybowska, K., & Łupicka, A. (2017). *Key competencies for Industry 4.0*. Volkson Press. 10.26480/icemi.01.2017.250.253

Gutiérrez, J. M., Mora, C. E., Diaz, B. A., & Marrero, A. G. (2017). Virtual technologies trends in education. *Eurasia Journal of Mathematics, Science and Technology Education*, 13(2), 469–486. 10.12973/eurasia.2017.00626a

Hamelink, C.J. (1997). *New information and communication technologies, social development and cultural change.*

Hassenzahl, M., Eckoldt, K., Diefenbac, S., Laschke, M., Len, E., & Kim, J. (2013). Designing Moments of Meaning and Pleasure. Experience Design and Happiness. *International Journal of Design*, 7(3), 21–31.

Hesket, J. (2002). *Toothpicks and Logos Design in Everyday Life*. Oxford University Press. 10.1093/oso/9780192803214.001.0001

Hoyer, W. D., Kroschke, M., Schmitt, B., Kraume, K., & Shankar, V. (2020). Transforming the customer experience through new technologies. *Journal of Interactive Marketing*, 51, 57–71. 10.1016/j.intmar.2020.04.001

Huang, T. C., Chen, C. C., & Chou, Y. W. (2016). Animating eco-education: To see, feel, and discover in an augmented reality-based experiential learning environment. *Computers & Education, 96*(1), 72-82. Elsevier Ltd. https://www.learntechlib.org/p/201462/

Hudson, S., Matson-Barkat, S., Pallamin, N., & Jegou, G. (2019). With or without you? Interaction and immersion in a virtual reality experience. *Journal of Business Research*, 100, 459–468. 10.1016/j.jbusres.2018.10.062

Itin, C. M. (1997). *The Orientation of Social Work Faculty to the Philosophy of Experiential Education in the Classroom.* [Unpublished Dissertation, University of Denver].

Jay, M. (2012). *Deneyim Şarkıları, Evrensel Bir Tema Üzerine Modern Çeşitlemeler. Çev: Barış Engin Aksoy.* Metis Yayınları, İstanbul.

Jensen, L., & Konradsen, F. (2018). A review of the use of virtual reality head-mounted displays in education and training. *Education and Information Technologies*, 23(4), 1–15. 10.1007/s10639-017-9676-0

Jonassen, D. (2000). Transforming Learning with Technology: Beyond Modernism and Post-Modernism or Whoever Controls the Technology Creates the Reality. *Educational Technology*, 40, 101–110. 10.1007/978-94-6209-269-3_7

Kee, T., Zhang, H., & King, R. (2023). An empirical study on immersive technology in synchronous hybrid learning in design education. *International Journal of Technology and Design Education.* Advance online publication. 10.1007/s10798-023-09855-5

Knihová, L., & Hronova, S. (2019). *Digital Entrepreneurship: Reskilling and Up-skilling with Mobile MOOCs.*

Liang, H. & Xiaoming, B. (2013). *Application Research of Virtual Reality Technology in Electronic Technique Teaching.* Springer. .10.1007/978-3-642-31656-2_22

Loke, S.-K. (2015). How do virtual world experiences bring about learning? A critical review of theories. *Australasian Journal of Educational Technology*, 31(1), 112–122. 10.14742/ajet.2532

Looser, J., Billinghurst, M., & Cockburn, A. (2004). Through the looking glass: The use of lenses as an interface tool for augmented reality interfaces. In *2nd intl. Conference on computer graphics and interactive techniques in Australasia and South East Asia* (pp. 204–211).

Macpherson, C., & Keppell, M. (1998). Virtual reality: What is the state of play in education? *Australasian Journal of Educational Technology*, 14(1), 60–74. 10.14742/ajet.1929

Mikropoulos, T. A. (2006). Presence: A unique characteristic in educational virtual environments. *Virtual Reality (Waltham Cross)*, 10(3-4), 197–206. 10.1007/s10055-006-0039-1

Milgram, P., & Kishino, F. (1994). A Taxonomy Of Mixed Reality Visual Displays. *IEICE Transactions on Information and Systems*, E77-D(12), 1–15.

Milgram, P., Takemura, H., Utsumi, A., & Kishino, F. (1994). Augmented reality: A class of displays on the reality-virtuality continuum. *In Telemanipulator and Telepresence Technologies* (p. 2351). 10.1117/12.197321

Miranda, J., Navarrete, C., Noguez, J., Molina-Espinosa, J. M., Ramírez, M. S., Navarro-Tuch, S. A., & Bustamante-Bello, M. R. (2021). The core components of education 4.0 in higher education: Three case studies in engineering education. *Computers & Electrical Engineering*, 93, 1–13. 10.1016/j.compeleceng.2021.107278

Mourtzis, D., Vlachou, K., Dimitrakopoulos, G., & Zogopoulos, V. (2018). Cyber-Physical Systems and Education 4.0 –The Teaching Factory 4.0 Concept. *Procedia Manufacturing*, 23, 129–134. 10.1016/j.promfg.2018.04.005

Murray, J. H. (1997). *Hamlet on the Holodeck: The Future of Narrative in Cyberspace* (1st ed.). MIT Press.

Murray, J. H. (2017). *Hamlet on the holodeck, updated edition: The future of narrative in cyberspace*. MIT Press.

Murti, K. G. K., Darma, G. S., Mahyuni, L. P., & Gordad, A. A. N. E. S. (2023). Immersive Experience in the Metaverse: Implications for Tourism and Business. *International Journal Of Applied Business Research*, 5(2).

Nussipova, G., Nordin, F., & Sörhammar, D. (2020). Value formation with immersive technologies: An activity perspective. *Journal of Business and Industrial Marketing*, 35(3), 483–494. 10.1108/JBIM-12-2018-0407

OECD. (2019). *OECD Future of Education and Skills 2030, OECD Learning Compass 2030. A Series of Concept Notes*. OECD. https://www.oecd.org

OEDC (2019). *OECD Future of Education and Skills 2030. OECD Learning Compass 2030. A Series of Concept Notes*. OECD.

Oprean, D. (2014). *Understanding the immersive experience: Examining the influence of visual immersiveness and interactivity on spatial experiences and understanding.* [Doctoral dissertation, University of Missouri].

Papanek, V. (2004). *Design for the Real World, Human Ecology and Social Change.* Thames & Hudson Ltd.

Patria, T. A., Hidayah, N., and Suherlan, H. (2023). Effect of Immersive Experience on Repurchase Intention of Virtual Heritage Tours among Gen-Z in Indonesia. *E3S Web of Conferences 388.* IEEE. 10.1051/e3sconf/202338804013

Perini, S., Luglietti, R., Maria, M., Fradinho Duarte de Oliveira, M., & Taisch, M. (2017). Training Advanced Skills for Sustainable Manufacturing: A Digital Serious Game. *Procedia Manufacturing*, 11, 1536–1543. 10.1016/j.promfg.2017.07.286

Pešikan, A., & Lalović, Z. (2017). *Education For Life: Key 21 St Century Competencies in Curricula in Montenegro.* UNICEF Montenegro.https://www.unicef.org

Pine, J., & Gilmore, J. H. (1999). *The experience economy.* Harvard Business School Press.

Pine, J., Gilmore, J. H. (2012) *Deneyim Ekonomisi.* Çeviren: Levent Cinemre. Optimist Yayınları.

Rauschnabel, P. A., Felix, R., Hinsch, C., Shahab, H., & Alt, F. (2022). What is XR? Towards a Framework for Augmented and Virtual Reality. *Computers in Human Behavior*, 133, 107289. 10.1016/j.chb.2022.107289

Robins, K. (2013). *İmaj. Görmenin Kültür ve Politikası,* İngilizceden Çeviren: Nurçay Türkoğlu, Ayrıntı Yayınları, 2. Basım.

Rüßmann, M., Lorenz, M., Gerbert, P., Waldner, M., Justus, J., Engel, P., & Harnisch, M. (2015). Industry 4.0: The future of productivity and growth in manufacturing industries. *Boston consulting group, 9*(1), 54-89.

Sarkar, S. (2012). *The Role of Information and Communication Technology (ICT) in Higher Education for the 21st Century.*

Schmitt, B. (2019). From atoms to bits and back: A research curation on digital technology and agenda for future research. *The Journal of Consumer Research*, 46(4), 825–832. 10.1093/jcr/ucz038

Schott, C., & Marshall, S. (2018). Virtual reality and situated experiential education: A conceptualisation and exploratory trial. *Journal of Computer Assisted Learning*, 34(6), 843–852. 10.1111/jcal.12293

Schwab, K. (2016). *The Fourth Industrial Revolution.* World Economic Forum.

Sharma, P. (2019). Digital Revolution of Education 4.0. *International Journal of Engineering and Advanced Technology*, 9(2), 3558–3564. 10.35940/ijeat.A1293.129219

Sherman, W., & Craig, A. B. (2003). *Understanding virtual reality: Interface, application, and design.* Morgan Kaufmann.

Slater, M., & Sanchez-Vives, M. (2016). Enhancing Our Lives with Immersive Virtual Reality. *Frontiers in Robotics and AI*, 3, 74. 10.3389/frobt.2016.00074

Slater, M., & Wilbur, S. (1997). A Framework for Immersive Virtual Environments (FIVE): Speculations on the Role of Presence in Virtual Environments. *Presence (Cambridge, Mass.)*, 6(6), 603–616. 10.1162/pres.1997.6.6.603

Sousa, M., & Rocha, Á. (2019). Digital learning: Developing skills for digital transformation of organizations. *Future Generation Computer Systems*, 91, 327–334. 10.1016/j.future.2018.08.048

Suh, A., & Prophet, J. (2018). The State of Immersive Technology Research: A Literature Analysis. *Computers in Human Behavior*, 86, 77–90. 10.1016/j.chb.2018.04.019

Szlapka, J., Ortega-Mier, M., Ordieres-Meré, J., & Facchini, F., & Mossa, G., & Lundquist, J. (2020). *Innovative methodologies and digital tools for higher education in industrial engineering and management.*

Turan, Z., Karabey, S. C. (2023). The use of immersive technologies in distance education: A systematic review. *Education and Information Technologies*. Springer.10.1007/s10639-023-11849-8

Wang, T. (2010). *A New Paradigm for Design Studio Education.* JADE:173-183

Witmer, B. G., & Singer, M. J. (1998). Measuring Presence in Virtual Environments: A Presence Questionnaire. *Presence (Cambridge, Mass.)*, 7(3), 225–240. 10.1162/105474698565686

World Economic Forum. (2020) *Schools of the Future: Defining New Models of Education for the Fourth Industrial Revolution.* WEF. https://www.weforum.org/publications/schools-of-the-future-defining-new-models-of-education-for-the-fourth-industrial-revolution/

Yu, S. (2022). The Research on the Characteristics and Forms of Immersive Experience in Art Exhibitions—Take "Van Gogh—the Immersive Experience" as an Example. *Journal of Education. Humanities and Social Sciences.*, (6), 154–159.

Zhang, C. (2020). The Why, What, and How of Immersive Experience. *IEEE Access : Practical Innovations, Open Solutions*, 8, 90878–90888. 10.1109/ACCESS.2020.2993646

Chapter 15
Exploring the Benefits and Challenges of IT–Enabled Learning in the Education Sector:
A Roadmap for Effective Use of Extended Reality

Shaina Arora
https://orcid.org/0000-0002-5998-6834
Chandigarh University, Mohali, India

Anand Pandey
Chandigarh University, Mohali, India

Kamal Batta
Chandigarh University, Mohali, India

Shad Ahmad Khan
https://orcid.org/0000-0001-7593-3487
University of Buraimi, Oman & INTI International University, Malaysia

ABSTRACT

In this chapter, the primary advantages, and problems of information technology (IT) enabled learning in the education sector are discussed. In addition, the effects of shifting from traditional classrooms to online learning environments are briefly discussed. This chapter is based on the perspective that the extended reality (XR) can be realized through the success of IT enable learning. The aim is to delve

DOI: 10.4018/979-8-3693-2432-5.ch015

into the significance of IT-enabled learning within today's educational landscape, examining the factors contributing to its rapid adoption. Drawing from existing research, the study discusses the implementation of IT-enabled learning technologies in educational environments. The key findings of this study include the benefits and drawbacks of moving from a traditional classroom setting to an online learning environment, including the frequency with which they arise, the different kinds of barriers that may be encountered, the possible advantages, the potential downsides, and security concerns.

INTRODUCTION

In recent years, the integration of extended reality (XR) technologies - encompassing virtual reality (VR), augmented reality (AR), and mixed reality (MR) - has been reshaping various industries (Jonathan et al., 2024). The education sector too has been undergoing the state of transformation (Khatri et al., 2024; Magd & Khan, 2024; Malik et al., 2024), these changes have a bigger implication in the form of online learning. The education sector has been witnessing change in terms of delivery, assessment, planning, accreditation, and improving learning experience (Naim et al., 2024a; 2024b). XR offers immersive and interactive experiences that have the potential to revolutionize traditional learning methods (Aguayo & Eames, 2023). XR could be a potential tool for the education sector, however, it cannot be realized without the implementation of IT enabled learning.

Online courses, hybrid learning, and online classrooms have brought about a dramatic change in the educational system throughout the globe in the last three to four years (Magd et al., 2023; Khan & Magd, 2021; Bocar et al., 2022). The introduction of distance learning options like MOOCs (Massive Open Online Courses) and hybrid formats prompted this shift. The globe around, people have noticed this change. This once-crucial shift is now seen differently around the world, with some places finding benefit and others seeing harm. This change might be seen positively or negatively depending on your location on the globe. This article will address the growth of information technology (IT) as well as the challenges and opportunities that have arisen for the educational sector as a direct consequence of this growth.

Although they have been around for a while, MOOCs are still considered a novel approach to distance education because they were put into practice before careful consideration of teaching and learning principles that are suitable for large numbers of online learning participants (Cleveland-Innes et al., 2019). Open Educational Resources (OER) may develop and share information between educationalists and the distribution and reuse of informative content can help shape the educational environment. Using OER supports ICT-based education, which enables flexible learning anywhere, anytime (Magd & Khan, 2022a;2022b). OERs may engage learners as Internet usage rises. In 2001, MIT began releasing free learning resources for use globally, sparking the OER movement. Many schools accept and promote OERs later. OERs provide free, excellent, reusable, and shareable educational materials. The Indian government launched many mission-mode initiatives to assist OER and ICT-enabled education, including NPTEL, SWAYAM, NROER, Digital Library Inflibnet, Swayam Prabha, eGyanKosh, and E-PG Pathshala.

To produce a profound and meaningful (collaborative-constructivist) learning experience, the Community of Inquiry (CoI) helps in the theoretical framework which can be utilized as a method that allows the development of three interdependent aspects. It is using a technique called a CoI learning community that this can be accomplished. Physical presence, social presence, and cognitive presence are the three pillars of the teaching presence. A person's "social presence" refers to their ability to interact meaningfully in an environment that trusts them, to build inter-personal relationships through the projection of their distinct personalities, and to be able to connect with the community (for example, through study), and it is defined as "the capacity of individuals to connect with the community (for example, course of study) "meaningfully interact in an environment that trusts them," and "build inter-personal(Garrison et al., 1999).

The term "teaching presence" is used to describe the teacher's intentionality in leading students through a learning process that results in content that is both personally relevant and academically acceptable. Presence in the classroom refers to the time spent planning, coordinating, and directing these activities(Anderson et al., 2019). When we speak of a learner's cognitive presence, we are referring to the extent to which they are able to continually reflect on their experiences and engage in discussion in order to develop and reaffirm meaning for themselves (Garrison et al., 2001)

Indian higher education is made up of 993 universities, 39,931 colleges, and 10,725 independent institutions that are located throughout the country.Among these figures, there aren't included the country's 15 open universities, which include IGNOU, the Indira Gandhi National Open University, and 14 state open universities located across the country.Nearly one-hundred & ten schools may be considered "dual-mode," since they provide both online and campus-based programmes to their students. India's higher education system has a college-dense average of 281. In India, 26.3% of people between the ages of 18 and 23 are enrolled in some kind of postsecondary education, according to the country's Gross Enrollment Ratio (GER). The United States has an equal percentage of men and women with GERs of 26.2% and 26.4%, respectively, between the ages of 18 and 24.It has been estimated that about 40% of all higher education enrollments in India are fulfilled by the country's robust distance learning and open learning systems. These systems account for 10.62% of the country's overall enrollment rate of 26.3%. A study found that 44.15 percent of college-bound women use online distance learning as a way of empowering themselves (Mohan, 2018).

Online education has several drawbacks compared to traditional physical teaching. These include limited social interaction and reduced opportunities for face-to-face discussions and networking (Magd & Khan, 2022b). Further, there are several technical challenges such as connectivity issues and digital literacy can hinder learning, while subjects requiring hands-on experience may be harder to replicate effectively online (Bocar et al., 2022). Self-motivation and time management are more crucial in online learning environments, and distractions at home can impact focus (Bocar et al., 2022). The quality of instruction and engagement can vary, and some students may feel isolated without the community atmosphere of a physical classroom (Magd & Khan, 2022b). Concerns about assessment integrity and digital fatigue are also prevalent, alongside unequal access to necessary resources, which can exacerbate educational disparities (Al Mulhim, 2023). XR is seen as a potential tool to overcome the shortfalls of the online education (Lee et al., 2024). The success of XRTop of FormBottom of Form is dependent on the adoption of the latest technology. The XR is expected to overcome the problems of make the online and hybrid education, hence, the relevance of this chapter becomes more important as it explores the ways IT enabled learning can play its role in education.

Online Learning and Blended Learning

There is mounting evidence that more and more learning is being delivered online (Bates, 2018) which is transforming higher education using the distribution of web-based information and interaction (Khan et al., 2024; Khan & Magd, 2023). Pond (2002), in his study, suggested that "neither the objective, the techniques, nor the population for whom education is meant now have any relation at all to those on which formal education is historically built." Neither the "people for whom education is designed today". There are many benefits to moving towards online learning and blended learning, such as the distribution of information, the facilitation of learning, and the engagement of students. The amount of information, experience, support, and leadership that is made accessible throughout the shift to this new method of learning is very important to the effectiveness of delivering education via online or hybrid methods. Furthermore, the fact that many faculty members do not have the necessary qualifications to teach has generated and continues to present an issue in the area of higher education about the quality of teaching. Additional work is required to employ online and blended learning while preserving or increasing education quality. This effort is necessary to get the benefits of online and hybrid education. Without the success of online and hybrid education, the success of XR cannot be realized. Thus, it is important for the HEIs and the supporting services to enhance online and hybrid education so that the technology acceptance level is enhanced among the audiences.

Massive Open Online Course (MOOCS)

The progress and dissemination of Massive Open Online Course (MOOC) is one recent effort aimed in this direction. Even though they have been around for a while, MOOCs (or massive open online courses) are still considered an innovative way of learning new information via the medium of the internet. Because of this, they were implemented before enough thought was given to adapting traditional pedagogical strategies for use with massive online student populations. Gasevic et al. (2014), noted a deficiency of pedagogical rigor in the initial growth of MOOCs in their study. They also claim it is difficult, if not impossible, to modify existing social learning frameworks to function in a massive open online course (MOOC). This is because of the rising popularity of massive open online courses (MOOCs). Many, however, believe that effective and scalable online learning environments may be built with the help of suitable learning activities. It is still feasible to teach, facilitate, and help a big group of pupils who are all engaged in the activity at hand (Liu & Yu, 2023). The (TEL) MOOC project's achievements may be utilized to support this hypothesis.

An Overview of the Diverse Educational Opportunities that Modern Technology Makes Possible Massive Open Online Course, which is also known as (TEL)MOOC, is a project that was developed as a result of a partnership between the Centre for Distance Education at Athabasca University, which is situated in Alberta, Canada, and the Commonwealth of Learning (COL), which has its headquarters in Burnaby, which is situated in British Columbia, Canada. Together, these two institutions collaborated to develop the Massive Open Online Course. Both establishments may be found in the country of Canada.

This MOOC is designed to include educators from all over the globe who teach at any level of education and are interested in learning more about how technology may be able to enhance education. Participants may teach at any level of education. Embedding the MOOC with XR is expected to enhance the learners experience and may enhance the learning engagement leading to effective learning.

PROBLEM STATEMENT

IT-enabled learning has been around for many years, but due to the COVID-19 pandemic, it has gained a lot of momentum in the educational sector. This has opened a wide range of opportunities and approaches to give a new boost to this industry. As XR is expected to overcome the problems of IT enabled/ online learning, the path to efficient implementation of XR can only be achieved if the level of acceptance of technology is enhanced in the education sector. Technology in educational institutions has been primarily focused on supporting traditional teaching and learning methods. However, the current education system requires instruction that applies, assesses, generates, and consolidates information. Recent studies have shown that technology is most effective when it is interactive, offers real-time feedback, and enables students to creatively apply and evaluate what they have learned. The key to success is the adaptation of this learning style that will lead to an effective implementation of the XR. Thus, a study that can check the primary advantages, and problems of IT Enabled Learning in the education sector is needed. This chapter presents the insights in this context through the review of literature so that the perspectives on the ways the XR can be realized through the success of IT enable learning.

Aim and Methodology of the Study

This study is based on a literature review of selected published articles and the qualitative data collected from participants who were mainly students that participated in the MOOC, the responses were gathered in the form of their feedback and reviews provided for the MOOC. As the initial interaction with the participants demonstrated a negligible awareness about the XR, the study focused on raising awareness about the advantages and challenges of IT-enabled learning and its scope in the current era of the digital world. Technology in the classroom allows children to adjust their learning pace. Students who require less assistance can move ahead, and those who need more time can take their time going through the activities until they fully understand them. It also provides the teacher with additional time to offer individualized assistance to those who require it. Principles of CoI as discussed in the introduction section was utilized as the main framework to address the objectives of this study. The same is also discussed extensively in the literature review section of this chapter.

LITERATURE REVIEW

Because of its accessibility and adaptability, the CoI theoretical framework (Garrison et al., 2001) has become the de facto standard for constructivist-based, technology-enabled learning design. Since then, Garrison, Anderson, and Archer have established the theoretical framework known as the CoI, which explains why this is the case. The CoI structure was created by Garrison, Anderson, and Archer. And this is the reason why. The evolved CoI theoretical framework may be traced back to the ideas of Garrison, Anderson, and Archer. All the above is the reasoning behind the statement. This is because the COI framework was originally developed by Garrison, Anderson, and Archer CoI. Why this is the case may be summed up as follows (Anderson, 2016). It was not only the main topic of discussion during the first week of the 2017 version of the Teaching English to Speakers of Other Languages Massive Open Online Course (TEL), but it also served as the foundation for the course's design and the guidance for many of the course's pedagogical techniques. Not only did it form the backbone of the course structure and guide the many pedagogical methods used, but it was also the principal topic of discussion throughout the first week's classes.

The CoI shines light on the teaching and learning process regardless of the delivery modality, and it offers support for both directed inquiry and deep, meaningful learning. Moreover, the CoI enlightens the teaching and learning process. This massive open online course makes use of a framework that was created by Garrison et al. (2001), to facilitate the dissemination of content and a variety of different learning activities.

The CoI (Anderson, 2016; Liu & Yu, 2023; Gasevic et al., 2014) theoretical framework may be used as a starting point for the development of MOOCs as an online distribution method. (Anderson, 2016; Anderson et al., 2019; Liu & Yu, 2023; Garrison et al., 2001; Gasevic et al., 2014) may be used for this purpose. To this end, references like (Anderson, 2016; Anderson et al., 2019; Liu & Yu, 2023; Gasevic et al., 2014) might be useful. In the studies conducted by (Anderson, 2016; Liu & Yu, 2023; Gasevic et al., 2014; Liu & Yu, 2023), it was explored that Learners participating in this inquiry-based massive open online course (iMOOC) are assisted in the form of three unique forms of teaching presence. The term "instructions" refers to the first type of materials. In this case, there will not be any chances for students to comment; rather, the content will be given like that of a modified lecture. This instruction may either be conveyed in the form of an audio recording or in written form. Using short movies in which information is presented, accompanied by a visual of the person presenting as well as slides or other visuals, is one method for accomplishing this goal. These videos may also be used in combination with other visual aids. The second way that teaching may be offered is via the demonstration of its subject matter using written words.

CoI framework can be useful for the studies on XR in education as well. Integrating the CoI framework with XR in education enhances learning by fostering cognitive engagement, social interaction, and effective teaching practices. XR facilitates deep cognitive involvement through immersive simulations and interactive experiences that promote critical thinking and practical application of knowledge. Social presence is strengthened as XR enables realistic, virtual interactions among students and instructors, fostering collaboration and community building. Teaching presence is enhanced through interactive teaching methods, personalized feedback, and the creation of engaging learning environments. By combining COI principles with XR, educational institutions can create enriching and interactive learning experiences that support diverse learning needs and improve overall learning outcomes.

To guarantee the long-term viability of OER at universities, (Luo et al., 2020) emphasized the need to build partnerships with instructional creators, e-learning experts, and academic librarians. For their 2011 study, Chakraborty and Ghosh analyzed the effectiveness of freely available textbooks and articles at Indian universities. The significance of India's open archival resources was further emphasized by Chakraborty and Ghosh. On this day and age of information technology, digital assets may serve as a source of knowledge that is easily available. Datt & Singh (2021) recommended opening up OERs to students with disabilities in poor regions of the globe. The collaborative nature of OERs and the opportunities for lifelong learning cited by (Henderson & Ostashewski, 2018) are highly valued by educators.

According to the report, open educational resources face challenges in the higher education sector of India due to factors like poverty, a lack of competent teachers, inadequate pedagogical and technological resources, and poor infrastructure (Dutta, 2016). In addition to this, Dutta praised the Indian government's National Mission on Education via Information and Communication Technology (NMEICT). These kinds of activities help to spread instructional content. (Kurelovic, 2016) explored academics' opinions on OERs and the sharing of learning resources in tiny countries with few OERs in the local or native language. Thakran and Sharma, two academics, assessed the use of open educational resources (OER) and the barriers to their broader implementation in India's higher education system in 2016. Furthermore, they examined existing programs to promote student access to education using OER to conclude relevant to the spread of OER in the context of higher education in India. Singh & Panigrahi (2018) researched attitudes about and usage of open educational resources (OERs) among Indian university students. They praised the usage, flexibility, and accessibility of OERs. Singh and Panigrahi's findings have far-reaching consequences for educational reform.

OBJECTIVES

We are conducting this study to explore the problems that exist in the field of education and to find solutions for them. The study has focused on the impact of IT-enabled learning on academics and academicians, the benefits and challenges of IT-enabled learning, and methods that can make online education less complicated and risky. Thus, this study checks the advantages and problems of IT Enabled Learning in the education sector. The second objective is also to bring forward perspectives on the ways the XR can be realized through the success of IT enable learning.

BENEFITS

The concept of working together was brought up in most of the participants' comments on the advantages. According to the responses, the CoI framework encouraged student collaboration, which in turn helped students "appreciate the value of studying together and helped them create connections and cooperation for a meaningful learning experience. "According to the statement of one more participant, "CoI gives the three-dimensional picture for the interaction of collaborative teaching and learning environment." This will result in students being able to learn more effectively as a result of this.

The replies indicate that an increase in accessibility and flexibility is the second most significant benefit and that this advantage is made possible by the CoI Teaching Presence. Because of this benefit, it is now feasible to engage in in-depth education regardless of the limits imposed by factors such as time and geography.

The third and fourth benefits brought forth by CoI are enhanced communication and knowledge acquisition. Students, instructors, and students' understanding of the subject matter all benefited from CoI with technology-enhanced learning, according to respondents. Others said that it gave students who would have been too shy to participate in class discussions the confidence they needed to speak out and make their voices heard in a traditional classroom setting. It's less likely that pupils will get disengaged when compared to huge in-person courses. The CoI has the potential to serve as a pedagogical crossroads where instructing professionals and their students may engage in meaningful dialogue. Students who may feel nervous while raising their hands or asking questions in a large group of their classmates may feel more at ease with CoI.

The potential of learners to project themselves socially and effectively into a CoI is the sixth benefit that was noted by the participants. This benefit is characterized as the ability of learners to have a social presence. One participant noted that "CoI will allow me to help my students comprehend the benefits of studying together and will assist them in improving connections and cooperation for a more meaningful learning experience."

One more person shared their thoughts, stating that "with remote learning, it is technology that allows these three presences to build a community where we socially engage, study, and get instruction." Distance doesn't have to get in the way of a dynamic social learning experience thanks to the CoI's ability to foster stronger relationships, communication, and cooperation between students and teachers. Student engagement, which may be characterized as the degree to which students demonstrate attention, curiosity, enthusiasm, optimism, and passion while they are learning, was the sixth most often mentioned advantage by the participants.

Most of the comments on increased engagement are related to building a community of learning and delivering an effective and meaningful education, as shown by the statement, "CoI might be an engaging activity for students, and this approach could contribute to the dialogue between students, thus creating the sense of belonging to a community." Of the seven most frequently cited benefits, "creating a strong social learning experience, increasing connection, communication, and collaboration between students and instructors with one another" stands out as particularly relevant because it allows students to share their ideas, thoughts, and experiences more freely in a risk-free setting.

Some Specific and Focused Benefits

Versatility

Employees have 24/7 access to digital classrooms and instructional materials. They are not obligated to attend standard classes at a set hour during the day. They can learn while they are on the go, whether it be during their daily commute, a layover at the airport, or even at home. Because of this, employees may make good use of their downtime and make sure that their education doesn't get in the way of completing their KRAs and departmental objectives.

Reasonably Priced

The trainer's tools or time are not used in this type of learning. Due to the availability of all necessary information and study materials in digital format, the costs associated with filling classrooms, holding lectures and courses, and travelling have been significantly reduced. For their learning, employees just need a Smartphone or other portable device with Internet access.

Self-Directed Education

The course modules are recorded and always accessible online. Employees don't need to learn as quickly or slowly as they would in a regular classroom. They can design a learning path that suits their preferences and learning styles.

CHALLENGES

The lack of a technological infrastructure to support learning that is facilitated by technology was the challenge that was mentioned the most often by those who responded. In this scenario, the examination of the CoI as a framework has been superseded by this dominant concern. Numerous studies identified a significant obstacle in the form of limited access to various forms of technology, including personal computers, laptops, tablets, and mobile phones (Vaportzis et al., 2017). Few studies observed that the issues are significant (Williamson & Eynon, 2020). Inadequate infrastructure is notable in a great number of the countries to the south of the Sahara (Calderón & Servén, 2010). Second, many areas with low median incomes have internet prices that are unaffordable for residents (Reddick et al., 2020). The selection of an efficient mode of instruction is the third consideration (Iqbal et al., 2022).

Participants ranked the difficulty in creating educational programs based on the pedagogical concepts of CoI as the second most important obstacle. Some people assumed it would take a lot of time to think up new educational activities, projects, and assignments and choose the proper medium. One learner said, "It may also be tricky to come up with the material, technology, and experience to ensure that the CoI is included in the learning throughout the complete course or curriculum," which suggests that doing so might be difficult. Others have cited difficulties in developing courses that adhere to proper pedagogical principles as the third most significant barrier that prevents the CoI from serving as an effective tool to facilitate technology-enabled learning. This is a method for making progress. According to the words of one of the attendees, "CoI challenges the design and execution of courses to be supported by technology in such a manner as to preserve the learner's core fascination with technology while continuing on to deep learning."

Participants' replies often mention cyber-malice as a difficulty. Cyberbullying includes remarks regarding academic dishonesty and unethical behavior. Cyberbullying was the top issue, followed by cheating and academic untruthfulness.

Lack of skills/support/training was the fourth most-cited obstacle. Instructors and/or students lacked training, assistance, or IT skills, according to the comments. As many participants hailed from impoverished countries, they thought instructors and students needed resources and expertise to implement technology-enabled learning.

DISCUSSION

Effective use of XR in the field of education requires a good and thorough implementation of IT enabled learning. XR could be a great tool for the education sector, however, it cannot be realized without the implementation of IT enabled learning. Thus, the framework of this study provided interesting insights into the implementation of IT enabled learning.

The participants in this research were given the unique chance to learn about and engage in a CoI during the duration of the study. Students, instructors, and material all benefitted from more communication and collaboration when CoI was combined with technology-enhanced learning. Children felt less self-conscious about speaking out in class and having conversations with their peers when they were in an environment conducive to learning like this one. A good number of participants enjoyed the conversational setting. The participants in this research were given the unique chance to learn about and engage in a CoI during the duration of the study CoI. Students, instructors, and material all benefitted from more communication and collaboration when CoI was combined with technology-enhanced learning. Like its face-to-face counterpart, is multi-functional, because of the multi-functionality of communication, the three main aspects of the CoI – cognitive presence, social presence, and teaching presence are intertwined." This finding provides further evidence of the significance of the benefits described above.

The students noticed that they were less reserved while talking to their classmates and those they learned more from these types of group discussions. The opportunity to interact with others while expanding their knowledge was also highly valued by many students. Teachers reported that students' critical thinking, creativity, and problem-solving skills improved, as well as the amount of time they spent studying, reflected upon learning, and used metacognition. (Xin, 2012) agrees that these benefits are significant when evaluating the CoI framework, and she writes, "online expression, like its face-to-face counterpart is multi-functional, [and] because of the multi-functionality of communication, the three main aspects of the CoI - cognitive presence, social presence, and teaching presence are intertwined.

The results not only emphasize the importance of access, but also the requirement for effective and efficient teacher professional development in the field of technology-enabled learning, and the application of conceptual frameworks like the CoI. Teachers' worries about students' lack of interest or motivation and their inability to acquire the necessary skills and knowledge around technology-enhanced learning are prevalent. A well-mapped course tends to boost learners' competence and confidence (Stodel et al., 2006).

Incorporating technological proficiency into course requirements may have heightened students' anxiety, especially among those students who started out with a lower level of technology competence. However, the fact that these students have demonstrated growth in this area suggests that they have become more at ease and are better able to handle the increased mental demand (Lambert & Fisher, 2013).

Consequently, more study, teaching, and training can only serve to diminish educator and student apprehensions equally if more of these activities are carried out. (Lambert & Fisher, 2013) concluding argument provides backing for the notion that more study is needed to "examine the effect of technical skill proficiency on students' ability to focus on the course content, to collaborate and communicate, and to develop a sense of community in online learning environments." This is of paramount importance in contexts like educational technology classes, where a broad range of cutting-edge technologies are employed in a single project.

It must be noted that XR can play a potential role in solving the issues in IT enabled learning or online learning. XR fosters social interaction through immersive virtual environments, facilitates hands-on learning via simulations and virtual labs, and enhances instructional quality with interactive, personalized experiences. XR also addresses isolation by creating virtual communities and supports secure assessments to maintain academic integrity. While not directly mitigating digital fatigue, XR's engaging nature can reduce distractions and improve focus. Although access to XR technology remains a consideration, advancements aim to make it more widely available, potentially reducing disparities in educational resources. Overall, integrating XR into online education shows promise in enriching learning experiences and overcoming traditional limitations. However, this integration would require the efficient implementation of IT-enabled learning in the education sector first.

CONCLUSION

Application of XR in the field of education requires a good and thorough implementation of IT enabled learning. On this account, this study is very relevant as it brings into account the issues that the education sector is facing on the front of

IT enabled learnings. XR could be a great tool for the education sector, however, it cannot be realized without the implementation of IT enabled learning.

This research studied the advantages and disadvantages of the CoI framework that is used in higher education institutions that are enabled by technology, as indicated by participants in iMOOCs. It contributes to the information that we already have base in a variety of senses. To begin, even in the year 2018, teachers in a broad variety of geographic areas agree that having access to technology is an essential, albeit inadequate, prerequisite for effective online learning.

According to the replies given by the participants, even though they are aware of the possible obstacles posed by the absence of a technological infrastructure, they believe that the advantages of cooperation, enhanced accessibility, flexibility, and interactivity exceed the limitations. Second, participants were able to experience an online setting thanks to MOOCs like the (TEL)MOOC, which were created with ideals of CoI in mind.

During the first week of the massive open online course (MOOC), which includes the study of the CoI framework, participants were allowed to evaluate the relevance of the CoI framework to their own educational context. This evaluation's findings are consistent with those of the CoI's previous research, providing more support for the notion that this iMOOC opportunity provides participants with a worthwhile learning experience.

Many of the learners experienced social presence, cognitive presence, and instructional presence for the first time in this course of study, which was grounded in constructivism as a design principle. As a result, chances occurred for the four cornerstones of the CoI model—self-reflection, active cognitive processing, participation, and peer instruction CoI. Because of this, participants not only gained a solid grounding in the framework's conceptual underpinnings, but also had the opportunity to put their newfound knowledge to use in a hands-on setting, paving the way for them to effectively incorporate the CoI framework into their own pedagogical routines.

REFERENCES

Aguayo, C., & Eames, C. (2023). Using mixed reality (XR) immersive learning to enhance environmental education. *The Journal of Environmental Education*, 54(1), 58–71. 10.1080/00958964.2022.2152410

Al Mulhım, E. N. (2023). Technology fatigue during the COVID-19 pandemic: The case of distance project-based learning environments. *Turkish Online Journal of Distance Education*, 24(1), 234–245. 10.17718/tojde.1034006

Anderson, T., Rourke, L., Garrison, R., & Archer, W. (2019). Assessing Teaching Presence in a Computer Conferencing Context. *Online Learning : the Official Journal of the Online Learning Consortium*, 5(2). Advance online publication. 10.24059/olj.v5i2.1875

Anderson. (2016). *Emergence and Innovation in Digital Learning: Foundations and Applications* (G. Veletsianos, Ed.). Athabasca University Press. 10.15215/aupress/9781771991490.01

Bates, T. (2018). The 2017 national survey of online learning in Canadian post-secondary education: Methodology and results. *International Journal of Educational Technology in Higher Education*, 15(1), 29. 10.1186/s41239-018-0112-3

Bocar, A. C., Khan, S. A., & Epoc, F. (2022). COVID-19 Work from Home Stressors and the Degree of its Impact: Employers and Employees Actions. *International Journal of Technology Transfer and Commercialisation*, 19(2), 270–291. 10.1504/IJTTC.2022.124349

Calderón, C., & Servén, L. (2010). Infrastructure and economic development in Sub-Saharan Africa. *Journal of African Economies*, 19(suppl_1), i13–i87. 10.1093/jae/ejp022

Cleveland-Innes, M., Gauvreau, S., Richardson, G., Mishra, S., & Ostashewski, N. (2019). Technology-Enabled Learning and the Benefits and Challenges of Using the Community of Inquiry Theoretical Framework. *International journal of e-learning & distance education, 34*(1), n1.

Datt, G., & Singh, G. (2021). Acceptance and Barriers of Open Educational Resources in the Context to Indian Higher Education. *Canadian Journal of Learning and Technology*, 47(3). 10.21432/cjlt28028

Dutta, I. (2016). Open Educational Resources (OER): Opportunities and Challenges For Indian Higher Education. *Turkish Online Journal of Distance Education*, 0(0). 10.17718/tojde.34669

Garrison, D. R., Anderson, T., & Archer, W. (1999). Critical Inquiry in a Text-Based Environment: Computer Conferencing in Higher Education. *The Internet and Higher Education*, 2(2–3), 87–105. 10.1016/S1096-7516(00)00016-6

Garrison, D. R., Anderson, T., & Archer, W. (2001). Critical thinking, cognitive presence, and computer conferencing in distance education. *American Journal of Distance Education*, 15(1), 7–23. 10.1080/08923640109527071

Gasevic, D., Kovanovic, V., Joksimovic, S., & Siemens, G. (2014). Where is research on massive open online courses headed? A data analysis of the MOOC Research Initiative. *International Review of Research in Open and Distance Learning*, 15(5). 10.19173/irrodl.v15i5.1954

Henderson, S., & Ostashewski, N. (2018). Barriers, incentives, and benefits of the open educational resources (OER) movement: An exploration into instructor perspectives. *First Monday*. 10.5210/fm.v23i12.9172

Iqbal, S. A., Ashiq, M., Rehman, S. U., Rashid, S., & Tayyab, N. (2022). Students' perceptions and experiences of online education in Pakistani Universities and Higher Education Institutes during COVID-19. *Education Sciences*, 12(3), 166. 10.3390/educsci12030166

Jonathan, H., Magd, H., & Khan, S. A. (2024). Artificial Intelligence and Augmented Reality: A Business Fortune to Sustainability in the Digital Age. In Singh, N., Kansra, P., & Gupta, S. L. (Eds.), *Navigating the Digital Landscape: Understanding Customer Behaviour in the Online World* (pp. 85–105). Emerald Publishing Limited. 10.1108/978-1-83549-272-720241005

Khan, S. A., & Magd, H. (2021). Empirical Examination of MS Teams in Conducting Webinar: Evidence from International Online Program conducted in Oman. *Journal of Content. Community and Communication*, 14(8), 159–175. 10.31620/JCCC.12.21/13

Khan, S. A., & Magd, H. (2023). New Technology Anxiety and Acceptance of Technology: An Appraisal of MS Teams. In *Advances in Distance Learning in Times of Pandemic* (pp. 105–134). CRC Press, Taylor and Francis. 10.1201/9781003322252-5

Khan, S. A., Narula, S., Kansra, P., Naim, A., & Kalra, D. (2024). Should Marketing and Public Relations be Part of the Institutional Accreditation Criterion of Business Schools? An Appraisal of Accreditation Criterion of Selected Accreditation Agencies. In Naim, A. (Ed.), *Accreditation Processes and Frameworks in Higher Education* (pp. 349–375). Nova Science Publishers. 10.52305/QUVJ6658

Khatri, B., Nandini, G., & Khan, S. A. (2024). Transition From Outcome-Based Learning to Global Accreditation of Top Universities of India: Elevating the Bar of Educational Excellence. In Naim, A., Saklani, A., Khan, S., & Malik, P. (Eds.), *Evaluating Global Accreditation Standards for Higher Education* (pp. 278–292). IGI Global. 10.4018/979-8-3693-1698-6.ch019

Kurelovic, E. (2016). *Advantages and Limitations of Usage of Open Educational Resources in Small Countries.*

Lambert, J. L., & Fisher, J. L. (2013). Community of Inquiry Framework: Establishing Community in an Online Course. *Journal of Interactive Online Learning*, 12(1). Www.Ncolr.Org/Jiol

Lee, S., Kim, D., Jeong, Y., & Ryu, J. (2024). Exploring Embodied Learning and XR Technologies in Online Education. In *Humanizing Online Teaching and Learning in Higher Education* (pp. 263–286). IGI Global. 10.4018/979-8-3693-0762-5.ch013

Liu, M., & Yu, D. (2023). Towards intelligent E-learning systems. *Education and Information Technologies*, 28(7), 7845–7876. 10.1007/s10639-022-11479-636532790

Luo, T., Hostetler, K., Freeman, C., & Stefaniak, J. (2020). The power of open: Benefits, barriers, and strategies for integration of open educational resources. *Open Learning*, 35(2), 140–158. 10.1080/02680513.2019.1677222

Magd, H., Jonathan, H., & Khan, S. A. (2023). Education Situation in Online Education before the Pandemic and in the Time of Pandemic. *In Advances in Distance Learning in Times of Pandemic (Eds.), 53-72.* CRC Press, Taylor and Francis. 10.1201/9781003322252-3

Magd, H., & Khan, S. A. (2022a). Strategic Framework for Entrepreneurship Education in Promoting Social Entrepreneurship in GCC Countries During and Post COVID-19. In Magd, H., Singh, D., Syed, R., & Spicer, D. (Eds.), *International Perspectives on Value Creation and Sustainability Through Social Entrepreneurship* (pp. 61–75). IGI Global. 10.4018/978-1-6684-4666-9.ch004

Magd, H., & Khan, S. A. (2022b). Effectiveness of using online teaching platforms as communication tools in higher education institutions in Oman: Stakeholders perspectives. *Journal of Content. Community and Communication*, 16, 148–160. 10.31620/JCCC.12.22/13

Magd, H., & Khan, S. A. (2024). Rationalizing the Online Learning in Higher Education in MENA Region: Reaching Education to Every Section of Society. In Naim, A., Saklani, A., Khan, S., & Malik, P. (Eds.), *Evaluating Global Accreditation Standards for Higher Education* (pp. 253–264). IGI Global. 10.4018/979-8-3693-1698-6.ch017

Malik, P. K., Naim, A., & Khan, S. A. (2024). Enhancing Higher Education Quality Assurance Through Learning Outcome Impact. In Naim, A., Saklani, A., Khan, S., & Malik, P. (Eds.), *Evaluating Global Accreditation Standards for Higher Education* (pp. 114–128). IGI Global. 10.4018/979-8-3693-1698-6.ch008

Mohan, M. (2018). AISHE Final Report 2018-19. *Ministry of Education.*

Naim, A., Malik, P. K., Khan, S. A., & Mohammed, A. B. (2024b). Mechanism of Direct and Indirect Assessments for Continuous Improvement in Higher Education. In Naim, A., Saklani, A., Khan, S., & Malik, P. (Eds.), *Evaluating Global Accreditation Standards for Higher Education* (pp. 200–216). IGI Global. 10.4018/979-8-3693-1698-6.ch013

Naim, A., Mohammed, A. B., Khan, S. A., & Malik, P. K. (2024a). Planning, Assessment, and Review of Program Educational Objectives in the Higher Education Systems. In Naim, A., Saklani, A., Khan, S., & Malik, P. (Eds.), *Evaluating Global Accreditation Standards for Higher Education* (pp. 241–252). IGI Global. 10.4018/979-8-3693-1698-6.ch016

Reddick, C. G., Enriquez, R., Harris, R. J., & Sharma, B. (2020). Determinants of broadband access and affordability: An analysis of a community survey on the digital divide. *Cities (London, England)*, 106, 102904. 10.1016/j.cities.2020.10290432921864

Stodel, E. J., Thompson, T. L., & MacDonald, C. J. (2006). Learners' Perspectives on what is Missing from Online Learning: Interpretations through the Community of Inquiry Framework. *International Review of Research in Open and Distance Learning*, 7(3). 10.19173/irrodl.v7i3.325

Vaportzis, E., Giatsi Clausen, M., & Gow, A. J. (2017). Older adults perceptions of technology and barriers to interacting with tablet computers: A focus group study. *Frontiers in Psychology*, 8, 1687. 10.3389/fpsyg.2017.0168729071004

Williamson, B., & Eynon, R. (2020). Historical threads, missing links, and future directions in AI in education. *Learning, Media and Technology*, 45(3), 223–235. 10.1080/17439884.2020.1798995

Xin, C. (2012). A Critique of the Community of Inquiry Framework. *International Journal of E-Learning & Distance Education / Revue Internationale Du e-Learning et La Formation à Distance*, 26(1). https://www.ijede.ca/index.php/jde/article/view/755

Chapter 16
Reality for Human Experience in AI in the Digital Economy

Nelloju Priyanka

Department of Information Technology, Teegala Krishna Reddy Engineering College, Meerpet, India

Smriti Sethi

Amity Institute of Psychology and Allied Sciences, Amity University, Noida, India

Anjali Sahai

https://orcid.org/0000-0002-2438-8682

Amity Institute of Psychology and Allied Sciences, Amity University, Noida, India

Akanksha Srivastava

School of Education, Sharda University, Greater Noida, India

M. Sambathkumar

https://orcid.org/0000-0003-2607-3454

Department of Mechanical Engineering, Kongu Engineering College, Erode, India

Sampath Boopathi

https://orcid.org/0000-0002-2065-6539

Department of Mechanical Engineering, Muthayammal Engineering College, Namakkal, India

ABSTRACT

Finance, decision-making, and AI interaction have been transferred to the digital economy due to the reduction of transaction costs and increase in security through blockchain technology. Integration of artificial intelligence (AI) and big data analytics with decision support systems (DSS), with a focus on risk assessment, predictive analytics, and strategic planning, has been explored. AI and DSS collaborated to deliver responsiveness and flexibility across several industries, leading to improved, data-driven decision-making. The current and future paths of AI with a focus on

DOI: 10.4018/979-8-3693-2432-5.ch016

finance, healthcare, and customer service, in addition to ethical problems, have also been discussed. Future developments in the digital economy, such as cybersecurity, decentralized banking, and quantum computing, have been explored to optimize benefits and reduce risks.

INTRODUCTION

The digital economy is revolutionizing the way individuals and organizations utilize technology, make decisions, manage finances, and anticipate trends. Fintech is revolutionizing the financial sector by offering cost-effective, practical, and efficient solutions. Important innovations in fintech include robo-advisors, mobile banking, and peer-to-peer financing, which are expanding access to financial services. Blockchain technology enhances security, transparency, and reliability in virtual financial systems, while decentralized finance (DeFi) solutions challenge traditional money and investing notions, reducing costs and improving operational efficiency (Boukherouaa et al., 2021). These modifications are broadening the range of financial services and encouraging economic growth.

Decision support systems (DSS) have been greatly upgraded by artificial intelligence and big data analytics. These technologies offer real-time information and predictive analytics to improve decision-making processes in a variety of companies. AI-powered DSS is useful in industries like banking, healthcare, and finance because it can see patterns and trends that human analysts would miss. This helps companies navigate complicated markets with confidence (Al-Sartawi, 2021).

The digital world is being completely transformed by artificial intelligence (AI), which makes repetitive work easier, personalizes customer interactions, and fosters creativity. Virtual assistants and chatbots lower operating expenses while raising client satisfaction. Medical AI systems detect disorders and suggest therapies, yet moral conundrums such as algorithmic bias and privacy issues still exist. Openness and accountability are essential to fostering trust and reducing unfavorable outcomes (Y. Zhou & others, 2022). DeFi, powered by cryptocurrencies and blockchain technology, is a significant advancement in the digital economy, opening up the financial system but raising regulatory concerns. Quantum computing, which solves complex problems at high speeds, could revolutionize fields like artificial intelligence and materials research. Cybersecurity is crucial as digital connections increase, as safeguarding sensitive data and ensuring system integrity are essential for trust and security in the digital economy(Mhlanga, 2020).

Financial services, innovation, and decision-making are all being revolutionized by digital technology, but these advantages need to be matched with strong legal and ethical frameworks. A smooth digital experience requires flexible solutions. AI, finance, and decision support are all being changed by the digital economy, which is also having an effect on human experience. We can create a future that is more varied, active, and productive by utilizing these technologies. Digital technology is developing quickly, improving human capacities while changing communication, healthcare, education, and entertainment (Huang, 2024).

Through social networking, instant messaging, and video conferencing systems, people can now share information and experiences in real time, revolutionizing communication. While this can promote inclusivity and transcend geographic barriers, it also raises questions about privacy, information overload, and the quality of human connections because digital communication could not have the same complexity and depth as face-to-face interactions (Ross & Liechtenstein, 2018).

Real-time health monitoring, virtual consultations, robotics, and AI-driven diagnostics are just a few of the ways that technology is transforming healthcare and extending patient lives. It also highlights how important strong cybersecurity is in order to safeguard private medical information. Particularly in underdeveloped areas, wearable technology, AI-driven diagnostics, and telemedicine platforms are expanding access to healthcare. Technology has also had a big influence on education, increasing access to knowledge and abilities through digital resources and online venues (J. Zhou et al., 2023). One of the biggest obstacles to inclusive and sustainable growth is the digital gap, which occurs when children do not have equitable access to digital resources.

Online gaming, streaming services, and virtual reality (VR) have all had a big impact on how people consume media and manage their time. These technologies are used to construct virtual worlds in the design, treatment, and training sectors. They provide dynamic, individualized experiences. Long-term screen usage, though, raises questions about addiction and mental health (J. Zhou et al., 2023). Automation, artificial intelligence, and remote work are just a few of the ways that technology is changing the workplace. While these innovations improve productivity and work-life balance, they also raise worries about job loss and the need for workers to upskill (Li et al., 2020). Technology and human experience have a complicated interaction that has benefits and drawbacks. Weighing the advantages of technological advancement against its effects on ethics, society, and the economy is critical because a well-considered strategy may promote a society that is more just, pleasant, and healthy(Mohanraj et al., 2024; Upadhyaya et al., 2024).

Scope

- Numerous technical fields, including biotechnology, nanotechnology, robotics, artificial intelligence, and telecommunications, will be the focus of the research. It will examine how technology affects work, communication, healthcare, education, and leisure, among other facets of human existence. In order to guarantee equitable and inclusive technological progress, the study will take into account viewpoints from impoverished communities and emerging economies by comprehending the worldwide effect of technology.

- In order to address concerns like algorithmic discrimination, digital inequality, privacy, data security, job loss, and mental health, the project investigates the social and ethical consequences of technology and the human experience. It also looks at how governance frameworks and policies for technology affect technological advancement and lessen risks related to digital rights, cybersecurity, data security, and intellectual property.

Objectives

- To explore how technology is transforming various aspects of human life(workplace, healthcare, education, entertainment, and communication).
- To discuss the potential benefits and drawbacks of integrating technology and human experience in dynamic environment.
- To increase understanding of the intricate relationships between technology and human behavior to encourage ethics for the benefit of society.

THE DIGITAL REVOLUTION IN FINANCE

The digital revolution in finance has totally changed how individuals and businesses manage their finances. The emergence of blockchain technology and fintech, or financial technology, is putting existing financial institutions under unprecedented danger. Peer-to-peer lending, mobile banking, robo-advisors, and other fintech innovations have made financial services more accessible and convenient for consumers worldwide. Furthermore, blockchain technology has completely changed the way transactions are carried out by providing improved efficiency, transparency, and security (Gupta et al., 2017). The financial landscape is being further transformed by cryptocurrencies, which are based on blockchain technology and have emerged as strong competitors to conventional currencies and investment vehicles. This introduction lays the groundwork for discussing the main forces behind the financial digital revolution and its ramifications, emphasizing how it has transformed people's lives, companies, and the world's financial markets(Sundaramoorthy et al., 2024).

Figure 1. Flowchart highlighting the digital revolution in finance

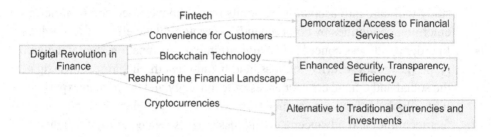

A flowchart illustrating the fintech and blockchain-driven digital transformation in finance is shown in Figure 1. Fintech has made financial services more accessible, while blockchain improves efficiency, security, and transparency. The financial environment has changed as a result of cryptocurrencies' emergence as alternatives to established currencies (Dab et al., 2016).

The emergence of the digital revolution has caused a seismic shift in the financial sector in recent years. Technology advancements that have challenged established financial conventions and given rise to the industry now known as financial technology, or fintech, have been a major factor in this change. Two major developments—the growth of fintech and the introduction of cryptocurrencies and blockchain technology—are at the center of this shift(Boopathi, 2024c).

Evolution of Fintech

Fintech is the fusion of technology and finance, utilizing advances in digital technology to improve financial processes and services. The introduction of online banking and payment methods in the early 2000s marked the beginning of fintech development. On the other hand, the fintech industry's expansion was actually spurred by the global financial crisis of 2008. The crisis brought attention to the shortcomings of the present financial system and increased demand for more innovative solutions (Ratajczak, 2022).

Since then, the fintech industry has rapidly grown to offer a variety of goods and services. Peer-to-peer lending platforms, robo-advisors, digital wallets, and mobile banking apps are examples of fintech technologies that have gained widespread usage. These technologies have made financial services more accessible to the general public, enabling individuals and businesses to handle their accounts with more ease and efficiency.

Fintech has also revolutionized traditional banking practices, bringing both cost and efficiency reductions. For example, the increased efficiency and security of financial transactions can be attributed to the decrease in the need for cash transactions due to digital payment systems. Similarly, investing has become more accessible to a larger group of people because to automated investment platforms that offer personalized portfolio management and inexpensive investment options.

Blockchain and Cryptocurrency

Once intended to serve as the foundation of Bitcoin, blockchain technology is currently upending the banking and other sectors of the economy. In essence, safe, transparent transactions may be facilitated by a distributed, decentralized ledger system like blockchain, which eliminates the need for middlemen. Cryptocurrencies, like Bitcoin, Ethereum, and Litecoin, are digital assets that employ blockchain technology to facilitate safe peer-to-peer transactions. Since cryptocurrencies are not governed by a single entity like traditional fiat currencies are, they are resistant to inflation and political manipulation (Kumar et al., 2023).

The rise of cryptocurrencies has challenged preconceived notions about money and investing. Cryptocurrencies have drawn financial interest and risen in popularity despite early opposition and regulatory scrutiny. Numerous financial institutions and organizations are looking at ways to incorporate blockchain technology and cryptocurrencies into their operations due to the potential cost and efficiency benefits(Kumar et al., 2023). In addition to cryptocurrencies, supply chain management, identity verification, and smart contracts are just a few areas where blockchain technology is being applied. The decentralized structure of the digital revolution offers opportunities for improved security, efficiency, and transparency across a range of industries (Maguluri et al., 2023; Sundaramoorthy et al., 2024).

Fintech, cryptocurrencies, and blockchain technology have revolutionized financial services, democratizing access and promoting transparency, security, and efficiency in international financial institutions.

Impact on Traditional Financial Institutions

The financial sector has undergone a significant transformation as a result of the unparalleled innovation and upheaval brought about by the digital revolution. Conventional financial institutions, including banks and insurance firms, risk going out of business if they don't swiftly adapt to the increasingly digital environment.

The main effects of the digital revolution on established financial institutions are examined in this article (Dhanya et al., 2023; Hussain et al., 2023).

The democratization of financial services is one of the primary effects of the digital revolution on established financial organizations. Digital platforms and fintech businesses have grown into strong rivals by providing a wide variety of financial services and products that were only available through traditional banks. Peer-to-peer lending platforms and mobile banking apps have drastically altered how consumers access and manage their accounts. These extra players have changed the nature of the game. To stay competitive in an increasingly crowded market, traditional financial institutions have been obliged to improve their digital services and streamline their procedures(Boopathi, 2024b; Kumar et al., 2023).

Furthermore, in light of the digital transformation, traditional financial institutions now need to reevaluate how they handle customer engagement and relationship management. Previously, face-to-face meetings and physical branches served as the primary means of contact between banks and their customers. But with the rise of digital channels like smartphone applications and online banking, the paradigm has shifted to prioritize digital-first interactions. Traditional banks must make investments in technology infrastructure and user-friendly interfaces to provide their customers with an impeccable online experience. Furthermore, data analytics and machine learning algorithms are being utilized to improve client retention rates and personalize product recommendations(Boopathi, 2024b).

The disruption of conventional payment methods is another important way that the digital revolution has affected traditional financial institutions. The emergence of digital wallets, contactless payments, and cryptocurrencies has put cash and conventional payment methods under pressure. The speed, security, and user-friendliness of digital payment options are attracting a growing number of customers. To remain relevant in the quickly changing payments environment, traditional financial institutions have had to adapt(KAV et al., 2023). They have accomplished this via adopting digital payment technology and looking into joint ventures with fintech businesses.

Blockchain technology is being increasingly utilized in trade financing, clearing, settlement, identity verification, and other traditional financial services due to the digital revolution. It enhances safety, transparency, and efficiency in peer-to-peer transactions without middlemen. Conventional financial institutions are exploring ways to enhance security, transparency, and operational efficiency through blockchain technology(Boopathi, 2024b).

To sum up, conventional financial institutions have been greatly impacted by the digital revolution and now need to adapt to the new technology landscape or risk falling behind. The financial industry is undergoing major and long-lasting changes as a result of the digital revolution, including the introduction of blockchain technology, the democratization of financial services, and the disruption of conventional payment methods(Pasumarthy et al., 2024). To stay competitive in an increasingly digital economy, traditional financial institutions need to embrace innovation and digital transformation.

DECISION SUPPORT SYSTEMS IN THE DIGITAL AGE

Figure 2. Use of digital decision support systems (DSS) for real-time insights

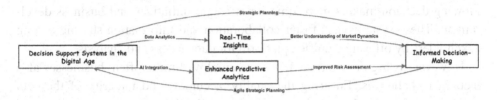

Figure 2 creates a flowchart showcasing the use of digital decision support systems (DSS) for real-time insights, their integration with artificial intelligence for enhanced predictive capabilities, and their ability to facilitate strategic planning through informed decision-making and a responsive feedback loop(Enyi, 2016).

The Role of Big Data and Analytics

Decision support systems (DSS) have become crucial tools for companies to make informed decisions based on data-driven insights. The advent of big data and analytics has significantly transformed the way businesses collect, manage, and evaluate vast amounts of data. Big data, generated from sources like social media, sensors, transactions, and online interactions, presents both opportunities and challenges for businesses. However, advancements in technology like cloud computing and distributed computing frameworks like Hadoop and Spark have enabled large and diverse datasets to be processed, analyzed, and stored at scale, making DSS essential for modern decision-making (O'Leary, 2008).

Analytics is the process of extracting useful information from data to aid in decision-making. It transforms raw data into actionable information, making it a crucial part of decision support systems. Descriptive analytics summarizes historical data, while diagnostic analytics identifies root causes of past events. Predictive analytics uses statistical algorithms and machine learning techniques to estimate future trends and outcomes, enabling proactive decision-making. Prescriptive analytics provides advice on achieving targeted outcomes, guiding decision-makers in the best course of action.

Big data and analytics integration into decision support systems can benefit businesses by enabling data-driven decisions based on unbiased research. Instantaneous database reviews can identify trends, patterns, and anomalies that human analysts might overlook. This allows companies to identify new opportunities, reduce risks, and respond quickly to changing market conditions, enhancing their ability to adapt to changing business environments.

Big data and analytics-driven decision support systems can enhance decision-making processes by automating tasks and providing useful information, allowing decision-makers more time for strategic initiatives and business development. These systems also foster collaboration and information sharing among stakeholders by offering a unified platform for data access and analysis.

However, as big data and analytics are employed more often, businesses also encounter challenges. Ensuring the quality, accuracy, and integrity of the data should come first. Inadequate data quality can lead to incorrect insights and subpar decision-making, which can undermine the credibility of decision support systems. Businesses must also manage concerns with data privacy, security, and compliance in order to safeguard sensitive information and adhere to legal requirements (Akkerman et al., 2019).

Big data and analytics are crucial in the development of modern decision support systems, enabling businesses to make data-driven decisions. These systems can improve decision-making, provide valuable data, and boost business performance. However, to fully utilize analytics-driven decision support systems, companies must address issues related to data security, privacy, and quality.

Integration of AI in Decision-Making

In the digital era, decision support systems (DSS) have undergone tremendous evolution, with advances in artificial intelligence (AI) being a major factor in boosting their capabilities. This paper examines how AI is incorporated into DSS decision-making procedures, emphasizing the revolutionary effects it has on a range of sectors and organizational roles(Hussain et al., 2023).

AI-powered decision support systems analyze massive amounts of data and extract valuable information by utilizing state-of-the-art machine learning and algorithms. By analyzing structured and unstructured data from a range of sources, such as social media, IoT devices, external market data, and internal databases, these systems let businesses make informed decisions in real-time. AI-driven DSS automate data collection, processing, and interpretation, saving time and effort during the decision-making process. This makes it possible for businesses to respond quickly to changing market conditions and rivalry issues(Boopathi, 2024c, 2024c).

One of the key benefits of integrating AI into decision support systems is the enhancement of forecasting and predictive analytics capabilities. Forecasts of future events may be more accurate if artificial intelligence (AI) systems were able to identify correlations, patterns, and trends in data sets that human analysts would have overlooked. For instance, by examining market trends, customer behavior, and risk indicators, AI-driven DSS in the financial services sector may be able to predict stock prices, spot fraudulent transactions, and enhance investment plans. In a similar vein, AI-powered DSS in the healthcare industry may assess patient data to predict the trajectory of a disease, identify individuals who are at high risk, and provide tailored treatment plans.

In a number of industries, risk assessment and mitigation strategies can also be more effective thanks to AI-driven decision support systems. Through the analysis of past data and the identification of risk indicators, artificial intelligence (AI) algorithms may help businesses anticipate potential risks and weaknesses. This gives them the ability to proactively reduce risks and prevent possible losses. For example, AI-powered DSS may assess insurance claims, spot fraudulent behavior, and expedite underwriting processes in the insurance industry to reduce risks and boost profitability. In a similar vein, supply chain management's AI-driven DSS may assess data to identify potential disruptions, optimize inventory levels, and enhance the efficiency of transportation.

AI integration into decision support systems allows for more strategic and data-driven decision-making processes. AI algorithms analyze large, complex data sets, providing insights and guidance to help decision-makers advance company goals. For example, AI-powered decision support systems can assess customer data in marketing and sales to identify target markets, customize advertising campaigns, and improve pricing strategies. AI-driven decision support systems in HR can identify skill gaps, improve hiring practices, and optimize workforce management strategies.

The digital age has seen a significant advancement in integrating artificial intelligence (AI) into decision support systems (DSS), enabling companies to make better data-driven judgments. AI-driven DSS uses advanced algorithms and machine learning techniques for accurate predictive analytics, risk assessment, and strategic decision-making across various industries. As AI advances, decision support systems will play a crucial role in helping firms achieve their strategic objectives and navigate uncertain environments.

Enhancing Predictive Analytics and Risk Assessment

The digital era has seen a significant transformation in decision support systems (DSS) due to the use of advanced technologies like big data analytics and AI, which are transforming decision-making across various industries (Zekrifa et al., 2023).

Predictive analytics is a crucial component of modern decision support systems. It is the act of looking at historical data to identify patterns and trends and project future outcomes. Because of advancements in AI and machine learning algorithms, predictive analytics models have become much more reliable and high-quality in the digital age. Through the analysis of enormous volumes of data from several sources, including both structured and unstructured data, these models may generate insights and forecasts in real time.

One field where predictive analytics is having a revolutionary impact is the financial services sector, where it is being used to forecast market patterns, identify investment opportunities, and assess credit risk. Predictive analytics models powered by artificial intelligence (AI) can lower the chance of financial losses and facilitate more intelligent investment choices by seeing patterns and correlations that humans might overlook when looking at historical market data. In order to help financial institutions, identify dubious behavior patterns and stop fraudulent transactions before they occur, predictive analytics is also used in fraud prevention and detection(Godwin Immanuel et al., 2024; Sonia et al., 2024; Sundar et al., 2024).

The healthcare industry is using predictive analytics to improve patient outcomes and save expenses. By analyzing genetic, medical imaging, and electronic health record data, predictive analytics models driven by artificial intelligence (AI) can identify individuals who are at risk of developing chronic diseases or experiencing negative medical occurrences. Healthcare professionals may save costs and improve patient outcomes by intervening early with targeted therapies and customized treatment plans.

Another area where predictive analytics is having a significant impact is supply chain management. Through the analysis of historical sales data, industry trends, and climatic patterns, AI-driven predictive analytics algorithms may be used to properly forecast product demand. Businesses may improve inventory levels, reduce stockouts, and minimize carrying costs by doing this, all of which boost the efficiency and profitability of the supply chain(Mohanty et al., 2023; Verma et al., 2024).

Risk assessment is just another crucial function of decision support systems in the digital age. Traditional risk assessment methods often rely on human judgment and past data, both of which may be biased or inaccurate. However, AI-powered risk assessment algorithms may be able to instantly examine enormous amounts of data from diverse sources in order to identify potential risks and opportunities (Boopathi, 2024a; Pasumarthy et al., 2024).

AI-driven risk assessment models are employed in the financial sector to evaluate operational, market, and credit risks. These models can produce more precise risk assessments and assist financial institutions in making more educated lending decisions by examining data from a variety of sources, such as financial statements, credit reports, and market indicators.

Digital-age decision support systems are enhancing risk assessment and predictive analytics in various businesses. These systems can analyze large data volumes in real-time, producing forecasts and insights using advanced technology like artificial intelligence and big data analytics. This transforms decision-making processes, driving innovation in the digital economy, improving investment decisions in finance, optimizing healthcare outcomes, and enhancing logistics supply chain efficiency(Ravisankar et al., 2024; S & Gopi, 2024; Vijaya Lakshmi et al., 2024).

Strategic Planning With Modern DSS Tools

This essay examines the strategic significance of decision support systems (DSS) in promoting efficient strategic planning and decision-making in the digital era. DSS tools utilize artificial intelligence and data analytics to provide valuable insights and suggestions to decision-makers, helping firms manage complexity and ambiguity in the rapidly changing business environment (Moormann & Lochte-Holtgreven, 1993).

A key procedure for businesses looking to accomplish their long-term goals and keep a competitive advantage in the marketplace is strategic planning. In the past, strategic planning required a lot of data collection, manual analysis, and subjective judgment. As a result of incomplete information and cognitive biases, judgments were frequently not ideal. Nevertheless, by automating data collection, processing, and visualization, contemporary DSS technologies have completely changed this process and allowed decision-makers to base their choices on real-time insights.

Contemporary DSS tools can handle large data volumes and identify significant patterns and trends, enabling them to identify correlations, anomalies, and forecast patterns those human analysts may miss. This data-driven approach to strategic planning helps organizations understand market dynamics, consumer behavior, and competitive threats, leading to more successful strategies(Boopathi, 2024a; Dhanalakshmi et al., 2024; Mohanraj et al., 2024).

Contemporary DSS technologies simplify scenario analysis and predictive modeling, enabling firms to project future results and assess potential effects. This helps decision-makers reduce hazards and make better judgments by modeling multiple scenarios and evaluating risks and rewards. Proactive strategic planning helps organizations become more resilient and agile in a dynamic and uncertain business environment (Chichernea, 2014).

Modern DSS technologies enable cooperative decision-making by providing a centralized platform for stakeholders to view and evaluate data. Cloud-based solutions facilitate communication between departments and locations, while interactive dashboards and visualization tools make complex data accessible, enabling decision-makers to effectively convey findings and agree on strategic goals.

Modern DSS technologies simplify strategic planning and enable businesses to track and assess their plans in real time. Decision-makers can monitor key performance indicators (KPIs) and metrics, identifying new trends, evaluating project results, and making necessary adjustments. This iterative approach to strategic management better equips organizations to respond to changing market conditions and explore new opportunities (Bose, 2001).

In the digital era, companies need access to advanced Decision Support Systems (DSS) tools, such as AI and data analytics, to facilitate efficient strategic planning and decision-making. These tools enable forecasting of future trends, practical insights, and increased cooperation, enabling organizations to navigate complexity and unpredictability, preparing them for long-term success in the fast-paced business world.

ARTIFICIAL INTELLIGENCE: CURRENT STATE AND FUTURE TRAJECTORY

The article explores the impact of artificial intelligence (AI) on various sectors, focusing on its applications in banking, healthcare, and customer service, and its current and future directions (Figure 3).

Figure 3. Artificial intelligence: Current state and future trajectory

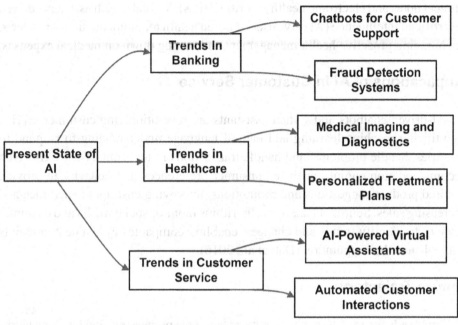

Applications of AI in Finance

AI is significantly advancing the banking industry in areas like investing strategies, fraud detection, and risk management. Large-scale financial data is analyzed by machine learning algorithms to find patterns and trends that improve risk assessment and predictive analytics. Artificial intelligence (AI)-driven chatbots and virtual assistants enhance client engagement and happiness by offering tailored financial advice and assistance to users(Venkateswaran et al., 2023; Zekrifa et al., 2023). Additionally, by using AI to execute transactions at blazing speed, algorithmic trading algorithms optimize investment portfolios and maximize profits for investors(Huang, 2024; Li et al., 2020).

Applications of AI in Healthcare

AI is transforming healthcare by increasing the precision of diagnoses, enhancing patient outcomes, and expediting administrative procedures. Medical imaging data, including MRIs and X-rays, are analyzed by machine learning algorithms to find anomalies and help radiologists diagnose patients more precisely. Healthcare professionals may identify high-risk patients and modify treatment strategies accordingly by using natural language processing (NLP) algorithms to extract insights from clinical notes and electronic health records (EHRs). Virtual health assistants driven by artificial intelligence (AI) give users tailored health recommendations and alerts, encouraging proactive health management and cutting down on medical expenses.

Applications of AI in Customer Service

AI-driven chatbots and virtual assistants are revolutionizing customer service by utilizing machine learning and natural language understanding to respond to inquiries, handle problems, and handle transactions in real-time. These AI-driven recommendation engines analyze consumer preferences and behavior to provide tailored product suggestions and promotions, improving customer experience and increasing sales. Sentiment analysis algorithms monitor social media and customer reviews to identify trends and changes, enabling companies to handle complaints and enhance their reputation (Dab et al., 2016).

Future Trajectory

Future advancements in robots, natural language processing, and machine learning are expected to be rapid. AI will play a significant role in finance, particularly in algorithmic trading, risk management, and regulatory compliance. Predictive analytics and AI-powered diagnostic technologies will revolutionize healthcare, enabling earlier diagnosis and personalized treatment. AI-powered virtual assistants in customer service will become more sophisticated, integrating seamlessly with other systems for tailored assistance (J. Zhou et al., 2023).

AI's widespread use has raised social and ethical concerns, including algorithmic unfairness, data privacy, and employment displacement. To ensure proper AI creation and usage, stakeholders, legislators, and ethicists must collaborate. AI has the potential to revolutionize industries like finance, medicine, and customer service, enhancing productivity, decision-making, and customer experiences. However, to fully realize its potential, ethical, legislative, and social implications must be carefully considered. This section explores the impact of Artificial Intelligence (AI) on various industries, focusing on its current and future directions, ethical issues, and the importance of AI governance and transparency, while also discussing the challenges and implications of AI.

Current State of AI

Artificial intelligence (AI) technologies, including machine learning, computer vision, robotics, and natural language processing, have significantly advanced in recent years. These advancements power applications like virtual assistants, medical diagnostics, autonomous vehicles, and recommendation systems, enhancing efficiency in industries like manufacturing, transportation, healthcare, and finance.

Ethical Considerations in AI

As AI becomes more integrated into our daily lives, ethical issues such as algorithmic discrimination, privacy violation, employment displacement, and autonomous decision-making become more significant. Algorithmic bias, where AI systems act unfairly due to unbalanced training data or flawed algorithms, can lead to unjust treatment based on factors like gender, race, or socioeconomic status. To address these ethical dilemmas and promote trust, AI systems must be made equitable, open, and responsible.

AI Governance and Transparency

Strong governance frameworks are crucial for responsible AI technology development and implementation. These frameworks should include rules, conventions, and regulations by governments, regulatory bodies, and industry groups. They should include data privacy, transparency, accountability, and cybersecurity. AI systems should provide clear, understandable processes for justifying decisions and actions, promoting accountability and trust among users(Sharma et al., 2024; Sundaramoorthy et al., 2024).

Future Trajectory of AI

Legal frameworks, cultural perspectives, and technical advancements will influence the direction of artificial intelligence. Ethics will remain crucial for developing AI systems prioritizing justice, safety, and human welfare. Governance frameworks will shift to address new challenges and ensure ethical use of AI technologies. Collaboration between policymakers, corporate executives, researchers, ethicists, and other stakeholders is essential for AI development that benefits society (Dhanya et al., 2023; Mohanty et al., 2023).

AI has great potential to promote creativity and tackle social issues, but strong governance structures and deep moral analysis are needed. Prioritizing ethics, openness, and accountability in AI research and deployment can maximize its advantages for humanity while minimizing risks and maximizing its revolutionary potential.

FUTURE TRENDS IN THE DIGITAL ECONOMY

The digital economy is constantly evolving due to rapid technological advancements and changing consumer habits. Key topics affecting the future include Decentralized Finance (DeFi), Quantum Computing's potential, cybersecurity's importance in a globalized society, and the impact of evolving technology on the digital economy (Pasumarthy et al., 2024; Vijaya Lakshmi et al., 2024).

Figure 4. Emerging developments in the digital economy

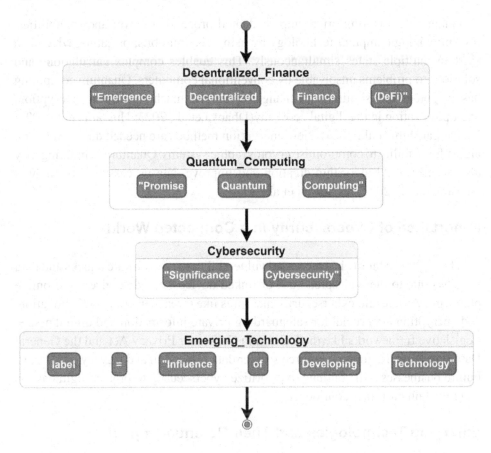

Figure 4 creates a state diagram that highlights emerging developments in the digital economy, including DeFi, the potential of quantum computing, the importance of cybersecurity, and the impact of evolving technologies.

The Rise of Decentralized Finance (DeFi)

Decentralized finance (DeFi) is a growing field that uses blockchain technology to create trustless financial networks, enabling peer-to-peer transactions and smart contracts. This eliminates the need for middlemen and reduces transaction costs. DeFi encompasses various financial operations like lending, borrowing, trading, and asset management on decentralized platforms. Its growth has the potential to revolutionize traditional banking procedures, advance financial inclusion, and expand financial services to a wider audience.

Potential of Quantum Computing

Quantum computing offers unprecedented processing power and capabilities, revolutionizing computer technology by using quantum bits, or qubits, which can exist in multiple states simultaneously. This enables complex calculations and solutions to problems unsolvable by conventional computers. Quantum computing has the potential to significantly change sectors like machine learning, encryption, and optimization in the digital economy(Dhanya et al., 2023; Hussain et al., 2023; Vijaya Lakshmi et al., 2024). New encryption methods are needed due to quantum algorithms' ability to compromise cryptographic systems. Quantum computing may also accelerate AI algorithm creation and improve data processing and analysis (Agrawal et al., 2023; Kalaiselvi et al., 2024).

Importance of Cybersecurity in a Connected World

The digital economy has increased vulnerability to ransomware attacks and data breaches due to the widespread use of linked devices, cloud services, and online platforms. As a result, cybersecurity measures like threat detection, authentication, and encryption are crucial for safeguarding private information and digital assets. Legislative frameworks like the California Consumer Privacy Act and the General Data Protection Regulation enforce stricter data protection and privacy guidelines. Future businesses will continue to prioritize cybersecurity to protect digital assets and maintain customer confidence.

Emerging Technologies and Their Potential Impact

Cybersecurity, quantum computing, and deFi are among the cutting-edge technologies that could significantly impact the digital economy. Other technologies include biotechnology, 5G networks, IoT, and AI. AI is expected to drive innovation in various sectors, while 5G networks will improve consumer experiences and streamline operations. Biotechnology innovations, like personalized medicine and gene editing, will transform healthcare and offer new treatment and therapy avenues.

The digital economy's future is influenced by rapid technological advancements, including DeFi, quantum computing, cybersecurity, and emerging technologies. Businesses must adapt to these trends and the evolving digital ecosystem to succeed in this dynamic environment, positioning themselves for success in the emerging digital economy.

IMPLICATIONS FOR HUMAN EXPERIENCE

The rapid advancement of digital technology is significantly altering human interaction and influencing various aspects of life. This section focuses on enhancing inclusion, balancing innovation with morality, and the impact of legislation and regulation on the future (Chichernea, 2014; Ratajczak, 2022).

Figure 5. Implications of digital technology on human experience

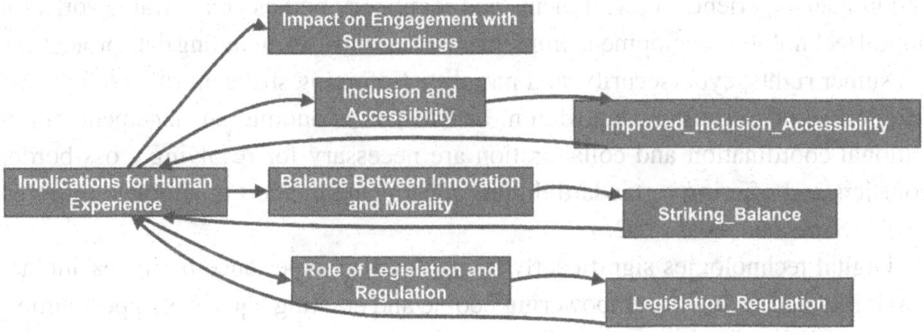

Figure 5 illustrate a flowchart outlining the implications of digital technology on human experience, its impact on engagement, focus on inclusion and accessibility, balancing innovation and morality, and the role of legislation in shaping the future.

Enhancing Accessibility and Inclusivity Through Digital Technologies

Digital technologies can create more inclusive environments for individuals with different backgrounds and abilities. Accessibility technologies like screen readers and voice recognition software enable people with impairments to access digital content and participate more actively in online activities. With widespread mobile devices and internet connectivity, more individuals have access to information and services. Prioritizing accessibility in digital product design can ensure equal access to opportunities and resources, improving the human experience for everyone.

Balancing Innovation With Ethical Considerations

Digital technology offers numerous benefits, but it also requires ethical considerations. To align with moral principles and social norms, concerns like algorithmic discrimination, data privacy, and automation's impact on employment must be thoroughly examined. Organizations should prioritize transparency, accountability, and fairness while balancing ethical concerns with innovation. A culture of ethical awareness and accountability among developers and consumers is crucial to minimize risks and maximize the positive benefits of digital advancements on human experience (Ratajczak, 2022).

The Role of Policy and Regulation in Shaping the Future

Policies and regulations are crucial for the advancement of digital technologies and human experience. Governments and regulatory bodies create frameworks for digital technology development, implementation, and use, including data protection, consumer rights, cybersecurity, and morality. Enforcing stringent rules safeguards people's rights, promotes innovation, and fosters economic advancement. International coordination and collaboration are necessary for resolving cross-border conflicts and offering a standard digital governance method in an interconnected world (Saravanan et al., 2022).

Digital technologies significantly impact human experience by increasing accessibility and inclusion, empowering people and creating equitable opportunities. However, balancing innovation with ethical concerns is crucial for ensuring these advancements align with moral norms and society's interests. Strong laws and regulations guide the development of digital technologies, guiding their development and serving society's interests. Addressing these concerns can leverage the transformative potential of digital technology, improving the human experience and creating a more ethical, ecological, and inclusive future.

CONCLUSION

The digital revolution, utilizing technologies like cybersecurity, decentralized banking, quantum computing, and artificial intelligence, is revolutionizing our lives, work, and communication. However, it raises moral questions. Balancing innovation with ethical standards, transparency, and accountability is crucial for ensuring accessibility, inclusivity, and efficiency while addressing ethical issues.

Regulation and policy are crucial for the development of digital technologies in the future. Cooperation between governments, regulatory agencies, and industry players is essential for responsible development, implementation, and use. Strong policy enforcement protects people's rights, encourages sustainable innovation, and stimulates the economy. The digital economy has the potential to improve human experiences and bring about positive change. Utilizing digital transformation, prioritizing morality, and tackling new issues will lead to a resilient, successful, and inclusive future.

REFERENCES

Agrawal, A. V., Shashibhushan, G., Pradeep, S., Padhi, S., Sugumar, D., & Boopathi, S. (2023). Synergizing Artificial Intelligence, 5G, and Cloud Computing for Efficient Energy Conversion Using Agricultural Waste. In *Sustainable Science and Intelligent Technologies for Societal Development* (pp. 475–497). IGI Global.

Akkerman, G., Buynosov, A., Dorofeev, A., & Kurganov, V. (2019). Decision support system for road transport management in the digital age. *International Scientific Siberian Transport Forum*, 773–781.

Al-Sartawi, M. (2021). *Big Data-Driven Digital Economy: Artificial and Computational Intelligence* (Vol. 974). Springer. 10.1007/978-3-030-73057-4

Boopathi, S. (2024a). Digital HR Implementation for Business Growth in Industrial 5.0. In *Convergence of Human Resources Technologies and Industry 5.0* (pp. 1–22). IGI Global. 10.4018/979-8-3693-1343-5.ch001

Boopathi, S. (2024b). Energy Cascade Conversion System and Energy-Efficient Infrastructure. In *Sustainable Development in AI, Blockchain, and E-Governance Applications* (pp. 47–71). IGI Global. 10.4018/979-8-3693-1722-8.ch004

Boopathi, S. (2024c). Sustainable Development Using IoT and AI Techniques for Water Utilization in Agriculture. In *Sustainable Development in AI, Blockchain, and E-Governance Applications* (pp. 204–228). IGI Global. 10.4018/979-8-3693-1722-8. ch012

Bose, R. (2001). An E-DSS for Strategic Planning of E-Commerce Website Development. *International Journal of the Computer, the Internet and Management, 9*(3), 1–21.

Boukherouaa, E. B., Shabsigh, M. G., AlAjmi, K., Deodoro, J., Farias, A., Iskender, E. S., Mirestean, M. A. T., & Ravikumar, R. (2021). *Powering the digital economy: Opportunities and risks of artificial intelligence in finance*. International Monetary Fund.

Chichernea, V. (2014). The Use Of Decision Support Systems (Dss) In Smart City Planning And Management. *Journal of Information Systems & Operations Management*, 8(2).

Dab, S., Ramachandran, S., Chandna, R., Hanspal, R., Grealish, A., & Peeters, M. (2016). The Digital Revolution in Trade Finance. *Boston Consulting Group*, 1–7.

Dhanalakshmi, M., Tamilarasi, K., Saravanan, S., Sujatha, G., Boopathi, S., & Associates. (2024). Fog Computing-Based Framework and Solutions for Intelligent Systems: Enabling Autonomy in Vehicles. In *Computational Intelligence for Green Cloud Computing and Digital Waste Management* (pp. 330–356). IGI Global.

Dhanya, D., Kumar, S. S., Thilagavathy, A., Prasad, D., & Boopathi, S. (2023). Data Analytics and Artificial Intelligence in the Circular Economy: Case Studies. In *Intelligent Engineering Applications and Applied Sciences for Sustainability* (pp. 40–58). IGI Global.

Enyi, E. P. (2016). *Accounting in the digital age: Creating values with paperless decision support systems.* Babcock University Inaugural Lecture Series.

Godwin Immanuel, D., Solaimalai, G., Chandrakala, B. M., Bharath, V. G., Singh, M. K., & Boopathi, S. (2024). Advancements in Electric Vehicle Management System: Integrating Machine Learning and Artificial Intelligence. In *Advances in Web Technologies and Engineering* (pp. 371–391). IGI Global. 10.4018/979-8-3693-1487-6.ch018

Gupta, M. S., Keen, M. M., Shah, M. A., & Verdier, M. G. (2017). *Digital revolutions in public finance.* International Monetary Fund.

Huang, H. (2024). Artificial Intelligence and Productivity Improvement in the Digital Economy. *Finance & Economics, 1*(5).

Hussain, Z., Babe, M., Saravanan, S., Srimathy, G., Roopa, H., & Boopathi, S. (2023). Optimizing Biomass-to-Biofuel Conversion: IoT and AI Integration for Enhanced Efficiency and Sustainability. In *Circular Economy Implementation for Sustainability in the Built Environment* (pp. 191–214). IGI Global.

Kalaiselvi, T., Saravanan, G., Haritha, T., Babu, A. V. S., Sakthivel, M., & Boopathi, S. (2024). A Study on the Landscape of Serverless Computing: Technologies and Tools for Seamless Implementation. In *Serverless Computing Concepts, Technology and Architecture* (pp. 260–282). IGI Global. 10.4018/979-8-3693-1682-5.ch016

Ka,. R. P., Pandraju, T. K. S., Boopathi, S., Saravanan, P., Rathan, S. K., & Sathish, T. (2023). Hybrid Deep Learning Technique for Optimal Wind Mill Speed Estimation. *2023 7th International Conference on Electronics, Communication and Aerospace Technology (ICECA)*, (pp. 181–186). IEEE.

Kumar, P. R., Meenakshi, S., Shalini, S., Devi, S. R., & Boopathi, S. (2023). Soil Quality Prediction in Context Learning Approaches Using Deep Learning and Blockchain for Smart Agriculture. In *Effective AI, Blockchain, and E-Governance Applications for Knowledge Discovery and Management* (pp. 1–26). IGI Global. 10.4018/978-1-6684-9151-5.ch001

Li, K., Kim, D. J., Lang, K. R., Kauffman, R. J., & Naldi, M. (2020). How should we understand the digital economy in Asia? Critical assessment and research agenda. *Electronic Commerce Research and Applications*, 44, 101004. 10.1016/j.elerap.2020.10100432922241

Maguluri, L. P., Arularasan, A., & Boopathi, S. (2023). Assessing Security Concerns for AI-Based Drones in Smart Cities. In *Effective AI, Blockchain, and E-Governance Applications for Knowledge Discovery and Management* (pp. 27–47). IGI Global. 10.4018/978-1-6684-9151-5.ch002

Mhlanga, D. (2020). Industry 4.0 in finance: The impact of artificial intelligence (ai) on digital financial inclusion. *International Journal of Financial Studies*, 8(3), 45. 10.3390/ijfs8030045

Mohanraj, G., Krishna, K. S., Lakshmi, B. S., Vijayalakshmi, A., Pramila, P. V., & Boopathi, S. (2024). Optimizing Trust and Security in Healthcare 4.0: Human Factors in Lightweight Secured IoMT Ecosystems. In *Lightweight Digital Trust Architectures in the Internet of Medical Things (IoMT)* (pp. 52–72). IGI Global. 10.4018/979-8-3693-2109-6.ch004

Mohanty, A., Venkateswaran, N., Ranjit, P., Tripathi, M. A., & Boopathi, S. (2023). Innovative Strategy for Profitable Automobile Industries: Working Capital Management. In *Handbook of Research on Designing Sustainable Supply Chains to Achieve a Circular Economy* (pp. 412–428). IGI Global.

Moormann, J., & Lochte-Holtgreven, M. (1993). An approach for an integrated DSS for strategic planning. *Decision Support Systems*, 10(4), 401–411. 10.1016/0167-9236(93)90070-J

O'Leary, D. E. (2008). The relationship between citations and number of downloads in Decision Support Systems. *Decision Support Systems*, 45(4), 972–980. 10.1016/j.dss.2008.03.008

Pasumarthy, R., Mohammed, S., Laxman, V., Krishnamoorthy, V., Durga, S., & Boopathi, S. (2024). Digital Transformation in Developing Economies: Forecasting Trends, Impact, and Challenges in Industry 5.0. In *Convergence of Human Resources Technologies and Industry 5.0* (pp. 47–68). IGI Global. 10.4018/979-8-3693-1343-5.ch003

Ratajczak, M. (2022). The state in the era of Digital Revolution and digital finance. In *Digital Finance and the Future of the Global Financial System* (pp. 93–108). Routledge. 10.4324/9781003264101-8

Ravisankar, A., Shanthi, A., Lavanya, S., Ramaratnam, M., Krishnamoorthy, V., & Boopathi, S. (2024). Harnessing 6G for Consumer-Centric Business Strategies Across Electronic Industries. In *AI Impacts in Digital Consumer Behavior* (pp. 241–270). IGI Global.

Ross, G., & Liechtenstein, V. (2018). Management of financial bubbles as control technology of digital economy. *Information Technology Science*, 96–103.

S, B., & Gopi, S. (2024). Crafting Effective HR Strategies for the Modern Workplace: Navigating the Digital Frontier. In *Convergence of Human Resources Technologies and Industry 5.0* (pp. 23–46). IGI Global. 10.4018/979-8-3693-1343-5.ch002

Saravanan, A., Venkatasubramanian, R., Khare, R., Surakasi, R., Boopathi, S., Ray, S., & Sudhakar, M. (2022). POLICY TRENDS OF RENEWABLE ENERGY AND NON. *Renewable Energy*.

Sharma, M., Sharma, M., Sharma, N., & Boopathi, S. (2024). Building Sustainable Smart Cities Through Cloud and Intelligent Parking System. In *Handbook of Research on AI and ML for Intelligent Machines and Systems* (pp. 195–222). IGI Global.

Sonia, R., Gupta, N., Manikandan, K., Hemalatha, R., Kumar, M. J., & Boopathi, S. (2024). Strengthening Security, Privacy, and Trust in Artificial Intelligence Drones for Smart Cities. In *Analyzing and Mitigating Security Risks in Cloud Computing* (pp. 214–242). IGI Global. 10.4018/979-8-3693-3249-8.ch011

Sundar, R., Srikaanth, P. B., Naik, D. A., Murugan, V. P., Karumudi, M., & Boopathi, S. (2024). Achieving Balance Between Innovation and Security in the Cloud With Artificial Intelligence of Things: Semantic Web Control Models. In *Advances in Web Technologies and Engineering* (pp. 1–26). IGI Global. 10.4018/979-8-3693-1487-6. ch001

Sundaramoorthy, K., Singh, A., Sumathy, G., Maheshwari, A., Arunarani, A., & Boopathi, S. (2024). A Study on AI and Blockchain-Powered Smart Parking Models for Urban Mobility. In *Handbook of Research on AI and ML for Intelligent Machines and Systems* (pp. 223–250). IGI Global.

Upadhyaya, A. N., Saqib, A., Devi, J. V., Rallapalli, S., Sudha, S., & Boopathi, S. (2024). Implementation of the Internet of Things (IoT) in Remote Healthcare. In *Advances in Medical Technologies and Clinical Practice* (pp. 104–124). IGI Global. 10.4018/979-8-3693-1934-5.ch006

Venkateswaran, N., Vidhya, K., Ayyannan, M., Chavan, S. M., Sekar, K., & Boopathi, S. (2023). A Study on Smart Energy Management Framework Using Cloud Computing. In *5G, Artificial Intelligence, and Next Generation Internet of Things: Digital Innovation for Green and Sustainable Economies* (pp. 189–212). IGI Global. 10.4018/978-1-6684-8634-4.ch009

Verma, R., Christiana, M. B. V., Maheswari, M., Srinivasan, V., Patro, P., Dari, S. S., & Boopathi, S. (2024). Intelligent Physarum Solver for Profit Maximization in Oligopolistic Supply Chain Networks. In *AI and Machine Learning Impacts in Intelligent Supply Chain* (pp. 156–179). IGI Global. 10.4018/979-8-3693-1347-3.ch011

Vijaya Lakshmi, V., Mishra, M., Kushwah, J. S., Shajahan, U. S., Mohanasundari, M., & Boopathi, S. (2024). Circular Economy Digital Practices for Ethical Dimensions and Policies for Digital Waste Management. In *Harnessing High-Performance Computing and AI for Environmental Sustainability* (pp. 166–193). IGI Global. 10.4018/979-8-3693-1794-5.ch008

Zekrifa, D. M. S., Kulkarni, M., Bhagyalakshmi, A., Devireddy, N., Gupta, S., & Boopathi, S. (2023). Integrating Machine Learning and AI for Improved Hydrological Modeling and Water Resource Management. In *Artificial Intelligence Applications in Water Treatment and Water Resource Management* (pp. 46–70). IGI Global. 10.4018/978-1-6684-6791-6.ch003

Zhou, J., San, O. T., & Liu, Y. (2023). Design and implementation of enterprise financial decision support system based on business intelligence. *International Journal of Professional Business Review*, 8(4), e0873–e0873. 10.26668/business-review/2023.v8i4.873

Zhou, Y. (2022). The application trend of digital finance and technological innovation in the development of green economy. *Journal of Environmental and Public Health*, 2022, 2022. 10.1155/2022/106455835865872

Chapter 17
Fostering Gratifying Customer Experiences Through the Art of Visual Content and Storytelling

Preeti Mehra
https://orcid.org/0000-0002-8979-9431
Campbell College, Edmonton, Canada

Pooja Kansra
https://orcid.org/0000-0003-2229-0662
Lovely Professional University, India

ABSTRACT

The human experience is what drives everything, notwithstanding the marketing sector's ongoing transformation. Through the use of narrative and visual content, brands can create experiences that touch people's emotions, ignite their imaginations, and leave a lasting impact. Storytelling that is both emotionally engaging and immersive leaves an impression. These strategies permanently modify consumers' perceptions and feelings while also raising engagement and conversion rates. A well-written tale has the ability to inspire, empower, and transform. It might make ordinary interactions with customers delightful, encouraging a sense of loyalty and community among them. Brands who embark on this path not only enhance their marketing tactics but also contribute to a larger narrative about how companies and consumers collaborate to shape the future. The current study investigates the capacity of narrative and visual content to construct timeless and cross-cultural narratives.

DOI: 10.4018/979-8-3693-2432-5.ch017

INTRODUCTION

In today's hyperconnected digital environment, when consumers are inundated with information from every direction, the skill of attracting and holding customers' attention has become a challenging problem for businesses. Since they have the ability to thoroughly engage viewers while also grabbing their attention, storytelling and visual content have emerged as crucial elements in this attempt. Businesses are being compelled to create an efficient visual content strategy due to the increased emphasis on brand communication on social media (Lim & Childs, 2020). Companies may connect with their audience through storytelling, which also helps brands engage with consumers by communicating their meaning and purpose (Whitler, 2008).

Brand storytelling has the ability to entertain, persuade, and leave a lasting impression on consumers, for branding because people create narratives about brands based on their interactions with them (Granitz and Forman, 2015; Solja et al., 2018).

THE IMPORTANCE OF NARRATIVE AND VISUAL CONTENT IN MODERN MARKETING

In a time when screens and smartphones are the norm, the influence of visuals has increased, transforming how people connect, communicate, and make decisions. With the development of captivating infographics and animations, as well as vivid images and engaging movies, visual information has become a universal language that transcends linguistic and cultural borders In the realm of modern marketing, captivating imagery is essential. In the realm of modern marketing, captivating imagery is essential. Visual content is now a major area of interest for publishers across all media channels due to the widespread availability of mass communication devices with enhanced visual capabilities (Manic, 2015).

The expansion of social networking websites, photo-sharing apps, and video-focused websites demonstrates how hungry modern consumers are for visual material. In a world filled with data and stimulation, visuals offer a way to stand out among the noise and leave a lasting impact on clients. Because of this, visual content has become a vital tool for companies trying to establish their corporate identity, deliver messages quickly, and create emotions.

Building Dynamic Consumer Experiences

The purpose of marketing is to provide customers with memorable and meaningful experiences. Visual elements and storytelling, which create narratives with both intellectual and emotional resonance, are used to create these experiences.

By incorporating visual elements with storytelling techniques, brands can develop storylines that connect with people on a very personal way. Storytelling constitutes a promising tool in destination brand communication (Pachuki et al., 2021).

The current study explores how visual content and narrative go above and beyond traditional marketing tactics and alter how brands engage with their audiences. It shall also explore the intricate connections between visual content, storytelling and user experiences and the cognitive mechanisms that drive engagement connect with their target customers on an emotional level.

INFLUENCE OF VISUAL CONTENT AND NARRATIVE IN THE DIGITAL AGE

This section attempts to explore the relationship of visual content and narratives in this digital age. In the digital age, where attention is a valuable resource and communication is increasingly more visual in character, the notions of "visual content" and "storytelling" have acquired significance in the field of marketing. Visual content may be described as the use of images, videos, graphics, and other visual components to communicate concepts, information, and narratives. These elements quickly and effectively communicate ideas by using images, which helps them get their point through to audiences who speak different languages. Marketing engagement through visual content is greatly aided by the significant effect of images and videos as well as the ease with which graphical content can now be produced.

On the other hand, presenting a tale involves developing narratives that relate to the emotions, experiences, and values of the audience. Both leadership and storytelling are performance arts, and like other performance arts, they entail doing as much as thinking. (Denning, 2005). This method transforms marketing from the basic presentation of products and benefits to a way of establishing connections by utilising the inborn human drive for narrative. The most effective storytellers frequently narrow their audience's attention to one key concept, and they can establish an emotional bond in as little as 30 seconds during a commercial (Monarth, 2014). By combining storytelling with visual content, marketing professionals can create an immersive experience that engages all of the senses and fosters a solid, long-lasting relationship with customers.

The Readability and Appeal of Visual Content

The appeal of visual content lies in its innate ability to amuse while also instructing. According to study, the brain processes visual information 60,000 times faster than text, demonstrating that humans have a natural predisposition for images and visuals (Palmer, 1999). Consumers can quickly develop impressions and grasp information thanks to this rapid processing in an era of information overload, making visual material a perfect medium for capturing attention.

Since the visual system is built from birth to perceive patterns, colours, and shapes, images and graphics can be utilised to transmit concepts quickly (Marr, 1982). This intuitive understanding makes it easier for customers to integrate information, which reduces cognitive load and enhances comprehension. A brand's organic reach is also increased by the shareability of visual content on social media platforms because it enables users to rapidly share engaging images with their networks.

The Power of Storytelling to Create Emotional Bonds

People are naturally drawn to stories since they have long played a significant role in human communication. In addition to being a method of distributing knowledge, storytelling is also a technique for cultivating empathy and creating emotional connections. According to (Bruner, 1991) makes the connection between autobiographical narrative modes and culture because culture offers linguistic and cognitive models that serve as narrative guides. When marketers utilise storytelling effectively, they develop plots that relate to the experiences, desires, and goals of their target market. By transcending logic and evoking sentiments instead, this emotional resonance strengthens the bond between the brand and the consumer.

When visual content is incorporated into a narrative, emotional involvement rises. Visuals have the capacity to instantly trigger emotions, whether through the use of hues that recall specific feelings or images that induce nostalgia. One intricate means of communication is colour. This component immediately affects the message's composition and the emotion that goes along with it at the level of artistic creation by influencing both formal characteristics and symbolic weight. When paired with an interesting story, these images intensify emotional responses and have a greater impact on the audience. Brands may encourage customer loyalty and trust by utilising narrative methods to provide their products and services a context that enables human connections.

In the sections that follow, the current study will go more deeply into the scientific underpinnings of visual engagement and study the cognitive mechanisms that give visual material its high effectiveness. The study will also examine how businesses produce memorable content by utilising storytelling and visuals.

THE SCIENCE OF VISUAL ENGAGEMENT

When it comes to efficiently processing visual data, the human brain is a wonder. Making sense of the world around us requires a complicated interaction between neurons and visual pathways, which is what visual perception entails. Our brains quickly absorb visual inputs and extract pertinent information when we are exposed to visual content, frequently in under a second (Marr, 1982). Some of the imperative issues that may be a part of this discussion may be the speed at which text-based information is processed and the role of visuals in aiding memory recall and decision making facilitation.

The Cognitive Processing of Text-Based Information More Quickly Than That of Visual Perception

The human brain is a marvel when it comes to effectively processing visual information. Visual perception involves a complex interaction between neurons and visual pathways that is necessary to make sense of the world around us. When exposed to visual content, our brains quickly process visual inputs and draw out relevant information, frequently in less than a second (Marr, 1982).

How Visual Information Affects Memory Retention and Recall

Strong links exist between memories and visuals. Studies have shown that people are more likely to remember visual content than text-based information. Verbal processes (inner speech) and nonverbal images are used as behavioral mediators and memory codes (Paivio, 2014). The "picture superiority effect," a phenomenon, emphasises the value of visual content. The ability of the human brain to recognise and recall images, particularly those that evoke powerful emotions or mental associations, is equally remarkable (Phelps, 2006). As it connects to emotions and tales, viewers are more likely to remember visual content with a strong narrative context. Visual content is crucial for creating a lasting impression on clients' thoughts because of its capacity for retention, which can significantly affect the brand recognition and recall.

How Memory Retention and Recall Are Affected by Visual Information

The relationship between memory and images is very strong. People are more likely to remember visual content than text-based information, according to studies (Paivio, 2014). The importance of visual content is emphasised by the "picture superiority effect," a phenomenon. The human brain is also remarkably adept in recognising and recalling images, particularly those that arouse strong feelings or mental associations. Emotion and cognition are linked from early perception to reasoning, according to research on the brain networks that underlie human behaviour. (Phelps, 2006). Visual content with a strong narrative context is more likely to be recalled by viewers because of its connection to feelings and stories. Due to its capacity for retention, visual material is an essential tool for leaving a lasting imprint on customers' minds, which can have a significant impact on brand recall and recognition.

How Visual Information Affects Memory Retention and Recall

The "picture superiority effect, "a phenomenon, emphasises the value of visual content. This connects to emotions and tales, viewers are more likely to remember visual content with a strong narrative context. Visual content is a crucial tool for making a long-lasting imprint on customers' thoughts because of its capacity for retention, which can significantly affect brand recall and recognition.

How Visuals Influence Emotions and Decision-Making

Emotions have a huge impact on how people behave and make decisions, and visual content can do this well. Visuals have the incredibly unique ability to instantaneously evoke a wide range of emotions due to their use of symbolism, colour, and arrangement. Whether they portray a joyful moment, a nostalgic sight, or a thought-provoking scenario, these emotional triggers have a significant impact on viewers and forge relationships that continue beyond the initial engagement. When narration and visual elements are combined, this emotional involvement is amplified.

Storytelling is more than just one tool; it's a wide range of tools that may be used to accomplish a number of goals, including inspiring people to take action, expressing who you are or our firm is, passing along values, disseminating knowledge, controlling the grapevine, and paving the way for the future (Denning, 2005). These narratives have a stronger emotional impact when they are visually conveyed. This emotional resonance effects decision-making because consumers are more likely to base purchases on emotional connections than just cognitive ones.

The cognitive processes involved in visual perception, as well as the better memory retention of visual content and its propensity to evoke emotions, serve as examples of the complex consequences of visual engagement on consumer experiences. Utilising these scientific insights, brands may create marketing strategies that are more convincing and engage people on a deeper level. Customers' brand experience, which is made up of all their thoughts, feelings, perceptions, and behavioral reactions to a brand, is influenced by compelling and well-crafted brand stories (Brakus et al., 2009). In the sections that follow, the present study will explore platforms and formats that can help with visual storytelling as well as the skill of using visual content to develop engaging brand narratives.

DEVELOPING POWERFUL BRAND NARRATIVES

In a world when there are a lot of products and services available, having the ability to tell a compelling story can help you stand out. By examining the heart of a company's mission, guiding values, and the emotional journey it promises to take its clients on, brand narratives go beyond straightforward marketing messaging.

Storytelling as a Method for Building a Brand Narrative

The brand narrative, the cornerstone of a brand's identity, impacts audience perceptions and emotions (Holt, 2004). Holt cautions against using traditional branding techniques, which emphasize advantages, brand personas, and emotional connections, to create symbols. Storytelling gives brands individuality and relatability. Instead of focusing solely on the characteristics of the product, a brand narrative weaves a tapestry of experiences, emotions, and objectives. Instead of just selling sportswear, a company that sells fitness apparel may encourage people to embrace their strength and embark on transformative fitness journeys in order to promote empowerment. Because it speaks to their dreams for empowerment and self-improvement, this story resonates to buyers who are searching for more than just garments.

Strengthening Brand Storytelling by Including Visual Elements

Imagine a luxury travel agency wishing to portray the thrill of discovery. The brand can transport viewers to breath-taking landscapes, fascinating cultures, and thrilling situations through well-chosen photos and videos. Instead of merely enhancing the brand narrative, these visuals strengthen its emotional resonance by becoming an integral part of it. In storytelling for a luxury hotel for example, linguistic features, such as the storyteller (third person vs. first person) or the number of words, can have an impact on consumer attention and response (Ryu et al., 2018). Although words are a powerful tool for storytelling, brand narratives are amplified when visual elements are added. Through visual content, audiences are able to enter the narrative universe and engage viscerally with the brand's story. By conjuring up scenarios that correspond to the experiences and goals of the viewers, images and films have the power to quickly evoke emotions.

Examples of Brand Narratives That Work Well and Connect With Consumers

Many brands have been successful in creating narratives that successfully engage emotionally with consumers by combining storytelling and visual content. One such example is Nike's "Just Do It" campaign. Through a combination of eye-catching ads and persuasive storytelling, Nike has created a brand narrative that is focused on tenacity, aspiration, and the relentless pursuit of perfection (Wheeler, 2009). By showing athletes overcoming obstacles and achieving their goals, Nike makes an emotional connection with people who are looking for inspiration and motivation. Another compelling argument is made by the Coca-Cola "Share a Coke" marketing campaign. Personalization and visual storytelling were successfully applied in this campaign, which urged customers to share a Coke with friends and loved ones, by swapping out popular names for the brand's symbol. The artwork on customised bottles not only highlighted diversity but also tapped into a universal need for connection and sharing. the design and implementation of storytelling in destination is a complex and integrated process that combines story content, storyteller and character, modality, and dissemination channels, involving collaboration among various stakeholders (Zhang and Ramayah, 2024).

These instances demonstrate the effectiveness of fusing narrative with visual material to create narratives that go beyond product and service marketing. By leveraging shared values, objectives, and emotions, brands can forge genuine connections with consumers that go beyond mere transactional interactions.

PLATFORMS AND FORMATS FOR VISUAL STORYTELLING

In the sections that follow, the study will look at the platforms and formats that provide a favourable environment for visual storytelling. It will also explore how companies may make use of these tools to design captivating immersive experiences for customers. Some interesting platforms being adopted by marketers are depicted in the Figure 1.

Figure 1. Platforms used by marketers for depicting brand narratives

Note. The figure explains the different platforms used by marketers to depict narratives about their brands.

Investigating the Viability of Social Media Sites as Visual Storytelling Platforms

In the digital age, social media platforms have transformed into engaging spaces for brands to share their narratives through visual content. Websites like Instagram, TikTok, Pinterest, and even Facebook offer a fully immersive setting where visual storytelling may take the lead. These platforms take use of people's inclination towards visual communication and provide opportunities for marketers to connect with consumers on a more intimate level. Instagram's concentration on photos and short videos has helped it grow into a dominant force in visual storytelling. Brands can utilise their profiles as virtual galleries to showcase their products, behind-the-scenes images, and user-generated content in order to construct a complicated narrative (https://blog.hootsuite.com/how-to-use-instagram-for-business/, 2023). While Pinterest's emphasis on photos makes it the ideal platform for businesses trying to inspire and develop creativity, TikTok's short-form video format enables imaginative storytelling that appeals to younger viewers.

Using Films, Infographics, Animations, and Visuals to Communicate Stories

For visual narrative, variety in format is crucial. Animations, infographics, films, and images all give brand stories a unique richness. Videos' dynamic movement and aural elements appeal to all of the senses, creating an immersive experience. They may effectively encapsulate the essence of a story, making them ideal for expressing emotions, humour, and essential ideas. They may express ideas, emotions, and moments in a single frame, images serve as the foundation of visual content. They give a quick synopsis of the narrative and let the audience to fill in the blanks with their imagination. Infographics combine visuals and data to create visually compelling narratives from complex information. Whether simple or intricate, animations give stories life, making them the ideal medium for illuminating abstract concepts, procedures, or historical events.

Adapting Visual Content for Different Platforms and Audience Preferences

Effective visual storytelling requires an understanding of the interests and behaviour of various audiences across various media. For each platform, there are particular user expectations, rhythms, and cultures. Brands must adapt their visual narratives to accommodate for these subtleties. For instance, using Instagram Stories might provide a short, in-the-moment glimpse into a brand's everyday activities, whereas using the grid can produce a coherent narrative that matches the brand's identity. Since longer videos allow for deeper narrative exploration, they are more suited for educational, in-depth storytelling, or brand documentaries on YouTube. Short-form videos for TikTok must tell stories that are punchy, compelling, and instantly resonant. The desires of different demographic groups should be considered when developing strategies. Gen Z, for instance, likes honesty, humour, and relatability. Millennials like learning narratives that align with their ideals.

IMMERSIVE CONTENT THROUGH VISUAL EXPERIENCES

In the parts that follow, the present study will delve into the world of immersive experiences made possible by visual content, looking at how brands may employ virtual reality (VR), augmented reality (AR), and interactive graphics to build long-lasting relationships with customers.

Virtual and Augmented Reality as Tools for Immersive Storytelling

As a result of technology improvements, virtual reality (VR) and augmented reality (AR) have made it possible for new visual narrative dimensions. These immersive technologies immerse people in stories and offer a level of engagement that was previously unheard of. While AR adds digital elements to the real world to blend real and virtual experiences, VR immerses users in entirely virtual environments. Businesses may create complete settings for people to explore, interact with, and receive a first-person view on tales in the virtual reality environment. This technology centres the story around the consumers by replicating a variety of scenarios, from historical recreations to product demos. Contrarily, augmented reality (AR) combines digital content with the actual world, enabling businesses to enhance physical venues, products, and experiences with contextual data and interactive elements. This involves a large class of `mixed reality' (MR) displays also (Milgram, et al., 1995). With realistic graphics, participatory storytelling, and multiplayer options, even virtual reality gaming keeps pushing the envelope as technology develops (Raji et al., 2024).

Increasing Consumer Engagement With Interactive Visual Content

Interactivity is the cornerstone of effective visual storytelling in the digital age. Customers are invited to participate, explore, and alter the story utilising interactive visual content. It makes inert viewers into active participants, strengthening the sense of connection and engagement. Interactive elements include things like clickable hotspots, 360-degree images, tests, and gamified experiences, to name a few. These features increase the amount of time users spend interacting with the information while also enabling them to delve deeper into it at their own pace. Interactive visual tales and personalised journeys improve understanding, create lasting impressions, and give the story a sense of ownership.

The automotive industry has also seen a rise in interest in immersive storytelling. Companies like Audi and Porsche that have employed virtual reality (VR) experiences to immerse clients in virtual showrooms, potential customers can now explore and customise vehicles as if they were physically present. With this approach, buying a car becomes a fun adventure that transcends the limitations of traditional dealerships. Fashion industry brands, like Gucci, have employed augmented reality to provide fun experiences for their clients. Users can virtually try on shoes by superimposing them on their actual environment using Gucci's augmented reality software (audi-mediacenter.com). This creative approach not only appeals to today's digital-first youth, but also makes trying on clothing a pleasurable and interesting experience.

PERSONALIZATION AND A CONNECTION WITH THE CONSUMER

As the study goes deeper, it investigates the significance of personalization in storytelling and visual material, revealing how modifying narratives to suit individual preferences strengthens ties between brands and consumers.

The Role Personalization Plays in Visual and Narrative Content

In the age of information overload, personalization has emerged as a potent strategy for businesses looking to cut through the noise and build strong relationships with customers. Personalization requires changing interactions and content to take into account user preferences, actions, and demographics. When utilised to produce visual content and convey tales, personalization delivers a level of relevance that strongly engages with customers. Artificial intelligence is being used to support personalized engagement marketing, as a strategy for developing, distributing, and communicating customized products to clients (Kumar, et al., 2019). Every customer is unique and has particular demands, interests, and ambitions, and personalization acknowledges this. By infusing customization into visual storytelling, brands transform one-size-fits-all communications into experiences that feel personalised and crafted for each individual.

Visual Narratives That are Specifically Created for Different Consumer Segments

Effective personalization requires an understanding of the diversity within a brand's audience and the development of visual tales that appeal to various client segments. These psychographics, psychographic traits, actions, or buying histories may be the basis for this categorization. By breaking down the audience into more manageable groupings, brands can create narratives that specifically target the particular wants and issues of each section. For instance, a tech corporation might design its visual content differently for users who aren't tech experts but are interested in user-friendly features and for tech enthusiasts searching for in-depth technical information. By customising the pictures to the distinct interests of each group, the brand boosts engagement and relevance.

The Benefits of Personalised Experiences for Boosting Brand Loyalty

Personalization provides many benefits in addition to the instant engagement and is essential for promoting brand loyalty. When customers feel cared for and heard, they are more likely to connect with a company. Personalised visual storytelling foster a sense of intimacy by making it appear as though the brand is communicating to consumers personally and attending to their specific needs. To facilitate consumer and engineer interaction with real-time, three-dimensional product representations, Silicon Graphics, for instance, opened the Visionar-ium Reality Center in June 1996 at its corporate headquarters in Mountain View, California. In addition to driving, walking, or flying, customers can see, hear, and touch a wide range of product options (Pine and Gilmore, 1998).

MEASUREMENT OF THE EFFECT ON CUSTOMER EXPERIENCES

As the study goes along, it discusses how to assess the value of storytelling and visual content as well as how data and analytics may be applied to strategy and user experience.

Measuring Tools for the Impact of Visual and Narrative Content

The capacity to assess the impact of narrative and visual content is crucial in the field of modern marketing. Brands may utilise data-driven insights to enhance their strategy and customer experiences by looking at how well these activities are received by customers. The vital considerations listed below can help decide how effective storytelling and visual material is for a business. Metrics, that are for measuring user engagement with the story and includes likes, shares, comments, and time spent interacting with visual content. Higher levels of engagement indicate that the audience is engaged with and responding to the content. Furthermore, Higher levels of engagement indicate that the audience is engaged with and responding to the content.

Reach and Impressions monitoring is another way. These figures demonstrate how far the visual story has spread in order to reach its intended audience. The more people who hear about the story, the greater exposure it will get. Reach and engagement metrics should be evaluated to see if the story is going beyond the surface level. Additionally, by monitoring customer sentiment using sentiment analysis techniques, brands can evaluate the emotional response the narrative produced. Positive emotions indicate that the narrative has been successful in eliciting the desired emotional reaction. Sentiment analysis identifies and extracts subjective information from the text using natural language processing and text mining (Wankhade et al., 2022).

Dwell time is a measurement of the amount of time users spend seeing a piece of visual content. Longer dwell times indicate that the content is interesting to the audience and may be luring them to continue exploring. Moreover, customer feedback gives businesses immediate access to the opinions and sentiments of consumers. Analysing comments, reviews, and direct communications can help find trends in how the story is being received and pinpoint areas that need improvement. Additionally, brands can track consumer sentiment regularly using sentiment analysis tools and identify changes in their emotional state over time

Continuous Improvement Using Data Insights

Impact measurement is not a target; it is a continuous process that motivates iterative improvements. When deciding what works and what doesn't for their visual content and storytelling initiatives, brands can make improvements based on data-driven insights. By examining measurements over time, businesses can identify trends, patterns, and anomalies. For instance, if a certain piece of visual content consistently receives greater interaction, marketers may look into ways to duplicate its success in upcoming stories. Similar to this, if conversion rates are low, changes can be made to the call-to-action in the story or its conformity to the target audience's preferences.

When a customer interacts with a product, brand, or individual, their psychological state is referred to as customer engagement (Brodie et al., 2011 and Zada et al., 2022). In the dynamic world of consumer preferences and habits, adaptation is essential. Customer perspectives regarding the advantages of a product or service and how demands are met are considered when a customer experiences and uses it (Amenuvor et al., 2019). Brands must be prepared to adjust their strategies in reaction to fresh data and trends. Continuous optimisation is a commitment to staying agile and responsive in order to preserve the effectiveness and relevance of visual content and storytelling strategies.

In conclusion, evaluating the impact of narrative and visual content combines art and science. It necessitates the use of both quantitative and qualitative data, in-depth understanding of client behaviour, and a willingness to adapt plans in light of new information. By rigorously analysing engagement, conversion rates, sentiment, and other relevant data, brands can enhance their strategies and create visual narratives that produce memorable consumer experiences.

POTENTIAL CHALLENGES AND THINGS TO PONDER

As the study comes to an end, the results demonstrate the ground-breaking impact that storytelling and visual material have had on contemporary marketing.

Addressing Potential Pitfalls in Storytelling and Visual Content

Although visual content and narrative have a great deal of promise to alter how customers connect with brands, they are not without challenges. Brands must avoid these errors to ensure that their tales are effective and well-received. Information overload: In a digital environment with lots of visual content, it's feasible for users to experience information overload. Brands need to strike a balance between providing relevant content and avoiding content overload. This necessitates meticulous curation and familiarity with the priorities of the audience.

Consumers respect authenticity and are quick to recognise falsehoods, which raises concerns regarding authenticity. Brands that prioritise a genuine relationship over exaggerated stories are more likely to build long-lasting trust with their audience. Overhyping stories may cause resentment if consumers think a brand is being dishonest.

Aligning Storytelling and Visual Content With Core Values

Storytelling and Visual content with core values must organically flow with a company's core values in order to ensure brand alignment and prevent misinterpretation. Misalignment may cause confusion and a decline in consumer confidence. Brands should: in order to avoid misconceptions and guarantee that stories have genuine resonance. Establish standards that describe the brand's visual identity, tone, and messaging.

There is a need to understand cultural sensitivities. Visual content that resonates with one culture might not do so with another. A thorough inquiry and the pursuit of multiple points of view might reduce this risk. Moreover, ambiguity in stories could lead to misunderstandings. Context is vital for ensuring listeners understand the intended message. Visual elements should support textual ones in order to create a cohesive and clear narrative.

Keeping Creativity and Clear Communication in Balance in Narratives

While inventiveness is crucial for creating compelling visuals and narratives, it must not come in the way of clear communication. Brands must find the right balance between creative self-expression and spreading a message that resonates with their target audience. A balance can be striked by adopting the following;

Creative examples and tales should help to make a point rather than confuse it. Ambiguity can lead to miscommunication and reduce the impact of the narrative. If the message is clear, it will be appropriately conveyed and understood. Additionally, a sample audience can be used to test a brand's narratives to assess how well the message is being received and understood. This procedure offers relevant data about probable trouble spots.

Consumers can draw the dots between different narrative pieces when there is visual consistency across all touchpoints. The narrative is improved and made more memorable by consistent graphic elements across all platforms, including the website, social media accounts, and marketing activities for the business. To sum up, storytelling and visual material both have their advantages and disadvantages for attracting customers' attention. Core values must be expressed through stories, potential dangers must be avoided and businesses must find a balance between creativity and clarity.

FUTURE DIRECTIONS FOR STORYTELLING AND VISUAL CONTENT

The realms of visual storytelling and content are expected to go through some exciting shifts in the next years. As technology advances and consumer habits change, several predictions for the future of these strategies emerge:

Predictions for the Growth of Narrative and Visual Content

Companies can generate experiences that are immersive. By fusing virtual reality (VR) and augmented reality (AR), immersive storytelling will be improved and customers will be able to engage with stories in entirely new ways. Brands will create virtual worlds that consumers can interact with, explore, and change. VR is said to be the type of video traffic that is expanding the fastest, so marketers may take advantage of this huge opportunity (Goh and Ping, 2014). Furthermore, hyper-personalization can be adopted. This will increase personalization by using AI and data analytics to create narratives that connect with people on a personal level.

Visual material will change in real time based on consumer preferences, actions, and context to deliver experiences that feel tailored.

Interactivity needs to be enhanced. More options for interaction need to be given besides just clicking and swiping. Brands will make advantage of gesture controls, speech recognition, and haptic feedback to produce more engaging and intelligible interactions. As the user explores the content, the story will be actively shaped by them.

How Emerging Technologies Affect Customer Experiences

How customers interact with products will radically change as a result of the integration of new technology and visual content. The following technical developments could have an impact.

Extended Reality (XR) which comprises virtual reality (VR), augmented reality (AR), and mixed reality (MR), will minimise the gap between the virtual and physical worlds by offering compelling and seamless narratives. Brands will employ XR to create hybrid experiences with a mix of digital and physical elements. There are more technologies in the operating model that supplement extended reality in the delivery model. These pairings give rise to the network or platform business models that serve as the models' bases (Wagner et al., 2022).

5G Connectivity is another significant development. The deployment of 5G networks would enhance the distribution of rich visual content by enabling faster streaming, lower latency, and more immersive experiences. Brands can create content that spontaneously adjusts to a variety of platforms and locations by utilising this technology. Moreover, advancements in neural interfaces will let users to engage directly with material using their brain signals. Despite being in its infancy, this technology offers a link between mind and experience, which has the potential to drastically alter how people interact with stories.

How AI and How Future Marketing Narratives Will Be Affected by Personalization

The future of marketing narratives will be shaped by artificial intelligence (AI), which will allow for unprecedented degrees of personalization and automation. It will be crucial to maintain a balance between human creativity and AI-generated material in order to assure authenticity. Intelligent assistant (AI) technologies are built on advanced machine learning and natural language processing techniques. Currently available intelligent assistants are Nina by Nuance, Google Assistant, Amazon Alexa and Siri. Likewise, chatbots and other virtual assistants are employed in marketing, customer support, content discovery, and data collection (Xu et al., 2017).

Marketing predictions can be done. AI will examine enormous volumes of customer data to forecast preferences and behaviours, assisting firms in developing stories that appeal to their target market. Furthermore, real-time personalization are also possible by AI by altering visual data in response to user interactions and context. This dynamic personalization will increase customer engagement and enjoyment by ensuring that storylines are always personal, interesting and relevant.

In conclusion, technological development, better engagement, and increased personalization will influence the direction of narrative and visual content in the future. Marketers will have access to powerful tools for telling tales that have a deep emotional connection with consumers as XR, 5G, neural interfaces, and AI evolve further. The secret to success will be using these technologies to create sincere, important, and lasting experiences that go beyond traditional marketing limitations.

CONCLUSION

In today's rapidly evolving digital environment, when consumer choices are plentiful and attention spans are short, the value of visual content and narrative is stronger than ever. This study has demonstrated the approaches' ground-breaking potential for developing emotionally powerful and engaging customer experiences.

Reiterating the Role That Narrative and Visual Material Have in the User Experience

Visual content has a greater impact on audiences than text-only content does. Because of its ability to effectively convey complex information, evoke emotions, and create long-lasting connections, it is a potent tool in the marketing professional's toolkit. When combined with storytelling, which plays on our irrational demand for stories, marketers may forge genuine connections with their audience that go beyond transactional encounters.

Stressing the Importance of Narrative and Visual Content to the User Experience

As the dynamics of consumer engagement evolve, businesses are called upon to embrace the power of visual content and storytelling. The call to action is clear: invest in creating compelling visual narratives that resonate with audiences on a deep level. Successful integration of visual content and storytelling requires a strategic approach. Brands must define their narratives, establish brand identities, and craft narratives that align with their values. They should leverage diverse formats, from images and videos to immersive experiences, adapting content to various platforms and audience preferences. Measuring impact through data-driven insights and continuously optimizing strategies ensures that narratives remain effective and relevant.

Immersive and Emotionally Resonant Storytelling's Long-Lasting Effects

Immersive and emotionally stirring storytelling has a long-lasting effect. These tactics not only increase engagement and conversion rates but also permanently alter consumer views and feelings. A masterfully constructed story has the capacity to uplift, empower, and transform. It may transform routine contacts into enjoyable experiences, fostering a sense of loyalty and affiliation among customers.

The goal of visual storytelling and content development is to connect people, give them meaning, and enhance their quality of life. Brands who embark on this path not only enhance their marketing tactics but also contribute to a larger narrative about how companies and consumers collaborate to shape the future. The human experience is what drives everything, notwithstanding the marketing sector's ongoing transformation. Through the use of narrative and visual content, brands can create experiences that touch people's emotions, ignite their imaginations, and leave a lasting impact.

Marketers must carry on with this study by utilising the strength of storytelling and visual material to create storylines that cut across boundaries and endure the test of time. The goal of visual storytelling and content development is to connect people, give them meaning, and enhance their quality of life. Brands that take part in this voyage not only enhance their marketing campaigns but also contribute to a larger story about the relationship between brands and consumers.

REFERENCES

Amenuvor, F., Owusu-Antwi, K., Basilisco, R., & Seong-Chan, B. (2019). Customer experience and behavioral intentions: The mediation role of customer perceived value. *International Journal of Science Research and Management*, 7(10), 1359–1374. 10.18535/ijsrm/v7i10.em02

Brakus, J. J., Schmitt, B. H., & Zarantonello, L. (2009). Brand experience: What is it? How is it measured? Does it affect loyalty? *Journal of Marketing*, 73(3), 52–68. 10.1509/jmkg.73.3.052

Brodie, R. J., Hollebeek, L. D., Juriae, B., & Iliae, A. (2011). Customer engagement: Conceptual domain, fundamental propositions, and implications for research. *Journal of Service Research*, 14(3), 252–271. 10.1177/1094670511411703

Bruner, J. (1991). The narrative construction of reality. *Critical Inquiry*, 18(1), 1–21. 10.1086/448619

Denning, S. (2005). *The leader's guide to storytelling: mastering the art and discipline of business narrative*. Jossey-Bass.

Feng, Y. (2018). Facilitator or inhibitor? The use of 360- degree videos for immersive Brand storytelling. *Journal of Interactive Advertising*, 18(1), 28–42. 10.1080/15252019.2018.1446199

Freeman, M. (2014). Advertising the yellow brick road: Historicizing the industrial emergence of transmedia storytelling. *International Journal of Communication*, 8, 2362–2381.

Gensler, S., Volckner, F., Liu-Thompkins, Y., & Wiertz, C. (2013). Managing brands in the social media environment. *Journal of Interactive Marketing*, 27(4), 242–256. 10.1016/j.intmar.2013.09.004

Goh, K. Y., & Ping, J. W. (2014). Engaging consumers with advergames: An experimental evaluation of interactivity, fit and expectancy. *Journal of the Association for Information Systems*, 15(7), 388–421. 10.17705/1jais.00366

Granitz, N., & Forman, H. (2015). Building self-Brand connections: Exploring brand stories through a transmedia perspective. *Journal of Brand Management*, 22(1), 38–59. 10.1057/bm.2015.1

Holt, J. (2004). *How brands become icons: The principles of cultural branding*. Harvard Business Press.

Kumar, V., Rajan, B., Venkatesan, R., & Lecinski, J. (2019). Understanding the Role of artificial intelligence in personalized engagement marketing. *California Management Review*, 61(4), 135–155. 10.1177/0008125619859317

Lim, H., & Childs, M. (2020). Visual storytelling on Instagram: Branded photo narrative and the role of telepresence. *Journal of Research in Interactive Marketing*, 14(1), 33–50. 10.1108/JRIM-09-2018-0115

Manic, M. (2015). Marketing Engagement Through Visual Content. *Bulletin of the Transilvania University of Brasov. Series V, Economic Sciences*, 57, 89.

Marr, D. (1982). *Vision: A Computational Investigation into the human representation and processing of visual information*. MIT Press.

Milgram, P., Takemura, H., Utsumi, A., & Kishino, F. (1995). Augmented reality: A class of displays on the reality-virtuality continuum. In *Proceedings of Tele-manipulator and Telepresence Technologies*. International Society for Optics and Photonics. 10.1117/12.197321

Monarth, H. (2014, March 11). The Irresistible Power of Storytelling as a Strategic Business Tool. *Harvard Business Review*. https://hbr.org/2014/03/the-irresistible-power-of-storytelling-as-a-strategic-business-tool

Newberry, C. (2023, January 5). *How To Use Instagram for Business in 2024: 6 Pro Tips*. Hootsuite. https://blog.hootsuite.com/how-to-use-instagram-for-business/

Pachucki, C., Grohs, R., & Scholl-Grissemann, U. (2022). No story without a storyteller: The impact of the storyteller as a narrative element in online destination marketing. *Journal of Travel Research*, 61(8), 1703–1718. 10.1177/00472875211046052

Paivio, A. (2014). *Imagery and verbal processes*. Psychology Press.

Palmer, S. (1999). *Vision science: Photons to phenomenology*. MIT Press.

Phelps, E. (2006). Emotion and cognition: Insights from studies of the human amygdala. *Annual Review of Psychology*, 57(1), 27–53. 10.1146/annurev.psych.56.091103.07023416318588

Pine, J. I. I., & Gilmore, J. H. (1998). Welcome to the experience economy. *Harvard Business Review*.10181589

Raji, M., Olodo, H., Oke, T., Addy, W., Ofodile, O., & Oyewole, A. (2024). Business Strategies in Virtual Reality: A Review of Market Opportunities and Consumer Experience. *International Journal of Management & Entrepreneurship Research*, 6(3), 722–736. 10.51594/ijmer.v6i3.883

Ryu, K., Lehto, X. Y., Gordon, S., & Fu, X. (2018). Compelling brand storytelling for luxury hotels. *International Journal of Hospitality Management*, 74, 22–29. 10.1016/j.ijhm.2018.02.002

Solja, E., Liljander, V., & Soderlund, M. (2018). Short brand stories on packaging: An examination of consumer responses. *Psychology and Marketing*, 35(4), 294–306. 10.1002/mar.21087

Wagner, R., & Cozmiuc, D. (2022). Extended reality in marketing—A multiple case study on internet of things platforms. *Information (Basel)*, 13(6), 6–278. 10.3390/info13060278

Wankhade, M., Rao, A. C. S., & Kulkarni, C. (2022). A survey on sentiment analysis methods, applications and challenges. *Artificial Intelligence Review*, 55(7), 5731–5780. 10.1007/s10462-022-10144-1

Wheeler, A. (2009). *Designing brand identity*. John Wiley & Sons, Inc.

Whitler, K. A. (2020). 3 Reasons Why Storytelling Should Be A Priority For Marketers. *Forbes*. https://www.forbes.com/sites/kimberlywhitler/2018/07/14/3-reasons-why-storytelling-should-be-a-priority-for-marketers/?sh=111624876758

Xu, A., Liu, Z., Guo, Y., Sinha, V., & Akkiraju, R. (2017). *A new chatbot for customer service on social media. In 2017 CHI conference on human factors in computing systems, association for computing machinery*, New York, NY, United States. 10.1145/3025453.3025496

Zada, M., Zada, S., Ali, M., Jun, Z. Y., Contreras-Barraza, N., & Castillo, D. (2022). How classy servant leader at workplace? linking servant leadership and task performance during the covid-19 crisis: A moderation and mediation approach. *Frontiers in Psychology*, 13, 810227. 10.3389/fpsyg.2022.81022735401384

Zhang, X., & Ramayah, T. (2024). Solving the mystery of storytelling in destination marketing: A systematic review. *Journal of Hospitality and Tourism Management*, 59, 222–237. 10.1016/j.jhtm.2024.04.013

KEY TERMS AND DEFINITIONS

Augmented Reality: Augmented reality, or AR, is a technology that allows users to enhance their experience in the actual world by superimposing visual, audio, or other sensory data. Retailers and other businesses can deploy creative marketing campaigns, promote goods and services, and gather specific consumer data by utilizing augmented reality.

Marketing Narratives: The multidisciplinary management of a brand's story that relates to the audience on an emotional level and motivates them to do desired actions is known as narrative marketing. It is accomplished by having consumers, employees, and the public co-create tales inside a carefully constructed story universe.

Storytelling: Using a narrative to convey a message is known as storytelling marketing. Everyone, from small businesses to larger corporations, can benefit from it. The objective is to evoke strong emotions in the audience, such as motivation to act and a greater sense of brand loyalty.

Visual Marketing: It is the process of communicating with your target audience and building your brand via the use of images, videos, and other multimedia content. It facilitates the depiction of some topics and ideas that would be more difficult to address with words alone as part of a more comprehensive marketing plan.

Compilation of References

Abdelfattah, F., Al-Alawi, A., Abdullahi, M. S., & Salah, M. (2023). Embracing the industrial revolution: The impact of technological advancements and government policies on tourism development in Oman. *Journal of Policy Research in Tourism, Leisure & Events*, 1–25. 10.1080/19407963.2023.2294789

Abidi, M. H., Alkhalefah, H., Moiduddin, K., Alazab, M., Mohammed, M. K., Ameen, W., & Gadekallu, T. R. (2021). Optimal 5G network slicing using machine learning and deep learning concepts. *Computer Standards & Interfaces*, 76, 103518. 10.1016/j.csi.2021.103518

Abraham, H. M., & Florian, S. (2021). Identifying Manipulative Advertising Techniques in XR Through Scenario Construction. *Conference on Human Factors in Computing Systems (CHI '21)*, Yokohama, Japan 10.1145/3411764.3445253

Adams, D. (1993). *Defining Educational Quality.* IEQ Publication 1: Biennial Report.

AEE (2023). *Defining Experiential Education: Challenge and experience followed by reflection, leading to learning and growth.* Association for Experiential Education (aee.org)

Agarwal, M., & Agarwal, R. (2021). Artificial Intelligence in Travel and Tourism Industry: A Case Study of SpiceJet, India. *International Journal of Management.*

Agrawal, A. V., Pitchai, R., Senthamaraikannan, C., Balaji, N. A., Sajithra, S., & Boopathi, S. (2023). Digital Education System During the COVID-19 Pandemic. In *Using Assistive Technology for Inclusive Learning in K-12 Classrooms* (pp. 104–126). IGI Global. 10.4018/978-1-6684-6424-3.ch005

Agrawal, A. V., Shashibhushan, G., Pradeep, S., Padhi, S., Sugumar, D., & Boopathi, S. (2023). Synergizing Artificial Intelligence, 5G, and Cloud Computing for Efficient Energy Conversion Using Agricultural Waste. In *Sustainable Science and Intelligent Technologies for Societal Development* (pp. 475–497). IGI Global.

Agrawal, S., Simon, A., Bech, S., Bærentsen, K., & Forchhammer, S. (2019). *Defining Immersion: Literature Review and Implications for Research on Immersive Audiovisual Experiences. (bildiri)*

Compilation of References

Aguayo, C., & Eames, C. (2023). Using mixed reality (XR) immersive learning to enhance environmental education. *The Journal of Environmental Education*, 54(1), 58–71. 10.1080/00958964.2022.2152410

Ahamed, B. S., Chakravarthy, K. S., Arputhabalan, J., Sasirekha, K., Prince, R. M. R., Boopathi, S., & Muthuvel, S. (2024). Revolutionizing Friction Stir Welding With AI-Integrated Humanoid Robots. In *Advances in Computational Intelligence and Robotics* (pp. 120–144). IGI Global. 10.4018/979-8-3693-2399-1.ch005

Akkerman, G., Buynosov, A., Dorofeev, A., & Kurganov, V. (2019). Decision support system for road transport management in the digital age. *International Scientific Siberian Transport Forum*, 773–781.

Akyazi, T., Goti, A., Oyarbide-Zubillaga, A., Alberdi, E., Carballedo, R., Ibeas, R., & Bringas, P. (2020). *Skills Requirements for the European Machine Tool Sector Emerging from Its Digitalization*. Metals - Open Access Metallurgy Journal., 10.3390/met10121665

Al Mulhim, E. N. (2023). Technology fatigue during the COVID-19 pandemic: The case of distance project-based learning environments. *Turkish Online Journal of Distance Education*, 24(1), 234–245. 10.17718/tojde.1034006

Alam, S. S., Susmit, S., Lin, C. Y., Mohammad, M., & Ho, Y. H. (2021). Factors Affecting Augmented Reality Adoption in the Retail Industry. *Journal of Open Innovation*, 7(142), 1–24. 10.3390/joitmc7020142

Ali, M. N., Senthil, T., Ilakkiya, T., Hasan, D. S., Ganapathy, N. B. S., & Boopathi, S. (2024). IoT's Role in Smart Manufacturing Transformation for Enhanced Household Product Quality. In *Advanced Applications in Osmotic Computing* (pp. 252–289). IGI Global. 10.4018/979-8-3693-1694-8.ch014

Alimamy, S., Deans, K., & Gnoth, J. (2017). An empirical investigation of augmented reality to reduce consumer perceived risk. *Academy of Marketing Science World Marketing Congress*, (pp. 127–135). Research Gate.

Al-Imamy, S., Gnoth, J. & Deans, K. (2019). *Decision-making and co-creation through AR technology*.

Al-Imamy, S., Gnoth, J., & Deans, K. (2018). The Role of Augmented Reality in the Interactivity of CoCreation. *International Journal of Technology and Human Interaction*, 14.

Aljapurkar, A. V., & Ingawale, S. D. (2024). Revolutionizing the Techno-Human Space in Human Resource Practices in Industry 4.0 to Usage in Society 5.0. In *Digital Transformation: Industry 4.0 to Society 5.0* (pp. 221–257). Springer.

Al-Sartawi, M. (2021). *Big Data-Driven Digital Economy: Artificial and Computational Intelligence* (Vol. 974). Springer. 10.1007/978-3-030-73057-4

Alzahrani, N. M. (2020). Augmented Reality: A Systematic Review of Its Benefits and Challenges in E-learning Contexts. *Applied Sciences (Basel, Switzerland)*, 10(16), 1–21. 10.3390/app10165660

Amenuvor, F., Owusu-Antwi, K., Basilisco, R., & Seong-Chan, B. (2019). Customer experience and behavioral intentions: The mediation role of customer perceived value. *International Journal of Science Research and Management*, 7(10), 1359–1374. 10.18535/ijsrm/v7i10.em02

Anderson. (2016). *Emergence and Innovation in Digital Learning: Foundations and Applications* (G. Veletsianos, Ed.). Athabasca University Press. 10.15215/aupress/9781771991490.01

Anderson, C. A., Smith, A., & Johnson, B. (2019). Enhancing Experiential Learning: The Impact of Virtual Reality Simulations in Education. *Journal of Educational Technology*, 42(3), 215–230.

Anderson, T., Rourke, L., Garrison, R., & Archer, W. (2019). Assessing Teaching Presence in a Computer Conferencing Context. *Online Learning : the Official Journal of the Online Learning Consortium*, 5(2). Advance online publication. 10.24059/olj.v5i2.1875

Anwar, Z. (2021). Privacy and Safety Issues With Facebook's New Metaventure. *Dark Reading*. https://www.darkreading.com/vulnerabilities-threats/privacy-and-safety-issues-with-facebook-s -new-metaventure-

Arif Ali, K., Sher, B., Peng, L., Muhammad, W., Bilal, K., Aakash, A., & Muhammad, A. A. (2022). Ethics of AI: A Systematic Literature Review of Principles and Challenges. *International Conference on Evaluation and Assessment in Software Engineering 2022 (EASE '22)*. ACM. 10.1145/3530019.3531329

Arora, M., Prakash, A., Mittal, A., & Singh, S. (2021). HR analytics and artificial intelligence-transforming human resource management. *2021 International Conference on Decision Aid Sciences and Application (DASA)*, (pp. 288–293). IEEE. 10.1109/DASA53625.2021.9682325

Arslan, A., Cooper, C., Khan, Z., Golgeci, I., & Ali, I. (2022). Artificial intelligence and human workers interaction at team level: A conceptual assessment of the challenges and potential HRM strategies. *International Journal of Manpower*, 43(1), 75–88. 10.1108/IJM-01-2021-0052

Assael, H. (2004). *Consumer Behavior. A Strategic Approach*. Houghton Mifflin Company.

Azis, N., Amin, M., Chan, S., & Aprilia, C. (2020). How smart tourism technologies affect tourist destination loyalty. *Journal of Hospitality and Tourism Technology*, 11(4), 603–625. 10.1108/JHTT-01-2020-0005

Azuma, R. (2019). Augmented Reality in Surgical Procedures: Real-Time Information for Precision. *Journal of Medical Technology*, 28(2), 123–137.

Babu, B. S., Kamalakannan, J., Meenatchi, N., Karthik, S., & Boopathi, S. (2022). Economic impacts and reliability evaluation of battery by adopting Electric Vehicle. *IEEE Explore*, 1–6.

Bahar, M., & Tenzin, D. (2021). A novel ethical analysis of educational XR and AI in literature. *Computers & Education: X Reality, 4*, 1-28. 10.1016/j.cexr.2024.100052

Bailenson, J. N. (2018). The Psychology of Virtual Interactions: Understanding Presence and Engagement in Virtual Reality Meetings. *Journal of Communication*, 36(4), 451–468.

Compilation of References

Baker, S. (2003). *New Consumer Marketing, Managing a Living Demand System*. Wiley and Sons.

Balakrishnan, J., Dwivedi, Y. K., Malik, F. T., & Baabdullah, A. M. (2023). Role of smart tourism technology in heritage tourism development. *Journal of Sustainable Tourism*, 31(11), 2506–2525. 10.1080/09669582.2021.1995398

Balcerak Jackson, M., & Balcerak Jackson, B. (2024). Immersive Experience and Virtual Reality. *Philosophy & Technology*, 37(1), 19. 10.1007/s13347-024-00707-1

Banaji, S., & Bhat, R. (2022). *Social media and hate*. Taylor & Francis. 10.4324/9781003083078

Bassellier, G., & Benbasat, I. (2004). Business competence of information technology professionals: Conceptual development and influence on IT-business partnerships. *Management Information Systems Quarterly*, 28(4), 673–694. 10.2307/25148659

Bates, T. (2018). The 2017 national survey of online learning in Canadian post-secondary education: Methodology and results. *International Journal of Educational Technology in Higher Education*, 15(1), 29. 10.1186/s41239-018-0112-3

Bayazıt, N. (2004). *Endüstriyel Tasarımcılar için Tasarlama Kuramları ve Metotları*. Birsen Yayınevi.

Beer, M., & Nohria, N. (2000). Cracking the code of change. *Harvard Business Review*, (May-June), 133–141.11183975

Behr, K. M., Nosper, A., Klimmt, C., & Hartmann, T. (2005). Some Practical Considerations of Ethical Issues in VR Research. *Presence (Cambridge, Mass.)*, 14(6), 668–676. 10.1162/105474605775196535

Belk, R. (2021). Ethical issues in service robotics and artificial intelligence. *Service Industries Journal*, 41(13–14), 860–876. 10.1080/02642069.2020.1727892

Ben, K. (2018). Virtual Reality: Ethical Challenges and Dangers: Physiological and Social Impacts. *IEEE Technology and Society Magazine*, 20–25. 10.1109/MTS.2018.2876104

Bennett, J., & Amanda Murphy, A. (2020) Skills for Immersive Experience Creation Barriers to Growth in the UK's Immersive Economy. StoryFutures.

Berkman, M. I. (2024). History of virtual reality. In *Encyclopedia of computer graphics and games*. Springer International Publishing. 10.1007/978-3-031-23161-2_169

Berthon, P. R., Pitt, L. F., Plangger, K., & Shapiro, D. (2012). Marketing meets Web 2.0, social media, and creative consumers: Implications for international marketing strategy. *Business Horizons*, 55(3), 261–271. 10.1016/j.bushor.2012.01.007

Bickley, S. J., Macintyre, A., & Torgler, B. (2021). Artificial intelligence and big data in sustainable entrepreneurship. *Journal of Economic Surveys*.

Bi, F., & Liu, H. (2022). Machine learning-based cloud IOT platform for intelligent tourism information services. *EURASIP Journal on Wireless Communications and Networking*, 2022(1), 59. 10.1186/s13638-022-02138-y

Biliavska, V., Castanho, R., & Vulevic, A. (2022). Analysis of the impact of artificial intelligence in enhancing the human resource practices. *J. Intell. Manag. Decis*, 1(2), 128–136. 10.56578/jimd010206

Billinghurst, M., & Dunser, A. (2012). Mixed Reality: Integrating Virtual and Physical Worlds. *IEEE Computer Graphics and Applications*, 32(2), 39–47.

Binder, J. K., & Belz, F.-M. (2015). Sustainable entrepreneurship: What it is. In *Handbook of entrepreneurship and sustainable development research* (pp. 30–72). Edward Elgar Publishing. 10.4337/9781849808248.00010

Binkley, M., Erstad, O., Herman, J., Raizen, S., Ripley, M., Miller-Ricci, M. & Rumble, M. (2011). *Defining Twenty-First Century Skills*. Springer. .10.1007/978-94-007-2324-5_2

Biocca, F., & Delaney, B. (1995). Immersive virtual reality technology. In Biocca, F., & Levy, M. R. (Eds.), *Communication in the age of virtual reality* (pp. 57–124). Lawrence Erlbaum Associates, Inc.

Blackwell, L., Ellison, N., Elliott-Deflo, N., & Schwartz, R. (2019). *Harassment in social virtual reality: Challenges for platform governance*. ACM HumanComputer Interaction New York. 10.1145/3359202

Block, B. (2018). *An innovative teaching approach in Engineering Education to impart reflective digitalization competencies*. IEEE. .10.1109/FIE.2018.8658604

Bocar, A. C., Khan, S. A., & Epoc, F. (2022). COVID-19 Work from Home Stressors and the Degree of its Impact: Employers and Employees Actions. *International Journal of Technology Transfer and Commercialisation*, 19(2), 270–291. 10.1504/IJTTC.2022.124349

Bogdanowicz, M. (2015). *Digital Entrepreneurship Barriers and Drivers. The need for a specific measurement framework*. (JRC Technical Report EUR 27679.) Institute for Prospective Technological Studies; 10.2791/3112

Bogdan, P., & Radu, D. V. (2022). Transhumanism as a Philosophical and Cultural Framework for Extended Reality Applied to Human Augmentation *13th Augmented Human International Conference (AH2022)*, Winnipeg, MB, Canada. 10.1145/3532525.3532528

Boopathi, S. (2022). Cryogenically treated and untreated stainless steel grade 317 in sustainable wire electrical discharge machining process: A comparative study. *Springer :Environmental Science and Pollution Research*, 1–10.

Boopathi, S. (2023). Deep Learning Techniques Applied for Automatic Sentence Generation. In *Promoting Diversity, Equity, and Inclusion in Language Learning Environments* (pp. 255–273). IGI Global. 10.4018/978-1-6684-3632-5.ch016

Compilation of References

Boopathi, S. (2023). Securing Healthcare Systems Integrated With IoT: Fundamentals, Applications, and Future Trends. In *Dynamics of Swarm Intelligence Health Analysis for the Next Generation* (pp. 186–209). IGI Global.

Boopathi, S. (2024). Digital HR Implementation for Business Growth in Industrial 5.0. In *Convergence of Human Resources Technologies and Industry 5.0* (pp. 1–22). IGI Global. 10.4018/979-8-3693-1343-5.ch001

Boopathi, S. (2024b). Balancing Innovation and Security in the Cloud: Navigating the Risks and Rewards of the Digital Age. In *Improving Security, Privacy, and Trust in Cloud Computing* (pp. 164–193). IGI Global.

Boopathi, S. (2024b). Energy Cascade Conversion System and Energy-Efficient Infrastructure. In *Sustainable Development in AI, Blockchain, and E-Governance Applications* (pp. 47–71). IGI Global. 10.4018/979-8-3693-1722-8.ch004

Boopathi, S. (2024b). Sustainable Development Using IoT and AI Techniques for Water Utilization in Agriculture. In *Sustainable Development in AI, Blockchain, and E-Governance Applications* (pp. 204–228). IGI Global. 10.4018/979-8-3693-1722-8.ch012

Boopathi, S. (2024a). Advancements in Machine Learning and AI for Intelligent Systems in Drone Applications for Smart City Developments. In *Futuristic e-Governance Security With Deep Learning Applications* (pp. 15–45). IGI Global. 10.4018/978-1-6684-9596-4.ch002

Boopathi, S., & Kanike, U. K. (2023). Applications of Artificial Intelligent and Machine Learning Techniques in Image Processing. In *Handbook of Research on Thrust Technologies' Effect on Image Processing* (pp. 151–173). IGI Global. 10.4018/978-1-6684-8618-4.ch010

Boopathi, S., & Khang, A. (2023). AI-Integrated Technology for a Secure and Ethical Healthcare Ecosystem. In *AI and IoT-Based Technologies for Precision Medicine* (pp. 36–59). IGI Global. 10.4018/979-8-3693-0876-9.ch003

Borthakur, P. G., & Das, B. B. (n.d.). *Future of Human Resource (HR) in Industry 5.0: Embracing Technology and Beyond-A Study.*

Bose, R. (2001). An E-DSS for Strategic Planning of E-Commerce Website Development. *International Journal of the Computer, the Internet and Management, 9*(3), 1–21.

Boukherouaa, E. B., Shabsigh, M. G., AlAjmi, K., Deodoro, J., Farias, A., Iskender, E. S., Mirestean, M. A. T., & Ravikumar, R. (2021). *Powering the digital economy: Opportunities and risks of artificial intelligence in finance.* International Monetary Fund.

Brakus, J. J., Schmitt, B. H., & Zarantonello, L. (2009). Brand experience: What is it? How is it measured? Does it affect loyalty? *Journal of Marketing, 73*(3), 52–68. 10.1509/jmkg.73.3.052

Bréchet, L. (2022). Personal Memories and Bodily-Cues Influence Our Sense of Self. *Frontiers in Psychology, 13*(855450), 855450. 10.3389/fpsyg.2022.85545035814046

Brey, P. A. E. (2012). Anticipating ethical issues in emerging IT. *Ethics and Information Technology*, 14(4), 305–317. 10.1007/s10676-012-9293-y

Brodie, R. J., Hollebeek, L. D., Juriae, B., & Iliae, A. (2011). Customer engagement: Conceptual domain, fundamental propositions, and implications for research. *Journal of Service Research*, 14(3), 252–271. 10.1177/1094670511411703

Bruner, J. (1991). The narrative construction of reality. *Critical Inquiry*, 18(1), 1–21. 10.1086/448619

Bruno, R. R., Wolff, G., Wernly, B., Masyuk, M., Piayda, K., Leaver, S., Erkens, R., Oehler, D., Afzal, S., Heidari, H., Kelm, M., & Jung, C. (2022). Virtual and augmented reality in critical care medicine: The patient's, clinician's, and researcher's perspective. *Critical Care*, 26(326), 1–13. 10.1186/s13054-022-04202-x36284350

Brussels. (2011). *Supporting growth and jobs – an agenda for the modernization of Europe's higher education systems*. Europea. https://eurlex.europa.eu/LexUriServ/LexUriServ.do?uri=COM:2011:0567:FIN:EN:PDF

Bruton, R. (2024). *The Rise of Immersive Technologies: Looking Back and Ahead.*

Brynjolfsson, E., & McAfee, A. (2014). *The second machine age: Work, progress, and prosperity in a time of brilliant technologies*. Norton & Co.

Buhr, D. (2015). *Social Innovation Policy for Industry 4.0*. Springer.

Bulchand-Gidumal, J., William Secin, E., O'Connor, P., & Buhalis, D. (n.d.). Artificial Intelligence's impact on hospitality and tourism marketing: Exploring key themes and addressing challenges. *Current Issues in Tourism*, 1–18. 10.1080/13683500.2023.2229480

Burdea, G., & Coiffet, P. (2003). Virtual Reality Technology. *Presence (Cambridge, Mass.)*, 12(6), 663–664. 10.1162/105474603322955950

Bye, K., Hosfelt, D., Chase, S., Miesnieks, M., & Beck, T. (2019). *The Ethical and Privacy Implications of Mixed Reality*. SIGGRAPH. 10.1145/3306212.3328138

Calderón, C., & Servén, L. (2010). Infrastructure and economic development in Sub-Saharan Africa. *Journal of African Economies*, 19(suppl_1), i13–i87. 10.1093/jae/ejp022

Calvet, L., Bourdin, P., & Prados, F. (2019). Immersive technologies in higher education: Applications, challenges, and good practices. *Proceedings of the 20193rd International Conference on Education and E-Learning*, (pp. 95–99). ACM. 10.1145/3371647.3371667

Camacho-Ruiz, M., Carrasco, R. A., Fernández-Avilés, G., & LaTorre, A. (2023). Tourism destination events classifier based on artificial intelligence techniques. *Applied Soft Computing*, 148, 110914. 10.1016/j.asoc.2023.110914

Camba, J. D., Soler-Dominguez, J., & Contero, M. (2017). *Immersive Visualization Technologies to Facilitate Multidisciplinary Design Education*. Springer. 10.1007/978-3-319-58509-3_1

Compilation of References

Cardenas-Robledo, L. A., Hernandez-Uribe, O., Reta, C., & Antonio, J. (2022). Extended reality applications in industry 4.0—A systematic literature review. *Telematics and Informatics*, 73, 101863. 10.1016/j.tele.2022.101863

Carmigniani, J., & Furht, B. (2011). Augmented Reality: An Overview. *Handbook of Augmented Reality*, 3–46. Springer. 10.1007/978-1-4614-0064-6_1

Carrozzi, A., Chylinski, M., Heller, J., Hilken, T., Keeling, D. I., & de Ruyter, K. (2019). What's mine is a hologram? How shared augmented reality augments psychological ownership. *Journal of Interactive Marketing*, 48, 71–88. 10.1016/j.intmar.2019.05.004

Carter, M., & Egliston, B. (2020). *Ethical Implications of Emerging Mixed Reality Technologies* (Faculty of Arts and Social Sciences, Issue. Chalmers, D. J. (2022). *Reality+*. Penguin Books Limited.

Castillo, M. J., & Taherdoost, H. (2023). The impact of AI technologies on e-business. *Encyclopedia*, 3(1), 107–121. 10.3390/encyclopedia3010009

Chander, B., Pal, S., De, D., & Buyya, R. (2022). Artificial intelligence-based internet of things for industry 5.0. *Artificial Intelligence-Based Internet of Things Systems*, 3–45.

Chandrika, V., Sivakumar, A., Krishnan, T. S., Pradeep, J., Manikandan, S., & Boopathi, S. (2023). Theoretical Study on Power Distribution Systems for Electric Vehicles. In *Intelligent Engineering Applications and Applied Sciences for Sustainability* (pp. 1–19). IGI Global. 10.4018/979-8-3693-0044-2.ch001

Chang, L. (2018). Media Communication and Application of "Immersive Experience" in the Visual Field [J]. *Design Art Research*, 8(01), 93–96.

Chaturvedi, R., Verma, S., Ali, F., & Kumar, S. (2023, August 09). Reshaping Tourist Experience with AI-Enabled Technologies: A Comprehensive Review and Future Research Agenda. *International Journal of Human-Computer Interaction*, 1–17. 10.1080/10447318.2023.2238353

Chen, Z., J., Wu, Gan, W., & Qi, Z. (2022). Metaverse Security and Privacy: An Overview, *2022 IEEE International Conference on Big Data (Big Data)*, (pp. 2950-2959). IEEE. 10.1109/BigData55660.2022.10021112

Chen, Y., Li, H., & Xue, T. (2023, October 26). Female Gendering of Artificial Intelligence in Travel: A Social Interaction Perspective. *Journal of Quality Assurance in Hospitality & Tourism*, 1–16. 10.1080/1528008X.2023.2275263

Cheriyan, A., Kumar, R., Joseph, A., & Kappil, S. R. (2022). Consumer Acceptance towards AI-enabled Chatbots; Case of Travel and Tourism Industries. *Journal of Positive School Psychology*, 6(3).

Chichernea, V. (2014). The Use Of Decision Support Systems (Dss) In Smart City Planning And Management. *Journal of Information Systems & Operations Management*, 8(2).

Chowdhury, S., Dey, P., Joel-Edgar, S., Bhattacharya, S., Rodriguez-Espindola, O., Abadie, A., & Truong, L. (2023). Unlocking the value of artificial intelligence in human resource management through AI capability framework. *Human Resource Management Review*, 33(1), 100899. 10.1016/j.hrmr.2022.100899

Christopoulos, A., Mystakidis, S., Pellas, N., & Jussi Laakso, M. (2021). ARLEAN: An Augmented Reality Learning Analytics Ethical Framework. *Computers*, 10(8), 92. 10.3390/computers10080092

Chuah, S. H. W., Marimuthu, M., Kandampully, J., & Bilgihan, A. (2017). What drives Gen Y loyalty? Understanding the mediated moderating roles of switching costs and alternative attractiveness in the value-satisfaction-loyalty chain. *Journal of Retailing and Consumer Services, 36*(July 2016), 124–136. 10.1016/j.jretconser.2017.01.010

Chuah, S. H.-W. (2018). Why and Who Will Adopt Extended Reality Technology? Literature Review, Synthesis, and Future Research Agenda. 10.2139/ssrn.3300469

Chuang, C. M. (2023). The conceptualization of smart tourism service platforms on tourist value co-creation behaviours: An integrative perspective of smart tourism services. *Humanities & Social Sciences Communications*, 10(1), 1–16. 10.1057/s41599-023-01867-9

Chylinski, M., Heller, J., Hilken, T., Keeling, D. I., Mahr, D., & de Ruyter, K. (2020). Augmented reality marketing: A technology-enabled approach to situated customer experience. *Australasian Marketing Journal*, 28(4), 374–384. 10.1016/j.ausmj.2020.04.004

Cleveland-Innes, M., Gauvreau, S., Richardson, G., Mishra, S., & Ostashewski, N. (2019). Technology-Enabled Learning and the Benefits and Challenges of Using the Community of Inquiry Theoretical Framework. *International journal of e-learning & distance education, 34*(1), n1.

Çöltekin, A., Lochhead, I., Madden, M., Christophe, S., Devaux, A., Pettit, C., Lock, O., Shukla, S., Herman, L., Stachoň, Z., Kubíček, P., Snopková, D., Bernardes, S., & Hedley, N. (2020). Extended reality in spatial sciences: A review of research challenges and future directions. *ISPRS International Journal of Geo-Information*, 9(7), 1–29. 10.3390/ijgi9070439

Coon, J. (2018). *Assisted reality: What it is, and how it will improve service productivity*. PTC. https://www.ptc.com/en/blogs/service/what-is-assisted-reality

Correia, A., & Kozak, M. (2016). Tourists' shopping experiences at street markets: Cross-country research. *Tourism Management*, 56, 85–95. 10.1016/j.tourman.2016.03.026

Coşkun, S., Kayıkçı, Y., & Gençay, E. (2019). Adapting Engineering Education to Industry 4.0 Vision. *Technologies*, 7(1), 10. 10.3390/technologies7010010

Cotton, M. (2021). *Virtual reality, empathy and ethics*. Springer Nature. 10.1007/978-3-030-72907-3

Creed, C., Al-Kalbani, M., Theil, A., Sarcar, S., & Williams, I. (2024). Inclusive AR/VR: Accessibility barriers for immersive technologies. *Universal Access in the Information Society*, 23(1), 59–73. 10.1007/s10209-023-00969-0

Compilation of References

Cummings, J. J., & Bailenson, J. N. (2016). How Immersive Is Enough? A Meta-Analysis of the Effect of Immersive Technology on User Presence. *Media Psychology*, 19(2), 272–309. 10.1080/15213269.2015.1015740

Dab, S., Ramachandran, S., Chandna, R., Hanspal, R., Grealish, A., & Peeters, M. (2016). The Digital Revolution in Trade Finance. *Boston Consulting Group*, 1–7.

Dahiya, V., & Dalal, S. (2018). Fog computing: A review on integration of cloud computing and internet of things. *2018 IEEE International Students' Conference on Electrical, Electronics and Computer Science (SCEECS)*, (pp. 1–6). IEEE.

Dahlbom, P., Siikanen, N., Sajasalo, P., & Jarvenpää, M. (2020). Big data and HR analytics in the digital era. *Baltic Journal of Management*, 15(1), 120–138. 10.1108/BJM-11-2018-0393

Dalgarno, B., & Lee, M. J. (2010). What are the learning affordances of 3-D virtual environments? *British Journal of Educational Technology*, 41(1), 10–32. 10.1111/j.1467-8535.2009.01038.x

Dang, T. D., & Nguyen, M. T. (2023). Systematic review and research agenda for the tourism and hospitality sector: Co-creation of customer value in the digital age. *Future Business Journal*, 9(1), 94. 10.1186/s43093-023-00274-5

Das, S., Lekhya, G., Shreya, K., Shekinah, K. L., Babu, K. K., & Boopathi, S. (2024). Fostering Sustainability Education Through Cross-Disciplinary Collaborations and Research Partnerships: Interdisciplinary Synergy. In *Facilitating Global Collaboration and Knowledge Sharing in Higher Education With Generative AI* (pp. 60–88). IGI Global.

Das, P., Ramapraba, P., Seethalakshmi, K., Mary, M. A., Karthick, S., & Sampath, B. (2024). Sustainable Advanced Techniques for Enhancing the Image Process. In *Fostering Cross-Industry Sustainability With Intelligent Technologies* (pp. 350–374). IGI Global. 10.4018/979-8-3693-1638-2.ch022

Dastane, O., Rafiq, M. & Turner, J.J. (2024). *Implications of metaverse, virtual reality, and extended reality for development and learning in organizations.* Development and Learning in Organizations. 10.1108/DLO-09-2023-0196

Datt, G., & Singh, G. (2021). Acceptance and Barriers of Open Educational Resources in the Context to Indian Higher Education. *Canadian Journal of Learning and Technology*, 47(3). 10.21432/cjlt28028

de Andreis, F., Comite, U., Gallo, A. M., Andone, D. M., & Ciaschi, G. (2024). Social business, artificial intelligence, and sustainability: An integrated approach for the future. *Sustainable Economies*, 2(1).

Deaky, B. A., & Parv, A. L. (2018, August). Virtual Reality for Real Estate–a case study. *IOP Conference Series. Materials Science and Engineering*, 399(1), 012013. 10.1088/1757-899X/399/1/012013

Dede, C. (2017). Augmented Reality in Education: Current Technologies and the Potential for Transformative Learning. *Educational Researcher*, 46(7), 56–63.

Deepa, R., Sekar, S., Malik, A., Kumar, J., & Attri, R. (2024). Impact of AI-focussed technologies on social and technical competencies for HR managers–A systematic review and research agenda. *Technological Forecasting and Social Change*, 202, 123301. 10.1016/j.techfore.2024.123301

Deepthi, B., & Bansal, V. (2023). Applications of Artificial Intelligence (AI) in the Tourism Industry: A Futuristic Perspective. In Tučková, Z., Dey, S. K., Thai, H. H., & Hoang, S. D. (Eds.), *Impact of Industry 4.0 on Sustainable Tourism* (pp. 31–43). Emerald Publishing Limited., 10.1 108/978-1-80455-157-820231003

Dengel, A. (2022). What Is Immersive Learning? *2022 8th International Conference of the Immersive Learning Research Network (iLRN)*. IEEE. 10.23919/iLRN55037.2022.9815941

Denning, S. (2005). *The leader's guide to storytelling: mastering the art and discipline of business narrative*. Jossey-Bass.

Dewey, J. (1938). *Education and experience*. Simon and Schuster.

Dhanalakshmi, M., Tamilarasi, K., Saravanan, S., Sujatha, G., Boopathi, S., & Associates. (2024). Fog Computing-Based Framework and Solutions for Intelligent Systems: Enabling Autonomy in Vehicles. In *Computational Intelligence for Green Cloud Computing and Digital Waste Management* (pp. 330–356). IGI Global.

Dhanya, D., Kumar, S. S., Thilagavathy, A., Prasad, D., & Boopathi, S. (2023). Data Analytics and Artificial Intelligence in the Circular Economy: Case Studies. In *Intelligent Engineering Applications and Applied Sciences for Sustainability* (pp. 40–58). IGI Global.

Dhillon, P. K. S., & Tinmaz, H. (2024). Immersive realities: A comprehensive guide from virtual reality to metaverse. *Journal for the Education of Gifted Young Scientists*, 12(1), 29–45. 10.17478/jegys.1406024

Dhirani, L. L., Mukhtiar, N., Chowdhry, B. S., & Newe, T. (2023). Ethical Dilemmas and Privacy Issues in Emerging Technologies: A Review. *Sensors (Basel)*, 23(3), 1–18. 10.3390/s23031115136772190

Di Vaio, A., Palladino, R., Hassan, R., & Escobar, O. (2020). Artificial intelligence and business models in the sustainable development goals perspective: A systematic literature review. *Journal of Business Research*, 121, 283–314. 10.1016/j.jbusres.2020.08.019

Diaz-Pacheco, A., Álvarez-Carmona, M. Á., Guerrero-Rodríguez, R., Chávez, L. A. C., Rodríguez-González, A. Y., Ramírez-Silva, J. P., & Aranda, R. (2022, December 13). Artificial intelligence methods to support the research of destination image in tourism. A systematic review. *Journal of Experimental & Theoretical Artificial Intelligence*, 1–31. 10.1080/0952813X.2022.2153276

Dick, E. (2021). Balancing User Privacy and Innovation in Augmented and Virtual Reality, *Information Technology & Innovation Foundation*, 1-27.

Dincelli, E., & Yayla, A. (2022). Immersive virtual reality in the age of the Metaverse: A hybrid-narrative review based on the technology affordance perspective. *The Journal of Strategic Information Systems*, 31(2), 101717. 10.1016/j.jsis.2022.101717

Compilation of References

Doborjeh, Z., Hemmington, N., Doborjeh, M., & Kasabov, N. (2022). Artificial Intelligence: A systematic review of methods and applications in hospitality and tourism. *International Journal of Contemporary Hospitality Management*, 34(3), 1154–1176. 10.1108/IJCHM-06-2021-0767

Doğan, S., & Niyet, İ. Z. (2024). Artificial Intelligence (AI) in Tourism. In Tanrisever, C., Pamukçu, H., & Sharma, A. (Eds.), *Future Tourism Trends* (Vol. 2, pp. 3–21). Emerald Publishing Limited. 10.1108/978-1-83753-970-320241001

Dogru, T., Line, N., Mody, M., Hanks, L., Abbott, J., Acikgoz, F., Assaf, A., Bakir, S., Berbekova, A., Bilgihan, A., Dalton, A., Erkmen, E., Geronasso, M., Gomez, D., Graves, S., Iskender, A., Ivanov, S., Kizildag, M., Lee, M., & Zhang, T. (2023). Generative Artificial Intelligence in the Hospitality and Tourism Industry: Developing a Framework for Future Research. *Journal of Hospitality & Tourism Research (Washington, D.C.)*, 10963480231188663, 10963480231188663. 10.1177/10963480231188663

Domakonda, V. K., Farooq, S., Chinthamreddy, S., Puviarasi, R., Sudhakar, M., & Boopathi, S. (2022). Sustainable Developments of Hybrid Floating Solar Power Plants: Photovoltaic System. In *Human Agro-Energy Optimization for Business and Industry* (pp. 148–167). IGI Global.

Domeke, A., Cimoli, B., & Monroy, I. T. (2022). Integration of network slicing and machine learning into edge networks for low-latency services in 5G and beyond systems. *Applied Sciences (Basel, Switzerland)*, 12(13), 6617. 10.3390/app12136617

Domínguez Vila, T., Alén González, E., & Darcy, S. (2019). Accessible tourism online resources: A Northern European perspective. *Scandinavian Journal of Hospitality and Tourism*, 19(2), 140–156. 10.1080/15022250.2018.1478325

Doshi, Y., Ramachandran, M., Dubey, A., Ankalagi, G., Raje, S., & Munshi, A. (2021). A Review of Opportunities, Applications, and Challenges of XR in Education. *International Journal of Innovative Research in Technology*, 7(9), 292–296.

Dr. Dávid, L. D., & Dadkhah, M. (2023). Artificial intelligence in the tourism sector: Its sustainability and innovation potential. *Equilibrium*, 18(3), 610–613. 10.24136/eq.2023.019

Duangruthai, V., & Leslie, K. (2018). Impact of Social Media on Consumer Behavior. *International Journal of Information and Decision Sciences.*, 11(3), 10014191. 10.1504/IJIDS.2019.10014191

Dunwill, E. (2016). *4 Changes That Will Shape The Classroom Of The Future: Making Education Fully Technological*. eLearning Industry. https://elearningindustry.com/4-changes-will-shape -classroom-of-the-future-making-education-fully-technological

Dutta, I. (2016). Open Educational Resources (OER): Opportunities and Challenges For Indian Higher Education. *Turkish Online Journal of Distance Education*, 0(0). 10.17718/tojde.34669

Edwards, B. (2008). *Understanding Architecture through Drawing*. The Cromwell Press. 10.4324/9780203882436

Enyi, E. P. (2016). *Accounting in the digital age: Creating values with paperless decision support systems*. Babcock University Inaugural Lecture Series.

Fabio, D. F., Cristina, D. L., Simona, D. C., & Antonella, P. (2023). Physical and digital worlds: Implications and opportunities of the metaverse. *Procedia Computer Science*, 217, 1744–1754. 10.1016/j.procs.2022.12.374

Femenia-Serra, F., Neuhofer, B., & Ivars-Baidal, J. A. (2019). Towards a conceptualisation of smart tourists and their role within the smart destination scenario. *Service Industries Journal*, 39(2), 109–133. 10.1080/02642069.2018.1508458

Feng, Y. (2018). Facilitator or inhibitor? The use of 360- degree videos for immersive Brand storytelling. *Journal of Interactive Advertising*, 18(1), 28–42. 10.1080/15252019.2018.1446199

Filieri, R., D'Amico, E., Destefanis, A., Paolucci, E., & Raguseo, E. (2021a). Artificial Intelligence (AI) for tourism: A European-based study on successful AI tourism start-ups. *International Journal of Contemporary Hospitality Management*, 33(11), 4099–4125. 10.1108/IJCHM-02-2021-0220

Findeli, A. (2001). Rethinking Design Education for the 21st Century: Theoretical, Methodological, and Ethical Discussion. *Design Issues*, 17(1), 5–17. 10.1162/07479360152103796

Finegold, D., & Notabartolo, A. S. (2010). 21st century competencies and their impact: An interdisciplinary literature review. *Transforming the US workforce development system, 19*, 19-56.

Fisk, P. (2017). *Education 4.0 … the future of learning will be dramatically different, in school and throughout life*. The Genius Works. http://www.thegeniusworks.com/2017/01/future-education-young-everyone-taught-together/

Flavian, C., Casalo, L., & Wang, D. (2021). Artificial intelligence in hospitality and tourism. *International Journal of Contemporary Hospitality Management*, 33(11).

Flavián, C., Sánchez, I. S., & Orús, C. (2019). The impact of virtual, augmented, and mixed reality technologies on the customer experience. *Journal of Business Research*, 100, 547–560. 10.1016/j.jbusres.2018.10.050

Fornell, C., & Larcker, D. (1981). Evaluating Structural Equation Models with Unobservable Variables and Measurement Error. *JMR, Journal of Marketing Research*, 18(1), 39–50. 10.1177/002224378101800104

Foster, N. (2023). In Foster, N., & Piacentini, M. (Eds.), *21st Century competencies: Challenges in education and assessment in Innovating Assessments to Measure and Support Complex Skills* (pp. 30–44). OECD Publishing.

Fox, D. (2022). Extended Reality (XR) Ethics and Diversity, Inclusion, And Accessibility, *The IEEE Global Initiative on Ethics of Extended Reality (XR) Report*, 1-24.

Fox, D., & Thornton, I. G. (2022). *The IEEE Global Initiative on Ethics of Extended Reality (XR) Report--Extended Reality (XR) Ethics and Diversity, Inclusion, and Accessibility*. IEEE. https://ieeexplore-ieee-org.ezproxy.ump.edu.my/servlet/opac?punumber=9727120

Compilation of References

Freeman, G., Zamanifard, S., Maloney, D., & Acena, D. (2022). Disturbing the Peace: Experiencing and Mitigating Emerging Harassment in Social Virtual Reality. *Proceedings of the ACM on Human-Computer Interaction*. ACM. 10.1145/3512932

Freeman, M. (2014). Advertising the yellow brick road: Historicizing the industrial emergence of transmedia storytelling. *International Journal of Communication*, 8, 2362–2381.

Gao, J., & Zhang, X. (2021). The Applications of Digital Extended Reality in Biomedicine. *Mini Review*, 6(3344), 1–3.

Garrison, D. R., Anderson, T., & Archer, W. (1999). Critical Inquiry in a Text-Based Environment: Computer Conferencing in Higher Education. *The Internet and Higher Education*, 2(2–3), 87–105. 10.1016/S1096-7516(00)00016-6

Garrison, D. R., Anderson, T., & Archer, W. (2001). Critical thinking, cognitive presence, and computer conferencing in distance education. *American Journal of Distance Education*, 15(1), 7–23. 10.1080/08923640109527071

Gasevic, D., Kovanovic, V., Joksimovic, S., & Siemens, G. (2014). Where is research on massive open online courses headed? A data analysis of the MOOC Research Initiative. *International Review of Research in Open and Distance Learning*, 15(5). 10.19173/irrodl.v15i5.1954

Gensler, S., Volckner, F., Liu-Thompkins, Y., & Wiertz, C. (2013). Managing brands in the social media environment. *Journal of Interactive Marketing*, 27(4), 242–256. 10.1016/j.intmar.2013.09.004

Gift, M. D. M., Senthil, T. S., Hasan, D. S., Alagarraja, K., Jayaseelan, P., & Boopathi, S. (2024). Additive Manufacturing and 3D Printing Innovations: Revolutionizing Industry 5.0. In *Technological Advancements in Data Processing for Next Generation Intelligent Systems* (pp. 255–287). IGI Global. 10.4018/979-8-3693-0968-1.ch010

Gill, M., & Mark. (2021). *White Paper-The IEEE Global Initiative on Ethics of Extended Reality (XR) Report--Extended Reality (XR) and the Erosion of Anonymity and Privacy* (Extended Reality (XR) and the Erosion of Anonymity and Privacy-White Paper). IEEE. https://ieeexplore.ieee.org/servlet/opac?punumber=9619997

Glaser, N., Schmidt, M., & Schmidt, C. (2022). Learner experience and evidence of cybersickness: Design tensions in a virtual reality public transportation intervention for autistic adults. *Virtual Reality (Waltham Cross)*, 26(4), 1–20. 10.1007/s10055-022-00661-3

Glaser, N., Thull, C., Schmidt, M., Tennant, A., Moon, J., & Ousley, C. (2023). Learning Experience Design and Unpacking Sociocultural, Technological, and Pedagogical Design Considerations of Spherical Video-Based Virtual Reality Systems for Autistic Learners: A Systematic Literature Review. *Journal of Autism and Developmental Disorders*. 10.1007/s10803-023-06168-338015318

Godwin Immanuel, D., Solaimalai, G., Chandrakala, B. M., Bharath, V. G., Singh, M. K., & Boopathi, S. (2024). Advancements in Electric Vehicle Management System: Integrating Machine Learning and Artificial Intelligence. In *Advances in Web Technologies and Engineering* (pp. 371–391). IGI Global. 10.4018/979-8-3693-1487-6.ch018

Goh, K. Y., & Ping, J. W. (2014). Engaging consumers with advergames: An experimental evaluation of interactivity, fit and expectancy. *Journal of the Association for Information Systems*, 15(7), 388–421. 10.17705/1jais.00366

Goldschmidt, G. (1992). Serial Sketching: Visual Problem Solving in Designing. *Cybernetics and Systems*, 23(2), 191–219. 10.1080/01969729208927457

Goo, J., Huang, C. D., Yoo, C. W., & Koo, C. (2022). Smart Tourism Technologies' Ambidexterity: Balancing Tourist's Worries and Novelty Seeking for Travel Satisfaction. *Information Systems Frontiers*, 24(6), 2139–2158. 10.1007/s10796-021-10233-635103046

Goralski, M. A., & Tan, T. K. (2020). Artificial intelligence and sustainable development. *International Journal of Management Education*, 18(1), 100330. 10.1016/j.ijme.2019.100330

Gorini, A., Capideville, C. S., Leo, G. D., Mantovani, F., & Riva, G. (2011). The role of immersion and narrative in mediated presence: The virtual hospital experience. *Cyberpsychology, Behavior, and Social Networking*, 14(3), 99–105. 10.1089/cyber.2010.010020649451

Granitz, N., & Forman, H. (2015). Building self-Brand connections: Exploring brand stories through a transmedia perspective. *Journal of Brand Management*, 22(1), 38–59. 10.1057/bm.2015.1

Greene, J. (2023). Ethical Design Approaches for Workplace Augmented Reality. *Communication Design Quarterly Review*, 10(4), 16–26. 10.1145/3531210.3531212

Grewal, D., Noble, S. M., Roggeveen, A. L., & Nordfält, J. (2020). The future of in-store technology. *Journal of the Academy of Marketing Science*, 48(1), 96–113. 10.1007/s11747-019-00697-z

Grewal, D., Roggeveen, A. L., & Nordfält, J. (2017). The Future of Retailing. *Journal of Retailing*, 93(1), 1–6. 10.1016/j.jretai.2016.12.008

Grosman, L. (2017). The future of retail: How we'll be shopping in 10 Years. *Forbes*. https://www.forbes.com/ sites/forbescommunicationscouncil/2017/06/20/the-future-of-retailhow-well-be-shoppingin-10- years/#21188bbe58a6

Grundner, L., & Neuhofer, B. (2021). The bright and dark sides of artificial Intelligence: A future perspective on tourist destination experiences. *Journal of Destination Marketing & Management*, 19, 100511. 10.1016/j.jdmm.2020.100511

Grzybowska, K., & Łupicka, A. (2017). *Key competencies for Industry 4.0.* Volkson Press. 10.26480/icemi.01.2017.250.253

Gupta, B. B., Gaurav, A., Panigrahi, P. K., & Arya, V. (2023). Analysis of artificial intelligence-based technologies and approaches on sustainable entrepreneurship. *Technological Forecasting and Social Change*, 186, 122152. 10.1016/j.techfore.2022.122152

Compilation of References

Gupta, K., Mane, P., Rajankar, O. S., Bhowmik, M., Jadhav, R., Yadav, S., Rawandale, S., & Chobe, S. V. (2023). Harnessing AI for strategic decision-making and business performance optimization. *International Journal of Intelligent Systems and Applications in Engineering*, 11(10s), 893–912.

Gupta, M. S., Keen, M. M., Shah, M. A., & Verdier, M. G. (2017). *Digital revolutions in public finance.* International Monetary Fund.

Gutiérrez, J. M., Mora, C. E., Diaz, B. A., & Marrero, A. G. (2017). Virtual technologies trends in education. *Eurasia Journal of Mathematics, Science and Technology Education*, 13(2), 469–486. 10.12973/eurasia.2017.00626a

Hair, J. F., Sarstedt, M., Hopkins, L., & Kuppelwieser, V. G. (2014). Partial least squares structural equation modeling (PLS-SEM): An emerging tool in business research. *European Business Review*, 26(2), 106–121. 10.1108/EBR-10-2013-0128

Hajli, N. (2014). A study of the impact of social media on consumers. *International Journal of Market Research*, 56(3), 387–404. 10.2501/IJMR-2014-025

Hajli, N. (2015). Social commerce construct and consumer's intention to buy. *International Journal of Information Management*, 35(2), 183–191. 10.1016/j.ijinfomgt.2014.12.005

Hamelink, C.J. (1997). *New information and communication technologies, social development and cultural change.*

Hanane, A., & Youssef, M. (2023). Exploring the Full Potentials of IoT for Better Financial Growth and Stability: A Comprehensive Survey. *Sensors (Basel)*, 23(19), 8015. 10.3390/s2319801537836845

Handa, M., & Aul, E. (n.d.). Immersive technology–uses, challenges and opportunities. *International Journal of Computing & Business Research.* http://researchmanuscripts.com/isociety2012/12.pdf

Hand, D. J. (2018). Aspects of Data Ethics in a Changing World: Where Are We Now? *Big Data*, 6(3), 176–190. 10.1089/big.2018.008330283727

Hang, Y., Li, Y., & Cai, Z. (2023). Security and Privacy in Metaverse: A Comprehensive Survey. *Big Data Mining and Analytics*, 6(2), 234–247. 10.26599/BDMA.2022.9020047

Hansdotter, Y. (2023). *The Affordances of Immersive Virtual Reality for Stimulating Prosocial Behaviour: A Mixed-Methods Pro-Environmental Intervention Study.* University College Dublin. Dublin. http://hdl.handle.net/10197/24360

Harikaran, M., Boopathi, S., Gokulakannan, S., & Poonguzhali, M. (2023). Study on the Source of E-Waste Management and Disposal Methods. In *Sustainable Approaches and Strategies for E-Waste Management and Utilization* (pp. 39–60). IGI Global. 10.4018/978-1-6684-7573-7.ch003

Hassenzahl, M., Eckoldt, K., Diefenbac, S., Laschke, M., Len, E., & Kim, J. (2013). Designing Moments of Meaning and Pleasure. Experience Design and Happiness. *International Journal of Design*, 7(3), 21–31.

Hawkins, D. I., Best, R. J., & Coney, K. A. (2004). *Consumer Behavior, Building Marketing Strategy*. McGraw-Hill.

Heikkilä, M. (2024). *VR headsets can be hacked with an Inception-style attack*. MIT Technology Review.

Henderson, S., & Ostashewski, N. (2018). Barriers, incentives, and benefits of the open educational resources (OER) movement: An exploration into instructor perspectives. *First Monday*. 10.5210/fm.v23i12.9172

Herdin, T., & Egger, R. (2018). Beyond the digital divide: Tourism, ICTs and culture - a highly promising alliance. *International Journal of Digital Culture and Electronic Tourism*, 2(4), 322. 10.1504/IJDCET.2018.092182

Hesket, J. (2002). *Toothpicks and Logos Design in Everyday Life*. Oxford University Press. 10.1093/oso/9780192803214.001.0001

Hilken, T., Keeling, D. I. K., de Ruyter, K., Mahr, D., & Chylinski, M. (2020). Seeing eye to eye: Social augmented reality and shared decision making in the marketplace. *Journal of the Academy of Marketing Science*, 48(2), 143–164. 10.1007/s11747-019-00688-0

Hirzle, T., Müller, F., Draxler, F., Schmitz, M., Knierim, P., & Hornbæk, K. (2023). When XR and AI Meet—A Scoping Review on Extended Reality and Artificial Intelligence. *Proceedings of the 2023 CHI Conference on Human Factors in Computing Systems*. ACM. 10.1145/3544548.3581072

Hollebeek, L. D., Clark, M. K., Andreassen, T. W., Sigurdsson, V., & Smith, D. (2020). Virtual reality through the customer journey: Framework and propositions. *Journal of Retailing and Consumer Services*, 55, 102056. 10.1016/j.jretconser.2020.102056

Holt, J. (2004). *How brands become icons: The principles of cultural branding*. Harvard Business Press.

Homayouni, C., & Zytko, D. (2023). Consensual XR: A consent-based design framework for mitigating harassment and harm against marginalized users in social VR and AR. *2023 IEEE International Symposium on Mixed and Augmented Reality Adjunct (ISMAR-Adjunct)*. IEEE. 10.1109/ISMAR-Adjunct60411.2023.00077

Ho, P.-T. (2022). Smart Tourism Recommendation Method in Southeast Asia under Big Data and Artificial Intelligence Algorithms. *Mobile Information Systems*, 2022, 1–11. 10.1155/2022/4047501

Hosfelt, D. (2019). *Making ethical decisions for the immersive web*. http://arxiv.org/abs/1905.06995

Hosseini, M. M., Hooshmandja, M., & Hosseini, T. M. (2023). Ethical Dilemmas of Mixed and Extended Reality. *Journal of Medical Education*, 22(1), 1–2. 10.5812/jme-133854

Hoyer, W. D., Kroschke, M., Schmitt, D. K., Kraume, V. S., & Shankar, V. (2020). Transforming the customer experience through new technologies. *Journal of Interactive Marketing*, 51, 57–71. 10.1016/j.intmar.2020.04.001

Hsiao, S. H., Wang, Y. Y., & Lin, T. L. (2024). The impact of low-immersion virtual reality on product sales: Insights from the real estate industry. *Decision Support Systems*, 178, 114131. 10.1016/j.dss.2023.114131

Huang, H. (2024). Artificial Intelligence and Productivity Improvement in the Digital Economy. *Finance & Economics, 1*(5).

Huang, T. C., Chen, C. C., & Chou, Y. W. (2016). Animating eco-education: To see, feel, and discover in an augmented reality-based experiential learning environment. *Computers & Education, 96*(1), 72-82. Elsevier Ltd. https://www.learntechlib.org/p/201462/

Huang, C. D., Goo, J., Nam, K., & Yoo, C. W. (2017). Smart tourism technologies in travel planning: The role of exploration and exploitation. *Information & Management*, 54(6), 757–770. 10.1016/j.im.2016.11.010

Huang, T.-L., & Liao, S.-L. (2017). Creating e-shopping multisensory flow experience through augmented-reality interactive technology. *Internet Research*, 27(2), 449–475. 10.1108/IntR-11-2015-0321

Hudson, S., Matson-Barkat, S., Pallamin, N., & Jegou, G. (2019). With or without you? Interaction and immersion in a virtual reality experience. *Journal of Business Research*, 100, 459–468. 10.1016/j.jbusres.2018.10.062

Hussain, Z., Babe, M., Saravanan, S., Srimathy, G., Roopa, H., & Boopathi, S. (2023). Optimizing Biomass-to-Biofuel Conversion: IoT and AI Integration for Enhanced Efficiency and Sustainability. In *Circular Economy Implementation for Sustainability in the Built Environment* (pp. 191–214). IGI Global.

Hu, T. (2017). Overview of augmented reality technology. [in Chinese]. *Computer Knowledge and Technology*, (34), 194196.

Iden, J., Bygstad, B., Osmundsen, K. S., Costabile, C., & Øvrelid, E. (2021). Digital platform ecosystem governance: Preliminary findings and research agenda. *Norsk IKT-Konferanse for Forskning Og Utdanning, 2*.

Ingle, R. B., Swathi, S., Mahendran, G., Senthil, T., Muralidharan, N., & Boopathi, S. (2023). Sustainability and Optimization of Green and Lean Manufacturing Processes Using Machine Learning Techniques. In *Circular Economy Implementation for Sustainability in the Built Environment* (pp. 261–285). IGI Global. 10.4018/978-1-6684-8238-4.ch012

Iqbal, M., Xu, X., Nallur, V., Scanlon, M., & Campbell, A. (2023). *Security, Ethics, and Privacy Issues in the Remote Extended Reality for Education*. Springer. 10.1007/978-981-99-4958-8_16

Iqbal, S. A., Ashiq, M., Rehman, S. U., Rashid, S., & Tayyab, N. (2022). Students' perceptions and experiences of online education in Pakistani Universities and Higher Education Institutes during COVID-19. *Education Sciences*, 12(3), 166. 10.3390/educsci12030166

Isensee, C., Griese, K.-M., & Teuteberg, F. (2021). Sustainable artificial intelligence: A corporate culture perspective. *Sustainability Management Forum| NachhaltigkeitsManagementForum, 29*(3), 217–230.

Itin, C. M. (1997). *The Orientation of Social Work Faculty to the Philosophy of Experiential Education in the Classroom.* [Unpublished Dissertation, University of Denver].

Jabeen, F., Al Zaidi, S., & Al Dhaheri, M. H. (2022). Automation and artificial intelligence in hospitality and tourism. *Tourism Review, 77*(4), 1043–1061. 10.1108/TR-09-2019-0360

Jaehnig, J. (2023, June 21). *The Intersections of Artificial Intelligence and Extended Reality.* ArPost. https://arpost.co/2023/06/21/intersections-artificial-intelligence-xr/

Jahid, A., Alsharif, M. H., & Hall, T. J. (2023). The convergence of blockchain, IoT and 6G: Potential, opportunities, challenges and research roadmap. *Journal of Network and Computer Applications, 217*, 103677. 10.1016/j.jnca.2023.103677

Janardhana, K., Singh, V., Singh, S. N., Babu, T. R., Bano, S., & Boopathi, S. (2023). Utilization Process for Electronic Waste in Eco-Friendly Concrete: Experimental Study. In *Sustainable Approaches and Strategies for E-Waste Management and Utilization* (pp. 204–223). IGI Global.

Jay, M. (2012). *Deneyim Şarkıları, Evrensel Bir Tema Üzerine Modern Çeşitlemeler. Çev: Barış Engin Aksoy.* Metis Yayınları, İstanbul.

Jeffrey, T. H., & Jeremy, N. B. (2021). The Social Impact of Deepfakes. *Cyberpsychology, Behavior, and Social Networking, 24*(3), 149–152. 10.1089/cyber.2021.29208.jth33760669

Jensen, L., & Konradsen, F. (2018). A review of the use of virtual reality head-mounted displays in education and training. *Education and Information Technologies, 23*(4), 1–15. 10.1007/s10639-017-9676-0

Jeong, M., & Shin, H. H. (2020). Tourists' Experiences with Smart Tourism Technology at Smart Destinations and Their Behavior Intentions. *Journal of Travel Research, 59*(8), 1464–1477. 10.1177/0047287519883034

Jessen, A., Hilken, T., Chylinski, M., Mahr, D., Heller, J., Keeling, D. I., & de Ruyter, K. (2020). The playground effect: How augmented reality drives creative consumer engagement. *Journal of Business Research, 116*, 85–98. 10.1016/j.jbusres.2020.05.002

Jeya, R., Venkatakrishnan, G. R., Rengaraj, R., Rajalakshmi, M., Pradeep Mohan Kumar, K., & Boopathi, S. (2023). Water Resource Managements in Soil and Soilless Irrigation Systems Using AI Techniques. In *Advances in Environmental Engineering and Green Technologies* (pp. 245–266). IGI Global. 10.4018/979-8-3693-0338-2.ch014

Joakim, L., Matti, M., & Matti, M. (2024). Ethics-based AI auditing: A systematic literature review on conceptualizations of ethical principles and knowledge contributions to stakeholders. *Information & Management, 61*(5), 103969. 10.1016/j.im.2024.103969

Compilation of References

Jobin, A., Ienca, M., & Vayena, E. (2019). The Global Landscape of AI Ethics Guidelines. *Nature Machine Intelligence*, 1(9), 389–399. 10.1038/s42256-019-0088-2

Johnson, L., & Keasler, T. (1993). An industry profile of corporate real estate. *Journal of Real Estate Research*, 8(4), 455–473. 10.1080/10835547.1993.12090732

Jonassen, D. (2000). Transforming Learning with Technology: Beyond Modernism and Post-Modernism or Whoever Controls the Technology Creates the Reality. *Educational Technology*, 40, 101–110. 10.1007/978-94-6209-269-3_7

Jonathan, H., Magd, H., & Khan, S. A. (2024). Artificial Intelligence and Augmented Reality: A Business Fortune to Sustainability in the Digital Age. In Singh, N., Kansra, P., & Gupta, S. L. (Eds.), *Navigating the Digital Landscape: Understanding Customer Behaviour in the Online World* (pp. 85–105). Emerald Publishing Limited. 10.1108/978-1-83549-272-720241005

Julia, A., Marta, B., Kathleen, R., & Benoit, B. (2023). *Extended Reality of socio-motor interactions: Current Trends and Ethical Considerations for Mixed Reality Environments Design*. ICMI '23 Companion: Companion Publication of the 25th International Conference on Multimodal Interaction, Paris, France. 10.1145/3610661.3617989

Ka,. R. P., Pandraju, T. K. S., Boopathi, S., Saravanan, P., Rathan, S. K., & Sathish, T. (2023). Hybrid Deep Learning Technique for Optimal Wind Mill Speed Estimation. *2023 7th International Conference on Electronics, Communication and Aerospace Technology (ICECA)*, (pp. 181–186). IEEE.

Kabha, R. (2019). Ethical Challenges of Digital Immersive and VR, *Journal of Content. Community & Communication*, 9(5), 41–49. 10.31620/JCCC.06.19/07

Kade, D. (2016). Ethics of Virtual Reality Applications in Computer Game Production. *Philosophies*, 1. .10.3390/philosophies1010073

Kaimara, P., Oikonomou, A., & Deliyannis, I. (2022). Could virtual reality applications pose real risks to children and adolescents? A systematic review of ethical issues and concerns. *Virtual Reality (Waltham Cross)*, 26(2), 697–735. 10.1007/s10055-021-00563-w34366688

Kalaiselvi, T., Saravanan, G., Haritha, T., Babu, A. V. S., Sakthivel, M., & Boopathi, S. (2024). A Study on the Landscape of Serverless Computing: Technologies and Tools for Seamless Implementation. In *Serverless Computing Concepts, Technology and Architecture* (pp. 260–282). IGI Global. 10.4018/979-8-3693-1682-5.ch016

Kamil, M. H. F. M., Yahya, N., Abidin, I. S. Z., & Norizan, A. R. (2021). Development of Virtual Reality Technology: Home Tour for Real Estate Purchase Decision Making. *Malaysian Journal of Computer Science*, 85–93. 10.22452/mjcs.sp2021no1.8

Kangrga, M., Dejan, N., Milena, S.-M., Ljiljana, R., Tatjana, K., Goran, D., & Milan, L. (2024). Recognizing the Frequency of Exposure to Cyberbullying in Children: The Results of the National HBSC Study in Serbia. *Children (Basel, Switzerland)*, 11(2), 172. 10.3390/children1102017238397284

Karthik, V. M. (2023). *The Ethics of Extended Realities: Insights from a Systematic Literature Review*. Uppsala University. https://www.diva-portal.org/smash/get/diva2:1773547/FULLTEXT01.pdf

Kavitha, C., Varalatchoumy, M., Mithuna, H., Bharathi, K., Geethalakshmi, N., & Boopathi, S. (2023). Energy Monitoring and Control in the Smart Grid: Integrated Intelligent IoT and ANFIS. In *Applications of Synthetic Biology in Health, Energy, and Environment* (pp. 290–316). IGI Global.

Kee, T., Zhang, H., & King, R. (2023). An empirical study on immersive technology in synchronous hybrid learning in design education. *International Journal of Technology and Design Education*. Advance online publication. 10.1007/s10798-023-09855-5

Keleko, A. T., Kamsu-Foguem, B., Ngouna, R. H., & Tongne, A. (2022). Artificial intelligence and real-time predictive maintenance in industry 4.0: A bibliometric analysis. *AI and Ethics*, 2(4), 553–577. 10.1007/s43681-021-00132-6

Ketaki, S., Soon, Y. O., & Jeremy, B. (2017). *Virtual Reality and Prosocial Behavior*. Cambridge University Press. 10.1017/9781316676202.022

Khan, M., Haleem, A., & Javaid, M. (2023). Changes and improvements in Industry 5.0: A strategic approach to overcome the challenges of Industry 4.0. *Green Technologies and Sustainability*, 1(2), 100020. 10.1016/j.grets.2023.100020

Khan, S. A., & Magd, H. (2021). Empirical Examination of MS Teams in Conducting Webinar: Evidence from International Online Program conducted in Oman. *Journal of Content. Community and Communication*, 14(8), 159–175. 10.31620/JCCC.12.21/13

Khan, S. A., & Magd, H. (2023). New Technology Anxiety and Acceptance of Technology: An Appraisal of MS Teams. In *Advances in Distance Learning in Times of Pandemic* (pp. 105–134). CRC Press, Taylor and Francis. 10.1201/9781003322252-5

Khan, S. A., Narula, S., Kansra, P., Naim, A., & Kalra, D. (2024). Should Marketing and Public Relations be Part of the Institutional Accreditation Criterion of Business Schools? An Appraisal of Accreditation Criterion of Selected Accreditation Agencies. In Naim, A. (Ed.), *Accreditation Processes and Frameworks in Higher Education* (pp. 349–375). Nova Science Publishers. 10.52305/QUVJ6658

Khatri, B., Nandini, G., & Khan, S. A. (2024). Transition From Outcome-Based Learning to Global Accreditation of Top Universities of India: Elevating the Bar of Educational Excellence. In Naim, A., Saklani, A., Khan, S., & Malik, P. (Eds.), *Evaluating Global Accreditation Standards for Higher Education* (pp. 278–292). IGI Global. 10.4018/979-8-3693-1698-6.ch019

Kim, M. J., Hall, C. M., Chung, N., Kim, M., & Sohn, K. (2023). Why do tourists use public transport in Korea? The roles of artificial intelligence knowledge are environmental, social, governance, and sustainability. *Asia Pacific Journal of Tourism Research*, 28(5), 467–484. 10.1080/10941665.2023.2247099

Compilation of References

Kipper, G., & Rampolla, J. (2012). *Augmented Reality: An Emerging Technologies Guide to AR.* Elsevier.

Kirtil, I. G., & Aşkun, V. (2021). Artificial Intelligence in Tourism: A Review And Bibliometrics Research. [AHTR]. *Advances in Hospitality and Tourism Research*, 9(1), 205–233. 10.30519/ahtr.801690

Knani, M., Echchakoui, S., & Ladhari, R. (2022). Artificial intelligence in tourism and hospitality: Bibliometric analysis and research agenda. *International Journal of Hospitality Management*, 107. 10.1016/j.ijhm.2022.103317

Knihová, L., & Hronova, S. (2019). *Digital Entrepreneurship: Reskilling and Upskilling with Mobile MOOCs.*

Koshariya, A. K., Khatoon, S., Marathe, A. M., Suba, G. M., Baral, D., & Boopathi, S. (2023). Agricultural Waste Management Systems Using Artificial Intelligence Techniques. In *AI-Enabled Social Robotics in Human Care Services* (pp. 236–258). IGI Global. 10.4018/978-1-6684-8171-4.ch009

Kotler, P., Kartajaya, H., & Setiawan, I. (2017). *Marketing 4.0: moving from traditional to digital.* Wiley: Harvard Business School Press.

Kotler, P., Kartajaya, H., & Setiawan, I. (2021). *Marketing 5.0: Technology for humanity.* John Wiley & Sons.

Kristensson, P. (2019). Future service technologies and value creation. *Journal of Services Marketing*, 33(4), 502–506. 10.1108/JSM-01-2019-0031

Ksentini, A., Jebalia, M., & Tabbane, S. (2021). IoT/Cloud-enabled smart services: A review on QoS requirements in fog environment and a proposed approach based on priority classification technique. *International Journal of Communication Systems*, 34(2), e4269. 10.1002/dac.4269

Ku, E. C. S., & Chen, C.-D. (2024). Artificial intelligence innovation of tourism businesses: From satisfied tourists to continued service usage intention. *International Journal of Information Management*, 102757, 102757. 10.1016/j.ijinfomgt.2024.102757

Kugler, L. (2022). Technology's Impact on Morality. *Communications of the ACM*, 65(7), 15–16. 10.1145/3516516

Kulkov, I., Kulkova, J., Rohrbeck, R., Menvielle, L., Kaartemo, V., & Makkonen, H. (2023). Artificial intelligence-driven sustainable development: Examining organizational, technical, and processing approaches to achieving global goals. *Sustainable Development.*

Kumar, A., & Singh, M. (2020). Leveraging Artificial Intelligence for Sustainable Tourism Development: A Case Study of Kerala, India. *International Journal of Recent Technology and Engineering.*

Kumar, M., Kumar, K., Sasikala, P., Sampath, B., Gopi, B., & Sundaram, S. (2023). Sustainable Green Energy Generation From Waste Water: IoT and ML Integration. In *Sustainable Science and Intelligent Technologies for Societal Development* (pp. 440–463). IGI Global.

Kumar, P. R., Meenakshi, S., Shalini, S., Devi, S. R., & Boopathi, S. (2023). Soil Quality Prediction in Context Learning Approaches Using Deep Learning and Blockchain for Smart Agriculture. In *Effective AI, Blockchain, and E-Governance Applications for Knowledge Discovery and Management* (pp. 1–26). IGI Global. 10.4018/978-1-6684-9151-5.ch001

Kumara, V., & Sharma, M. D., Samson Isaac, J., Saravanan, S., Suganthi, D., & Boopathi, S. (2023). An AI-Integrated Green Power Monitoring System: Empowering Small and Medium Enterprises. In *Advances in Environmental Engineering and Green Technologies* (pp. 218–244). IGI Global. 10.4018/979-8-3693-0338-2.ch013

Kumar, V., Rajan, B., Venkatesan, R., & Lecinski, J. (2019). Understanding the Role of artificial intelligence in personalized engagement marketing. *California Management Review*, 61(4), 135–155. 10.1177/0008125619859317

Kumlu, S. T., Samancıoğlu, E., & Özkul, E. (2024). Reality Technologies (AR, VR, MR, XR) in Tourism. Tanrisever, C., Pamukçu, H. and Sharma, A. (eds.) *Future Tourism Trends Volume 2 (Building the Future of Tourism)*. Emerald. 10.1108/978-1-83753-970-320241007

Kunkel, N., & Soechtig, S. (2017). *Mixed reality: Experiences get more intuitive, immersive and empowering*. Deloitte University Press. https://www2.deloitte.com/uk/en/insights/focus/tech-trends/2017/mixed-reality-applications-potential.html

Kurelovic, E. (2016). *Advantages and Limitations of Usage of Open Educational Resources in Small Countries*.

Lai, W. (2024). *Application of Computer VR Technology in Digital Media System Design*. Springer. 10.1007/978-981-99-9299-7_28

Lambert, J. L., & Fisher, J. L. (2013). Community of Inquiry Framework: Establishing Community in an Online Course. *Journal of Interactive Online Learning*, 12(1). Www.Ncolr.Org/Jiol

Lawson, R. (2000). Consumer Behavior. In *Marketing Theory*. Research Gate.

Lee, H., Lee, J., Chung, N., & Koo, C. (2018). Tourists' happiness: Are there smart tourism technology effects? *Asia Pacific Journal of Tourism Research*, 23(5), 486–501. 10.1080/10941665.2018.1468344

Lee, S., Kim, D., Jeong, Y., & Ryu, J. (2024). Exploring Embodied Learning and XR Technologies in Online Education. In *Humanizing Online Teaching and Learning in Higher Education* (pp. 263–286). IGI Global. 10.4018/979-8-3693-0762-5.ch013

Lemmens, J. S., Simon, M., & Sumter, S. R. (2022). Fear and loathing in VR: The emotional and physiological effects of immersive games. *Virtual Reality (Waltham Cross)*, 26(1), 223–234. 10.1007/s10055-021-00555-w

Compilation of References

Le, V. H., Nguyen, H. T. T., Nguyen, N., & Pervan, S. (2020). Development and validation of a scale measuring hotel website service quality (HWebSQ). *Tourism Management Perspectives*, 35, 100697. 10.1016/j.tmp.2020.100697

Liang, H. & Xiaoming, B. (2013). *Application Research of Virtual Reality Technology in Electronic Technique Teaching*. Springer. .10.1007/978-3-642-31656-2_22

Ligthart, S., Meynen, G., Biller-Andorno, N., Kooijmans, T., & Kellmeyer, P. (2021). Is Virtually Everything Possible? The Relevance of Ethics and Human Rights for Introducing Extended Reality in Forensic Psychiatry. *AJOB Neuroscience*, 13(3), 144–157. 10.1080/21507740.2021. 189848933780323

Li, K., Kim, D. J., Lang, K. R., Kauffman, R. J., & Naldi, M. (2020). How should we understand the digital economy in Asia? Critical assessment and research agenda. *Electronic Commerce Research and Applications*, 44, 101004. 10.1016/j.elerap.2020.10100432922241

Lim, H., & Childs, M. (2020). Visual storytelling on Instagram: Branded photo narrative and the role of telepresence. *Journal of Research in Interactive Marketing*, 14(1), 33–50. 10.1108/JRIM-09-2018-0115

Lindholm, A. L., Gibler, K., & Leväinen, K. (2006). Modeling the value-adding attributes of real estate to the wealth maximization of the firm. *Journal of Real Estate Research*, 28(4), 445–476. 10.1080/10835547.2006.12091187

Liu, X., Wang, D., & Gretzel, U. (2022). On-site decision-making in smartphone-mediated contexts. *Tourism Management, 88*, 104424. 10.1016/j.tourman.2021.104424

Liu, Y., Zhao, J., Xiong, Z., Niyato, D., Yuen, C., Pan, C., & Huang, B. (2020). Intelligent reflecting surface meets mobile edge computing: Enhancing wireless communications for computation offloading. *arXiv Preprint arXiv:2001.07449*.

Liu, H.-Y., & Sobocki, V. (2022). Influence, Immersion, Intensity, Integration, Interaction: Five Frames for the Future of AI. *Law & Policy*, 35, 541–560. 10.1007/978-94-6265-523-2_27

Liu, M., & Yu, D. (2023). Towards intelligent E-learning systems. *Education and Information Technologies*, 28(7), 7845–7876. 10.1007/s10639-022-11479-636532790

Loke, S.-K. (2015). How do virtual world experiences bring about learning? A critical review of theories. *Australasian Journal of Educational Technology*, 31(1), 112–122. 10.14742/ajet.2532

Looser, J., Billinghurst, M., & Cockburn, A. (2004). Through the looking glass: The use of lenses as an interface tool for augmented reality interfaces. In *2nd intl. Conference on computer graphics and interactive techniques in Australasia and South East Asia* (pp. 204–211).

López, B. R. (2024). *Ethics of Virtual Reality*. Springer Nature. 10.1007/978-3-031-48135-2_6

Lüdeke-Freund, F. (2020). Sustainable entrepreneurship, innovation, and business models: Integrative framework and propositions for future research. *Business Strategy and the Environment*, 29(2), 665–681. 10.1002/bse.2396

Luhmann, N. (2000). Familiarity, confidence, trust: Problems and alternatives. Trust. *Making and Breaking Cooperative Relations*, 6(1), 94–107.

Lu, J., Li, L., Chen, G., Shen, D., Pham, K., & Blasch, E. (2017). Machine learning based intelligent cognitive network using fog computing. *Sensors and Systems for Space Applications X*, 10196, 149–157.

Luo, T., Hostetler, K., Freeman, C., & Stefaniak, J. (2020). The power of open: Benefits, barriers, and strategies for integration of open educational resources. *Open Learning*, 35(2), 140–158. 10.1080/02680513.2019.1677222

Lv, H., Shi, S., & Gursoy, D. (2022). A look back and a leap forward: A review and synthesis of big data and artificial intelligence literature in hospitality and tourism. *Journal of Hospitality Marketing & Management*, 31(2), 145–175. 10.1080/19368623.2021.1937434

Macpherson, C., & Keppell, M. (1998). Virtual reality: What is the state of play in education? *Australasian Journal of Educational Technology*, 14(1), 60–74. 10.14742/ajet.1929

Madary, M., & Metzinger, T. K. (2016). Real virtuality: A Code of Ethical Conduct. Recommendations for Good Scientific Practice and the Consumers of VR-Technology. *Frontiers in Robotics and AI*, 3(3), 1–23.

Maddikunta, P. K. R., Pham, Q.-V., Prabadevi, B., Deepa, N., Dev, K., Gadekallu, T. R., Ruby, R., & Liyanage, M. (2022). Industry 5.0: A survey on enabling technologies and potential applications. *Journal of Industrial Information Integration*, 26, 100257. 10.1016/j.jii.2021.100257

Magd, H., Jonathan, H., & Khan, S. A. (2023). Education Situation in Online Education before the Pandemic and in the Time of Pandemic. *In Advances in Distance Learning in Times of Pandemic (Eds.), 53-72.* CRC Press, Taylor and Francis. 10.1201/9781003322252-3

Magd, H., & Khan, S. A. (2022a). Strategic Framework for Entrepreneurship Education in Promoting Social Entrepreneurship in GCC Countries During and Post COVID-19. In Magd, H., Singh, D., Syed, R., & Spicer, D. (Eds.), *International Perspectives on Value Creation and Sustainability Through Social Entrepreneurship* (pp. 61–75). IGI Global. 10.4018/978-1-6684-4666-9.ch004

Magd, H., & Khan, S. A. (2022b). Effectiveness of using online teaching platforms as communication tools in higher education institutions in Oman: Stakeholders perspectives. *Journal of Content. Community and Communication*, 16, 148–160. 10.31620/JCCC.12.22/13

Mageswari, D. U., Kareemullah, H., Jithesh, K., Boopathi, S., Rachel, P. M. P. P., & Ramkumar, M. S. (2024). Experimental investigation of mechanical properties and multi-objective optimization of electronic, glass, and ceramic waste–mixed concrete. *Environmental Science and Pollution Research International*. 10.1007/s11356-024-33751-738806982

Maguluri, L. P., Ananth, J., Hariram, S., Geetha, C., Bhaskar, A., & Boopathi, S. (2023). Smart Vehicle-Emissions Monitoring System Using Internet of Things (IoT). In *Handbook of Research on Safe Disposal Methods of Municipal Solid Wastes for a Sustainable Environment* (pp. 191–211). IGI Global.

Maguluri, L. P., Arularasan, A., & Boopathi, S. (2023). Assessing Security Concerns for AI-Based Drones in Smart Cities. In *Effective AI, Blockchain, and E-Governance Applications for Knowledge Discovery and Management* (pp. 27–47). IGI Global. 10.4018/978-1-6684-9151-5.ch002

Maheswari, B. U., Imambi, S. S., Hasan, D., Meenakshi, S., Pratheep, V., & Boopathi, S. (2023). Internet of things and machine learning-integrated smart robotics. In *Global Perspectives on Robotics and Autonomous Systems: Development and Applications* (pp. 240–258). IGI Global. 10.4018/978-1-6684-7791-5.ch010

Maimela, C. & others. (2024). *Artificial Intelligence and its Impact on Library Staff Learning and Development.*

Majid, G. M., Tussyadiah, I., Kim, Y. R., & Pal, A. (2023). Intelligent automation for sustainable tourism: A systematic review. *Journal of Sustainable Tourism*, 31(11), 2421–2440. 10.1080/09669582.2023.2246681

Majumdar, M. (2022). *A Comprehensive Framework for AR/VR Technology in India.*

Malathi, J., Kusha, K., Isaac, S., Ramesh, A., Rajendiran, M., & Boopathi, S. (2024). IoT-Enabled Remote Patient Monitoring for Chronic Disease Management and Cost Savings: Transforming Healthcare. In *Advances in Explainable AI Applications for Smart Cities* (pp. 371–388). IGI Global.

Maloney, D., Freeman, G., & Robb, A. (2021). Social Virtual Reality: Ethical Considerations and Future Directions for An Emerging Research Space, *2021 IEEE Conference on Virtual Reality and 3D User Interfaces Abstracts and Workshops*. IEEE. , 271-277. 10.1109/VRW52623.2021.00056

Mamedov, O., Tumanyan, Y., Ishchenko-Padukova, O., & Movchan, I. (2018). Sustainable economic development and post-economy of artificial intelligence. *Entrep. Sustain*, 2018(2), 6. 10.9770/jesi.2018.6.2(37)

Manic, M. (2015). Marketing Engagement Through Visual Content. *Bulletin of the Transilvania University of Brasov. Series V, Economic Sciences*, 57, 89.

Marcolin, B. L., Compeau, D. R., Munro, M. C., & Huff, S. L. (2000). Assessing User Competence: Conceptualization and Measurement. *Information Systems Research*, 11(1), 37–60. 10.1287/isre.11.1.37.11782

Marr, D. (1982). *Vision: A Computational Investigation into the human representation and processing of visual information*. MIT Press.

Matt, C. (2018). Fog computing: Complementing cloud computing to facilitate industry 4.0. *Business & Information Systems Engineering*, 60(4), 351–355. 10.1007/s12599-018-0540-6

Mauri, M., Rancati, G., Riva, G., & Gaggioli, A. (2024). Comparing the effects of immersive and non-immersive real estate experience on behavioral intentions. *Computers in Human Behavior*, 150, 107996. 10.1016/j.chb.2023.107996

Mazurchenko, A., & Maršíková, K. (2019). Digitally-powered human resource management: Skills and roles in the digital era. *Acta Informatica Pragensia*, 8(2), 72–87. 10.18267/j.aip.125

Méndez-Picazo, M.-T., Galindo-Martín, M.-A., & Castaño-Martínez, M.-S. (2021). Effects of sociocultural and economic factors on social entrepreneurship and sustainable development. *Journal of Innovation & Knowledge*, 6(2), 69–77. 10.1016/j.jik.2020.06.001

Mer, A., & Srivastava, A. (2023). Employee engagement in the new normal: Artificial intelligence as a buzzword or a game changer? In *The Adoption and Effect of Artificial Intelligence on Human Resources Management, Part A* (pp. 15–46). Emerald Publishing Limited.

Metz, R. (2014). Google Glass Is Dead; Long Live Smart Glasses. *MIT Technology Review*. https://www.technologyreview.com/2014/11/26/169918/google-glass-is-dead-long-live-smart-glasses/

Mhlanga, D. (2020). Industry 4.0 in finance: The impact of artificial intelligence (ai) on digital financial inclusion. *International Journal of Financial Studies*, 8(3), 45. 10.3390/ijfs8030045

Mhlanga, D. (2021). Artificial intelligence in the industry 4.0, and its impact on poverty, innovation, infrastructure development, and the sustainable development goals: Lessons from emerging economies? *Sustainability (Basel)*, 13(11), 5788. 10.3390/su13115788

Middleton, M. (2022). Business, Finance, and Economics. *The IEEE Global Initiative on Ethics of Extended Reality (XR) Report--Business, Finance, and Economics*, (pp. 1-30). IEEE. https://ieeexplore-ieee-org.ezproxy.ump.edu.my/servlet/opac?punumber=9740584

Mikropoulos, T. A. (2006). Presence: A unique characteristic in educational virtual environments. *Virtual Reality (Waltham Cross)*, 10(3-4), 197–206. 10.1007/s10055-006-0039-1

Milgram, P., & Kishino, F. (1994). *A Taxonomy of Mixed Reality Visual Displays*. Institute of Electronics, Information and Communication Engineers (IEICE) Transactions on Information and Systems. https://search.ieice.org/bin/summary.php?id=e77-d_12_1321. https://search.ieice.org/bin/summary.php?id=e77-d_12_1321

Milgram, P., Takemura, H., Utsumi, A., & Kishino, F. (1994). Augmented reality: A class of displays on the reality-virtuality continuum. *In Telemanipulator and Telepresence Technologies* (p. 2351). 10.1117/12.197321

Milgram, P., & Kishino, F. (1994). A Taxonomy Of Mixed Reality Visual Displays. *IEICE Transactions on Information and Systems*, E77-D(12), 1–15.

Milgram, P., & Kishino, F. (1994). A Taxonomy of Mixed Reality Visual Displays. *IEICE Transactions on Information and Systems*, E77-D(12), 1321–1329.

Miljkovic, I., Shlyakhetko, O., & Fedushko, S. (2023). Real estate app development based on AI/VR technologies. *Electronics (Basel)*, 12(3), 707. 10.3390/electronics12030707

Millard, D. E., Hewitt, S., O'Hara, K., Packer, H., & Rogers, N. (2019). The Unethical Future of Mixed Reality Storytelling. *Proceedings of the 8th International Workshop on Narrative and Hypertext*, Hof, Germany. https://doi.org/10.1145/3345511.3349283

Compilation of References

Minna, V., Sami, P., & Liubov, V. (2021). A Systematic Literature Review on Extended Reality: Virtual, Augmented and Mixed Reality in Working Life. *The International Journal of Virtual Reality: a Multimedia Publication for Professionals*, 21(2), 1–28. 10.20870/IJVR.2021.21.2.4620

Miranda, J., Navarrete, C., Noguez, J., Molina-Espinosa, J. M., Ramírez, M. S., Navarro-Tuch, S. A., & Bustamante-Bello, M. R. (2021). The core components of education 4.0 in higher education: Three case studies in engineering education. *Computers & Electrical Engineering*, 93, 1–13. 10.1016/j.compeleceng.2021.107278

Mir, U. B., Sharma, S., Kar, A. K., & Gupta, M. P. (2020). Critical success factors for integrating artificial intelligence and robotics. *Digital Policy. Regulation & Governance*, 22(4), 307–331. 10.1108/DPRG-03-2020-0032

Mitchell, A., & Khazanchi, D. (2012). Ethical Considerations for Virtual Worlds. *Proceedings of the Eighteenth Americas Conference on Information Systems*, Seattle, Washington.

Mittal, A. (2024). Impact of Negative Aspects of Artificial Intelligence on Customer Purchase Intention: An Empirical Study of Online Retail Customers Towards AI-Enabled E-Retail Platforms. In R. Verma, P. Kumar, S. Goyal, & S. Dadwal (Eds.), *Demystifying the dark side of AI in business* (1st ed., Vol. 1, pp. 159–173). IGI Global. 10.4018/979-8-3693-0724-3.ch010

Mohan, M. (2018). AISHE Final Report 2018-19. *Ministry of Education*.

Mohanraj, G., Krishna, K. S., Lakshmi, B. S., Vijayalakshmi, A., Pramila, P. V., & Boopathi, S. (2024). Optimizing Trust and Security in Healthcare 4.0: Human Factors in Lightweight Secured IoMT Ecosystems. In *Lightweight Digital Trust Architectures in the Internet of Medical Things (IoMT)* (pp. 52–72). IGI Global. 10.4018/979-8-3693-2109-6.ch004

Mohanty, A., Venkateswaran, N., Ranjit, P., Tripathi, M. A., & Boopathi, S. (2023). Innovative Strategy for Profitable Automobile Industries: Working Capital Management. In *Handbook of Research on Designing Sustainable Supply Chains to Achieve a Circular Economy* (pp. 412–428). IGI Global.

Mokni, M., Yassa, S., Hajlaoui, J. E., Chelouah, R., & Omri, M. N. (2022). Cooperative agents-based approach for workflow scheduling on fog-cloud computing. *Journal of Ambient Intelligence and Humanized Computing*, 13(10), 4719–4738. 10.1007/s12652-021-03187-9

Monarth, H. (2014, March 11). The Irresistible Power of Storytelling as a Strategic Business Tool. *Harvard Business Review*. https://hbr.org/2014/03/the-irresistible-power-of-storytelling-as-a-strategic-business-tool

Moormann, J., & Lochte-Holtgreven, M. (1993). An approach for an integrated DSS for strategic planning. *Decision Support Systems*, 10(4), 401–411. 10.1016/0167-9236(93)90070-J

Moreno, A., & Redondo, T. (2016). Text analytics: The convergence of big data and artificial intelligence. *IJIMAI*, 3(6), 57–64. 10.9781/ijimai.2016.369

Mourtzis, D., Vlachou, K., Dimitrakopoulos, G., & Zogopoulos, V. (2018). Cyber-Physical Systems and Education 4.0 –The Teaching Factory 4.0 Concept. *Procedia Manufacturing*, 23, 129–134. 10.1016/j.promfg.2018.04.005

Muhanna, M. A. (2015). Virtual reality and the CAVE: Taxonomy, interaction challenges and research directions. *Journal of King Saud University. Computer and Information Sciences*, 27(3), 344–361. 10.1016/j.jksuci.2014.03.023

Mundin, F. (2024). *Emerging Legal Issues in Virtual Reality: Exploring the Intersection of Law and Immersive Technology in 2024*. LawCrossing.

Munir, A., Kansakar, P., & Khan, S. U. (2017). IFCIoT: Integrated Fog Cloud IoT: A novel architectural paradigm for the future Internet of Things. *IEEE Consumer Electronics Magazine*, 6(3), 74–82. 10.1109/MCE.2017.2684981

Murray, J. H. (2017). *Hamlet on the holodeck, updated edition: The future of narrative in cyberspace*. MIT Press.

Murray, J. H. (1997). *Hamlet on the Holodeck: The Future of Narrative in Cyberspace* (1st ed.). MIT Press.

Murti, K. G. K., Darma, G. S., Mahyuni, L. P., & Gordad, A. A. N. E. S. (2023). Immersive Experience in the Metaverse: Implications for Tourism and Business. *International Journal Of Applied Business Research, 5*(2).

Naim, A., Khan, S.A., Mohammed, A., Sabahath, A., & Malik, P. K. Achieving performance and Reliability in predicting the Marketing Price of Bitcoins through Blockchain Technology. *Pacific Asia Journal of the Association for Information Systems*. https://aisel.aisnet.org/pajais _preprints/23/]

Naim, M. F. (2023). Reinventing workplace learning and development: Envisaging the role of AI. In *The adoption and Effect of artificial intelligence on human resources management, Part A* (pp. 215–227). Emerald Publishing Limited.

Nannelli, M., Capone, F., & Lazzeretti, L. (2023). Artificial intelligence in hospitality and tourism. State-of-the-art and future research avenues. *European Planning Studies*, 31(7), 1325–1344. 10.1080/09654313.2023.2180321

Narmeen, R., Almadhor, A., Alkhayyat, A., & Ho, P.-H. (2024). Secure Beamforming for Unmanned Aerial Vehicles Equipped Reconfigurable Intelligent Surfaces. *IEEE Internet of Things Magazine*, 7(2), 30–37. 10.1109/IOTM.001.2300238

Narwal, M., & Sachdeva, G. (2013). Impact of Information Technology (IT) On Consumer Purchase Behavior. *Journal of Art, Science & Commerce*.

Nassar, A., & Yilmaz, Y. (2021). Deep reinforcement learning for adaptive network slicing in 5G for intelligent vehicular systems and smart cities. *IEEE Internet of Things Journal*, 9(1), 222–235. 10.1109/JIOT.2021.3091674

Compilation of References

Nath, S. B., Gupta, H., Chakraborty, S., & Ghosh, S. K. (2018). A survey of fog computing and communication: Current researches and future directions. *arXiv Preprint arXiv:1804.04365*.

Nativi, S., Mazzetti, P., & Craglia, M. (2021). Digital ecosystems for developing digital twins of the earth: The destination earth case. *Remote Sensing (Basel)*, 13(11), 2119. 10.3390/rs13112119

Naveeenkumar, N., Rallapalli, S., Sasikala, K., Priya, P. V., Husain, J., & Boopathi, S. (2024). Enhancing Consumer Behavior and Experience Through AI-Driven Insights Optimization. In *AI Impacts in Digital Consumer Behavior* (pp. 1–35). IGI Global. 10.4018/979-8-3693-1918-5.ch001

Neuhofer, B., Buhalis, D., & Ladkin, A. (2013). Experiences, Co-Creation and Technology: A conceptual approach to enhance toruism. *Tourism and Global Change: On the Edge of Something Big*, 546–555.

Newberry, C. (2023, January 5). *How To Use Instagram for Business in 2024: 6 Pro Tips*. Hootsuite. https://blog.hootsuite.com/how-to-use-instagram-for-business/

Neyret, S., Oliva, R., Beacco, A., Navarro, X., Valenzuela, J., & Slater, M. (2020). An embodied perspective as a victim of sexual harassment in virtual reality reduces action conformity in a later milgram obedience scenario. *2019 IEEE International Symposium on Olfaction and Electronic Nose (ISOEN)*. IEEE. 10.1038/s41598-020-62932-w

Ng, K. S. P., Wong, J. W. C., Xie, D., & Zhu, J. (2023). From the attributes of smart tourism technologies to loyalty and WOM via user satisfaction: The moderating role of switching costs. *Kybernetes*, 52(8), 2868–2885. 10.1108/K-09-2021-0840

Nikolić, D., Maftei, L., & Whyte, J. (2019). Becoming familiar: How infrastructure engineers begin to use collaborative virtual reality in their interdisciplinary practice. *Journal of Information Technology in Construction*, 24, 489–508. 10.36680/j.itcon.2019.026

Ning, Z., Huang, J., & Wang, X. (2019). Vehicular fog computing: Enabling real-time traffic management for smart cities. *IEEE Wireless Communications*, 26(1), 87–93. 10.1109/MWC.2019.1700441

No, E., & Kim, J. K. (2015). Comparing the attributes of online tourism information sources. *Computers in Human Behavior*, 50, 564–575. 10.1016/j.chb.2015.02.063

Novakova, H., & Starchon, P. (2021). Creative Industries: Challenges And Opportunities in XR Technologies, SHS Web of Conferences 115. *Current Problems of the Corporate Sector*, 2021, 1–9. 10.1051/shsconf/202111503011

Nuno Verdelho, T., Alfredo, F., João Madeiras, P., & Sérgio, O. (2023). Extended reality in AEC. *Automation in Construction*, 154, 105018. 10.1016/j.autcon.2023.105018

Nussipova, G., Nordin, F., & Sörhammar, D. (2020). Value formation with immersive technologies: An activity perspective. *Journal of Business and Industrial Marketing*, 35(3), 483–494. 10.1108/JBIM-12-2018-0407

O'Donovan, P., Gallagher, C., Leahy, K., & O'Sullivan, D. T. (2019). A comparison of fog and cloud computing cyber-physical interfaces for Industry 4.0 real-time embedded machine learning engineering applications. *Computers in Industry*, 110, 12–35. 10.1016/j.compind.2019.04.016

O'Hagan, J., Saeghe, P., Gugenheimer, J., Medeiros, D., Marky, K., Khamis, M., & McGill, M. (2022). Privacy-Enhancing Technology and Everyday Augmented Reality: Understanding Bystanders' Varying Needs for Awareness and Consent. *Proceedings of the ACM on Interactive, Mobile, Wearable and Ubiquitous Technologies*, 6(4), 1–35. 10.1145/3569501

O'Leary, D. E. (2008). The relationship between citations and number of downloads in Decision Support Systems. *Decision Support Systems*, 45(4), 972–980. 10.1016/j.dss.2008.03.008

Obschonka, M., & Audretsch, D. B. (2020). Artificial intelligence and big data in entrepreneurship: A new era has begun. *Small Business Economics*, 55(3), 529–539. 10.1007/s11187-019-00202-4

Odeleye, B., Loukas, G., Heartfield, R., Sakellari, G., Panaousis, E., & Spyridonis, F. (n.d.). *Virtually Secure: A taxonomic assessment of cybersecurity challenges in virtual reality environments.*

OECD. (2019). *OECD Future of Education and Skills 2030, OECD Learning Compass 2030. A Series of Concept Notes*. OECD. https://www.oecd.org

OEDC (2019). *OECD Future of Education and Skills 2030. OECD Learning Compass 2030. A Series of Concept Notes*. OECD.

Oliveira, R., Arriaga, P., Santos, F. P., Mascarenhas, S., & Paiva, A. (2021). Towards prosocial design: A scoping review of the use of robots and virtual agents to trigger prosocial behaviour. *Computers in Human Behavior*, 114, 106547. 10.1016/j.chb.2020.106547

Oprean, D. (2014). *Understanding the immersive experience: Examining the influence of visual immersiveness and interactivity on spatial experiences and understanding.* [Doctoral dissertation, University of Missouri].

Oun, A., Hagerdorn, N., Scheideger, C., & Cheng, X. (2024). Mobile Devices or Head-Mounted Displays: A Comparative Review and Analysis of Augmented Reality in Healthcare. *IEEE Access : Practical Innovations, Open Solutions*, 12, 21825–21839. 10.1109/ACCESS.2024.3361833

Ozdemir, O., Dogru, T., Kizildag, M., & Erkmen, E. (2023). A critical reflection on digitalization for the hospitality and tourism industry: Value implications for stakeholders. *International Journal of Contemporary Hospitality Management*, 35(9), 3305–3321. 10.1108/IJCHM-04-2022-0535

P21. (2019) *Framework*. P21. https://static.battelleforkids.org/documents/p21/P21_Framework_DefinitionsBFK.pdf

Pachucki, C., Grohs, R., & Scholl-Grissemann, U. (2022). No story without a storyteller: The impact of the storyteller as a narrative element in online destination marketing. *Journal of Travel Research*, 61(8), 1703–1718. 10.1177/00472875211046052

Paez, A. (2017). Gray literature: An important resource in systematic reviews. *Journal of Evidence-Based Medicine*, 10(3), 233–240. 10.1111/jebm.1226628857505

Compilation of References

Paivio, A. (2014). *Imagery and verbal processes*. Psychology Press.

Paliwal, M., Chatradhi, N., Singh, A., & Dikkatwar, R. (2022). Smart tourism: Antecedents to Indian traveller's decision. *European Journal of Innovation Management*. 10.1108/EJIM-06-2022-0293

Palmas, F., & Klinker, G. (2020). *Defining Extended Reality Training: A Long-Term Definition for All Industries*. 2020 IEEE 20th International Conference on Advanced Learning Technologies (ICALT), Tartu, Estonia. 10.1109/ICALT49669.2020.00103

Palmer, S. (1999). *Vision science: Photons to phenomenology*. MIT Press.

Pandey, S. (2020). Exploring the role of Artificial Intelligence (AI) in transforming HR functions: An Empirical Study in the Indian Context. *International Journal of Scientific Research and Engineering Development*.

Papanek, V. (2004). *Design for the Real World, Human Ecology and Social Change*. Thames & Hudson Ltd.

Parsons, T. D. (2021). Ethical Challenges of Using Virtual Environments in the Assessment and Treatment of Psychopathological Disorders. *Journal of Clinical Medicine*, 10(3), 1–16. 10.3390/jcm1003037833498255

Pasumarthy, R., Mohammed, S., Laxman, V., Krishnamoorthy, V., Durga, S., & Boopathi, S. (2024). Digital Transformation in Developing Economies: Forecasting Trends, Impact, and Challenges in Industry 5.0. In *Convergence of Human Resources Technologies and Industry 5.0* (pp. 47–68). IGI Global. 10.4018/979-8-3693-1343-5.ch003

Pathak, S., & Solanki, V. K. (2021). Impact of internet of things and artificial intelligence on human resource development. *Further Advances in Internet of Things in Biomedical and Cyber Physical Systems*, 239–267.

Patria, T. A., Hidayah, N., and Suherlan, H. (2023). Effect of Immersive Experience on Repurchase Intention of Virtual Heritage Tours among Gen-Z in Indonesia . *E3S Web of Conferences 388*. IEEE. 10.1051/e3sconf/202338804013

Patricia, P., Samuel, N.-M., & Jose, L. (2022). Extended reality for mental health: Current trends and future challenges. *Frontiers of Computer Science*, 4, 1034307. 10.3389/fcomp.2022.1034307

Paul, A., & Thilagham, K. KG, J.-, Reddy, P. R., Sathyamurthy, R., & Boopathi, S. (2024). Multi-criteria Optimization on Friction Stir Welding of Aluminum Composite (AA5052-H32/B4C) using Titanium Nitride Coated Tool. *Engineering Research Express*.

Pawankumar, S., & Bibhu, D. (2022). The digital carbon footprint: Threat to an environmentally sustainable future. *International Journal of Computer Science and Information Technologies*, 14(3), 25. 10.5121/ijcsit.2022.14302

Peckham, J. B. (2021). The ethical implications of 4IR. *Journal of Ethics in Entrepreneurship and Technology*, 1(1), 30–42. 10.1108/JEET-04-2021-0016

Pereira, V., Hadjielias, E., Christofi, M., & Vrontis, D. (2023). A systematic literature review on the impact of artificial intelligence on workplace outcomes: A multi-process perspective. *Human Resource Management Review*, 33(1), 100857. 10.1016/j.hrmr.2021.100857

Perini, S., Luglietti, R., Maria, M., Fradinho Duarte de Oliveira, M., & Taisch, M. (2017). Training Advanced Skills for Sustainable Manufacturing: A Digital Serious Game. *Procedia Manufacturing*, 11, 1536–1543. 10.1016/j.promfg.2017.07.286

Pešikan, A., & Lalović, Z. (2017). *Education For Life: Key 21 St Century Competencies in Curricula in Montenegro*. UNICEF Montenegro.https://www.unicef.org

Phelps, E. (2006). Emotion and cognition: Insights from studies of the human amygdala. *Annual Review of Psychology*, 57(1), 27–53. 10.1146/annurev.psych.56.091103.07023416318588

Philipp, R., Reto, F., Chris, H., Hamza, S., & Florian, A. (2022). What is XR? Towards a Framework for Augmented and Virtual Reality. *Computers in Human Behavior*, 133, 1–18. 10.1016/j.chb.2022.107289

Pietro C., Irene A., Mariano A., & Giuseppe R. (2018). *The Past, Present, and Future of Virtual and Augmented Reality Research: A Network and Cluster Analysis of the Literature.*

Pillai, R., Sivathanu, B., Zheng, Y., Wu, Y., Pai, C. K., Liu, Y., Kang, S., & Dai, A. (2020). An investigation of how perceived smart tourism technologies affect tourists' well-being in marine tourism. *Sustainability (Switzerland)*, 18, 1–19. 10.3390/su12166592

Pine, J., Gilmore, J. H. (2012) *Deneyim Ekonomisi*. Çeviren: Levent Cinemre. Optimist Yayınları.

Pine, J. I. I., & Gilmore, J. H. (1998). Welcome to the experience economy. *Harvard Business Review*.10181589

Pine, J., & Gilmore, J. H. (1999). *The experience economy*. Harvard Business School Press.

Pitchai, R., Guru, K. V., Gandhi, J. N., Komala, C. R., Kumar, J. R. D., & Boopathi, S. (2024). Fog Computing-Integrated ML-Based Framework and Solutions for Intelligent Systems: Digital Healthcare Applications. In *Technological Advancements in Data Processing for Next Generation Intelligent Systems* (pp. 196–224). IGI Global. 10.4018/979-8-3693-0968-1.ch008

Pizzi, G., Scarpi, D., Pichierri, M., & Vannucci, V. (2019). Virtual reality, real reactions?: Comparing consumers' perceptions and shopping orientation across physical and virtual-reality retail stores. *Computers in Human Behavior*, 96, 1–12. 10.1016/j.chb.2019.02.008

Pleyers, G., & Poncin, I. (2020). Non-immersive virtual reality technologies in real estate: How customer experience drives attitudes toward properties and the service provider. *Journal of Retailing and Consumer Services*, 57, 102175. 10.1016/j.jretconser.2020.102175

Prabhuswamy, M., Tripathi, R., Vijayakumar, M., Thulasimani, T., Sundharesalingam, P., & Sampath, B. (2024). A Study on the Complex Nature of Higher Education Leadership: An Innovative Approach. In *Challenges of Globalization and Inclusivity in Academic Research* (pp. 202–223). IGI Global. 10.4018/979-8-3693-1371-8.ch013

Compilation of References

Prahalad, C. K., & Ramaswamy, V. (2002). The Co-creation connection. *Strategy & Business.*

Pramila, P., Amudha, S., Saravanan, T., Sankar, S. R., Poongothai, E., & Boopathi, S. (2023). Design and Development of Robots for Medical Assistance: An Architectural Approach. In *Contemporary Applications of Data Fusion for Advanced Healthcare Informatics* (pp. 260–282). IGI Global.

Pranav, P., Shireen, P., Nivedita, P., & Manan, S. (2020). Systematic review and meta-analysis of augmented reality in medicine, retail, and games. *Visual Computing for Industry, Biomedicine, and Art,* 3(21), 21. 10.1186/s42492-020-00057-732954214

Pratono, A. H. (2022). Reinterpreting excellence for sustainable competitive advantage: The role of entrepreneurial culture under information technological turbulence. *Measuring Business Excellence,* 26(2), 180–196. 10.1108/MBE-04-2021-0056

Puranik, T. A., Shaik, N., Vankudoth, R., Kolhe, M. R., Yadav, N., & Boopathi, S. (2024). Study on Harmonizing Human-Robot (Drone) Collaboration: Navigating Seamless Interactions in Collaborative Environments. In *Cybersecurity Issues and Challenges in the Drone Industry* (pp. 1–26). IGI Global.

Putera, N., Saripan, H., Bajury, M., & Ya'cob, S. (2022). Artificial Intelligence in the Tourism Industry: A Privacy Impasse. *ENVIRONMENT-BEHAVIOUR PROCEEDINGS JOURNAL,* 7(17), 433–440. 10.21834/ebpj.v7iSI7.3812

Qi, X., & Li, X. (2022). Extraction Method of Tourism Sustainable Development Path under the Background of Artificial Intelligence + Smart City Construction. *Journal of Interconnection Network.* 10.1142/S0219265921430271

Quatman-Yates, C. C., Paterno, M. V., Strenk, M. L., Kiger, M. A., Hogan, T. H., Cunningham, B., & Reder, R. (2019). A model for cultivating a culture of continuous learning and improvement: An ethnographic report. In *Structural Approaches to Address Issues in Patient Safety* (pp. 197–225). Emerald Publishing Limited. 10.1108/S1474-823120190000018009

Rafiq, M., Farrukh, M., Mushtaq, R., & Dastane, O. (2023). *Exploring the Intersection of AI and Human Resources Management.* IGI Global. 10.4018/979-8-3693-0039-8

Rahamathunnisa, U., Sudhakar, K., Padhi, S., Bhattacharya, S., Shashibhushan, G., & Boopathi, S. (2024). Sustainable Energy Generation From Waste Water: IoT Integrated Technologies. In *Adoption and Use of Technology Tools and Services by Economically Disadvantaged Communities: Implications for Growth and Sustainability* (pp. 225–256). IGI Global.

Raji, M., Olodo, H., Oke, T., Addy, W., Ofodile, O., & Oyewole, A. (2024). Business Strategies in Virtual Reality: A Review of Market Opportunities and Consumer Experience. *International Journal of Management & Entrepreneurship Research,* 6(3), 722–736. 10.51594/ijmer.v6i3.883

Ramudu, K., Mohan, V. M., Jyothirmai, D., Prasad, D., Agrawal, R., & Boopathi, S. (2023). Machine Learning and Artificial Intelligence in Disease Prediction: Applications, Challenges, Limitations, Case Studies, and Future Directions. In *Contemporary Applications of Data Fusion for Advanced Healthcare Informatics* (pp. 297–318). IGI Global.

Rao, S., Chitranshi, J., & Punjabi, N. (2020). Role of artificial intelligence in employee engagement and retention. *Journal of Applied Management-Jidnyasa*, 42–60.

Ratajczak, M. (2022). The state in the era of Digital Revolution and digital finance. In *Digital Finance and the Future of the Global Financial System* (pp. 93–108). Routledge. 10.4324/9781003264101-8

Ratcliffe, J., Soave, F., Bryan-Kinns, N., Tokarchuk, L., & Farkhatdinov, I. (2021). Extended Reality (XR) Remote Research: A Survey of Drawbacks and Opportunities. *CHI*, 21(May), 8–13. 10.1145/3411764.3445170

Rauschnabel, P. A. (2018). Virtually enhancing the real world with holograms: An exploration of expected gratifications of using augmented reality smart glasses. *Psychology and Marketing*, 35(8), 557–572. 10.1002/mar.21106

Ravisankar, A., Sampath, B., & Asif, M. M. (2023). Economic Studies on Automobile Management: Working Capital and Investment Analysis. In *Multidisciplinary Approaches to Organizational Governance During Health Crises* (pp. 169–198). IGI Global.

Ravisankar, A., Shanthi, A., Lavanya, S., Ramaratnam, M., Krishnamoorthy, V., & Boopathi, S. (2024). Harnessing 6G for Consumer-Centric Business Strategies Across Electronic Industries. In *AI Impacts in Digital Consumer Behavior* (pp. 241–270). IGI Global.

Raymundo, O. (2016). Tim Cook: Augmented reality will be an essential part of your daily life, like the iPhone. *Macworld*. https://www.macworld.com/article/3126607/tim-cook-augmented-reality-will-be-an-essential-part-of-your-daily-life-like-the-iphone.html

Rebecca, B., Kumar, K. P. M., Padmini, S., Srivastava, B. K., Halder, S., & Boopathi, S. (2024). Convergence of Data Science-AI-Green Chemistry-Affordable Medicine: Transforming Drug Discovery. In *Handbook of Research on AI and ML for Intelligent Machines and Systems* (pp. 348–373). IGI Global.

Rebecca, H., Juliana, Z., Stephen, R. Z., Desiree, S., & Leon, S. (2021). The association of mobile touch screen device use with parent-child attachment: A systematic review. *Ergonomics*, 64(12), 1606–1622. 10.1080/00140139.2021.194861734190030

Reddick, C. G., Enriquez, R., Harris, R. J., & Sharma, B. (2020). Determinants of broadband access and affordability: An analysis of a community survey on the digital divide. *Cities (London, England)*, 106, 102904. 10.1016/j.cities.2020.10290432921864

Reddy, M. A., Reddy, B. M., Mukund, C., Venneti, K., Preethi, D., & Boopathi, S. (2023). Social Health Protection During the COVID-Pandemic Using IoT. In *The COVID-19 Pandemic and the Digitalization of Diplomacy* (pp. 204–235). IGI Global. 10.4018/978-1-7998-8394-4.ch009

Reiners, D., Davahli, M. R., Karwowski, W., & Cruz-Neira, C. (2021). The combination of Artificial Intelligence and Extended Reality: A Systematic Review. *Frontiers in Virtual Reality*, 2, 721933. 10.3389/frvir.2021.721933

Reiserer, M., Jones, M., & Johnson, L. (2021). The Societal Impact of Extended Reality: Democratizing Access to Experiences. *Journal of XR Studies*, 10(1), 45–62.

Revathi, S., Babu, M., Rajkumar, N., Meti, V. K. V., Kandavalli, S. R., & Boopathi, S. (2024). Unleashing the Future Potential of 4D Printing: Exploring Applications in Wearable Technology, Robotics, Energy, Transportation, and Fashion. In *Human-Centered Approaches in Industry 5.0: Human-Machine Interaction, Virtual Reality Training, and Customer Sentiment Analysis* (pp. 131–153). IGI Global.

Riva, G., Wiederhold, B. K., & Mantovani, F. (2020). Virtual Reality in Medical Education: How Virtual Reality May Change Medical Students' Education. *Cyberpsychology, Behavior, and Social Networking*, 23(3), 151–152.

Robins, K. (2013). *İmaj. Görmenin Kültür ve Politikası*, İngilizceden Çeviren: Nurçay Türkoğlu, Ayrıntı Yayınları, 2. Basım.

Roche, C. (2022). *Ethics and diversity in artificial intelligence policies, strategies and initiatives.* Springer.

Rosário, A. T., & Dias, J. C. (2022). Sustainability and the digital transition: A literature review. *Sustainability (Basel)*, 14(7), 4072. 10.3390/su14074072

Rosário, A. T., & Dias, J. C. (2024). Exploring the Landscape of Smart Tourism : A Systematic Bibliometric Review of the Literature of the Internet of Things. *Administrative Sciences*, 14(22), 1–26. 10.3390/admsci14020022

Ross, G., & Liechtenstein, V. (2018). Management of financial bubbles as control technology of digital economy. *Information Technology Science*, 96–103.

Rubio-Tamayo, J. (n.d.). Immersive environments and virtual reality: Systematic review and advances in communication, interaction and simulation. *Multimodal Technologies and Interaction.* MDPI. https://www.mdpi.com/2414-4088/1/4/21

Rueda-Esteban, N. R. (2019). Technology as a tool to rebuild heritage sites: The second life of the Abbey of Cluny. *Journal of Heritage Tourism*, 14(2), 101–116. 10.1080/1743873X.2018.1468762

Rüßmann, M., Lorenz, M., Gerbert, P., Waldner, M., Justus, J., Engel, P., & Harnisch, M. (2015). Industry 4.0: The future of productivity and growth in manufacturing industries. *Boston consulting group, 9*(1), 54-89.

Ryu, K., Lehto, X. Y., Gordon, S., & Fu, X. (2018). Compelling brand storytelling for luxury hotels. *International Journal of Hospitality Management*, 74, 22–29. 10.1016/j.ijhm.2018.02.002

S, B., & Gopi, S. (2024). Crafting Effective HR Strategies for the Modern Workplace: Navigating the Digital Frontier. In *Convergence of Human Resources Technologies and Industry 5.0* (pp. 23–46). IGI Global. 10.4018/979-8-3693-1343-5.ch002

Sahlin, J., & Angelis, J. (2019). Performance management systems: Reviewing the rise of dynamics and digitalization. *Cogent Business & Management*, 6(1), 1642293. 10.1080/23311975.2019.1642293

Saleem, M., Kamarudin, S., Shoaib, H. M., & Nasar, A. (2021). Retail Consumers' Behavioral Intention to Use Augmented Reality Mobile Apps in Pakistan. *Journal of Internet Commerce.* 10.1080/15332861.2021.1975427

Samala, N., Katkam, B. S., Bellamkonda, R. S., & Rodriguez, R. V. (2022). Impact of AI and robotics in the tourism sector: A critical insight. *Journal of Tourism Futures*, 8(1), 73–87. 10.1108/JTF-07-2019-0065

Samara, D., Magnisalis, I., & Peristeras, V. (2020). Artificial intelligence and big data in tourism: A systematic literature review. *Journal of Hospitality and Tourism Technology*, 11(2), 343–367. 10.1108/JHTT-12-2018-0118

Samikannu, R., Koshariya, A. K., Poornima, E., Ramesh, S., Kumar, A., & Boopathi, S. (2022). Sustainable Development in Modern Aquaponics Cultivation Systems Using IoT Technologies. In *Human Agro-Energy Optimization for Business and Industry* (pp. 105–127). IGI Global.

Sampath, B., Pandian, M., Deepa, D., & Subbiah, R. (2022). Operating parameters prediction of liquefied petroleum gas refrigerator using simulated annealing algorithm. *AIP Conference Proceedings*, 2460(1), 070003. 10.1063/5.0095601

Sandhya, M., & Prasad, M. V. N. K. (2017). *Biometric template protection: A systematic literature review of approaches and modalities*. Springer. 10.1007/s10676-018-9452-x

Sangeetha, M., Kannan, S. R., Boopathi, S., Ramya, J., Ishrat, M., & Sabarinathan, G. (2023). Prediction of Fruit Texture Features Using Deep Learning Techniques. *2023 4th International Conference on Smart Electronics and Communication (ICOSEC)*, 762–768.

Sarah, D. R., & Radiah, R. Ville Mäkelä, & Florian, A. (2023). *Challenges in Virtual Reality Studies: Ethics and Internal and External Validity*. Augmented Humans International Conference 2023 (AHs '23), Glasgow, United Kingdom.

Sarango-Lalangui, P., Santos, J. L. S., & Hormiga, E. (2018). The development of sustainable entrepreneurship research field. *Sustainability (Basel)*, 10(6), 2005. 10.3390/su10062005

Sara, Q., Park, T., Kelly, D. M., Scott, W., & Robert, W. P. (2022). Digital technologies: Tensions in privacy and data. *Journal of the Academy of Marketing Science*, 50(6), 1299–1323. 10.1007/s11747-022-00845-y35281634

Compilation of References

Saraswathi, P. A. S., Pavithra, A., Kowsalya, J., Priya, S. K., Jayasree, G., & Nandhini, T. K. (2020). *An emerging immersive technology-a survey.* Research Gate. https://www.researchgate.net/profile/Pavithra-A/publication/338819764_An_Emerging_Immersive_Technology-A_Survey/links/5e2c1d3c4585150ee780fca1/An-Emerging-Immersive-Technology-A-Survey.pdf

Saravanan, A., Venkatasubramanian, R., Khare, R., Surakasi, R., Boopathi, S., Ray, S., & Sudhakar, M. (2022). POLICY TRENDS OF RENEWABLE ENERGY AND NON. *Renewable Energy.*

Sarkar, S. (2012). *The Role of Information and Communication Technology (ICT) in Higher Education for the 21st Century.*

Satav, S. D., Lamani, D., Harsha, K., Kumar, N., Manikandan, S., & Sampath, B. (2023). Energy and Battery Management in the Era of Cloud Computing: Sustainable Wireless Systems and Networks. In *Sustainable Science and Intelligent Technologies for Societal Development* (pp. 141–166). IGI Global.

Satav, S. D., Hasan, D. S., Pitchai, R., Mohanaprakash, T., Sultanuddin, S., & Boopathi, S. (2023). Next generation of internet of things (ngiot) in healthcare systems. In *Sustainable Science and Intelligent Technologies for Societal Development* (pp. 307–330). IGI Global.

Saydam, M. B., Arici, H. E., & Koseoglu, M. A. (2022). How does the tourism and hospitality industry use artificial intelligence? A review of empirical studies and future research agenda. *Journal of Hospitality Marketing & Management, 31*(8), 908–936. 10.1080/19368623.2022.2118923

Sayed Fayaz, A., & Heesup, H. (2023). Impact of artificial intelligence on human loss in decision making, laziness and safety in education. *Humanities & Social Sciences Communications, 10*(1), 311. Advance online publication. 10.1057/s41599-023-01787-837325188

Schmitt, B. (2019). From atoms to bits and back: A research curation on digital technology and agenda for future research. *The Journal of Consumer Research, 46*(4), 825–832. 10.1093/jcr/ucz038

Schöne, B., Kisker, J., Lange, L., Gruber, T., Sylvester, S., & Osinsky, R. (2023). The reality of virtual reality. *Frontiers in Psychology, 14,* 1093014. 10.3389/fpsyg.2023.109301436874824

Schott, C., & Marshall, S. (2018). Virtual reality and situated experiential education: A conceptualisation and exploratory trial. *Journal of Computer Assisted Learning, 34*(6), 843–852. 10.1111/jcal.12293

Schroeder, R. (2007). An overview of ethical and social issues in shared virtual environments. *Futures, 39*(6), 704–717. 10.1016/j.futures.2006.11.009

Schwab, K. (2016). *The Fourth Industrial Revolution.* World Economic Forum.

See, Z. S., & Cheok, A. D. (2015). Virtual reality 360 interactive panorama reproduction obstacles and issues. *Virtual Reality (Waltham Cross), 19*(2), 71–81. 10.1007/s10055-014-0258-9

Selvakumar, S., Adithe, S., Isaac, J. S., Pradhan, R., Venkatesh, V., & Sampath, B. (2023). A Study of the Printed Circuit Board (PCB) E-Waste Recycling Process. In *Sustainable Approaches and Strategies for E-Waste Management and Utilization* (pp. 159–184). IGI Global.

Senthil, T., Puviyarasan, M., Babu, S. R., Surakasi, R., Sampath, B., & Associates. (2023). Industrial Robot-Integrated Fused Deposition Modelling for the 3D Printing Process. In *Development, Properties, and Industrial Applications of 3D Printed Polymer Composites* (pp. 188–210). IGI Global.

Sethi, A. (2022). Security and Privacy in Metaverse: Issues, Challenges, and Future Opportunities. *Cyber Security Insights Magazine*, 2, 1–4.

Shahab, H., Shahzad, F., & Yasin, G. (2022). Virtual Reality as a Marketing Tool to Drive Consumer Decision-Making. *Pakistan Journal of Social Research*, 4(1), 664–677. 10.52567/pjsr.v4i1.933

Shandilya, G., Srivastava, P., & Jana, A. (2024). Industry Experts and Business Consultants' Takes on India's Readiness for Metaverse: A Review of the Retail Industry. In Singla, B., Shalender, K., & Singh, N. (Eds.), *Creator's Economy in Metaverse Platforms: Empowering Stakeholders Through Omnichannel Approach* (pp. 132–147). IGI Global. 10.4018/979-8-3693-3358-7.ch008

Sharma, D. M., Ramana, K. V., Jothilakshmi, R., Verma, R., Maheswari, B. U., & Boopathi, S. (2024). Integrating Generative AI Into K-12 Curriculums and Pedagogies in India: Opportunities and Challenges. *Facilitating Global Collaboration and Knowledge Sharing in Higher Education With Generative AI*, 133–161.

Sharma, D. M., Ramana, K. V., Jothilakshmi, R., Verma, R., Maheswari, B. U., & Boopathi, S. (2024). Integrating Generative AI Into K-12 Curriculums and Pedagogies in India: Opportunities and Challenges. *Facilitating Global Collaboration and Knowledge Sharing in Higher Education With Generative AI*.

Sharma, D. M., Ramana, K. V., Jothilakshmi, R., Verma, R., Maheswari, B. U., & Boopathi, S. (2024). Integrating Generative AI Into K-12 Curriculums and Pedagogies in India: Opportunities and Challenges. *Facilitating Global Collaboration and Knowledge Sharing in Higher Education With Generative AI*. Springer.

Sharma, P. (2019). Digital Revolution of Education 4.0. *International Journal of Engineering and Advanced Technology*, 9(2), 3558–3564. 10.35940/ijeat.A1293.129219

Sherman, W. R., & Craig, A. B. (2003). *Understanding virtual reality*. Morgan Kauffman.

Sherman, W. R., & Craig, A. B. (2018). *Understanding virtual reality: Interface, application, and design*. Morgan Kaufmann.

Shuqiong, L., Di, Z., & Lucas, K. (2024). A systematic review of research on xReality (XR) in the English classroom: Trends, research areas, benefits, and challenges. *Computers & Education: X Reality, 4*.

Sineviciene, L., Hens, L., Kubatko, O., Melnyk, L., Dehtyarova, I., & Fedyna, S. (2021). Socio-economic and cultural effects of disruptive industrial technologies for sustainable development. *International Journal of Global Energy Issues*, 43(2–3), 284–305. 10.1504/IJGEI.2021.115150

Compilation of References

Singh, M., & Saxena, P. (2020). The Role of Artificial Intelligence in Transforming Public Transportation in the Tourism Industry: A Case Study of Delhi Metro. *International Journal of Research in Management, Economics and Commerce*.

Singhania, V. (2018). *Augmented & Virtual Reality Apps: The Legal Angle*. Law School Policy Review.

Singh, S. K., Salim, M. M., Cha, J., Pan, Y., & Park, J. H. (2020). Machine learning-based network sub-slicing framework in a sustainable 5g environment. *Sustainability (Basel)*, 12(15), 6250. 10.3390/su12156250

Skulmowski, A. (2023). Ethical issues of educational virtual reality, *Computers & Education: X Reality*, 2, 1-8.

Slater, M. (2021). Beyond Speculation About the Ethics of Virtual Reality: The Need for Empirical Results. *Frontiers in Virtual Reality*, 2, 687609. Advance online publication. 10.3389/frvir.2021.687609

Slater, M., Gonzalez-Liencres, C., Haggard, P., Vinkers, C., Gregory-Clarke, R., Jelley, S., Watson, Z., Breen, G., Schwarz, R., Steptoe, W., Szostak, D., Halan, S., Fox, D., & Silver, J. (2020). The Ethics of Realism in Virtual and Augmented Reality. *Frontiers in Virtual Reality*, 1, 1. Advance online publication. 10.3389/frvir.2020.00001

Slater, M., & Sanchez-Vives, M. (2016). Enhancing Our Lives with Immersive Virtual Reality. *Frontiers in Robotics and AI*, 3, 74. 10.3389/frobt.2016.00074

Slater, M., & Wilbur, S. (1997). A Framework for Immersive Virtual Environments (FIVE): Speculations on the Role of Presence in Virtual Environments. *Presence (Cambridge, Mass.)*, 6(6), 603–616. 10.1162/pres.1997.6.6.603

Solja, E., Liljander, V., & Soderlund, M. (2018). Short brand stories on packaging: An examination of consumer responses. *Psychology and Marketing*, 35(4), 294–306. 10.1002/mar.21087

Song, J. H., & Zinkhan, G. M. (2008). Determinants of perceived Web site interactivity. *Journal of Marketing*, 72(2), 99–113. 10.1509/jmkg.72.2.99

Soni, N., Sharma, E. K., Singh, N., & Kapoor, A. (2019). Impact of artificial intelligence on businesses: From research, innovation, market deployment to future shifts in business models. *arXiv Preprint arXiv:1905.02092*.

Sonia, R., Gupta, N., Manikandan, K., Hemalatha, R., Kumar, M. J., & Boopathi, S. (2024). Strengthening Security, Privacy, and Trust in Artificial Intelligence Drones for Smart Cities. In *Analyzing and Mitigating Security Risks in Cloud Computing* (pp. 214–242). IGI Global. 10.4018/979-8-3693-3249-8.ch011

Soni, V. (2023). Impact of Generative AI on Small and Medium Enterprises' Revenue Growth: The Moderating Role of Human, Technological, and Market Factors. *Reviews of Contemporary Business Analytics*, 6(1), 133–153.

Sony, M. (2018). Industry 4.0 and lean management: A proposed integration model and research propositions. *Production & Manufacturing Research*, 6(1), 416–432. 10.1080/21693277.2018.1540949

Sousa, M., & Rocha, Á. (2019). Digital learning: Developing skills for digital transformation of organizations. *Future Generation Computer Systems*, 91, 327–334. 10.1016/j.future.2018.08.048

Southgate, E., & Smith, S. (2017). *Asking ethical questions in research using immersive virtual and augmented reality technologies with children and youth*. IEEE. https://ieeexplore.ieee.org/abstract/document/7892226/

Sreedhar, P. S. S., Sujay, V., Rani, M. R., Melita, L., Reshma, S., & Boopathi, S. (2024). Impacts of 5G Machine Learning Techniques on Telemedicine and Social Media Professional Connection in Healthcare. In *Advances in Medical Technologies and Clinical Practice* (pp. 209–234). IGI Global. 10.4018/979-8-3693-1934-5.ch012

Srinivas, B., Maguluri, L. P., Naidu, K. V., Reddy, L. C. S., Deivakani, M., & Boopathi, S. (2023). Architecture and Framework for Interfacing Cloud-Enabled Robots. In *Handbook of Research on Data Science and Cybersecurity Innovations in Industry 4.0 Technologies* (pp. 542–560). IGI Global. 10.4018/978-1-6684-8145-5.ch027

Srivastava, Praveen, Mishra, N., Srivastava, S., & Shivani, S. (2024). Banking with Chatbots: The Role of Demographic and Personality Traits. *FIIB Business Review*. 10.1177/23197145241227757

Srivastava, P. (2023). Tech Driven Dining : How ICT Innovation Can help Achieve Sustainable Development Goals. In Nadda, P. T. V., Tyagi, P. K., & Vieira, R. M. (Eds.), *Sustainable Development Goal Advancement Through Digital Innovation in the Service Sector* (pp. 57–63). IGI Global. 10.4018/979-8-3693-0650-5.ch005

Srivastava, P., Srivastava, S., & Mishra, N. (2023). Impact of e-servicescape on hotel booking intention: Examining the moderating role of COVID-19. *Consumer Behavior in Tourism and Hospitality*, 18(3), 422–437. 10.1108/CBTH-03-2022-0076

Stackpole, B. (2023). *The business impact of extended reality*. MIT. https://mitsloan.mit.edu/ideas-made-to-matter/business-impact-extended-reality

Stahl, B. C., Flick, C., & Timmermans, J. (2017). Ethics of Emerging Information and Communication Technologies-On the implementation of RRI. *Science & Public Policy*. 10.1093/scipol/scw069

Stanney, K. M., Archer, J., Skinner, A., Horner, C., Hughes, C., Brawand, N. P., Martin, E., Sanchez, S., Moralez, L., Fidopiastis, C. M., & Perez, R. S. (2022). Performance gains from adaptive eXtended Reality training fueled by artificial intelligence. *The Journal of Defense Modeling and Simulation*, 19(2), 195–218. 10.1177/15485129211064809

Statista. (2023). *AR & VR: market data & analysis, Market Insights reports*. Statista. https://www.statista.com/study/125081/arandvr-market-report/

Compilation of References

Steele, P., Burleigh, C., Kroposki, M., Magabo, M., & Bailey, L. (2020). Ethical Considerations in Designing Virtual and Augmented Reality Products—Virtual and Augmented Reality Design with Students in Mind: Designers' Perceptions. *Journal of Educational Technology Systems*, 49(2), 1–20. 10.1177/0047239520933858

Stendal, K., & Bernabe, R. D. (2024). Extended Reality—New Opportunity for People With Disability? Practical and Ethical Considerations. *Journal of Medical Internet Research*, 26(1), e41670. 10.2196/4167038349731

Steve, M., Silvia, M., Todd, S., & Venkat, V. (2022). *Meet Me in the Metaverse: The continuum of technology and experience, reshaping business.* Accenture. https://www.accenture.com/content/dam/accenture/final/industry/insurance/document/Accenture-Insurance-Technology-Vision-2022.pdf#zoom=40

Stodel, E. J., Thompson, T. L., & MacDonald, C. J. (2006). Learners' Perspectives on what is Missing from Online Learning: Interpretations through the Community of Inquiry Framework. *International Review of Research in Open and Distance Learning*, 7(3). 10.19173/irrodl.v7i3.325

Su, C.-J., & Huang, S.-F. (2018). Real-time big data analytics for hard disk drive predictive maintenance. *Computers & Electrical Engineering*, 71, 93–101. 10.1016/j.compeleceng.2018.07.025

Suh, A., & Prophet, J. (2018). The State of Immersive Technology Research: A Literature Analysis. *Computers in Human Behavior*, 86, 77–90. 10.1016/j.chb.2018.04.019

Sulistyaningsih, E. (2023). Improving Human Resources Technology Innovation as a Business Growth Driver in the Society 5.0 Era. *ADI Journal on Recent Innovation*, 4(2), 149–159.

Sundar, R., Srikaanth, P. B., Naik, D. A., Murugan, V. P., Karumudi, M., & Boopathi, S. (2024). Achieving Balance Between Innovation and Security in the Cloud With Artificial Intelligence of Things: Semantic Web Control Models. In *Advances in Web Technologies and Engineering* (pp. 1–26). IGI Global. 10.4018/979-8-3693-1487-6.ch001

Sung, E., Bae, S., Han, D.-I. D., & Kwon, O. (2021). Consumer engagement via interactive artificial intelligence and mixed reality. *International Journal of Information Management*, 60(June), 102382. 10.1016/j.ijinfomgt.2021.102382

Syamala, M., Komala, C., Pramila, P., Dash, S., Meenakshi, S., & Boopathi, S. (2023). Machine Learning-Integrated IoT-Based Smart Home Energy Management System. In *Handbook of Research on Deep Learning Techniques for Cloud-Based Industrial IoT* (pp. 219–235). IGI Global. 10.4018/978-1-6684-8098-4.ch013

Szlapka, J., Ortega-Mier, M., Ordieres-Meré, J., & Facchini, F., & Mossa, G., & Lundquist, J. (2020). *Innovative methodologies and digital tools for higher education in industrial engineering and management.*

Taj, I., & Zaman, N. (2022). Towards industrial revolution 5.0 and explainable artificial intelligence: Challenges and opportunities. *International Journal of Computing and Digital Systems*, 12(1), 295–320. 10.12785/ijcds/120128

Tärneberg, W. (2019). *The confluence of Cloud computing, 5G, and IoT in the Fog.*

Terán-Yépez, E., Marín-Carrillo, G. M., del Pilar Casado-Belmonte, M., & de las Mercedes Capobianco-Uriarte, M. (2020). Sustainable entrepreneurship: Review of its evolution and new trends. *Journal of Cleaner Production*, 252, 119742. 10.1016/j.jclepro.2019.119742

Theodoraki, C., Dana, L.-P., & Caputo, A. (2022). Building sustainable entrepreneurial ecosystems: A holistic approach. *Journal of Business Research*, 140, 346–360. 10.1016/j.jbusres.2021.11.005

Thierer, A., & Camp, J. (2017). *Permissionless Innovation and Immersive Technology Public Policy for Virtual and Augmented Reality-innovation-virtual-reality-VR 3 Permissionless Innovation and Immersive Technology: Public Policy for Virtual and Augmented Reality.* Mercatus. https://www.mercatus.org/permissionless-innovation-virtual

Thomas, F. (2021). *In defence of the human being: Foundational questions of an embodied anthropology.* Oxford University Press. 10.1093/oso/9780192898197.001.0001

Thomas, P., Andrea, G., & Giuseppe, R. (2020). Extended Reality for the Clinical, Affective, and Social Neurosciences. *Brain Sciences*, 10(12), 992. 10.3390/brainsci1012092233339175

Torabi, Z. A., Pourtaheri, M., Hall, C. M., Sharifi, A., & Javidi, F. (2023). Smart Tourism Technologies, Revisit Intention, and Word-of-Mouth in Emerging and Smart Rural Destinations. *Sustainability (Basel)*, 15(14), 1–21. 10.3390/su151410911

Torabi, Z. A., Rezvani, M. R., Hall, C. M., & Allam, Z. (2023). On the post-pandemic travel boom: How capacity building and smart tourism technologies in rural areas can help - evidence from Iran. *Technological Forecasting and Social Change*, 193(May), 122633. 10.1016/j.techfore.2023.12263337223653

Tuo, Y., Ning, L., & Zhu, A. (2021). How Artificial Intelligence Will Change the Future of Tourism Industry: The Practice in China. In Wörndl, W., Koo, C., & Stienmetz, J. L. (Eds.), *Information and Communication Technologies in Tourism 2021* (pp. 83–94). Springer International Publishing. 10.1007/978-3-030-65785-7_7

Turan, Z., Karabey, S. C. (2023). The use of immersive technologies in distance education: A systematic review. *Education and Information Technologies.* Springer. 10.1007/s10639-023-11849-8

Ugandar, R., Rahamathunnisa, U., Sajithra, S., Christiana, M. B. V., Palai, B. K., & Boopathi, S. (2023). Hospital Waste Management Using Internet of Things and Deep Learning: Enhanced Efficiency and Sustainability. In *Applications of Synthetic Biology in Health, Energy, and Environment* (pp. 317–343). IGI Global.

Ullah, F., Sepasgozar, S. M., & Wang, C. (2018). A systematic review of smart real estate technology: Drivers of, and barriers to, the use of digital disruptive technologies and online platforms. *Sustainability (Basel)*, 10(9), 3142. 10.3390/su10093142

Um, T., & Chung, N. (2021). Does smart tourism technology matter? Lessons from three smart tourism cities in South Korea. *Asia Pacific Journal of Tourism Research*, 26(4), 396–414. 10.1080/10941665.2019.1595691

Compilation of References

Upadhyaya, A. N., Saqib, A., Devi, J. V., Rallapalli, S., Sudha, S., & Boopathi, S. (2024). Implementation of the Internet of Things (IoT) in Remote Healthcare. In *Advances in Medical Technologies and Clinical Practice* (pp. 104–124). IGI Global. 10.4018/979-8-3693-1934-5.ch006

van Herpen, E., van den Broek, E., van Trijp, H. C., & Yu, T. (2016). Can a virtual supermarket bring realism into the lab? Comparing shopping behavior using virtual and pictorial store representations to behavior in a physical store. *Appetite*, 107, 196–207. 10.1016/j.appet.2016.07.03327474194

Vaportzis, E., Giatsi Clausen, M., & Gow, A. J. (2017). Older adults perceptions of technology and barriers to interacting with tablet computers: A focus group study. *Frontiers in Psychology*, 8, 1687. 10.3389/fpsyg.2017.0168729071004

Veeranjaneyulu, R., Boopathi, S., Kumari, R. K., Vidyarthi, A., Isaac, J. S., & Jaiganesh, V. (2023). *Air Quality Improvement and Optimisation Using Machine Learning Technique*. IEEE.

Veeranjaneyulu, R., Boopathi, S., Narasimharao, J., Gupta, K. K., Reddy, R. V. K., & Ambika, R. (2023). Identification of Heart Diseases using Novel Machine Learning Method. *IEEE- Explore*, (pp. 1–6). IEEE.

Veeranjaneyulu, R., Boopathi, S., Narasimharao, J., Gupta, K. K., Reddy, R. V. K., & Ambika, R. (2023). *Identification of Heart Diseases using Novel Machine Learning Method*. IEEE.

Venkatasubramanian, V., Chitra, M., Sudha, R., Singh, V. P., Jefferson, K., & Boopathi, S. (2024). Examining the Impacts of Course Outcome Analysis in Indian Higher Education: Enhancing Educational Quality. In *Challenges of Globalization and Inclusivity in Academic Research* (pp. 124–145). IGI Global.

Venkateswaran, N., Vidhya, K., Ayyannan, M., Chavan, S. M., Sekar, K., & Boopathi, S. (2023). A Study on Smart Energy Management Framework Using Cloud Computing. In *5G, Artificial Intelligence, and Next Generation Internet of Things: Digital Innovation for Green and Sustainable Economies* (pp. 189–212). IGI Global. 10.4018/978-1-6684-8634-4.ch009

Venkateswaran, N., Kiran Kumar, K., Maheswari, K., Kumar Reddy, R. V., & Boopathi, S. (2024). Optimizing IoT Data Aggregation: Hybrid Firefly-Artificial Bee Colony Algorithm for Enhanced Efficiency in Agriculture. *AGRIS On-Line Papers in Economics and Informatics*, 16(1), 117–130. 10.7160/aol.2024.160110

Venkateswaran, N., Vidhya, R., Naik, D. A., Raj, T. M., Munjal, N., & Boopathi, S. (2023). Study on Sentence and Question Formation Using Deep Learning Techniques. In *Digital Natives as a Disruptive Force in Asian Businesses and Societies* (pp. 252–273). IGI Global. 10.4018/978-1-6684-6782-4.ch015

Vennila, T., Karuna, M., Srivastava, B. K., Venugopal, J., Surakasi, R., & Sampath, B. (2022). New Strategies in Treatment and Enzymatic Processes: Ethanol Production From Sugarcane Bagasse. In *Human Agro-Energy Optimization for Business and Industry* (pp. 219–240). IGI Global.

Verhoef, P. C., Lemon, K. N., Parasuraman, A., Roggeveen, A., Tsiros, M., & Schlesinger, L. A. (2009). Customer experience creation: Determinants, dynamics and management strategies. *Journal of Retailing*, 85(1), 31–41. 10.1016/j.jretai.2008.11.001

Verma, D., Kansra, P., & Khan, S. A. (2024). Apparent Advantages and Negative Facet of Block Chain in Banking Sector: An Innovative Theoretical Perspective. In rfan, M., Muhammad, K., Naifar, N., Khan, M.A. (eds), *Applications of Block Chain technology and Artificial Intelligence: Lead-ins in Banking, Finance, and Capital Market* (pp. 19-27). Cham: Springer International Publishing. 10.1007/978-3-031-47324-1_2

Verma, R., Christiana, M. B. V., Maheswari, M., Srinivasan, V., Patro, P., Dari, S. S., & Boopathi, S. (2024). Intelligent Physarum Solver for Profit Maximization in Oligopolistic Supply Chain Networks. In *AI and Machine Learning Impacts in Intelligent Supply Chain* (pp. 156–179). IGI Global. 10.4018/979-8-3693-1347-3.ch011

Vermesan, O., Bröring, A., Tragos, E., Serrano, M., Bacciu, D., Chessa, S., Gallicchio, C., Micheli, A., Dragone, M., & Saffiotti, A. (2022). Internet of robotic things–converging sensing/actuating, hyperconnectivity, artificial intelligence and IoT platforms. In *Cognitive Hyperconnected Digital Transformation* (pp. 97–155). River Publishers. 10.1201/9781003337584-4

Vidushi, M. (2018). *Artificial intelligence policy in India: A framework for engaging the limits of data-driven decision-making. Philosophical Transactions of the Royal Society a Mathematical.* Physical and Engineering Sciences. 10.1098/rsta.2018.0087

Vijaya Lakshmi, V., Mishra, M., Kushwah, J. S., Shajahan, U. S., Mohanasundari, M., & Boopathi, S. (2024). Circular Economy Digital Practices for Ethical Dimensions and Policies for Digital Waste Management. In *Harnessing High-Performance Computing and AI for Environmental Sustainability* (pp. 166–193). IGI Global., 10.4018/979-8-3693-1794-5.ch008

Vijayakumar, G. N. S., Domakonda, V. K., Farooq, S., Kumar, B. S., Pradeep, N., & Boopathi, S. (2024). Sustainable Developments in Nano-Fluid Synthesis for Various Industrial Applications. In *Adoption and Use of Technology Tools and Services by Economically Disadvantaged Communities: Implications for Growth and Sustainability* (pp. 48–81). IGI Global.

Vorobeva, D., Costa Pinto, D., António, N., & Mattila, A. S. (n.d.). The augmentation effect of artificial Intelligence: Can AI framing shape customer acceptance of AI-based services? *Current Issues in Tourism*, 1–21. 10.1080/13683500.2023.2214353

Vrontis, D., Christofi, M., Pereira, V., Tarba, S., Makrides, A., & Trichina, E. (2022). Artificial intelligence, robotics, advanced technologies and human resource management: A systematic review. *International Journal of Human Resource Management*, 33(6), 1237–1266. 10.1080/09585192.2020.1871398

Wagner, R., & Cozmiuc, D. (2022). Extended reality in marketing—A multiple case study on internet of things platforms. *Information (Basel)*, 13(6), 6–278. 10.3390/info13060278

Wang, T. (2010). *A New Paradigm for Design Studio Education*. JADE:173-183

Wang, K., & Lin, C. L. (2012). The adoption of mobile value-added services: Investigating the influence of IS quality and perceived playfulness. *Managing Service Quality*, 22(2), 184–208. 10.1108/09604521211219007

Wang, K., Zhou, Y., Wu, Q., Chen, W., & Yang, Y. (2021). Task offloading in hybrid intelligent reflecting surface and massive MIMO relay networks. *IEEE Transactions on Wireless Communications*, 21(6), 3648–3663. 10.1109/TWC.2021.3122992

Wang, N. (2022). Application of DASH client optimisation and artificial Intelligence in managing and operating big data tourism hotels. *Alexandria Engineering Journal*, 61(1), 81–90. 10.1016/j.aej.2021.04.080

Wang, P. (2021). Connecting the parts with the whole: Toward an information ecology theory of digital innovation ecosystems. *Management Information Systems Quarterly*, 45(1), 397–422. 10.25300/MISQ/2021/15864

Wang, T. (2023). Exploration of User Acceptance Behavior of Hotel Artificial Intelligence Technology Based on Experience Quality. *Journal of Artificial Intelligence Practice*, 6(5). 10.23977/jaip.2023.060505

Wankhade, M., Rao, A. C. S., & Kulkarni, C. (2022). A survey on sentiment analysis methods, applications and challenges. *Artificial Intelligence Review*, 55(7), 5731–5780. 10.1007/s10462-022-10144-1

Wassan, S. (2021). How artificial intelligence transforms the experience of employees. [TURCOMAT]. *Turkish Journal of Computer and Mathematics Education*, 12(10), 7116–7135.

Wedel, M., Bigne, E., & Zhang, J. (2020). Virtual and augmented reality: Advancing research in Consumer marketing. *International Journal of Research in Marketing*, 37(3), 443–465. 10.1016/j.ijresmar.2020.04.004

Wheeler, A. (2009). *Designing brand identity*. John Wiley & Sons, Inc.

Whitler, K. A. (2020). 3 Reasons Why Storytelling Should Be A Priority For Marketers. *Forbes*. https://www.forbes.com/sites/kimberlywhitler/2018/07/14/3-reasons-why-storytelling-should-be-a-priority-for-marketers/?sh=111624876758

Wijethilaka, S., & Liyanage, M. (2021). Survey on network slicing for Internet of Things realization in 5G networks. *IEEE Communications Surveys and Tutorials*, 23(2), 957–994. 10.1109/COMST.2021.3067807

Williamson, B., & Eynon, R. (2020). Historical threads, missing links, and future directions in AI in education. *Learning, Media and Technology*, 45(3), 223–235. 10.1080/17439884.2020.1798995

Witmer, B. G., & Singer, M. J. (1998). Measuring Presence in Virtual Environments: A Presence Questionnaire. *Presence (Cambridge, Mass.)*, 7(3), 225–240. 10.1162/105474698565686

Wiyata, L. I., & Liu, H. (n.d.). THE POTENTIAL FUTURE OF ARTIFICIAL IN LIGENCE IN FOSTERING SUSTAINABLE ENTREPRENEURSHIP WITHIN THE CREATIVE ECONOMY. *Fostering Sustainable Entrepreneurship In Emerging Market: An Interdisciplinary Perspective*, 173.

World Economic Forum. (2020) *Schools of the Future: Defining New Models of Education for the Fourth Industrial Revolution*. WEF. https://www.weforum.org/publications/schools-of-the -future-defining-new-models-of-education-for-the-fourth-industrial-revolution/

Wright, D. (2011). A framework for the ethical impact assessment of information technology. *Ethics and Information Technology*, 13(3), 199–226. 10.1007/s10676-010-9242-6

Wu, G., Xu, T., Sun, Y., & Zhang, J. (2022). Review of multiple unmanned surface vessels collaborative search and hunting based on swarm intelligence. *International Journal of Advanced Robotic Systems*, 19(2), 17298806221091885. 10.1177/17298806221091885

Xiang, Z., Magnini, V. P., & Fesenmaier, D. R. (2015). Information technology and consumer behavior in travel and tourism: Insights from travel planning using the internet. *Journal of Retailing and Consumer Services, 22*(2014), 244–249. 10.1016/j.jretconser.2014.08.005

Xie, D., & He, Y. (2022). Marketing Strategy of Rural Tourism Based on Big Data and Artificial Intelligence. *Mobile Information Systems*, 2022, 1–7. 10.1155/2022/9154351

Xin, C. (2012). A Critique of the Community of Inquiry Framework. *International Journal of E-Learning & Distance Education / Revue Internationale Du e-Learning et La Formation à Distance, 26*(1). https://www.ijede.ca/index.php/jde/article/view/755

Xi, N., Chen, J., Gama, F., Korkeila, H., & Hamari, J. (2024). Acceptance of the metaverse: A laboratory experiment on augmented and virtual reality shopping. *Internet Research*, 34(7), 82–117. 10.1108/INTR-05-2022-0334

Xiong, J., Hsiang, E. L., He, Z., Zhan, T., & Wu, S.-T. (2021). Augmented reality and virtual reality displays: Emerging technologies and future perspectives. *Light, Science & Applications*, 10(1), 216. 10.1038/s41377-021-00658-834697292

Xu, A., Liu, Z., Guo, Y., Sinha, V., & Akkiraju, R. (2017). *A new chatbot for customer service on social media*. In *2017 CHI conference on human factors in computing systems, association for computing machinery*, New York, NY, United States. 10.1145/3025453.3025496

Xu, J., Shi, P. H., & Chen, X. (2024). Exploring digital innovation in smart tourism destinations: Insights from 31 premier tourist cities in digital China. *Tourism Review*, (December). 10.1108/ TR-07-2023-0468

Yaghmaie, P., & Vanhaverbeke, W. (2020). Identifying and describing constituents of innovation ecosystems: A systematic review of the literature. *EuroMed Journal of Business*, 15(3), 283–314. 10.1108/EMJB-03-2019-0042

Yang, C., Lin, C., & Fan, X. (2022). Cultivation model of entrepreneurship from the perspective of artificial intelligence ethics. *Frontiers in Psychology*, 13, 885376. 10.3389/ fpsyg.2022.88537635846706

Yim, M., Chu, S., & Sauer, P. (2017). Is Augmented Reality Technology an Effective Tool for E-commerce? An Interactivity and Vividness Perspective. *Journal of Interactive Marketing, 39*, 89–103. 10.1016/j.intmar.2017.04.001

Yin, D., Ming, X., & Zhang, X. (2020). Sustainable and smart product innovation ecosystem: An integrative status review and future perspectives. *Journal of Cleaner Production, 274*, 123005. 10.1016/j.jclepro.2020.123005

Yoo, C. W., Goo, J., Huang, C. D., Nam, K., & Woo, M. (2017). Improving travel decision support satisfaction with smart tourism technologies: A framework of tourist elaboration likelihood and self-efficacy. *Technological Forecasting and Social Change, 123*, 330–341. 10.1016/j.techfore.2016.10.071

Yupapin, P., Trabelsi, Y., Nattappan, A., & Boopathi, S. (2023). Performance improvement of wire-cut electrical discharge machining process using cryogenically treated super-conductive state of Monel-K500 alloy. *Iranian Journal of Science and Technology. Transaction of Mechanical Engineering, 47*(1), 267–283. 10.1007/s40997-022-00513-0

Yu, S. (2022). The Research on the Characteristics and Forms of Immersive Experience in Art Exhibitions—Take "Van Gogh—the Immersive Experience" as an Example. *Journal of Education. Humanities and Social Sciences.*, (6), 154–159.

Zada, M., Zada, S., Ali, M., Jun, Z. Y., Contreras-Barraza, N., & Castillo, D. (2022). How classy servant leader at workplace? linking servant leadership and task performance during the covid-19 crisis: A moderation and mediation approach. *Frontiers in Psychology, 13*, 810227. 10.3389/fpsyg.2022.81022735401384

Zaheer, H., Breyer, Y., & Dumay, J. (2019). Digital entrepreneurship: An interdisciplinary structured literature review and research agenda. *Technological Forecasting and Social Change, 148*, 119735. 10.1016/j.techfore.2019.119735

Zakarneh, B., Annamalai, N., Alquqa, E. K., Mohamed, K. M., & Al Salhi, N. R. (2024). Virtual Reality and Alternate Realities in Neal Stephenson's "Snow Crash". *World Journal of English Language, 14*(2), 244–252. 10.5430/wjel.v14n2p244

Zakrzewski, P. (2022). *Extended Reality Experience Design: The Multimodal Rhetorical Framework for Creating Persuasive Immersion.* Emerald Publishing Limited. 10.1108/978-1-80262-365-920221005

Zehir, C., Karaboğa, T., & Başar, D. (2020). The transformation of human resource management and its impact on overall business performance: Big data analytics and AI technologies in strategic HRM. *Digital Business Strategies in Blockchain Ecosystems: Transformational Design and Future of Global Business*, 265–279.

Zekrifa, D. M. S., Kulkarni, M., Bhagyalakshmi, A., Devireddy, N., Gupta, S., & Boopathi, S. (2023). Integrating Machine Learning and AI for Improved Hydrological Modeling and Water Resource Management. In *Artificial Intelligence Applications in Water Treatment and Water Resource Management* (pp. 46–70). IGI Global. 10.4018/978-1-6684-6791-6.ch003

Zhang, C. (2020). The Why, What, and How of Immersive Experience. *IEEE Access : Practical Innovations, Open Solutions*, 8, 90878–90888. 10.1109/ACCESS.2020.2993646

Zhang, H., Song, M., & He, H. (2020). Achieving the success of sustainability development projects through big data analytics and artificial intelligence capability. *Sustainability (Basel)*, 12(3), 949. 10.3390/su12030949

Zhang, X., & Ramayah, T. (2024). Solving the mystery of storytelling in destination marketing: A systematic review. *Journal of Hospitality and Tourism Management*, 59, 222–237. 10.1016/j.jhtm.2024.04.013

Zhang, Z., Jiang, T., & Yu, W. (2022). Learning based user scheduling in reconfigurable intelligent surface assisted multiuser downlink. *IEEE Journal of Selected Topics in Signal Processing*, 16(5), 1026–1039. 10.1109/JSTSP.2022.3178213

Zhao, R., Zhang, Y., Zhu, Y., Lan, R., & Hua, Z. (2021). Metaverse: Security and Privacy Concerns. *Journal of Latex Class Files*, 14(8), 1–7.

Zheng, Y., & Wu, Y. (2023). An investigation of how perceived smart tourism technologies affect tourists' well-being in marine tourism. *PLoS ONE, 18*, 1–19. 10.1371/journal.pone.0290539

Zheng, K., Kumar, J., Kunasekaran, P., & Valeri, M. (2022). Role of smart technology use behaviour in enhancing tourist revisit intention: The theory of planned behaviour perspective. *European Journal of Innovation Management*. 10.1108/EJIM-03-2022-0122

Zhou, J., San, O. T., & Liu, Y. (2023). Design and implementation of enterprise financial decision support system based on business intelligence. *International Journal of Professional Business Review*, 8(4), e0873–e0873. 10.26668/businessreview/2023.v8i4.873

Zhou, Y. (2022). The application trend of digital finance and technological innovation in the development of green economy. *Journal of Environmental and Public Health*, 2022, 2022. 10.1155/2022/106455835865872

Ziker, C., Truman, B., & Dodds, H. (2021). Cross Reality (XR): Challenges and Opportunities Across the Spectrum. *Springer Briefs in Statistics*. Springer. 10.1007/978-3-030-58948-6_4

Zizic, M. C., Mladineo, M., Gjeldum, N., & Celent, L. (2022). From industry 4.0 towards industry 5.0: A review and analysis of paradigm shift for the people, organization and technology. *Energies*, 15(14), 5221. 10.3390/en15145221

About the Contributors

Sathish Arumbi Saravanan holds a bachelor's degree in Statistics and master's in business administration specialised in Marketing. Started his career as a management trainee with M/s. Nutrine Confectionery Company Private Limited for a period of 5 years with the designation as Officer – Exports. Dr. Sathish A S is a Professor at VIT Business School, Vellore Institute of Technology, Vellore, India, and a fellow FDP from IIM Ahmedabad. His research interests include Marketing, Retailing, Branding, Services Marketing and Customer Experience. He guided four Ph.D scholars successfully and published more than 30 peer-reviewed journals, five case studies and two books to his credit.

Shaina Arora, Assistant Professor, Chandigarh University, India pursuing Ph.D in Commerce, M.Com from Panjab University and MBA HR-Marketing from LPU. She has earned many awards, published many National-International research papers, also worked on National-International Patents and coordinated, completed & attended many National and International conferences/FDPs/Workshops/ Short term courses to her work credit. She has also an achiever in conferences as presenter, reviewer and key-note speaker. She has awarded with many award certificates, also gained many online learning certificates from different platforms.

Zeeshan Asim is a distinguished faculty member at the University of Buraimi, where he specializes in Supply Chain and Operations Management. His research focuses on optimizing supply chain processes and enhancing operational efficiency.

R. Indradevi is currently working as a Professor in the Department of Commerce, School of Social Sciences and languages, Vellore Institute of Technology, Vellore. She is basically a literature Graduate and has done her PG in Management Studies with specialization in HR. Her area of interest is Human Resource management, Organizational Behaviour, Emotional Intelligence, Leadership, and Change management. She has to her credit published around 65 research papers in peer reviewd, Scopus and ABDC indexed journals. She has published eleven case studies in the European Case Clearing House. Dr.Indradevi has received Distinguished Women Academician Award, from Research Education Solution, Dr.Sarvepalli Radhakrishnan distinguished Professor and Researcher Award in Human Resource Management from IMRF Institute of Higher Education and Research, India and Asia pacific HRM congress award as "BEST PROFESSOR IN HRM" from Times Ascent.

Kamal Batta, Assistant Professor, Chandigarh University, India pursuing Ph.D in Business Management, MBA Marketing-Finance and having twelve years of teaching and non-teaching experience. He has worked on many National and International publications & patents, also successfully completed/ attended more than fifteen National-International FDPs, workshops & seminars and streamed profile as presenter, reviewer and key-note speaker. He has awarded with many award certificates from renowned organizations, also gained many online certifications from Elsevier, LinkedIn Learning, Facebook and Alison.

Sampath Boopathi is an accomplished individual with a strong academic background and extensive research experience. He completed his undergraduate studies in Mechanical Engineering and pursued his postgraduate studies in the field of Computer-Aided Design. Dr. Boopathi obtained his Ph.D. from Anna University, focusing his research on Manufacturing and optimization. Throughout his career, Dr. Boopathi has made significant contributions to the field of engineering. He has authored and published over 230 research articles in internationally peer-reviewed journals, highlighting his expertise and dedication to advancing knowledge in his area of specialization. His research output demonstrates his commitment to conducting rigorous and impactful research. In addition to his research publications, Dr. Boopathi has also been granted one patent and has three published patents to his name. This indicates his innovative thinking and ability to develop practical solutions to real-world engineering challenges. With 17 years of academic and research experience, Dr. Boopathi has enriched the engineering community through his teaching and mentorship roles.

Celal Murat Kandemir graduated from Anadolu University, Department of Electrical and Electronics Engineering in 1995 and started to work as a Research Assistant at Eskişehir Osmangazi University, Faculty of Engineering and Architecture, Department of Electrical and Electronics Engineering. He completed her master's and Ph.D. degrees in 2002 and 2009 respectively. Kandemir, who works as an Assistant Professor at Eskisehir Osmangazi University Faculty of Education, Department of Instructional Design, has international and national publications in his field.

Ozge Kandemir graduated from Eskisehir Osmangazi University, Department of Architecture in 1999 and started to work as a lecturer at Anadolu University, Faculty of Fine Arts, Department of Interior Design, where she joined the Master's Program in 2001. She completed her master's degree in 2004 and the Proficiency in Art Program in 2013 in the field of Interior Design at the same university. Kandemir, who works as an Associate Professor at Eskisehir Technical University, Faculty of Architecture and Design, Department of Interior Design, has many international and national publications and awards in her field.

Shad Ahmad Khan is serving as Assistant Professor in College of Business, University of Buraimi in Sultanate of Oman. He is an active researcher who has a professional strength in the area of Business Management and Marketing. He has a vast experience of organizing international events like conferences and seminars. His area of interest is Data Sciences, green practices, entrepreneurship, administration sciences and marketing.

Mudassar Mahmood, a Lecturer at the University of Buraimi, specializes in Mathematics, with a focus on mathematical theories and their practical applications.

Preeti Mehra is a Business Faculty with Campbell College working in collaboration with Portage College Continuing Education, a public board-governed college based in Alberta, Canada and is focussed on providing the definitive educational experience for international learners. Additionally, she is a Sessional Instructor (Marketing) with Keyano College, Alberta and is teaching students pursuing business programs. She is a doctorate from Guru Nanak Dev University, Amritsar, India and her specialisation is marketing. She has an experience of 15 years in Corporate and Academics and was a professor in marketing with a leading private university in India. She is dedicated to imparting knowledge and is passionate about research and e-content development. She has an expertise in public speaking, academic instruction, and research management. She offers an history of delivering marketing advancements and developing substantial university curricula and is devoted to creating future field leaders through education and mentoring. She specialises in Micro Branding, Sachet Marketing, Gesture Recognition, Rural Marketing Strategy, Services Marketing and Brand Management. Her research work focusses on expressively enriching organizational reach and market share through the application of robust strategies, effective pricing and excellent client relationship management. She has contributed towards distinguished journals of national and international repute like Emerald, Sage and has participated and presented in many national and international conferences. She has acted as editor of several books and has contributed towards many book chapters in the field of marketing. She has acted as an external trainer in many workshops and Faculty Development Programmes related to marketing and research methodology. She has several copyrights and patents to her credit and has supervised several doctorate students.

About the Contributors

Arun Mittal is Assistant Professor (AL-12) at Birla Institute of Technology, Mesra Ranchi, Noida Campus. He holds a PhD, MBA in MPhil, and ECPDM from IIM-Kashipur. He has 16 years of experience teaching consumer behaviour, marketing research, marketing analytics, and multivariate data analysis. He has published about 25 research papers in Scopus, SSCI indexed, ABDC ranked, and UGC CARE journals and presented papers in around 25 conferences and seminars. He has authored/co-authored five books in the field of management. He has successfully supervised four PhD. He has conducted many FDPs, MDPs, and workshops on digital marketing, business analytics, and research methodology. He is the Project Director and Co-Director in a major project sponsored by ICSSR and MGNCRE. He is a life member of ICA and ISTD.

Devarajanayaka Muniyanayaka, an Assistant Professor at the University of Buraimi, Oman, specializes in Business Administration, with a focus on strategic management and organizational behavior.

M. Sureshkumar completed his undergraduate in Mechanical Engineering and postgraduate in the field of Engineering Design. He completed his Ph.D. from Anna University, Chennai, Tamil Nādu, India.

Tawheed Nabi is currently Assistant Professor at Mittal School of Business ACBSP USA, Accredited, Lovely Professional University, Punjab (India). Dr. Nabi received his PhD degree from DOS in Economics, Karnatak University, Dharwad and has been UGC-UPE research fellow. His expertise entails areas like International Trade, Agriculture Economics and Business Models.

P. B. Narendra Kiran is currently working as an assistant professor in School of Business and Management, Christ University, Bengaluru, Karnataka (India). He has done his M.B.A. from JNTU Kakinada and M.Phil., Ph.D. from Andhra University, Visakhapatnam. He has 14 years of experience in academics, research and teaching diverse student groups. More than 500+ students were guided with their capstone projects in their academic and professional life. His area of interest in teaching is Entrepreneurship, HR Analytics, Talent Acquisition, Design Thinking, and Organisational Behaviour. He has published 10 patents and authored two Textbooks on the Fundamentals of HRM and HR Analytics. He has more than 50+ FDP/Seminars/workshops attended, conducted, and organized on his expertise and presented his research at reputed National and International conferences in different parts of the country. He has authored seventeen research papers in Scopus/Wos/UGC. He has three professional memberships from reputed professional bodies.

Stanzin Padma is a research scholar at the Mittal School of Business, Lovely Professional University, India. She also serves as an Assistant Professor of Economics at Government Degree College Nobra, University of Ladakh, India, and has seven years of teaching experience in economics. She has done her M.Phil in Economics from Jawaharlal Nehru University, Delhi and has been a Junior Research Fellow. Her research interests are in tourism, labour economics and informal sector studies. She can be reached at padmastanzin123@gmail.com.

Anand Pandey is having more than 3 years of teaching experience in the field of computer application and Information Technology. Currently he is working as an Assistant Professor at Chandigarh University. He has a vast knowledge in the area Artificial intelligence, IOT, Machine Learning and Leading softwares used in the organizations. Moreover, he has filled two International patents and published one National patent in the area IOT and Artificial Intelligence. Multiple conferences/FDPs/Workshops/Conclaves have been attended by him and also presented in them. He has recently published a national book on "Internet of Things for Beginners-A Practical Approach".

Gautam Shandilya is Assistant Professor in the Department of Hotel Management, BIT Mesra, Ranchi and has served in industry and academia for more than 23 years. He has several research papers, books, edited books, and book chapters to his credit. His interests lie in Tourism, Fast Food, Relationship Marketing, Entrepreneurship. He is Associate Editor of Journal of Hospitality Application and Research (JOHAR), an ABDC indexed Journal. He has presented research papers at several national and international conferences. He has edited and Co-Authored 3 books on Hotel and Hospitality industry and published several articles in journals. He is a proactive lecturer and researcher with more than 16 years of experience in teaching courses like Food Production, Food & Beverage Services, Event management, Communication Skills & Tourism at undergraduate & postgraduate level. He is skilled in food & beverage production, event organization & Microsoft Office. Apart from academics and research he is also very much active in taking administrative challenges at his university and has organized various theme lunches, food festivals and provided support in events of national repute like 34th National Games, BITOTSAV as Faculty Coordinator and Science and Technology Festival during Azadi ka Amrit Mahotsav as Hospitality Coordinator. He has taken additional assignments like hostel warden, NSS Program Officer and served in various committees during Convocation, Athletic Meets, Induction Programs, Institute Foundation Day, Delegate's visits, PANTHEON, VAJRA, Jharkhand Science and Environment Festival, Anti-ragging Squad, Value Education Cell, IKS programs, Central Mess Purchase, BITWS Corpus, Staff Club etc.

Praveen Srivastava is an Experienced Academician with a demonstrated history of working in the education management industry for more than 20 years. Skilled in Tourism, Hospitality, MOOC Courses, Customer Relationship Management, ICT, Training and Marketing Research. He has authored two books and several journal articles. Strong educational professional degree from IHM Bhopal and Ph.D. from Ranchi University. He is also a certified instructor for "Managing Front Office Operation" and "Leadership and Management in the Hospitality Industry" by American Hotel and Lodging Association (AH&LA), USA, Michigan, and recipient of "Award of Excellence" by IIT Mumbai for being amongst the top performer of the Faculty Development Program on "Use of ICT in Education for Online and Blended learning ".in 2016. In the year 2018, IIT Mumbai awarded him with the Top Performer badge again in two-week Faculty Development Program (FDP 301X) on "Mentoring Educators in Educational Technology". He was also selected as a Mentor in the AICTE approved Two Faculty Development Program (FDP101x and FDP201x) on Pedagogy for Online and Blended Teaching-Learning Process conducted by the Indian Institute of Technology (IIT) Mumbai from August 3, 2017, to September 7, 2017, and from September 14, 2017, to October 12, 2017, respectively. He is currently serving as Associate Dean of Student Affairs at BIT Mesra and Editor-In-Chief for the journal JOHAR, which is indexed in ABDC Journal Quality List, and he is associated with Department of Hotel Management and Catering Technology as an Assistant Professor

Gökhan Ulusoy, graduated from Anadolu University, Faculty of Architecture and Design, Department of Interior Design undergraduate program in 2015 and Anadolu University Institute of Fine Arts, Department of Interior Design master's program in 2019. He continues his education at the Anadolu University Institute of Fine Arts, Department of Interior Design Proficiency in Art Program, which he started in the same year. In 2015, he was appointed as a research assistant to Anadolu University, Faculty of Architectural and Design, Department of Interior Design Since 2015, he has been working as a research assistant at Eskisehir Technical University, Faculty of Architecture and Design, Department of Interior Design, with the assignment of higher education.

Asokan Vasudevan an Associate Professor at Inti International University, specializes in Operations Management, focusing on optimizing business processes and improving operational efficiency.

K.P. Venkataswamy is currently working as Assistant Professor in School of Management Studies, REVA University, Bangalore. He has done his MBA with HR and Marketing Specialisation and did Ph.D. at Visvesvaraya Technological University, Belagavi. He has 18 years of experience in Teaching, Research and Industry. He has published papers in the National Journals and he has also published papers in Edited Books. He has completed Online Course on IPR at IISC Bangalore. He was honoured with Academic Excellence Award by Indian Institute of Production Management, Odisha.

Yusri Yosof, an Associate Professor at Universiti Tun Hussein Onn Malaysia, specializes in Manufacturing Engineering, focusing on advanced manufacturing processes and mechanical systems.

Index

238, 244, 247, 255, 256

M

machine learning 48, 119, 121, 127, 131, 133, 134, 141, 153, 163, 173, 174, 175, 176, 177, 179, 180, 186, 187, 188, 194, 196, 197, 198, 199, 202, 204, 232, 233, 234, 235, 236, 238, 241, 244, 248, 254, 255, 259, 260, 261, 262, 263, 265, 266, 267, 268, 271, 277, 279, 282, 284, 286, 289, 290, 294, 298, 300, 301, 302, 304, 312, 313, 314, 315, 316, 321, 380, 381, 382, 383, 384, 387, 388, 389, 392, 397, 400, 417

Marketing Narratives 417, 423
Modern Workplace 257, 399
Multidisciplinary Applications 2, 7, 9

N

Network Slicing Architectures 260, 261, 262, 272, 275, 277, 279, 282, 284

P

Perceived Risk 97, 100, 105, 106, 112, 114, 115
Perceived Trust 100, 101, 105, 106, 111, 112, 114
Perceived Value 420
performance management 173, 176, 179, 208, 232, 233, 234, 236, 237, 238, 242, 243, 248, 251, 252, 257
Predictive Analytics 118, 120, 176, 177, 179, 186, 189, 208, 211, 212, 213, 232, 233, 234, 236, 238, 239, 241, 249, 251, 261, 263, 265, 266, 267, 277, 294, 298, 300, 307, 374, 375, 381, 383, 384, 385, 387, 388

R

real estate business 81, 82, 83, 84, 86, 87, 88, 89, 90, 91, 92, 93
Real-Time Analytics 275, 293, 298, 300,

302, 303, 304, 305
Resource Optimization 202, 265, 266, 279, 299
Risk Assessment 374, 383, 384, 385, 387

S

semi-immersive virtual reality [SIVR] 81, 82, 83, 84, 85, 86, 88, 89, 90, 91, 92, 93
Service-Dominant Logic 135
SmartPLS 147, 155, 159, 160, 161, 163, 164
Smart Tourism Technology (STT) 147, 148, 149, 150, 151, 152, 153, 154, 156, 160, 161, 162, 163, 164, 165, 166, 167, 169
sociology 217, 218, 219
Storytelling 2, 3, 6, 8, 12, 39, 45, 67, 140, 338, 340, 401, 402, 403, 404, 406, 407, 408, 409, 410, 411, 412, 413, 414, 415, 416, 418, 419, 420, 421, 422, 423
Strategic Planning 185, 233, 374, 381, 385, 386, 396, 398
sustainable entrepreneurship development 201, 204, 209, 210, 211, 213

T

Three-dimensional (3D) 18, 97, 364, 413
Tourist Satisfaction 138, 147, 148

V

Virtual Content 28
Virtual reality (VR) 2, 3, 4, 5, 6, 7, 8, 14, 16, 18, 20, 21, 24, 26, 29, 35, 36, 37, 38, 39, 40, 41, 42, 43, 44, 45, 46, 47, 48, 49, 51, 54, 55, 60, 61, 62, 63, 65, 67, 69, 70, 71, 72, 73, 74, 75, 77, 79, 80, 81, 82, 83, 84, 85, 86, 88, 89, 90, 91, 92, 93, 94, 95, 97, 99, 117, 128, 133, 134, 138, 144, 189, 193, 198, 236, 253, 289, 315, 318, 320, 324, 336, 337, 338, 339, 348, 349, 351, 352, 353, 354, 357, 376, 410, 411, 416, 417, 421

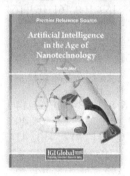
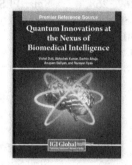

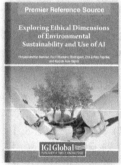

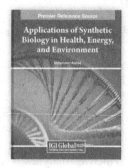

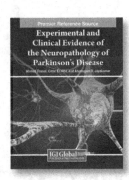
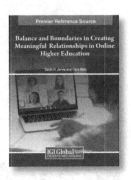

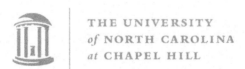

Printed in the United States
by Baker & Taylor Publisher Services